ALCOHOLIC BEVERAGES

ECONOMIC MICROBIOLOGY

Series Editor

A. H. ROSE

Volume 1. Alcoholic Beverages

In preparation

Volume 2. Primary Products of Metabolism

Volume 3. Secondary Products of Metabolism

Volume 4. Microbial Cell Material: Biomass

Volume 5. Enzymes and Enzymic Conversions

Volume 6. Biodegradation

ECONOMIC MICROBIOLOGY
Volume 1

ALCOHOLIC BEVERAGES

edited by

A. H. ROSE

School of Biological Sciences
University of Bath,
Bath, England

1977

ACADEMIC PRESS

LONDON   NEW YORK   SAN FRANCISCO

A Subsidiary of Harcourt Brace Jovanovich, Publishers

ACADEMIC PRESS INC. (LONDON) LTD.
24/28 Oval Road
London NW1

United States edition published by
ACADEMIC PRESS INC.
111 Fifth Avenue
New York, New York 10003

Library of Congress Catalog Card Number: 77-77361
ISBN: 0-12-596550-8.

Printed in Great Britain at the Spottiswoode Ballantyne Press
by William Clowes & Sons Limited, London, Colchester and Beccles

CONTRIBUTORS

F. W. BEECH University of Bristol, Research Station, Long Ashton, Bristol, England.

J. G. CARR University of Bristol, Research Station, Long Ashton, Bristol, England.

ROBIN W. GOSWELL John Harvey and Sons Limited, Bristol, England.

ANDRZEJ JARCZYK Department of Food Technology, Agricultural University of Warsaw, Warsaw, Poland.

K. KODAMA Kodama Brewing Co. Ltd., Iitagawa, Akita Prefecture, Japan.

RALPH E. KUNKEE Department of Viticulture and Enology, University of California, Davis, California, U.S.A.

M. LEHTONEN Research Laboratories of the State Alcohol Monopoly (ALKO), Box 350, SF-00101 Helsinki 10, Finland.

T. P. LYONS Biocon Limited, Eardiston, Near Tenbury Wells, Worcestershire, England.

ANNA M. MacLEOD Department of Brewing and Biological Sciences, Heriot-Watt University, Edinburgh, Scotland.

A. H. ROSE Zymology Laboratory, School of Biological Sciences, Bath University, Bath, England.

A. C. SIMPSON Research and Development Department, International Distillers and Vintners Limited, Harlow, Essex, England.

H. SUOMALAINEN Research Laboratories of the State Alcohol Monopoly (ALKO), Box 350, SF-00101 Helsinki 10, Finland.

WIESLAW WZOREK Department of Food Technology, Agricultural University of Warsaw, Warsaw, Poland.

K. YOSHIZAWA The National Research Institute of Brewing, Tokyo, Japan.

PREFACE TO THE SERIES

Controlling and exploiting the World's flora and fauna have been fundamental to Man's colonization of this planet. His ability to regulate the activities, both pathogenic and saprophytic, of micro-organisms, and to go on to harness microbial activity in the manufacture of foods and chemicals represents a truly outstanding achievement especially when one remembers that microbes represented an invisible activity or agent until microbiology became established as a science during the latter half of the last Century. Only then did it become apparent that Man's very existence depends on microbial activity.

This multi-volume series aims to provide authoritative accounts of the many facets of exploitation and control of microbial activity. The first volume describes production of alcoholic beverages, and in the second and third volumes there are accounts of the microbiological production of commercially important chemicals. Production of microbial biomass is the subject of the fourth volume, and in the fifth there are accounts of production of enzymes from micro-organisms and of industrially-important chemical conversions or reactions mediated by microbes. Later volumes will deal with biodeterioration caused by microbes, sewage purification and the microbiology of foods. Throughout the volumes, emphasis is placed on the chemical activities of micro-organisms for it is these activities which affect with such impact the activities of man. It is hoped that the series will provide an adequate testimony to the unique relationship which Man has forged with his smallest servants.

January, 1977   ANTHONY H. ROSE

PREFACE TO VOLUME 1

Any historical perspective of Man's control and exploitation of microbial activity must grant pride of place to production of alcoholic beverages. Exactly when a yeast fermentation was first used to make a potable alcoholic beverage will never be known, but it must have been several thousands of years B.C. It is known however that, by purely empirical techniques, the ancient brewers in Egypt brought about a detectable improvement in the purity of their yeast, and this surely attests to the skills which these early craftsmen had acquired. The art of distilling came later, almost certainly having been pioneered by the alchemists. With their ancient history, brewing of beverages and distilling of spirits are inextricably interwoven into Man's social development over the ages, not least because the beverages and spirits concerned have, over the years, played a not inconsiderable part in creative activities in the realms of literature, music and rhetoric.

The number of different alcoholic beverages made throughout the World must run into many hundreds. However, three groups can be clearly defined, based on their alcoholic content, namely beers and wines, fortified wines, and distilled spirits. The volume describes the microbiology and biochemistry of production of major representatives in these groups. There is, unfortunately, one omission, namely brandy where despite the most strenuous efforts I was unable to persuade an author to submit a manuscript. The accounts here presented show clearly that some beverages, such as beers, have been much more intensively researched from a microbiological and biochemical stand-point than others.

I should like to thank all of the contributors who have written for this first volume in the Economic Microbiology series. I am sure that their authoritative accounts do full justice to these most ancient and venerable of Man's exploitations of microbial activity.

January, 1977   ANTHONY H. ROSE

CONTENTS

1. History and Scientific Basis of Alcoholic Beverage Production
A. H. ROSE

2. Beer
ANNA M. MacLEOD

3. Cider and Perry
F. W. BEECH and J. G. CARR

4. Table Wines
RALPH E. KUNKEE and ROBIN W. GOSWELL

5. Fruit and Honey Wines
ANDRZEJ JARCZYK and WIESLAW WZOREK

6. Saké
K. KODAMA and K. YOSHIZAWA

7. Fortified Wines
ROBIN W. GOSWELL and RALPH E. KUNKEE

8. Gin and Vodka
A. C. SIMPSON

9. Rum
M. LEHTONEN and H. SUOMALAINEN

10. Whisky
T. P. LYONS and A. H. ROSE

NOTES

Abbreviations

The abbreviations used for chemical and biochemical compounds in this book are those recommended by the International Union of Pure and Applied Chemistry—International Union of Biochemistry Commission on Biochemical Nomenclature, and summarized in the *Biochemical Journal* (1976; *153*, 1-24).

Nomenclature of Yeasts

Except where otherwise indicated, the nomenclature used for strains of yeast is that recommended by J. Lodder in *The Yeasts, A Taxonomic Study* (1970; North-Holland Publishing Co., Amsterdam).

Alcoholic Strength of Beverages

There are several ways of expressing quantitatively the alcoholic strength of a beverage, and manufacturers of a particular class of beverage frequently use one way in preference to others. The various ways used are described in Chapter 1, pages 34–36.

1. History and Scientific Basis of Alcoholic Beverage Production

ANTHONY H. ROSE

School of Biological Sciences, Bath University,
Bath, England

I. INTRODUCTION

This volume brings together chapters which describe the microbiological and biochemical bases of the commercial production of alcoholic beverages, which include non-distilled beverages and distilled spirits. Alcoholic-beverage and potable-spirit industries operate in almost all countries of the world, and together they represent one of the most economically stable sectors in modern-day commerce. At the same time, they are among the most diverse of today's industries because of the tremendous variety of beverages and spirits which they produce. The stability of these industries, and the obvious

1

popularity which their products have with mankind throughout the World, have not gone unnoticed by governments many of whom have been quick to exploit the popularity as a source of tax revenue. It has to be admitted, however, that the popularity of non-distilled as well as distilled alcoholic beverages has not been an unqualified benefit to governments, since it has brought with it sociological problems to the extent that some governments, often temporarily, have legislated against production and consumption of these beverages and spirits.

Individual chapters in the volume deal with the production of different classes of alcoholic beverages. Clearly, with the vast range of different beverages produced in the World, it has not been possible to describe in detail each and every product; indeed many are not even mentioned. Inevitably, emphasis has been placed on those beverages whose production has been studied, in greater or lesser detail, from a microbiological and biochemical standpoint.

All alcoholic-beverage industries are based on the production of ethanol, and a wide range of other quantitatively minor but organoleptically very important compounds, by fermentation of a cereal, fruit or vegetable extract by strains of yeast. The yeasts involved are almost invariably strains of *Saccharomyces* particularly *Sacch. cerevisiae* and *Sacch. uvarum*. Van der Walt, writing in Lodder (1970), includes in the latter species strains which were previously known as *Sacch. carlsbergensis* despite the widespread lack of enthusiasm amongst industrial microbiologists who continue to refer to the species as *Sacch. carlsbergensis*. Strains of *Saccharomyces* are endowed with a capacity to effect a very efficient alcoholic fermentation of sugars (monosaccharides and small oligosaccharides). The fermentable sugar may be in the aqueous extract of the raw material (such as grapes and other fruits) used to make the alcoholic beverage whereas, in other processes, such as brewing of beer and saké, the sugars are furnished by hydrolytic breakdown of polysaccharides. A further subdivision of the alcoholic beverage industries arises from the fact that some products of the fermentation process are consumed more or less as such, whereas in other industries the fermented product is distilled to form the consumable product.

II. HISTORY OF ALCOHOLIC BEVERAGES

A. Non-Distilled Beverages

Exploiting the ability of certain yeasts to produce a potable and stimulating beverage by alcoholic fermentation dates back to very early times, certainly to several thousands of years B.C. It is hardly surprising to discover therefore that the first occasions on which beverages resembling what we now know as beer, cider and wine were made are not documented (Hardwick, 1975). In all likelihood, the first wine was made from fruit, possibly grape, juice quite inadvertently, since juices extracted from most types of fruit are contaminated with microbes, including yeasts, that form the surface flora or 'bloom' on the fruit, with the result that the juices are susceptible to alcoholic fermentation provided that the environmental temperature is conducive. Nor can it be stated where the first wines were made, although many authorities believe that it was probably in the valley of what we now know as the River Tigris in Iraq.

With some reservations, historians believe that beer production, which involves hydrolytic breakdown of starch in cereal extracts, was invented in Egypt some 5,000–6,000 years B.C. (Huber, 1926; Corran, 1975). Interestingly, the brewing process, in its early stages of development, resembled the baking of bread. Barley was placed in an earthenware vessel and buried in the ground until germination began. Then it was crushed, made into a dough, and baked until a crust formed. Finally, the cake of dehydrated dough was soaked in water until fermentation was complete. The acid beer so produced was called *boozah*, a term that is now used in a quite different sense in Britain to describe the location of beer drinking rather than the product (King, 1947).

For many centuries after these early beginnings, production of both wine and beer gradually developed as an art and a craft, in of course the complete absence of any scientific knowledge of the basis of the processes. It is worth noting, however, that improvements seemingly were made in the technology of beer brewing. Microscopic examination of beer urns found during excavations of a wealthy estate at Thebes revealed what almost certainly are yeast cells. Moreover, one researcher claims that he could trace a decided improvement in the purity of the yeast in sediments dating from 1,440 B.C. compared with those of 3,400 B.C. Brewing of beer and production of wine took their place in the primitive societies that were evolving (Smith and Ferdinand, 1940), documentation of which is delightfully illustrated in the marvellously preserved and exquisitely constructed models of a bakery and a brewery in an estate of the XIth Dynasty unearthed at Thebes. Both processes also began to be chronicled in religious and other literatures of the early civilizations. One of the earliest treatises, probably the earliest, on brewing of beer was written by Zosimos of Panopolis, Upper Egypt, in the latter part of the Third Century, A.D. (Sarton, 1927).

Centuries later, in 1680, the Dutchman Antonie van Leeuwenhoek, a draper living in Delft, Holland, was the first person to see a yeast cell when he examined drops of fermenting beer with his primitive microscope (Chapman, 1931). The drawings which Leeuwenhoek made, and which he submitted to the Royal Society in London, leave no doubt that he was able to examine the yeast cell in some detail. But this discovery of the yeast cell was soon forgotten, and it was not until 1837 that there appeared publications which can be said to have initiated the concept of a causal relationship between alcoholic fermentation and the activity of yeast cells. The concept was advanced independently by three workers, namely Cagniard-Latour, Schwann and Kützing, mainly on the basis of microscopic examination of fermenting liquids. In 1837, Schwann dubbed yeast the causative agent, 'Zuckerpilz', from which the name 'Saccharomyces' or 'sugar fungus' originates. But the ridicule which was heaped upon these reports by publications, both anonymous and signed, from Liebig, Wöhler and Berzelius, effectively prevented any serious consideration of such a causal relationship. The situation was finally resolved by the epic-making discoveries and publications of Louis Pasteur, which are well documented in the biographies of Vallery-Radot (1902) and Dubos (1950) and reviewed by Dubos (1960) and Porter (1972). Pasteur's main contributions came in the form of two publications, firstly his *Études sur le Vin*, published in 1866, and *Études sur la Bière* which appeared in 1876. In the second of these publications, Pasteur concluded that living yeast cells cause fermentations when they are obliged to live in the absence of air, and that, during the fermentation, the yeast converts sugar into ethanol and carbon dioxide. Conant (1952) compiled a valuable case history of Pasteur's studies on fermentation, which merits perusal by the serious student of the history of alcoholic beverages.

One important question remained unanswered, namely the exact cause of decomposition of the sugar molecule, and in particular whether the sugar molecule is decomposed inside the yeast cell or as a result of transference of 'decomposing activity' from the cell plasm to the sugar molecule, which was the alternative suggestion coming from the proponents of the 'chemical fermentation theory'. The answer was provided in 1897 by the Buchner brothers and Hahn when they discovered that, by grinding yeast cells with a mixture of kieselguhr and sand, it was possible to obtain a juice that brought about an alcoholic fermentation of a sugar solution in the absence of intact cells, so showing that fermentation results from action of substances contained within the yeast cell. The importance of this discovery in relation to the biochemistry of alcoholic fermentation is discussed more fully in Section III.B (p. 21) of this chapter.

The microbiology of brewing made a significant advance over the microbiology of wine making when, starting around 1880, the Danish botanist Emil Christian Hansen began publishing some epoch-making investigations into the morphology and physiology of yeasts (Jørgensen, 1948). Hansen, who worked at the Carlsberg Laboratory at Copenhagen in Denmark, focused attention on problems that arise in the brewing of beer as a result of the activities of yeasts that differ from the prime fermenting organisms, yeasts which are dubbed 'wild yeasts' by the brewer. To put his theories into practice, Hansen isolated pure cultures of brewing yeast which he then used in the brewing process. Gradually the practice of using pure cultures of *Saccharomyces cerevisiae* and *Sacch. carlsbergensis* (as they were then known, see p. 8) became acceptable in the brewing industry, and today is commonplace, but not so until very recently in the manufacture of wines and ciders. For many years, grape and other fruit juices were, and indeed often still are, fermented by yeasts that make up the natural flora or 'bloom' which occurs on the surfaces of these fruits.

Not long after Hansen made his contribution through the introduction of 'pure-culture' brewing, Oivid Winge, working also in the Carlsberg Laboratory in Copenhagen, was laying the foundations of yeast genetics. It might have been expected that the brewing microbiologist would extend these pioneer advances by attempting to breed yeasts specially for brewing. Strangely, this did not happen, and it has only been in recent years that the possibilities of breeding yeasts for brewing purposes have been seriously examined (Clayton *et al.*, 1972; Anderson and Martin, 1975).

B. Distilled Spirits

The history of distilling potable spirits is far shorter than that of making non-distilled alcoholic beverages. There are nevertheless several very early references which can be taken to indicate that a potable spirit was known many thousands of years ago. The earliest reference to production, and official warnings regarding excessive consumption, of potable distilled spirits appear to have come from China, some 1,000 years B.C. (Legge, 1893; Simon, 1948). Aristotle later mentions purifying sea water by evaporation, and also a 'wine which produces a spirit'. For centuries, the art of distilling remained firmly in the hands of the alchemist. Herbs had long been thought to cure various maladies—agrimony for jaundice, foxglove for blisters— and it would seem that the alchemists argued that, if the juice of one of these herbs could be, say, quadrupled in strength, then the efficiency of the cure would be multiplied fourfold (Layton, 1968). The alchemists were responsible for many improvements in the art of distilling. The first treatise on distilling was written by the French chemist Arnold de Villeneuve, probably sometime around 1310 although it is known that the book was printed in 1478 in Venice. The Spaniard, Raymond Lully, did much to disseminate knowledge about distilling in Europe in the 13th Century, while a comprehensive text on the subject by a physician named Ryff appeared in 1556 in Frankfurt am Main.

It was not until around the 15th Century that the enjoyment of distilled spirits as beverages came to be widely appreciated. The events leading up to this realization are, hardly surprisingly, far from clear. It has been suggested that distilled spirits were consumed as palliatives during the Black Death of 1347–1351 in Europe, and in the 16th Century in mines in Hungary to protect against cold and damp. Distilling fermented grape juice to give brandy first became widespread in France in the 17th Century, partly because the low-quality wines produced at that time in the Charente region were not very popular.

After production of distilled spirits began to pass out of the hands of the alchemist, improvements were gradually made in two areas of the art of distilling. Firstly, in a purely pragmatic fashion, the distiller learned to collect from the still just those fractions that have the desirable organoleptic qualities, and to reject those that contain compounds with undesirable flavours and odours. Secondly, considerable advances were made in the construction of stills.

The early processes of distillation utilized alembics, which consist of closed containers in which the fermented liquid is heated, and in which the vapours that are produced are transferred through a tube to a separate cooling chamber where they condense. Alembics were usually made of copper iron or tin; lead and silver were known to produce undesirable distillates. Developments to these early alembics involved encasing the vessel in clay or brick boxes, and using a long coiled tube or crane neck to connect the vessel and the cooling coil. The stills used today in many Scotch malt whisky and French brandy distilleries are basically of this type. During the 19th Century, many other improvements in still design were made, some of the more important being associated with the names of the Frenchman Edouard Adam, and the Dublin-born Aeneas Coffey. In 1801, Adam designed the prototype of a charge still. He used egg-shaped vessels to hold the fermented liquid through which vapours from the kettle are passed. Continuous stills had been designed in the early years of the 19th Century, and one was patented by the Englishman Wyatt although it was rejected by the Bureau of Excise on the grounds that its use would encourage illegal distilling. But the still designed by Coffey in 1830 was accepted. It consists of two columns, in the first of which alcohol and other volatile compounds are removed from the fermented liquid using steam while, in the second, the vapours are condensed to give a high-proof spirit (94–96% v/v ethanol). The original Coffey still has undergone several design modifications, but many of the stills nowadays used to produce potable spirits do not differ appreciably in basic design from the original Coffey still.

III. MICROBIOLOGY AND BIOCHEMISTRY OF ALCOHOLIC BEVERAGE PRODUCTION

A. Microbiology

The alcoholic beverages described in this volume, as well as the alcoholic liquids which are distilled to yield potable spirits, have in common that they are produced by the alcoholic fermentation of sugar-containing nutrient solutions by species of the yeast *Saccharomyces*. The source of the sugar in the liquid varies with the nature of the beverage. With some, such as wines made from grapes or other fruits, the sugar is present as such in the raw material. In others, it is formed following the hydrolysis of polysaccharides in the raw material. The availability of free sugars for alcoholic fermentation by species of *Saccharomyces* is essential, since none of the species that are used to ferment alcoholic beverages has the capacity to produce extracellular enzymes capable of catalysing hydrolysis of polysaccharides.

1. *The Genus* Saccharomyces

The genus *Saccharomyces* is just one of the 39 genera of single-celled fungi or yeasts recognized in the standard taxonomic treatise on yeasts edited by Lodder (1970). Van der Walt (1970), who wrote the contribution on the genus *Saccharomyces* in Lodder's treatise, recognized 41 species in the genus, a number that has since been extended to 44 in the text of Barnett and Pankhurst (1974) which modified Lodder's (1970) approach to yeast taxonomy.

The generic name *Saccharomyces* was introduced by Meyen in 1838, and the genus first defined some years later by Reess (1870). From the inception of yeast systematics, it has been realized that this taxon is phylogenetically very heterogeneous, to the point that the presently recognized demarcation of the genus is essentially utilitarian. Moreover, such has been the extent of genetic manipulation of species in the genus (see p. 19) that no attempt can be made at present to consider the taxonomic position in the genus of these laboratory artefacts (Van der Walt, 1970). Detailed historical accounts of the genus *Saccharomyces* can be found in the texts by Stelling-Dekker (1931), Lodder and Kreger-Van Rij (1952) and Kudriavzev (1939, 1960).

The principal characteristics of yeasts placed in the genus *Saccharomyces* are vegetative production of spherical, ellipsoidal or more rarely cylindrical cells by multilateral budding. Pseudomycelium is rarely, and true mycelium never, formed. Species of *Saccharomyces* are ascosporogenous yeasts, and the one to four ascospores formed in each ascus are not spontaneously released when the asci reach maturity (Fowell, 1969). A property which all species of *Saccharomyces* possess, and which is seminal to their role in the production of alcoholic beverages, is the capacity to bring about an efficient alcoholic fermentation of sugars. This is an energy-yielding process in which ATP, the energy supply for biosynthetic reactions, is produced along with certain three-carbon compounds that are used in the synthesis of new yeast cell constituents. The process, which is described more fully in Section III.B (p. 21) of this chapter, is, in biochemical terms, a true *fermentation* in that an organic compound (a monosaccharide) is the electron donor, and an organic compound (pyruvate) the electron acceptor.

There are four main subdivisions of *Saccharomyces* species (Van der Walt, 1970). As far as production of alcoholic beverages is concerned, the most important of these groups is the first, which includes species closely related to the type species of the genus, namely *Saccharomyces cerevisiae* Hansen. Species in this first group, which are the so-called *Saccharomyces cerevisiae sensu strictu* (Van der Walt, 1970) are, when isolated from natural environments, stabilized predominantly in the diploid phase. Another important characteristic of species in the group is that they are invariably interfertile, which explains many of the difficulties and much of the confusion which surround the taxonomy of species in the group, particularly of industrially important species. When isolated from natural environments, many of the species in this group are unable to utilize the sugar maltose, although they can readily acquire this ability after prolonged maintenance in media which contain the sugar (Scheda and Yarrow, 1966, 1968). Acquiring the ability to utilize maltose is of more than academic interest in view of the fact that several alcoholic beverages are manufactured by fermentation of extracts that contain maltose. Yet another characteristic of strains of *Saccharomyces* in this first group is their ability to form *petite* or respiratory-deficient mutants, especially following treatment with the mutagen acriflavin (Bulder, 1964).

The second group in the subdivision of *Saccharomyces* spp. includes strains closely related to *Sacch. bailli*, a yeast which is probably identical with *Zygosaccharomyces acidofaciens* described by Nickerson (1943). The third group includes species which Stelling-Dekker (1931) originally assigned to the genus *Torulaspora*, and which Kudriavzev (1960) placed in the genus *Debaryomyces*.

The fourth group is even more of a rag bag, and includes species for which there is little or no evidence of a phylogenetic connection or relationship.

The vast majority of yeasts which are used in the manufacture of alcoholic beverages are classified by Van der Walt (1970) as strains of *Sacch. cerevisiae* or *Sacch. uvarum*. These names are the latest appellations to be used for these strains (Van der Walt, 1970). Traditionally, strains of yeast (the so-called top-fermenting strains) used for producing ale-type beers were dubbed *Sacch. cerevisiae*, and those used for making bottom-fermentation beers or lagers as *Sacch. carlsbergensis*. These strains are differentiated by the ability of the latter strains, as distinct from *Sacch. cerevisiae*, to hydrolyse the disaccharide melibiose. However, Van der Walt (1970) preferred to include strains previously recognized as *Sacch. carlsbergensis* in the species *Sacch. uvarum*, a redesignation which has been very unenthusiastically received by the principal users of strains of *Sacch. carlsbergensis*, namely the brewing fraternity. Yeasts that are principally responsible for the fermentation of grape juice to make wines were originally known, dating from the description of Reess (1870), as *Sacch. ellipsoideus*. Van der Walt (1970) was even less convinced of the need for a distinction to be made between these wine yeasts and strains of *Sacch. cerevisiae*, and he included them in the same species without any varietal distinction. Even more confusion surrounds the name *Sacch. beticus*, strains of which are traditionally associated with production of the fortified wine, sherry. The name was first used to describe strains isolated from Spanish wines by Marcilla *et al.* (1936), the specific epithet *beticus* being derived from the Roman word Baetica (Andalusia). It came to be held that strains of *Sacch. beticus* are responsible, in part at least, for the characteristic flavour of Spanish sherry. Then Lodder and Kreger-Van Rij (1952) preferred to call this species *Sacch. fermentati*, while Van der Walt (1970) refused to recognize the species at all, and included all strains which had hitherto been known as *Sacch. beticus* in *Sacch. cerevisiae*. But events are coming to full cycle, for Barnett and Pankhurst (1974) recognize *Sacch. beticus* as a separate species.

Yeast taxonomists, in common with other microbiologists who set out to classify groups of micro-organisms, strive to place organisms in genera and species that reflect their phylogenetic relationships. It is just unfortunate that the strains of *Saccharomyces* that are used to produce alcoholic beverages and potable spirits happen to be yeasts whose properties have yet to be fully evaluated from a phylogenetic standpoint. Nor is the prognosis for a more stable state of affairs at all propitious for, as industrially important strains of *Saccharomyces* are subjected to greater genetic manipulation, the chances of arriving at an agreed and lasting classification cannot be reckoned to be very great.

2. Important Properties of Strains of Saccharomyces Used in Production of Alcoholic Beverages

Strains of *Saccharomyces* employed in the manufacture of alcoholic beverages have a number of properties in common which make them useful in these industries, and demark them from related groups of yeasts and other micro-organisms.

a. *Ability to effect an efficient alcoholic fermentation of sugars.* Reference has already been made to this fundamentally important property required of strains of *Saccharomyces* used in the manufacture of alcoholic beverages and potable spirits. The bio-chemical basis of the property is discussed in Section III.B (p. 21) of this chapter. From a microbiological standpoint, it is of interest in that it is a property not possessed to anything like the same degree by other groups of micro-organisms which might conceivably, taking into consideration other requirements (such as lack of patho-genicity), be used to manufacture beverages. Certain bacteria produce ethanol as a fermentation end-product, but along with other fermentation products which would render any beverages produced by these bacteria totally unacceptable.

Despite the importance of the fermenting ability of strains of *Saccharomyces*, very few quantitative studies have been made on this property. The fermenting ability of strains of *Saccharomyces* cannot be assessed simply by comparing their behaviour during production of alcoholic beverages and liquids, because the conditions under which they are acting—conditions such as sugar concentration, availability of other nutrients, and temperature—differ even when considering just one type of beverage. It is however possible to compare the fermenting ability of strains when these are examined under strictly defined laboratory conditions. So far, this has only been attempted to any great extent for strains used in the brewing of beer. Thorne (1954) introduced the term *fermentation velocity* which he defined as the number of millilitres of carbon dioxide at N.T.P. evolved by one gram wet weight of yeast in one hour, using a standard nitrogen-free substrate solution containing 10% (w/v) glucose under strictly defined conditions. The rate of gas production is measured in a fermentometer apparatus, shaken at constant speed (120 cycles per minute) and maintained at 20°C. Thorne (1954) reported a wide 'variation in the fermentation velocities of a collection of brewing yeasts, ranging from as little as 5 to as much as 35 ml carbon dioxide per gram of yeast per hour. A later publication from Thorne (1961) related the fermentation velocity of a strain to the nitrogen content of the cells, and he defined the ratio of these two values as the *fermentation efficiency* of a strain. Surveying the fermentation efficiencies of a collection of yeasts, which included some 250 strains of bottom-fermenting yeasts and 150 strains of top-fermenting yeasts, Thorne (1961) found that the latter group have significantly higher fermentation efficiencies (14.1 ± 0.1) compared with top yeasts (12.2 ± 0.2). Distillery yeasts in the collection had higher fermentation efficiencies (13.8 ± 0.4) compared with ale yeasts (12.6 ± 0.3).

Despite these attempts by Thorne to bring some uniformity into measurements of the fermenting ability of strains of *Saccharomyces*, he has attracted few fellow travellers. This is probably because most industrial users of yeasts wish only to compare a range of strains for a particular fermentation process, and so use conditions for measuring fermenting ability that resemble those that the strains will encounter under production conditions. An example of this more pragmatic approach to comparing the fermenting abilities of yeasts came recently in a report of a study on hybridizing strains of brewer's yeasts to produce improved strains for beer production. In this study, Anderson and Martin (1975) used fermentation ability as one of their more important characteristics. They quoted values for parent and hybrid strains in the range 5–10 μl carbon dioxide produced/min/mg dry weight at pH 5.0 and 25°C, and employed a Gilson apparatus to measure the rate and as substrate either ale wort (specific gravity, 1.060) or glucose or maltose each at 6% (w/v). As the efficiency of pure cultures of *Sacch. cerevisiae* assumes greater importance in the production of alcoholic beverages, more attention will undoubtedly be paid to assessing quantitatively the fermenting ability of strains of this yeast.

b. *Ethanol tolerance.* Closely related to the ability of strains of *Saccharomyces* to bring about an efficient alcoholic fermentation of sugars is the requirement to remain viable and also to grow and to ferment in the presence of concentrations of ethanol which may reach 16% (v/v) or even higher. Despite the obvious importance of this property, strangely little research has been carried out on it. There has however been a recent upsurge of interest in this property in strains of *Sacch. cerevisiae* because many brewers have begun to appreciate the economic advantages that could come from producing beers with a high content of ethanol (of the order of 8–9%, v/v) and then diluting these high-gravity beers to give the marketed product.

The importance of ethanol tolerance was first appreciated over half a century ago when Guilliermond and Tanner (1920) found that differences between the fermenting ability of various species of *Saccharomyces*, as well as between different strains of one species, were attributable to differences in their capacity to tolerate the presence of ethanol. Thereafter, research on ethanol tolerance in yeasts proceeded in a decidedly desultory fashion. Gray, in a series of papers in the 1940s, was the only person until quite recently to show any interest in the problem. He (Gray, 1941) confirmed that ethanol tolerances differ considerably among various species of yeast, including species outside the genus *Saccharomyces*, a finding which has more recently been confirmed specifically for strains of *Sacch. cerevisiae* by Ismail and Ali (1971a). The latter workers reported however that none of the 20 strains that they studied was capable of growing in the presence of 12% (v/v) ethanol. Gray (1945) also showed that ethanol tolerance in *Sacch. cerevisiae* is influenced by environmental factors, including the concentration of sugar in the growth medium as well as by the lipid and protein contents of the yeast (Gray, 1948).

Ethanol is an amphipathic molecule, and it is difficult to believe that its primary toxic effects on the yeast cell are not at the plasma membrane. Nevertheless, in spite of the wealth of data that are available on the lipid composition of *Sacch. cerevisiae* (Hunter and Rose, 1971; Rattray *et al.,* 1975), studies on the effect of ethanol on the plasma membrane of *Sacch. cerevisiae*, particularly in so far as action of the alcohol may be influenced by the lipid composition of the plasma membrane, have yet to be reported. Of some significance in this connection is a recent publication by Hayashida *et al.* (1974) who showed that unsaturated fatty acids, when incorporated into anaerobically-grown *Sacch. saké* (recognized as a strain of *Sacch. cerevisiae*; Lodder, 1970), enhanced the ethanol tolerance of their strain of yeast.

Apart from the report by Ismail and Ali (1971b), data on the genetic basis of ethanol tolerance in *Sacch. cerevisiae* are not available. These workers claim, somewhat predictably, that the genetic basis of ethanol tolerance is complex, and certainly involves a wide variety of genes. It would be of interest to know how ethanol tolerance is altered in mutants of *Sacch. cerevisiae* that have genetic lesions which affect properties of the plasma membrane.

c. *Production of organoleptically desirable compounds.* The taste, flavour and bouquet of an alcoholic beverage are attributable in only small part to the ethanol content of the drink. The main attraction of an alcoholic beverage to the palate and to the sense of smell, and more importantly the principal components which distinguish one beverage from another, are a wide variety of compounds present in the drink at fairly low concentrations, some of which are produced by action of the yeast on one or more components of the sugar-containing raw material. The Herculean task of identifying these compounds in various alcoholic beverages and potable spirits is as yet far from complete. Section III.B.2 (p. 28) of this chapter describes some of the compounds that are known to contribute to the organoleptic qualities of beverages and spirits.

Over the ages, the brewer, wine-maker and distiller have many times discovered quite empirically that some yeasts produce a beverage or spirit that is particularly acceptable and attractive. There can be no doubt that at least some of the desirable qualities conferred by a yeast are attributable to the ability of the strain or mixture of strains to excrete in sufficient quantity certain organic compounds that affect the taste and smell of the beverage or spirit, and as such this is a microbiologically desirable property in a strain of *Sacch. cerevisiae* used for making beverages or spirits. However not until more data are available on the chemical nature of these organoleptically desirable compounds, and on factors which influence their secretion by yeasts, will it be possible to select strains of *Saccharomyces* on this basis for use in the production of specific beverages and spirits.

d. *Strain stability and viability.* The fact that alcoholic beverages, and fermented liquids that are subsequently distilled, have been produced with the aid of yeasts for many centuries shows that the strains of *Saccharomyces* which brought about these fermentations must have been reasonably stable micro-organisms. The knowledge of yeast physiology acquired over the past century, and the advances in fermentation technology that have occurred in more recent times, have permitted a detailed assessment to be made of strain stability among species of industrially important yeasts, and at the same time have paradoxically made the problem less important because industrial microbiologists have been persuaded to pay more attention to it. Nevertheless, even today some alcoholic beverages (such as certain ciders and table wines) are produced under conditions where the source of the principal strain of yeast is poorly understood, with the strain emerging as a result of a complex sequence of ecological changes in the flora of the fermenting juice. Such strains of *Saccharomyces* must have a very pronounced survival capacity. In recent years, industrial microbiologists have paid more attention to the conditions under which yeast, which is to be used in the production of alcoholic beverages, is cultured or harvested, and maintained, so that problems of strain stability are less frequently encountered although they are now far better appreciated.

Instability in a yeast strain can range from a tendency to lose viability after being harvested from a fermentation and stored, to the loss of ability to produce in low concentration one or more compounds that contribute to the organoleptic qualities of a beverage or spirit. Manifestation of any type of instability must reflect changes in the yeast genome. Unfortunately, almost nothing is known about the genetic basis of the more subtle properties of commercial yeast strains, especially the ability to excrete organoleptically desirable compounds.

However, a few data are available on the retention of viability in strains of *Saccharomyces*. Death of a micro-organism usually follows quite rapidly when the organism is deprived of nutrients. This is a situation which yeast used in industry frequently encounters, as for example when stored after being harvested from a brewery fermentation or when pressed into a cake to be used in the production of potable spirits. Death of a cell, which to the microbiologist means inability to reproduce sufficiently to yield a clone or colony, can follow the development of any one of a great variety of metabolic lesions.

At the centre of any discussion on retention of microbial viability is the ability of a cell to produce ATP. Even when growing and dividing, but much more so when not growing, there is a continual turnover of microbial cell constituents, that is a breakdown followed by an ATP-requiring resynthesis of the cell components. The energy or ATP required to keep a cell alive, without leading to reproduction of the cell, is known as the maintenance energy, and values for this requirement have been calculated for a number of micro-organisms. When a micro-organism is deprived of nutrients, the ability of that cell to retain the ability to multiply will depend on the speed at which the lytic enzymes act to break down cell constituents, and the extent to which the organism can call upon intracellular energy reserves and mobilize these reserve compounds to produce ATP. Not much is known about the activities of lytic enzymes in strains of *Saccharomyces*, or of the manner in which these activities are manifested when a yeast cell is deprived of nutrients. It is known however that several lytic activities in actively growing cells of *Sacch. cerevisiae* are located in intracellular structures often referred to as vacuoles. The first report of this intracellular location of lytic enzyme activities described the presence of nucleases and proteases in yeast vacuoles and, when reporting this discovery, Matile and Wiemken (1967) made the prescient comment that yeast vacuoles may function as the yeast lysosome. There have since been several other reports of lytic enzymes present in yeast vacuoles, and the list now includes glucanases (Matile *et al.*, 1971; Cortat *et al.*, 1972), as well as mannanases and lipases (Cartledge *et al.*, 1976). Moreover, it has been suggested that, during the cell cycle in *Sacch. cerevisiae*, the vacuole fragments to give a population of smaller vesicles, which become located in the region of envelope growth and are thought to be concerned in the growth process (Sentandreu and Northcote, 1969). Research at the Eidgenössische Technische Hochschule in Zurich (Cortat *et al.*, 1972; Matile *et al.*, 1972) and in my own laboratory (Cartledge *et al.*, 1976) has led to the separation of fractions rich in vacuoles or small vesicles, and further characterization of their enzymic and lipid composition. Presumably, when a yeast cell encounters starvation conditions, the enzymes contained in these vacuoles (which are more accurately described as large vesicles) and small vesicles escape from these structures and catalyse breakdown of cell constituents which, when the cell is unable to synthesize ATP, cannot be resynthesized.

Strains of *Saccharomyces* are known to synthesize two carbohydrate energy reserves, namely the disaccharide trehalose and the polysaccharide glycogen, and to store appreciable amounts of both compounds (Manners, 1971). Chester (1963, 1964) reported that the amounts of trehalose and glycogen present in several brewing strains of *Sacch. cerevisiae* differed quite widely, although in general the glycogen content accounted for about 10% of the cell dry weight while the amounts of trehalose present were much smaller (Stewart *et al.*, 1950). When cells of *Saccharomyces* spp. encounter starvation conditions, ATP can be produced by catabolism of trehalose, which involves action of the enzyme trehalase to yield glucose, and of glycogen, breakdown of which is catalysed by a phosphorylase and an amylo-1,6-glucosidase. There is evidence, too, that RNA can be used as a source of ATP by yeasts when they are subjected to starvation conditions (Day *et al.*, 1975). Strains of *Sacch. cerevisiae* (Higuchi and Uemura, 1959) and *Sacch. carlsbergensis* (Lewis and Phaff, 1964) both degrade RNA when incubated under nutrient-free conditions, and excrete ultraviolet-absorbing compounds. Ribonucleic acid is most likely used as a source of ATP when the reserves of trehalose and glycogen have been exhausted.

Recently, research by Atkinson and his colleagues has begun to clarify the extent to which micro-organisms can be deprived of ATP before they lose the ability to multiply. This work has introduced the concept of the *energy charge* or *adenylate charge* of a population of micro-organisms (Atkinson, 1968), which is calculated by measuring the concentrations of AMP, ADP and ATP in the population, and using the equation:

$$\text{Energy charge} = \frac{0.5[\text{ADP}] + 2[\text{ATP}]}{[\text{AMP}] + [\text{ADP}] + [\text{ATP}]}$$

Values for the energy charge, as calculated from this formula, fall in the range 1.0–0.0. Actively growing micro-organisms possess an energy charge in the range 0.7–0.8. When the energy charge of a suspension of *Escherichia coli* falls below about 0.5, the bacteria lose their viability (Chapman *et al.*, 1971). The situation is however different with *Sacch. cerevisiae*, the energy charge of which can fall to as low as 0.15 without any impairment to cell viability (Ball and Atkinson, 1975). This discovery would seem to explain, to some extent at least, how strains of *Sacch. cerevisiae* have been successfully maintained over the centuries for production of alcoholic beverages.

e. *Flocculation.* In the production of alcoholic beverages and of alcoholic liquids for subsequent distillation, a prime requirement is an efficient but at the same time controlled conversion of sugar into ethanol and carbon dioxide by the yeast used as an inoculum or by the strains of *Saccharomyces* that become the principal members of the microbial flora. Some strains of *Saccharomyces* have a tendency, in the later stages of a batch fermentation, to agglomerate and to form flocs which settle to the bottom of the fermentation vessel. This phenomenon, which is known as *flocculation*, has for long been recognized as a very important one in production of alcoholic beverages. In order to achieve maximum conversion of sugar into ethanol and carbon dioxide, it is essential for the yeast to remain suspended in the fermenting liquid and not to flocculate. At the same time, the ability of the yeast to flocculate when the fermentation has been completed, or reached the desired stage, is an advantage to the manufacturer of alcoholic beverages because it greatly assists in the removal of yeast from the beverage. In other words, the yeast should ideally flocculate only at the desired stage in a fermentation, a stage that varies with different beverages and with different types of any one beverage. Much also depends on the type of vessel in which the fermentation is being carried out. This is well illustrated in the brewing of beer, where the flocculation characteristics of a yeast used in open fermenting vessels may be quite unsuitable for producing beer in the recently introduced cylindro-conical vessels. The required flocculation characteristics of a yeast vary, therefore, not only with the type of beverage being produced, but also with the design of the vessel in which it is being produced. With fermentations from which the yeast is not removed, such as those used in the manufacture of distilled spirits, flocculation of the yeast is on the whole an undesirable property, since the aim is to keep the yeast in suspension until the fermented liquid is distilled.

Although the importance of yeast flocculation in the manufacture of alcoholic beverages has been appreciated for almost a century, yeast physiologists are still profoundly ignorant of the biochemical basis of flocculation (Rainbow, 1966; Stewart, 1975). At present, the consensus of opinion is that anionic groups already present, or produced in the stationary phase of growth, in the yeast wall form salt bridges with counterpart groups in other cells through calcium ions. Additional secondary bonds may also be involved in the cell-cell adhesion. The major unsolved problems in flocculation are the nature of the anionic groups that participate—some workers (Lyons and Hough, 1970a, b; 1971) believe that these are phosphodiester linkages in the wall mannan while others (Stewart et al., 1975; Jayatissa and Rose, 1976) contend that they are carboxyl groups in the acidic wall protein—and the manner in which flocculating ability becomes manifest only at the end of a brewery fermentation. The sheer complexity of the cell wall in Saccharomyces strains suggests that these questions will remain unanswered for some years to come. Meanwhile, it is pleasing to note that attention is being given to the complex genetics of flocculation in Sacch. cerevisiae (Lewis et al., 1976).

f. Strain improvement. Attempts are continually being made to improve the performance of micro-organisms that are used industrially to manufacture various chemicals, such as organic acids and antibiotics (see volume 2 of this series). The techniques used are many and varied, and range from selection of variants from the parent strain to sophisticated mutagenesis programmes. Manufacturers of alcoholic beverages have also striven to acquire better performing strains of Saccharomyces, although by comparison with other fermentation industries, such as those concerned with antibiotic production, their efforts have been rather puny. The reason for this comparative lack of interest in strain improvement is that the properties required of a strain of Saccharomyces used in, say, brewing of beer are so multifarious that an enhancement in one property may be undesirable because it is not matched or balanced by an appropriate adjustment in the expression of other interconnected properties of the strain. Nevertheless, some efforts have been made at strain improvement, particularly in recent years.

There are four main ways in which the composition of a microbial genome can be changed, namely mutation, conjugation, transformation and transduction. Dealing with strains of Saccharomyces, only three of these methods have been contemplated, because there has not so far been any evidence reported for the existence of a yeast phage or virus which would allow transduction to be used in strain improvement. Double-stranded viruses have been reported to infect strains of Sacch. cerevisiae during mating (Lhoas, 1972), but this does not lead to transduction since there is no evidence that the viral genomes are expressed in the yeast host.

Transformation is a well established phenomenon among several groups of bacteria, but whether this method for changing the composition of a genome can be used with strains of *Saccharomyces* is still much in dispute. Some years ago, Oppenoorth (1959, 1961) claimed that transformation can be effected with strains of *Saccharomyces*, although reports confirming and developing Oppenoorth's claim did not subsequently appear in the literature. The issue has recently been resurrected following the publication of somewhat more rigorous evidence for transformation in genetically labelled strains of *Saccharomyces* by Khan and Sen (1974). It will be interesting to see to what extent this latest claim can be substantiated.

Strains of *Saccharomyces* are tremendously popular organisms in studies in the basic cell biology of eukaryotic organisms, and these studies have been assisted extensively by the large numbers of mutant strains of *Saccharomyces* that have been isolated. Many collections of *Saccharomyces* mutants have been assembled, and a list of some of the better characterized mutants available has been compiled by Plischke *et al.* (1976). Techniques for obtaining mutant strains of *Saccharomyces* have been described by Kilbey (1975). The mutant strains of *Saccharomyces* isolated using these methods are necessarily haploid, since mutant strains from cells of higher ploidy are almost impossible to obtain. This fact makes application of mutation in any programme for improving industrial strains of *Saccharomyces* of little value, since these strains are almost invariably diploid, aneuploid or polyploid.

To date, the only method for altering the composition of the genome in *Saccharomyces* spp. which has been successfully applied to industrial strains is conjugation. Strains of *Saccharomyces* are members of the Ascomycetaceae, and diploid strains have the capacity to produce asci containing four (or often fewer) haploid ascospores. Unfortunately, sporulating ability is often poorly manifested in industrially important strains of *Saccharomyces* (Fowell, 1969; Emeis, 1958), added to which the few spores that are formed often have low viability or fertility. A number of techniques have been advocated for overcoming these problems, particularly for separating the small proportion of spores from vegetative cells by oil flotation (Gutz, 1958) or electrophoresis (Resnick *et al.*, 1967). Hybridization has been successfully applied in programmes designed to obtain improved strains of baker's yeast (Burrows and Fowell, 1961a, b), of strains of *Saccharomyces* with ability to produce greater quantities of ethanol (Kosikov, 1963), and of strains used in brewing beer (Gilliland, 1951; Anderson and Martin, 1975). Currently, many other users of industrial strains of *Saccharomyces* are exploring the possibilities of using hybridization to improve their strains.

B. Biochemistry

1. Alcoholic Fermentation

a. *Embden–Meyerhof–Parnas pathway*. The principal biochemical process in the production of alcoholic beverages is the catabolism by strains of *Saccharomyces* of simple sugars to yield a mixture of ethanol and carbon dioxide. The stoicheiometry of the process was known well over a century and a half ago, and was described in 1815 by the famous Gay-Lussac equation:

$$C_6H_{12}O_6 \rightarrow 2C_2H_5OH + 2CO_2$$

But research into the reactions involved in the conversion of sugars into ethanol and carbon dioxide could not commence until it was possible to carry out an alcoholic fermentation in the absence of living yeast cells. It has already been noted that this event occurred in 1897, when the Buchner brothers and Hahn (Buchner *et al.*, 1897) demonstrated that sugars can be fermented in the absence of yeast cells by a juice expressed from the cells (see p. 5). This discovery virtually gave birth to the science of biochemistry, and paved the way for a most exciting half century of research during which the details of the dozen biochemical reactions that are involved in the conversion of glucose into ethanol and carbon dioxide were unravelled. Many workers were involved, but the major contributions came from the laboratories of Gustav Embden in Frankfurt, Otto Meyerhof in Heidelberg, and Jacób Karol Parnas in Lwow (now in the Ukraine, U.S.S.R.), which explains why the pathway is usually known as the *Embden–Meyerhof–Parnas* (E.M.P.) pathway. The intermediates on the E.M.P. pathway are shown in Figure 1, and the enzymes involved are listed in Table 1. The book by Harden (1932) and the review by Nord and Weiss (1958) give much of the

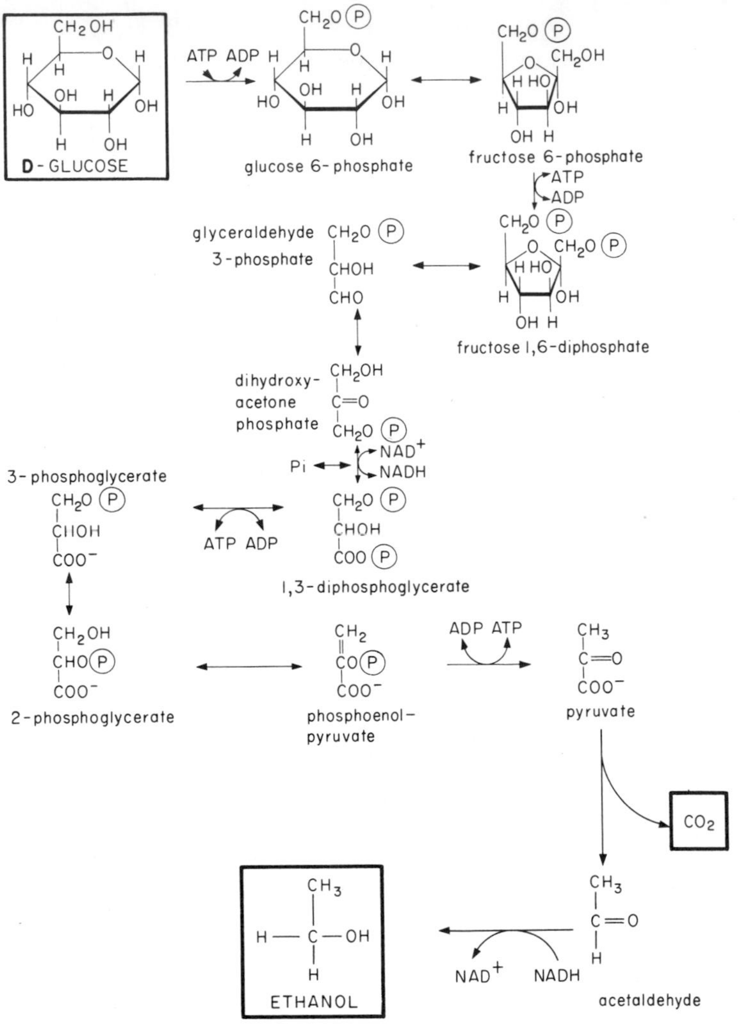

Fig. 1. The Embden–Meyerhof–Parnas pathway.

interesting background to the charting of this glycolytic pathway, while more up-to-date information on it has come from Sols *et al.* (1971).

The first reaction involves phosphorylation of glucose to give glucose 6-phosphate, a reaction catalysed by hexokinase. A very active glucosephosphate isomerase catalyses the second reaction, and maintains an equilibrium of glucose 6-phosphate and fructose 6-phosphate in the ratio of about 3:1. Phosphorylation of fructose

Table 1

Data on reactions involved in conversion of glucose to ethanol and carbon dioxide by strains of *Saccharomyces* via the Embden–Meyerhof–Parnas pathway

Reaction number	Reaction catalysed	Name of enzyme involved	Cofactors
1	Glucose + ATP → glucose 6-phosphate + ADP	Hexokinase	Mg^{2+}
2	Glucose 6-phosphate ⇌ fructose 6-phosphate	Glucosephosphate isomerase	
3	Fructose 6-phosphate + ATP → fructose 1,6-diphosphate + ADP	Phosphofructokinase	Mg^{2+}
4	Fructose 1,6-diphosphate ⇌ glyceraldehyde 3-phosphate + dihydroxyacetone phosphate	Aldolase	Zn^{2+} (enzyme-bound)
5	Dihydroxyacetone phosphate ⇌ glyceraldehyde 3-phosphate	Triosephosphate isomerase	
6	Glyceraldehyde 3-phosphate + NAD^+ + Pi ⇌ 1,3-diphosphoglycerate + NADH	Glyceraldehyde 3-phosphate dehydrogenase	
7	1,3-Diphosphoglycerate + ADP ⇌ 3-phosphoglycerate + ATP	Phosphoglycerate kinase	Mg^{2+}
8	3-Phosphoglycerate ⇌ 2-phosphoglycerate	Phosphoglycerate mutase	2,3-diphosphoglycerate
9	2-Phosphoglycerate ⇌ phosphoenolpyruvate + H_2O	Enolase	Mg^{2+}
10	Phosphoenolypyruvate + ADP → pyruvate + ATP	Pyruvate kinase	
11	Pyruvate → acetaldehyde + CO_2	Pyruvate decarboxylase	Thiamin pyrophosphate; Mg^{2+}
12	Acetaldehyde + NADH ⇌ ethanol + NAD^+	Alcohol dehydrogenase	Zn^{2+} (enzyme-bound)

6-phosphate to yield fructose 1,6-diphosphate is catalysed by phosphofructokinase, a reaction that is virtually irreversible *in vivo*. An
aldolase catalyses cleavage of fructose 1,6-diphosphate into a mixture
of dihydroxyacetone phosphate and glyceraldehyde 3-phosphate.
This is the key reaction on the pathway, and explains why the
pathway has also been referred to as the *hexose diphosphate
pathway*. Interconversion of these two cleavage products is catalysed
in reaction 5 by a triose phosphate isomerase. The equilibrium is
displaced in favour of dihydroxyacetone phosphate but, as glyceraldehyde 3-phosphate is removed in the next step on the pathway,
the reaction during glycolysis proceeds in the direction of glyceraldehyde 3-phosphate formation. Oxidation of glyceraldehyde
3-phosphate to give 1,3-diphosphoglycerate is catalysed by glyceraldehyde 3-phosphate dehydrogenase. In the next reaction, catalysed
by phosphoglycerate kinase, 1,3-diphosphoglycerate is converted
into 3-phosphoglycerate, the high-energy acyl phosphate bond of the
substrate being transferred to ADP. 3-Phosphoglycerate is converted
into 2-phosphoglycerate in a reaction catalysed by phosphoglycerate
mutase, which requires for activity catalytic amounts of
2,3-diphosphoglycerate. Dehydration of 2-phosphoglycerate to yield
phosphoenolpyruvate is catalysed by enolase, in a reaction in which a
low-energy phosphate bond is converted into a high-energy phosphate bond. Pyruvate kinase then catalyses cleavage of phosphoenolpyruvate into pyruvate in a reaction in which a high-energy
phosphate bond is transferred to ADP. In the penultimate step on
the pathway, pyruvate is decarboxylated to yield acetaldehyde and
carbon dioxide, in a reaction catalysed by pyruvate decarboxylase.
Finally, the acetaldehyde formed is reduced to ethanol by $NADH^+$ in
a reaction catalysed by alcohol dehydrogenase, thereby regenerating
NAD.

Rarely, if ever, is glucose the only sugar available for fermentation
by yeasts in production of alcoholic beverages and potable spirits. It
is, however, present in appreciable concentrations in most of the raw
material extracts used in these fermentations, either as a sugar
derived from breakdown of starch or one present in a fruit juice.
Glucose enters the yeast cell by way of one or more transport
proteins located in the plasma membrane. A wide range of other
sugars are available to the yeast cell for fermentation in the
production of most beverages and spirits. Fructose, which is com-

monly found in fruit juices, can be phosphorylated by hexokinase to give fructose 6-phosphate which enters the E.M.P. pathway in reaction 2 (Table 1). Two disaccharides, sucrose and maltose, are frequently made available to yeasts during production of alcoholic beverages and potable spirits. Sucrose is often found in fruit juices, including apple juices used to make cider. This disaccharide is hydrolysed to a mixture of glucose and fructose by the enzyme invertase (β-fructofuranosidase) which is a mannan-protein located in the walls of *Saccharomyces* spp. When starchy raw materials are used, starch is degraded prior to fermentation to maltose together with smaller amounts of oligosaccharides that include maltotriose and maltotetraose (Manners, 1971). Maltose is hydrolysed to glucose by the yeast enzyme maltase. The efficiency of a yeast fermentation is enhanced when the strain can utilize maltotriose and maltotetraose to yield fermentable sugars. Not all strains of *Saccharomyces* have this property, and it is one which is highly desirable in strains, such as those used in brewing beer, which are used to ferment raw materials derived from starchy substrates.

As an energy-yielding process, the E.M.P. pathway is woefully inefficient. The maximum amount of energy obtainable from conversion of a glucose molecule into two molecules of pyruvate, that is the standard free energy change or $\Delta G'_0$ value of the reaction, is $-47,000$ cal/mole. Since the net energy yield from one molecule of glucose is two molecules of ATP, and the standard free energy of the two high-energy phosphate bonds formed in the ATP molecules is 7,300 cal/mole, the E.M.P. pathway is only about 30% efficient as an energy-yielding process.

b. *Other anaerobic glycolytic pathways used by* Saccharomyces *strains.* Like all other micro-organisms, yeasts have to use the available sources of carbon and energy (in the case of yeasts furnished by one compound, namely glucose) to produce: (a) metabolic energy in the form of ATP; (b) low molecular-weight intermediates used in the synthesis of new cell components; and (c) reducing power, in the form of NADH and NADPH, since yeast constituents are on average in a more reduced state than the nutrient sugar. In view of these requirements, it is easy to predict that not all of the glucose fermented by strains of *Saccharomyces* is catabolized to ethanol and carbon dioxide by the E.M.P. pathway. Certain of the intermediates on the E.M.P. pathway, such as pyruvate, are used in the biosynthesis of cell constituents. Moreover, some of the NADH generated in reaction 6 of the pathway can also be used in the synthesis of new cell constituents. But, if either or both of these compounds are so used, the E.M.P. pathway will quickly cease to operate because of a lack of NAD^+. If reaction 12 is not operative, regeneration of NAD^+ can be effected in yeast by an alternative reaction, namely reduction of dihydroxyacetone phosphate to glycerol 3-phosphate:

$$
\begin{array}{l}
CH_2OH \\
| \\
C = O \\
| \\
CH_2O.PO_3H_2
\end{array}
\quad
\begin{array}{cc}
NADH & NAD^+ \\
\end{array}
\quad
H^+
$$

$$
\begin{array}{l}
CH_2OH \\
| \\
CHOH \\
| \\
CH_2O.PO_3H_2
\end{array}
\quad Pi \quad
\begin{array}{l}
CH_2OH \\
| \\
CHOH \\
| \\
CH_2OH
\end{array}
$$

The glycerol phosphate formed is hydrolysed by a specific phosphatase to yield glycerol which in turn is excreted by the cell (Gancedo *et al.*, 1968). The classical studies of Carl Neuberg first showed that small amounts of glycerol are produced in most alcoholic fermentations carried out by yeasts. Regeneration of NAD^+ in this way is thought to operate at the beginning of a glucose fermentation when the amount of acetaldehyde available to the cell is insufficient to support efficient activity of the ethanol dehydrogenase in step 12 (Holzer *et al.*, 1963).

However, the yeast cell cannot rely exclusively on reduction of dihydroxyacetone phosphate to regenerate NAD^+ since this would denude the cell of low molecular-weight compounds, such as pyruvate, required for synthesis of new cell constituents. Instead, strains of *Saccharomyces* use another glycolytic pathway to generate reducing power required to synthesize cell components. This pathway is the *hexose monophosphate* (H.M.P.) or *Warburg-Dickens* pathway. Details of this pathway can be found in any of the basic texts on microbial biochemistry (Mandelstam and McQuillen, 1973; Rose, 1976a). Estimates have been made, using radioactively labelled glucose as substrate, of the relative extent to which the E.M.P. and H.M.P. pathways are used in catabolism of glucose by strains of

Saccharomyces. These have shown (Blumenthal *et al.*, 1954) that, when *Sacch. cerevisiae* is grown anaerobically, up to 95% of the glucose assimilated is metabolized by the E.M.P. pathway. This contrasts with aerobically growing *Sacch. cerevisiae* which metabolizes only 70% of glucose assimilated via the E.M.P. pathway.

c. *Regulation of energy-yielding metabolism in* Saccharomyces *strains*. While production of ethanol and carbon dioxide by strains of *Saccharomyces* is accompanied by synthesis of ATP, it has to be remembered that these micro-organisms are facultative aerobes, and that they have the ability when oxygen is available to oxidize pyruvate completely using reactions of the tricarboxylic acid cycle. Much has been written on the manner in which anaerobic and aerobic pathways of catabolism are regulated in yeasts. Louis Pasteur discovered the inhibition of yeast fermentation by respiration, a phenomenon which represented the first observation on metabolic regulation and one which has intrigued microbial physiologists ever since (Racker, 1974). While a complete explanation of the *Pasteur effect* has yet to be forthcoming, it would seem that at least three processes are involved, namely feedback inhibition of isocitrate dehydrogenase activity by AMP, of phosphofructokinase activity by ATP and citrate, and of the activity of glucose-transport proteins by glucose 6-phosphate. This last process leads to a decreased rate of glucose transport into the cell, a quite 'rational' regulatory measure since the yield of ATP by oxidation of pyruvate greatly exceeds the yield from the E.M.P. pathway (Sols *et al.*, 1971).

There is also an inhibition of respiration by fermentation in strains of *Saccharomyces*. This regulatory process, which was first studied by Ephrussi *et al.* (1956), has been termed the *Crabtree effect* because the phenomenon was first observed in tumours by Crabtree (1929). Since one of the main aims of the manufacturer of alcoholic beverages and potable spirits is to bring about an efficient fermentation of sugars into ethanol and carbon dioxide using strains of *Saccharomyces*, operation of the Crabtree effect is clearly important in these strains. The effect is probably brought about by a combination of catabolite repression, caused by the presence in yeast fermentations of high concentrations of sugars, and the virtual absence of functional mitochondrial structures in yeast cells growing under conditions of near anaerobiosis that obtain in these fermentations (Sols *et al.*, 1971).

2. Production of Organoleptically Important Compounds

It has already been stressed (Section III.A, p. 14) that the organoleptically desirable properties of an alcoholic beverage or distilled
spirit are only in small part attributable to the content of ethanol in
the drink. Many of the physiological effects, as well as the distinctive
taste and aroma of a beverage or spirit, are ascribed to the presence
in the drink of low concentrations of organic compounds that
include among others alcohols, aldehydes, acids, esters and sulphur-
containing compounds. The availability of sophisticated analytical
methods, particularly the gas-liquid chromatograph often coupled up
to a mass spectrometer, has made identification of these compounds
a relatively straightforward task, although a time-consuming one
because of the extremely large number of compounds involved.
Suomalainen and Nykänen (1968) have reviewed the analytical
methods employed. Individual chapters in this volume refer to
compounds that are thought to be responsible for the characteristic
flavour and aroma of the beverage or spirit which forms the subject
of the chapter, and the reader should turn to these chapters for a
fuller account of the appropriate organoleptic compounds. Some
workers, notably A. Dinsmoor Webb at the University of California
at Davis, and Heikki Suomalainen and his colleagues at the Laboratories of the State Alcohol Monopoly in Helsinki, Finland, have
made comparative studies on the types and concentrations of
flavour-producing compounds in different beverages and spirits, and
have shown that, although some compounds are peculiar to a
particular drink or type of drink, in general the compounds that are
responsible for flavour and bouquet in beverages and spirits are of
the same types irrespective of the nature of the drink. It has
moreover been established that, while the flavouring compounds in a
drink may be present in concentrations as high as milligrams per litre,
or as low as micrograms per litre, the contribution which the
compounds make to the flavour of the drink cannot be predicted
from the concentration present, since the taste threshold values for
compounds differ very considerably. Moreover, the taste threshold
values for a particular compound can be changed when that compound is present along with other organoleptic compounds. Importantly, too, it has been shown that the taste threshold of a
compound may be altered by the presence of ethanol (Rankine,

1967). The metabolic origin of these organoleptically important compounds has been the subject of intensive study for many years, and there is now an extensive amount of data on this problem. Some organoleptically important compounds are present in the raw-material extract used to manufacture the beverage or spirit, and remain unaltered during the fermentation and distillation to contribute to the flavour and aroma of the final drink. Other compounds in the extract may be changed chemically by the yeast or during distillation to produce derivatives that influence the flavour and aroma of the product. During fermentation, yeast excretes other compounds which also add to the spectrum of organoleptically desirable compounds in the drink. Finally, other compounds may appear in the drink as a result of its being stored in wooden casks.

The remainder of this section of the chapter deals briefly with the main classes of organoleptically important compounds that have been detected in alcoholic beverages and distilled spirits, with some discussion of their origin. Authoritative reviews on the subject have come from Margalith and Schwartz (1970), Webb and Muller (1972) and Suomalainen et al. (1974).

a. *Higher alcohols.* Quantitatively, and in terms of their flavour-producing effects, the most important group of compounds present in beverages and spirits are the higher alcohols, often referred to as fusel alcohols or fusel oils. These compounds are usually detected in drinks in concentrations of the order of milligrams per millilitre. In beers and wines, organoleptically the most important higher alcohols are amyl and isoamyl alcohols, together with 2-phenethanol a compound with a strong rose-like odour (Engan, 1974). The concentrations of these compounds is higher in red as compared with white wines (Guymon and Heitz, 1952). Distilled spirits have a rather different range of higher alcohols, which include butanols and pentanols.

Higher alcohols are synthesized from oxo acids, which are decarboxylated to yield aldehydes that are in turn reduced to alcohols. Formally, these reactions are analogous to the synthesis of ethanol from pyruvate via acetaldehyde (see Fig. 1). The oxo acids may be formed during carbohydrate metabolism by the yeast, or by deamination or transamination of an amino acid (Webb and Ingraham, 1963). Some examples of the reactions that lead to formation of higher alcohols from amino acids are given in Figure 2.

Strains of *Saccharomyces* have been reported to contain a single enzyme which catalyses transamination reactions that lead to formation of the various oxo acids, as well as just one species of decarboxylase for converting oxo acids to aldehydes (SentheShanmuganathan, 1960). However, Kunkee and Singh (1975) recently reported that there are probably several different alcohol dehydrogenases responsible for formation of the individual higher alcohols from the corresponding aldehydes.

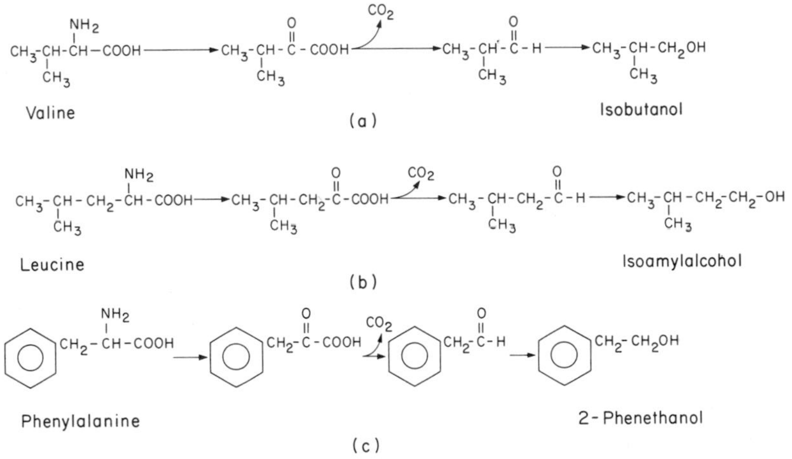

Fig. 2. Examples of pathways which lead to formation of higher alcohols from amino acids.

The polyhydric alcohol glycerol is present in almost all alcoholic beverages and spirits, and in wines there may be as much as 1% (w/v) glycerol. Glycerol gives 'body' to a drink. It has already been noted (see p. 26) that this compound arises as a result of reduction of dihydroxyacetone phosphate, and subsequent hydrolysis of the glycerol phosphate formed.

b. *Aldehydes and ketones.* Aldehydes are formed by decarboxylation of oxo acids during the formation of higher alcohols, and it is likely that many of the aldehydes that have been detected in alcoholic beverages and spirits arise in this way. Many of these aldehydes have low taste threshold values. They include saturated straight-chain aldehydes ranging from formaldehyde to hexanal, as well as iso-aldehydes. Acetaldehyde is one of the commonest, and in beers it has been shown to be produced mainly during the early stages of fermentation and later to disappear (Sandegren and Enebo,

1961). The diketone diacetyl, and to a lesser extent 2,3-pentanedione, are extremely important organoleptic compounds in alcoholic beverages and spirits (Wainwright, 1973). Diacetyl has a flavour which has been variously described as resembling 'butter', 'butterscotch' and 'toffee', and it has a taste threshold concentration of 0.1–0.5 mg/l depending on the beverage. The overwhelming evidence is in favour of diacetyl being formed from α-acetolactate, itself an intermediate on the pathway for synthesis of the amino acids leucine and valine from pyruvate (Rose, 1976a), although some workers believe that an alternative pathway, involving a reaction between hydroxy-ethylthiamin pyrophosphate, may also operate. Many strains of *Saccharomyces* can reduce diacetyl to acetylmethyl carbinol.

c. *Organic acids.* A very wide range of organic acids have been detected in beverages and spirits, and these include both short-chain and long-chain acids. Among the shorter chain acids, acetic, lactic and *n*-butyric acids are the most abundant, while among the longer chain acids that are commonly detected are caproic, capric and lauric acids. Scotch whisky is worth mentioning in this context since it, among potable distilled spirits, is unique in containing detectable amounts of palmitoleic acid (Suomalainen *et al.*, 1974). The metabolic origins of these acids have not been researched to any great extent. Acetic acid could well arise from acetyl-CoA, an intermediate in both synthesis and degradation of long-chain fatty acids in yeasts. Shorter chain acids might be formed by β-oxidation of long-chain (C_{16} or C_{18}) acids, which takes place even during active growth of the yeast. The longer chain acids are most likely produced from their coenzyme-A esters which are involved in synthesis of phospholipids, triacylglycerols and sterol esters (Rose, 1976b).

d. *Esters.* A wide variety of esters, corresponding to and probably synthesized from the alcohols and organic acids already referred to, have been reported to occur in alcoholic beverages and potable spirits. Of these, ethyl acetate is present in organoleptically important concentrations in very many drinks, as are to a lesser extent ethyl formate and isoamyl acetate (Margalith and Schwartz, 1970). It must be presumed, in the absence of definite information, that these esters are synthesized in reactions that involve the alcohol and the coenzyme-A ester of the acid, and which are catalysed by acyl transferases.

e. *Sulphur-containing compounds.* Many compounds, both

inorganic and organic, which contain the sulphur atom are well known to smell, often pungently. Alcoholic beverages and potable spirits frequently contain low concentrations (of the order of μg per litre) of certain sulphur-containing compounds which can contribute to the flavour and aroma of the drink. By the same token, when these compounds are present in higher concentrations, they may give rise to obnoxious flavours and aromas. Because they usually occur in beverages and spirits in low concentrations, information on the nature of many of these sulphur-containing compounds, and the precise concentration at which they occur, is far from complete, although considerable progress has been made in recent years following the introduction of sensitive sulphur-specific detectors which can locate these compounds as they emerge from gas-liquid chromatographic columns. Profound ignorance also surrounds the metabolic origin of many of these organoleptically important compounds.

Although they are detectable in most beverages and potable spirits, our understanding of the nature of the sulphur-containing compounds that influence the taste and bouquet of drinks is most extensive for beers. Hydrogen sulphide has been detected in a wide range of beers in concentrations that range from over 100 μg/litre to as little as 1 μg/litre (Anderson and Howard, 1974). Various organic mercaptans and sulphides have also been reported to be present in beers (Sinclair et al., 1969). Interestingly, a claim has recently been made that dimethyl sulphide makes an important contribution to the flavour of lager beer (Anderson et al., 1975).

Wainwright (1972) has reviewed available information on the metabolic origins of organoleptically important sulphur-containing compounds. Some of these compounds, or precursors of them, arise from the malt and hops used to brew beer, while others would seem to be minor metabolic products of strains of Saccharomyces. These metabolic products presumably arise as a result of small but significant lesions arising on pathways that are concerned with metabolism of sulphur-containing amino acids and with dissimilatory sulphate reduction by yeast strains. Little is known about the finer aspects of metabolic regulation on these pathways, and this information must be available before the brewing microbiologist can begin to explain the origin of many of the sulphur-containing compounds that affect the taste and aroma of beers.

IV. WORLD-WIDE PRODUCTION OF ALCOHOLIC BEVERAGES

A. Range of Beverages and Spirits Produced

The alcoholic beverages described in this volume—and they include beers, wines made from grapes, apples and other fruits, fortified wines as well as saké—are those whose production methods have been most extensively researched both microbiologically and biochemically. Together they account for the major part of the total volume of alcoholic beverages produced in the World. However, as anyone travelling to, or spending a vacation in, some of the less well developed countries knows, there are scores of other alcoholic beverages produced in the World, usually on a fairly small scale and for largely local consumption. Very little is usually known of the microbiology and biochemistry of their manufacture. In future years, some of these beverages will undoubtedly offer a formidable challenge to the fermentation microbiologist. For example, further research on the microbiological and biochemical changes that take place in the manufacture of palm wines (Ahmad *et al.*, 1954; Simonart and Laudelot, 1951) is now attracting some attention (Okafur, 1972). But such research is only justified when the data obtained can be expected to lead to a greater efficiency in the production process and in control over the quality of the drink.

The present work is less expansive when describing the production of potable spirits, dealing as it does with only gin, vodka, rum and whisky. The scores of other spirits which are distilled for human consumption are manufactured on a smaller scale, and largely for local consumption. Johnson's (1969) delightfully produced book is one of the few sources of information on lesser known distilled spirits. Again, because of the small scale of production, little has been discovered about the scientific basis of the manufacture of these spirits. Many of these less well known potable spirits resemble neutral spirits, and their production cannot be very different from that used to manufacture gins and vodkas. Brazilian pinga would seem to be in this category. But other distilled spirits have much more character of their own. Again, one might give as an example arracks, which are produced by distillation of palm wines.

Although the final arbiters of the quality of any alcoholic beverage or potable spirit are the human palate and sense of smell, such is the importance of these drinks as sources of tax revenue in almost all countries of the World that a variety of methods have been devised for indicating quantitatively the alcoholic strength (not necessarily indicative of the quality), or some value which can be taken as a measure of the alcoholic strength, of a beverage or spirit. Legislation in several countries, particularly in Europe, makes it mandatory for manufacturers of alcoholic beverages to indicate on the label the content of alcohol in the beverage. Elegant and accurate methods are available for measuring the content of ethanol in a beverage or spirit (Tate, 1930). For convenience, hydrometers have traditionally, and indeed still are, used for measuring this value. Hydrometers measure the specific gravity of a liquid, a value which depends on the temperature. This temperature dependence of specific gravity is the cause of much of the confusion which has existed with regard to measuring the alcoholic strength of beverages and spirits. Tables are available for relating the specific gravity of a beverage or spirit to the alcohol content at a particular temperature. Adjustments need to be made if the gravity is measured at a temperature different from that on which the table was constructed. Many countries, France for example, quote the alcohol contents of their wines as per cent by volume, on a scale that runs from 0% (water) to 100% (absolute alcohol). An older method uses the same scale but in degrees rather than percentages; these are degrees Gay-Lussac, named after the French physicist. The Tralles system used in Austria, Italy and Russia is very similar, but at 60°F rather than 59°F. Other countries, such as West Germany, quote the alcohol content of their wines as per cent by weight (Windisch system) and not by volume.

While the strength of beers can be quoted in terms of the alcohol content of the drink, traditionally brewers throughout the World have used a variety of other scales, a practice which has occasioned a considerable amount of confusion. When a medium containing a moderately high concentration of sugar is fermented by a strain of *Saccharomyces*, conversion of sugars into ethanol leads to a drop in the specific gravity of the culture medium. But brewers very rarely refer to specific gravity, but simply to the 'gravity' of their wort or beer, which is the value for the specific gravity multiplied by 1,000. For example, a beer with a final gravity of 1008 is one which has been fermented to a specific gravity of 1.008. Moreover, the brewers have introduced this terminology into their manufacturing processes. When they refer to an original gravity of, for example ten forty, they mean that the malt wort which was used to brew the beer had a specific gravity of 1.040.

Since it is impossible to draw up accurate tables relating the specific gravity of brewer's malt wort and the percentage sugar composition, simply because of the heterogeneous nature of wort composition, brewers resorted to a system in which they related the specific gravity of the wort, measured using various types of hydrometer but usually referred to as saccharometers, to the notional content of cane sugar (sucrose) in the wort. Tables describing this relationship were published in 1843 by von Balling, with the result that the strength of brewer's malt worts came to be measured in degrees Balling. There were slight inaccuracies in Balling's tables, and more accurate tables were published in Germany in 1900 by F. Plato. The use of degrees Plato to describe the strength of worts is still common in several countries. Nor is this the end of the story, for the Brix and Baumé tables were later constructed also relating the solute content of extracts or worts to their specific gravity. Brix values relate grams of cane sugar to 100 grams of solution from specific gravities measured at 20°C; they are still used widely, notably in the table wine industries of many countries (see Chapter 4, p. 338). Baumé tables are based on salt solutions, and are related to the tables of Plato by use of a modulus. Tables relating these various scales for measuring wort strength can be found in Bates *et al.* (1942).

The alcoholic strength of some potable spirits is quoted using the terms already described, but not so in the Scotch and American whisky industries. Again, the reasons for these industries adopting different systems are historical. Before hydrometers came into general use, a rough and ready standard for the strength of a whisky was that it should contain 50% (v/v) alcohol, and *proof* that this standard had been attained was made by dampening gunpowder with the spirit. If the gunpowder still ignited, the alcohol content was satisfactory; if not, the spirit was said to be 'under proof' and contained excess water. The increasing importance to governments of the revenue which came from duty on sale of potable spirits called for the setting up of more exact standards of measurement, and the

Spirits Act of 1916 in Britain adopted Sikes's hydrometer for official purposes and gave the first definition of proof spirit. Further legal revisions followed, and the Customs and Excise Act of 1952 in Great Britain stated 'Spirits shall be deemed to be proof if the volume of the ethylalcohol contained therein made up to the volume of the spirits with distilled water has a weight equal to that of 12/13ths of a volume of distilled water equal to the volume of the spirits, the volume of each liquid being computed at 51°F'. This means that, at 51°F (equal to 10.5°C), British proof spirit (that is spirit of 100 degrees proof) contains 48.24% by weight or 57.06% by volume of alcohol. The proportions are often quoted at 60°F (15.5°C) instead of 51°F, when they become 49.28% by weight and 57.1% by volume. On the scale of Sikes's hydrometer, absolute ethanol is 175.1 degrees proof. In the United States of America, 100 degree proof spirit is taken to contain 50% alcohol by volume at 60°F, rather than the awkward British value of 57.1%. Readers should consult Chapter 11 (p. 635) for more information on proof spirit as applied to British and American whiskies.

B. Present Size and Future Prospects

Largely because of the great variety of alcoholic beverages and potable spirits produced in the World, efforts to collect reliable production data for any one year for a particular drink usually fail. Regular attempts are, however, made, for example by the International Union of Pure and Applied Chemistry, whose two latest reports have been published (World Survey of Fermentation Industries, 1963, 1971). Individual chapters in this volume comment on the scale of production for the beverages or spirits described, some more extensively than others. Data from the various sources show that annual production of beers now approaches almost three quarters of a million hectolitres, while annual production of wines of various types is approaching half a million hectolitres. Total annual production of potable spirits in the World is probably around 50,000 hectolitres.

World-wide production of all types of beverage and spirit rises steadily each year, which attests the buoyant condition of the producing industries. Future prospects must therefore be extremely rosey. But whether future expansion will be along the lines already taken—with the same types of beverage and spirit being produced—or whether the lesser known drinks will become more popular, especially in the larger consuming countries, is a matter for speculation.

C. Problems

While consumption of alcoholic beverages and potable spirits has on the whole given tremendous pleasure to mankind over the centuries, and has often contributed materially to the literary and musical expression of the human spirit, it has to be admitted that drinking alcoholic beverages and spirits can with some individuals become compulsive and uncontrolled. The disease of alcoholism, which this is, is now a major sociological problem—sometimes admitted by governments, sometimes not—in very many countries of the World. The literature on alcoholism is voluminous—and one journal, the *Quarterly Journal of Studies on Alcohol*—deals exclusively with the disease and related problems. Manufacturers of alcoholic beverages and potable spirits are required to keep a careful watch on the problems of alcoholism as they are manifested in the areas of the World in which their products are retailed.

V. ACKNOWLEDGEMENTS

I should like to thank my many friends and colleagues in the alcoholic beverage industries, in many countries of the World, who over the years have patiently dealt with the many questions put to them in my efforts to probe the scientific basis of their profession.

REFERENCES

Ahmad, M., Chaudhury, A. R. and Ahmad, K. U. (1954). *Mycologia* 46, 708.
Anderson, R. J. and Howard, G. A. (1974). *Journal of the Institute of Brewing* 80, 357.
Anderson, R. J. and Martin, P. A. (1975). *Journal of the Institute of Brewing* 81, 242.
Anderson, R. J., Clapperton, J. F., Crabb, D. and Hudson, J. R. (1975). *Journal of the Institute of Brewing* 81, 208.
Atkinson, D. E. (1968). *Biochemistry, New York* 7, 4030.

Ball, W. J. and Atkinson, D. E. (1975). *Journal of Bacteriology* 121, 975.
Barnett, J. A. and Pankhurst, R. J. (1974). 'A New Key to the Yeasts', 273 pp. North-Holland Publ. Co., Amsterdam.
Bates, F. J., Bowman, N. L., Brawns, D. H., Brewster, J. F., Cragoe, C. S., Frush, H. L., Golden, P. E., Hammond, L. D., Hubbell, M. L., Isabell, H. S., Jackson, R. F., McDonald, E. J., Phelps, F. P., Pigman, W. W., Proffitt, M. J., Saunders, J. B., Snyder, C. F. and Tool, A. Q. (1942). 'Polarimetry, Saccharimetry and the Sugars', 810 pp. National Bureau of Standards Circular No. C440. Washington, D.C.
Blumenthal, H. J., Lewis, K. F. and Weinhouse, S. (1954). *Journal of the American Chemical Society* 76, 6093.
Buchner, E., Buchner, H. and Hahn, M. (1897). 'Die Zymasegärung.' R. Oldenberg, Munchen, West Germany.
Bulder, C. J. E. A. (1964). *Antonie van Leeuwenhoek* 30, 1.
Burrows, S. and Fowell, R. R. (1961a). *British Patent* 868, 621.
Burrows, S. and Fowell, R. R. (1961b). *British Patent* 868, 633.
Cartledge, T. G., Belk, D. M. and Rose, A. H. (1976). *Journal of Bacteriology* in press.
Chapman, A. C. (1931). *Journal of the Institute of Brewing* 37, 433.
Chapman, A. G., Fall, L. and Atkinson, D. E. (1971). *Journal of Bacteriology* 108, 1072.
Chester, V. E. (1963). *Biochemical Journal* 86, 153.
Chester, V. E. (1964). *Biochemical Journal* 92, 318.
Clayton, E., Howard, G. A. and Martin, P. M. (1972). *Proceedings of the Annual Meetings of the American Society of Brewing Chemists* 78.
Conant, J. B., ed. (1952). *Harvard Case Histories in Experimental Science, Case 6.* Harvard University Press, Cambridge, Mass.
Corran, H. S. (1975). 'A History of Brewing', 303 pp. David and Charles, London.
Cortat, M., Matile, P. and Wiemken, A. (1972). *Archiv für Mikrobiology* 82, 189.
Crabtree, H. G. (1929). *Biochemical Journal* 23, 536.
Day, A., Anderson, E. and Martin, P. A. (1975). *Proceedings of the European Brewing Convention, Nice*, 377.
Dubos, R. (1950). 'Louis Pasteur, Free Lance of Science', 418 pp. Little Brown, Boston, Mass., U.S.A.
Dubos, R. (1960). 'Pasteur and Modern Science', 159 pp. W. H. Heinemann, London.
Emeis, C. C. (1958). *Naturwissenschaften* 45, 441.
Engan, S. (1974). *The Brewers Digest* August, 52.
Ephrussi, B., Slonimski, P. P., Yotsuyanagi, Y. and Tavlitski, J. (1956). *Compte Rendus des Traveaux du Laboratoire Carlsberg, Series Physiologique* 26, 87.
Fowell, R. R. (1969). *In* 'The Yeasts' (A. H. Rose and J. S. Harrison, eds.), Vol. 1, pp. 303-383. Academic Press, London.
Gancedo, C., Gancedo, J. M. and Sols, A. (1968). *European Journal of Biochemistry* 5, 165.
Gilliland, R. B. (1951). *Proceedings of the European Brewing Convention, Brighton*, 35.
Gray, W. D. (1941). *Journal of Bacteriology* 42, 561.
Gray, W. D. (1945). *Journal of Bacteriology* 49, 445.

Gray, W. D. (1948). *Journal of Bacteriology* 55, 53.

Guilliermond, A. and Tanner, F. W. (1920). 'The Yeasts.' 424 pp. John Wiley and Sons, New York.

Gutz, H. (1958). *Brauerei Wissenschaft Beilage* 11, 149.

Guymon, J. F. and Heitz, J. E. (1952). *Journal of the Science of Food and Agriculture* 6, 359.

Harden, A. (1932). 'Alcoholic Fermentation', 243 pp. Longmans, Green and Co., London.

Hardwick, W. A. (1975). *Technical Quarterly of the Master Brewers Association* 12, 90.

Hayashida, S., Feng, D. D. and Hongo, M. (1974). *Agricultural and Biological Chemistry* 38, 2001.

Higuchi, M. and Uemura, T. (1959). *Nature, London* 184, 1381.

Holzer, H., Bernhardt, W. and Schneider, S. (1963). *Biochemische Zeitschrift* 336, 495.

Huber, E. (1926). *'Bier und Bierbereitung bei dem Völkern Urzeit'*, Berlin.

Hunter, K. and Rose, A. H. (1971). *In* 'The Yeasts' (A. H. Rose and J. S. Harrison, eds.), Vol. 2, pp. 211-270. Academic Press, London.

Ismail, A. A. and Ali, A. M. (1971a). *Folia Microbiologica* 16, 346.

Ismail, A. A. and Ali, A. M. (1971b). *Folia Microbiologica* 16, 350.

Jayatissa, P. M. and Rose, A. H. (1976). *Journal of General Microbiology* 96, 165.

Johnson, H. (1969). 'The World Atlas of Wine', 272 pp. Mitchell Beazley, London.

Jørgensen, A. (1948). 'Micro-organisms and Fermentation', 15th edition. Trans. by A. Hansen. Charles Griffin and Co. Ltd., London.

Khan, N. C. and Sen, S. P. (1974). *Journal of General Microbiology* 83, 237.

Kilbey, B. J. (1975). *In* 'Methods in Cell Biology' (D. M. Prescott, ed.), Vol. 12, pp. 209-231.

King, F. A. (1947). 'Beer has a History', 180 pp. Hutchinson's Scientific and Technical Publications, London.

Kosikov, K. V. (1963). *Mikrobiologiya* 32, 1052.

Kudriavzev, V. I. (1939). *Mikrobiologiya* 8, 393.

Kudriavzev, V. I. (1960). 'Die Systematik den Hefen', Berlin, West Germany.

Kunkee, R. E. and Singh, R. (1975). *Journal of the Institute of Brewing* 81, 214.

Layton, T. A. (1968). 'Cognac and Other Brandies', 153 pp. Harper Trade Journals, London.

Legge, J. (1893). 'Chinese Classics', Vol. 3, p. 274.

Lewis, C. W., Johnston, J. R. and Martin, P. A. (1976). *Journal of the Institute of Brewing* 82, 158.

Lewis, M. J. and Phaff, H. J. (1964). *Journal of Bacteriology* 87, 1389.

Lhoas, P. (1972). *Nature, New Biology* 236, 86.

Lodder, J., ed. (1970). 'The Yeasts, a Taxonomic Study', 1385 pp. North-Holland Publishing Co., Amsterdam, The Netherlands.

Lodder, J. and Kreger-Van Rij, N. J. W. (1952). 'The Yeasts, a Taxonomic Study', Amsterdam, The Netherlands.

Lyons, T. P. and Hough, J. S. (1970a). *Journal of the Institute of Brewing* 76, 564.

Lyons, T. P. and Hough, J. S. (1970b). *The Brewers Digest* 45 (8), 52.

Lyons, T. P. and Hough, J. S. (1971). *Journal of the Institute of Brewing* 77, 30.

Mandelstam, J. and McQuillen, K. (1973). 'Biochemistry of Bacterial Growth', 2nd edition, 582 pp. Blackwells Scientific Publications, Oxford.

Manners, D. J. (1971). *In* 'The Yeasts' (A. H. Rose and J. S. Harrison, eds.), Vol. 2, pp. 419–439. Academic Press, London.

Marcilla, J., Alas, G. and Feduchy, E. (1936). *Anals Centro de Investigacione Vinicultural* 1, 1.

Margalith, P. and Schwartz, Y. (1970). *Advances in Applied Microbiology* 12, 35.

Matile, P. and Wiemken, A. (1967). *Archiv für Mikrobiologie* 58, 201.

Matile, P., Cortat, A., Wiemken, A. and Frey-Wyssling, A. (1971). *Proceedings of the National Academy of Sciences of the United States of America* 68, 636.

Meyen, J. (1838). *Wiegmann Archives für Naturgeschichte 4, Bd.* 2, 100.

Nickerson, W. J. (1943). *Mycologia* 35, 66.

Nord, F. F. and Weiss, S. (1958). *In* 'The Chemistry and Biology of Yeasts' (A. H. Cook, ed.), pp. 323–368. Academic Press, New York.

Okafur, N. (1972). *Journal of the Science of Food and Agriculture* 23, 1399.

Oppenoorth, W. F. F. (1959). *Proceedings of the European Brewing Convention, Rome* 180.

Oppenoorth, W. F. F. (1961). *Proceedings of the European Brewing Convention, Vienna* 172.

Pasteur, L. (1866). 'Etudes sur le Vin', 387 pp. Masson, Paris.

Pasteur, L. (1876). 'Etudes sur la Bière', 387 pp. Gauthier-Villars, Paris.

Plischke, M. E., von Borstel, R. C., Mortimer, R. K. and Cohn, W. E. (1976). *In* 'Handbook of Biochemistry and Molecular Biology' (G. D. Fasman, ed.), 3rd edition, Chemical Rubber Company Press, Cleveland, Ohio.

Porter, J. R. (1972). *Science, New York* 178, 1249.

Racker, E. (1974). *Molecular and Cellular Biochemistry* 5, 17.

Rainbow, C. (1966). *Process Biochemistry* 1, 489.

Rankine, B. C. (1967). *Journal of the Science of Food and Agriculture* 18, 583.

Rattray, J. B. M., Schibeci, A. and Kidby, D. K. (1975). *Bacteriological Reviews* 39, 197.

Reess, M. (1870). 'Botanische Untersuchungen über die Alkoholgäraungspilze'. Leipzig, Germany.

Resnick, M. A., Tippetts, R. D. and Mortimer, R. K. (1967). *Science, New York* 158, 803.

Rose, A. H. (1976a). 'Chemical Microbiology', 3rd edition, Butterworths Scientific publications, London.

Rose, A. H. (1976b). *In* 'The Filamentous Fungi' (J. Smith and D. R. Berry, eds.), Vol. 2, pp. 308–327. Edward Arnold, London.

Sandegren, E. and Enebo, L. (1961). *Wallerstetin Laboratories Communications* 24, 269.

Sarton, J. (1927). 'An Introduction to the History of Science', Vol. 1. Carnegie Institute of Washington Publication No. 376. Williams and Wilkins Co., Ltd., Baltimore, Md.

Scheda, R. and Yarrow, D. (1966). *Archiv für Mikrobiologie* 55, 209.

Scheda, R. and Yarrow, D. (1968). *Archiv für Mikrobiologie* 61, 310.

Sentandreu, R. and Northcote, D. H. (1969). *Journal of General Microbiology* 55, 393.

SentheShanmuganathan, S. (1960). *Biochemical Journal* 74, 568.

Simon, A. (1948). 'Drink', 272 pp. Burke Publishing Co. Ltd., London.

Simonart, P. and Laudelot, H. (1951). *Bulletin de l'Institut Royal Colonial Belge* 22, 383.

Sinclair, A., Hall, R. D. and Thorburn-Burns, D. (1969). *Proceedings of the European Brewing Convention, Interlaken*, 427.

Smith, W. H. and Ferdinand, C. H. (1940). 'Liquor, the Servant of Man', Little Brown and Co., Boston, Mass.

Sols, A., Gancedo, S. and Gancedo, G. (1971). *In* 'The Yeasts' (A. H. Rose and J. S. Harrison, eds.), Vol. 2, pp. 271–301. Academic Press, London.

Stelling-Dekker, H. M. (1931). Die Sporogenen Hefen. *Yerhandelingen der K. academie van Wetenschappen Section II* 28, 1.

Stewart, G. G. (1975). *The Brewers Digest* 42.

Stewart, G. G., Russell, I. and Garrison, I. F. (1975). *Journal of the Institute of Brewing* 81, 248.

Stewart, L. C., Richtmeyer, N. K. and Hudson, C. S. (1950). *Journal of The American Chemical Society* 72, 2059.

Suomalainen, H. and Nykänen, L. (1968). *Wallerstein Laboratories Communications* 31, 5.

Suomalainen, H., Nykänen, L. and Eriksson, K. (1974). *American Journal of Enology and Viticulture* 25,179.

Tate, F. G. H. (1930). 'Alcoholometry', London.

Thorne, R. S. W. (1954). *Journal of the Institute of Brewing* 60, 227.

Thorne, R. S. W. (1961). *The Brewers Digest* 38.

Vallery-Radot, R. (1902). 'The Life of Pasteur', Vols. 1 and 2. Archibald Constable and Co. Ltd., London.

Van der Walt, J. P. (1970). *In* 'The Yeasts, a Taxonomic Study' (J. Lodder, ed.), pp. 555–718. North-Holland Publishing Co., Amsterdam, The Netherlands.

Wainwright, T. (1972). *The Brewers Digest* 47, 78.

Wainwright, T. (1973). *Journal of the Institute of Brewing* 79, 451.

Webb, A. D. and Ingraham, J. L. (1963). *Advances in Applied Microbiology* 5, 317.

Webb, A. D. and Muller, C. J. (1972). *Advances in Applied Microbiology* 15, 75.

World Survey of Fermentation Industries (1963). *Pure and Applied Chemistry* 13, 405.

World Survey of Fermentation Industries (1971). *International Union of Pure and Applied Chemistry Information Bulletin. Technical Report No. 3.* International Union of Pure and Applied Chemistry, Oxford.

2. Beer

ANNA M. MACLEOD

Department of Brewing and Biological Sciences,
Heriot-Watt University, Edinburgh, Scotland

I. INTRODUCTION

The definition of beer in the Pocket Oxford Dictionary as 'an alcoholic beverage made from fermented malt, etc., flavoured with hops, etc.' has the merit of being comprehensive; it names, directly or by implication, the four essential normal contributors to all types of beer, namely water, malt, hops and yeast, and leaves considerable scope for the inclusion of other ingredients. Malt similarly rates a generously broad definition as 'barley or other grains prepared by steeping and germination or otherwise, for brewing and distilling'. Acceptance of these two definitions implies that any liquid which is a fermented hop-flavoured cereal product can be classed as beer. Conversion of barley by means of added enzymes is not precluded, as the essential attributes of beer are the use of cereals as at least a partial source of fermentables, the characteristic flavour derived from hops and the final production of an alcoholic solution. This definition of beer provides a convenient frame of reference for this chapter.

II. HISTORICAL ASPECTS OF BREWING

A. Prehistoric and Early Historic

Although the origins of brewing are lost in prehistory there is little doubt that barley, the principal ingredient of beer throughout the ages, is one of the oldest of man's cultivated plants (Zohary, 1969). There is now general agreement that the ancestor of modern cultivated barleys is the wild two-rowed brittle *Hordeum spon-taneum* and, among the earliest finds of cultivated cereals, the barleys from Jarmo (6750 ± 250 B.C.) resemble *H. spontaneum* but show evidence of a tougher, less brittle, spike which would allow harvesting to be accomplished without shattering of the ear. As discussed by Helbaek (1959), six-rowed barleys appear later in the archaeological record, and the introduction of primitive cultivars to man-made habitats has been associated with spontaneous hybridiz-ation followed by continued gene-flow from wild local barleys to the cultivated forms. Selection, whether 'natural' or inadvertently humanly-controlled, must have been largely on agronomic grounds. The concept of barley specifically designed for malting is a relatively recent one, though different types of barley are recommended for different qualities of beer in early Babylonian texts (Hartman and Oppenheim, 1950).

Two major technological steps are required to complete the transformation of the raw material into the finished product, namely controlled germination (i.e. malting) which allows the ultimate production of a fermentable extract through the activities of enzymes formed during seedling growth, and fermentation. Malting improves the digestibility and palatability of raw grain, and a parallel development of the technologies of baking and brewing seems likely to have occurred long before the invention of writing and the possibility of a historical record, i.e. before 3000 B.C. Certainly the use of cakes of crushed malt which were crumbled into water to provide either a nutritious gruel or a fermentable extract is well attested in early Egyptian records (see, for example, Wild, 1966) and the use of beer-bread in the other major brewing centre of antiquity, Mesopotamia, though less well documented, also seems probable (Hartman and Oppenheim, 1950). Although it is difficult to fill in the millenia between the domestication of barley and the first permanent records of brewing, it is noteworthy that Braidwood *et al.* (1953) suggest the possibility of beer ante-dating bread in a paper provocatively entitled *Did Man Once Live by Beer Alone?* Corran (1975) has confirmed the feasibility of baking malt bread at Egyptian summer temperatures and subsequently fermenting the mash made by crumbling the loaf into warm water; the resulting unfiltered beer contained 3–5% alcohol.

Fermentation must initially have been fortuitous, but the importance ascribed to the brewer's conical vat in early pictograms and to the dregs therein in early texts attests the realization that some extraneous agent was required to transform the sweet, bland malt mash to a more interesting drink. The part played by the yeast cell was not properly appreciated before the work of Pasteur in the 19th Century; the brewster of antiquity (for the profession was a female one in Old Babylonian times) derived divine protection from the goddess Siris, who doubtless assumed some responsibility for the mysterious and desirable transformations performed by the yeast.

Various aromatic herbs were used to flavour beer in early historic times, and there have been suggestions (Bickerdyke, 1886) that hops were cultivated and used in brewing in Babylonia at the time of the captivity, though their use does not seem to have been general.

Details of processing of beer in early historic times are not easy to come by. Filtration does not seem to have been practised in Mesopotamia, and fermented mash, including husks, was imbibed communally through tubes from knee-high conical containers (see, for example, cylinder seal impressions in Hartman and Oppenheim, 1950). In ancient Egypt, however, various types of filter including a horse-hair sieve were in vogue, and packaging of beer was into clay bottles sealed by baked clay stoppers (Wild, 1966). Wild also comments that brewing technology in Egypt showed very little change in procedure between the Vth and the XVIIIth Dynasties, a period of over one thousand years.

Finally, it comes as no surprise to learn that, even in ancient Mesopotamia, beer was subjected to legislation with regard to quality, and to taxation in the form of tribute, in kind, to the temple authorities (Kramer, 1958).

B. Brewing in Europe

To the Greeks, beer was a barbarian (i.e. foreign) drink, and wine was the preferred alcoholic beverage of the Romans, though Helbaek (1964) provides good evidence for the existence of a maltings, and so presumably a brewery, in the Roman legionary fortress at Caerleon in Wales, where spelt (*Triticum spelta*), rye and a small proportion of six-rowed barley were carbonized and so preserved in an identifiable form as a result of a kiln fire.

Although cereal-based fermented beverages found little favour in the two major civilizations of classical antiquity, it is clear from the writings of Dioscorides, Pliny and Tacitus that beer was the standard drink of most other European countries—Germany, Gaul, Spain and Britain—though mead was also popular. Much has been written elsewhere about the technological and social history of beer in Europe, and only reference to some key works need be given here.

The early history of brewing in England is well covered by King (1947) and by Monckton (1966). Hoffman (1956) provides a useful account of developments in brewing in Germany, and Nordland (1969) has surveyed traditional brewery equipment used throughout the ages in Norway.

Apart from the gradual acceptance of hops as a standard flavouring (and, possibly, preservative) agent for beer, there have been few major changes in the ingredients used in brewing. The earliest European record of a hop garden appears to be at Hallertau in 736 (Corran, 1975) and hops slowly, and not without objections largely from vested interests, replaced the traditional 'gruit' of mediaeval brewers—a mixture of aromatic herbs such as eyebright, coriander, rosemary, yarrow and bog myrtle. The brewing of hopped beer spread from Germany to the Netherlands and thence to England where there was prolonged opposition to the 'foreign' drink attempting to supplant 'honest English ale'. Bickerdyke (1886) gives an entertaining account of this centuries-long conflict between ale and beer. That hopped beer emerged triumphant is at least partly attributable to the fact that large numbers of Flemish immigrants settled in Kent in 1524, and there introduced the cultivation of hops, so initiating the earliest English hop gardens. However, old customs die hard in brewing, and, as late as 1860, bog myrtle (*Myrica gale*) was regularly used in brewing in Sweden in place of hops (von Hofsten, 1960).

The use of sugar in brewing was first legally permitted in England in 1847 and, with the exception of Bavaria where the Reinheitsgebot of 1516 which restricts brewing materials to malt, hops and yeast still prevails, sugar and syrups are now familiar components of fermentable extracts in most parts of the world.

Though brewing materials of today would be recognized by the mediaeval brewer, brewing plant would not. Corran (1975), in a fascinating survey of changing brewing technology which he considers in terms of materials of vessel construction from the clay period of the Ancient World via the wooden period, which is still partly with us, to the metal period of today, gives a very full account of the introduction of now-familiar items of brewing equipment ranging from thermometers to sparging systems and wort-coolers—all undreamed of in the 17th Century. Readers are referred to Corran's (1975) book for a complete account of the development of brewing technology over the past three hundred years.

To complement this general account, reference must also be made to histories of individual brewing companies usually commissioned to commemorate some anniversary. These histories provide a wealth of detail on types of beer and on local innovations in the brewing process: see, for example, Denison (1955), Pudney (1971), Serocold (1949) and Strong (1957).

III. OUTLINE OF THE BREWING PROCESS

The principal operations carried out in brewing are illustrated schematically in Figure 1. In the controlled germination, or malting, of barley the main objective is to produce enzymes which serve, either during malting or later, to hydrolyse polymerized reserve materials of the grain and so allow the extraction of, *inter alia*, fermentable sugars and amino acids. The changes in grain texture accompanying malting are described as 'modification' and they, and enzyme action, are arrested by kiln drying.

Mashing of the crushed grain with water at temperatures of up to $67°C$ causes rapid degradation of solubilized starch, and less extensive hydrolysis of other high-molecular substances, and is followed by a leaching process (sparging) which completes the separation of the solutes from the spent grains. The resulting 'sweet wort' is boiled in a copper, or kettle, traditionally with hops, and a further separation is then required of spent hops and precipitated high-molecular material (the trub) from the hopped wort, which is then cooled. The specific gravity of wort rises as increasing amounts of sugars are extracted, and reference to appropriate tables allows transformation of values for specific gravity to 'extract', either as a percentage (de Clerck, 1958) or as pounds per quarter of malt (Recommended Methods of Analysis, Institute of Brewing, 1971).

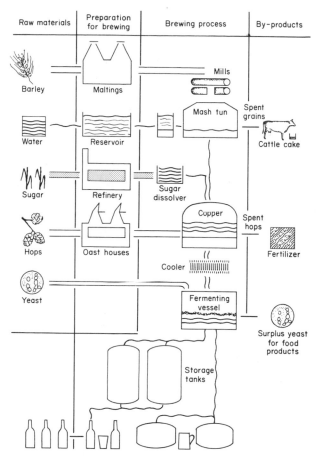

Fig. 1. Schematic outline of operations carried out in the brewing process. Reproduced by courtesy of the Institute of Brewing.

After adjustment to the desired specific gravity, the wort is 'pitched' with a selected strain of yeast. As the yeast grows and ferments the sugars of the wort, the gravity falls, a process known as attenuation. When fermentation has reached near the attenuation limit, the yeast is separated from the immature or 'green' beer, which is allowed to mature for an appropriate period and, after filtration, pasteurization and possibly other treatments, the beer is ready for despatch as draught or tank beer or for packaging into kegs, bottles or cans.

Brewing plant and brewing technology have developed by a

process of industrial evolution, with trial and error and survival of
the fittest, over at least 4,000 years, but only over the last century
has there arisen any real understanding of the scientific principles—
biological, biochemical and physico-chemical—underlying the use of
techniques which experience has shown to yield a product which is
satisfactory, economically as well as organoleptically. The evolution
of brewing from a cottage craft via an industrial art to a science-
based technology is not yet complete, but recent developments in
plant design, in automation and above all, in scientific understanding
of the raw materials and of the operations required to transform
them to beer, have gone a long way towards making brewing a
scientific process. The remainder of this chapter will therefore
concentrate on current understanding of the basis of present-day
brewing technology.

IV. MALTING

A. Suitability of Barley for Brewing

The domestication of barley and wheat initially led to their use in
agriculture-based crafts, but the survival of barley as a major
ingredient of the brewer's mash-tun is not wholly due to the innate
conservatism of the practitioners of an ancient art. There are at least
three attributes of the barley grain which make it peculiarly suitable
to the brewing process as we know it today.

First the husk, which surrounds the caryopsis, appears to afford
considerable microbiological protection during large-scale malting.
Compared with huskless cereals such as wheat, germinating barley is
normally reasonably free from mould growth, though undesirable
medical effects of unacceptable levels of fungal growth on malting
barley have occasionally been reported (Riddle *et al.*, 1968).
Secondly, the husk of barley provides a useful filter aid during
traditional methods of wort separation. Thirdly, and more important than either of the first two points, the gelatinization temperature of malt starch (Table 1) is lower than that at which α-amylase
(one of the principal agents involved in the production of fermentable sugars) is inactivated. This, together with the presence of
significant amounts of β-amylase in barley and in barley malt, make

Table 1

Temperature range for gelatinization of cereal
starches. From Brenner (1972)

Cereal	Gelatinization range ($^\circ$C)
Barley	52–59
Wheat	58–64
Rye	57–70
Maize	62–72
High-amylose maize	67–>80[a]
Rice	68–77
Sorghum	68–77

[a] Gelatinization is incomplete at 100°C.

it possible for solubilization and hydrolysis of malt starch to be
accomplished economically in one operation. New methods of
processing may invalidate some of these reasons for the pre-eminence
of barley and barley malt in brewing, and there is no reason (apart
from restrictive legislation) why advantage should not be taken of
other economically desirable sources of starch, provided such starch
sources are without deleterious effects on beer properties.

B. The Malting Process

The principal objectives of malting are: (i) to promote synthesis by
the grain of hydrolytic enzymes including endo-β-glucanase,
α-amylase and peptidases; (ii) to secure solubilization of the walls of
the endosperm cells and then enzymic degradation of the soluble
constituents to materials of low molecular-weight; (iii) to allow
degradation of the reserve protein to an appropriate mixture of
polypeptides and amino acids; and (iv) to accomplish operations i–iii
as rapidly and as economically as possible.

The ungerminated grain contains β-amylase, part of which is
readily extractable in salt solutions and part only in the presence of
sulphydryl agents (LaBerge and Meredith, 1971). Alpha-amylase is
virtually absent from ungerminated barley, and its synthesis and that
of certain other hydrolytic enzymes is accomplished by the aleurone
cells (Fig. 2) in response to the hormone gibberellic acid (GA), which

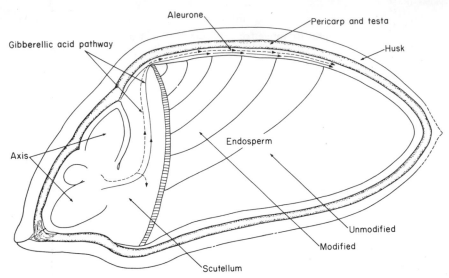

Fig. 2. Longitudinal section through a barley grain. After Palmer (1969).

is secreted from the embryo to the aleurone, within the first 24 hours after the grain has imbibed water and has access to oxygen (MacLeod and Millar, 1962; MacLeod and Palmer, 1966; Palmer, 1974). The rate of formation of certain GA-controlled hydrolytic enzymes is shown in Figure 3.

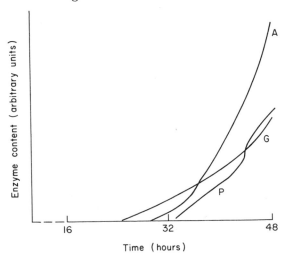

Fig. 3. Formation of the principal hydrolytic enzymes during malting of barley. A indicates α-amylase; G, endo-β-glucanase; P, peptidase. Isolated endosperms treated with gibberellic acid (0.5 p.p.m.) show a similar pattern of enzyme formation, though production of enzymes starts 8–10 hours sooner (MacLeod et al., 1964).

The endosperm cell walls contain insoluble and water-soluble β-linked glucan and pentosan, and the amounts of the soluble polymers (β-glucan particularly) rise during the early stages of malting, a rise which is associated with an increase in viscosity of extracts of the grain (Fig. 4). Though the mechanisms involved in the

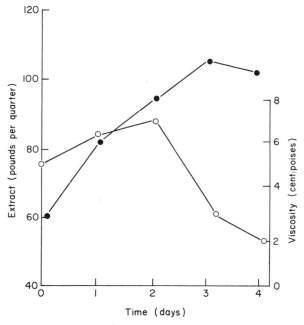

Fig. 4. Changes in wort viscosity (open circles) and in extract (solid circles) during a laboratory malting of barley at 18°C. Unpublished data from the author's laboratory.

initial solubilization of the walls are not fully known (see Bathgate *et al.*, 1974, for a detailed discussion of the problem), endo-β-glucanase activity, as measured by the fall in viscosity of a solution of barley β-glucan, certainly rises during malting (Manners and Marshall, 1969) and is effective in degrading the soluble β-glucan. By the end of malting it is desirable that the content of high molecular-weight soluble β-glucan be as low as possible. Pentosans and pentosanases follow a similar pattern to β-glucans and β-glucanases though at a lower level (Preece and Hoggan, 1957). The net action of the amylases during malting is to digest the small starch granules preferentially (Bathgate and Palmer, 1973); the major action of the amylases, however, takes place during mashing.

The best characterized of the peptidases which are active during malting is a carboxypeptidase (Mikola *et al.*, 1972) which increases some twenty-fold in activity during malting and is located in the starchy endosperm of the malt. The net result of proteolytic activity during malting is that, as initially shown by Bishop (1929), approximately 40% of the nitrogen-containing compounds are rendered soluble (Fig. 5) to yield: (a) amino acids which are essential for yeast nutrition; and (b) large polypeptides which may later be involved in maintaining foam stability and, in conjunction with polyphenols, in potential haze formation.

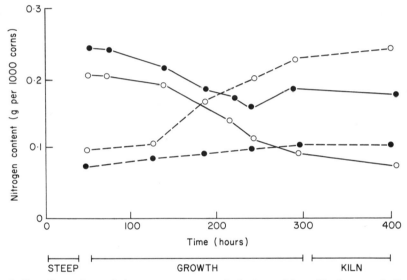

Fig. 5. Transformations of nitrogenous compounds during malting of barley. ●—● indicates changes in the content of glutelin; ○—○ of hordein; ●- - -● of albumin and globulin; and ○- - -○ in non-protein nitrogen (amino acids and polypeptides). After Bishop (1929).

The transformations effected by malting can best be appreciated by comparing electron micrographs of the endosperm of unmalted and malted barley (Fig. 6) in which elimination of the cell walls and small starch granules and the general cleaning-up of the intracellular matrix are apparent. These cellular and subcellular changes are responsible for modification of tough barley corns to the friable malt required by the brewer.

The fuller understanding of the physiology and biochemistry of malting which has developed during the last two decades has

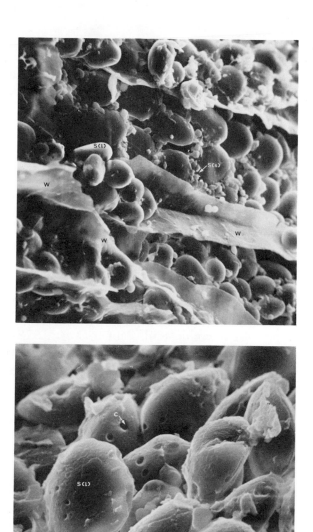

Fig. 6. Scanning electron micrographs of the endosperm of the barley grain (upper photograph) and of malt (lower photograph). Note the disappearance of (i) cell walls and (ii) small starch granules during malting. Note also the corrosion pits in malt starch granules. See Palmer (1972). W denotes a cell wall; S(l), large (25 μm) starch granules; S(s) small (5 μm) starch granules; and C a corrosion pit. The photographs are reproduced by courtesy of Dr G. H. Palmer, of the Brewing Research Foundation, Nutfield, Surrey, England.

encouraged the science-based development of improved malting techniques. Thus, an appreciation of the role of gibberellic acid (GA) in normal germination has justified adding GA at casting from the steep to augment the natural supplies of the hormone. The most recent development in accelerated malting has involved abrasion of the grains to remove a small amount of material (0.3% of the dry weight) from the distal (non-embryo) end of the grain, so that gibberellic acid added in the last steep can enter the grain more readily, and modification takes place from both ends simultaneously (Palmer *et al.*, 1970). Seedling growth is not sought for during malting; it is merely a natural concomitant of the conditions which are needed to secure the gibberellin-mediated synthesis of enzymes. Techniques for 'killing' the seedling without impairing the enzymic transformations which are required in the endosperm have been suggested. These include re-steeping the grain after 3–4 days of malting (Pollock, 1960) and treatment of abraded grains with dilute sulphuric acid in the second steep coupled with the use of an extraneous supply of gibberellic acid (Palmer *et al.*, 1972).

Limitation or abolition of seedling growth results in analytical differences in the finished malt (Table 2) since hydrolysis products of endospermic reserves are no longer remetabolized by the seedling.

Table 2

Effect of abrasion and acid treatment on the properties of barley after three days' malting. After Palmer *et al.* (1972)

	Extract (lb/quarter)	Nitrogen content (%, w/v)	Root growth (%, w/w)
Control	91.4	0.54	1.88
Treated barley[a]	103.5	0.60	0.30

[a] The treatment involved eight hours in steep water, followed by 16 hours in air and eight hours in 0.006 N H_2SO_4. Gibberellic acid (0.5 p.p.m.) was added after eight and 16 hours.

For example, the level of α-amino nitrogen is higher in acidulated gibberellin-treated malts, and allowances have to be made for this in preparing the grist for mashing; furthermore, development of colour on the kiln may be difficult to restrain to the desired limits.

The degree of success achieved in applying results of scientific studies of malting made over the past 25 years can best be appreciated by comparing the time taken, commercially, to prepare malt in the immediate post-war years and at present. In the 1940s, 11 days, exclusive of kilning, was not uncommon; today six-day malting is routinely encountered and, with abraded gibberellic acid-treated malt, 3–4 day malting schedules are in operation (Northam and Button, 1973).

There is still, however, a large gap in our understanding of the effects of barley properties on the properties of the final beer, and the complexities of the changes which occur between the raw materials and the end product are such that it is not yet possible to draw up a full specification for malting barley, as plant breeders know only too well. Any new cultivar has to be tested empirically, in pilot maltings and pilot brewings, before it can be generally accepted for brewing; see, for example, Narziss (1974) for an account of the procedures used. Minor alterations to malting variables, such as temperature, moisture content of the grain and the nature of the ambient gas mixture, can have significant effects on the malt (Narziss, 1969) and a full explanation of these effects is not yet available.

One technique which shows promise as a means of predicting some of the effects of barley on beer quality is that of iso-electric focusing (Drawert et al., 1973) as by its use the history of individual protein fractions can be followed through the whole brewing process. By use of these and other methods, analysis of new cultivars may eventually be refined to such a pitch that it can replace the trial and error procedures which have to be used today.

C. Kilning

When malting is judged to be complete, seedling growth must be arrested and the development of micro-organisms must be inhibited to allow storage of the finished malt. The requirements are fulfilled by kiln drying which has the additional effect of promoting, through the Maillard reaction (see, for example, Hodge, 1967; Greenshields and MacGillivray, 1972), formation of amino acid-carbonyl compounds which undergo further transformations to yield the coloured, aromatic, incompletely characterized compounds known as melanoidins. Inevitably, some decline in the activities of hydrolytic enzymes occurs during kilning and, in passing, one may wonder whether modern technology could not improve on the current procedure of adding water to grain to allow enzyme formation, removing that water at considerable expense, and inactivating some of the newly formed enzymes, merely to permit storage prior to mixing the crushed grain with water yet once again in the mash tun.

1. Enzyme Inactivation

Some control of enzyme inactivation is accomplished by regulation of draught and air temperature and, obviously, the moister the grain the more vulnerable its enzymes are to heat inactivation. However, as Isebaert (1965) has shown, it is possible to kiln dry to 8% moisture at a temperature of 65°C and obtain malt in which 75% of the grains retain the capacity for further growth, thus implying that there has been at least partial survival of all essential enzymes. In most commercial practice, however, not only is there complete elimination of the possibility of future growth but also a considerable diminution in the activity of the hydrolytic enzymes whose action will later be required in the mash tun. The destruction of enzymic potential is particularly marked during the final curing storage, when air temperatures rise from 65°C to 85°C or more, and moisture contents fall from about 8% to 2.5% or less. The hydrolytic enzymes vary in their sensitivity to high temperature. For example, Preece (1954) has shown that, whereas the α-amylase activity of commercial malts suffered an average decline of only approximately 4% during the final stage of curing, β-amylase levels declined to about one-third of those of malt which had not been heated above 60°C. For endo-β-glucanase activity, Preece and Hoggan (1957) found a decline of about one-third during kilning. Carboxypeptidases, however, which according to Mikola et al. (1972) are the most important of the peptidases active during malting and mashing, suffered only a minor degree of inactivation of 10-20% during the whole of kilning. Finally, there is a decrease in phytase activity (Essery, 1951) to between 20 and 40% of that found in the green malt. All of these values must be subject to considerable variation according to the kilning technique used; they are illustrative of what may happen in an 'average' kilning procedure rather than of general applicability.

2. *Development of Colour and Aroma*

The activity of hydrolytic enzymes continues during the early stages of kilning so long as the grain is moist, with the production of, *inter alia*, amino acids and reducing sugars which can condense to yield an assortment of coloured compounds of characteristic aroma. For the production of pale malts, this colour formation is minimized by rapid removal of water following forced draught at low temperatures, whereas for dark malts it is encouraged by 'stewing' in moist air on the kiln at temperatures of 50–55°C. Present knowledge of mechanisms involved in the 'browning' reaction during malting has recently been reviewed by Bathgate (1973) and it is clear that much yet remains to be learnt about the details of formation of the characteristic coloured aromatic components of malt. There is even some uncertainty about how extensively, and by what means, malt flavour contributes to beer flavour, though recent assessments by flavour profile (Clapperton, 1973) suggest that the flavour potential of the malt used may be of considerable importance in determining the typical, though chemically elusive, lager flavour *vis-a-vis* ale flavour of different types of beer. Certainly one group of compounds formed during kilning (1-valino, 1-alanino and 1-glycino derivatives of 1-deoxy-D-fructose) have been shown unequivocally to contribute to the malty flavour of beer (Yoshida *et al.*, 1972) and it is to be hoped that further studies will provide additional chemical links between malt properties and beer flavour.

V. MASHING

A. Brewing Liquor

For every hectolitre of finished beer emerging from a brewery, ten or more hectolitres of water may be consumed though, according to Meyer (1973), it should be possible to lower this figure by half. Water economy, effluent treatment and re-use of treated water are obviously of great economic importance to the brewing industry, but for the present purpose only the properties and treatment of that fraction of a brewery's water requirements which enters into the composition of the finished beer will be considered.

The location of breweries is historically related to the availability and mineral content of the local natural water supply. In Britain, for example, Burton-on-Trent and Edinburgh developed as brewing centres at least partly because of the properties of the available underground water supplies. Nowadays, however, the successful use of water-treatment systems has made the siting of a brewery largely independent of the chemical constitution of the available water, though the volume of potable water required is still an important consideration. The liquor used in mashing exercises its effect through its ionic content, especially that of Ca^{2+} and HCO_3^-. These ions influence the pH value in the mash tun (which in turn affects wort composition) as follows.

Calcium ions interact with phosphate ions to yield, *inter alia*, the insoluble tertiary salt, removal of which from solution induces a shift to the right in the system:

$$\begin{array}{ccccccc}
 & H^+ & & H^+ & & H^+ & \\
 & \nearrow & & \nearrow & & \nearrow & \\
H_3\,PO_4 & \rightleftharpoons & H_2\,PO_4 & \rightleftharpoons & H\,PO_4 & \rightleftharpoons & PO_4 \\
 & \nwarrow & & \nwarrow & & \nwarrow & \Big\downarrow \\
 & H^+ & & H^+ & & H^+ & \\
 & & & & & & Ca_3\,(PO_4)_2
\end{array}$$

Three H^+ ions are thus set free, with a consequent lowering of the pH value of the mash. Magnesium ions act in a similar manner but they are less efficacious because of the greater solubility of secondary and tertiary magnesium phosphates. The phosphate involved in this reaction is derived from the grain being mashed and, though the scheme presented above implies that the phosphate is inorganic, this is an oversimplification and phytate (inositol hexaphosphate) and its products of degradation by phytase during malting must also be involved in reactions with Ca^{2+} ions.

The lowering of the pH value of the mash from approximately 6.0, the value obtained when malt is mashed with distilled water (Hopkins, 1925), to 5.4 is associated with an increase in the fermentable extract of the wort, because of the imposition of more appropriate conditions for the activity of amylolytic and other enzymes. Although acid treatment of the mash may accomplish the same effect, the use of liquor containing 5–9 m-equiv. of Ca^{2+} per litre can be responsible for a worthwhile drop in pH value during mashing. Bicarbonate ions act in the opposite sense to Ca^{2+}. At the temperature of mashing, and to a greater extent during wort boiling, H_2CO_3 is lost as carbon dioxide and the shifting ionic equilibrium:

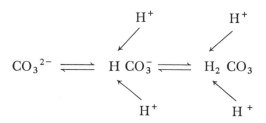

involves the uptake of H^+ ions with a consequent rise in pH value. The effect of calcium bicarbonate in brewing liquor is thus to raise the pH value of the mash since more H^+ ions are removed in the transition from CO_3^{2-} to H_2CO_3 than are set free by the precipitation of $Ca_3(PO_4)_2$.

Brewing liquor is therefore treated, if necessary, to remove bicarbonate, and calcium salts are added in amounts appropriate to the type of beer being produced. For bitter beers, calcium sulphate is the principal salt which is added (at a concentration of approximately 250 p.p.m.) because of the contribution of SO_4^{2-} to a drier, more bitter flavour. For mild ales, salt addition is at lower concentrations and, to enhance the sweeter flavour of the mild ale, a sulphate:chloride ratio of about 2:3 is aimed at.

Much has been written about the effects of different ions on beer flavour, magnesium ions conferring a sour/bitter flavour, sodium a sour/saline note, and chloride being associated with a sweeter flavour. The scientific basis of such flavour effects has not been established but the practical effects seem to be real.

Certain ions are undesirable in brewing liquor. Nitrate is regarded with disfavour not only because it may be indicative of pollution of the liquor supply but also because it is potentially toxic to yeast, and high concentrations of Fe^{2+} or Fe^{3+} (which are unlikely to be present in typical brewing water) also have a deleterious effect on yeast. Bacteriological standards for brewing liquor are the same as those required for potable waters. A detailed account of brewing water is given by Hough et al. (1971), and reviews by Comrie (1967) and Case (1973) deal with, respectively, salt effects and analysis of brewing liquor.

B. Mash-Tun Ingredients Other Than Malt

In addition to malted barley, the grist used in the mash tun may contain substantial proportions (30% or more) of unmalted cereals including preparations of rice, maize, wheat or barley. Basically these cereals are used as less expensive sources of starch compared with malt. Harris (1968a) has given comparative costs of various mash-tun adjuncts at a time when World prices were more stable than is the case today; maize grits then appeared to be the most competitive adjunct in the brewery concerned. Owing to the high gelatinization points of their starches (Table 1, p. 51) maize and rice must be precooked before incorporation in the mash, so that allowance has to be made for fuel and labour costs, as well as for the extractability of the starch, in arriving at a realistic price for the contribution derived from an adjunct.

In addition to giving direct economies, cereal adjuncts offer a second advantage. They allow the use of malts made from the generally less expensive barleys of higher nitrogen content. Some adjuncts offer a further bonus. The use of maize, according to Harris (1968a), is associated with better shelf-life, presumably as a consequence of lower levels of high molecular-weight nitrogenous compounds in the beer, and wheat flour, possibly owing to its content of a glycoprotein (Anderson and Harris, 1963), has beneficial effects on head retention.

In pilot-plant trials, the extraction rate for wheat flour and even more for barley flakes was significantly lower than for the maize products (Harris, 1968a) and both wheat and barley may be associated with protracted wort separation owing to their propensity for yielding intractable 'fines'—the amorphous particles of residual unsolubilized material which tend to block mash filters (Crabb and Bathgate, 1973). Barleys with a high content of β-glucan may exacerbate separation difficulties not only because of the innate viscosity of the glucan solutions but also because the glucan tends to gum the 'fines' together, to give an impermeable grain bed. Bourne and Pierce (1970) have shown that β-glucan content may be a varietal factor, and choice of barley adjuncts on the basis of low β-glucan content could be worthwhile. Furthermore, the demonstration by Morgan (1971) that β-glucan undergoes a diminution in molecular size, and thus in its solution viscosity, when it is heated above 85°C, may be an important consideration in the brewing of certain stouts where roasted barley forms a significant proportion of the grist. The deleterious effects of wheat flour on wort separation may be associated with its content of pentosans. Though the connection has not been unequivocally established, the fines from mashes containing wheat flour certainly contain high proportions of pentosan (G. N. Bathgate, personal communication).

In the last analysis, any adjunct must be judged by its effect on beer flavour. Harris (1968a) rated beers brewed with 25–30% maize as highly as all-malt beers, though beers based on substantial quantities of wheat flour were slightly less well regarded. On the other hand, Scully and Lloyd (1965) could not find flavour defects attributable to the use of substantial amounts of wheat flour in the grist; clearly, the effect of an adjunct on flavour must vary in different brewing systems and with different types of beer.

What emerges from laboratory studies as well as from brewery usage is that maize products, and, indeed, rice in appropriate economic situations, are wholly acceptable as brewing material. Economically, the high-yielding nature of maize and the value of the easily separated non-brewing part of the grain, the embryo, as a source of corn oil, make it on a World basis a more attractive brewing adjunct than barley. In north-temperate zones, however, where barley is plentiful and maize cannot be grown, it might be advantageous to examine means for separating barley starch commercially, for the potential defects of barley as an adjunct are associated not with the starch granules but with other endosperm constituents. This technology remains to be developed.

C. Mashing Systems

There are two widely contrasting systems of mashing: (i) infusion mashing which is characterized by the biochemical conversion of the grist at a uniform temperature (approximately 65°C) in a single vessel which serves for extraction and filtration; and (ii) decoction mashing in which conversion starts at a lower temperature which is eventually raised, sometimes by the removal, boiling and return of part of the mash (and any adjuncts used), the whole mash finally being transferred to a separate vessel, the lauter tun, for filtration. Infusion mashing evolved in Britain in conjunction with the use of well modified malt, coarsely ground, whereas decoction, the typical lager mashing system of continental Europe, uses a finer grind and less well modified malt. To do justice to the different processes, and their variants, would require a chapter in itself, and readers are referred to Hough *et al.* (1971) for a detailed description of types of plant used.

Clearly, in infusion mashing the malt enzymes take their chance in a somewhat unfavourable environment as far as temperature is concerned, though the possibility of their survival in an active form is enhanced by the use of thick mashes of about 2.5 parts of liquor to one of grist, compared with the five-to-one ratio of most lager mashes. In theory at least, decoction mashing offers a more versatile procedure, adjustable to suit different types of malt and, in biochemical terms, the low-temperature stand must favour activity of the more heat-labile enzymes such as proteinases, β-glucanases and β-amylase.

The behaviour of the goods (i.e. the cereal mix) differs in the two mashing systems. In the unstirred thick infusion mash, the goods float on the surface of wort which rapidly increases in gravity as starch conversion proceeds; flotation is aided by occluded air and there is little segregation of fines. At run-off, infusion worts therefore have initially to traverse only a thin layer of sedimented spent grains. In the thin decoction system, stirring, and heating of the mash, favour physical separation of differently sized particles and, in the lauter tun, an impermeable layer of fines may form on the surface of the sedimented bed, imposing considerable resistance to filtration. Rotating knives are used to cut the bed to allow wort separation to proceed. The different behaviour of static and transferred mashes is discussed and illustrated photographically by Harris (1968b) who also gives a detailed analysis of the factors which govern diffusion of solutes from mash particles and subsequent leaching by the sparge liquor.

With a traditional mash-tun operating at optimal efficiency, four brews are possible per day, the bottleneck in production being run-off time (Royston, 1968). To improve throughput, the obvious need is to adopt the common biological solution of increasing the surface area of the straining system without concomitant increase in vessel size. Proposed solutions along these lines include the Valley

Bottom tun (see Scott, 1967) in which increased surface area is achieved by corrugation, and the Nooter tun or Strainmaster (see Smith, 1965) in which groups of tubes, pear shaped in section, are immersed in the mash which is filtered with suction. The former procedure allows for 8–10 brews per day, and the latter for 11–13. The intensive scouring in the Strainmaster causes greater than normal extraction of phospholipid (Edwards and Thompson, 1968) which may have a marked effect on the head-forming propensities of the fermenting wort.

D. Enzymolysis in the Mash Tun

1. Amylolysis

Quantitatively, the most important objective of mashing is to produce fermentable sugars, largely through the amylolytic degradation of solubilized starch. The joint action of α- and β-amylases on the two components of starch, amylose and amylopectin, results in the approximate proportions of the different sugars and dextrins indicated in Table 3. The endo-enzyme, α-amylase, is unable to

Table 3

Products of mash-tun amylolysis

Component (g/100 ml wort)	Danish lager (Gjertsen, 1955)	English pale ale (Harris et al., 1951)
Glucose	0.91	1.00
Maltose	5.24	3.89
Maltotriose	1.28	1.14
Maltotetraose	0.26	0.20
Higher dextrins	2.13	2.32
Percent fermentable	75.6	70.5

attack amylopectin at points nearer than two-to-three linkages from an α-1,6 branch point. Beta-amylase, a sulphydryl-dependent exo-enzyme which attacks amylose and the external straight-chain branches of amylopectin from the non-reducing ends to yield maltose, has limited stability at infusion mashing temperatures, but it is to some extent protected by the thick mash and the essentially reducing conditions prevailing therein. In addition to fermentable sugars, mash-tun amylolysis therefore yields considerable quantities of unfermentable α-linked dextrins, whose structure has recently been intensively studied by Enevoldsen (1969) and Enevoldsen and Schmidt (1973). These dextrins persist to the finished beer, where it is unlikely that they make any useful contribution, other than adding to its calorific content.

The pH value attained in the mash tun cannot be expected to be optimal for all of the simultaneously proceeding enzymic reactions. The compromise value of 5.4 frequently attained in infusion mashing has been shown by Hopkins (1925) to yield maximal fermentable extract.

As Meddings and Potter (1971) have shown, α-amylolysis proceeds very rapidly within the mash particle. Hydration, heat transfer, starch gelatinization, liquefaction, scission of the macromolecules and diffusion of the products of hydrolysis to the ambient fluid are well advanced within five minutes at 67°C, especially with a finely ground malt, which, as Diedering (1955) suggested, expedites amylolytic action by promoting rapid penetration of water. With simple infusion mashing systems, however, fine grinding may cause difficulties in subsequent separations.

The carbohydrate composition of the wort, and especially the ratio of dextrins to simple sugars, and hence fermentability, is greatly influenced by mashing temperature (Table 4) and considerable care is therefore taken to secure the desired final temperature in mixing the

Table 4

Effect of mashing temperature on the carbohydrate composition of wort. After MacWilliam (1968)

Component (g/100 ml wort)	Mashing temperature (°C)		
	62.2	65.5	68.8
Monosaccharides	1.12	0.98	0.81
Sucrose	0.40	0.40	0.45
Maltose	4.30	4.19	3.92
Maltotriose	1.49	1.55	1.63
Higher dextrins	2.03	2.24	2.52
Percent fermentable	78.3	76.1	72.3

mash, allowance being made for the specific heat and slaking heat of the malt used, both of which vary with moisture content (Hopkins and Carter, 1933).

Finally, it has recently been shown (Bathgate *et al.*, 1973) that any small starch granules which survive malting, or are introduced as barley adjunct, are resistant to α-amylolysis even after they have been boiled, possibly because of their relatively massive occluding coat of protein. In decoction mashing, the initial low-temperature stand might be expected to favour action of the heat-labile β-amylase, but the only substrate available for β-amylase at temperatures of about 50°C will be the ready-formed dextrins of the malt, and massive β-amylolysis cannot be expected to occur until liquefaction and rapid production of additional end groups by the action of α-amylase take place during the saccharification stage of temperature-programmed mashes.

2. *Products of Mashing Other Than Fermentable Sugars*

Although about 90% of the fermentable sugars of wort are derived from enzymic action during mashing, much of the amino-acid complement, essential for yeast nutrition and important in relation to beer flavour, is already present in the malt and requires only simple dissolution. The malting methods employed have a marked effect on the amino-acid complement of the malt; for example, application of bromate (Macey and Stowell, 1961) restricts proteolysis whereas high-nitrogen barley and treatment with gibberellic acid are associated with high levels of amino acids (Jones and Pierce, 1963); gibberellic acid-treated malts are also relatively low in proline.

Although the proteolytic enzymes which are active in mashing have not been comprehensively identified, there is no doubt that, particularly in decoction-type mashing (Sandegren *et al.*, 1954), with its 'protein rest' but also in infusion mashing (Jones and Pierce, 1963; Barrett and Kirsop, 1971), there is a substantial production of amino acids and of simple peptides (Clapperton, 1971). Table 5 illustrates the range and proportions of amino acids resulting from the combined processes of malting and mashing.

Other mash-tun reactions, quantitatively less important than the production of sugars and amino acids, none the less have significant effects on fermentation and on the finished beer. These reactions

Table 5
Amino-acid composition of wort

Component (mg/100 ml wort)	Type of wort		
	American lager (Robbins et al., 1964)	Swedish lager (Enebo and Johnsson, 1965)	British infusion (Jones and Pierce, 1964)
Alanine	6.3	6.1	8.0
Arginine	8.8	12.0	10.8
Aspartic acid	5.8	5.3	6.1
Glutamic acid	3.0	9.5	7.8
Glycine	2.2	1.9	2.7
Histidine	3.6	4.6	3.2
Isoleucine	3.6	5.7	4.9
Leucine	7.5	11.0	12.1
Lysine	6.3	7.9	9.1
Methionine	2.0	2.1	2.6
Phenylalanine	6.5	11.0	9.0
Threonine	3.5	4.7	—
Tryptophan	4.1	4.7	5.7
Tyrosine	5.4	7.7	4.6
Valine	6.9	8.6	10.1
Serine + amides	12.9	16.6	14.8
Proline	20.5	52.5	36.2
Total	108.9	171.9	147.7

include simple extraction of vitamins (Table 6), inorganic ions (Table 7), fatty acids, organic acids (Table 8), tannins and lipids. Nucleotides are dephosphorylated to nucleosides and, in low-temperature mashing, further degraded to free bases (Harris and Parsons, 1958).

Residual β-glucan is solubilized and, although barley endo-β-glucanase is inactivated within five minutes in an infusion mash at 65°C (Bourne and Pierce, 1970), some β-glucan degradation can occur during this brief period of enzyme activity. Endo-β-glucanase is active during the low-temperature stand of decoction mashing (Erdal and Gjertsen, 1967) but, in spite of this, decoction worts tend to be more viscous than infusion worts, a reflection possibly of the less well modified malts used in the former. Phytase is also active in decoction mashes (Sandegren, 1948) so increasing the phosphate and inositol contents of the worts.

Table 6

Vitamin contents of some worts. From MacWilliam (1968)

Vitamin	Concentration in wort (μg per 100 ml)	Wort type	Reference
Biotin	0.85	English ale	Lynes and Norris (1948)
Inositol	6000.0	German lager	Weinfurtner et al., (1966)
Nicotinic acid	1000.0	American lager	Laufer et al. (1943)
Pantothenic acid	98	American lager	Laufer et al. (1943)
Pyridoxin	58	English ale	Hopkins and Pennington (1947)
Riboflavin	45	English ale	Hopkins and Wiener (1944)
Thiamin	33	Irish stout	Tullo and Stringer (1945)

Table 7

Some inorganic constituents of Canadian
lager wort. From Latimer et al. (1966)

Constituent	Concentration (p.p.m.)
Na	20
K	450
Ca	40
Fe	0.37
Mg	100
Cl	360
PO_4 [a]	883

[a] Attributable to both inorganic and phytate phosphate.

Mashing occupies a central position in the brewing process, and changes in mashing conditions, including the type of malt and adjuncts used, length and temperature of conversion, pH value, fineness of grind and ratio of liquor to grist, have profound effects on later stages of production. Piendl (1973) has provided a detailed analysis of the effects of these variables on the carbohydrate spectrum of wort, and Hudson (1973a) has surveyed all major mash-tun reactions in relation to beer properties.

Table 8

Some organic acids of wort. From Enebo
et al. (1955)

Organic acid	Concentration in wort (mg/litre)
Pyruvic	4
Fumaric	13
Succinic	11
α-Oxoglutaric	16
Malic	44
Citric	86

E. Sparging

As the sweet wort is drawn off from the mash tun or lauter tun into a vessel called an underback, the goods are washed with water at a temperature of about 75°C. This procedure ensures dissolution of all residual soluble materials and the almost complete inactivation of any remaining enzymes; traces of α-amylase activity may survive. Silicates and tannins, largely from the husk (Stone and Gray, 1948), which may later be implicated in formation of beer hazes, are concentrated in the poorly buffered final sparge and, as noted earlier, excess phospholipid can be removed by over-vigorous washing. According to Royston (1968), the average gravity value for final spargings from British mash tuns is 1.001; for continental Europe comparatative figures are 1.004 and for North America 1.008. Clearly, the traditional British system secures the maximum value from its mash, but at a cost of a very much less rapid turnover. The spent grains with approximately 20% protein on a dry-weight basis are a valuable by-product for compounding cattle-feed (Garscadden, 1973).

In the interests of clarity, mashing, wort separation and sparging have been discussed as if they were isolated processes. In most modern breweries, however, though the underlying biochemical and physicochemical principles remain unchanged, advances in plant design have resulted in integration of the separate processes into a single automated block system.

VI. DIRECT CONVERSION OF BARLEY TO WORT

Not surprisingly, with the advent of reasonably priced commercial enzymes, attempts have been made to circumvent the laborious and costly procedures of malting and kilning and transform barley directly into a fermentation medium suitable for the production of beer. Successful methods for the preparation of barley syrups have been described by Macey *et al.* (1966a) and by Crisp and East (1971); analytically the composition of these syrups matches wort remarkably well, and acceptable beers were produced from them.

Protein degradation is probably the most critical of the enzymic transformations required in converting raw barley to wort because of the major contribution of the malting process to the production of amino acids which merely require extraction in a malt mash. Nielsen (1971), as part of a comprehensive study of barley conversion with extraneous enzymes, has provided a comparative account of the behaviour of six bacterial peptidases acting on barley flour at various temperatures. One hour's conversion at 45–50°C generally seemed to give an appropriate degree of proteolysis and an amino-acid spectrum resembling that of a malt mash. Surprisingly, when starch was gelatinized prior to the addition of proteolytic enzymes at 45°C, the amount of amino nitrogen was greatly decreased (in one instance from 125 to 76 mg per litre); one wonders whether a similar effect operates with malt peptidases.

Amylolysis presents few problems in barley conversions. Microbial α-amylase acting at 65°C, together with the β-amylase from the barley or from the late addition at a lowered temperature (62°C) of 10% of highly diastatic malt (which also contributes free amino acids), give the normal range of wort carbohydrates. However, in spite of the analytical similarity to malt wort, barley conversions frequently show lower fermentability (Klopper, 1969a). Nielsen (1971) found that addition of pullulanase from *Aerobacter aerogenes*, which hydrolyses the α-1,6 linkages in dextrins (Enevoldsen, 1970), improved fermentability very considerably.

As with all innovations in brewing, the quality of the beer must be the major criterion in deciding on the implementation of the new technique on a commercial scale. The only flavour defect regularly reported (Macey *et al.*, 1967; Klopper, 1969b) appears to be a slightly harsh after-taste, probably associated with the barley husk. According to Nielsen (1971) the most successful procedure for eliminating this undesirable feature was that recommended by J. Hoggan (personal communication to Nielsen), namely reduction of wort pH value to 4.9 before boiling.

A technological problem which had to be overcome was that of milling the barley which is too hard for the crushing action of a normal malt mill. Wet-milling (Fig. 7), which toughens the husk, has

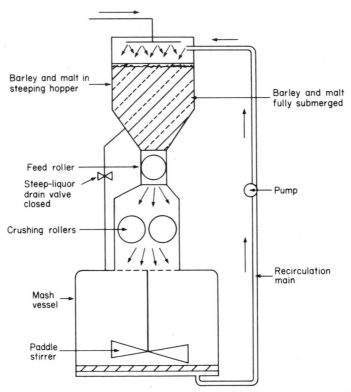

Fig. 7. Equipment for wet milling of 50% barley with 50% malt and enzymes. The arrows show the path of the recirculated water. From Button and Palmer (1974).

proved satisfactory provided additional flutings are made in the mill roller (Button and Palmer, 1974). These workers found that steeping to about 25% moisture with water between 10°C and 14°C gave the highest extracts, whereas Pfenninger *et al.* (1971) preferred a 20 minute steep at 45°C; clearly trial and error must play a large part in the development of this relatively new technology. Button and

Palmer (1974), using 70% barley and 30% malt, and extraneous enzymes, initially encountered the problem of low fermentability referred to above, and overcame it by an extended mashing time with programmed temperature rests (Fig. 8).

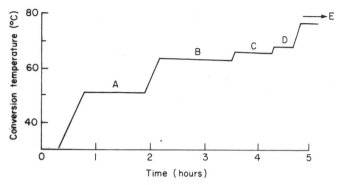

Fig. 8. Conversion of a mixture of 50% barley and 50% malt with proteolytic and amylolytic enzymes. The A period indicates 60 min at 50°C; B, 75 min at 63°C; C, 40 min at 65°C; D, 20 min at 68°C; and E, pump-to-lauter time. From Button and Palmer (1974).

It is difficult to make a realistic general assessment of the economies which can be secured by direct conversion procedures. Nielsen (1971) suggests a possible saving of between 7 and 17% when 10% malt is used with barley and added enzymes. Button and Palmer (1974) merely state that 'the economic benefits are considerable'.

VII. WORT BOILING AND COOLING

A. General

The objectives of wort boiling are easily though possibly superficially stated as: (i) inactivation of any enzymes which have survived sparging; (ii) sterilization of the wort; (iii) completion of ionic interactions which are conducive to a drop in pH value, i.e. removal of carbon dioxide from bicarbonate and precipitation of calcium phosphate; (iv) concentration of the wort; (v) denaturation and precipitation of proteins; (vi) dissolution of any additional sugars used; (vii) isomerization of hop α-acids; and (viii) volatilization and removal of unwanted flavour components. Objectives (i) and (ii) are attained with one-to-two minutes of boiling but precipitation of proteins continues for at least three hours (Bremner, 1963) and the longer boil may be associated with better shelf-life of the beer, for example 16 weeks freedom from haze for a two-hour boil compared with nine weeks for a 30-minute boil (Hudson and Birtwistle, 1966). Practical brewers have long advocated 'a good rolling boil', and the results of Hudson and Birtwistle suggest that movement, for example by stirring, is more important than temperature in securing the elimination of unwanted high molecular-weight material. Carragheen (Irish moss), the dried fronds of the red alga *Chondrus crispus*, can be added at a rate of about 5 g/hl to the copper to improve flocculation of proteins. According to Vickers and Ballard (1972) over 3% more nitrogen is removed from the wort by treatment with carragheen, and clearer worts may be obtained. There is, however, no evidence that wort clarity is closely related to immediate beer clarity; certainly, the turbid worts resulting from 30 minutes' boiling (above) gave beer of acceptable clarity. Moreover, Rennie (1972) has shown that temperature conditioning of wort, for example at 85°C for 90 minutes, can produce an acceptably bright beer and, indeed, can introduce the possibility (Rennie, 1973) of adjusting certain flavour qualities at will. Thus, the 'malty' full-bodied flavour of the beer declines, and sharper notes are enhanced with rising temperature of heat treatment.

Although it is not necessarily an objective of boiling, an inevitable concomitant of this stage of processing is further development of colour, by mechanisms similar to those which operate during kilning. An increase in wort colour by 50% and, if the wort is aerated, of up to 75% is normal (Bremner, 1963), and the magnitude of the increase is related to the content of permanently soluble nitrogen in the wort.

Though copper has traditionally been used for fabricating wort-boiling plant, heat transfer being better from copper than from stainless steel, use of the latter is becoming more common. Directly-fired coppers are now rare. The normal practice is to use either steam or high-pressure hot water, and the heating panels are arranged to give localized boiling with, as a result, vigorous circulation of the worts. Considerable attention is paid to heat recovery as, according to Royston (1971), 75% recovery of heat from the products of evaporation will produce about 5 m^3 of wash water at 85°C for every 10 m^3 of wort boiled.

1. *Sugars and Syrups*

It is usual at the copper-boiling stage to introduce additional fermentable carbohydrate either as simple sugars, such as glucose, sucrose or invert sugar, or as syrups prepared by acid-enzyme or enzyme-enzyme treatment of maize or wheat starch. With the commercial availability of different microbial amylolytic enzymes, it is possible to produce more or less tailor-made carbohydrate syrups (Maiden, 1970) and the brewer can choose a product which, apart from the absence of sucrose and fructose, shows the normal carbohydrate spectrum of wort (dextrins included, for what they are worth) or syrups which contain predominantly maltose or predominantly glucose. Not only do these copper adjuncts provide economies in plant utilization and in the actual cost of fermentables (Harris, 1968a), they also dilute the nitrogenous components of the wort. The use of excessive proportions of carbohydrate syrups (as of starch adjuncts in mashing) could lead to deficiencies in the amounts of amino acids available for yeast growth. However, at suitable concentrations in relation to the analytical properties of the malt, and with regard to the mashing conditions used, these convenient products have no detrimental effects on fermentation or on the palate of the finished beer.

B. Hops and Hopping

It is at the copper-boiling stage that hops, whole or powdered, are traditionally introduced to the beer, though post-fermentation bittering with chemically isomerized extracts is becoming increasingly common and is likely in the not too distant future (Verzele, 1971) to replace the crude older methods completely.

The part of the hop plant (*Humulus lupulus*) used in brewing is the cone or strobilus (Fig. 9) which bears resin-containing lupulin glands on the infolded bases of the bracteoles and on the fruits (the hop seed of commerce). To produce these strobili, an annual growth of 5–6 m of vegetative bine, supported on strings and wirework, is required. To provide hop-bittering material is thus a costly enterprise, for the crop is used only in brewing. Small wonder, then, that brewers take great interest in the economics of hop cultivation and in

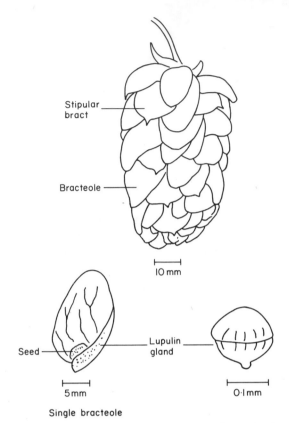

Stipular
bract

Bracteole

10 mm

Seed

Lupulin
gland

5 mm

0·1 mm

Single bracteole

Fig. 9. Drawings of the strobilus of the hop plant (*Humulus lupulus*).

the efficient use of the hop resins for, in the last analysis, the
brewing industry has to bear the cost of growing massive amounts of
plant material to secure the presence in beer of 20–50 p.p.m. of
bittering substances and traces of the essential oils which impart a
hoppy aroma to the beer.

The chemistry of the hop resins is an organic chemist's dream—or
nightmare, according to one's point of view—and the 52-page review
by Stevens (1967) gives an excellent account of the complexities of
hop chemistry. For the present purpose, however, only the broad
principles of hop bittering and hop aroma will be dealt with.

The bittering potential of fresh hops is derived almost entirely
from the α-acids (Fig. 10) which are precipitable with lead acetate
from a hexane extract of total resins. This property of the α-acids
formed the basis of the first, gravimetric, method of estimating the

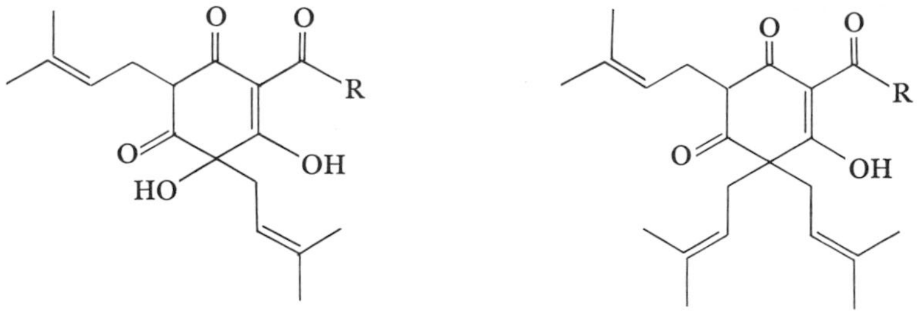

α-Acids	R	β-Acids
HUMULONE	$CH_2CH(CH_3)_2$	LUPULONE
COHUMULONE	$CH(CH_3)_2$	COLUPULONE
ADHUMULONE	$CH(CH_3)CH_2CH_3$	ADLUPULONE

Fig. 10. Structural formulae of the α-acids (humulones) and β-acids (lupulones) of hops.

brewing value of hops (Ford and Tait, 1932) and has led to the introduction of a useful, though not wholly specific, simple conductometric titration (Goedkoop and Hartong, 1957). Accurate measurement of total α-acids can be made by a polarimetric method introduced by Salac and Dyr (1943) and further developed by, for example, Verzele (1957), or by ion-exchange chromatography (Otter et al., 1972). The α-acids comprise three principal and two minor analogues which can be separated by countercurrent distribution (Rigby and Bethune, 1953).

There are considerable varietal differences in total α-acids content (Table 9) and, indeed, in the proportions of cohumulone in the mixture (Howard and Tatchell, 1957), and breeders are active in developing suitable new varieties of hops with a high content of α-acids coupled with suitable agronomic properties, particularly in relation to disease resistance (Thompson and Neve, 1972).

Humulone and its analogues are not themselves bitter and they have very limited solubility in wort. During boiling, however, they are transformed to the soluble, bitter iso-α-acids (Fig. 11), though the overall utilization of α-acids in the conditions prevailing in the copper and throughout fermentation is regrettably low, rarely exceeding 35%.

When hops are stored, there is a decline in the content of α-acids (Burgess and Tatchell, 1950) which, as would be expected from their structure, readily undergo autoxidation. Stored hops are not as deficient in bittering ability as polarimetric analysis would suggest

Table 9

Mean contents of alpha-acids at harvest for different cultivars of hops. Data from
Hudson (1972, 1973b, 1974)

Cultivar	Percent content of alpha-acids		
	1971	1972	1973
Alliance	3.89	3.93	4.58
Bullion	5.95	7.41	8.28
Fuggles	3.78	4.10	4.39
Goldings	4.47	4.20	5.17
Northern Brewer	6.15	6.48	5.88
Wye Challanger	—	6.86	7.36
Wye Northdown	7.37	7.69	8.32
Wye Target	—	—	9.87

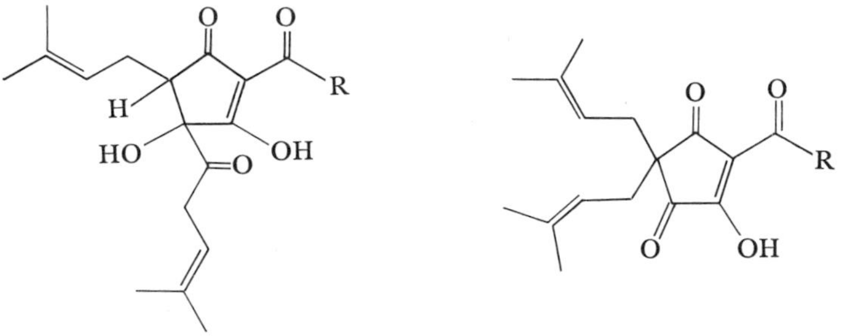

ISO-α-ACIDS (From α-ACIDS)   HULUPONES
R as in Figure 10   R as in Figure 10
Major source of bitterness   Minor source of bitterness

Fig. 11. Structural formulae of some bitter transformation products of α-acids and β-acids
found in beer.

(Birtwistle *et al.*, 1963) because some of the oxidation products of
various resin fractions, for example hulupones, derived from β-acids
and tricyclodehydroisohumulone (Laws, 1973) derived from
humulone, are themselves bitter. The most useful practical guide for
estimating hop rates involves determining lead conductance values of
a toluene extract at harvest, and making an empirical allowance of
5% for loss of bittering potential per annum; the gain in bittering
value from oxidized compounds (some of which react in the
conductometric analysis) counterbalances the disappearance of true
α-acids.

Much used to be heard about the preservative value of hops, and elaborate formulae based on α- and β-acid values were devised to quantify this elusive property (see Hudson, 1960). However, although resin-derived material does exhibit bacteriostatic power towards lactic-acid bacteria (Kulka, 1958), the species of *Lactobacillus* encountered in beer rapidly develop tolerance to hop substances (Richards and Macrae, 1964) and good hygiene is now preferred to reliance on a somewhat dubious antiseptic, especially since hop rates have declined to values as low as 200 g of whole hops (equivalent possibly to 8 g of α-acid) per hectolitre.

The essential oils which are responsible for the characteristic aroma of hops are a complex mixture, including monoterpenes (for example myrcene), sesquiterpenes (for example humulene) and various oxygenated compounds, including esters, acids, ketones and alcohols. Different varieties of hops have characteristic aromas and, indeed, it has been suggested (Buttery and Ling, 1966) that the identity of an unknown sample of hops may be determined from a chromatogram of its oils, though changes which the essential oils undergo during storage (De Mets and Verzele, 1968) may make such identifications rather hazardous. Surprisingly, few of the essential oils which are undoubtedly present in hops can be detected in beer (Buttery *et al.*, 1967), and it seems possible that much of the hoppy aroma of beer emanates from degradation products of hop resins (Verzele, 1967).

Oil composition is correlated with resin composition (Howard and Slater, 1957) in that, as would be expected from their biogenetic pathways (Harris, 1967), hops with a high content of myrcene also have higher proportions of cohumulone and colupulone in the α- and β-acids fractions, respectively. American hops, which are typically high in cohumulone (35% of α-acids), have a characteristic 'catty' aroma which is disliked by European brewers, whereas Hallertau and Saaz hops are low in cohumulone (about 20%). The principle underlying the choice of a copper hop must involve selection of a high α-acid cultivar with that proportion of α-acid analogue which is associated with the organoleptic qualities desired in a particular beer. Most of the volatile hop constituents are certainly lost in the boil, though the practice of reserving a proportion of the 'finer' hops for a late addition may contribute, disproportionately, to flavour.

There has been considerable controversy on the question of seeded versus seedless hops. British hops are grown with free access to male plants, and so contain 15% or more of seeds, whereas Continental 'seedless' hops contain less than 1%. The hop seeds are rich in oil, but Harrison (1971) could find no adverse effects of macerated hop seeds on beer flavour, unless the beers were bottled with excessively high air contents (10–15 ml head space air). However, in a large-scale collaborative trial in which lagers were brewed with seeded and seedless growths of the same hop (Northern Brewer), flavour differences could be detected (Virden, 1972) and, although the 'seedless' beer was preferred, the 'seeded' was perfectly acceptable to the tasting panel.

Hop extracts suitable for addition to the copper are available (Mitchell, 1970), but their utilization is little better than that of whole hops, and the future of hop extracts must surely be with the pre-isomerized extracts which are suitable for post-fermentation bittering.

C. Wort Clarification and Cooling

At the end of boiling, which may last for up to two hours to ensure maximal isomerization of α-acids, the spent hops and the trub are separated from the wort which, after cooling, goes forward for fermentation. The traditional British hop-back, a vessel with a slotted false bottom which allows clear wort to percolate, after recirculation, through a bed of spent hops which also retains the trub, is becoming a thing of the past. Removal of spent hops from a hop-back is messy and labour-intensive; a hop bed 0.3 m thick is needed for efficient working (Royston, 1971) so that present hop rates, further diminished by the use of isomerized extracts, do not provide this depth and, finally, the operation in the hop-back is too slow to accommodate modern intensive brewing schedules. The hop-back is therefore being superseded by hop strainers, which have long been used in Germany and in the United States of America. These devices allow wort to pass forward complete with trub. The spent hops are retained in a wirework basket or on a perforated plate and, after sparging and compression, are removed, frequently by means of an Archimedean screw. Losses of wort may be greater in hop strainers than in the classical hop-back.

The hot trub can be removed by solid-bowl or automatic desludging centrifuge or in the increasingly popular whirlpool tank whose operating cost, according to Nielsen and · True (1968), is only one-third of that of a self-ejecting centrifuge. The whirlpool is a beautifully simple device, a cylindrical vessel into which hot wort is pumped tangentially through a pipe situated about one metre above the base. The rotating wort forms a vortex, and the pressures developed are such that the particles tend to collect in a firm cone on the bottom of the vessel. Velocity and angle of entry are, to some extent, determined by trial and error for different types of wort, but carragheen (van Gheluwe and Dadic, 1972) does seem to promote formation of a firm deposit, especially when hop powders are used.

The clear wort emerging from the hop back, centrifuge or whirlpool is cooled, normally by means of a plate heat exchanger in which useful supplies of hot water are generated by running the hot wort counter-current to the cold liquor. Further precipitations occur during cooling, which are enhanced by the turbulent conditions prevailing in the heat exchanger and, on occasions, by the injection of air.

The importance of wort cooling was first emphasized by Brown (1913) who showed that, if reasonable flocculation was not achieved, fermentations would be sluggish. Detailed laboratory studies have suggested that there may be a critical length of time for wort cooling and Clendinnen (1936) and Shimwell et al. (1938) have demonstrated that worts vary in optimal period of cooling. Whatever the theoretical explanation (and it is by no means fully established), the fact remains that modern heat exchangers deal very satisfactorily with cooling, aeration and clarification of a wide range of different types of wort.

From this stage onwards, sterility is essential as wort bacteria, such as *Enterobacter aerogenes*, which do not survive fermentation, can produce detectable amounts of undesirable volatile compounds such as dimethyl sulphide which persist to the finished beer (Anderson *et al.*, 1971).

VIII. FERMENTATION

A. Brewing Yeasts

In recent years, yeast has had a good press biochemically speaking (see, for example, Holzer, 1968; Suomalainen, 1968; Rainbow, 1970;

Wainwright, 1971a) and no attempt will be made here to cover all facets of yeast biochemistry. As far as beer is concerned, the physical performance of yeast in a fermentation and the effect on it of wort constituents including hop-derived materials have important technological implications, and the presence of the minor metabolic by-products of yeast, such as diacetyl, may determine whether a beer is acceptable or not. Attention will therefore be concentrated on those aspects of yeast biochemistry and behaviour which are known to exercise a major influence on the production and characteristics of the end product.

Of the two species of yeast used in brewing, *Saccharomyces cerevisiae* is typically an ale yeast and *Sacch. carlsbergensis* (now known as *Sacch. uvarum*) a lager yeast. Distinction between the two species is readily made biochemically by their behaviour towards the trisaccharide raffinose; *Sacch. cerevisiae* can ferment only one-third of the molecule, whereas *Sacch. carlsbergensis* ferments it completely. The two species can also be distinguished immunologically (Campbell and Brudzynski, 1966) though strains of *Sacch. carlsbergensis* are not antigenically identical (Sandula *et al.*, 1964). In fermentation systems, *Sacch. cerevisiae* often behaves as a 'top' yeast and forms a copious head on the surface of the wort towards the end of fermentation, while *Sacch. carlsbergensis*, a 'bottom' yeast, tends to settle at the foot of the vessel. This distinction is far from absolute (Walkey and Kirsop, 1969) and strains of *Sacch. cerevisiae* which yield a top crop in two metre-deep fermentations may behave largely as bottom yeasts in six metre-deep cylindroconical tanks, especially on sudden chilling (Thompson, 1970).

Diagnosis only to the species level is far too blunt an instrument for the selection of brewing yeasts and, just as cultivated barley was selected by agronomic and harvesting pressures, so culture yeasts have for many centuries been subjected to the selection pressures of fermentation performance and flavour contributions to the beer. More recently, deliberate introductions have been made of chosen strains of yeast from one country with a high reputation for its beer to another in which the brewing industry was a new development. Brewing in the United States of America, for example, was founded on the immigration of German brewers with their characteristic bottom-fermentation yeasts.

With the introduction of pure-culture methods to lager brewing at the end of the 19th Century by Hansen, scientific appraisal of yeast properties became a possibility. Top-fermentation brewers in Britain were slow to accept the undoubted advantage of the new techniques, possibly owing to unfortunate experiences in situations where the mixed nature of the brewery yeast was not appreciated and replacement by a single strain, albeit one free from contaminating micro-organisms, did not prove as satisfactory as the previous rule-of-thumb system of yeast management. In some cases, industrial selection pressures may, unknown to the brewer concerned, achieve the same results as a laboratory-based system of strain selection. Thus, in an examination of 39 pitching yeasts used in British breweries, Hough (1959) found that 12 contained only a single strain, 16 had two major strains, and the remainder had three or more components. Comparison of the fermentation efficiencies of yeasts in brewery use with yeasts in general, made by Thorne (1958), also illustrates the selective power of the industrial process (Fig. 12).

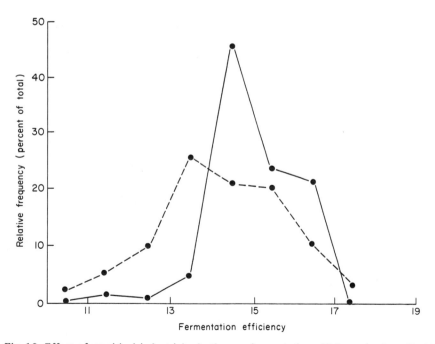

Fig. 12. Effect of empirical industrial selection on fermentation efficiency (carbon dioxide production/nitrogen content) of yeast. •---• indicates behaviour of all bottom strains (mean = 14.1 ± 0.11); •—•, bottom strains in industrial use (mean = 15.1 ± 0.06). From Thorne (1958).

It is possible for a brewery to draw up a specification for its 'ideal' yeast (Helm and Thorne, 1955; Thorne, 1973). Requirements will vary according to the fermentation system used, the method of yeast separation employed, and the beer characters aimed at, but criteria which would appear in such a specification might include flocculating power, ability to ferment maltotriose, head-forming potential, fermentation efficiency, interaction with isohumulones, response to finings, and propensities for producing important individual flavour components. These characteristics will be discussed in greater detail later.

The search for the ideal strain usually begins in a brewery's own pitching yeast. Thus Seed (1952) describes how a satisfactory pure culture was selected from the twelve types found in the existing brewery yeast, and Gilliland (1951) reports a similar analysis which revealed the presence of four different flocculating types (see p. 95). Later, Stevens (1966) based a selection procedure on flocculation properties, pH value and yeast count at racking, haze levels 24 hours after fining, and results of taste-panel evaluations. Ferguson *et al.* (1972) chose attenuative power as a first criterion and also examined, *inter alia*, the production in tall-tube fermentation tests (Dixon, 1967) of the principal fusel alcohol components of beer, and of ethyl acetate. They concluded that this type of laboratory screening could provide the brewery, if required, with a more attenuative yeast which did not produce higher than normal amounts of fusel oils and esters; for final evaluation, particularly of flavour, large-scale trials were necessary.

Up to the present, strain selection from existing brewery yeasts and from the British National Collection of Yeast Cultures (Walkey and Kirsop, 1969) or other national collections has proved more rewarding than hybridization partly, at least, because of the poor sporulating ability of brewers' yeasts and the low viability of the ascospores which do form (Winge, 1944; Clayton *et al.*, 1972). Windisch and Emeis (1969), however, have patented a highly-attenuative yeast derived from *Sacch. carlsbergensis* x *Sacch. diastaticus*, and Clayton *et al.* (1972) consider that, since recent developments in brewing technology may require a yeast with properties rather different from those of traditional brewing yeasts, hybridization, however frustrating it may be, is worth further exploration.

B. Biochemical Events During Brewing Fermentations

1. General

Some of the many changes which take place during the fermentation of wort are shown in Figure 13. In the example chosen (Maule *et al.*, 1966), the wort was aerated to 75% saturation and pitched with a

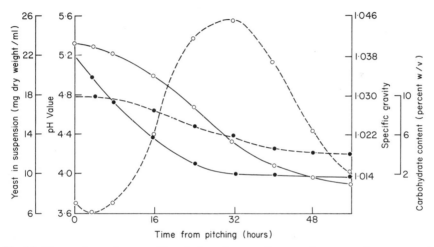

Fig. 13. Changes in wort composition during a brewery fermentation. ○- - -○ denotes yeast in suspension (mg/10 ml); ●—●, pH value; ○—○, wort gravity; and ●- - -●, total carbohydrate. After Maule *et al.* (1966).

top-fermentation industrial brewing yeast at a rate of 0.375 kg dry weight per hectolitre. It has subsequently been shown (e.g. Haukeli and Lie, 1973) that, if initial oxygen concentrations are significantly below 75% saturation, yeast growth is impaired and ethanol production is low (Fig. 14). However, the previous history of the yeast affects its requirements for oxygen; aerobically-grown yeast ferments satisfactorily in de-aerated wort whereas anaerobically grown yeast performs poorly, though ergosterol can substitute for oxygen in anaerobic conditions (David and Kirsop, 1973). The initial absorption of oxygen may thus be associated with sterol synthesis, or with the formation of inducible enzymes.

In the example shown in Figure 13, dissolved oxygen had vanished

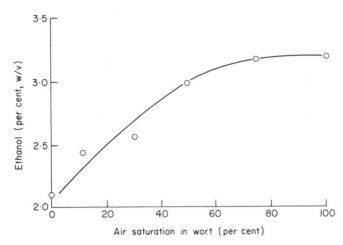

Fig. 14. Concentration of ethanol as a function of percentage of initial air saturation in malt wort, fermented by *Saccharomyces carlsbergensis* for 150 hours at 10°C. From Haukeli and Lie (1973).

from the fermenting wort within one and a half hours. During the eight-hour lag phase, absorption of amino acids, especially of lysine, though not of carbohydrates, had begun, and the wort pH value had fallen from 5.16 to 4.71. Clearly, yeast is not metabolically inert during the lag phase. Ester production and higher alcohol (fusel oil) formation can be related, broadly, to yeast growth and, rather surprisingly in view of its metabolic importance in the yeast cell, pyruvic acid is also excreted by growing yeast to the wort (Coote *et al.*, 1973). Many other acids contribute to the drop in pH value, notably acetic acid formed by oxidation of acetaldehyde (Nordström, 1968). Indeed, Owades and Dono (1965) found that the concentrations of volatile acids more than doubled during the first two days of fermentation and then fell off gradually.

Finally (Fig. 13) the decline in the concentration of suspended yeast cells after about 32 hours is related to flocculation and separation of yeast to the head. Biochemical events in the brewery fermentation are virtually complete in two to three days but, in older types of system, several days are then allowed for 'cleansing' (i.e. deposition or flotation) of the yeast from the fermented wort.

Lager fermentations are traditionally performed at lower temperatures (8°C) pitched at about 0.25 kg dry weight per hectolitre, and maintained at temperatures not greatly exceeding 10°C. Fermentation therefore lasts for up to 14 days, and the general changes occurring in the wort resemble those taking place in an ale fermentation, but at a more leisurely pace.

2. Carbohydrate Metabolism

Energy for yeast growth comes mainly from fermentation of carbohydrates by the Embden–Meyerhof–Parnas pathway with, according to Blumenthal (1968), a 10% contribution from the pentose phosphate pathway. Sucrose, hydrolysed by the invertase of the yeast cell wall, glucose and fructose are the first sugars to be absorbed from the wort and their entry to the cell is by facilitated diffusion.

For uptake of maltose, the principal sugar of wort, an induced maltose permease is required (Harris and Millin, 1963) so there may be a delay during which the permease is synthesized. A similar situation exists with regard to maltotriose which is absorbed only after the maltose of wort has been substantially depleted and, according to Griffin (1970), formation of the maltose permease is the major biochemical factor determining whether a strain of yeast will ferment wort rapidly, as internal cell maltase is always present in adequate amounts. The delay in production of maltose permease is due not only to the time required for its synthesis but also to the fact that glucose inhibits or destroys (Masschelein, 1967) the permease so that, in glucose-supplemented wort, there can be a further delay in maltose utilization, despite the presence of adequate amounts of the appropriate inducing sugar. Kirsop and Brown (1972) have suggested, however, that many strains of yeast in common use in breweries may possess a constitutive maltose permease system.

Most brewery yeasts can absorb maltotriose after permease induction, and therefore hydrolyse and ferment it, though different strains (Walkey and Kirsop, 1969) ferment maltotriose at different rates. However, loss of ability to utilize maltotriose is a not uncommon mutation, especially, according to Thorne (1970), in continuous fermentations accomplished by *Sacch. carlsbergensis*. Non-fermenters of maltotriose are also occasionally contaminants of top-fermentation pitching yeast (Gilliland, 1969) and may even replace the culture yeast if they crop well.

A small number of strains of brewing yeasts from the National Collection of Yeast Cultures (Clapperton and MacWilliam, 1971) proved to be capable of fermenting maltotetraose; all of these strains fell into Class 5 (Walkey and Kirsop, 1969) which contains the fast fermenters and extensive attenuaters.

3. Amino-Acid Assimilation

Much of our recent understanding of amino-acid assimilation from wort fermented by *Sacch. cerevisiae* is based on the extensive studies of Jones and Pierce (see, for example, Jones and Pierce, 1964; Jones *et al.*, 1969). Amino acids are selectively absorbed by *Sacch. cerevisiae* in an orderly sequence, and four amino-acid groups can be distinguished (Fig. 15) according to their relative rates of disappearance from the wort. Amino acids in Group A are eliminated early,

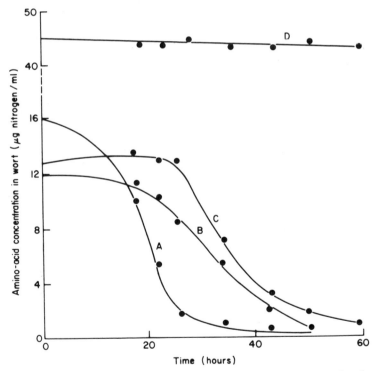

Fig. 15. Classification of amino acids according to their speed of absorption from wort under brewery conditions. *Group A* includes arginine, asparagine, aspartic acid, glutamic acid, glutamine, lysine, serine and threonine. *Group B*, histidine, isoleucine, leucine, methionine and valine. *Group C*, alanine, ammonia, glycine, phenylalanine, tyrosine and tryptophan. *Group D* includes only proline. From Jones and Pierce (1964).

those in Group B are removed more slowly, while those in Group C (which also harbours ammonia) are absorbed only after a lag period whose termination coincides with the disappearance of Group A amino acids. Proline, which is the sole member of Group D, is taken up very slowly indeed though it can be metabolized, especially under aerobic conditions. In lager (*Sacch. carlsbergensis*) fermentations at 8-9°C, a similar orderly pattern of uptake was found by Palmqvist and Äyräpää (1969); here again, substantial amounts of proline (350-400 mg per litre) remained in the finished beer.

These results can be related to the activities of a permease (Surdin *et al.*, 1965) or permeases (Grenson, 1966) with amino acids (for example those in Groups A and C) competing for the appropriate permease. Shortage or excess of an individual amino acid thus does not affect the sequence of uptake (Jones and Pierce, 1969) though the rate of uptake is proportional to the concentration of the amino acid in the wort.

Once they have entered the cell, the amino acids participate in a complex series of reactions including transaminations, and work with labelled amino acids (Jones *et al.*, 1969) has shown that ^{15}N becomes randomly distributed throughout all of the amino acids. There is little interconversion of the carbon skeletons of the amino acids, but simple sugars may also contribute to the oxo-acid pool for protein synthesis. During a brewery fermentation, however, some amino acids (for example, lysine) normally derive all of their carbon skeletons from the parent amino acids of the wort, and it is desirable that these amino acids be present in the accustomed proportions, as alteration of normal patterns of interconversion may alter the production of by-products, such as fusel alcohols, and affect final beer flavour. It is interesting to note that, in the conversions with bacterial enzymes described by Nielsen (1971), the concentrations of these 'critical' amino acids agreed well with values for a malt mash, suggesting that no untoward flavour need be expected, from this source, from brewing with barley plus enzymes.

4. Metabolic By-Products

Some of the quantitatively minor products of yeast metabolism have a disproportionate effect on the character of the final beer and, though the pathways responsible for formation of these trace constituents are moderately well understood, the complexity of wort, the operation of various control systems within the yeast cell, the potential production of some metabolic by-products by more than one biochemical route and the effects of different yeast strains operating in different types of fermentation system all combine to make generalization an unusually hazardous procedure.

For example, formation of certain higher alcohols (for example 3-methylbutanol) is closely related to the amino-acid metabolism of the yeast cell (Fig. 16) but the oxo-acids involved in their synthesis (α-oxo-isocaproic acid in the case of 3-methylbutanol) can also be

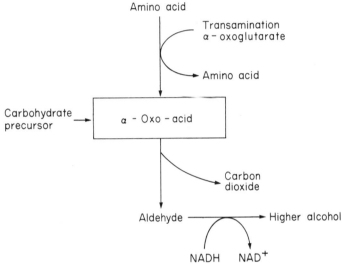

Fig. 16. Schematic representation of the formation of higher alcohols by brewer's yeast.

derived from carbohydrate precursors. As was shown by Äyräpää (1971), formation of many (though not all) of the higher alcohols including 3-methylbutanol, is negatively correlated with available nitrogen, except at very low concentrations but, after the nitrogen source has been exhausted, formation of the higher alcohol continues and, in the case of 3-methylbutanol, increases. It must therefore be concluded that the yeast cannot halt the formation of carbon skeletons which previously took part in transamination reactions leading to synthesis of the relevant amino acid.

A number of useful empirical observations which have been made on the fusel alcohol content of beer (for example Hough and Stevens, 1961; Hudson and Stevens, 1960) may eventually be related to the more recent understanding of the biosynthetic pathways involved, especially in view of the great advances in methods for determining individual higher alcohols, but there is a long way to go before an explanation can be given of the effects of yeast strain and fermentation system on this facet of beer composition.

A second group of compounds whose formation is related to the amino-acid metabolism of yeast are the vicinal diketones, notably diacetyl, a compound which has an aroma reminiscent of slightly rancid butter. Inadequate supplies of the amino acid valine are associated with overproduction of diacetyl (Owades *et al.*, 1959) because α-acetolactate, which is involved during valine biosynthesis, escapes into the wort where it breaks down, chemically, to yield diacetyl (Fig. 17).

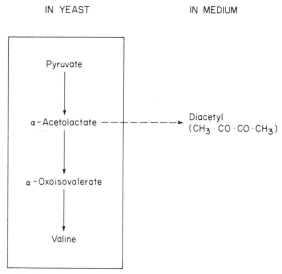

Fig. 17. Pathway for formation of diacetyl by brewer's yeast After Wainwright (1973).

Many other examples could be given of side-effects of an anomalous amino-acid composition of wort. A deficiency of methionine (which could be caused by inadequate supplies of pantothenate in the wort) is associated with unacceptable levels of hydrogen sulphide (Wainwright, 1971b) and excess threonine has a similar effect. Careful control of the amino-acid composition of wort is a prudent biochemical gesture rather than a desire to adhere blindly to tradition.

The last group of minor constituents formed by yeast to which reference will be made are the esters (Fig. 18), with ethyl acetate the predominant member of the group. As amply demonstrated by Nordström (1965), ester formation involves condensation of acyl-CoA esters with alcohols, and conditions which favour ester production include, high-gravity brewing followed by dilution, ample supplies of assimilable nitrogen and relatively high concentrations of alcohol. Metabolic reactions can rarely be considered usefully in isolation, however; since increasing concentrations of assimilable nitrogen are associated with lowered production of higher alcohols (Äyräpää,

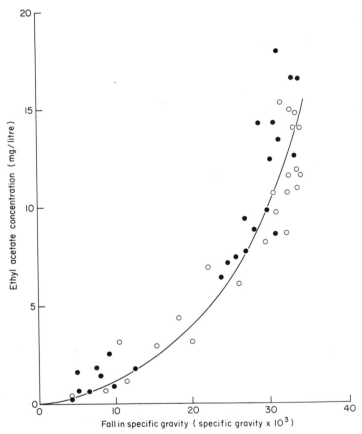

Fig. 18. Relationship between extent of fermentation (fall in specific gravity) and ethyl acetate formation during stirred (○) and unstirred (●) fermentations by various yeast strains. From Anderson and Kirsop (1974).

1971) while total ester content increases at higher nitrogen concentrations, some individual components (for example isopentyl acetate) may not alter significantly in concentration.

5. *Wort Deficiencies*

According to Kirsop and Brown (1972) minor essential wort constituents, other than amino acids, are normally present in an all-malt wort in at least twofold excess, and certainly inspection of the list of wort constituents compiled by MacWilliam (1968) suggests that, nutritionally, most worts must be more than adequate for the known requirements of *Sacch. cerevisiae* or *Sacch. carlsbergensis*. Occasional instances have been reported, however, of worts which proved to be deficient in specific nutrients required in trace amounts. For example, Brightwell *et al.* (1968) found that a continuous-fermentation system initially operated satisfactorily but, after 23 days, attenuation was poor and the yeast had turned pink, which is a typical symptom of biotin deficiency. Additions of biotin (or of wort sediment) produced a spectacular recovery and, surprisingly, further work suggested that the New Zealand barley which provided the malt had an unusually low content of biotin.

A second, possibly more frequent, deficiency in wort may be with regard to zinc. Bishop (1971) has described some work carried out in the 1940s in which the addition of 0.75 p.p.m. of zinc to a defective brewery fermentation gave an instant improvement, and a yeast head over two metres high!

Bishop, incidentally, also suggests that zinc may be removed with the wort sediment. Caution must, of course, be exercised in adding zinc to brewery fermentations as concentrations above 1 p.p.m. are toxic (Densky *et al.*, 1966).

C. Physical Behaviour of Yeast

1. *Head Formation*

In traditional ale fermentations, yeast cells, in association with bubbles of carbon dioxide, collect on the surface of the wort, a process which has been described in detail, in prose and photographically, by Bishop (1938). From this yeast head, or barm, an appropriate fraction is used to pitch the next fermentation and, in the past, ability to form a satisfactory head was a desirable, indeed an essential, feature of a top-fermentation yeast. As will be seen later, changing techniques of fermentation and yeast collection (Harris, 1969) are rapidly modifying this requirement.

Strains of *Sacch. cerevisiae* vary in their ability to adhere to the bubbles of carbon dioxide which transport them to the surface and, as Dixon and Kirsop (1969) have shown, accumulation of yeast cells in the bubble surfaces tends to stabilize the foam; *Sacch. carlsbergensis*, as might be expected, shows poor bubble adhesion.

Wort constituents also affect yeast head formation. In their series of model experiments, Dixon and Kirsop (1969) showed that more stable heads could be formed from wholly fermented than from partly fermented wort, and that some direct-conversion barley syrups were defective as head-forming media. Isohumulones promote head formation (Dixon, 1967) and some yeasts have such poor head-forming abilities in unhopped wort that it is impossible to collect sufficient yeast by skimming to pitch a subsequent fermentation.

Though isohumulones participate in head formation, owing to their surface activity, they are partly removed with the yeast head or, more precisely, on the foam associated with the head (Dixon, 1967). Fermentation losses of isohumulones incurred in this way may be quite substantial and, as suggested by Lloyd (1969), the greater losses of bittering materials observed when high-gravity wort is fermented may be associated with enhanced production of fermentation gases.

Many other surface-active wort constituents must influence the behaviour of the yeast head during fermentation, and Thompson *et al.* (1965) found that sparging the surface of the fermentation with recirculated wort offered a convenient means of diminishing the height of the foam. Reference has already been made to wort phospholipids in this context, and deliberate addition of sorbitan monolaurate (Button and Wren, 1972) can equally result in a decline in foam levels to one-third of untreated controls. Silicones (Hall, 1972a; Hall and Evans, 1972) have a similar effect, and give a marked improvement in hop utilization. These foam-controlling additives are adsorbed on filter materials (or removed by finings) so they do not impair the foam-stability of the beer, and they offer obvious advantages in the form of better plant utilization.

2. *Flocculation*

In addition to their diverse abilities to participate in the formation of a stable yeast head, yeast strains also differ in flocculating power, i.e. in the tendency to clump together in groups which then separate from the main body of the wort, subsiding to the bottom of the vessel or, buoyed up with entrained carbon dioxide, collecting in the yeast head. Not all yeast strains flocculate; powdery yeasts remain in suspension as individuals while fermentation proceeds. With a powdery yeast it is therefore possible to attenuate the beer to the limit in the primary fermentation and, if so desired, to obtain complete removal of all fermentable sugars from the wort. In contrast, a highly flocculent yeast may aggregate and start to separate from the fermentation well before the utilizable sugars are exhausted. Gilliland (1951) has distinguished four classes of yeast with respect to flocculating ability (Table 10) and, if a mixture of

Table 10

Yeast classification according to flocculation characteristics. From Gilliland (1951)

CLASS I	Does not flocculate; cells remain in suspension until final attenuation limit is reached.
CLASS II	Flocculates after about two-thirds of the fermentable sugars have been utilized, leaving the beer relatively clear of yeast, and fermentation complete.
CLASS III	Starts to flocculate about the same point as strains in Class II but comes out of suspension very rapidly forming 'caseous' masses, and leaving fermentable sugar in the wort.
CLASS IV	Flocculates very early; newly formed cells fail to separate. Smaller clumps of cells are produced than with strains in Class III, so a better 'head' results though fermentation is incomplete.

strains is used, care has to be taken to ensure that the desired proportion of each is present in the yeast collected for pitching; early collection will favour the more flocculent yeast and result in progressively poorer attenuations (Bremner, 1942).

The ability to flocculate is genetically controlled (Thorne, 1951; Gilliland, 1951) but physical expression of the phenomenon depends on the condition of the wort and on the physiological state of the yeast. When a yeast is added to wort, the cells become fully dispersed, whatever the flocculating potential of the strain concerned, because the presence of maltose (Lindquist, 1953) prevents flocculation; as the maltose concentration declines, so flocculation is favoured. Calcium ions promote flocculation, and Mill (1964) has suggested that salt bridges are formed by Ca^{2+} linking carboxyl groups on adjoining cells. Taylor and Orton (1973), however, consider that the ionic interactions involved are less simple than Mill suggests. It is reasonably certain that the cell-wall constituents of yeast are concerned in flocculation. Eddy and Rudin (1958) demonstrated that isolated walls have the same flocculation characteristics as their parent cells, but the precise part played by the phosphomannan-protein of the wall remains a question for argument. Gross analyses of cell walls of flocculent and non-flocculent yeasts do not indicate any consistent differences between the two types but, as shown by Lyons and Hough (1970), some genetically non-flocculent yeasts contain lower levels of phosphate in a mannan-rich fraction of the wall; these authors postulate that the glycoprotein phosphate complexes with calcium in the initiation of clumping and that powdery yeasts may contain insufficient available phosphate to allow formation of stable salt bridges.

The technological importance of flocculation is self-evident, and a critical discussion of possible mechanisms involved is given by Rainbow (1970).

D. Fermentation Systems

Over the past quarter of a century, changes in fermentation technology have probably been more extensive than in all of the previous millenia of beer brewing. At present we have a mixture of old and new systems, small and large installations, batch processes and continuous processes; all can produce excellent beers, and the future pattern of development may depend as much on the economics of distribution as on the efficiency of the fermentation system employed. Thus, the economies of scale could well be annulled by the cost of fuel for transport, and forward planning with regard to siting of fermentation units is at present no easy task. With a product which is about 95% water, the possibility of fermenting wort of very high initial gravity and later diluting, as required, near the site of consumption, offers interesting possibilities (excise laws permitting) and results of work at present in progress (Anderson and Kirsop, 1974) suggest that this attractive possibility is likely to be evaluated rather critically in the near future.

1. Traditional Batch Systems

a. *Top-fermentation skimming systems and their successors.* The skimming system, which is well described by Lloyd-Hind (1948), is the traditional ale fermentation whose genesis can be traced back to prehistoric times. In the modern enclosed vessel, usually constructed of stainless steel, with wall attemperation, collection points for carbon dioxide and facilities for in-place cleaning, progress of a fermentation proceeds as shown in Figure 13 (p. 85). Elimination of the expensive delay caused by the 'natural' cleansing of the yeast can readily be achieved by centrifugation when the essential biochemical changes have been completed. In any event, enclosure of the vessel introduces difficulties in operating a skimming system because many yeast heads do not easily move across the beer surface to the manhole (Ricketts, 1971). In the older skimming systems, rousing of the yeast (i.e., blowing air through the wort to keep the yeast in suspension) was regularly practised; this is rare today both because it is incompatible with the engineering simplicity required for efficient automated cleaning and because selection of a suitable yeast strain, which need not be a head former, makes rousing redundant. Operating a batch fermentation with yeast collection by skimming contributes to making fermentation the highest basic cost in brewing as far as labour is concerned and, as Harris (1969) has shown, centrifugal collection of yeast introduces substantial economies. Selection of an appropriate strain of yeast along the lines previously discussed must naturally accompany such a change in plant operation.

b. *Yorkshire stone squares.* In this variant of the skimming system, there is a deck or platform (with a manhole and interconnecting pipe) slightly below the level of the wort. Vigorous rousing of the highly flocculent yeast employed is required to allow the fermentation to go to completion and, on desisting from rousing, the yeast collects on the deck, leaving clear beer below. Although the original stone squares were, as their name implies, constructed from local slate, modern versions are available in stainless steel.

c. *Burton Unions*. In contrast to the Yorkshire Squares, Burton Unions have evolved in conjunction with the use of a non-flocculent yeast which could not be removed by skimming. In this system the fermenting wort is transferred after about 36 hours to a row of casks each provided with a swan-neck tube which opens into a common inclined trough above the set of casks. Carbon dioxide, yeast and beer drop in large blobs into the trough, which may be cooled to promote yeast settlement and allow drainage of the beer. Within the casks, cooling coils are used to control fermentation and, eventually, to ensure sedimentation of the yeast, and the beer, with a fairly standard low population of yeast, is removed through a tube which projects above the level of sediment.

As can be imagined, cleaning costs are formidably high, as are figures for losses of beer. Ricketts (1971) quotes a value of 5% and, though a room full of Burton Unions is indeed a noble sight, economic considerations suggest that, in the none too distant future, Burton Unions will become a mere memory enshrined in the annals of brewing archaeology. Detailed descriptions of Yorkshire Stone Squares and Burton Unions and their operation are provided by Lasman *et al.* (1955).

d. *Lager fermentations*. A typical lager fermentation differs from an ale fermentation in the species of yeast used (a sedimentary or powdery strain of *Sacch. carlsbergensis*) and in the fermentation temperature which is not usually allowed to exceed 10°C. The wort is pitched, frequently in open vessels, at about 0.25 kg dry weight per hectolitre and, though no persistent yeast head is formed, foam to a height of at least 50 cm can be expected. Many lager brewers run the fermenting wort into a second closed vessel after about 40 hours of fermentation, leaving the sludge behind, and fermentation continues for up to 14 days. Cooling to 4°C assists yeast sedimentation and, as in ale brewing, centrifugation may be used to hasten the removal of yeast. A surface layer of undesirable bitter material is removed before the 'green' beer, containing some fermentable sugar, is transferred to lagering tanks for a more, or less, extended period of conditioning.

2. *Continuous Fermentations*

Although methods suitable for the continuous fermentation of wort have been discussed, and patented, and examined on the laboratory or pilot-plant scale since the beginning of the Century, it was not until the 1960s that continuously fermented beer became common-place commercial reality, with New Zealand particularly advanced in this development (Coutts, 1961a, b). Successful continuous fermentation is intimately linked with satisfactory microbiological control, with adequate instrumentation and, particularly in the development stage, with the availability of analytical methods which are sufficiently precise to allow comparison of the beer with the batch product, for matching with an existing beer rather than the introduction of a new line has been the objective of most ventures into continuous fermentation.

Theoretical aspects of continuous fermentation are fully discussed elsewhere (see, for example, Herbert, 1961; Portno, 1968a) and the present account will be limited to a consideration of the major types of continuous fermentation which are known to be in current use.

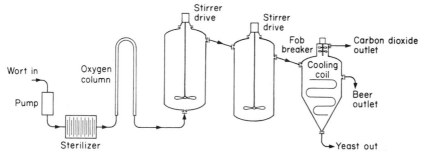

Fig. 19. A diagram of a stirred-tank continuous fermentation system. From Bishop (1970a).

One such system (Fig. 19) described by Bishop (1970a) involves the use of two stirred vessels followed by a smaller settling vessel; yeast escapes with the beer so this is an 'open' system. The mechanics of ensuring suitable supplies of wort can be difficult, so provision is made for storage of wort at 2°C; up to 14 days' storage is apparently practicable. Oxygenation of the wort is carefully controlled to allow satisfactory yeast growth in the first vessel; over-oxygenation has been found to result in the development of cells of aberrant morphology. Under steady-state conditions, the wort is fermented to half gravity in the first vessel and, in the second, further attenuation is achieved with only a small increase in the yeast population. The patented cooling system in the settling vessel ensures adequate yeast separation so that the emerging beer contains fewer than 7.5 million cells per ml. Both analytically and on taste-testing assessment, the beers produced in this continuous fermentation system 'matched' the batch products satisfactorily. Of paramount importance for this system is the choice of a suitable strain of yeast; it must flocculate well only after full attenuation and possess the correct flavour attributes.

Economic advantages of the system include saving of labour costs, easy collection of pure carbon dioxide, minimal losses of duty-paid beer, and a reduction in the loss of isohumulones on the greatly diminished foam.

A second successful continuous system which accommodates fermentation and yeast separation within a single vessel is the tower fermentor (Fig. 20). Here again the attributes of the yeast are important; it must be a highly flocculent sedimentary type, able to overcome the upward movement of beer and carbon dioxide against the density gradient imposed by the transformation of wort to beer. Early studies with tower fermentors (Klopper et al., 1965) suggested that yeast growth was negligible, but more recent work (Ault et al., 1969) has shown that multiplication of yeast approximates to that in a batch fermentation. Again, aeration is critical, as unacceptably high concentrations of esters are found in conditions of deficient oxygen supply. From the results of extensive biochemical studies on the metabolism of yeast within the tower, Ault et al. (1969) conclude that satisfactory matching with batch-fermented beer is possible but, whereas batch fermentation requires 72 hours, residence time in the tower can be as little as four to six hours.

Despite the unequivocal demonstration by Thorne (1970) that deleterious mutations of Sacch. carlsbergensis can be expected when a continuous fermentation system is operated over a prolonged period, little trouble seems to have been experienced from detectable alterations in yeast behaviour. In this connection, it is interesting to note that Hall (1970) found that strains of Sacch. carlsbergensis showed a much greater degree of instability than did Sacch. cerevisiae, though lager and ale both appear to have been successfully produced by the two continuous systems described.

Invasion of a continuous-fermentation system by a 'killer yeast'

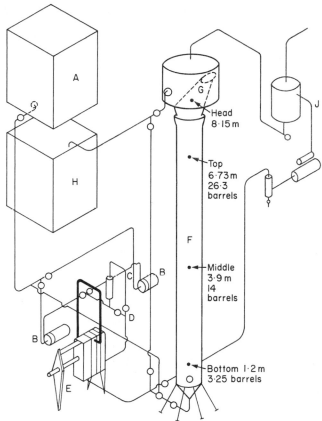

Fig. 20. Diagram of a production-tower fermentor and ancillary plant. A indicates the wort-collecting vessel; B, impellor-type pump; C, flowmeter; D, control valve; E, flash pasteurizer; F the tower; G, yeast separator; H, beer receiver; and J, carbon dioxide collecting vessel. From Ault *et al.* (1969).

has, however, been reported (Maule and Thomas, 1973); 80% of the culture yeast died within 24 hours, necessitating a close down and sterilization of the plant.

The latest introduction to the field of continuous fermentation is the plug fermentor (Narziss and Hellich, 1971) in which clear de-oxygenated wort is pumped through a mixture of lager yeast and kieselguhr. Yeast growth does not take place, there is little uptake of amino nitrogen, fusel alcohols and esters in the beer are slightly lower than normal and, though diacetyl develops to an unacceptably high concentration during storage, a preliminary conditioning for two-to-four days in the presence of yeast suffices to lower diacetyl concentrations to a satisfactory extent. Trials with *Sacch. cerevisiae*

(Baker and Kirsop, 1973) have shown that this system can be equally effective with ale yeasts; in this case, the problems posed by development of diacetyl were solved by heating the beer emerging from the plug to expedite the transformation to diacetyl of its precursor, α-acetolactate, and then removing the diacetyl, which is readily reduced by yeast, by passing the heated beer through a second plug. Plug fermentation of wort can legitimately be called continuous, but the life expectation of the plug is only about one week, as it gradually becomes occluded with colloidal material from the wort.

3. Cylindro-conical Tank Fermentations

The increasingly popular cylindro-conical fermentation vessels appear to owe their genesis to the ideas of Nathan (1930) who appreciated the potential merits of a single, tall vessel used for fermentation and then for conditioning by purging from the base with carbon dioxide. Nathan's ideas, however, were not actively followed up until the early 1960s, and since then many installations have been developed ranging in size from a modest 870-hectolitre capacity (Thompson, 1970) up to the giant 4,800-hectolitre outdoor tank described by Ulenberg et al. (1972). The jacketted lagged tank described by Thompson (1970) has a domed cover with a combined pressure release and vacuum break valve which serves as an outlet for carbon dioxide, facilities for sterile sampling, and separate attemperation of the basal cone. A strain of Sacch. cerevisiae is used which, apart from its sedimentary behaviour, resembles that used in the brewery's batch fermentations. Fermentation takes 60 hours. Little foam is formed so that hop rates can be decreased by up to 20%; yeast, encouraged by cooling, settles in the cone whence it is drawn off for a subsequent fermentation, and beer is racked through the same port.

The 4,800-hectolitre tank requires about 16 hours for filling, and contains 10 brews but, apart from the logistics of management, no insurmountable difficulties have emerged in controlling the fermentation. As discussed by Ladenburg (1968) the formation of bubbles of carbon dioxide in the depths of the vessel, and their subsequent rising and expansion, drag up the wort to provide a regular circulation throughout the tank and, rather surprisingly, the content of carbon dioxide in beers stored in such tanks (for they can also be used for conditioning) is fairly uniform throughout. Analyses of the yeast during fermentation and of the final beer produced in a giant tank showed no major deviations from control fermentations (Harada *et al.*, 1972). It appears, therefore, that the only limitations to size lie in the ability to attemperate the large volumes at a reasonable rate, and in the microbiological expertise of the operators, for a massive wort infection could have rather serious consequences.

IX. BEER TREATMENTS

A. Maturation and Conditioning

Before it is ready for consumption, freshly fermented beer must undergo a number of changes, including the elimination of certain volatile fermentation products, super-saturation with carbon dioxide, separation of yeast cells, and removal of some of the polyphenolic and other materials which will eventually give rise to turbidity in the beer.

In the past, and especially in lager brewing, prolonged storage at low temperatures (up to 9 months at 2°C) accomplished most of these objectives. The enclosed lagering tanks were vented to allow escape of the undesirable volatiles. Yeast slowly fermented the residual sugars with, if necessary, addition of 'krausen' (partly fermented wort) to expedite conditioning and, in the fullness of time, yeast cells settled slowly and polymerized polyphenols associated with large polypeptides came out of solution and improved the prospects of obtaining a haze-free product with extended shelf life.

In ale brewing, conditioning was, and often still is, secured much more rapidly by adding a 'priming' sugar which has the double function of sweetening the beer and allowing a secondary fermentation to take place in cask or other container. Not only culture yeasts but, in the days of high-gravity beers, wild yeasts such as *Brettanomyces* spp. (Claussen, 1904) used to participate in the after-fermentation, and were believed to contribute to the luscious, winey, 'unmistakable English character' of the stock beers. Be that as it may, Shimwell (1947a) has amply demonstrated the undesirable effects of this infecting organism in beers of original gravity below 1060°.

Settlement of yeast in the cask can be aided by treatment with isinglass finings, which is a preparation of collagen derived from the swim-bladders of various fish; the origin of this practice is as obscure as the effect is beneficial. The viscous, positively charged collagen molecules coprecipitate with the negatively charged yeast cells (Leach, 1967) leaving the supernatant beer completely clear. Finings, incidentally, have a valuable subsidiary action in precipitating head-negative materials such as phospholipids and silicones which usefully control foam during the fermentation, but would adversely affect the head-forming properties of the beer.

Two developments have combined to shorten the time required for maturation and conditioning of both ales and lagers. The first is the replacement of natural, that is yeast-induced, conditioning with artificial carbonation, and the second is the greater knowledge which has accumulated of the chemical events taking place during storage and the development of sound methods of analysis, both pre-requisites of adequate control.

A plant-scale comparison of beer which had been carbonated mechanically to 0.5–0.6% carbon dioxide with similar beer which was naturally conditioned by krausening (Posada et. al., 1969) showed that the two beers did not differ analytically except for lower concentrations of acetaldehyde and hydrogen sulphide in the carbonated beer. It seems unlikely that there can be any deleterious effect of artificial carbonation, provided it is adequately controlled.

Acetaldehyde and hydrogen sulphide are two of the compounds associated with a 'green' beer flavour (Hartong, 1966), and the efficacy of yeast in functioning as a reducing agent towards acet-aldehyde is uncontested. Prolonged contact with residual or krausening yeast during lagering must contribute to the elimination of acetaldehyde; interestingly, the 'plug' conditioner studied by Baker and Kirsop (1973) lowered acetaldehyde concentrations from 40 p.p.m. to 4 p.p.m. as well as removing over 80% of the diacetyl.

It is considerably simpler, however, as for example Devreux (1971) has shown, to store beer for two days at an elevated temperature (14°C or more) to allow simple volatilization of undesirable fermentation products, and Devreux doubts the efficacy of carbon dioxide as a scouring agent. With concentrations of hydrogen sulphide decreased to below 20 μg per litre, three days at −2°C sufficed to precipitate the chill haze material before carbonating the finished beer. In this case, changes in techniques of maturation and conditioning decreased production time from two months to ten days.

B. Haze Prevention

Understanding and, as a result, control of the formation of haze in stored beer has been one of the success stories of the past decade. Because of its content of polyphenolic compounds and polypeptides of high molecular weight (loosely referred to, respectively, as tannins and proteins), together with trace quantities of metallic ions, it is inevitable that polymerized polyphenols in association with protein will eventually come out of solution. Copper and iron catalyse the formation of haze, and warm storage and molecular oxygen expedite it (de Clerck, 1934). The brewer's problem is to arrange his production methods to ensure that the onset of haze is deferred until the slowest moving sample of the beer concerned has been consumed.

Two types of protein-tannin haze can be distinguished. These are chill haze and permanent haze which, in addition to appearing at different stages and temperatures of storage, differ in appearance in the electron microscope (Claesson and Sandegren, 1963). Chill haze appears, earlier than permanent haze, when beer is cooled to about 3°C and it redissolves on warming. Common sense therefore demands that, after the chilling of lager beers, they be filtered without any rise in temperature. Equally, avoidance of post-fermentation contact with oxygen is mandatory, not only in relation to haze but, as will be seen later, for considerations of flavour. Permanent haze, whose amorphous particles probably represent an aggregation of the small isodiametric chill-haze species, eventually forms at temperatures of, for example, 20°C and does not redissolve in beer. Brewing practice can, often unwittingly, affect the length of time a beer is free from haze. Thus Curtis and Clark (1959) found that, with different bottlings of pale ale, the time taken for development of an unacceptable haze ranged from 18 to over 440 days, with peaks of haze formation at 46 and 124 days.

On the basis of amino-acid analysis, the protein component of hazes from various types of beer has been shown to be derived from all of the original barley proteins (Djurtoft, 1965) and not exclusively from some specific fraction though recent work on isofocusing (Savage and Thompson, 1973) may modify this view. The composition and development of the polyphenolic moiety has attracted a great deal of attention (see, for example, Gramshaw 1967, 1968), and the broad picture seems to be that polyphenols may polymerize slowly in mild acid conditions, as in beer, and rapidly in the presence of oxygen. After polymerization to at least a dimer (Eastmond, 1974), association with protein leads to the inevitable formation of aggregates too large to remain in solution.

It is against this background of understanding of events involved in haze formation that rational methods of haze deferment have developed, though empirical procedures for prolonging shelf life have been used satisfactorily by generations of brewers who were completely unaware of the niceties of polymerization and condensation and, indeed, of the very presence of polyphenols in their beers.

For haze prevention, control methods can be aimed at either, or both, of the major components of beer haze, and the point of treatment depends on, *inter alia*, the volume of precipitate produced by the treatment. Thus papain, used at a concentration of 3g of crude enzyme per hectolitre (Urion, 1965), hydrolyses the protein moiety leaving no insoluble residue, and can most effectively be introduced to the bright beer tank, though it probably exercises its maximal effects during pasteurization (Gray *et al.*, 1963). Tannic acid, on the other hand, whose use at about 10 g per hectolitre is strongly advocated by de Clerck (1970), is employed as a protein precipitant in the conditioning tank, and the tannin-protein complex is removed during subsequent processing. Bentonite, an aluminium silicate, is another non-specific protein adsorbent which effectively stabilizes beer, though the resulting voluminous precipitate is slow to settle, and its lack of specificity can impair foam stability (Schimpf and Runkel, 1962). Thus, Willox (1970) reported that a 50% decrease in bentonite addition gave an increased head retention of 12%, though this increase was at the expense of a 36% decrease in predicted stability. Certain proprietary types of silica gel, however, are more specific and faster acting than bentonite (Raible, 1961).

Attacking the haze problem from the polyphenol end by adsorption on polyamides has proved highly successful. Nylon 66 was the first polyamide to be used commercially (Curtis and Clark, 1960); it has now been replaced by polyvinylpyrrolidone (Polyclar AT) which was first suggested by McFarlane and Bayne (1961), and which has a lesser effect than Nylon 66 on foam stability. Polyclar AT can be added to beer and then removed together with adsorbed polyphenols, but it can also be used as a column or even incorporated in filter sheets (Keller, 1963).

With such an armoury of weapons available to attack the haze-forming material before any damage is done, it is not surprising that packaged beers today have a very long physical shelf-life. Excessive zeal in applying stabilizing treatments can, however, produce beer of very thin palate (Narziss et al., 1968). Furthermore, each treatment carries a cost addition to the final product. It is not too difficult to produce, at considerable expense, a bland, stable product of poor foaming quality and minimal flavour, but this is not the objective of sensible stabilization treatment. A commercially successful procedure should involve a minimal treatment consistent with adequate shelf life, rather than bad brewing practice followed by expensive remedial treatment which carries with it impairment of some of the desirable qualities of beer.

Let it not be thought, however, that the ultimate has been reached in the control of haze formation. Thus, Nummi et al. (1969) have demonstrated that acidic proteins have a greater tendency than the more basic fractions to promote haze formation, and Savage and Thompson (1973), confirming this observation by using electro-focusing techniques for protein separation, have shown that alterations to mashing procedures (for example aeration) can diminish the contents of such compounds in wort. Although addition of form-aldehyde to wort (Macey et al., 1966b) enhances the stability of beer by causing early polymerization of polyphenols and alterations in nitrogenous components, the prospect of haze control by a modification of processing procedures without the use of additives is encouraging.

C. Yeast Removal

Centrifugation and filtration are the normal procedures for removing residual yeast and assorted detritus from conditioned beer. Beer centrifuges occupy a minimum amount of space but, unless they are hermetically sealed, there is a danger of ingress of air which is particularly undesirable at a point when the yeast population in the beer is diminishing. With chilled beer, care must be taken to avoid any rise in temperature lest the material deposited previously redissolve, only to come out of solution at a later stage when the beer is in trade.

Filtration may be through pulp, kieselguhr, composite filter sheets or more rarely, through cellulose ester membranes. Though it can produce a stable beer, pulp filtration is labour-intensive and it has largely been superseded by some form of kieselguhr filter followed, possibly, by pasteurization. The kieselguhr is deposited on a support, a coarse grade being first applied as a pre-coat which bridges the gaps in the support, followed by a finer grade. The concentration of the metered body-feed kieselguhr which accompanies the beer is related to the amount of accompanying particulate matter.

Table 11

Acceptable biological standards for different beers. These values gave adequate biological stability for the given beers in normal trade in the United Kingdom. From Harris (1968b)

Beer type	Organisms permitted (after filtration) per ml of beer
Beer for cellar tanks	0–10
Canned and bottled beer, subsequently pasteurized in container	100
Beer for bottling and canning, subsequently sterile-filtered	100
Keg beer, subsequently flash pasteurized	250

Types of support include the sheet filter used in the traditional plate and frame, wire-mesh leaf filters and systems of superimposed stainless-steel rings arranged in columns. These are all well described by Johnstone and Whitmore (1971) and related to the type of beer being filtered by Martin (1973). The theoretical background to kieselguhr filtration is discussed by Wylie (1962) and by Harris (1968b).

Composite sheet filters contain a mixture of chrysolite asbestos, cellulose and kieselguhr and can be obtained in various grades with the finest, at 10 μm pore size, acting as a sterilizing filter. The positively charged asbestos fibres adsorb negatively charged micro-organisms as well as removing particles by simple sieving but, as sterilizing filters are easily overloaded, they are normally used as a second-stage filter (Osgood, 1969).

The number of yeast cells which can be tolerated in beer emerging from the filters will depend on the further treatment, if any, designed for that beer (Table 11), and the best compromise of ease of operation, economy and microbiological security has to be determined for each beer by each individual brewery.

D. Pasteurization

Although sterile filtration followed by aseptic filling is sometimes the only microbiological protection provided, most beers are subjected to the minimum heat treatment consistent with freedom of the treated beers from subsequent growth of micro-organisms. Calculation of the optimal time-temperature regime is important because pasteurization flavour can result with overtreatment, especially in the presence of oxygen. The commonest procedure for bulk beer is flash pasteurization in which the entering beer flows countercurrent, first to hot pasteurized beer and then to steam, until it reaches a holding area where it remains for approximately 20 sec at 70°C before cooling and packaging.

Tunnel pasteurizers are used with bottled or canned beer and, as their name implies, the containers travel through an enclosed area in which they are sprayed with hot water, left for an appropriate time, and then treated with a cold-water spray. These and other methods of pasteurization are critically discussed by Portno (1968b).

Sterile filling may function satisfactorily for a time and then succumb to infection, as is shown in a most interesting case history reported by Brightwell (1972). Here, after four years' trouble-free operation, the products of a high-speed bottling line suddenly showed evidence of growth of a non-culture strain of *Sacch. cerevisiae* which, because of its propensities for flocculating in large lumps, was resistant to cold sterilants such as the heptyl ester of

p-hydroxybenzoic acid and survived 10 min heating at 65°C, though it could be destroyed by tunnel pasteurization. Though its point of entry was not established, it had become entrenched in all parts of the bottling hall and, despite rigorous cleaning, the only solution was ultimately to replace sterile filling with tunnel pasteurization. Despite occasional setbacks like this, interest in sterile filling of flash-pasteurized beer continues (van den Bogart *et al.*, 1967; Posada *et al.*, 1973).

E. Post-Fermentation Bittering

As will have been appreciated from the brief discussion of hop utilization, the economics of adding whole hops to the copper leaves much to be desired. Not only is the pH value of the wort unfavourable for isomerization, but subsequent losses, especially in foam, are considerable. With the development of convenient methods for manufacturing reasonably pure isomerized extracts (see, for example, Koller, 1969; Hartl, 1971; Hildebrand *et al.*, 1973), post-fermentation bittering has become an increasingly attractive proposition. Most preparations of isomerized bittering substances, however, contain substantial amounts of hop components other than iso-α-acids, and qualitative examination by thin-layer chromatography (Aitken *et al.*, 1967) followed by spectrophotometric estimation of iso-α-acids (Wood *et al.*, 1968) must be carried out before metering-in the bitter material to the beer.

The addition even of pure isomerized preparations to beer is accompanied by some degree of haze formation, particularly when high local concentrations of iso-α-acids are allowed to develop because of a failure to ensure rapid intimate mixing with the beer. The haze can be removed in the final sheet filter though it tends to cause blockage, and Whitear and Button (1971) have preferred to introduce the isomerized extract before kieselguhr filtration. A less pure and consequently cheaper extract with a greater tendency to form haze could then be successfully monitored in to the beer stream.

The economics of post-fermentation bittering are naturally related to the cost of the product and to the success a brewer has in hopping by conventional means, and this varies greatly from brewery to brewery. Not least among the advantages of using isomerized extracts, however, is the ability to control bitterness to any desired level, a matter of increasing importance when a company has breweries in different areas which are striving to produce an identical brand of beer.

X. BEER PROPERTIES

A. Colour and Clarity

As was mentioned earlier, melanoidins from kilned malt introduce colour to beer though there appears to be no quantitative relationship, at least for pale malts, between malt colour and subsequent beer colour (Siegfried, 1955). Roasted barley is also used as a source of colour, in particular for stouts where it may constitute 6% of the grist. As well as providing colour, roasted barley makes a characteristic contribution to the flavour and head retention of stout.

Adjustment of colour can also be made by adding caramel either in the copper or, if the exact colour match has not been achieved by that stage, in the conditioning tank. Certain preparations of caramel tend to come out of solution, and determination of the isoelectric point of a caramel by paper electrophoresis (Greenshields et al., 1969) can help to predict its behaviour on addition to beer.

It is fairly easy to increase the amount of colour in beer—though beer colour is physically complex (see, for example, Trolle et al., 1951)—but the regular production of a very pale beer requires care in early stages of processing, though use of adjuncts such as maize which do not contribute free amino-nitrogen to the wort offers a useful method of colour control.

With satisfactory methods available for manipulating the poly-peptide-polyphenol haze-forming precursors (see p. 105), control of beer clarity is now not difficult, and reference need only be made to a few rather rare causes of haze induction. Metal hazes can occur. Tin, for example, causes an instantaneous production of flocculum when it is added to bottled beer at 2 p.p.m. and slightly slower precipitation at 0.2 p.p.m. (Michel et al., 1956), but the tin content of bottled beers rarely exceeds 0.005 p.p.m. (Steiner and Oliver, 1963). In some canned beers, however, concentrations of tin may rise during storage to approach 0.1 p.p.m. (Rooney, 1963).

The slow development of oxalate haze is associated with the use of brewing liquor which is low in calcium, so that calcium oxalate escapes precipitation during brewing (Burger and Becker, 1949). Silica hazes (Stone and Gray, 1948) may result from excessive sparging of barley husks, and polysaccharide haze attributable to the deposition of β-glucan (Erdal and Gjertsen, 1967) can be related to the use of under-modified barley. Starch haze (Helm, 1939) is, one hopes, a thing of the past.

In short, it can be said that, although maintenance of clarity demands constant vigilance, it can be, and almost always is, achieved in well controlled breweries today.

B. Foam

A firm, white, persistent, well-textured head on a glass of beer is generally regarded as aesthetically satisfying, as is the 'lacing' effect of the foam which adheres to the glass when the beer is drunk. Klopper's phrase (1954) 'for each draught, a ring' beautifully describes the changing appearance, during consumption, of a glass of beer which has good foam adhesion properties, and undoubtedly adequate head-retention and satisfactory cling are desiderata of all beers.

The amount of foam formed on a beer is directly related to its carbon dioxide content (Helm and Richardt, 1936) and to the method of pouring, whereas head retention and foam cling depend on those surface-active constituents of beer which become concentrated on the surface of the bubbles comprising the foam, *viz.* the high molecular-weight nitrogenous materials and the iso-α-acids. Though Grabar and Daussant (1971) have demonstrated immuno-electrophoretically that the proteins of beer foam have more or less the same composition as those participating in haze, Bateson and Leach (1969) found that the more basic proteins have a greater foam-stabilizing effect, so the possibility exists, as Savage and Thompson (1973) have shown, of adjusting brewing procedures to minimize the carry-forward of haze-promoting proteins without affecting those principally involved in foam stabilization. Not surprisingly, over-enthusiastic stabilizing treatments with the protein precipitant, tannic acid (Klopper, 1955), or with proteolytic enzymes (Posada *et al.*, 1971) adversely affect foam stability.

The iso-α-acids are particularly implicated in the ability of beer foam to cling to the glass (Klopper, 1955), a phenomenon which is also manifested when iso-α-acids are added to peptone solutions (Klopper, 1973; Bishop, 1974). In a detailed study of the action of iso-α-acids as foam stabilizers and promoters of foam cling, Bishop (1974) has shown that metal salts of iso-α-acids are present in foam in quantities which exceed their solubility limits; the bubble surface, he suggests, therefore carries a 'solid' or 'solid-reinforced' film, and it is the stiffening of this film, in association with proteins, which promotes foam adhesion.

A number of ill-characterized foam-destructive substances are present in beer (see Cook, 1971, for a general discussion). The higher fatty acids are most likely to be implicated here, as Klopper (1973) found that the threshold values for foam inhibition by linoleic acid and oleic acid (0.1 p.p.m.) could be exceeded by their concentrations in beer.

Finally, the condition of the glass containing the beer is highly important in relation to head stability. The presence of traces of grease or of residual quaternary ammonium compounds, which are used in glass washing, can have a deleterious effect on foam, however satisfactory the foaming potential of the beer may have been when it left the brewery.

C. Flavour and Aroma

Assessment of beer flavour can be made from either of two extreme positions: detailed chemical analysis, aimed at measuring all possible contributors to flavour, and organoleptic, or sensory, evaluation of the product as a whole or of some individual attribute of its impact on the human sense organs. Both approaches, and hybrids between them, have their uses. To all but the most discriminating consumers, however, recognition of a specific component often implies an off-flavour, unless an unfamiliar brand is being sampled, when the presence of some unexpected characteristic may cause comment, even though the compound responsible for it is well within the quality-control specification of the brand concerned.

Many results of analyses of different groups of flavour compounds have been reported in recent years (Suomalainen and Ronkainen,

1968; Palamand and Hardwick, 1969; Harrison, 1970; Meilgaard and
Moya, 1970; Meilgaard *et al.*, 1970; Palamand *et al.*, 1971; Engan,
1972) and a small selection of some of the findings is given in Figure
21 and in Table 12 where various compounds are assigned flavour

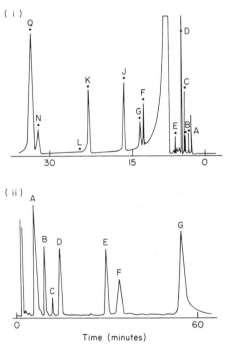

Fig. 21. (i) Typical gas-liquid chromatogram of beer head-space vapour. A indicates
acetaldehyde; B, ethyl formate; C, acetone; D, ethyl acetate; E, ethyl propionate; F,
propanol; G, iso-amyl acetate; J, isobutanol; L, ethyl hexoate; N, active amyl alcohol; Q,
iso-amyl alcohol. (ii) Typical gas-liquid chromatogram of the esterified α-oxo-acids of beer.
A denotes methyl pyruvate; B, ethyl pyruvate; C, methyl-α-oxo-butyrate; D, methyl-α-
oxo-isovalerate; E, methyl-α-oxo-β-methyl valerate; F, methyl-α-oxo-isocaproate; G is
methyl-α-oxo-caproate, added as a reference standard. From Harrison (1970).

threshold values, i.e. concentrations at which the given compound
can just be detected in beer. Caution is required in using these
threshold values, not only because individuals differ in their abilities
to detect different compounds but also because interactions, both
synergistic and antagonistic, can cause complications. Thus, sub-
threshold levels of acetaldehyde depress aroma and introduce a
sweet, estery note, and a combination of isobutyraldehyde and
methylglyoxal gives an earthy, musty aroma which is not apparent
when either is added individually (Palamand and Hardwick, 1969).

Table 12

Concentrations of some flavour constituents of beer

Component	Content (p.p.m.) in			
	Irish beer (Harrison, 1970)	Norwegian lager (Engan, 1972)	English pale ale (Morgan, 1965)	Threshold value
Acetic acid	100	—	—	200
Pyruvic acid	200	—	—	250
Caprylic acid	5	2.8	—	4
Iso-amyl alcohol	60	44	47–61	50–75
Phenethyl alcohol	25	18	36–53	40–75
Acetaldehyde	10	9.8	—	25–50
Ethyl acetate	15	14.6	14–23	15
Iso-amyl acetate	2	1.6	1.4–3.3	1.4–3.3
Diacetyl	0.05	0.12	—	0.1
Dimethyl sulphide	0.02	0.03	—	0.6

Combinations of alcohols or esters may have an additive effect so that, if several compounds of the same class are present in beer each below its threshold value, there may still be a marked effect on flavour (Engan, 1972). A similar additive effect was found by Wheeler et al. (1971) for carbonyl compounds. On the other hand, volatile amines seem to have a general dampening effect on the palate of the beer (Slaughter and Uvgard, 1971).

With the complexity of beer flavour revealed by chemical analysis, the more subjective organoleptic approach of flavour-profile assessment has become increasingly popular, and increasingly useful. Palamand and Hardwick (1969), Wren (1972) and Clapperton (1973, 1974) have all made successful use of this approach. It involves training a team to use a common vocabulary for describing a large number of individual items of aroma and flavour, and scoring each item, after consultation, on a scale of, usually, 0 to 5. The 'profile' which results can be reasonably consistent, from team to team and from week to week with a given beer, and it offers a useful technique for 'matching' beers or for monitoring changes which are being made in a given beer quality. Whether beers will eventually all be described by number with each digit standing for an agreed parameter remains to be seen, though Thorne (1973) has suggested such a system for describing lager yeast strains.

The sweetness of a beer is, naturally, related to its sugar content, which is usually rather carefully controlled with any necessary additions being made at the end of conditioning. Treatment with amyloglucosidase may be used to yield additional glucose from dextrins during conditioning. It is hoped that the enzyme will be inactivated by pasteurization, so that the glucose content of the beer does not continue to increase in trade. Chloride ion is reputed to enhance sweetness and it also may be monitored. Some values of sugar contents for different beers are shown in Table 13.

Table 13

Sugar contents of some commercial beers. From Otter and Taylor (1967)

Type of beer	Sugar Content (%, w/v) of				
	Pale ale	Brown ale[a]	Lager	Lager[b]	Stout[c]
Original gravity	1.050	1.032	1.052	1.040	1.044
Fructose	nil	1.0	trace	0.18	nil
Glucose	0.06	1.0	0.15	0.49	nil
Sucrose	nil	trace	nil	nil	nil
Maltose	0.54	trace	0.13	nil	nil
Maltotriose	0.28	0.2	0.16	nil	trace
Maltotetraose	0.04	0.4	0.14	nil	nil
Total	0.92	2.6	0.58	0.67	trace

[a] The sucrose added as a priming sugar has been inverted during storage.
[b] Enzymic treatment applied to degrade dextrin: 'diabetic' lager.
[c] Naturally conditioned.

Finally, some hop aroma may be introduced into cask beer by adding a handful of hops, or a hop pellet, or a preparation of lupulin glands (Bishop, 1970b). Hop oils prepared by distillation do not seem to give the same effect as dry-hopping but, in any event, hop aroma appears to be a vanishing attribute of modern beer.

D. General Composition and Dietary Value of Beer

The amount of ethanol in beer is related to the amount of fermentable sugars in the wort and to the degree of attenuation achieved by the yeast. It is normal practice to describe beer strength in terms of the original gravity of the wort, though in some parts of the world a value for Degrees Proof spirit is quoted in beer specifications. Alcohol contents have fallen over the past century or more, possibly in an inverse relation to the taxation imposed. For example, Brown and Morris (1889) quote analyses of two beers, one a strong ale of 1888 and the other brewed in 1798, and discovered in a cellar 90 years later; the original gravities, were respectively, 1.11088 and 1.10358 and the alcohol contents 10.8 and 9.7% (w/v). Today alcohol contents are likely to range from a rare 8.0% down to 2.0%.

The calorific value of beer is almost wholly derived from the alcohol and the residual carbohydrates and, in a study of the nutritional value of beers, Vanbelle *et al.* (1972) quote figures of 230–770 calories per litre, with 'table' beers at the lowest level and Belgian 'Trappiste' at the highest. These figures are between 8% and 30% of the daily calorific requirements of an adult male.

Their extensive removal by yeast (Fig. 15, p. 88) means that beer is a relatively poor source of amino acids though, surprisingly, Vanbelle *et al.* (1972) found that one litre of beer could contribute between 10 and 32% (according to the original gravity) of the

Table 14

Some vitamin-B constituents of beers

| | Content (μg/l) of | | | |
Origin of beers	Thiamin	Riboflavin	Nicotinic acid	Reference
Australia	13–66	119–340	7,400–11,500	Bottomley and Lincoln (1958)
United States of America	15–20	227–330	7,830–8,680	Laufer *et al.* (1942)
Germany	25–60	118–420	6,500–10,500	Just and Herbst (1954)
Daily requirement (μg) of an adult male	1800	2700	18,000	Vanbelle *et al.* (1972)

averaged daily requirements of six essential amino acids; isoleucine was the amino acid in poorest supply.

Similarly (Table 14), beer makes some contribution to vitamin-B requirements, especially of riboflavin and nicotinic acid, though thiamin is extensively removed by the yeast during fermentation. Finally, the salt content of beer, which lies between 97 and 176 mg sodium chloride per litre (Norris, 1946), makes beer an appropriate replacement liquid in situations which cause extensive losses of water and salts by sweating.

Beer is not, however, consumed for its calorific value or for its vitamin content or even for its alcohol content (most of the beverages described in this volume have more to offer in this last respect), but a discussion of the psychological and sociological effects of beer lies outwith this chapter.

XI. BEER DEFECTS

A. Gushing

When a bottle of beer is opened, the contents may occasionally erupt violently with considerable losses of foam and liquid. Outbreaks of 'wild' or 'gushing' beer occur sporadically—an interesting study of such an outbreak is described by Thorne and Helm (1957)—and the fundamental causes of gushing have not been easy to establish. Factors which promote gushing include metal ions, particularly Ni^{2+} which requires the presence of isohumulones for its effect (Rudin and Hudson, 1958) and Fe^{3+} (Gray and Stone, 1956), microcrystals of calcium oxalate (Brenner, 1957), and hop resin oxidation products which may be present in some isomerized hop extracts (Laws and McGuinness, 1972). Malt made from weathered barley which harboured the field fungus *Fusarium* was found by Prentice and Sloey (1960) and by Gjertsen *et al.* (1964) to be associated with gushing, and the latter workers extracted an unidentified gushing factor from the malts concerned. Recently, Amaha *et al.* (1973) have characterized the factor as a peptide containing 14 amino-acid residues, and have shown that it can be formed by various fungi including *Rhizopus* sp. and *Fusarium graminearum* grown in culture as well as in association with barley.

Irrespective of the factors which contribute to gushing, the operative mechanism must be related to the energetics of bubble formation in a supersaturated solution which contains an assortment of surface-active substances in colloidal solution. Essentially, gushing is an uncontrolled loss of supersaturation and, as first suggested by Krause (1936) and recently reviewed by Gardner (1973), it appears to be a nucleation phenomenon analogous to the results of 'seeding' supersaturated salt solutions.

Gushing can be suppressed by humulone or by higher unsaturated fatty acids such as linoleic acid (Carrington et al., 1972). Hop-oil components, especially caryophyllene, effectively inhibit gushing (Gardner et al., 1973) and, unlike linoleic acid, they have no adverse effect on the foam characters of normal beers.

The position thus seems to be that beer normally contains both promoters and inhibitors of gushing, and the balance between the effects of the two groups of compounds on the bubble surface merits physico-chemical investigation. In the meantime, in addition to avoiding agitation of beer, careful selection of barley, checking of isomerized hop extracts and, possibly, addition of hop oil (with as a result a re-establishment of hop aroma) offer some prospects of control of gushing.

B. Microbiological Spoilage

Owing to its low pH value (about 4.0), beer is an inhospitable medium for most bacteria though many wild (i.e. non-culture) yeasts can thrive in it. When Pasteur (1879) examined pitching yeasts, his observations doubtless fascinated and possibly horrified the brewers concerned, but whether his observation on the 'occult power of diseased ferments' was acted on is another matter. Certainly, 60 years later, Shimwell (1936) deplored the fact that there was not a single beer-disease organism in the British National Culture Collection, an omission which he soon rectified by depositing therein cultures of *Lactobacillus pastorianus* and *Acetobacter capsulatum* (now *Acetomonas oxydans*). Though tribute is always, and rightly, paid to Pasteur, scientific brewing bacteriology really began with Shimwell; the acetic-acid bacteria (*Acetobacter* spp. and *Acetomonas* spp.) and the lactic acid-forming (*Lactobacillus* spp. and *Pediococcus* spp.) are still probably the commonest beer spoilage organisms, and to them must be added *Zymomonas anaerobia*, also isolated from beer by Shimwell (1937).

The metabolism and nomenclature of bacteria associated with brewing and methods suitable for their cultivation and identification have recently been reviewed by Ault (1971), so discussion here will be restricted to their effects on beer.

Since the acetic-acid bacteria are aerobic, their growth is restricted to the surface of beer and results in the development of a characteristic vinegary aroma and flavour. *Acetomonas oxydans*, which can tolerate very low levels of oxygen, produces gelatinous capsules which, to the naked eye, appear as voluminous 'ropy' strands; this objectionable slimy material is formed from the beer dextrins (Shimwell, 1947b).

With the rigorous cleaning and microbiological control that operates in breweries today, trouble is rarely experienced with acetic-acid bacteria in pasteurized bottled beer, though vigilance is required with draught beer in cask which, if carelessly managed in trade, may absorb sufficient oxygen to support growth of species of *Acetobacter* or *Acetomonas*.

Brewery lactobacilli such as *Lactobacillus pastorianus* or *L. lindneri*, the latter of which, according to Ault (1971), is commoner in lager fermentations, are more troublesome than the acetic-acid bacteria because they are facultative anaerobes. Though they are nutritionally fastidious, many beers contain sufficient residual amino acids to support their growth. Some lactic acid-forming cocci (for example *Pediococcus damnosus*) also produce large amounts of diacetyl, so giving rise to turbid, acid, evil-smelling beer. None of these organisms should survive pasteurization. Finally, the soil organism, *Zymomonas anaerobia*, which produces acetaldehyde and hydrogen sulphide during fermentation of glucose to give a smell reminiscent of rotten parsnips, may gain access to primed cask beer during conditioning or in trade, and cause spoilage within 2– 3 days (Dadds and Martin, 1973).

In recent years, wild yeasts which are capable of growing in beer to produce turbidity have increasingly attracted attention as beer spoilage organisms. Wiles (1953) described classical methods suitable for identification of such infecting organisms but, for rapid control, immunofluorescent techniques (Campbell and Allan, 1964; Richards and Cowland, 1967) are desirable. Richards (1969) has developed this technique to a point at which one 'wild' *Saccharo-myces* cell per million culture cells can be detected and, as Ellison and Doran (1961) had found that this order of contamination sufficed to produce a haze by a 'non-fining' *Sacch. cerevisiae*, the technique is clearly a useful one.

One of the most obnoxious wild-yeast contaminants is *Sacch. diastaticus* (Andrews and Gilliland, 1952). This yeast can ferment the dextrins of beer and simultaneously produce off-flavours; one cell per bottle is enough for trouble.

This brief picture of the microbiological hazards to which beer is exposed should not leave the reader too gloomy; control methods are adequate, and organisms pathogenic for Man are known not to survive in beer.

C. Oxidation Flavour, Stale Flavour and Other Off-Flavours

In a review of the control of oxygen concentration during beer processing, Nielsen (1973) has suggested that one-third of the World's beer production is consumed in a more or less oxidized state, with the characteristic bread-like palate which oxidation induces. Though low concentrations of air in bottle (5 ml or less per litre) are now usual, absorption of oxygen prior to bottling, during carbonation or filtering for example, can negate all of the advantages of careful bottling. Anti-oxidants like ascorbic acid (Gray and Stone, 1939) may act as 'oxygen scavengers' but, in Nielsen's opinion, the best anti-oxidant is yeast itself, actively metabolizing in the conditioning tank. Naturally conditioned bottled beer, with its residual yeast population, may have an advantage to offer here.

The isolation from beer of trans-2-nonenal (Jamieson *et al.*, 1969; Jamieson and van Gheluwe, 1970) and the recognition that remarkably low concentrations of this compound (one part per thousand million) can be responsible for a cardboard-like stale flavour has stimulated research into the origin of this and other carbonyl compounds. Drost *et al.* (1971) who found that, in addition to the nonenal, a similar concentration of 2-methyl furfural was required to impart an authentic stale flavour to fresh beer, have shown that nonenal is derived from linoleic acid, which is introduced into wort from the malt. Other carbonyl compounds which are associated with the ageing of beer are oxidation products of higher alcohols, such as butyraldehyde. As Hashimoto (1972) has shown, melanoidins, which overall function as reducing agents, catalyse this oxidation, and molecular oxygen expedites it, presumably as a result of transformation of the reduced melanoidin to the active oxidized state. Oxidation products of carotenoids may also contribute to stale flavour (Strating and van Eerde, 1973).

In common with haze formation, staling would thus seem to be a natural characteristic of beer. Elimination of oxygen during the final stages of processing, minimal pasteurization—for pasteurization flavours have much in common with aged flavour (Wheeler et al., 1971)—and attention to stock control in trade seem at present to be the best guarantees of a reasonable flavour stability.

It is difficult to generalize about other off-flavours because different beers can accommodate different amounts of compounds which have intense flavour effects. Diacetyl, for example, is detectable in lager at 0.2 p.p.m. and tends to mask other sensory attributes whereas, at this concentration in ale, it cannot be detected, though its presence is associated with greater palate-fullness (Clapperton, 1974). Other off-flavours may be caused by inappropriate storage of bottled beer. The 'skunky' or sunstruck flavour which develops rapidly in beer exposed to light has been attributed by Kuroiwa and Hashimoto (1961) to isopentenyl mercaptan; photolysis of iso-humulone yields 3 methylbut-2-enyl radicals which react with hydrogen sulphide or any available thiol, to form this offensive compound.

Minor changes in processing may have major effects on flavour. An interesting—and biochemically predictable—example has been described by Otter and Taylor (1971) with regard to acetaldehyde. A wide range of acetaldehyde contents was found in beers of similar type; in primed beers, for example, values ranged from 3 to 37 p.p.m.—and the taste threshold is 25 p.p.m. The high values were associated with the practice of adding bisulphite as a preservative while yeast was still metabolizing vigorously. Acetaldehyde, formed normally in fermentation, was bound by sulphite and accumulated instead of being reduced to ethanol.

Let it not be thought that off-flavours are common features of commercially-produced beer. They are not. To savour the full range of possible beer defects, personal experience suggests that one should act as a judge in a home-brewing contest.

XII. THE STATE OF THE INDUSTRY

A. Types of Beer Brewed

1. Ale and Lager

Throughout this chapter, reference has been made to ale and lager without any serious attempt to discriminate between the two, apart from allusion to the different production procedures which are traditionally employed. Most consumers would have no difficulty in identifying extreme examples of either beer, but the contributions made by the different procedural steps are not easy to quantify. Use of an appropriate species (and strain) of yeast is generally regarded as the most important determinant of ale/lager flavour (Hall, 1972b), though recent work by Crabb (1974) suggests that the typical sulphury aroma of lager may originate in the malt. Although Sinclair et al. (1969) found that dimethyl sulphide concentrations in Continental lagers were higher than in British ales, it seems a little simplistic to look for a single specific cause of the flavour of a particular beer type. Other compounds which may affect the ale/lager flavour include tryptophol, which Szlavko (1973) found to be higher in Canadian ales (8 p.p.m.) than in lagers ($<$ 1 p.p.m.); committed ale drinkers preferred the lagers to which tryptophol had been added compared with untreated lager. Reference has already been made to the higher diacetyl content of ales and to the 'burnt' malty flavours associated with more intensive kilning (Yoshida et al., 1972); these, and other factors, must all contribute to the ultimate flavour differences.

Lagers can range from the pale highly-hopped Pilsener to the dark, aromatic less bitter Munich type, and English ale includes well-bittered pale ales and darker, sweeter mild ales of low gravity and restrained bitterness.

2. Stout

The most obvious characteristic of stout, as a genus, is the characteristic dark colour which is conferred on it by inclusion in the grist of roasted barley (6% or more) or caramel. Within the genus there are sweet stouts, and dry, highly hopped stouts with a characteristic 'grainy' flavour and particularly good head-retention properties.

3. Beer for Sale

The packaging of beer lies outwith the realm of this chapter, though it is an operation which generates a very high labour cost in a modern brewery (Harris, 1969). Canning and bottling machinery grows in speed and in sophistication and, with the greater awareness of the dangers of oxygenation and infection, elimination of air at filling and maintenance of sterility are prime considerations in plant selection and operation.

The traditional container for draught beer, the oak cask, has largely been superseded by the more hygienic metal keg or cask or cellar tank, and dispensing of the filtered conditioned draught beer frequently by means of a top pressure of carbon dioxide is usually the only operation required at the retail outlet. No completely foolproof method of avoiding over-carbonation at the point of sale seems yet to have been devised.

There is still a demand (possibly in a connoisseur's market) for beers which have been naturally conditioned in bottle. Here care is needed to ensure that, at bottling, there is the correct amount of active yeast and priming sugar to make certain that the desired content of carbon dioxide (about 2.6 vol) is eventually achieved; freedom of the conditioning yeast from infective micro-organisms is, of course, mandatory. Porter (1973) has described the necessary precautions involved in processing one type of naturally conditioned beer.

B. World Beer Production

Detailed statistical analyses of all facets of beer production, in West Germany in particular but also in other parts of the World, are assembled in the *Statistischer Bericht des Deutschen Brauer-Bundes*. In 1972 (see Horst, 1973) World beer production was approximately 683 million hectolitres, an increase of about 3% from 1971. The classical brewing countries (Germany, Britain and Belgium) showed some levelling-off in output whereas, in other parts of the World (for example Japan, Africa and the U.S.A.), there was a continuing upwards trend. Within the European Economic Community, Germany and Britain account for about 70% of beer production

Table 15

Sales of beer in Great Britain by type of beer
Reproduced, with permission, from The Brewers Society
Statistical Handbook (1974)

	Sales (per cent of total)	
Category	1971	1972
Draught		
Mild	17.6	15.9
Premium-priced bitter and stout	17.4	17.8
Ordinary bitter	31.3	31.1
Lager	7.1	8.6
Packaged		
Light, pale and export:		
Returnable packages	9.4	9.2
Non-returnable packages	2.0	2.2
Lager		
Returnable packages	1.9	1.9
Non-returnable packages	0.9	1.2
Brown		
Returnable packages	3.9	3.7
Non-returnable packages	0.2	0.2
Stout		
Returnable packages	6.8	6.5
Non-returnable packages	0.3	0.3
Strong ales and barley wine (O.G. 1060° and above);		
returnable and non-returnable packages	0.6	0.7
Party containers (4, 5 and 7 pints capacity)	0.6	0.7
Total	100.0	100.0

(Simmonds, 1973). The structure of the industry in these two countries differs, however, in that in 1971 there were 1680 independent brewing companies in West Germany over half of which, according to Puderbach (1973), produced less than 10,000 hectolitres per annum, compared with 92 in Britain, where six major groups provide some 75% of the total production.

Britain differs from the rest of the brewing world in that ale, of one type or another, accounts for 75% of sales (Table 15). Draught beers (ale, lager and stout) are more popular than packaged beers in Britain but, in the U.S.A. according to Katz (1973), sales of draught beer are a mere 12.5% of the total production, essentially of lager. Stout is a characteristic English and Irish beer, but the brewing of stout has spread to Australia, Africa and Malaysia. The figures in Table 15 have their counterparts elsewhere, with different countries dominated by different types of beer and, in most, some variety introduced by the production of local specialties.

It would be foolish to speculate extensively on possible future developments in the industry. It does seem probable, however, that carefully designed quality control, both chemical and micro-biological, and fundamental research into the raw materials of brewing and the techniques of production will continue to con-tribute to the quality and consistency of the product in the future as they have done in the past.

XIII. ACKNOWLEDGEMENTS

The author would like to express her thanks to individuals and to publishers who have generously given permission to use data pub-lished elsewhere.

REFERENCES

Aitken, R. A., Bruce, A., Harris, J. O. and Seaton, J. C. (1967). *Journal of the Institute of Brewing* 73, 528.

Amaha, M., Kitabatake, K., Nakagawa, A., Yoshida, J. and Harada, T. (1973). 'Proceedings of the European Brewery Convention Congress, Salzburg, p. 381. Elsevier, London.

Anderson, F. B. and Harris, G. (1963). *Journal of the Institute of Brewing* 69, 383.

Anderson, R. G. and Kirsop, B. H. (1974). *Journal of the Institute of Brewing* 80, 48.

Anderson, R. J., Howard, G. A. and Hough, J. S. (1971). 'Proceedings of the European Brewery Convention Congress, Estoril, p. 253. Elsevier, London.

Andrews, J. and Gilliland, R. B. (1952). *Journal of the Institute of Brewing* 58, 189.

Ault, R. G. (1971). *In* 'Modern Brewing Technology' (W. P. K. Findlay, ed.), Chapter 7. Macmillan Press, London and Basingstoke.

Ault, R. G., Hampton, A. N., Newton, R. and Roberts, R. H. (1969). *Journal of the Institute of Brewing* 75, 260.

Äyräpää, T. (1971). *Journal of the Institute of Brewing* 77, 266.

Baker, D. A. and Kirsop, B. H. (1973). *Journal of the Institute of Brewing* 79, 487.

Barrett, J. and Kirsop, B. H. (1971). *Journal of the Institute of Brewing* 77, 42.

Bateson, J. B. and Leach, A. A. (1969). 'Proceedings of the European Brewery Convention Congress, Interlaken, p. 161. Elsevier, London.

Bathgate, G. N. (1973). *Brewers' Digest* (April) 60.

Bathgate, G. N., Clapperton, J. F. and Palmer, G. H. (1973). 'Proceedings of the European Brewery Convention Congress, Salzburg, p. 183. Elsevier, London.

Bathgate, G. N. and Palmer, G. H. (1973). *Journal of the Institute of Brewing* 79, 402.

Bathgate, G. N., Palmer, G. H. and Wilson, G. (1974). *Journal of the Institute of Brewing* 80, 278.

Bickerdyke, J. (1886). 'The Curiosities of Ale and Beer—An Entertaining History.' The Leadenhall Press, London.

Birtwistle, S. E., Hudson, J. R. and Whitear, A. L. (1963). *Journal of the Institute of Brewing* 69, 239.

Bishop, L. R. (1929). *Journal of the Institute of Brewing* 35, 323.

Bishop, L. R. (1938). *Journal of the Institute of Brewing* 44, 69.

Bishop, L. R. (1970a). *Journal of the Institute of Brewing* 76, 172.

Bishop, L. R. (1970b). 'Proceedings of the American Society of Brewing Chemists, p. 145.

Bishop, L. R. (1971) *Journal of the Institute of Brewing* 77, 12.

Bishop, L. R. (1974) *Journal of the Institute of Brewing* 80, 68.

Blumenthal, H. J. (1968). *Wallerstein Laboratories Communications* 31, 171.

Bottomley, R. A. and Lincoln, G. J. (1958). *Journal of the Institute of Brewing* 64, 50.

Bourne, D. T. and Pierce, J. S. (1970). *Journal of the Institute of Brewing* 76, 328.

Braidwood, R. J., Sauer, J. D., Helbaek, H., Mangelsdorf, P. C., Cutler, H. C., Coon, C., Linton, R., Stewart, J. and Oppenheim, L. (1953). *American Anthropologist* 55, 515.

Bremner, T. S. (1942). *Journal of the Institute of Brewing* 48, 17.

Bremner, T. S. (1963). *Journal of the Institute of Brewing* 69, 406.

Brenner, M. W. (1957). 'Proceedings of the American Society of Brewing Chemists', p. 5.

Brenner, M. W. (1972). 'Proceedings of the Twelfth Convention of the Australia and New Zealand Section of the Institute of Brewing', p. 154.

Brightwell, R. W. (1972). 'Proceedings of the Twelfth Convention of the Australia and New Zealand Section of the Institute of Brewing', p. 209.

Brightwell, R. W., George, P. M. and Oliver, A. P. (1968). 'Proceedings of the Twelfth Convention of the Australia and New Zealand Section of the Institute of Brewing', p. 133.

Brown, H. T. (1913). *Journal of the Institute of Brewing* 19, 84.

Brown, H. T. and Morris, G. H. (1889). *Transactions of the Laboratory Club* (later: *Journal of the Institute of Brewing*) 3, 81.

Burger, M. and Becker, K. (1949). 'Proceedings of the American Society of Brewing Chemists', p. 169.

Burgess, A. H. and Tatchell, A. R. (1950). 'Annual Report of the Department of Hop Research, Wye College', p. 21.

Buttery, R. G., Black, D. R., Lewis, M. J. and Ling, L. (1967). *Journal of Food Science* 32.

Buttery, R. G. and Ling, L. C. (1966). *Brewers' Digest* (August) 77.

Button, A. H. and Palmer, J. R. (1974). *Journal of the Institute of Brewing* 80, 206.

Button, A. H. and Wren, J. J. (1972). *Journal of the Institute of Brewing* 78, 443.

Campbell, I. and Allan, A. M. (1964). *Journal of the Institute of Brewing* 70, 316.

Campbell, I. and Brudzynski, A. (1966). *Journal of the Institute of Brewing* 72, 556.

Carrington, R., Collett, R. C., Dunkin, I. R. and Halek, G. (1972). *Journal of the Institute of Brewing* 78, 243.

Case, A. C. (1973). *The Brewer* (May) 237.

Claesson, S. and Sandegren, E. (1963). 'Proceedings of the European Brewery Convention Congress, Brussels', p. 221. Elsevier, London.

Clapperton, J. F. (1971). *Journal of the Institute of Brewing* 77, 171.

Clapperton, J. F. (1973). *Journal of the Institute of Brewing* 79, 495.

Clapperton, J. F. (1974). *Journal of the Institute of Brewing* 80, 164.

Clapperton, J. F. and MacWilliam, I. C. (1971). *Journal of the Institute of Brewing* 77, 519.

Claussen, N. H. (1904). *Journal of the Institute of Brewing* 10, 308.

Clayton, E., Howard, G. A. and Martin, P. A. (1972). 'Proceedings of the American Society of Brewing Chemists', p. 78.

Clendinnen, F. W. J. (1936). *Journal of the Institute of Brewing* 42, 567.

de Clerck, J. (1958). 'A Textbook of Brewing' (English translation by K. Barton-Wright), Vol. II. Chapman and Hall, London.

de Clerck, J. (1934). *Journal of the Institute of Brewing* 40, 407.

de Clerck, J. (1970). *Technical Quarterly of the Master Brewers Association of America* 7, 1.

Comrie, A. A. D. (1967). *Journal of the Institute of Brewing* 73, 335.

Cook, A. H. (1971). 'Proceedings of the European Brewery Convention Congress, Estoril', p. 469. Elsevier, London.

Coote, N., Kirsop, B. H. and Buckee, G. K. (1973). *Journal of the Institute of Brewing* 79, 298.

Corran, S. (1973). *Journal of the Institute of Brewing* 79, 83.

Corran, S. (1975). 'A History of Brewing', pp. 303. David and Charles, Newton Abbot.

Coutts, M. W. (1961a). *British Patents* 872,391–872,400.

Coutts, M. W. (1961b). 'Proceedings of the Ninth Convention of the Australian Section of the Institute of Brewing', p. 1.

Crabb, D. (1974). *Journal of the Institute of Brewing* 80, 229.

Crabb, D. and Bathgate, G. N. (1973). *Journal of the Institute of Brewing* 79, 519.

Crisp, J. W. M. and East, E. (1971). 'Proceedings of the European Brewery Convention Congress, Estoril', p. 185. Elsevier, London.

Curtis, N. S. and Clark, A. G. (1959). *Brewers Guild Journal* 186.

Curtis, N. S. and Clark, A. G. (1960). *Journal of the Institute of Brewing* 66, 226.

Dadds, M. J. S. and Martin, P. A. (1973). *Journal of the Institute of Brewing* 79, 386.

David, M. H. and Kirsop, B. H. (1973). *Journal of the Institute of Brewing* 79, 20.

De Mets, M. and Verzele, M. (1968). *Journal of the Institute of Brewing* 74, 74.

Denison, M. (1955). 'The Barley and the Stream—The Molson Story.' McClelland & Stewart, Toronto.

Densky, H., Gray, P. J. and Buday, A. (1966). 'Proceedings of the American Society of Brewing Chemists', p. 93.

Devreux, A. (1971). *Fermentatio* 67, 55.

Diedering, P. L. (1955). *Die Brauerei* 9, 561.

Dixon, I. J. (1967). *Journal of the Institute of Brewing* 73, 488.

Dixon, I. J. and Kirsop, B. H. (1969). *Journal of the Institute of Brewing* 75, 200.

Djurtoft, R. (1965). *Journal of the Institute of Brewing* 71, 305.

Drawert, F., Radola, B., Müller, W., Görg, A. and Bednar, J. (1973). 'Proceedings of the European Brewery Convention Congress, Salzburg', p. 463. Elsevier, London.

Drost, B. W., van Eerde, P., Hoekstra, S. F. and Strating, J. (1971). 'Proceedings of the European Brewery Convention Congress, Estoril', p. 451. Elsevier, London.

Eastmond, R. (1974). *Journal of the Institute of Brewing* 80, 188.

Eddy, A. A. and Rudin, A. D. (1958). *Journal of the Institute of Brewing* 64, 139.

Edwards, R. and Thompson, C. C. (1968). *Journal of the Institute of Brewing* 74, 251.

Ellison, J. and Doran, A. J. (1961). 'Proceedings of the European Brewery Convention Congress, Vienna', p. 224. Elsevier, London.

Enebo, L. and Johnsson, E. (1965). 'Proceedings of the European Brewery Convention Congress, Stockholm', p. 172. Elsevier, London.

Enebo, L., Blomgren, G. and Johnsson, E. (1955). *Journal of the Institute of Brewing* 61, 408.

Enevoldsen, B. (1969). 'Proceedings of the European Brewery Convention Congress, Interlaken', p. 205. Elsevier, London.

Enevoldsen, B. S. (1970). *Journal of the Institute of Brewing* 76, 546.

Enevoldsen, B. S. and Schmidt, F. (1973). 'Proceedings of the European Brewery Convention Congress, Salzburg', p. 135. Elsevier, London.

Engan, S. (1972). *Journal of the Institute of Brewing* 78, 33.

Erdal, K. and Gjertsen, P. (1967). 'Proceedings of the European Brewery Convention Congress, Madrid', p. 295. Elsevier, London.

Essery, R. E. (1951). *Journal of the Institute of Brewing* 57, 125.

Ferguson, B., Richards, M. and Rainbow, C. (1972). 'Proceedings of the Twelfth Convention of the Australia and New Zealand Section of the Institute of Brewing', p. 169.

Ford, J. S. and Tait, A. (1932). *Journal of the Institute of Brewing* 38, 351.

Gardner, R. J. (1973). *Journal of the Institute of Brewing* 79, 278.

Gardner, R. J., Laws, D. R. and McGuinness, J. D. (1973). *Journal of the Institute of Brewing* 79, 209.

Garscadden, B. A. (1973). *Brewing Review* 88, 655.

Gilliland, R. B. (1951). 'Proceedings of the European Brewery Convention Congress, Brighton', p. 35. Elsevier, London.

Gilliland, R. B. (1969). 'Proceedings of the European Brewery Convention Congress, Interlaken', p. 303. Elsevier, London.

Gjertsen, P. (1955). 'Proceedings of the European Brewery Convention Congress, Baden-Baden', p. 37. Elsevier, London.

Gjertsen, P., Trolle, B. and Andersen, K. (1964). 'Proceedings of the European Brewery Convention Congress, Brussels', p. 320. Elsevier, London.

Goedkoop, W. and Hartong, B. D. (1957). *Journal of the Institute of Brewing* 63, 386.

Grabar, P. and Daussant, J. (1971). *Journal of the Institute of Brewing* 77, 544.

Gramshaw, J. W. (1967). *Journal of the Institute of Brewing* 73, 258, 455.

Gramshaw, J. W. (1968). *Journal of the Institute of Brewing* 74, 20.

Gray, P. P. and Stone, I. (1939). *Wallerstein Laboratories Communications* 2, 24.

Gray, P. P. and Stone, I. (1956). 'Proceedings of the American Society of Brewing Chemists', p. 83.

Gray, P. P., Saletan, L. T. and Gantz, C. S. (1963). 'Proceedings of the European Brewery Convention Congress, Brussels', p. 288. Elsevier, London.

Greenshields, R. N., Hunt, P. B., Feasey, R. and Macgillivray, A. W. (1969). *Journal of the Institute of Brewing* 76, 542.

Greenshields, R. N. and MacGillivray, A. W. (1972). *Process Biochemistry* (December) 11.

Grenson, M. (1966). *Biochimica et Biophysica Acta* 127, 339.

Griffin, S. R. (1970). *Journal of the Institute of Brewing* 76, 41.

Hall, J. F. (1970). *Journal of the Institute of Brewing* 76, 522.

Hall, R. D. (1972a). *Journal of the Institute of Brewing* 78, 364.

Hall, R. D. (1972b). *Brewers' Guardian* 101, 121.

Hall, R. D. and Evans, J. I. (1972). *British Patent* 1,290,444.

Harada, T., Nakagawa, A. and Amaha, M. (1972). 'Proceedings of the Twelfth Convention of the Australia and New Zealand Section of the Institute of Brewing', p. 39.

Harris, G., Barton-Wright, E. C. and Curtis, N. S. (1951). *Journal of the Institute of Brewing* 57, 264.

Harris, G. and Millin, D. J. (1963). 'Proceedings of the European Brewery Convention Congress, Brussels', p. 400. Elsevier, London.

Harris, G. and Parsons, R. (1958). *Journal of the Institute of Brewing* 64, 308.

Harris, J. O. (1967). *Journal of the Institute of Brewing* 73, 386.

Harris, J. O. (1968a). *Brewers' Guardian* (May) 81.

Harris, J. O. (1968b). *Journal of the Institute of Brewing* 74, 500.

Harris, J. O. (1969). *Journal of the Institute of Brewing* 75, 243.

Harrison, G. A. F. (1970). *Journal of the Institute of Brewing* 76, 486.

Harrison, J. (1971). *Journal of the Institute of Brewing* 76, 350.

Hartl, A. (1971). 'Proceedings of the European Brewery Convention Congress, Estoril', p. 115. Elsevier, London.

Hartman, L. F. and Oppenheim, A. L. (1950). Beer and Brewing Techniques in Ancient Mesopotamia. *Journal of the American Oriental Society, Supplement* 10.

Hartong, B. D. (1966). *Mallasjuomat* (Finland) 76.

Hashimoto, N. (1972). *Journal of the Institute of Brewing* 78, 43.

Haukeli, A. D. and Lie, S. (1973). *Journal of the Institute of Brewing* 79, 55.

Helbaek, H. (1959). *Science, New York* 130, 365.

Helbaek, H. (1964). *New Phytologist* 63, 158.

Helm, E. (1939). *Journal of the Institute of Brewing* 45, 80.

Helm, E. and Richardt, O. C. (1936). *Journal of the Institute of Brewing* 42, 413, 419.

Helm, E. and Thorne, R. S. W. (1955). *Brewers' Digest* (October) 53.

Herbert, D. (1961). 'Continuous Culture of Micro-organisms.' Society of Chemical Industry Monograph No. 12. S.C.I. London.

Hildebrand, R. P., Clarke, B. J., Lance, D. G. and White, A. W. (1973). 'Proceedings of the European Brewery Convention Congress, Salzburg', p. 125. Elsevier, London.

Hodge, J. E. (1967). 'The Chemistry and Physiology of Flavour' (W. H. Schultz *et al.*, eds.). Avi Publishing Co., New York.

Hoffman, M. (1956). '5000 Jahre Bier.' Metzner, Frankfurt.

Holzer, H. (1968). *In* 'Aspects of Yeast Metabolism' (A. K. Mills, ed.), p. 155. Blackwell Scientific Publications, Oxford and Edinburgh.

Hopkins, R. H. (1925). *Journal of the Institute of Brewing* 31, 399.

Hopkins, R. H. and Carter, W. A. (1933). *Journal of the Institute of Brewing* 39, 59.

Hopkins, R. H. and Pennington, R. J. (1947). *Journal of the Institute of Brewing* 53, 251.

Hopkins, R. H. and Wiener, S. (1944). *Journal of the Institute of Brewing* 50, 124.

Horst Report (1973). Coburg, Germany. Privately published.

Hough, J. S. (1959). *Journal of the Institute of Brewing* 65, 479.

Hough, J. S., Briggs, D. E. and Stevens, R. (1971). 'Malting and Brewing Science', pp. 678. Chapman and Hall, London.

Hough, J. S. and Stevens, R. (1961). *Journal of the Institute of Brewing* 67, 488.

Howard, G. A. and Slater, C. A. (1957). *Journal of the Institute of Brewing* 63, 491.

Howard, G. A. and Tatchell, A. R. (1957). *Journal of the Institute of Brewing* 63, 138.

Hudson, J. R. (1960). 'Development of Brewing Analysis—a Historical Review.' The Institute of Brewing, London.

Hudson, J. R. (1972). *Journal of the Institute of Brewing* 78, 65.

Hudson, J. R. (1973a). 'Proceedings of the European Brewery Convention Congress, Salzburg', p. 157. Elsevier, London.

Hudson, J. R. (1973b). *Journal of the Institute of Brewing* 79, 33.

Hudson, J. R. (1974). *Journal of the Institute of Brewing* 80, 81.

Hudson, J. R. and Birtwistle, S. E. (1966). *Journal of the Institute of Brewing* 72, 46.

Hudson, J. R. and Stevens, R. (1960). *Journal of the Institute of Brewing* 67, 471.

Isebaert, L. (1965). 'Proceedings of the European Brewery Convention Congress, Stockholm', p. 35. Elsevier, London.

Jamieson, A. M., Chen, E. C. and van Gheluwe, J. E. A. (1969). 'Proceedings of the American Society of Brewing Chemists', p. 123.

Jamieson, A. M. and van Gheluwe, J. E. A. (1970). 'Proceedings of the American Society of Brewing Chemists', p. 192.

Johnstone, J. T. and Whitmore, D. J. (1971). *In* 'Modern Brewing Technology' (W. P. K. Findlay ed.), Chapter 10. The Macmillan Press, London and Basingstoke.

Jones, M. and Pierce, J. S. (1963). 'Proceedings of the European Brewery Convention Congress, Brussels', p. 101. Elsevier, London.

Jones, M. and Pierce, J. S. (1964). *Journal of the Institute of Brewing* 70, 307.

Jones, M. and Pierce, J. S. (1969). 'Proceedings of the European Brewery Convention Congress, Interlaken', p. 151. Elsevier, London.

Jones, M., Pragnell, M. J. and Pierce, J. S. (1969). *Journal of the Institute of Brewing* 75, 520.

Just, F. and Herbst, A. (1954). *Brauerei Wissenschaftlichen Beilage* 7, 123.

Katz, P. C. (1973). *Brewers' Digest* 48 (October), 28.

Keller, K. (1963). *Brauwissenschaft* 16, 262.

King, F. A. (1947). 'Beer Has a History.' Hutchisons Scientific and Technical Publications, London.

Kirsop, B. H. and Brown, M. L. (1972). *Journal of the Institute of Brewing* 78, 1.

Klopper, W. (1954). *Journal of the Institute of Brewing* 60, 217.

Klopper, W. J. (1955). *Wallerstein Laboratories Communications* 18, 123.

Klopper, W. J. (1969a). *Brauwelt* 109, 753.

Klopper, W. J. (1969b). *Bulletin de l'Association des Ancients Etudients de Brasserie, Louvain* 65 (2), 57.

Klopper, W. J. (1973). 'Proceedings of the European Brewery Convention Congress, Salzburg', p. 363. Elsevier, London.

Klopper, W. J., Roberts, R. H., Royston, M. G. and Ault, R. G. (1965). 'Proceedings of the European Brewery Convention Congress, Stockholm', p. 238. Elsevier, London.

Koller, H. (1969). *Journal of the Institute of Brewing* 75, 175.

Kramer, S. N. (1958). 'History Begins at Sumer.' Thames and Hudson, London.

Krause, B. (1936). *Svenska Bryggareforeningens Manadsflad* 51, 221.

Kulka, D. (1958). *Journal of the Institute of Brewing* 64, 331.

Kuroiwa, Y. and Hashimoto, N. (1961). 'Proceedings of the American Society of Brewing Chemists', p. 28.

LaBerge, D. E. and Meredith, W. O. S. (1971). *Journal of the Institute of Brewing* 77, 436.

Ladenburg, K. (1968). *Technical Quarterly of the Master Brewers Association of America* 5, 81.

Lasman, W. C., Peard, G. T. and Peet, E. G. (1955). *Journal of the Institute of Brewing* 61, 192.

Latimer, R. A., Lakshminarayanan, K., Quittenton, R. C. and Dennis, G. E. (1966). 'Proceedings of the 9th Conference of the Australia and New Zealand Section of the Institute of Brewing', p. 111.

Laufer, S., Davis, C. F. and Saletan, L. T. (1943). *American Brewer* 52.

Laufer, S., Swartz, R. and Laufer, L. (1942). *Food Research* 7, 306.

Laws, D. R. (1973). *Journal of the Institute of Brewing* 79, 437.

Laws, D. R. and McGuinness, J. D. (1972). *Journal of the Institute of Brewing* 78, 302.

Leach, A. A. (1967). *Journal of the Institute of Brewing* 73, 8.

Lindquist, W. (1953). *Journal of the Institute of Brewing* 59, 59.

Lloyd, R. O. V. (1969). 'Proceedings of the Tenth Convention of the Australia and New Zealand Section of the Institute of Brewing', p. 41.

Lloyd-Hind, H. (1948). 'Brewing Science and Practice', Vol. II. Chapman and Hall Ltd., London.

Lynes, K. J. and Norris, F. W. (1948). *Journal of the Institute of Brewing* 54, 150, 207.

Lyons, T. P. and Hough, J. S. (1970). *Journal of the Institute of Brewing* 75, 504.

Macey, A. and Stowell, K. (1961). 'Proceedings of the European Brewery Convention Congress, Vienna', p. 85. Elsevier, London.

Macey, A., Stowell, K. and White, H. B. (1966a). 'Proceedings of the European Brewery Convention Congress, Madrid', p. 283. Elsevier, London.

Macey, A., Stowell, K. C. and White, H. B. (1966b). *Journal of the Institute of Brewing* 72, 29.

Macey, A., Stowell, K. C. and White, H. B. (1967). 'Proceedings of the European Brewery Convention Congress, Estoril', p. 283. Elsevier, London.

McFarlane, W. D. and Bayne, P. D. (1961). 'Proceedings of the European Brewery Convention Congress, Vienna', p. 278. Elsevier, London.

MacLeod, A. M., Duffus, J. H. and Johnston, C. S. (1964). *Journal of the Institute of Brewing* 70, 521.

MacLeod, A. M. and Millar, A. S. (1962). *Journal of the Institute of Brewing* 68, 322.

MacLeod, A. M. and Palmer, G. H. (1966). *Journal of the Institute of Brewing* 72, 580.

MacWilliam, I. C. (1968). *Journal of the Institute of Brewing* 74, 38.

Maiden, A. M. (1970). 'Glucose Syrups and Related Carbohydrates' (G. G. Birch, L. F. Green and C. B. Coulson, eds.), p. 3. Elsevier Publishing Co.

Manners, D. J. and Marshall, J. (1969). *Journal of the Institute of Brewing* 76, 550.

Martin, E. C. B. (1973). *Brewers' Guardian* 102 (August) 31.

Masschelein, C. A. (1967). *Technical Quarterly of the Master Brewers Association of America* 4, 159.

Maule, A. P. and Thomas, P. D. (1973). *Journal of the Institute of Brewing* 79, 137.

Maule, D. R., Pinnegar, M. A., Portno, A. D. and Whitear, A. L. (1966). *Journal of the Institute of Brewing* 72, 488.

Meddings, P. J. and Potter, D. E. (1971). *Journal of the Institute of Brewing* 77, 246.

Meilgaard, M., Elizondo, A. and Moya, E. (1970). *Technical Quarterly of the Master Brewers Association of America* 7, 143.

Meilgaard, M. and Moya, E. (1970). *Technical Quarterly of the Master Brewers Association of America* 7, 135.

Meyer, H. (1973). 'Proceedings of the European Brewery Convention Congress, Salzburg', p. 429. Elsevier, London.

Michel, G., Gagnaire, B. and Lebreton, P. (1956). *Bulletin de la Société de Chimie Biologique* 38, 931.

Mikola, J., Pietila, K. and Enari, T.-M. (1972). *Journal of the Institute of Brewing* 78, 384, 388.

Mill, P. J. (1964). *Journal of General Microbiology* 35, 61.

Mitchell, W. (1970). *Brewers' Guardian* (March) 51.

Monckton, H. A. (1966). 'A History of English Ale and Beer.' The Bodley Head Ltd., London.

Morgan, K. (1965). *Journal of the Institute of Brewing* 71, 166.

Morgan, K. (1971). *Journal of the Institute of Brewing* 77, 509.

Narziss, L. (1969). 'Proceedings of the European Brewery Convention Congress, Interlaken', p. 77. Elsevier, London.

Narziss, L. (1974). *Journal of the Institute of Brewing* 80, 259.

Narziss, L. and Hellich, P. (1971). *Brauwelt* 111, 1491.

Narziss, L., Rusitzka, P. and Fulda, C. (1968). *Brauwelt* 108, 1833.

Nathan, L. (1930). *Journal of the Institute of Brewing* 36, 536.

Nielsen, E. B. (1971). 'Proceedings of the European Brewery Convention Congress, Estoril', p. 149. Elsevier, London.

Nielsen, H. (1973). *Journal of the Institute of Brewing* 79, 147.

Nielsen, H. and True, H. (1968). *Brauwissenschaft* 21, 342.

Nordland, O. (1969). 'Brewing and Beer Traditions in Norway.' Universitets-
    forlaget, Oslo.
Nordström, K. (1965). 'Proceedings of the European Brewery Convention
    Congress, Stockholm', p. 195. Elsevier, London.
Nordström, K. (1968). *Journal of the Institute of Brewing* 74, 192.
Norris, F. W. (1946). *Journal of the Institute of Brewing* 52, 74.
Northam, P. B. and Button, A. H. (1973). 'Proceedings of the European Brewery
    Convention Congress, Salzburg', p. 99. Elsevier, London.
Nummi, M., Loisa, M. and Enari, T.-N. (1969). 'Proceedings of the European
    Brewery Convention Congress, Interlaken', p. 349. Elsevier, London.
Osgood, G. (1969). *Brewers Guild Journal* 55, 298.
Otter, G. E. and Taylor, L. (1967). *Journal of the Institute of Brewing* 73, 570.
Otter, G. E. and Taylor, L. (1971). *Journal of the Institute of Brewing* 77, 467.
Otter, G. E., Silvester, D. J. and Taylor, L. (1972). *Journal of the Institute of
    Brewing* 78, 57.
Owades, J. L. and Dono, J. M. (1965). 'Proceedings of the American Society of
    Brewing Chemists', p. 157.
Owades, J. L., Maresca, L. and Rubin, G. (1959). 'Proceedings of the American
    Society of Brewing Chemists', p. 22.
Palamand, S. R. and Hardwick, W. A. (1969). *Technical Quarterly of the Master
    Brewers Association of America* 6, 117.
Palamand, S. R., Markl, K. S. and Hardwick, W. A. (1971). 'Proceedings of the
    American Society of Brewing Chemists', p. 211.
Palmer, G. H. (1969). *Journal of the Institute of Brewing* 75, 536.
Palmer, G. H. (1972). *Journal of the Institute of Brewing* 78, 326.
Palmer, G. H. (1974). *Journal of the Institute of Brewing* 80, 13.
Palmer, G. H., Barrett, J. and Kirsop, B. H. (1970). *Journal of the Institute of
    Brewing* 76, 65.
Palmer, G. H., Barrett, J. and Kirsop, B. H. (1972). *Journal of the Institute of
    Brewing* 78, 81.
Palmqvist, U. and Äyräpää, T. (1969). *Journal of the Institute of Brewing* 75,
    181.
Pasteur, L. (1879). 'Etudes sur la Bière' (English translation by F. Faulkner and
    D. C. Robb). Macmillan & Co., London.
Pfenninger, H. G., Schur, F. and Wieg, A. J. (1971). 'Proceedings of the
    European Brewery Convention Congress, Estoril', p. 171. Elsevier, London.
Piendl, A. (1973). *Brewers' Digest* (September) 58.
Pollock, J. R. A. (1960). *Journal of the Institute of Brewing* 66, 22.
Porter, A. M. (1973). *Brewers' Guardian* (October Supplement) 17.
Portno, A. D. (1968a). *Journal of the Institute of Brewing* 74, 55.
Portno, A. D. (1968b). *Journal of the Institute of Brewing* 74, 291.
Posada, J., Almenar, J. and Garcia Galindo, J. (1971). 'Proceedings of the
    European Brewery Convention Congress, Estoril', p. 379. Elsevier, London.
Posada, J., Candela, J., Almenar, J. and Palomero, F. L. (1969). 'Proceedings of
    the European Brewery Convention Congress, Interlaken', p. 253. Elsevier,
    London.
Posada, J., Galindo, J. G. and Palomero, F. L. (1973). 'Proceedings of the
    European Brewery Convention Congress, Salzburg', p. 399. Elsevier, London.
Preece, I. A. (1954). 'The Biochemistry of Brewing', pp. 393. Oliver & Boyd,
    Edinburgh.

Preece, I. A. and Hoggan, J. (1957). 'Proceedings of the European Brewery Convention Congress, Copenhagen', p. 72. Elsevier, London.

Prentice, N. and Sloey, W. (1960). 'Proceedings of the American Society of Brewing Chemists', p. 28.

Puderbach, K. (1973). *The Brewer* (February) 74.

Pudney, J. (1971). 'A Draught of Contentment: The Story of the Courage Group.' New English Library, London.

Raible, K. (1961). *Monatsschrift für Brauerei* 14, 80.

Rainbow, C. (1970). *In* 'The Yeasts' (A. H. Rose and J. S. Harrison, eds.), Vol. 3, p. 147. Academic Press, London.

Recommended Methods of Analysis of the Institute of Brewing (1971). *Journal of the Institute of Brewing* 77, 181.

Rennie, H. (1972). *Journal of the Institute of Brewing* 78, 162.

Rennie, H. (1973). *Journal of the Institute of Brewing* 79, 85.

Richards, M. (1969). *Journal of the Institute of Brewing* 75, 476.

Richards, M. and Cowland, T. W. (1967). *Journal of the Institute of Brewing* 73, 552.

Richards, M. and Macrae, R. M. (1964). *Journal of the Institute of Brewing* 70, 484.

Ricketts, R. W. (1971). *In* Modern Brewing Technology' (W. P. K. Findlay, ed.), p. 83. Macmillan Press, London.

Riddle, H. F. Y., Channell, S., Blyth, W., Weir, D. M., Lloyd, M., Amos, W. M. G. and Grant, I. W. B. (1968). *Thorax* 23, 271.

Rigby, F. L. and Bethune, J. L. (1953). 'Proceedings of the American Society of Brewing Chemists', p. 119.

Robbins, G. S., Farley, M. and Burkhard, B. A. (1964). 'Proceedings of the American Society of Brewing Chemists', p. 34.

Rooney, R. C. (1963). *Analyst, London* 80, 959.

Royston, M. (1968). *Process Biochemistry* 3, 16.

Royston, M. A. (1971). *In* 'Modern Brewing Technology' (W. P. K. Findlay, ed.), Chapter 3. The Macmillan Press, London.

Rudin, A. D. and Hudson, J. R. (1958). *Journal of the Institute of Brewing* 64, 317.

Salac, V. and Dyr, J. (1943). *Gambrinus* 4, 253.

Sandegren, E. (1948). *Journal of the Institute of Brewing* 54, 200.

Sandegren, E., Enebo, L. Guthenberg, H. and Ljungdahl, L. (1954). 'Proceedings of the American Society of Brewing Chemists', p. 63.

Sandula, J., Kockova-Kratochvilova, A. and Zameknikova, M. (1964). *Brauwissenschaft* 17, 130.

Savage, D. J. and Thompson, C. C. (1973). 'Proceedings of the European Brewery Convention Congress, Salzburg', p. 33. Elsevier, London.

Schimpf, F. W. and Runkel, U. D. (1962). *Monatsschrift für Brauerei* 15, 53.

Scott, P. M. (1967). *Brewers' Guild Journal* 53, 339.

Scully, P. A. S. and Lloyd, M. J. (1965). *Journal of the Institute of Brewing* 71, 156.

Seed, B. V. S. (1952). *Journal of the Institute of Brewing* 58, 124.

Serocold, W. P. (1949). 'The Story of Watneys', pp. 130. Vernon & Co., St. Albans.

Shimwell, J. L. (1936). *Journal of the Institute of Brewing* 42, 585.

Shimwell, J. L. (1937). *Journal of the Institute of Brewing* 43, 191.

Shimwell, J. L. (1947a). *American Brewer* 80 (May) 21, 56.

Shimwell, J. L. (1947b). *Journal of the Institute of Brewing* 53, 280.

Shimwell, J. L., Kirkpatrick, M. F. and Baylis, P. H. (1938). *Journal of the Institute of Brewing* 44, 270.

Siegfried, H. (1955). *Schweizer Brauerei Rundschau* 66, 7.

Simmonds, D. (1973). *International Bottler and Packer* (August) 48

Sinclair, A., Hall, R. D. and Thorburn-Burns, D. (1969). 'Proceedings of the European Brewery Convention Congress, Interlaken', p. 427. Elsevier, London.

Slaughter, J. C. and Uvgard, A. R. A. (1971). *Journal of the Institute of Brewing* 77, 446.

Smith, G. R. (1965). *Brewers' Digest* 40, 56.

Steiner, R. L. and Oliver, R. T. (1963). 'Proceedings of the American Society of Brewing Chemists', p. 111.

Stevens, R. (1967). *Chemical Reviews* 67, 19.

Stevens, T. J. (1966). *Journal of the Institute of Brewing* 72, 369.

Stone, I. and Gray, P. P. (1948). *Wallerstein Laboratories Communications* 11, 311.

Strating, J. and van Eerde, P. (1973). *Journal of the Institute of Brewing* 76, 414.

Strong, L. A. G. (1957). 'A Brewer's Progress—A Survey of Charringtons Brewery on the Occasion of its Bicentenary.' The Curwen Press, London.

Suomalainen, H. (1968). *In* 'Aspects of Yeast Metabolism' (A. K. Mills, ed.), p. 1. Blackwell Scientific Publications, Oxford and Edinburgh.

Suomalainen, H. and Ronkainen, P. (1968). *Technical Quarterly of the Master Brewers Association of America* 5, 119.

Surdin, Y., Sly, W., Sire, A. W., Bordes, A. M. and de Robichon-Szulmajster, H. (1965). *Biochimica et Biophysica Acta* 107, 546.

Szlavko, C. (1973). *Journal of the Institute of Brewing* 79, 283.

Taylor, N. W. and Orton, W. L. (1973). *Journal of the Institute of Brewing* 79, 294.

Thompson, C. C. (1970). *Brewers' Guild Journal* 56, 509.

Thompson, C. C., Curtis, N. S., Gough, P. E. and Ralph, D. J. (1965). 'Proceedings of the European Brewery Convention Congress, Stockholm', p. 305. Elsevier, London.

Thompson, F. C. and Neve, R. A. (1972). *Journal of the Institute of Brewing* 78, 156.

Thorne, R. S. W. (1951). 'Proceedings of the European Brewery Convention Congress, Brighton', p. 21. Elsevier, London.

Thorne, R. S. W. (1958). *Journal of the Institute of Brewing* 64, 411.

Thorne, R. S. W. (1970). *Journal of the Institute of Brewing* 76, 555.

Thorne, R. S. W. (1973). *Brewers' Guardian* (September) 39.

Thorne, R. S. W. and Helm, E. (1957). *Journal of the Institute of Brewing* 63, 415.

Trolle, B., Nyborg, P. and Buchmann-Olsen, B. (1951). *Journal of the Institute of Brewing* 57, 347.

Tullo, J. W. and Stringer, W. J. (1945). *Journal of the Institute of Brewing* 51, 86.

Ulenberg, G. H., Gerritsen, H. and Huisman, J. (1972). 'Proceedings of the Twelfth Convention of the Australia and New Zealand Section of the Institute of Brewing', p. 47.

Urion, E. (1965). *Brasserie* 20, 293.

Vanbelle, M., de Clerck, E. and Vervack, W. (1972). *Bulletin de l'Association Royale des Anciens Etudients en Brasserie, Louvain* 68, Part 3 (September) 6.

van den Bogart, X., Hassan, S. and Quesada, F. (1967). 'Proceedings of the European Brewery Convention Congress, Madrid', p. 227. Elsevier, London.

van Gheluwe, J. E. A. and Dadic, M. (1972). *Brewers' Digest* (September) 120.

Verzele, M. (1957). *Wallerstein Laboratories Communications* 20, 7.

Verzele, M. (1967). 'Proceedings of the European Brewery Convention Congress, Madrid', p. 77. Elsevier, London.

Verzele, M. (1971). 'Proceedings of the European Brewery Convention Congress, Estoril', p. 95. Elsevier, London.

Vickers, J. W. and Ballard, G. P. (1972). 'Proceedings of the Twelfth Convention of the Australia and New Zealand Section of the Institute of Brewing', p. 111.

Virden, J. (1972). *Journal of the Institute of Brewing* 78, 399.

von Hofsten, N. (1960). *Bog Myrtle and Other Substitutes for Hops in Former Times. Acta Academiae Regiae Gustavi Adolphi* XXXVI.

Wainwright, T. (1971a). *In* 'Modern Brewing Technology' (W. P. K. Findlay, ed.), Chapter 6. MacMillan, London and Basingstoke.

Wainwright, T. (1971b). 'Proceedings of the European Brewery Convention Congress, Estoril', p. 437. Elsevier, London.

Wainwright, T. (1973). *Journal of the Institute of Brewing* 79, 451.

Walkey, R. J. and Kirsop, B. H. (1969). *Journal of the Institute of Brewing* 75, 393.

Weinfurtner, F., Eschenbecker, F. and Hettmann, K. H. (1966). *Brauwissenschaft* 19, 174.

Wheeler, R. E., Pragnell, N. J. and Pierce, J. S. (1971). 'Proceedings of the European Brewery Convention Congress, Estoril', p. 423. Elsevier, London.

Whitear, A. L. and Button, A. H. (1971). 'Proceedings of the European Brewery Convention Congress, Estoril', p. 129. Elsevier, London.

Wild, H. (1966). *Bulletin de l'Institut Francais d'Archeologie Orientale* 64, 95.

Wiles, A. E. (1953). *Journal of the Institute of Brewing* 59, 265.

Willox, I. (1970). *Brewers' Guardian* (*Bottling & Canning Supplement*) (October) 24.

Windisch, S. and Emeis, C. C. (1969). *West German Patent* No. 1442311.

Winge, Ø. (1944). *Comptes rendus Laboratoire Carlsberg. Série Physiologique* 24, 31.

Wood, S. A., Lloyd, R. O. V. and Whitear, A. L. (1968). *Journal of the Institute of Brewing* 74, 510.

Wren, J. J. (1972). *Journal of the Institute of Brewing* 78, 69.

Wylie, D. M. (1962). *Brewers' Guild Journal* 48, 456.

Yoshida, T., Horie, Y. and Kuroiwa, Y. (1972). *Report of the Research Laboratories of the Kirin Brewery Co. Ltd.* 15, 45.

Zohary, D. (1969). *In* 'The Domestication and Exploitation of Plants and Animals' (P. J. Acko and G. W. Dimbleby, eds.). Duckworth & Co., London.

3. Cider and Perry

F. W. BEECH AND J. G. CARR

University of Bristol, Research Station, Long Ashton,
Bristol, England

I. INTRODUCTION

A. Definition of Cider and Perry

In this chapter, the term 'cider' is used to describe the fermented juice of the apple (*Malus pumila*). Cyder is an alternative form; both terms have been used since at least 1631 (Markham, 1631). The same two terms are used in Australia but have different meanings. There, cider is the alcoholic beverage, whereas cyder is usually apple juice or a non-alcoholic beverage (apple drink).

The terms 'fresh', 'sweet' or 'farm' cider are used in the U.S.A. to describe unfermented juice bought straight from the press or held refrigerated prior to sale. Sorbic acid is also sometimes added to increase the shelf-life of the juice. The product is rather oxidized in colour and flavour and still contains some fruit solids (Luce, 1973). Apple juice is the product made by any process that largely prevents appearance of the oxidized character, for example heating, addition of ascorbic acid or clarification. However, 'pure natural apple juice' is similar in appearance to farm cider, but is stabilized by pasteurization. Deposit formation is prevented but the cloudy appearance retained in another process (La Belle, 1973).

The fermented juice, called cider in England, is known as 'hard cider' in the U.S.A. It is defined in para. 240.544 of Chapter 1 of the Internal Revenue Service Department of the Treasury (Title 26. Internal Revenue) as being the 'non-effervescent product of normal alcoholic fermentation of apple juice only'. In para. 4.10e of Part 4, Title 27, wine, whatever its source, is defined as 'containing not less than 7 per cent and not more than 24 per cent alcohol by volume'. In Quebec, Canada, cider may not be sold with more than 13% of alcohol by volume (Gagnon, 1971). A similar situation occurs in Nova Scotia in Canada, but two apple wines are sold at 7% and 14% (v/v) alcohol, respectively.

In Europe, fermented apple juice is known as 'cidre' (France), 'sidre' (Italy), 'sidra' (Spain), 'apfelwein' (Germany and Switzerland). In each of these countries, the name for the unfermented product is clearly distinguished as apple juice (Tavernier, 1960a). In the E.E.C. Customs Classifications, Heading No. 22.07 is for ciders with more than 2.5% (v/v) alcohol and 22.02 for those with less.

Three attempts have been made to define English cider precisely and to list approved cidermaking techniques. The first was the Ministry of Agriculture's National Mark Scheme for Cider (Statutory Rules and Orders 1931, No. 168). This described the requirements that had to be met for using the official National Mark Label on bottled cider (see Table 1). Select cider (Champagne Process) had to be a pure-juice cider made from apples, or a blend of apples and pears, that could be sweetened with sucrose, and had to be carbonated in bottle by the champagne process. Addition of water as sugar

Table 1

Requirements to be fulfilled for labelling bottled cider as Select Cider
(Champagne) Process. From the Ministry of Agriculture Statutory Rules
and Orders, 1931, No. 168

To be made from clean sound cider apples only or from a blend (including
pears).

No sweetness other than cane or beet sugar.

No additions of: concentrate or other fruit juices, foreign acids, artificial essences
or artificial carbonation.

To the undiluted juice or battery diffusion juice may be added not more than
25% of its own volume of a syrup made from pure cane or beet sugar. The
original gravity of the pure juice and cider to which the syrup was added must
not be less than 1.040 at 15°C.

No preservatives or colouring matter prohibited by the Public Health (Preservatives etc. in Food) Regulations.

Acetic acid not be discernible on the palate and volatile acidity not to exceed
0.15%. To be free of disorders.

The last stages of fermentation must take place in the bottle and the deposit
removed by disgorging.

---

syrup or diffusion juice was allowed under specified conditions.
Select cider differed in that tartaric or citric acid could be added, and
there were no provisions concerning the method of carbonation.
Subsequently the limit for volatile acidity was increased from 0.15 to
0.2% (w/v) as acetic acid (Statutory Rules and Orders, 1935, No.
705). There was also a dispensation for the use of concentrated juice
as a medium for cultivation of the yeast inoculum.

The National Mark Scheme was discontinued in the late 1930s.
The second attempt (Anon, 1962c) to characterize cider was Resolution No. 7, adopted on the proposal of the Committee on Cider
and Other Fermented Beverages, at the European Conference of the
National Associations concerned with Wine, Spirits, Beer and Cider,
held under the auspices of the Consultative Assembly of the Council
of Europe in Strasbourg from 29th November to 1st December,
1962 (Table 2). Objections were registered to the Resolution. The
French delegation wished the word 'mousseux' to be reserved for
cider (perry) carbonated naturally, maintained that all ciders (and
perries) should contain a minimum of 5% (v/v) total alcohol (actual
+ potential), objected to the use of ferrocyanide for the removal of
iron, to the use of sugar or dilute concentrate, but favoured the use
of concentrated juice for sweetening purposes. According to the

Table 2

Draft Regulation on Cider and Perry. Resolution 7.
Council of Europe, Strasbourg, 30th November 1962
(A.S./Agr/V.Sp (14) 10 Rev)

I. *Definitions*

Cider—Beverage obtained by the complete or partial fermentation of the
juice of fresh apples or a mixture of the juice of fresh apples and fresh
pears, with or without the addition of drinking water.

Perry—Beverage obtained by the complete or partial fermentation of the
juice of fresh pears or a mixture of the juice of fresh pears and fresh
apples, with or without the addition of drinking water.

Pure juice cider or perry—Cider or perry obtained without the addition of
water.

Sparkling cider or perry—Cider (Perry) charged with pure carbon dioxide
which effervesces more or less protractedly when uncorked [described].
Each Contracting Party shall fix the maximum authorized pressure for
effervescent cider (perry).

II. *Cider or Perry fit for consumption, characteristics*

		Pure juice cider (perry)	Other cider (perry)
Actual + potential alcohol by volume	Minimum	5%	4%
Total dry extract, without sugar less 1 gramme	Minimum per litre	16 g	13 g
		Both	
Volatile acid	Maximum	1.4 g/l as acetic acid (23.3 m.eq.)	
Iron	Maximum	10 mg/l as acetic acid (23.3 m.eq.)	
Ethanol	Maximum	150 mg/l as acetic acid (23.3 m.eq.)	

III. *Authorized practices* [Lists 22]

IV. *Forbidden treatments or practices*

Use of colouring matter except caramel, any practices intended to alter
the composition with a view to deceiving the purchaser of the true
nature or origin of the product or to disguise its deterioration.

[   ] Contain authors' summaries.

British delegation, any prohibition on the use of sugar for sweetening
or fermentation would prohibit the production of 99% of all cider
(perry) made in Great Britain. The Resolution, with the Objections,
was sent to the Committee of Governmental Experts appointed by
the Committee of Ministers of the Council of Europe, where it has
remained ever since.

Recognizing that, unlike other European countries, there were no authorized standards for cider (perry) made in the United Kingdom, the National Association of Cidermakers drafted Standards for British Cider and Perry (Anon, 1970f). The definition of cider now reads 'complete or partial fermentation of juice of the apple or a mixture of the juice of apples and pears, with or without the addition of water, sugars or concentrated apple or pear juices, provided always that not more than 25% of the juice shall be pear juice'. In the definition of perry, the words apple and pear were transposed. A clear distinction was made between sparkling (artificially carbonated) and champagne (carbon dioxide naturally produced during fermentation). The minimum *actual* alcohol strength was to be 4% by volume and the sugar-free extract 13 g/l.

The opposing attitudes are understandable bearing in mind that, in the 1960s, the United Kingdom had a shortage of cider apples whereas there was an enormous surplus in France. As described in Section I.C (p. 147), the position is liable to change in the future.

The National Association of Cidermakers' Standards have not been registered by the Ministry of Agriculture, Fisheries and Food as a permitted Code of Practice, largely because the current and contemplated changes in food legislation cover most of the points with much greater precision. At present, there are no discussions within the E.E.C. to define cider (perry), but the Codex Alimentarius Commission, under the Joint F.A.O./W.H.O. Food Standards Programme, has issued 'Recommended International Standards for Apple Juice preserved exclusively by physical means'—CAC/RS 48—1971 (Codex Alimentarius Commission, 1974a). The standard for concentrated apple juice (CAC/RS 63—1972) has been published (Codex Alimentarius Commission, 1974b). Undoubtedly these will set the pattern for future standards and legislation.

B. Outline of the Process of Cidermaking

English cider is made from fresh fruit and concentrated juice (Carr, 1964a; Fig. 1). The fruit is a mixture of home grown and French cider apples and outgraded English dessert and culinary apples. True cider apples, also called bittersweets, are distinguished by a higher concentration of phenolic components than is present in table apples

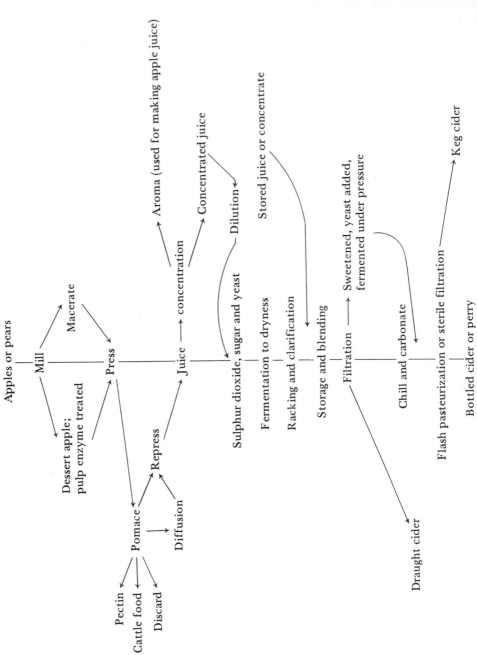

Fig. 1. Flow sheet for the process of cidermaking.

(see Section II.A.e, p. 172). These components give a characteristic bitter character to the cider made in the South West of England, North West France and Spain. Concentrated apple juice, whether made from cider or non-cider apples, is imported from France, Switzerland, Austria, Germany, Canada and Australia.

The fruit is milled to a pulp and the juice extracted by hydraulic pressure or by centrifugal force. Concentrated juice is diluted to its original gravity. In the larger factories, the composition of the juice may be standardized by addition of sugar and malic acid; the nutrient status may also be increased. Spoilage yeasts and bacteria, and oxidizing enzymes, are inhibited by the controlled addition of sulphur dioxide. After the appropriate period for equilibration, it is usual to add a pure yeast culture. Temperature of fermentation is rarely controlled and fermentation may be completed in one to four weeks depending on the ambient temperature. The fully fermented cider is then clarified by fining, centrifugation or kieselguhr filtration. Storage out of contact with air is followed by blending to produce ciders of standard composition. These are then stabilized by sterile filtration or flash pasteurization prior to packaging.

Most ciders produced in factories in Britain are sweetened, carbonated, bottled or canned, but a proportion is sold unsweetened or 'dry'. Both types are also sold from keg dispensers. The ciders are carbonated by direct injection with carbon dioxide prior to filling. Their alcohol contents range between 4 and 5% v/v; there is a more restricted sale of ciders of 6 to 7% alcohol. Ciders of greater strength, 7.5–8%, are sold in champagne bottles; these are highly carbonated, either artificially or by retention of their fermentation gas. The latter is called 'champagne cider' in Britain but 'cidre mousseux' in France. Some cider is sold uncarbonated or 'still', sometimes in bottle but more usually in glass jars, or plastic containers fitted with dispensing taps. The trade in wooden barrels has almost disappeared over the last decade (Allcott, 1968).

Ciders made in smaller factories or on the farms are popular locally and with visitors to the West Country in Britain. They are usually uncarbonated, clear or cloudy; they may be pasteurized in their container or be sterilized by filtration. A proportion is sold hazy, straight from the barrel, usually only to local customers, since in warm weather it can soon turn vinegary or start to referment unless kept cool.

Similarly, perry is made from special types of pears in England and Switzerland. The fruit used is astringent to the taste and usually full of stone cells. Perry from ripe dessert pears is rarely successful unless the natural acetate esters of the fruit are removed. Pear wine from unripe dessert pears has a considerable sale in the U.S.A.

The manufacture of English perry is very similar to that described for cider except that the true perry pears contain a proportion of leucoanthocyanins which need to be removed by storing the pulp or fining the perry with gelatin. It is usual to mix in some acid apples because of the high pH value of most pear juices, a practice described by Worlidge in 1678. Special problems also occur from the acetaldehyde and citric acid present in the juice. Perry is usually sold at 5% (v/v) alcohol for the artificially carbonated produce or 8.4% (v/v) for a very popular speciality perry.

1. Materials Coming into Contact with Cider

Formerly wood, cloth and stone were virtually the only materials used in cidermaking. Even here problems were experienced with lead as described in Section I.C (p. 147). Nowadays cadmium- and zinc-plated equipment must not come in contact with cider as their soluble salts are also harmful to humans.

Although their salts are less harmful, the use of equipment made of copper and non-stainless iron must be avoided. Some of the metals dissolve in cider causing it to turn green or black when exposed to air. The flavour is spoilt by an astringent disagreeable metallic taste. These metals have been used when tin- or silver-plated but constant care had to be exercised to maintain the integrity of the coating (Charley, 1949).

Now there is a wide array of materials from which beverage equipment is constructed (Sudraud and Cassignard, 1963), not all of which are suitable for contact with apple juice, cider or its allied products (Charley, 1934; Tavernier, 1958). Where wood is still in use, it must be non-resinous, such as oak or chestnut. Sometimes flexibility is also needed, such as in press racks, when ash or acacia wood is employed. Findlay (1959) has written of the properties and treatment of timber for brewing, and Singleton (1972) has prepared a similar account for wine timbers. A brief note on the practical treatment of wooden cider barrels and vats was given by Pollard and Beech (1957).

For a number of years, concrete tanks lined with sheets of special bitumastic or glass tiles were used for cidermaking. Their installation ceased in the 1960s because of unfavourable decisions on local tax ratings and the emergence of reliable linings for steel (Ricketts and Stott, 1965; Niedt, 1970). Overseas, concrete tanks have been lined with epoxy-resin; sometimes trouble has been experienced with solvents, or the movement of moisture through the concrete walls of underground tanks has caused flaking of the lining. Steel tanks are commonly lined with sprayed-on, solvent-free epoxy-resin coatings. It is done by specialist companies since preparation of the steel surface, the accurate heating, mixing and metering of the hardener and liquid are critical (Anon, 1970b, 1973a). Tanks can be delivered already lined, and these linings can also be of furnace-cured enamel or 'glass', or they may be built from sheet steel *in situ* and lined on site.

Very pure aluminium has also been used (Bryan, 1948) and, although slowly dissolved, the cider does not suffer any obvious defects. Its use is now confined to equipment in which storage is very brief, and it has largely been superseded by stainless steel. For this purpose, molybdenum- and titanium-containing grades are essential, especially for tanks or evaporators with air spaces and in the presence of sulphur dioxide. Titanium stainless steels are not normally considered so reliable for such arduous duties (Charley, 1934; Daepp and Verde, 1968, 1970; Henry *et al.*, 1972). In some countries, such as Australia, the price of stainless steel and epoxy-lined steel tanks are very similar so that the former is the material of choice.

For the last 15 years plastics have been widely adopted by the cider industry in common with the food industry generally. While high-density polyethylene and nylon are very suitable, all suppliers of equipment made of plastic (British Plastics Federation, 1974) should now be able to assure users that the material is not only satisfactory with regard to its mechanical properties but also that it does not cause: (a) a taint in the product; (b) leaching of heavy metals or potential carcinogens; or (c) oxygen to diffuse in or carbon dioxide to diffuse out (Davis, 1968; de Leiris, 1970; Anon, 1970c).

C. Historical Aspects

According to the Shorter Oxford English Dictionary the name 'cider' evolved from the Hebrew shēkār. Originally this meant any strong drink but, eventually, it was applied to a drink made from apples. The Greek word was *sikera*, which in Latin became *sicera*, in Old French *sidre* (now *cidre*) leading to the Middle English *sidre* (see also Lethbridge, 1900). Perry has a less ancient etymology being derived from the Latin *pirium*, a pear, which in late Latin was *pera*. In Old French it was rendered as *pere* or *perey*, the forerunner of the Middle English, *pereye*. Much of the information in this section of the chapter comes from the Herefordshire Pomona (Hogg and Bull, 1876–1885), but similar conditions prevailed in the Western cider counties in Britain (Marshall, 1789, 1796; Le Couteur, 1813; Coulson, 1898; Lethbridge, 1900).

The apple was one of the first fruits mentioned in the Biblical book Genesis. The event is said to be celebrated anatomically by Adam, unable to swallow the forbidden fruit, being left evermore with the protuberance showing from his throat. The apple plays a major role in legend (Burgess, 1897), saga and folk lore as a reward for valour or for its health-giving properties, but it is its product and that of the pear that should be examined here. According to Sir George Birdwood (Radcliffe Cooke, 1898), 'the apple tree was known and beloved by the Aryan races of Northern Europe . . . the apple tree is distinctly their source of wine . . . as the vine of the Persians, Greeks and Romans. Cowley (Hogg and Bull, 1876–1885) speaks of 'The . . . of pears and apples next succeed . . . they serve for grapes and make the Northern wine'. Certainly the apple tree has been cultivated in England for as far back as there are records. The Druids gave particular reverence to the apple, the orchards being planted next to the sacred oak groves. Sprigs of apple blossom were awarded for excellence in song (Hogg and Bull, 1876–1885). They continued to grow them after the Roman invasion, even as late as the 6th century, A.D.

The Elder Pliny in his description of the 29 sorts of apple, talks of 'some woodland apples with but little that is pleasant in the way of taste and even less so in point of smell, which is highly pungent. They have a marked peculiarity of bitterness and enough acidity to turn the edge of a sword'. Of crabs and wildings (chance seedlings) he says 'and for their harsh sourness they have many a foul word and shrewd curse given them'. Are these the progenitors of our cider and cooking apples? In Pliny's Chapter 15 which deals with pears and grafting, he describes wine being made by doctors from apples and pears, using wine and water, to make cooling drinks for the treatment of the sick.

Although neither Caesar nor Tacitus describes apples in England, the crab was indigenous and they were aware that the soil and climate were suitable for fruit trees. The Romans also brought over their own fruit trees, including pears, and the planting of these imported species gradually spread out from the new settlements. As the native inhabitants retreated before the invaders, they carried their varieties of apples into the more remote areas of Wales. Eventually the refugees travelled to the north-west coast of France, then called Armorica, but later, because so many came, Brittany. They are said to have taken their apple trees with them, and there are records of at least two parties of monks planting extensive acreages of apple orchards. Tradition has it that one of the orchards at Dôle, which was three miles in extent and lasted into the 12th Century A.D., first led to the manufacture of cider in Normandy. Following this, extensive plantings took place between the 13th and 16th Centuries. The Normans may, of course, have another version of the origin of their industry. A further impetus to its development was during the period when phylloxera was devastating the vineyards.

In England, from the conversion of the Anglo Saxons to Christianity and up to the 14th Century, cultivation of fruit was carried on chiefly by monks. These orchards and gardens were walled and always given the most favourable sites. Having connections with their parent houses on the European Continent, the best varieties of fruit, vegetables and medicinal herbs were grown. However, it is more than probable that apples and pears were cultivated long before cider and perry were made. The early inhabitants probably drank ale or mead, although there was one variation of the latter, namely *cyser*, made from apple juice and honey. The first record of cider was in 1205 in payment to the Exchequer of 200 pearmains and four hogsheads of wine made from pearmains. From then on, more references are available so that cider was made wherever apples could be grown.

Pears appear less frequently; in fact there are no references to pears for some 400–500 years after the Roman invasion, although they must have been cultivated in monastery gardens. The pears most esteemed in the 13th Century had a very hard texture, were long keeping and suitable for baking. In Britain, Worcester, but not Hereford, became celebrated for its pear orchards, and 'three pears sable' were added to the town's coat of arms at the direction of Queen Elizabeth I in 1575 (Williams, 1963). By 1597 the position had changed. Gerard (Herball) describes Hereford as having '. . . in the pastures and hedgerows . . . so many (apple) trees of all sorts that the servants drink for the most part no other sort, but that which is made of apples ... the Parson hath for tithe many hogsheads of syder'. Again '. . . the stock or kindred of pears not to be numbered, every county hath its peculiar fruit. The tame peare trees be planted in orchards as be the apple trees. Much longer lived than the apple and much less liable to decay'. He talks of 'a hit' as being a year of extra heavy pear crops. It was probably some time in the 14th and 15th Centuries when the soil of Hereford was found to be so suitable for growing apples and pears.

The planting of orchards in the 17th Century was accelerated not only by the loss of the French Provinces by England but also by the Continental Wars following the English Civil War, when wine imports virtually ceased. Men, such as Lord Scudamore, made Hereford like an orchard. He is said to have found the seedling which was the famous Redstreak or Redstrake, pre-eminent in its day of all other cider apples. He is also said to have introduced apples from Northern France, known here as Normans. These were noted for their greater and more consistent cropping. Later, any new seedling was described as Norman if it was a bittersweet (Marshall, 1789), in spite of the strictures of the learned.

Cider was made from juice of the first pressing. In a dry season, water would be added to give moisture during grinding. Makers were admonished not to add too much as the cider would be spoiled. The residual press cake was remilled with water and repressed (Charley, 1940). The cider made from this extract was known as *ciderkin* or *purr*, and it was consumed in almost unlimited quantities during haytime and harvest. It was probably the forerunner of an ambiguously named beverage, non-alcoholic cider.

In 1664 it was calculated that some 22.73×10^6 litres of cider were consumed within a 32 km circle around Hereford. The author (Beale, 1664) goes on to say that 'few cottagers, yea very few of our wealthiest yeomen, do taste any other drink in the family, except at some special festivals, twice or thrice in the year and that for variety rather than choice'. By constant trial and error, a method was evolved for making a first class cider which commanded a high price. The information was disseminated in books (Markham, 1631; Evelyn, 1664; Worlidge, 1678), pamphlets and even in the form of poems (Phillips, 1708; Lethbridge, 1900). Not everything was idyllic however. A number of writers (Field, 1789; Ham, 1827; Bulmer in Hogg and Bull, 1876–1885; Lethbridge, 1900) have described a disease that first appeared in Devon in 1757. It was caused by the use of lead in the roller mill, on the bed of the press, and as white lead to caulk leaky casks or for pipes through which cider was drawn from the cellar to the bar. Usually scrupulous cleanliness, discarding of the first running of juice or cider, prevented excessive solution of the heavy metal by the acid of the cider. Where these principles were not observed, then the symptoms of Devonshire colic appeared. They were described graphically in its other names such as the colic of Poitou (which suggests it was also known in France), dry gripes or dry bellyache; at worst it gave rise to paralytic complaints. Once the cause was understood, lead was used with much greater circumspection until it was abandoned entirely for these purposes. At one stage, a similar scare occurred with arsenic in beer, which originally was derived from the anthracite fuel used for direct fired malt kilns.

In the aftermath of the Napoleonic Wars, corn growing and cattle raising became more profitable. Orchards and cidermaking received less and less skilled attention. Fallen trees were replaced with worthless seedlings, and the enormous volumes of cider and perry produced were now of indifferent quality, and caused depressed prices. Even worse, much of the cider trade was given over to cider merchants, who bought everything wholesale at their own price. The hogsheads of cider and perry were blended, fined, flavoured and fortified and sold in Bristol and London. The best was filled into bottles while the remainder is said to have re-appeared as Hamburg port and sherry, or hock or champagne, according to the prevailing demand.

During the 19th Century, imports of Continental and American apples and pears appeared on the market in Britain. The better prices received for this well graded and packed produce stimulated production of what had been called pot fruit, that is dessert or cooking apples packed in square wicker baskets or pots holding 29 kg (Gaunt, 1939). Cider apples were grafted over to the table sorts and, eventually, this led to the growth of the specialized table apple industry. It was also thought that the making of cider could be revived as a manufacturing industry, although for years its sale and that of pot fruit had still provided the livelihood of many smallholders of land. It was realized that any such revival would need basic information on pomology and fermentation. The first was provided by the efforts of the Woolhope Club who sponsored an illustrated Pomona (Hogg and Bull, 1875–1885) and obtained and distributed graft wood of the best English and French sorts. Mr R. Neville Grenville arranged for experiments to be carried out on cidermaking from 1893 to 1903 by Mr F. J. Lloyd (1897, 1903) under the sponsorship in Britain of the Bath and West and Southern Counties Society, and with small grants from the Board of Agriculture. Mr Lloyd's report (1903) encouraged the Board to set up an Institute for research and instruction in cidermaking. The Institute came into being on 26th October 1903, financed jointly by the Board, the Society and the County Councils of Devon, Gloucester, Hereford, Somerset, Worcester and Monmouth. The objects of the Institute were to investigate and demonstrate the best methods of growing fruit and vegetables, of making cider and perry, to improve the cultivars by breeding, and to disseminate the knowledge by teaching and publishing instructional literature (Brooke-Hunt, 1904). In 1912 it was made an Agricultural Research Institute and a Department of Agriculture and Horticulture in the University of Bristol in England. Its remit was enlarged to carry out research on problems of fruit culture and the practical control of diseases and pests of fruit trees (Wallace and Marsh, 1953). The research work of the Institute (Wallace and Barker, 1953) has helped in the development of cidermaking from what was essentially a farm-based process to the industrialized procedures known today (Beech, 1972a). Similar research centres were established at Caen in France (later transferred to Rennes) and Wädenswil in Switzerland.

Mention must be made of the empirical cidermaking method, evolved in the 17th Century, which persisted to some extent in England in the late 1940s. It was practised extensively in France (Tavernier, 1952), and can still be seen on the smaller farms of Normandy and Brittany. Its success depended on the maker giving his closest personal attention to every stage of production. The fruit came from his own orchards, the vintage qualities of the cultivars used and their blending requirements had been learnt by experience (Rich, 1897; Barker, 1953). The fruit was divided into three classes: (1). Those to be made into summer cider, which was fermented dry and drunk within a month of making; (2). Table fruit giving a pleasant but not long lasting dry cider; traditionally the barrel was not tapped until after the first frost; (3). Varieties that gave the best, richest and longest keeping, sweet cider which would not be broached for 9-12 months and would keep 4-5 years. Originally it was bottled when it was two years old but, during the 19th Century, this was reduced to the spring following the making.

Apples were allowed to fall naturally, and gathered at intervals until all the crop had been harvested. The branches might be shaken to speed the harvest but cider made from fruit gathered in this manner was not considered to be as good. Cultivars in classes 1 and 2 (above) were crushed and pressed straight away but the others, the true bittersweets and bittersharps, were gathered in shallow heaps. Under the best conditions, the fruit would be kept off the ground on hurdles and covered in straw (Barker, 1911). It was crushed in late December when the seeds were black; it had the maximum amount of aroma and the flesh could be depressed easily with the thumb. This practice may have been a carry-over from the time when apples were crushed by being pounded with pestles, since Marshall (1796) describes the heaps of apple being kept 'until they be sufficiently "come", that is until the *brown rot* has begun to take place'. Badly rotted fruit would be removed prior to crushing, which originally meant smashing the apples or pears in wooden or stone troughs with heavy wooden pestles having nails driven into their ends (Worlidge, 1678). Indeed, even today, the room in which the apples and pears are milled and pressed may be called the Pound House. Following this was the use of the horse-drawn circular mill wheel or 'runner' running on its edge in a circular stone trough or 'chase'. The necessary sandstone or millstone grit came from the Forest of Dean and, for several years, there was a considerable industry at Lydney and Blakeney in trimming and cutting the millstones and the stone vats in which the pressed-out juice collected (Williams, 1963). At first, one mill would serve a district but later each large farm had its own. In 1678, Worlidge described his Ingenio, a hand-operated moveable iron mill, modelled on a Cuban sugar mill. In England it was introduced first in Somerset, then Devon, Gloucester and finally Hereford, where the stone mill was very widely used. The American grater mill was introduced towards the end of the 19th Century. Power-driven screw presses were also available then but the hydraulic press did not come into use until 1909 (Barker, 1953). Following the Industrial Revolution, a traction engine drawing the mill and press

would be driven into the orchard. It would crush and press all of the
fruit, ripe or unripe; the barrels would be filled and the cavalcade
move to the next farm. Needless to say, because of the lack of
attention to fruit maturity, the quality of the cider was not
particularly good.

In the traditional process, the carefully ripened fruit would be
crushed to a fine pulp and then placed in open vessels where it would
be left for 24 to 48 hours. This macerated pulp would then be built
up in layers between reeds or clean straw or, in Hereford, horse-hair
cloths (Le Couteur, 1813) and pressed slowly in a screw or lever
press. It might be 24 or 48 hours in the press, with the screw or lever
being raised at intervals, the side chopped square with a hay knife,
the loose choppings put in the middle, and pressure re-exerted.
Because of the large amount of pulp and straw particles present, the
juice would be collected and held in tall open-topped barrels called
keeves (Knight, 1809). The fine pulp collected on the surface would
be scooped off sometimes but normally it was left (Barker, 1907). At
times it would be re-inforced by the formation of a thick brown jelly
and the juice would 'drop bright'. This natural clarification was
exploited by the French cidermakers who called it 'défécation',
enabling them to produce naturally sweet cider with more certainty
(Tavernier and Jacquin, 1946; Jacquin and Tavernier, 1953; Tavernier *et al.*, 1955).

Eventually the floating mass would dry out, crack and begin to
fall. If the process had been carried out successfully, the partly
fermented cider would be clear and could be syphoned off from
between the crust and the lower deposit or lees. When run into clean
barrels, treated with isinglass and kept cool under an air lock, it
virtually ceased to ferment, although still containing sugar. In the
early spring, it was racked into the purchaser's casks or bottled in
champagne bottles, corked and stored. Eventually a slow fermentation carbonated the cider with the formation of only a small yeast
deposit, which was removed by disgorging. This system was used for
years in one of the early cider factories (Alwood, 1903). The
scientific basis of the défécation process, which depended on removal
of a yeast crop with a calcium pectate clot, has been investigated and
described (Kieser and Pollard, 1952; Beech and Challinor, 1951;
Beech, 1958a).

Perry making differed in that often the liquid would not clear satisfactorily, when it had to be syphoned off from the fermentation cask. Filtration through bags of coarse flax was advocated prior to fining with isinglass.

D. Production Statistics

It is difficult to find consistent figures for production of cider apples and ciders; those given in this section for England have been published in the main by the Statistics Division of the Ministry of Agriculture, Fisheries and Food and the Department of Trade (M.A.F.F. Agricultural Statistics: England and Wales; Agricultural Statistics: United Kingdom; Agricultural Censuses and Production; Agricultural Returns; H.M.S.O.). Figures for total World production of commercial cider are not available but are probably less than 500 million litres. It is impossible to estimate how much is made on farms.

Since the end of the 19th Century, cider-fruit growing in England has changed from numerous small multi-purpose orchards to the more recent development of large intensively grown orchards producing fruit under contract to the makers. At the same time, a drink consumed largely in the West Country is now produced almost entirely in a very few factories selling nationally.

Consider first the growing of the fruit. In the Board of Agriculture Returns for 1880, the cropped area of arable or grassland used for fruit trees of any kind was 70,900 hectares. The counties of Hereford, Devon and Somerset each had 10–11,000 hectares, the orchards consisting almost entirely of cider apples and perry pears. The state of the industry during the First World War was described by Le Rouzic et al. (1916), and after the Second World War in Ministry of Agriculture and Fisheries Economic Series No. 50 (M.A.F., 1949). In 1949 there were 20.4 thousand hectares, falling to 17.2 in 1951 and remaining relatively constant until 1957 (Fig. 2). Thereafter a steady loss of some 800 hectares took place annually, the decline only being halted in the middle 1960s with the planting of new orchards based on contracts with the cider manufacturers. In these, the cost of the first three establishment years are recovered from the sale of fruit to the maker. This was a departure from their previous practice when, even from the 1920s onwards, the manu-

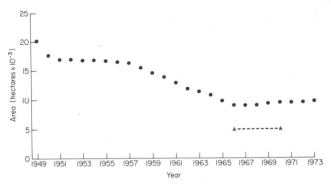

Fig. 2. Changes in the area occupied by cider-apple orchards in England and Wales over the period 1949–1973. ● indicates the total cropped area; ▲ the area occupied by commercial orchards. From data supplied by the Ministry of Agriculture, Fisheries and Food of Great Britain.

facturers had schemes for the supply, planting and after-care of cider trees. The new method was more akin to that used by food manufacturers for supplies of horticultural crops on contract.

The necessity for the manufacturers to bring about this change had been foreseen as the best solution for the future by Pollard (1956) in his review of cider-fruit production. The earlier Ministry of Agriculture and Fisheries Survey (M.A.F., 1949) had also called for the planting of large orchards, and central grading and distribution centres for table apples to allow for better utilization of the entire crop. At that time 81% of the holdings were of between 0.5 and 4.0 hectares. These views illustrate the change in attitude since 1919, when Barker (1920) had advocated a revival of the small farm orchard growing a mixture of good quality eating and vintage cider apples.

The fruit censuses of 1966 and 1970 revealed that, of the modest 9,200 hectares, only half consisted of commercially viable orchards (Table 3). The planting of intensive orchards began in Hereford in 1965; 1,200 hectares should have been planted by 1979. In Somerset it will amount to 400 hectares; plantings were carried out prior to 1965 but on a smaller scale. In January 1957, 6.95% of the total cropped area was planted with trees under seven years old and, in November 1962, 4.44% were under five years old, bearing in mind these percentages are based on the larger cropped area. It is clear that, even over the short period 1966–70, Hereford emerged as the major cider-apple growing county in England, with over 11% of the

Table 3

Cropped area of commercially viable orchards of cider apples in England and Wales

Region	1966		1970		
	Cropped area (ha)	Per cent with trees less than four years old on a regional basis	Cropped area (ha)	Per cent with trees less than four years old on a regional basis	Per cent with trees less than eight years old on a national basis
Devon	934	6.63	823	3.49	1.76
Gloucestershire	293	2.21	253	3.67	0.31
Herefordshire	2,214	8.65	2,342	17.95	11.88
Shropshire	150	6.76	69	1.18	0.21
Somerset	1,261	14.95	1,192	6.18	5.09
Worcestershire	248	9.46	357	29.11	2.47
Wales	66	0.61	51	27.20	0.27
Miscellaneous	63	12.82	64	2.33	0.19
Total	5,229	9.83	5,151	12.66	22.19

Data obtained from M.A.F.F. Agricultural Statistics: England and Wales.

orchard cropped area planted with young trees. Somerset lost its pre-eminent position in the same period. Worcestershire is now an area of new plantations whereas Devon has only a minor replant programme. The Southern Welsh Counties, Dorset, Cornwall, Suffolk, Sussex and Wiltshire now supply insignificant quantities of cider apples. Contrast this with 1949 (M.A.F., 1949) when Devon, Somerset, Dorset and Cornwall produced nearly 53% of the crop.

The annual tonnage of fruit, that is the harvested production, varies over a wide range (Fig. 3) with years of low crops in 1955,

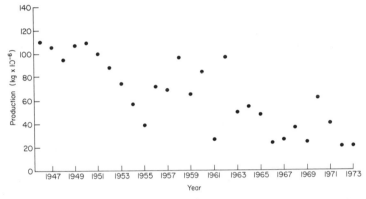

Fig. 3. Annual production of cider apples over the period 1946–1973 in England and Wales. Average production in the period 1934–1973 was 82 million kg, and in the period 1947–1971, 66 million kg. From data supplied by the Ministry of Agriculture, Fisheries and Food of Great Britain.

1961 and 1966 to 1969. The trend is influenced by the decline in cropped area previously described, although this can be compensated for by calculating yield in kg per hectare (Table 4). The time intervals are not constant, having been chosen to illustrate the periods, pre-Second World War, the war years, the static period of orchard cropped area (1949–50), the years of decline (1957–66) and the slow recovery (1967–70). The values for yield depend entirely on the interpretation of 'cropped area', the criterion chosen having changed over the years, the only true value being that for 1967–70. Here removal of derelict orchards and improved new orcharding has doubled the yield, leading, it is hoped, to 20–25 thousand kg per hectare. The term 'cider fruit' is difficult to interpret; undoubtedly it still includes pot and cull fruit. According to the M.A.F. (1949), culls formed 19% of the fruit intake of the cider factories from 1924 to

Table 4

Changes in yields of cider apples in England and Wales

	Years					
	1934/1939	1940/1948	1949/1956	1957/1966	1967/1970
Average weight ($kg \times 10^{-3}$)	72,745.6	77,713.8	82,275.2	62,372.2	44,460.2
Cropped area (ha)	27,115 (for 1936)	24,006 (for 1946)	17,495	12,764	9,340 or 5,070
Yield (kg/ha)	2,683	3,237	4,703	4,887	4,760 or 8,769

Data were obtained from M.A.F.F. Agricultural Statistics: England and Wales.

1935, and 18% in 1936–37. Pollard (1956) estimated that 14–19% of the 1939 intake and 23% over the years 1948 to 1958 were culls. Recent estimates are not available, but if, in an average year, there were from 5% to 10% of the total dessert and culinary apple crop available as culls, this would yield between 20 and 40 million kg of fruit.

The price received for cider apples reflects the change from glut to shortage conditions. In the immediate post-war years £14/tonne was usual, falling to £10–11 in the 1950s, rising slowly in the 1960s to £15. The price in 1971 rose to £17.75 to encourage new plantings. In that year, the French growers withheld a considerable proportion of their fruit so that the price of French apples delivered in England rose from £24/tonne to over £60/tonne in one season. Since then such fruit has cost between £45 and £55/tonne. English cider apples varied in price from £24/30 in 1973 and reached £30 in 1974. Over the last two years, the price for processing grade Bramley's Seedling has moved from £12–14/tonne to £24–28/tonne due to competition for this quality fruit between manufacturers of apple juice and makers of individual fruit pies. High fruit prices and a low selling price had the effect of decreasing sales of French cider from 245 to 123 million litres between 1958 and 1972.

Importation of early cider apples from Normandy and Brittany has helped to sustain the falling production of English cider apples and the rising sales of cider (Table 5). Imports of apples, cider or

Table 5

Importation of French cider apples into England

Year	kg	Year	kg	Year	kg
1961	158,496	1965	5,221,224	1969	32,918,400
1962	15,783,560	1966	14,938,248	1970	5,813,552
1963	150,368	1967	35,356,800	1971	13,206,984
1964	6,858,000	1968	28,498,800	1973	14,186,408

Data were obtained from publications of the Department of Trade and Industry, Great Britain, and from Fruit: a review (Commonwealth Secretariat, 1925 *et seq.*).

concentrate are necessary since, if English cider orchards produced adequate crops even in poor years, there would be glut crops in most seasons and cider-apple growing would be unprofitable (Pollard, 1956). The total of fruit from both sources averaged 61.5 million kg over the period 1961–71. However, imported apples will decline in importance, not just because of the very high prices, but because they arrive when the factories are in the middle of pressing the English crop. None were imported in 1974. The apple crop of 1971 was disastrous throughout the Northern Hemisphere and showed the need for importing a more stable raw material, concentrated apple juice, from a much wider area than previously. Again, because of shortages in 1971 and the great increase in exports to the U.S.A. for manufacture of flavoured wine (160 million litres juice equivalent in 1971–2), the price of concentrated juice rose from 22 to 66 pence per litre. In 1974 there was a surplus once more and the price fell to ca. 55p/litre. The extensive use of concentrate has brought a new dimension to cider making since it can be diluted and fermented as part of a planned production throughout the year. The scale of the imports could only be gauged from the Returns of the Statistical Office of H.M. Customs and Excise for Great Britain for 1973, when the values for concentrated apple and pear juice were reported separately from other concentrated juices. In that year, 7,034,580 litres of the two products were imported from all sources. In the 1960s an average of 4,100,000 litres of French cider were imported per annum (Returns of the Customs and Excise); in 1973 it was 1,765,000 litres (Dept. of Trade and Industry of Great Britain) or 1,833,000 (Syndicat du Commerce d'Exportation des vins, Cidres, Spirit neux et Liqueurs de France). Makers are turning more and more to concentrate because: (a) its smaller volume means lower transport and storage charges; and (b) the quality of the final product is more easily controlled.

At the beginning of the Century, the sales of English cider were stated variously as being 250 or 4,050 million litres, depending on whether the speaker was including an estimate for farm production or not (Barker, 1911). Production diminished over the years falling to 91 million litres between 1946 and 1965. Thereafter sales have increased as cider and perry makers have spent more than £1 million sterling per annum on advertising (Retail Business, 1974). These changes are shown in Fig. 4; production is expected to reach 182 million litres in 1978.

In France there has been a decline in cider-fruit production from 3,050 million kg in 1965 to just over 1,000 million in the 1970s (average 2,014,220,000; 1,422 million kg in 1973). Only a small

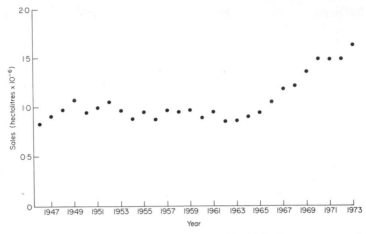

Fig. 4. Sales of English cider over the period 1946–1973. From data supplied by the National Association of Cidermakers (Brewer's Society, 1973).

Table 6

Utilization of French cider apples

	1952 (kg x 10⁻³)	1971 (kg x 10⁻³)
Left on farms	2,000,000	800,000
State alcohol production	800,000	100,000
Commercial cider production	500,000	200,000
Calvados production	94,000	130,000
Apple juice production	67,056	80,000
Production of concentrated juice	145,146	200,000
Total	3,606,202	1,510,000

Data were obtained from M. Denoly, *Les March de l'Ouest,* 22nd July, 1972.

proportion of this fruit is used in commercial cider factories (Table 6). Half of the fruit is never used commercially, a decreasing percentage is bought by the State for conversion into alcohol, and sales of commercial cider are diminishing rapidly (in 1,000 millions of litres, 254 in 1958, 208 in 1961, 143 in 1970 and 1972). Sales of calvados are increasing with the shortage of grape brandy and the imposition of standards (appellation contrôlée and régelementée; see Section III.F.2.a, p. 290). Sales of apple juice and concentrate have increased under the influence of the Government's anti-alcohol campaigns (Pollard and Beech, 1966a). Volumes of cider produced throughout the world are given in Table 7.

Table 7

Production of commercial cider in various countries during 1973

Country	Production (litres x 10^{-3})
Australia[a]	13,638
Canada	15,161
Finland	3,282
France	140,926
Norway[b]	536
Spain	77,282
Switzerland[c]	31,145
West Germany	70,000
United Kingdom[d]	156,532

[a] indicates that the production figure is an estimate.
[b] The production figure is an average for 1971 and 1972, and includes perry and mead production.
[c] The production figure is for cider and perry.
[d] The production figure is for the output of members of the National Association of Cider Makers in Great Britain.

The early cropped areas of perry pears are not as well documented as those for apples. By 1947 there were just under 1,820 hectares which then declined slowly (Fig. 5). Beginning in 1959, plantings of some 200 hectares were made in Somerset in Great Britain, a non-traditional area for this fruit, but they have not been sufficient to stem the decline in commercial orcharding (Table 8). Hereford can no longer be considered the premier perry country in Great Britain and by the end of the decade Somerset will contain the only commercial perry orchards in the United Kingdom.

From 1946 onwards, the annual output of perry pears in Great Britain has averaged 3,556,000 kg with little change in yield per hectare until the last few years. The latter apparent improvement only comes about by neglecting the area of non-commercial orchards (Table 9). The time intervals are those used for comparing the average yield

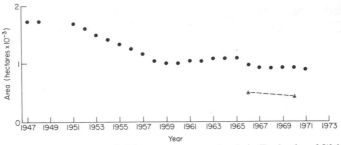

Fig. 5. Changes in the area occupied by perry-pear orchards in England and Wales over the period 1947–1973. ● indicates the total cropped area; ▲ the area occupied by commercial orchards. From data supplied by the Ministry of Agriculture, Fisheries and Food of Great Britain.

of cider apples. If time intervals illustrating the changes in the cropped area of perry orcharding are chosen instead, the yields become:

1951–59	1960–71	1966–70
Years of decline	Little apparent	Based on commercial
506 kg/hectare	change	orcharding
	572	1,217

Both sets of values confirm that commercial orchards give a better yield, but this is still well below a truly profitable value.

The deficiency in supplies is made up by importations of concentrated pear juice, mainly from Switzerland, where the fruit has a similar chemical composition to English perry pears. The only indication of the annual production of perry can be obtained from the difference between the volume of sales of cider and perry (Business Monitor, 1973) and those for cider alone (Ministry of Agriculture, Fisheries and Food) giving an annual sale of 20 million litres for 1973. Even in this, an assumption has to be made that the two estimates of cider production have been based on the same set of statistics.

The quantity of perry pears grown in France is not reported separately. Jacquin (1955) stated that some 152.4 million kg were grown, of which some 30.5 million kg were processed in the cider factories. Monsieur J. F. Drilleau, Director of the Cider Research Station at Rennes, estimated that in 1972 (J. F. Drilleau, personal communication) perry pears formed about 5% of the 'apple' crop, which would give a value of about 8.64 million kg. These were processed with the apples or made into concentrate for export.

Table 8

Cropped area of commercially viable orchards of perry pears in England and Wales

Region	October 1966		October 1970		
	Cropped area (ha)	Per cent with trees less than four years old on a regional basis	Cropped area (ha)	Per cent with trees less than four years old on a regional basis	Per cent with trees less than eight years old on a national basis
Gloucestershire	93	1.74	76	0.53	0.50
Herefordshire	142	2.86	104	4.67	2.19
Somerset	189	37.69	193	29.98	31.71
Worcestershire	40	–	29	–	–
Miscellaneous	38	4.30	5	7.69	0.50
Total	502	15.67	407	15.61	34.89

The source of these data was the M.A.F.F. Agricultural Statistics: England and Wales.

Table 9

Changes in yields of perry pears in England and Wales

	Year			
	1940/1948	1949/1956	1957/1966	1967/1970
Average weight (kg)	7,274,560	3,870,960	3,616,960	3,434,080
Cropped area (ha)	(for 1947) 1,780	1,473	1,060	(for 1970) 923 or 407
Yield (kg/ha)	4,087	2,628	3,412	3,720 or 8,435

The data were abstracted from the M.A.F.F. Agricultural Statistics: England and Wales.

Switzerland grows a very considerable weight of pears, between 102 and 205 million kg per annum. They are processed into unfermented and fermented juice. As stated above, much of the crop, particularly in glut years, is concentrated and exported to England.

II. COMPOSITION

A. Juice

1. Chemical Composition

a. *General considerations.* For convenience, cider apples are divided into four groups based upon flavour, and these groupings are reflected in the analysis figures for the various juices. The two flavour components used to define the different categories are the acids and tannins. It is a curious fact, however, that the terminology of this classification uses the word sweet, which in this particular application has nothing to do with sugar.

The first of the flavour descriptions is *sweet*, meaning that the juice is low in tannins and acids (Carr, 1970a). The juice is bland and, therefore, suitable for blending with more strongly flavoured juices. The second category is that of *bittersweet* and, as the name implies, these are high in tannins but low in acid. It is these apples which give cider the tang which remains on the palate. Such apples are typical of the south western part of England and are also to be found in Britanny and Normandy. *Bittersharps*, as the name implies, are high in both acid and tannins. Some of the milder apples of this category can be used to make ciders of single varieties (cultivars) but this would be an unusual procedure in commercial practice where juices are usually blended. The fourth category are the *sharps*, being low in tannin and high in acid. These are genuine cider varieties but culinary fruit is used to boost the acidity of ciders. Table 10 shows examples of the four flavour groups and includes some culinary and dessert cultivars.

Apple juice is mainly water. As a rough guide, the percentage

Table 10

Analysis of apple cultivars

Cultivar	Type	Flavour category	Acidity (% w/v malic acid)	Tannin (%, w/v)
Yarlington Mill	Cider	Bittersweet	0.22	0.32
Dabinett	Cider	Bittersweet	0.18	0.29
Sweet Coppin	Cider	Sweet	0.20	0.14
Kingston Black	Cider	Bittersharp	0.58	0.19
Stoke Red	Cider	Bittersharp	0.64	0.31
Tom Putt	Cider	Sharp	0.68	0.14
Brown's Apple	Cider	Sharp	0.67	0.12
Bramley's Seedling	Culinary	Sharp	0.85	0.08
Cox's Orange Pippin	Dessert	Sharp	0.60	0.07
Worcester Pearmain	Dessert	Bittersharp	0.50	0.12
Golden Delicious	Dessert	Mild Sharp	0.45	0.06

soluble solids is about equal to the specific gravity divided by a factor of four. Thus, a juice of specific gravity 1.040 would have about 10% soluble solids. Juices only occasionally have a specific gravity greater than 1.060 so that a maximum figure for soluble solids would be in the region of 15%. Of these, four-fifths is sugar and the remainder consists of organic acids, nitrogenous compounds, phenolics, aroma compounds, B group vitamins and mineral salts.

b. *Sugars.* Apples contain three major sugars, namely sucrose, glucose and fructose. In juice, fructose occurs in the greatest concentration, being in the region of 6% (w/v), whereas glucose is usually at a concentration of 1.5–2.0% (w/v), while sucrose is between 2.5 and 3.5% (w/v). When a juice is expressed from the fruit, inversion is brought about by the acid conditions so that stored unfermented apple juice will in due time contain no sucrose at all.

There are several other sugars or sugar-like compounds that may be found in apple juice, one of these being D(+)-xylose which is present at a concentration of 0.05% (w/v) (Whiting, 1961). Other minor constituents are galactose, arabinose, ribose, rhamnose, sorbose and inositol. The last compound is present at a concentration of 0.04% (w/v) (Whiting, 1961).

The major sugars of pear juices are substantially the same as those of apples but they are present in slightly different proportions. Fructose is the most abundant, but glucose is likely to exceed the amount of sucrose, thus reversing the situation found in apples. Fructose occurs at a concentration of about 7.0% (w/v) whereas glucose is of the order of 2–2.5% (w/v) with sucrose about 1% (w/v). There is one sugar-like compound found in perry-pear juices which is significantly higher in concentration than in apple juice. This is sorbitol, present in a concentration ranging from 1 to 5% (w/v). Since this compound is not fermented by yeasts, it remains after fermentation and serves to boost the specific gravity of what in reality is a 'dry' perry. Xylose is also present in perries in quantities greater than in the apple and can reach as high as 0.2% (w/v). Other sugars and related compounds tentatively identified in perries are galactose, arabinose, ribose and inositol. According to Whiting (1961) these, together with an unidentified oligosaccharide, make up about 0.04% (w/v) of the total sugars and related compounds.

c. *Organic acids.* The organic acids of cider-apple and perry-pear juices have been investigated in England by Phillips *et al.* (1956) and Whiting and Coggins (1960c), and in Switzerland by Rentschler and Tanner (1954a, b). By the use of paper chromatography, ion-exchange resins and silica-gel columns, it has been possible to show that apple and pear juices contain the range of organic acids shown in Table 11.

The Table shows that the range of malic acid is much greater in apples than in pears. The lower concentration was that found in a

Table 11

Comparison of organic-acid contents in cider-apple and perry-pear juice

Acids	Cider apples (%)	Perry pears (%)
Malic	0.10–1.36	0.45–0.88
Quinic	0.04–0.46	0.05–0.13
Citric	nil–0.02	trace–0.8
Citramalic	trace–0.05	trace
Latic	nil–trace	nil–trace
Succinic	nil–trace	nil–trace
Shikimic	trace–0.015	trace
Galacturonic	trace	trace
Chlorogenic	trace–0.30	trace–0.10
p-Coumarylquinic	trace–0.05	trace
Caffeic	trace	nil

bittersweet cultivar called Dabinett, while the higher figure was derived from an acid cultivar with the name Frederick. Perhaps the most noticeable difference between the two fruits is the relatively small amount of citric acid in apples in contrast to some pears which contain very substantial quantities. This is not important in the initial juice stages but becomes so during fermentation and storage when lactic-acid bacteria may be present. The metabolism of citric acid which can have a profound effect upon flavour will be mentioned later.

Having examined a number of cider-apple and perry-pear cultivars Phillips *et al.* (1956) noted a difference in the spread of the pH values. Pears produce juices with pH values within the range 3.6–3.8. Below this value the number of cultivars gradually declined until there were none at a pH value below 3.2. From pH 3.8 upwards, there was a similar decline particularly in the range pH 4.0–4.2. Finally they tailed off until there was none above pH 4.6. In contrast, the apple cultivars divided into two peaks, a large number falling within the range 3.2–3.4, tailing off until there were none below pH 3.0. Very few cultivars fell within the range 3.6–3.8, but there was a fresh peak at pH 3.8–4.2 which gradually tailed off until there were none above pH 4.4. During the course of fermentation and storage, the organic acids undergo a number of changes due to bacterial activity, which are controlled by pH value. The lower limit for the growth of most juice bacteria is pH 3.2.

In addition to the major acids there are those, such as caffeic and chlorogenic acid, which are of great interest in their role as metabolites for certain lactic-acid bacteria, which will be discussed later in this chapter.

One organic acid not listed or discussed is ascorbic acid. Under the usual conditions of cidermaking, this acid is usually oxidized and therefore disappears. Addition of sulphur dioxide creates reducing conditions and, in the presence of this compound, ascorbic acid will be retained for a longer period. It has been reported that ascorbic acid occurs in cider apples up to a concentration of 34 mg/100 g which is somewhat higher than the concentrations reported for culinary and dessert varieties which do not exceed a value of about 23 mg/100 g (Pollard et al., 1946; Kieser and Pollard, 1947a). It has been reported by Whiting and Coggins (1960a) that dehydroascorbic acid, which is the oxidation product of ascorbic acid, is converted to L-xylosone in the presence of sulphur dioxide. L-Xylosone is a compound that will bind sulphur dioxide strongly.

d. *Nitrogenous compounds*. Burroughs (1957a, 1958), who studied the nitrogenous compounds in apple juices, found that they could be divided into three categories. These were alcohol-insoluble, alcohol-soluble that were adsorbed on to Zeokarb-225, and alcohol-soluble that appeared in the percolate from this resin. The first of these was protein which varied in amount according to the apple variety. The portion adsorbed on to Zeokarb-225 contained the free amino acids whereas the percolate probably contained pyrimidines and nitrate.

We know little about the proteins since, once they are liberated when the fruit cells are ruptured, they become denatured by combination with tannins. The category about which most is known is the amino acids which play an important role in supporting growth of yeasts and bacteria during and after fermentation.

The amounts of soluble nitrogen that occur in cider apples can vary from as little as 4.4 to 33 mg/100 ml but even the highest concentration is not as high as those of other fermented beverages such as beers and wines. Higher concentrations of nitrogenous compounds can, however, be expected since cider-apple trees now receive fairly large additions of nitrogenous fertilizer to increase yield.

Table 12 shows the types of amino acids in cider apples with their

Table 12

Amino acids in cider-apple juices

Amino acid	Concentration range (mg nitrogen/100 ml)
Asparagine	0.19–17.5
Aspartic acid	0.35–1.5
Glutamic acid	0.21–0.31
Serine	0.04–0.65
α-Alanine	0.03–0.18
γ-Aminobutyric acid	trace
Valine	trace
Leucine + isoleucine	trace

upper and lower concentrations. In addition to those listed, traces of the following have also been found in some juices: proline, methyl-hydroxyproline, pipecolinic acid, glycine, threonine, arginine, gluta-mine and β-alanine.

The amino-acid pattern of the true perry pears is somewhat different from that of apples. True perry pears are analogous to cider apples, that is to say suitable for making perry but rarely fitted for culinary or dessert use. In these it is unusual to find a nitrogen content exceeding 10 mg/100 ml, and the pattern is somewhat different from apples.

Table 12 shows that the three main amino acids in the apple are aspartic acid, asparagine and glutamic acid. While it is true to say that these form a fairly substantial proportion of the amino acids in pears, they are not present in such high concentrations as in the apple. Burroughs (1958) showed that the amino acid occurring in greatest quantity in pears is proline, a compound only present in trace amounts in apples. There is one amino acid occurring in substantial quantities in some pears but only as a minute trace in apples. Its identity was unknown until Burroughs (1957b) identified it as 1-amino-cyclopropane-1-carboxylic acid. Although known as an amino acid that had been synthesized in the laboratory, this was the first time it had ever been isolated from a natural source.

Amino acids play an important part in the nutrition of all micro-organisms that are found in apple juices. During fermentation and other microbial activity many changes occur among the concen-tration of these amino acids.

e. *Tannins*. Originally this was a term used to describe those substances that tanned protein. It is now known that only one group of these is capable of combining with protein and should more precisely be called procyanidins. Because they all contain within their molecules a phenol structure, a much more suitable collective description for the compounds herein described is apple phenolics. These are the compounds associated with bitterness and astringency. These two sensations, which are quite separate, are often confused because in most bitter cider-apple cultivars they occur together. Astringency is a tactile sensation characterized by an overall dry shrivelled feeling in the mouth. Bitterness is that flavour which is not salty, sweet or acidic and is detected most intensely on the sides of the tongue at the rear. The reason for detecting astringency is well understood since it is caused by a combination of phenolics with proteins of the cells lining the walls of the mouth. Bitterness in cider apples is not due to the usual plant bitter compounds (for example, caffeine in tea) and, as yet, no single compound has been identified that is able to reproduce this flavour.

The term 'phenolics' is used because these groupings are part of the whole molecule and they are used to estimate the amounts present. For the purposes of routine analysis they are measured by a permanganate titration. This method only measures those compounds containing phenol groups with two or more hydroxy groups in *ortho*- or *para*-positions on the phenol molecule, and is therefore at best somewhat inaccurate (Williams, 1953).

Table 13 lists those substances that Lea (1974) includes in the phenolics of cider-apple juices. It should be noted that the phenolics

Table 13

Phenolic compounds present in cider-apple juices

Compound	Example
Phenolic acids	Chlorogenic acid
Phloretin derivatives	Phloridzin
Simple catechins	(−) Epicatechin
Condensed procyanidins	B2
Minor constituents	{ Flavonol glycosides { Anthocyanins

of the whole fruit are not the same as those of the juice since some occur in the skin, where they remain during juice extraction, and there are those that are oxidized when released from the fruit tissues.

Lea (1974) lists four major categories of phenolics as follows:

i. Phenolic acids. These are usually present as esters of quinic acid, the most important being chlorogenic acid; it is usually accompanied by *p*-coumaryl quinic acid. The structure of the former is illustrated in Figure 6. In addition, smaller amounts of *p*-coumaric and caffeic acids are also to be found. The structure of *p*-coumaric acid is illustrated in Figure 6. Caffeic has the same structure with the exception of an extra hydroxyl group on C-5. Esters such as chlorogenic acid are metabolized by certain strains of lactic-acid bacteria; this will be described later in this chapter.

ii. Phloretin derivatives. Perhaps the most important derivative is phloridzin which is present in a number of rosaceous plants including *Malus* species. It was shown to be present in apples by Johnson *et al.* (1968) and later by Timberlake (1971, 1972) to occur in cider apples. Its structure is given in Figure 6.

iii. Simple catechins. These substances were first noted in apples by Lavollay *et al.* (1944) and later by Williams (1953) in cider apples. They contain (+) catechin and (−) epicatechin, the latter usually being present in the greater amount. There are some exceptions, an example being the cider apple cultivar Medaille d'Or in which the two compounds occur in equal proportion. The structure of (−)-epicatechin is shown in Figure 6. The (+)-catechin is similar in general structure to that of (−)-epicatechin except that the hydroxyl group indicated by the arrow in Figure 6 is above the plane of orientation rather than below.

iv. Condensed procyanidins. When (−)-epicatechin or (+)-catechin molecules link together in pairs or greater numbers, they form procyanidins. Since there are several isomeric forms of these molecules it necessarily follows that, when they link to form procyanidins, there is the possibility of a variety of configurations each with differing properties. Figure 6 shows the structure of a dimeric procyanidin.

The form of isomerism usually encountered in the natural products is at the hydroxyl group on C-3. This can either be above or below the plane of orientation giving (+)-catechin and (−)-epicatechin respectively. For the formation of a dimer, there are a

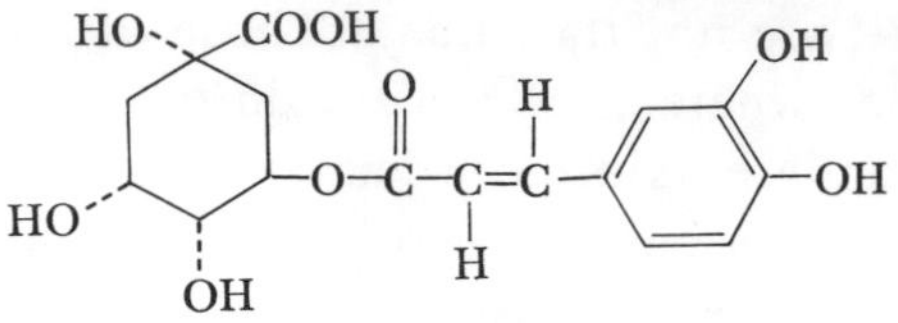

Chlorogenic acid

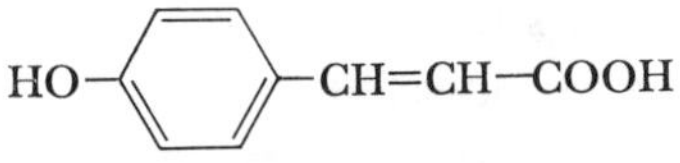

p-Coumaric acid

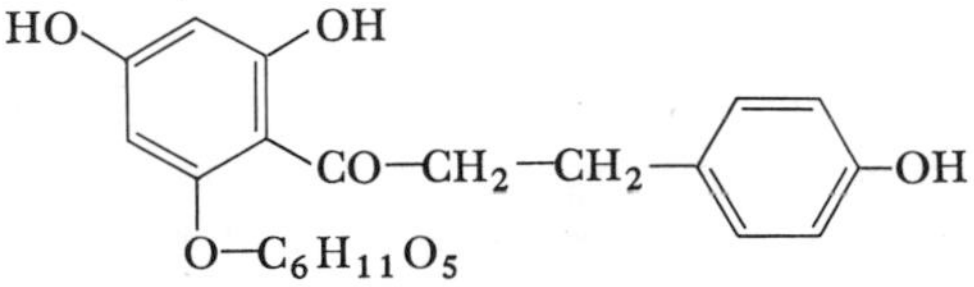

Phloridzin

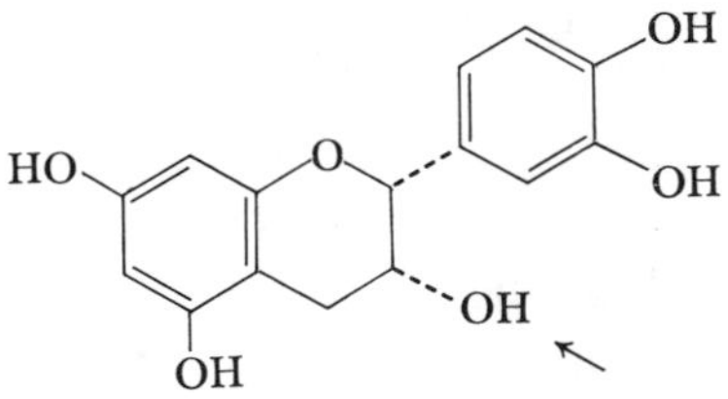

(−)-Epicatechin

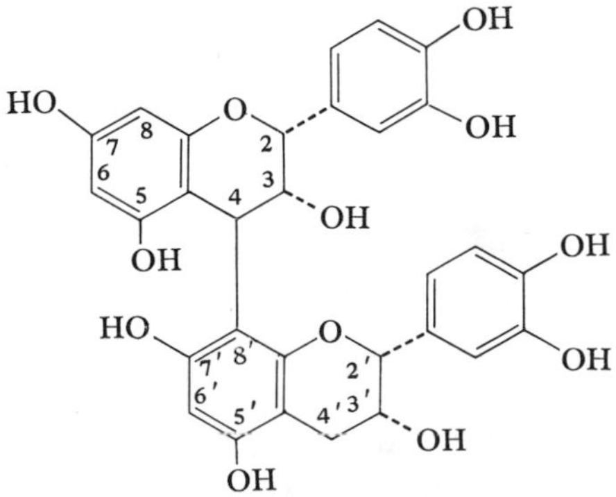

A dimeric procyanidin (B2)

Fig. 6. Structural formulae of some phenolic compounds that occur in apples.

number of possibilities which include (−)-epicatechin plus (+)-cate-
chin, or (−)-epicatechin plus (−)-epicatechin designated respectively
B1 and B2 (see Fig. 6). The nature of the link between C-4 and C-8 is
unknown but is such that it too can alter the structure and give rise
to another dimer that has been called B5. Recently Lea and
Timberlake (1974) have confirmed the presence in cider of procyanidins B1, B2 and B5 and two trimers based on (−)-epicatechin.

When these compounds are tasted in the concentration in which
they occur in ciders, they are not astringent. If, however, they are
tasted in higher concentrations the astringency becomes apparent. It
is thought that the intense astringency of some cider-apple juices
may be due to the presence of tetramers and even larger procyanidins. This is confirmed by the observation that, after extraction
of smaller molecules from the procyanidin fractions, the astringency
remains. It is clear that more work is required to establish which of
the phenolics are responsible for bitterness as there seems little doubt
that cider apples are rather special in lacking the compounds that
usually render plant tissues bitter. There is also a need to discover
what size procyanidin molecule gives the intense astringency found
in some cider apples, and finally to elucidate the mechanism of
colour formation. It is also possible that the larger molecules are
responsible for the colour. It may be, however, that this is not just a
function of the larger procyanidins alone but rather that they are
linked with other compounds such as proteins to form the brown
colours.

v. Minor components. The flavonal glycosides and anthocyanins
are mainly associated with apple skins where they usually remain
during the process of juice extraction.

f. *Aroma compounds*. Until the advent of gas-liquid chromatography (g.l.c.), little more was known about these compounds than
that they were responsible for aromas that immediately informed the
discerning taster whether a juice was, for example, derived from pears
or apples. The difficulty in handling these compounds was due to
their extreme volatility and low concentrations, making it hard to
identify them by conventional chemical methods. The sensitivity of
g.l.c. has revealed how numerous these odorous volatile compounds
are. In doing so it has posed the question: which are the compounds
responsible for the true fruit aroma?

Recently A. A. Williams (personal communication) compared

volatile aroma compounds of apples belonging to the four traditional flavour categories. Details of the cultivars and their analyses are listed in Table 14. The best known of the volatile compounds may be described as the low-temperature boiling compounds and have been arbitrarily defined by Williams as those that emerge from the g.l.c.

Table 14

Analyses of the cider-apple cultivars examined for aroma compounds.
Unpublished data of A. A. Williams

Cultivar	Acidity (% malic acid, w/v)	Tannin (%, w/v)	Class
Yarlington Mill	0.24	0.31	Bittersweet
Sweet Coppin	0.20	0.07	Sweet
Kingston Black	0.50	0.14	Bittersharp
Bramley's Seedling	1.10	0.09	Sharp

column before hexenol. A selection is shown in Table 15. From this it is possible to see that they differ in amount rather than kind between the four cultivars chosen for examination.

Table 15

Selected alcohols and esters of cider apples

Substance	Level (p.p.m.) in			
	Yarlington Mill	Sweet Coppin	Kingston Black	Bramley's Seedling
n-Propanol	0	0.6	0.5	3
n-Butanol	35	16	40	8
Isobutanol	0	1	0	2
n-Pentanol	0.05	0.2	0.5	0.1
2- and 3-Methylbutanol	2	1	9	8
n-Hexanol	4	0.3	11	6
2-Hexenol	1	1	0.1	0.3
Ethyl acetate	2	1	1	2
Isobutyl acetate	—	—	—	0.03
Ethyl butyrate	0.3	0.01	0.2	0.3
2- and 3-Methylbutyl acetate	0.15	0.02	0.2	0.1
Ethyl-2-methylbutyrate	0.0006	—	0.01	0.04
Hexyl acetate	0.6	0.3	0.2	0.3

The major differences between the juices occur in the higher-boiling compounds which emerge after hexenol. These compounds are often present in very small concentrations but nevertheless they may be able to influence the aroma in a manner disproportionate to their concentration. The identity of such compounds is largely unknown. The traces they make on the chromatogram indicate that Yarlington Mill contains a fair number of these minor components, whereas Sweet Coppin has virtually none; Kingston Black and Bramley's Seedling are in an intermediate position. It is by no means certain yet which volatile compounds present in apples can be said to impart the true aroma of this fruit. Experiments have shown that, even using a pure yeast culture in single cultivar juices, considerable changes take place amongst the volatiles during fermentation, which will be described later. In a commercial cider such changes must be even more complex since the starting material consists of a blend of many different kinds of apple, and the fermenting juice probably contains several yeasts and probably bacteria.

g. *B-Group vitamins.* Little work has been done on the concentrations of this important group of compounds in cider apple juices. According to Beech (1972a), the B-group vitamins in apples are present in the following amounts per 100 g of fresh whole fruit: biotin, 0.25 μg; pantothenic acid, 50 μg; riboflavin, 5–50 μg; thiamin, 20–60 μg; and myo-inositol, 24 μg. Goverd (1973a, b) showed that there can be considerable variation between apple cultivars and even between the same cultivars grown on different sites (Table 16).

Goverd (1973a, b) has also shown that juices from the same cultivars in two consecutive years give different results for their vitamin concentrations. Thiamin, for example, showed some degree of consistency among the cultivars chosen for study. The smallest difference between two seasons was found in the cultivar Michelin where there was only a 3.5% difference between years 1 and 2 being represented by 8.6 and 8.3 μg/100 ml. The largest percentage difference, namely 24.2%, was in the cultivar Crimson King. Amongst the other cultivars chosen for study, the percentage differences ranged between 3.5 and 7.14%. The results for nicotinic acid showed bigger percentage differences from one year to another, the lowest being Bramley's Seedling at 12% and the highest Brown Snout at 33.0%. The differences for pantothenic acid were somewhat

Table 16

Vitamin concentrations in nine apple juices of different flavour categories

Cultivar	Flavour group	Concentration (μg/100 ml)			
		Thiamin	Nicotinic acid	Pantothenic acid	Riboflavin
Sweet Alford	Sweet	2.8	77	116	1.5
Sweet Coppin (A)	Sweet	4.4	47	75	0.9
Sweet Coppin (B)	Sweet	4.4	57	114	0.55
Crimson King	Sharp	6.6	102	94	1.5
Bramley's Seedling	Sharp[a]	13.2	75	71	1.3
Cox's Orange Pippin	Sharp[b]	6.1	70	64	0.33
Brown Snout	Bittersweet	6.4	79	70	1.6
Michelin	Bittersweet	8.6	150	94	2.6
Stoke Red	Bittersharp	7.2	37	47	1.9

[a] Culinary apple.
[b] Dessert apple.

intermediate between the two years, analyses showing Sweet Alford at 23.3% and the smallest for Brown Snout at 10%. There was no consistent trend. None of the vitamins examined was either consistently higher or lower in the second year over the range of cultivars examined.

When James (1948) examined some of the B-group vitamins of apple juice, she showed some correlation between contents of nitrogenous compounds and of pantothenic acid. The results obtained by Goverd (1973a, b) do not lend much support to this correlation. Two cultivars of Sweet Coppin from different sites do, however, show that the one with the higher level of nitrogenous compounds (7.49 mg/100 ml) had a pantothenic content of 114 μg/100 ml compared with a lower content of nitrogenous compounds of 3.91 mg/100 ml and a pantothenic acid content of 75 μg/100 ml. It will be seen later (p. 197) that B-group vitamins play an important part in controlling the growth of yeasts and bacteria, and that the concentrations remaining in the finished cider are lower than those in the juice.

h. *Mineral salts.* Reference to the mineral content of ciders or cider apples is very sparse in the literature. Jacquin (1958a, b) states that cider apples contain 10–19 mg/100 g of Ca and 5.9–6.1 mg/100 g of Mg which fall within the ranges given for these elements in other apple cultivars. Most of the measurements have been carried out on apple flesh, few workers having examined the expressed juice. A notable exception was the work of Ayres and Fallows (1951) who measured the phosphorus and nitrogen contents of dessert and culinary apple juices from fruit taken off the same trees over a period of five years. In the first four of these years, the phosphorus content remained fairly constant, giving a mean of 12.5 mg/100 ml (measured as P_2O_5). In the fifth year, this value rose to 21.8 mg/100 ml. The content of nitrogenous compounds in fruit from the same trees fluctuated from 16 mg/100 ml to 38 mg/100 ml.

As those nitrogen figures just quoted imply, levels of mineral salts in apples fluctuate from one season to another in the same cultivar or even in the same tree. Indeed, such fluctuation is just as great as that between different cultivars. This is well illustrated in what is perhaps the most comprehensive survey on the minerals of apples by Chatt (1968). He has drawn from many sources including one as early as 1891 (Table 17).

Table 17

Contents of mineral elements in apples

	Content (mg/100 g)			
	K	Ca	Mg	P
Min-Max	44–163	1.5–23	1.5–18	3.5–26

2. Microflora

a. *Yeasts*. There have been several reports of yeast surveys of orchards by Miller and Webb (1954), Adams (1961), Bowen (1962), Bowen and Beech (1964, 1967), Davenport (1968), Beech and Davenport (1970). These surveys reveal that there are a large number of yeasts associated with the soil, vegetation, animals and air of the orchard. They are represented by the following genera of yeasts and yeast-like organisms: *Aureobasidium, Saccharomyces, Hansenula, Torulopsis, Pichia, Candida, Debaryomyces, Rhodotorula, Sporobolomyces, Trichosporon, Kloeckera, Saccharomycodes.*

Most of the yeasts are of interest only to the ecologist rather than the cidermaker. Of the organisms listed above, the only ones of significance in cidermaking are the fermenting yeasts of the genus *Saccharomyces* and the weakly fermenting *Kloeckera apiculata*. In addition, the large-celled and weakly fermenting yeast *Saccharomycodes ludwigii* can be of considerable importance as the cause of a disorder, but that will be discussed later (p. 215). *Kloeckera apiculata* can be found in juices and will grow very rapidly indeed. Its presence is detrimental to flavour but fortunately it rarely reaches the fermentation stage in modern cidermaking as it succumbs readily to addition of sulphur dioxide. It is an organism that can increase in numbers fairly rapidly, and Beech and Davenport (1970) reported that it can increase from as few as 50 cells/g of apple tissue to 45,000/g when the fruit is in store. Damaged fruit is, of course, very susceptible to microbial growth since the juices so released can support growth of a wide variety of yeasts and bacteria, giving rise to a series of unwanted sulphite-binding compounds, an account of which will be given later (p. 183).

Although *Saccharomyces* species have been referred to, their occurrence is sporadic and quite rare. This poses the question as to how these yeasts, so rare in the orchard, become an integral part of the process of making cider. The obvious means of transport of the *Saccharomyces* spp. into the factory is on the fruit yet, when Beech (1959) studied fruit of the cultivar Kingston Black, he only found representatives of the genera *Candida*, *Torulopsis* and *Hansenula*. Later Davenport (1968) showed that *Saccharomyces* spp. were to be found most consistently and in greatest numbers on mummified fruit that had not dried out completely. He speculated that the small amount of ethanol produced by fermentation might act as an insect attractant, and thus, facilitate spread of these yeasts. Davenport (1968) also showed that *Saccharomyces* spp. could be found within the loculi of sound apples. These organisms could have reached the fruit either during the act of insect pollination, and then have become enclosed in the developing apple, or they could have been transported through the eye of mature fruit by small insects. Either of these vectors could act as sporadic introducers of *Saccharomyces* spp.

When the fruit is milled and pressed, yeasts of the following genera may be found: *Kloeckera*, *Candida*, *Cryptococcus*, *Torulopsis*, *Hansenula*, *Pichia*, *Rhodotorula* and *Saccharomyces*. It has been shown that, in factories where a strict regime of hygiene is maintained, the flora of the juice contains those organisms previously listed with the exception of the *Saccharomyces* spp. (Beech and Davenport, 1970). These are the organisms of the orchard and the apple and are therefore constantly coming into the factory with the fruit. The fact that the *Saccharomyces* spp. disappear when a high standard of cleanliness is maintained means that they grow somewhere on the equipment. Indeed, Marshall and Walkley (1951) showed a large increase of *Saccharomyces* spp. during a day of pressing. The numbers increased so that, at the end of the day there were, 8×10^3 yeasts/cm^2 of press cloth, enough to give 8×10^2 yeasts/ml juice. There seems little doubt that, in the traditional method of cidermaking, the fermenting yeasts come from the pressing equipment. It is perhaps paradoxical that those factories which are the least hygienic are more likely to have a vigorous naturally occurring yeast fermentation than those with a stricter regime.

The effect of the more recently introduced presses on the yeast population is not well known. However, one set of data from the same batch of fruit pressed partly by the traditional rack and cloth method, and partly through a screw press made entirely of stainless steel, show marked differences in composition of the yeast flora. Table 18 shows these differences.

Such information is not available for the Bucher Guyer press but, because of its construction, it is thought that the effect on the composition of the yeast flora would be more like that revealed in the right-hand column in Table 18 than the left.

b. *Bacteria*. The bacteria of apple juices and ciders must of necessity be tolerant of acid and alcohol. These somewhat stringent conditions, therefore, restrict the bacteria to a few genera as follows: *Acetobacter, Acetomonas, Lactobacillus, Leuconostoc, Pediococcus, Zymomonas*. These bacteria are all able to grow at a pH value of 4 and most at pH values considerably lower than 4.0. They can be said to be truly acid tolerant.

In a survey of cider apple orchards, Carr (1964b) examined a number of cultivars for the presence of bacteria on apples hanging on the trees. In addition, bacteriological examinations were made of fruit on the ground, after harvesting, and during storage at the factory before processing. The occurrence of acid-tolerant bacteria

Table 18

Difference in the yeast composition of apple juice extracted by
two methods of pressing

Species	Number of yeasts/ml	
	Screw press	Hydraulic press
Kloeckera apiculata	360,000	160,000
Saccharomyces spp.	—	23,000
Pichia spp.	5,000	23,000
Torulopsis spp.	—	2,030,000
Candida pulcherrima	—	23,000
Carotenoid-containing yeasts	—	23,000

on apples hanging on the tree was extremely rare. Indeed they were
only found on two cultivars, named Tremlett's Bitter and Court
Royal, both of which carried very large populations of non-acid-
tolerant bacteria. The relative numbers were 10.2×10^4 non-acid-
tolerant bacteria per gram of apple tissue compared with 0.1×10^4
acid-tolerant bacteria on the cultivar Tremlett's Bitter, while the
respective figures for Court Royal were 55.9×10^4 and 0.1×10^4
bacteria per gram. Only after three weeks' storage was it possible to
detect any significant numbers of acid-tolerant bacteria (3.8×10^4/g)
on undamaged hand-harvested fruit. In contrast, the same fruit
mechanically harvested and damaged by the machinery in the process
carried 430×10^4 acid-tolerant bacteria per gram. Thus, the condition
of the fruit can greatly influence the numbers of bacteria that get
into the juice. This was later confirmed by Carr and Passmore
(1971a), who showed that the number of isolates of acetic-acid
bacteria from unsound local fruit was six times less than unsound fruit
that had been shipped from France and which had, therefore, been in
store and transit for a longer period. Although the acid-tolerant
bacteria occur in small numbers on fruit hanging on the tree, it must
be concluded that these small reservoirs of infection are sufficient to
grow into the much larger numbers on fruit during storage. In very
badly damaged fruit, the presence and activity of micro-organisms
become obvious from the smell of acetic acid and the marked rised in
temperature.

What type of bacteria can be found on the fruit and in the pulp?
The ones most frequently encountered are the aerobic acetic acid

bacteria represented by such species as *Acetomonas oxydans, Aceto-bacter aceti* and *Acetobacter xylinum*. Growth of the first named organism is of the utmost importance since, although they can utilize ethanol, little of this compound is present prior to yeast fermentation. They metabolize, therefore, the available carbohydrates of which the most abundant is fructose. From this sugar they produce 2,5-D-*threo*-hexodiulose (5-oxofructose) which has the capacity to bind sulphur dioxide and render it inactive as an antimicrobial agent. The discovery of this activity goes most of the way to explain the observation that a juice made from a poor quality fruit has a higher sulphur dioxide-binding capacity than one from good quality apples.

Acetic-acid bacteria can be isolated from the juice but tend to disappear when yeast fermentation starts. Their fate will be considered further when fermentation is discussed. Several different lactic-acid bacteria can be isolated from the fruit and juice. Carr and Passmore (1971a) isolated *Lactobacillus* and *Leuconostoc* spp. from apples, and it was noted that the latter were present in greater numbers than the former. This was not surprising since it had been shown earlier by Carr (1970b) that the lactic-acid bacteria occurring most frequently in juice running from the press of a commercial cidermaker were a *Leuconostoc* sp. Other lactic-acid bacteria found on this occasion were strains of the homofermenter *Lactobacillus plantarum* and a similar isolate. This latter proved to be weakly catalase-positive and different from *L. plantarum* in a number of properties, and was subsequently named *L. mali* (Carr and Davies, 1970). One other organism, a heterofermentative lactic rod formerly called *L. pastorianus* var. *quinicus*, is also a fairly frequent inhabitant of the juice. Recently the name of this organism has been changed to *L. collinoides* (Carr and Davies, 1972, 1974). Once the juice has been expressed from the fruit, changes begin to occur which make it into cider. It is during fermentation that the most intense yeast and bacterial activity takes place.

B. Fermentation and Storage

1. Chemical Composition and Change

a. *Sugars.* Due to inversion, sucrose is unlikely to be present in any significant quantity at the beginning of fermentation. The two major sugars are, therefore, glucose and fructose. These are fermented by yeasts by the Embden–Meyerhof–Parnas pathway to ethyl alcohol and carbon dioxide. This accounts for the majority of the sugars and is the main concern of the cidermaker. During fermentation, other side effects may be observed such as accumulation of pyruvic acid. This occurs most readily under conditions of thiamin deficiency since pyruvate decarboxylase requires thiamin pyrophosphate as a coenzyme and its absence causes pyruvate to build up significantly. G. C. Whiting (personal communication) observed concentrations of pyruvate as high as 0.17% (w/v) in ciders with extreme thiamin deficiency. Pyruvate in such concentrations provides other micro-organisms, for example lactic-acid bacteria, with a metabolic intermediate which is diverted to end-products different from the required ethyl alcohol and carbon dioxide.

Lactic-acid bacteria sometimes grow with the yeasts and, in doing so, metabolize the sugars to lactic acid and other end-products. One group, the homofermenters, produce lactic acid only from glucose or fructose. They do so by means of a slightly modified Embden–Meyerhof–Parnas pathway. In yeasts, pyruvate is decarboxylated to acetaldehyde and carbon dioxide as illustrated in equation (1):

$$CH_3CO . COOH \rightarrow CH_3CHO + CO_2 \tag{1}$$

Acetaldehyde is then reduced to ethyl alcohol as shown in equation (2):

$$CH_3CHO + 2H \rightarrow CH_2CH_2OH \tag{2}$$

In the homofermentative lactic-acid bacteria the decarboxylation step does not operate so that a direct reduction of pyruvate takes place giving lactic acid, as shown in equation (3):

$$CH_3CO . COOH + 2H \rightarrow CH_3CHOH COOH \tag{3}$$

The other group of lactic-acid bacteria are called heterofermenters and, as the name implies, they produce several end-products from glucose, namely, lactic acid, ethyl alcohol, carbon dioxide and some acetic acid. The glycolytic pathway of these organisms is usually called the hetero-lactic pathway, and while it involves some steps of the Embden–Meyerhof–Parnas pathway in the later stages, the early steps are quite different. The glucose is split into C_5 and C_1 fragments the latter being released as carbon dioxide. The C_5 fragment is then split again into C_3 and C_2 moieties which give rise, respectively, to lactic acid and ethanol. The end-products from metabolism of fructose are similar. However, heterofermentative lactic-acid bacteria use fructose for two purposes, first as an energy source giving rise to the end-products already mentioned, and second as a hydrogen acceptor. The reduction product of fructose is mannitol, which, being a fairly stable compound, accumulates. At one time mannitol formation was thought to be a disorder in wines and many of the older papers on this topic contain references to mannitic wines. These pathways have been described in detail elsewhere by Carr (1968a). Thus, the fermentation of the major sugars in apple juice may result in production of lactic acid as well as ethyl alcohol and carbon dioxide. Other compounds produced as a direct result of sugar metabolism are the polysaccharides which are dealt with later in this chapter (p. 207) under the heading of disorders.

After fermentation has ceased, the cider is racked off the lees and left in storage. It is then said to be 'dry', i.e. devoid of sugar. This, however, is not strictly true since there are a number of sugars and sugar-like compounds that yeasts do not metabolize left in the dry cider. There are even traces of glucose and fructose which disappear during storage, probably due to the activity of lactic-acid bacteria. Whiting (1961) has shown that, of the non-yeast fermentable substances, xylose can be present in quantities of about 0.05% (w/v). In addition, hexitols, which include mannitol derived from bacterial activity and sorbitol, which is naturally present, can be present in concentrations over the range 0.35–0.75% (w/v). In dry perries, the sorbitol content can be in excess of 4% (w/v). Traces of other sugars and related compounds such as arabinose and glycerol can be found in dry ciders and perries, and may act as energy sources for bacteria during storage. For example, arabinose and xylose, if not attacked by lactic-acid bacteria during fermentation, are likely to be utilized during storage. Given favourable conditions for growth, acetic-acid bacteria will convert sorbitol to sorbose and eventually to 5-oxo-fructose (Carr and Whiting, 1971), a compound that has been mentioned previously as an important binder of sulphur dioxide.

One group of substances not previously mentioned are those derived from pectin. Pollard and Kieser (1958) reported that pectin in the juice was demethylated by a naturally occurring methyl esterase, which was subsequently broken down by a yeast containing a polygalacturonase to mono-, di- and trigalacturonic acids.

b. *Organic acids*. Probably the most important change that takes place during fermentation or storage is breakdown of malic acid to lactic acid, ensuring that cider rarely contains any malic acid in the finished product. In view of the importance of the malo-lactic fermentation, it has been described under a separate heading. The other changes that take place are of great scientific interest but are perhaps less important in practical cidermaking.

One change in the organic acids of perries which is of rather more than academic interest is the metabolism of citric acid. According to Whiting and Coggins (1964) citrate is metabolized in the following manner:

$$2 \text{ citrate} \rightarrow 2 \text{ oxaloacetate} + 2 \text{ acetate}$$

$$2 \text{ oxaloacetate} \rightarrow 2 \text{ pyruvate} + CO_2$$

$$2 \text{ pyruvate} \rightarrow \text{lactate} + \text{acetate (heterofermentative lactobacilli)}$$

$$2 \text{ pyruvate} \rightarrow \text{acetoin} + 2 CO_2 \text{ (homofermentative lactobacilli)}$$

The heterofermentative cocci, i.e. leuconostocs, show a combination of these characteristics, namely, production of lactate and acetoin. Thus, with the significant amounts of citrate contained in pear juice, it is possible for acetification to take place anaerobically and for the flavour to be tainted.

Certain hetero- and homofermentative lactobacilli and also a few leuconostocs can metabolize quinic acid. Generally this takes place in storage after malic acid has been converted to lactic acid. It was first reported by Carr *et al.* (1957) and has been mentioned on subsequent occasions (Whiting and Coggins, 1969; Carr and Whiting, 1971). More recently, Whiting and Coggins (1974) published data on the enzymology of one of the homofermentative pathways, and it is from that paper that the scheme shown in Figure 7 is taken.

Metabolism of quinate by the heterofermentative rod, now known as *Lactobacillus collinoides* (Carr and Davies, 1972), covers stages I–V when it ceases. In contrast, the homofermentative cider organism *Lactobacillus plantarum* metabolizes quinate by way of the intermediates shown in Figure 7 where it ceases at stage XII. This is, however, only one of two end products that *L. plantarum* produces, the other being catechol. It is thought to branch away from the scheme shown in Figure 7 at shikimate, although the divergence

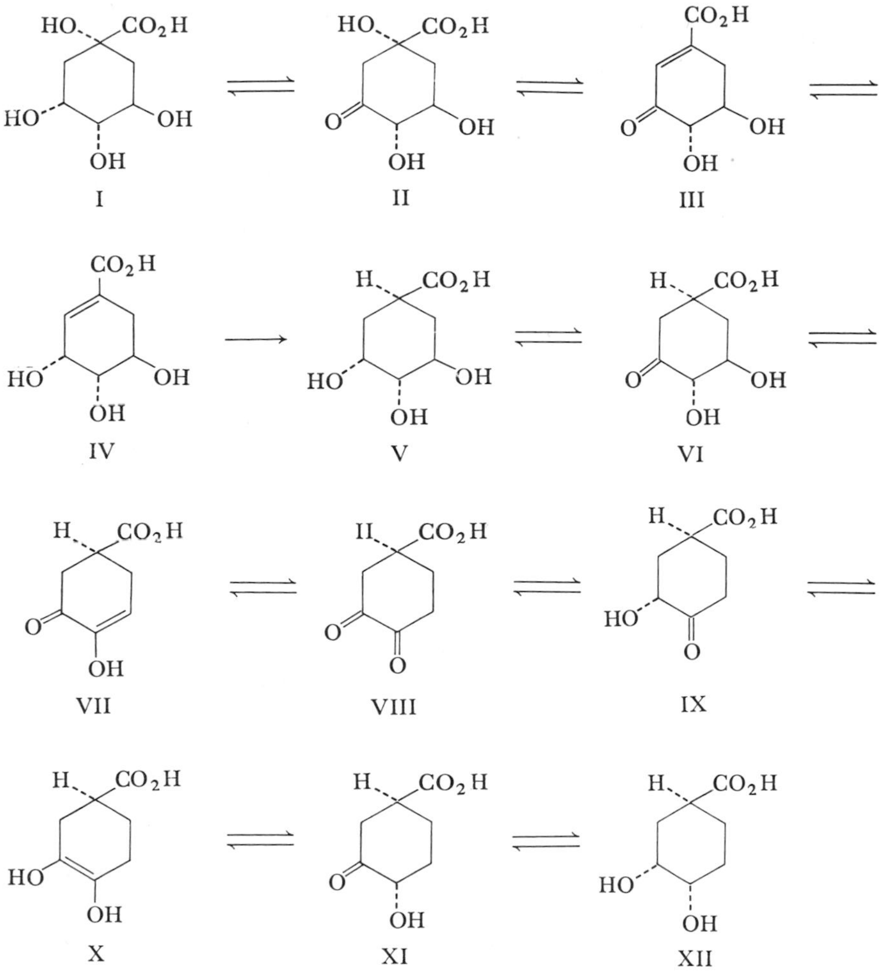

Fig. 7. Pathway for reduction of (−)-quinate to (−)t-3,t-4-dihydroxycyclohexane-c-1-carboxylate. The key to the compounds is: I, (−)-quinate; II, (−)-3-dehydroquinate; III, (−)-3-dehydroshikimate; IV, (−)-shikimate; V, (−)-dihydroshikimate; VI, (−)t-4,c-5-dihydroxy-3-oxocyclohexane-c-1-carboxylate; VII, 4-hydroxy-3-oxocyclohex-4-ene-c-1-carboxylate; VIII, 3, 4-dioxocyclohexane-c-1-carboxylate; IX, t-3-hydroxy-4-oxocyclo-hexane-c-1-carboxylate; X, 3,4-dihydroxycyclohex-3-ene-c-1-carboxylate; XI, 4-hydroxy-3-oxocyclohexane-c-1-carboxylate; XII, (−)-t-3,t-4-dihydroxycyclohexane-c-1-carboxylate.

could take place earlier at compound III. Before catechol is reached there are several stages which are shown in Figure 8.

The precise role of these chemical changes is not fully understood, but what does seem clear is that they provide hydrogen acceptors for the bacteria, as illustrated by the following examples (Whiting and

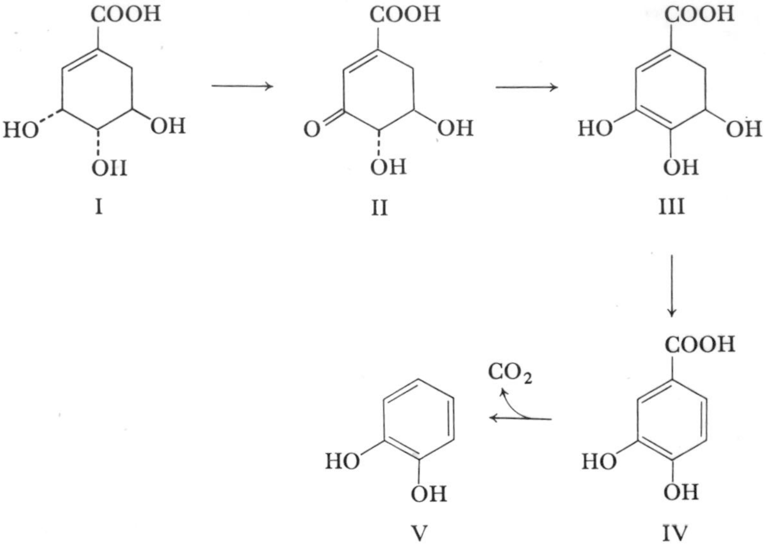

Fig. 8. Metabolism of shikimate by *Lactobacillus plantarum*. The key to the compounds is: I, (−)-shikimate; II, (−)-3-dehydroshikimate; III, the enol form of compound II; IV, protocatechuate; V, catechol.

Coggins, 1969; Carr and Whiting, 1971; Whiting and Coggins, 1971). Using the heterofermentative *L. collinoides* (formerly called *L. pastorianus*), it was possible to show the effect of the presence of shikimate or fructose and lactate:

3 fructose → 2 mannitol + lactate + acetate + CO_2
fructose + 4 shikimate → 4 dihydroshikimate + acetate + 2 CO_2
lactate → no metabolism
lactate + 2 shikimate → 2 dihydroshikimate + acetate + CO_2

Should either the first or second reaction occur, there would be an immediate increase in the concentration of acetic acid. With fructose in the presence of shikimate (or quinate), there would be a six-fold (600%) increase and for lactate a 100% increase. Both of these effects would cause a tainted flavour. Furthermore, the presence of catechol would also tend to give an off-flavour.

Another transformation of organic acids is that of chlorogenic acid by *L. collinoides* (Whiting and Carr, 1957, 1959). The acid is hydrolysed into quinic and caffeic acids. Quinic acid is then metabolized to dihydroshikimate by way of the pathway shown in Figure 7. The other compound produced during the hydrolysis, caffeic

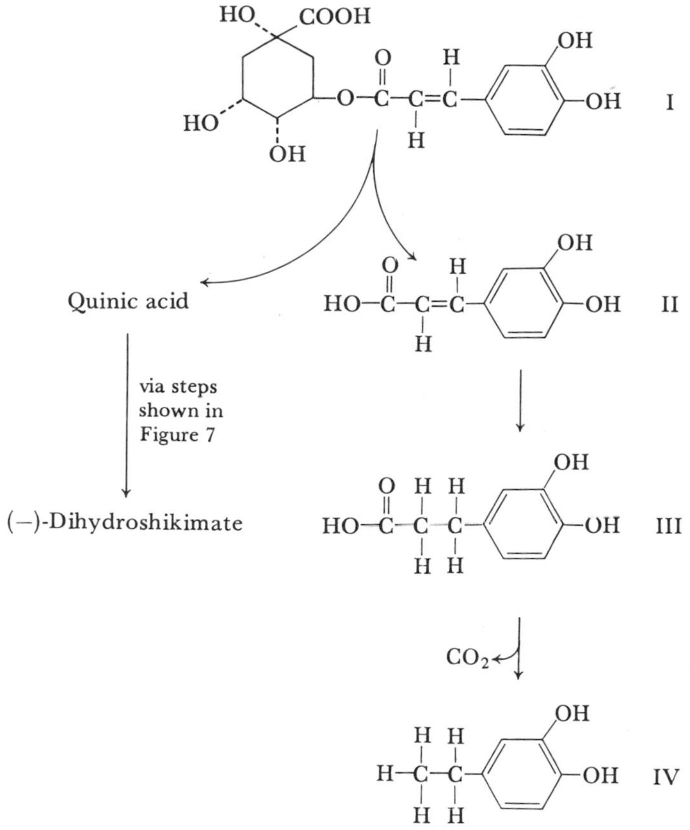

Fig. 9. Metabolism of chlorogenic acid by *Lactobacillus collinoides*. The key to the compounds is: I, chlorogenic acid; II, caffeic acid; III, dihydrocaffeic acid; IV, ethyl catechol.

acid, is metabolized by the bacterium as shown in Figure 9. Production of ethyl catechol could be the cause of off-flavours since this compound has a somewhat unpleasant aroma.

The changes in concentrations of organic acids so far described have been under anaerobic conditions and brought about by the lactic-acid bacteria. Acetic-acid bacteria can also cause certain oxidative changes. For example, members of the genus *Acetomonas* form acetic acid by oxidation of malic acid. From quinic, shikimic or dihydroshikimic acid, they bring about a series of analogous oxidative changes (Carr and Whiting, 1971) as shown in Figure 10. If these occur, it is most likely that they will take place after fermentation and during storage.

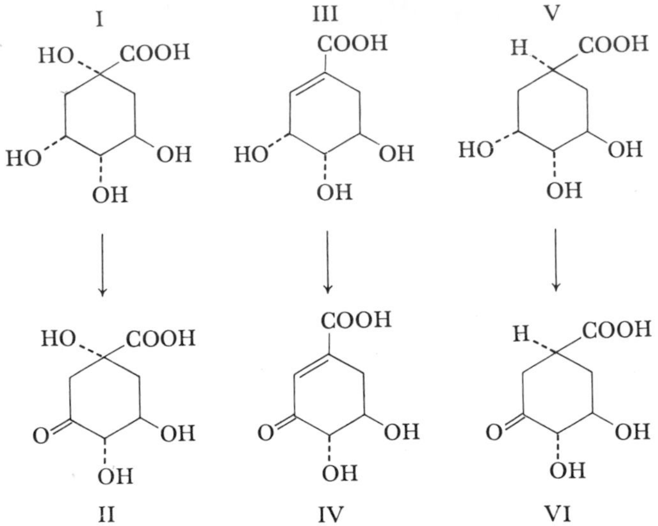

Fig. 10. Oxidation of quinic acid and related acids by *Acetomonas* spp. The key to the compounds is: I, quinic acid; II, 3-dehydroquinic acid; III, shikimic acid; IV, 3-dehydroshikimic acid; V, dihydroshikimic acid; VI, 4-5-dihydroxy-3-oxocyclohexane-1-carboxylate.

Several other organic acids have been identified in ciders which probably arise as a result of yeast fermentation (Whiting and Coggins, 1960c). These are 2-methyl-2:3-dihydroxybutyric acid, 2:3-dihydroxy-*iso*-valeric acid, 2-ethyl-2:3-dihydroxybutyric acid and 3-ethyl-2:3-dihydroxybutyric acid. They only occur in low concentrations but their effect may be disproportionately large compared with their concentrations. The second acid can act as a precursor for valine which is an amino acid present in low concentrations in ciders. Many cider lactic-acid bacteria have an absolute requirement for this compound (Carr, 1956) and it is possible that the presence of this dihydroxy acid could serve as an additional source of valine for the bacteria.

c. *Nitrogenous compounds.* Amino acids are amongst the most easily detected of the nitrogen-containing compounds and, therefore, more is known about them than any others. During fermentation they tend to disappear and later to re-appear in smaller quantities but in a greater variety as a result of yeast excretion and autolysis. This is well illustrated in Table 19 which shows the content of amino acids at various stages of a cider fermentation. The work of Burroughs and Carr (1957) showed that fluctuation of the content of amino acids affected the ability of certain test lactic-acid bacteria to grow in sterilized cider removed at certain stages during fermentation.

Table 19 shows that, although the concentrations of amino acids are considerably higher in the juice than the dry cider, the variety of these compounds is greater at the end of the fermentation. Whereas at the beginning of the fermentation there were 15 amino acids and related compounds present, by day 113 there were 21 present. The six additional compounds were glycine, arginine, lysine, phenyl-alanine, tyrosine and an unknown peptide. According to Burroughs (1957a) the amino acids typical of yeast autolysis are the leucines, lysine, arginine, phenylalanine and tyrosine.

Table 19

Changes in content of amino-acids during fermentation of apple juice

	Days of fermentation				
	0	5	16	57	113
Specific gravity	1,056	1,044	1,024	1,005	1,001
Soluble nitrogen (mg N/100 ml)	4.94	2.13	2.03	2.00	2.53
Alcohol-soluble nitrogen (mg N/100 ml)	4.58	1.90	1.82	1.89	2.29
Volume of juice or cider on chromatogram	5 ml	20 ml	20 ml	20 ml	20 ml
Amino acids[a]					
Aspartic acid	10	1	1	tr.	2
Asparagine	10	1	tr.	0	tr.
Glutamic acid	10	3	1	1	2
Serine	8	2	1	2	4
Glycine	0	tr.	tr.	1	1
Threonine	2	0	0	tr.	1
α-Alanine	4	tr.	tr.	2	6
β-Alanine	1	tr.	0	0	tr.
γ-Aminobutyric acid	3	tr.	0	tr.	2
Valine	2	0	0	tr.	2
Leucines	2	0	0	tr.	3
Proline	tr.	0	0	0	tr.
Methyl-hydroxyproline	small	med.	med.	med.	med.
Arginine	0	0	0	0	1
Lysine	0	tr.	tr.	tr.	3
Pipecolinic acid	tr.	2	1	1	1
Phenylalanine	0	0	0	0	1
Tyrosine	0	0	0	0	tr.
Unknown (near proline)	1	2	2	3	2
Peptide (near arginine)	1	1	1	tr.	1
Peptide (near glutamine)	0	3	2	1	2

[a] Contents of amino acids are listed on a scale (0–10) based on a visual assessment of chromatograms; tr. indicates a trace. Leucine and isoleucine are not separated by the solvent system used. The amino acids are listed in descending order of concentration in juices.

There is no doubt (Burroughs and Carr, 1957) that the disappearance of these amino acids from the fermentation is due to yeast activity which renders the fermenting juice a less favourable substrate to support growth of lactic-acid bacteria, as shown in Table 20. This shows that the test bacteria are less able to grow in the cider after 5 and 15 days' fermentation than before the start of yeast activity.

Table 20

Growth of lactic-acid bacteria in sterile filtered apple juices and ciders

Days of fermentation	Specific gravity	Growth (%) of organisms			
		A	B	C	D
0	1.056	100	100	100	100
5	1.044	33	36	27	67
16	1.024	33	36	18	42
57	1.005	67	43	42	50
113	1.001	100	50	68	33

A indicates growth of *Leuconostoc mesenteroides* (non-slime-forming); B of *Lactobacillus pastorianus* var. *quinicus*, now known as *L. collinoides*; C of *Lactobacillus pastorianus* var. *quinicus* (slime-forming strain), probably *L. collinoides*; and D of *Lactobacillus plantarum* (atypical).

Most increase their ability to grow in the cider at days 57 and 113 with the exception of organism D, which seems to show something of an anomalous result in the final sample. Further, while the bacteria do not show their best growth in the dry cider, they are able to grow better as the result of the presence of yeast autolysis products. The fact that the concentration of amino acids continues to increase if the dry cider is left on the lees has been amply confirmed by Burroughs (1957a). He showed that, after a period of some three months on the lees, the amino acids of the cider may double or treble in concentration.

Burroughs and Carr (1957) not only showed that the yeasts could remove and replace amino acids, but also demonstrated that the lactic-acid bacteria showed similar behaviour. Organisms C and D shown in Table 20 were allowed to grow in the sterile juice used in the investigation, and the results obtained are shown in Table 21. It will be noted that both bacteria showed a similar uptake of amino acids, which is in accord with the work of Carr (1956) who reported that glutamic acid and valine were essential for growth of some 35 lactic acid bacteria which included leuconostocs, hetero- and homo-fermentative lactic acid bacteria. It has been suggested by Burroughs and Carr (1957) that valine could have been the factor controlling growth of organisms shown in Table 19. It will be noted that, on days 5 and 16 when the ability of the bacteria to grow in the ciders was at its lowest (Table 20), valine could not be detected (Table 19).

Tables 19 and 21 show that there is a constant interchange of amino acids brought about by yeasts and bacteria. This may also apply to the other nitrogenous constituents of ciders and perries about which much remains to be learnt.

Table 21

Changes in the contents of amino acids caused by growth of lactic-acid bacteria in sterile filtered apple juice

Organism	Utilized	Excreted
Lactobacillus pastorianus var. *quinicus*	Aspartic acid Asparagine Glutamic acid Serine Valine Isoleucine	α-Alanine Phenylalanine Three not identified
Lactobacillus plantarum	Asparagine Glutamic acid Serine Valine Isoleucine	α-Alanine

d. *Tannins*. At present our knowledge of the fate of phenolic compounds is somewhat sparse. In Section II.B.1.b (p. 186) it has been shown that certain phenolic acids, such as chlorogenic acid, can be broken down by lactic-acid bacteria, but little is yet known of the fate of the more complex phenolic compounds. Indeed, it is only recently that the occurrence and identity of some of these compounds have been elucidated. From the tannin permanganate titration, it would appear that little change takes place, since the titre changes only slightly, if at all, in the juice as compared with the finished cider. However, it is reported in Section II.A.1.e (p. 172) that this titration only accounts for some of the phenolics, and changes could take place that would leave the permanganate value unaltered. Only when more is known about the phenolics of the juice will it be possible to see if they change in concentration during fermentation and storage.

e. *Aroma compounds*. A knowledge of the fate of aroma compounds is based upon experiments with juices from the cultivars Yarlington Mill, Sweet Coppin, Kingston Black and Bramley's Seedling. Sterilized samples of each juice inoculated with *Saccharomyces cerevisiae* (AWY 350R) were examined for volatile aroma components before and after fermentation. At the same time, a nutrient medium containing glucose was prepared, inoculated with the same yeast, and fermented in parallel with the juices to provide a comparison between a substrate containing no initial aroma compounds and the juices which contained a considerable spectrum of these compounds.

Table 22 shows the amounts of certain higher alcohols present before and after fermentation. It can be seen that *n*-propanol increases considerably in concentration in all apple juices. In contrast, *n*-butanol diminishes in concentration in all apple juices in spite of the fact that the yeast is able to synthesize small quantities in the semisynthetic medium. The other alcohols produced in the semisynthetic medium, namely, isobutanol, 2- and 3-methylbutanols and 2-phenethanol, all show similar or greater increases in the fermented juices. There seems to be no doubt that the appearance and disappearance of these alcohols during the fermentation period is not a simple process.

Generally, esters are present in smaller concentrations than alcohols (Table 23), with the notable exception of ethyl acetate and 2- and 3-methylbutyl acetates which, in Yarlington Mill juice, increase 200-fold during fermentation. The concentrations shown in the tables should be taken as a guide, since it is not quite certain how some compounds are affected by extraction procedures. Nothing is yet known about chemical changes taking place during the period of storage, but it seems likely that many do occur during this time.

The results obtained so far, while being a useful guide, only approximate to reality for, in the industrial situation, many apple cultivars are mixed together during processing. The fermentation juice can often contain more than one yeast, each of which probably has its own pattern of volatile-compound production and modification. Added to this is the presence of bacteria whose activities as

Table 22

The major higher alcohols in apple juices and ciders

Substance	Content (p.p.m.) in									
	Yarlington Mill		Sweet Coppin		Kingston Black		Bramley's Seedling			
	juice	cider	juice	cider	juice	cider	juice	cider	sugar fermentation
n-Propanol	0	52	0.6	46	0	34	3	44	80
n-Butanol	35	2	16	1	40	34	8	6	0.5
Isobutanol	0	6	1	6	0.5	6	2	25	8
n-Pentanol	0.05	0.01	0.2	tr.	0.5	0.3	0.1	0.1	—
2- and 3-Methylbutanols	2	96	1	107	9	105	8	90	81
Hexanol	4	4	3	1	11	9	6	4	—
2-Hexanol	1	0.05	1	0.05	0.1	0.2	0.3	0.1	—
2-Phenethanol	0	19	0	34	0	30	0	19	9

Table 23

Concentrations of the major esters in apple juices and ciders

Ester	Content (p.p.m.) in								
	Yarlington Mill		Sweet Coppin		Kingston Black		Bramley's Seedling		Sugar fermentation
	juice	cider	juice	cider	juice	cider	juice	cider	
Ethyl acetate	2	35	1	20	1	17	2	15	33
Isobutyl acetate	–	0.2	–	0.003	–	0.1	0.03	0.3	0.02
Ethyl butyrate	0.3	–	0.01	0.01	0.2	0.4	0.3	0.1	0.3
2- and 3-Methylbutyl acetates	0.15	30	0.02	3	0.2	4	0.1	0.9	1
Ethyl 2-methyl butyrate	0.006	–	–	–	0.01	–	0.04	–	–
Hexyl acetate	0.6	6	0.3	0.1	0.2	1.5	0.3	0.7	–
Ethyl hexanoate	–	2	–	0.02	–	0.6	–	0.9	2
2- and 3-Methylbutyl octanoates	–	4	–	0.1	–	0.7	–	0.01	0.1

regards the volatiles are as yet unknown. There remains, therefore, a great deal of investigation into the fate of these compounds finally responsible for the aroma of ciders.

f. *B-Group vitamins.* Goverd (1973a, b) studied changes in the four B-group vitamins thiamin, nicotinic acid, pantothenic acid and riboflavin in juices derived from two cultivars, namely Cox's Orange Pippin and Bramley's Seedling. Of these two, the Cox's Orange Pippin was higher in nitrogen content than the Bramley's Seedling. The analyses were achieved by inoculating the sterilized juices with the yeast *Saccharomyces uvarum*, and taking samples at intervals for nitrogen content and vitamin assay. The initial concentration of the high-nitrogen juice was 26.8 mg/100 ml, and this diminished to 8.0 mg/100 ml at the end of the experiment. The low-nitrogen juices started with 10.4 mg of nitrogen/100 ml and finished at a concentration of 3.9 mg/100 ml. Some of Goverd's (1973a, b) results are summarized in Table 24. The thiamin followed the pattern of

Table 24

Fate of four B-group vitamins in fermenting low- and high-nitrogen apple juices. From Goverd (1973a, b)

Cultivar	Vitamin	Vitamin concentration (mg/100 ml)		No. of days to reach minimum vitamin concentration
		Initial	Final	
Cox's Orange Pippin	Thiamin	25.6	3.0	5
Bramley's Seedling		9.5	2.8	14
Cox's Orange Pippin	Nicotinic acid	85	42	6
Bramley's Seedling		60	50	12
Cox's Orange Pippin	Pantothenic acid	50	75	2
Bramley's Seedling		76	162	0
Cox's Orange Pippin	Riboflavin	2.4	6.4	0
Bramley's Seedling		3.6	6.2	0

changes in the nitrogen since high nitrogen was always associated with high thiamin, and *vice versa*. Although not shown in the table, the rate of fermentation was considerably faster in the high-nitrogen juice. This is reflected in the time taken to reach the minimum concentration of the vitamin. In both ciders, thiamin was completely consumed but very soon afterwards some was released by the yeast so that the final concentrations in the two ciders were very similar.

Nicotinic acid showed the same initial pattern of concentration as thiamin, namely, that the higher-nitrogen juice contained the greater concentration of vitamin. As described previously, the high-nitrogen juice fermented faster than the lower-nitrogen juice, this again being reflected in the number of days it took to reach the minimum concentration of nicotinic acid. Unlike thiamin, nicotinic acid was never completely depleted and, as the fermentation slowed down, it was released into the medium. It is interesting to note that, although the Bramley juice started with less nicotinic acid than Cox juice, when the final concentrations were measured the position was reversed.

The concentration of pantothenic acid in the lower-nitrogen Bramley juice exceeded that in the Cox juice and this was the situation at the end of the fermentation. A further interesting point is that, in the high-nitrogen juice, there was a drop in concentration for two days and from thereon an increase. This is perhaps explainable by suggesting that the high content of nitrogen allowed a very rapid growth of yeast which caused a temporary depletion of the vitamin and that, after a while, it began to be synthesized. In the low-nitrogen juice, there was a slower increase in yeast-cell number, no rapid initial depletion of pantothenic acid concentration, and only a steady increase. Thus, the minimum concentration occurs at zero time as recorded in Table 24.

Riboflavin showed the same reversal as pantothenic acid, the higher initial concentration occurring in the juice with the lower content of nitrogen. Both juices showed their minimum concentration at zero time and, from thereon, increased in amount so that finally they had very similar concentrations of riboflavin present.

These experiments were supplemented by others (K. A. Goverd, personal communication) in which two strains of *Saccharomyces cerevisiae*, named Champagne and AWY 350R, showed similar results with pantothenate, namely, that there was more present after fermentation than before it. They differed in their behaviour towards nicotinic acid since strain AWY 350R appeared to synthesize this vitamin while Champagne depleted it.

The removal and addition of these B-group vitamins during fermentation may well dictate what happens during storage when the fermenting yeasts have died. Since lactic-acid bacteria are more exacting nutritionally than the yeasts, they are more sensitive to the presence or absence of B-group vitamins. Carr (1958) showed that

without exception cider lactic-acid bacteria had an absolute requirement for pantothenate and nicotinic acid, and that thiamin was most
important in the growth of the heterofermentative rods.

There seems little doubt that uptake and release of B-group
vitamins must play a great role in the interaction of yeasts and
bacteria and of growth of the latter in stored ciders. Since each
commercial factory has its own yeast, and probably its own bacterial,
flora much remains to be learned about how these distinct groups of
organisms are involved with the B-group vitamins under fermentation
conditions.

2. Microflora

a. *Yeasts.* The kind of yeasts that occur in fermenting cider are
largely determined by the condition of the fruit and the state of
hygiene in the factory. If the fruit is poor and the factory where it is
handled not under a particularly good sanitation regime, then the
numbers and different kinds of yeast will be high. This was the
situation in the past and, in those days, fermentation might have
been expected to start with *Kloeckera apiculata*. Being a yeast that
grows rapidly, it would form the major part of the microflora and
fermentation would begin. Since it is not very tolerant of alcohol, it
would die out when a concentration of 2–5% (v/v) ethanol was
reached. The slowing down of the growth of *K. apiculata* and its
eventual death were accompanied by growth of the *Saccharomyces*
spp. of which there could be several. In the very early stages of
fermentation, it might be possible to find other weakly fermenting
yeasts such as *Metschnikowia pulcherrima, Saccharomycodes
ludwigii* and perhaps even species of *Brettanomyces*. During the
latter part of the fermentation, the main fermenting yeast gradually
died out and, by the time the fermentable sugar has been depleted,
most fermenting yeasts would be dead or moribund. In the stored
cider, these yeasts continue to die and, although they would no
longer bring about any changes as living cells, the process of autolysis
releases the amino acids and B-group vitamins discussed in previous
sections of this chapter.

Even if the yeasts were left in the stored cider, they would not
survive, mainly due to the lack of sugar and presence of ethanol. One
that can survive, however, is *Saccharomycodes ludwigii*, because it

can utilize lactic acid which, by this stage, is usually present in abundance owing to the activities of lactic-acid bacteria. Film yeasts will also grow during storage if the cider is exposed to air. Such a situation may be found in the premises of a small cidermaker who is still using wooden casks, but growth of these yeasts on the large scale is minimal compared with the volume stored. Furthermore, the standards of factory hygiene are more stringent on the large scale and sulphur dioxide is used more frequently.

Adding sulphur dioxide at the start of fermentation kills off such yeasts as *M. pulcherrima* and *K. apiculata* although, if the latter is present in very large numbers, it may only be suppressed and not eliminated completely. Addition of this preservative gives the *Saccharomyces* spp. more opportunity to grow. In a cider made from sulphited juice, these yeasts may belong to a single species or a combination of them. The commonest, and the one said to be the true cider yeast, is *Saccharomyces uvarum*, but this may be replaced by or be in company with *Sacch. florentinus* and *Sacch. cerevisiae*. One yeast which is not often found but which has the capacity to survive sulphiting is *Saccharomycodes ludwigii*.

Waiting for *Saccharomyces* spp. to develop naturally after sulphiting is often a lengthy process, so that most large manufacturers grow a pure yeast culture of their own choosing and add it to the sulphited cider. The reason for choosing a yeast may be several. Speed of growth, ease of removal, production of aroma compounds may all be taken into consideration (see Section III, p. 250). Different yeast strains produce different aroma compounds (Beech and Davenport, 1970), and it is possible in due time that yeasts may be chosen to produce ciders with particular flavours. As one of the characteristics of a yeast to be used for this purpose is fermentation vigour, then it is likely to outgrow any of the yeasts that are naturally present and impose upon the cider those characteristics thought to be desirable. It is possible for a situation to arise in which one of the naturally occurring yeasts could outgrow the one that had been added. This is probably rare and, for all practical purposes, the efficient use of sulphur dioxide and an adequate amount of yeast is almost as good as the employment of pure-culture techniques.

The establishment of a dominant yeast is probably the most widely used method of inoculation amongst the larger cidermakers. With certain special products, however, pure yeast cultures may be inoculated into sterile juice. The products most likely to receive such treatment would probably be the champagne ciders and perries. With these high-quality drinks, the price is sufficient to cover the cost of initial sterilization of the juice and subsequent sterile handling.

b. *Bacteria.* Lactic-acid bacteria are most suited to survive in the anaerobic conditions of fermentation. They are micro-aerophilic, can utilize the residual sugars and seem to be able to withstand the intense competition from yeasts. Microscopic examination of a fermenting cider will invariably reveal lactic-acid bacteria along with yeasts. In the early stages, these may be homofermenters like *Lactobacillus plantarum* and *L. mali* (Carr and Davies, 1970). Later these disappear giving way to *L. collinoides* (Carr and Davies, 1972) which is a heterofermentative rod. During this period, they utilize the available sugars from which the principal end-product is lactic acid. They may also attack malic acid at this stage breaking it down to carbon dioxide and lactic acid. In the absence of yeast, malo-lactic fermentation proceeds fastest when there are sugars present. However, in a fermenting cider, the competition may be such that this particular activity is deferred until yeast fermentation has ceased. There is evidence to show (Carr *et al.*, 1972) that certain yeasts, notably *Saccharomyces uvarum*, are markedly inhibitory towards development of some lactic-acid bacteria.

Generally it is the rods that are found during fermentation, and this could be a reflection of their temperature responses. These bacteria have an optimum of 30°C which is never reached in cider, although a temperature of 25°C is sometimes achieved during vigorous yeast fermentation. It may be that the elevated temperature encourages growth of rods during this period.

The bacteria, unlike the yeasts, can survive and indeed grow in stored ciders. It is probably true to say that the lactic-acid bacteria most often found in stored 'dry' ciders are the heterofermentative cocci which are *Leuconostoc* spp. In a survey of ciders collected from various manufacturers, Carr and Davies (1972) noted that, in those ciders where the use of fairly high concentrations of sulphur dioxide was usual, the predominant organisms were *Leuconostoc* spp. whereas, in the ciders from factories where little or no sulphur dioxide was used, the predominant bacteria were rods. Experiments on a strain of *L. plantarum* in a model system suggest that bacterial resistance to sulphur dioxide may be much greater than hitherto believed.

Although leuconostocs can be found during fermentation, they are more likely to be encountered in the cooler conditions of dry stored cider, where they will attack malic acid if it has not already been metabolized at an earlier stage. On the factory scale, the advent of malo-lactic fermentation is dependent upon the environmental temperature. Where large vats are deliberately kept cool, a minimum temperature of about 15°C in the cider must be reached before malic acid begins to disappear. Thus it can be well into the summer before acid breakdown takes place. Large vats present problems because it is possible for the upper layers to be sufficiently warm for a malo-lactic fermentation to take place whereas, at lower levels, no such activity is in progress. The ability to break down malic acid is almost universal amongst cider lactic-acid bacteria, whereas the capability of metabolizing quinic acid is rarer. It is restricted to hetero-fermentative rods of the species *L. collinoides* and to a few strains of *Leuconostoc*. If one of these organisms metabolizes malic acid in a 'dry' cider, it does not attack quinic acid until all malic acid has disappeared. The mechanism that prevents the two activities from being concurrent is unknown. Although a dry cider is assumed to be devoid of sugar, it contains traces of fructose, glucose and xylose that disappear during a malo-lactic fermentation.

One organism mentioned previously which is encountered only rarely is *Pediococcus cerevisiae* (Carr, 1970c), a homofermentative coccus. It plays little part in cider making but can be a nuisance because some strains form slime. Like most lactic-acid bacteria it can break down malic acid.

It might be thought that, because acetic-acid bacteria are aerobic, they are unable to survive the intense anaerobic conditions of cider fermentation. This is not so for Carr (1959a) showed that acetic-acid bacteria can grow in a juice before yeast fermentation starts, survive fermentation until storage, and then show a resurgence of growth. Passmore (1972) later confirmed that this persistence in fermenting ciders is a characteristic of several species. Both Carr (1959b) and Passmore (1972) isolated *Acetomonas* spp., *Acetobacter mesoxy-dans, A. xylinum, A. rancens* and, in addition, Passmore (1972) reported the occurrence of *A. aceti*. By using pure cultures of acetic-acid bacteria in a pure-culture yeast fermentation, Passmore

Table 25

Survival of bacteria in controlled cider fermentation

Incubation time (days)	Acetobacter aceti Jar 1	Acetobacter lovaniense Jar 2	Acetobacter mesoxydans Jar 3	Acetomonas sp. Jar 4	Acetobacter rancens Jar 5	Acetobacter xylinum Jar 6	All six cultures together Jar 7
3	+++	+++	+++	++	++	++	+++ (1, 2, 3, 4, 5, 6 survive)
6	+++	+++	+++	—	+++	++	+++ (1–6)
11	+++	++	+++	—	+++	+	+++ (1, 3, 5, 6)
24	++	—	+++	—	++	—*	+ (1, 5, 6)
36	++	—	+++	—	++	—	+ (1, 5)a
Analysis:							
Sp. gr. (15°C)	1.011	1.001	1.002	1.001	1.207	0.999	1.010
Ethanol (% v/v)	4.6	6.6	5.6	8.8	4.4	7.8	4.7
45	+++	—	++	—	++	—	+ (1, 5)
Ethanol (% v/v)	3.9	6.6	5.9	not tested	2.9	7.9	5.1

Incubation conditions: aerobic, 25°C.

Yeast culture: *Saccharomyces cerevisiae* AWY 350R.

Initial juice: sterile Cox's Orange Pippin: pH 3.42; sp. gr. 1.060.

+ + + = > 10^4 bacteria/ml; + + = < 10^4 but > 10^3 bacteria/ml; + = < 10^3 bacteria/ml; — = no colonies on isolation plates; → = duration of visible fermentation.

a Indicates that bacteria were not isolated but the jar had a viable leathery pellicle of *Acetobacter xylinum*. Reproduced from Passmore (1972).

(1972) was able to show that certain acetic-acid bacteria could readily survive the fermentation. This is shown in Table 25. From this it is possible to see that certain species not only survived fermentation but increased in numbers. This is particularly noticeable in jar 5 where growth of *A. rancens* slowed the fermentation to such an extent that the final specific gravity was 1.027. A similar process took place in jar 1 containing *A. aceti*, and also in jar 7 containing all of the test bacteria. Even *A. mesoxydans* in jar 3 survived the whole fermentation but its presence does not appear to have inhibited the yeast.

Both the lactic- and acetic-acid bacteria interact with yeasts and, as yet, the factors controlling these activities are little understood.

C. Disorders

These may be defined as any change in cider which makes the appearance of flavour unacceptable to the consumer. Disorders can be due to micro-organisms or to chemical changes. There is a third category which encompasses both, namely, hazes, which can be caused either by micro-organisms or by chemical reactions.

1. Microbiological Disorders due to Bacteria

a. *Cider sickness.* Although this disorder was first described by Barker (1908), it was probably known amongst cidermakers for a considerable time before this. In his description, Barker (1908) describes all of the salient features of the disorder, namely, that it can be transmitted from one cider to another by inoculation of a sound cider with a sick one, that it is most likely to occur in a slowly fermenting cider, and that not all ciders are equally susceptible. Only sweet ciders having a high acidity are immune. Finally, an elevated temperature aids progress of the disorder. What Barker did not say in 1907 was that the organism causes a milky whiteness due to production of acetaldehyde which combines with polyphenols in the cider. It is the excess aldehyde that characterizes the disorder due to its sweetish pungent smell and aroma. Many aspects of the disorder have been described by Barker and Ettle (1912), Barker (1913, 1946, 1949, 1952), Grove (1915, 1917, 1924), Spiers (1915), Tutin (1926) and Barker *et al.* (1950, 1952). However, the first paper to describe the causal organism was by Barker and Hillier (1912) in which the following properties were listed: a motile non-sporing rod able to cause an alcoholic fermentation of glucose and fructose but not of sucrose, maltose or lactose; the optimum temperature was described as being close to 30°C.

It was not until the work of Millis (1951, 1956) that the organism was named. She studied the bacteriological and technological characteristics of the organism and these are shown in Table 26. Millis (1951, 1956) proposed that the name of the cider sickness organism should be *Zymomonas anaerobia* var. *pomaceae*. The generic name was derived from a similar organism isolated from pulque by Lindner (1928). The latter named the organism *Termobacterium mobile* but it was subsequently renamed *Pseudomonas lindneri* by Kluyver and Hoppenbrouwers (1931) and changed once more to *Zymomonas mobile* by Kluyver and van Neil in 1936. The specific name, *anaerobia*, Millis derived from a similar organism discovered in beer by Shimwell in 1937, which he then called *Achromobacter anaerobium*, but later renamed *Saccharomonas anaerobium* (Shimwell, 1950). Present knowledge indicates that the differences between *Z. mobilis* and *Z. anaerobia* are too small to justify two species, and it has been suggested independently by Dadds *et al.* (1973) and Richards and Corbey (1974) that there should be the single species, namely *Z. mobilis*.

This multiplicity of names suggests that the zymomonads are unusual organisms whose precise relationship with other bacteria cannot be decided easily. Indeed, the 8th edition of Bergey's Manual does not attempt to group them with any other bacteria since such relationships remain obscure. They are unusual bacteria as they carry out an alcoholic fermentation. This they do by the Entner–Doudoroff pathway which, at the fourth step, gives rise to the unusual compound 2-oxo-3-deoxy-6-phosphogluconate which is cleaved into pyruvate and glyceraldehyde 3-phosphate, which in turn is converted to pyruvate by way of the later steps of the Embden–Meyerhof–Parnas pathway. It has already been mentioned that the acetaldehyde formed after pyruvate tends to accumulate to give the typical symptoms of the disorder. This is usually described as a 'rotten lemon' or 'banana skin' type aroma. In France, where the disorder is prevalent due to their practice of storing low-acid sweet

Table 26

Biochemical and other properties of various strains of *Zymomonas*

	Carr and Passmore (1971b)	Results recorded by Millis (1956)	
Test applied	Response of culture	Cider sickness	*Termobacterium mobile*
Production of catalase	+	+	+
Production of hydrogen sulphide	+	+	+
Growth at 15°C	+ (after 11 days)	NR	NR
25°C	+ (within 72 h)	NR	NR
30°C	+ (between 24 and 48 h)	optimum	optimum
40°C	− (after 11 days)	NR	NR
Fermentation of:			
Ribose	−	NR	NR
Arabinose	−	−	−
Glucose	gas	gas	gas
Fructose	gas	gas	gas
Lactose	−	−	−
Sucrose	−	−	gas
Maltose	−	−	−
Melibiose	−	NR	NR
Raffinose	−	−	+ 1/3
Sorbitol	−	W 2/3	+ 3/3

+ = positive reaction or growth; − = negative reaction or no growth; gas = gas but not acid produced; + 1/3 = one out of three cultures tested positive; W = weak growth; NR = not recorded.

ciders, the name *framboisé* is applied, yet it is difficult to identify a raspberry flavour with the aroma of a sick cider.

Table 26 shows that this organism can only utilize glucose and fructose, and that a pH value of 3.7 or less is unfavourable. These two characters have been utilized in English cidermaking for measures to prevent severe outbreaks of the disorder. It is, therefore, customary to ferment the cider to dryness as quickly as possible and to keep the pH value below 3.7. Since zymomonads are resistant to sulphur dioxide in excess of the permitted level of 200 p.p.m., strong competition from a rapid yeast fermentation is essential. Because zymomonads can only derive energy from glucose and fructose, conversion of these two sugars to alcohol by yeast fermentation prevents growth of the bacterium. It can truly be said that the current method of cidermaking in England, i.e. fermentation to dryness and storage of dry cider, is due directly to the existence of *Zymomonas anaerobia*.

One of the mysteries surrounding this organism is where it survives when not growing in cider. Until recently it had never been found anywhere but in 'sick cider'. It had always been assumed that the organism was introduced into the factory on the fruit and, if the conditions were suitable, it could grow and cause the disorder. No evidence existed for this. However, Carr and Passmore (1971b) isolated *Z. anaerobia* from apple pulp before the juice was extracted from it. The fact that the organism was isolated from the dis-integrated fruit tends to support the idea that these bacteria are introduced on the apples. It is interesting to note that the bacterium was unable to grow under factory conditions and that cider sickness did not occur. In spite of this additional evidence, the question still remains where the organism lives out most of its existence. It would be reasonable to assume that it lives in the soil or in association with plant material, but this remains to be proven.

b. *Ropiness or oiliness*. This is a disorder common to ciders, beers and wines, but is not necessarily caused by the same organism in each of the beverages. It is characterized by a gradual thickening of the consistency of the drink until its texture becomes like that of thin lubricating oil at which stage it is called oiliness. If, however, the consistency becomes even thicker to such an extent that, by placing a finger on the liquid surface a thread of slime can be drawn up, then it is known as ropiness. At this stage, it tends to pour like golden syrup, and its unpleasant feature is not due to any particular off-flavour but to the production of a slimy sensation on the palate resembling that of raw egg white. The particular sensation arouses a powerful feeling of revulsion in most people.

There are three known causes of the disorder, of which the most common is a heterofermentative lactic rod which has never been named, but which resembles quite closely the species called *Lactobacillus collinoides* (Carr and Davies, 1972) as shown in Table 27. The

Table 27

The characteristics of *Lactobacillus collinoides*. From Carr and Davies (1972)

Test		Response
	Colony morphology	Irregular (see text for full description)
	Cell morphology	Rods 0.73 μm x 4.0 μm many long filaments (see text for fuller description)
	Fermentation type	Heterofermentative
	Growth in 5% (w/v) NaCl	Few strains grow
Hydrolysis of	{ Aesculin	Split by most
	Arginine }	Hydrolysed by most
	Growth at 15°C	All strains grow
	Growth at 40°C	Some strains grow
Fermentation of	{ Arabinose	All strains ferment these sugars
	Xylose }	
Fermentation of	{ Ribose	
	Glucose	
	Fructose	Most strains ferment these sugars
	Galactose	
	Maltose }	
Fermentation of	{ Rhamnose	
	Lactose	
	Sucrose	
	Trehalose	
	Cellobiose	
	Raffinose	
	Melezitose	Most strains do not ferment these sugars
	Inulin	
	Glycerol	
	Mannitol	
	Dulcitol	
	Salicin	
	α-Methylglucoside }	
Fermentation of	{ Mannose	
	Sorbose	No strains ferment these sugars
	Sorbitol }	
Metabolism of	{ Malic acid	
	Citric acid	Most strains ferment these acids
	Quinic acid }	

organism was first described by Millis (1951) and later by Carr (1957, 1959c). Millis (1951) showed that this rod could produce slime and acid from glucose, fructose and maltose and, in addition, could produce acid from arabinose and xylose. These observations were later confirmed by Carr (1957) who noted that, of all the sugars tested, arabinose was attacked preferentially, a characteristic of many heterofermentative lactic rods. Some light was thrown on the structure of the polysaccharide by Barker et al. (1958), who showed that glucose, galactose, arabinose and mannose all occurred in the products of its hydrolysis.

Two cocci have been reported as the cause of ropiness in ciders. The first of these was described by Millis (1951). It was isolated from a cider with a high pH value (4.2) in which the typical symptoms of oiliness had developed. When cultured on an apple-juice agar it produced colonies of about 0.75 mm diameter after 17 days' incubation anaerobically at 25°C. The feature of these colonies was that, in spite of their small size, they pulled up into slimy strings about 8 cm long. The colonies yielded Gram-positive cocci about 0.7 μm in diameter. When re-inoculated into apple juice, the phenomenon of ropiness was reproduced. Millis (1956) showed that this organism could produce acid from glucose, fructose, sucrose, xylose and raffinose, and that its optimum pH value and temperature range were 4.6–5.6 and 25–31°C, respectively. Millis (1951) concluded that the organism belonged to the genus Leuconostoc, and tentatively suggested that it might belong to the species Leuc. mesenteroides. However, it does not seem likely it can be a member of this species since typical members cleave sucrose, utilize the fructose for energy and build glucose into a polysaccharide. This particular organism produces acid mainly from sucrose, and slime not at all from this sugar. Unfortunately the organism loses its ability to produce slime, and eventually dies out in subculture. Since that time, many leuconostocs have been isolated from ciders but none has possessed the ability to produce slime. It seems probable that Millis's (1951) slimy coccus was unique, and that with the extensive use of sulphur dioxide and the tendency to use juices of lower pH value the chance of finding it again are remote.

One slime-forming organism that has been isolated from outbreaks of ropiness more than once is the tetrad-forming Pediococcus cerevisiae which was described by Carr (1970c). When cultured, two forms of this organism occurred, a slimy and non-slimy form. There was little difference between them except in the slime-forming ability which, of course, influenced their colony form. There always seemed to be a proportion of non-slimy colonies amongst the slimy organisms. Since the properties of this organism have been fully documented elsewhere (Carr, 1970c), it is not intended to describe its bacteriological properties. It was possible to show however that, in the presence of carbon dioxide, slime production was enhanced and also that, if the pediococcus was grown in the presence of certain weakly and non-fermenting yeasts, for example *Candida krusei*, slime production was likewise increased. These bacteria are very similar to the slime-forming cocci of beer which are known either as *Pediococcus* spp. or *Streptococcus damnosus*.

In the early 1950s, the most prevalent type of ropiness was that caused by lactic rods. With the improvement in cidermaking methods over the last two decades, this disorder has ceased to be a major problem. However, outbreaks which have been investigated more recently have been due to the coccus *Pediococcus cerevisiae* rather than the rod.

c. *Acetification*. The previous disorders are due to micro-aerophilic bacteria, whereas acetification is an oxidative activity brought about by aerobic organisms belonging to the genera *Acetobacter* and *Acetomonas* (*Gluconobacter*). The earliest occasion on which acetification might occur is in bruised and damaged fruit where juice leaks out, undergoes alcoholic and possibly lactic fermentation, followed by oxidation of ethanol to acetic acid by members of either of these groups. In very extreme cases of damaged and neglected fruit, acetification and other exothermic microbial activities becomes so intense that there is a rise in temperature causing the fruit to heat. It has been mentioned already that fructose is converted by some acetomonads into 2,5-D-*threo*-hexodiulose (5-oxofructose; Carr and Whiting, 1971). This, in itself, does not constitute a disorder, but the fact that it can nullify the effect of sulphur dioxide means that sulphur dioxide-sensitive disorder-producing micro-organisms can flourish in conditions under which they would normally be suppressed.

Acetic-acid bacteria show little activity during fermentation, yet these aerobic organisms are not killed by the intensely anaerobic conditions of fermentation (Carr, 1959a). During this phase, they seem to be relatively inactive and only appear in large numbers during storage. Many years ago, ciders were stored in numerous small wooden vessels. This meant that such vessels, partially full, presented a large surface area-to-volume ratio, and that acetifying bacteria could grow readily on the surface, imparting a vinegary flavour. Indeed, it was not uncommon when emptying small wooden casks for a sheet of tannin-stained cellulose produced by the growth of *Acetobacter xylinum* to slop out of the bunghole. Today wooden vats are still in use, but their capacity is so large, compared with their surface area, that the risk of acetification is minimal. Acetic-acid bacteria may grow in the small inspection port of these large wooden vats but the amount of acetic acid produced is minute when compared with the total volume, which might be 180,000 litres or more. About 100 p.p.m. of acetic acid can be detected by aroma and flavour. Acetyl-CoA combines with ethanol to form ethyl acetate, a phenomenon which seems to enhance the intensity of the acetic aroma and flavour. Although the methods of storage, i.e. exclusion of air and addition of sulphur dioxide, control acetification quite effectively, it is nearly always possible to isolate acetic-acid bacteria from ciders and cidermaking materials. Indeed, in a survey carried out by Passmore (1973), she showed that there was no single aspect of cidermaking in which acetic-acid bacteria could not be found. The species she identified were *Acetobacter aceti, A. xylinum, A. rancens, A. mesoxydans* and *Acetomonas* spp. She also isolated *Acetobacter ascendens* from effluent water in a cider-factory sewage sump. Her examination of a cidermaking plant that had not been used since the preceding pressing season revealed only moulds and yeasts. The same sites sampled one week after fruit processing had started in the new season revealed the presence of *Acetobacter mesoxydans, A. xylinum* and *Acetomonas* spp.

Modern methods of factory hygiene, together with the use of more easily cleanable vessels made of stainless steel and acid-resistant lined steel, have decreased the incidence of acetification. However, it is true to say that, in spite of these measures, acetic-acid bacteria are present and, if presented with the right conditions, can develop and cause the disorder.

While this is the obvious form of acetic-acid production in ciders, there are other organisms which, under different conditions, can produce acetic acid. These have been reviewed extensively by

Whiting (1973) and are discussed on page 186 of this chapter. One example of acetification brought about by lactic-acid bacteria was first mentioned by Müller-Thurgau and Osterwalder (1913) and was referred to by them as anaerobic acetification. This is due to breakdown of citrate to oxaloacetate and acetate with the subsequent conversion of oxaloacetate to pyruvate which is then dismutated to acetate and lactate as shown below:

$$citrate \longrightarrow oxaloacetate + acetate$$

$$oxaloacetate \longrightarrow pyruvate + CO_2$$

$$2\ pyruvate + H_2O \longrightarrow acetate + lactate + CO_2$$

This conversion of citrate is of little importance in apple juices because they contain so little of this acid, whereas perries can contain up to 0.7% (Phillips *et al.*, 1956) which is a potential source of acetic acid.

d. *Mousiness*. Caged mice have a very distinctive and unpleasant aroma which is very similar to that which emerges from a bottle of crude acetamide. For many years, acetamide has been quoted as the classical example of mousiness but, in fact, the pure substance is odourless. Tucknott and Williams (1973) showed that a condensation product of acetamide, 2,4,6-trimethyl-1,3,5-triazine, has a mousy smell. The structure is shown in Figure 11.

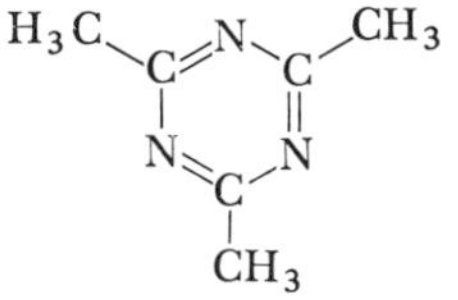

Fig. 11. Structural formula of 2,4,6-trimethyl-1,3,5-triazine.

Experiments with mousy cider have shown that this compound is not implicated although it is possible that the taint might be caused by one of similar structure. It is, however, possible to produce it at will. Certain lactic-acid bacteria can produce the taint and, with the strain used by O. G. Tucknott and P. A. Davies (personal communication), it seems the presence of a yeast is necessary for the taint of mousiness to develop. In contrast, however, this off-flavour can be produced by certain strains of *Brettanomyces*. The active compound is extremely elusive, and none of the several groups working on the disorder have as yet been able to produce an answer. It is, of course, possible that mousiness of cider is due to a compound quite unrelated to trimethyltriazine and yet can elicit the same sensation on the palate and in the nose.

All individuals differ in sensitivity to many aromas, but mousiness is an extreme example of a compound that affects people in different ways. There are those who can detect the smell and flavour of this taint in very low concentrations and others who can only just detect it at concentrations at which sensitive people find it intolerable. It can be detected by aroma, but its most unpleasant feature lies in its flavour. The taste of a mousy cider is not immediately apparent but it builds up gradually in intensity after a short initial delay.

2. Microbiological Disorders due to Yeasts

a. *Fermentation of concentrate.* One way in which the cider-maker can spread his fermentations over the whole year, instead of having them all set up immediately after pressing, is to concentrate the juice and store it in this condition. In theory the low water activity in a juice concentrated to about one-sixth or one-seventh of its original volume ought to prevent microbial activity. This is not so, for there are a number of yeasts that can grow under such conditions. Perhaps the most important of these is *Saccharomyces rouxii*, some strains of which can grow in and ferment concentrates with as much as 68–70% (w/v) of sucrose. *Saccharomyces bailii* var. *bailii* and *Sacc. bailii* var. *osmophilus* are found increasingly to be the cause of fermenting concentrated juice, especially those contain-ing preservatives. Their activity is very insidious since the fermen-tation is so slow that it may not be detected for months or even years. This is considered a disorder because the yeasts bring about a fermentation in a substrate that has been specifically prepared to be microbiologically stable and, secondly, they are not very good fermenters should the concentrate be diluted to its original strength. Some species, for example, *Sacch. bailii* var. *bailii*, produce acetic acid and, therefore, not only produce an uncontrolled fermentation but an undesirable off-flavour as well.

Concentrates arc hygroscopic and take in water from the atmos-phere to form a surface film. This film has a lower sugar content which allows a group of osmotolerant yeasts to grow; these yeasts include members of the following genera: *Candida, Hanseniaspora, Pichia* and *Saccharomyces*. Once the osmophilic yeasts have started to lower the sugar content, growth of the osmotolerant yeasts can follow.

Both kinds of yeasts are found in nature wherever there are high concentrations of sugars such as in honey, plant exudates and mummified fruit, and are carried by insects that feed on sugary solutions. How they infect concentrated juices is not known precisely, but it is thought that they enter cider factories as part of the annual yeast influx and that they are present in undetectably low levels, only being noticed when they have initiated a fermentation.

b. *Yeasts growing during fermentation.* During fermentation in non-sulphited ciders, several different kinds of yeasts can grow. One group which grows rapidly during the first 5° drop in specific gravity are collectively known as the apiculate yeasts, of which *Kloeckera apiculata* is a principal component. These are small, lemon-shaped yeasts, which grow rapidly and can ferment. Beech (1959) showed that the apiculate yeasts that grew during the first 5° drop in specific gravity could still be detected after a drop of some 35°, in spite of competition from the more numerous, strongly fermenting *Saccharomyces* spp. He also showed that, in the same sulphited juice, the apiculate yeasts disappeared during the first 5° drop in gravity. Apiculate yeasts not only ferment sugars to ethanol and carbon dioxide but also produce acetaldehyde and acetic acid, both of which spoil the flavour. At present, the use of sulphur dioxide keeps these undesirable yeasts in check but, if the present legislative pressures to decrease the use of sulphur dioxide succeed, some other means of preventing growth of apiculate yeasts, such as pasteurizing or sterile filtration, will have to be used.

c. *Growth of yeasts in bottle.* This can be disastrous for any cidermaker, since his aim is to prolong the shelf life of a bottled cider for as long as possible. It is usually achieved, either by subjecting the cider to a sterile filtration procedure, or by the application of heat by way of a heat exchanger. If there is a breakdown in a filter, it is customary for the bottles to become contaminated with the yeast normally used for fermentation and, possibly, any bacteria that may also be present. This type of in-bottle infection shows itself as a cloudiness in the bottled cider and an increase in pressure. The first of these is unpleasant because, although some draught-cider drinkers are prepared to accept 'cloudy' cider, consumers of the bottled product expect a clear drink. Secondly, as most bottled ciders are sweet and, therefore, contain sugar, there is the danger of bottles, designed only to withstand normal carbonation pressures, exploding. A similar situation can arise if the cider is normally heated and there is a malfunctioning of the pasteurizing or cooling equipment. This type of trouble usually arises in a hot summer when the demand for cider increases. The speed of production is such that perhaps the various sterilization procedures are carried out more hastily and less efficiently than usual, and the higher ambient temperatures encourage growth of micro-organisms.

Another form of in-bottle infection is caused by the yeast *Saccharomycodes ludwigii*. This is a large apiculate yeast which exhibits bipolar budding and is the sole member of its genus. It is a slow growing, slow fermenting yeast which is highly resistant to sulphur dioxide and, because its cells cling together, resistant to heating. This yeast has the ability to live in pipe-lines and, as the liquid flows through, an occasional piece of yeast growth breaks off which usually ends up in a bottle. It may be some time before an infection by this yeast is noticed because it does not produce a haze but grows on the bottom of bottles, forming a coherent but friable film. As soon as the bottle is inverted, the film breaks up producing a snowflake appearance. Explosion of bottles is less likely to be a danger with this yeast because it ferments rather slowly. It is very difficult to eradicate and only a very strict programme of hygiene is likely to get rid of the organism. According to Beech and Davenport (1970) *S'codes ludwigii* can be found in small numbers associated with the developing fruit in the dormant flower buds and mummified fruit. It has been found in juice and concentrated juices and may be isolated from fermenting juice and stored ciders. In any of these situations, it plays an insignificant role but once it gets into the plant it is exceedingly dangerous.

One other form of yeast contamination in bottles ought, with the use of different closures, to be disappearing. That is contamination through the use of screw-stoppered bottles. These bottles still persist in the cider industry in the form of flagons which have an internal screw thread into which can be screwed a plastic stopper. To effect the seal, the stopper has a rubber ring. If the stoppers are not properly sterilized, yeasts can lodge behind the rubber rings and contaminate bottles. The likely contaminants from such a situation are *Saccharomyces* spp. and even members of the genus *Hansenula* have been known to produce estery off-flavours from the bottle closures.

The types of yeast contamination already described are often due to inadequate sterilization and dirty conditions in factories. One further example of contamination in bottles comes from pieces of apparatus that can be found in all cider factories using sterilizing filters. These are the sight glasses and pressure gauges situated on the sterile side of the filter. If yeasts get into these devices, then no amount of steaming will kill all of the organisms, so that the survivors leak out into the 'sterile' cider causing extensive contamination. It is in this sort of situation that *S'codes ludwigii* might be found. Only special sterilization of sight glasses and pressure gauges will free them of contaminating organisms.

3. Disorders of Minor Importance

a. *Film yeasts.* Such yeasts as *Pichia membranaefaciens* and *Candida valida* (formerly *C. mycoderma*) can often be found growing on the surface of ciders stored in wooden vats, particularly in the area of the inspection hole. Like acetic-acid bacteria they can be suppressed by excluding air; their major oxidative activity is the conversion of ethanol to carbon dioxide and water. They are, however, so restricted in distribution as not to constitute a major disorder.

b. *Hazes.* The cause of hazes are many, but two of the commonest are the combination of polyphenols with protein and the occurrence of dextran. These hazes are often so fine as to constitute a colloidal suspension which readily passes through the normal filters and remains unaltered in chemical composition.

III. TECHNOLOGY

The greatest changes in the history of the cider industry have occurred during the last decade. Formerly, in England, it consisted of a group of relatively small companies with little control over the type of fruit it bought and competed to sell in retail outlets belonging to the brewers. Now it is a vertically integrated industry controlling, or having under contract, supplies of fruit and juice concentrate and selling nationwide in association with the brewers. In addition, there are many more off-licences and licensed supermarkets, and a determined effort is being made to enter this market also. Most of the cider is produced by a few large companies who possess the necessary technical and marketing skills which enable them to make significant increases in sales (Roberts, 1974). The smaller makers have prudently withdrawn from this very competitive arena and find a more profitable market in selling, either direct or through speciality shops, to discerning local cider drinkers or visitors to the English West Country.

A. Fruit Supply

The changes in marketing techniques have required the industry always to have a guaranteed supply of raw material, irrespective of the vagaries of factors such as crop size. This has meant planting, or encouraging the planting, of profitable intensive cider-apple orchards of those varieties having a suitable tannin composition. Again, the policy of buying concentrated juice has been changed. Formerly concentrate was only bought when there was a shortage of fresh apples and then only at the lowest price. The concentrate manufacturers, without a guaranteed market, considered supplies for this market as a salvage operation, and did not give a great deal of attention to the production methods. Now forward contracts are signed with producing countries in both the northern and southern hemispheres, guaranteeing prices and product quality. Such concentrates can be stored safely for two or three years and buffer any marked variations in the size of the fresh fruit crop.

1. Orcharding

The state of the English cider orchards prior to these changes was summarized by Williams (1966). The committee on whose activities Williams (1966) reported was concerned about the continuing decline of the acreage and the low average yield of fruit per acre (see Section I.D., p. 155). The only exception was Hereford, where the planting schemes initiated by Messrs H. P. Bulmer Limited were balancing the loss of orchards of standard trees that had finished their useful lives (50–100 years). Large mixed profitable farms producing cider apples, hops, black currants, beef cattle and sheep were peculiar to the county, largely because of its strong grassland tradition. Similar schemes were available for pears in Somerset (Williams, 1961).

However, all of the major cidermakers were agreed that insufficient of the best high-yielding apple varieties were being grown, and that the use of large standard trees was inconsistent with modern concepts of economics. To persuade growers rather than farmers to plant the new orchards needed considerable persuasion, since the fruit could only have one very small group of customers. Again, unlike cash crops which can be switched according to market requirements, an orchard needs to be in bearing for at least 20 years in order to realize a sufficient return on capital. The committee compared, therefore, the costs of a traditional cider apple-stock grazing orchard with one devoted to specialized cider-apple production, preference being given to a farm already producing hops or other fruit so that equipment such as spray machinery could be used more efficiently. They reached a number of conclusions, as follows: (a) If the profit from a mature orchard could not be raised to a level comparable with other farm crops it should be grubbed; (b) Varieties planted in the new orchards should be confined to heavy bitter-sweets; (c) The growers would need 'protection against the effects of pricing in a market of oligopolistic buyers and competitive sellers'. A similar situation used to exist with the growing of vegetables and soft fruits for canning and freezing, but has been overcome by the manufacturer buying at higher prices under contract and the use of very stringent quality-control standards.

The outcome was that two manufacturers offered contracts for a minimum of 20 years, guaranteeing to take all of the crop at agreed prices, the costs of establishing the orchard over the first three years to be met out of returns received for the fruit. The manufacturers also raised the trees, planted them and maintained them for the three year period. In itself this was insufficient unless a high yield of 20–25 thousand kg/hectare could also be guaranteed. The committee, therefore, examined all the varieties on the previous Recommended List (Anon., 1957) and finally selected several which it was considered could be grown anywhere, whose pomological characteristics were consistent with the requirements for intensive cultivation, and which gave high and consistent yields. These were Michelin, Dabinett and, in frost-prone areas, Vilberie. A second group consisted of Tremlett's Bitter, Taylors, Chisel Jersey, Somerset Red Streak and Brown Snout. The first group now form some 70–75% of the orchards that were planted, the remainder being chosen from the second group. Even these are not entirely free from faults, and might benefit from alterations in their genetic make-up with irradiation treatment. Thus, a more compact form of Vilberie is needed, Dabinett is susceptible to potash deficiency, the propensity of Tremlett's Bitter to form breast wood needs eliminating, and Michelin requires a rigid anti-mildew programme. Improved yield was ensured by using heat-treated planting material and a semi-dwarfing habit induced with the MM106 and 111 rootstocks. Slowly more and more of these dwarf bush orchards are being planted; there are 862 hectares so far, with another 755 projected over the next five years. Potentially these could supply some 40 million kg of fruit or just over half the total amount used at present in England. Not unnaturally all of these pomological changes have caused changes in juice composition, the extent of which has now to be re-investigated.

To some extent the plantings of semi-dwarfing trees were an act of faith on the part of the cidermakers, since they were using the experience gained with dessert and not cider apples. At first, attempts were made to raise catch crops or to use zero grazing between the rows of trees during the establishment period before cropping commenced. Such efforts have now been virtually abandoned, as they delayed development of the tree and the onset of cropping. Hence research is in progress on improving regularity of cropping, to produce trees more cheaply by eliminating rootstocks, and to try and 'spread' the harvest season beyond the one month as it will be at present. This could be done, either by bringing in new varieties, or by the use of synthetic growth substances to advance or retard fruit maturity and drop. However, the more difficult problem for the future will be the mechanical harvesting of apples, for which no real precedent exists.

In France there have been limited plantings of cider apples as bush trees, i.e. large trees with short instead of long trunks (Auclair, 1957), but these are totally insufficient to replace the decaying population of existing trees. It is expected that the supply of cider apples for commercial processing will become critical by 1980 at the latest. There is resistance to planting on the part of the growers because of unsatisfactory prices in the past. Cidermakers have very little finance to spare for subsidizing plantings because of the drastically lowered cider sales.

The perry-pear orchards of bush trees planted in the 1960s in Somerset, England, have been virtually the only revival of such orcharding since the time of Queen Anne. When the new orchards were established, the available information on growing pears in this form was very meagre, and it was not known how to get the trees into cropping early on in their life. Added to this, pears had never been grown on any scale in the county previously. For whatever of these reasons, they have neither flourished nor produced a significant tonnage of fruit so far.

2. Mechanical Harvesting

As has been experienced already in the cider industry with the operation of hydraulic presses, there is a move by labour away from seasonal jobs carried out under uncongenial conditions (Cargill and Rossmiller, 1969). At first, labour could be retained for apple harvesting by raising the wage rates, but it became clear that people just did not like bending down all day harvesting fallen apples in the cold, wet early winter months. Hence, even in standard orchards, some form of mechanical harvester became necessary (U.S.D.A., 1965; Tennes et al., 1971; Williams, 1972; Rudkin et al., 1973).

The first was the Hedgehog, a simple spiked roller, pushed by hand through the fallen fruit. It picked reasonably well but was tiring to use and the receiver buckets had to be emptied manually so often that the speed of harvesting was seriously retarded. Puncturing the skins did not cause any serious damage in the early maturing varieties, provided they were processed quickly; failure to do so led to extensive rotting. With the late season fruit, the wound sealed off and they could be matured normally (Beech, 1963a). A tractor-mounted and a larger, independently motorized version, were produced but in each case were handicapped by having small, batch fruit-holding systems. They could still be used by owners of small orchards without the need for seasonal labour.

The Cacquaval machine, using a contra-rotating reel, was developed for use in French cider-apple orchards. There is both a small self-propelled version, which is very popular in France, and a much larger model, the Super 2500, mounted on the front of a tractor. The first has only a small fruit holder; the second is somewhat complex mechanically. It needs a wide alleyway and branches well clear of the floor. Leaves and grass are removed to some extent as the harvested material passes over a series of rollers before being conveyed to a truck or trailer. The third, the Tuthill-Temperley Harvester, exists only in prototype form and is still under development. It consists of fingers rotating on a horizontal bar inside a 1.8 m-wide nozzle. There is a high-speed fan mounted inside the throat of the nozzle which projects leaves and grass over the back while apples are conveyed into an integral gondola. A mechanized arm in front of the machine sweeps the fruit from between the trees into the alleys so that it can be picked up.

In spite of attempts to clean the fruit, all of these machines are also liable to pick up a certain amount of mud and trash. This puts a greater Biochemical Oxygen Demand load in the effluent from the water-conveying systems of the factory's storage silos. Again, in the orchards of the English South West, the higher rainfall leads to replacement of the original herbage by shallow-rooting, spreading *Agrostis* grass. This tends to be rolled up like a carpet by harvesters picking fruit off the ground. However, the fact remains that only this type of machine is suitable when there are a large number of small orchards planted with a limited number of varieties and scattered over a wide area. The fruit can be left in the cool grass for up to three weeks without harm until arrival of the harvester. Even in intensive orchards, some fruit always falls before the main crop is due for harvesting, so two types of machine are necessary.

In contrast, orchards with large cropping areas in close proximity need a different type of machine, one capable of harvesting large areas in a short time. An over-the-row harvester would probably be most suitable for this purpose. The Penn State over-the-row harvesting machine, similar in concept to grape and blackcurrant harvesters, and using apples grown as a tall narrow hedgerow, has been tried in the U.S.A. and abandoned. It requires a new and difficult-to-manage tree shape and the level of damage (30%) in dessert apples was unacceptable. Another method, the shake and catch system, is used for harvesting products such as nuts and peaches in the U.S.A. Designed for very large trees, the independently motorized catching frame(s) is placed under the tree canopy, the trunk vibrated mechanically, and the fruit caught on the cushioned bars of the frame. This type of machine is already being used in the U.S.A. to harvest dessert apples intended for processing, but the damage caused as the fruit hits the intervening branches prevents the harvesting of apples intended for store or for sale as fresh fruit. However, a limited degree of bruising of cider fruit processed a few hours after harvesting would not be important. Experiments will be carried out from 1974 season onwards to see what modifications are necessary to enable the smaller and more numerous trees of the intensive orchard to be harvested at a satisfactory rate with a continuous shake-catch system (Williams, 1974). Development costs must be kept small since the potential market for the machine is also small.

It is important to remember that the harvester cannot be considered in isolation; for example, the shape of the tree should be modified to allow the harvester to be used with maximum efficiency. The sward of the orchard must also be examined; maximum canopy size means minimum light for the grass, which is a better surface for a machine in wet weather than bare soil. Herbage must be found capable of growing in such conditions, but its leaf length must be controllable, for example with maleic hydrazide, to minimize time spent on mowing. For machines picking off the ground there is also an additional need for deep-rooted rather than short surface-rooting grasses. The use of ripeners and stickers to allow successive blocks of orchards to be harvested in turn has already been mentioned. Even the layout of varieties within rows and in adjacent orchards must be considered in relation to the problem of harvesting the fruit.

The length of the apple stalk is important when using the shaking system, since short-stalked fruit require less energy to detach them than long-stalked ones. A synthetic growth hormone controlling stalk abscission independently of ripening would be invaluable. Needless to say, means must be found for producing the optimum size of crop consistently. It is clear that the culture of cider apples, as with much of our horticultural and agricultural produce, is moving into the realms of biological engineering, when the animal or plant is modified to fit in with the method of processing and production.

3. *Fruit Reception*

Modern published information on the reception of cider apples at commercial cider factories is virtually non-existent. The only detailed publication refers to French practice some 20 years ago (Charley *et al.*, 1953). Until the 1950s nearly all farms and factories received fruit in hessian sacks, holding approximately 50 kg, which were stood, either on the ground or on concrete slabs, around the press house. The larger factories then adopted the Continental system of having the bagged fruit emptied into silos. Factories having rail access would use dump trucks and silos below the lines. In the 1960s more and more fruit was delivered by tipper-type lorries. Eventually container lorries, holding up to 20 thousand kg of fruit, became common. Such vehicles are now used for moving fruit from the eastern to the western counties, from Normandy to England or from California to Washington or British Columbia. The advent of mechanical harvesting will demand very efficient systems for handling and processing large volumes of fruit in a relatively short period of time.

The original silos were of two types. The first was designed for the reception of cull dessert and culinary apples, hand picked straight from the tree and outgraded without contact with the soil. These could be handled dry using a conveyor and roofed bins for holding the fruit until ripe. Reversal of the conveyor took the fruit direct to the mill without fear of breaking it with stones or other hard adventitious debris. The second consisted of roofed or unroofed silos with steep sloping sides. Underneath ran a concrete channel through which water could be circulated moving the apples to a central pond. The channel was normally covered with wooden slats which had to be removed at intervals in order to discharge the fruit into the flowing water. Subsequently, the slopes were made less steep and one or more manholes provided to give access to channels underground. Fruit was then forced into the manholes using water cannon supplied from the recirculated water main. In the final development, the ground was flat so that a calfdozer could be used instead of a water cannon. Alternatively, the silos could be opened at the base and the fruit received on conveyor belts made of stainless steel slats. From the pond, the fruit would be lifted by a slatted elevator or archimedian screw. Systems also exist for washing the fruit and storing it in covered silos ready for conveying by belt to the mill. Modern installations of the latter type can empty 20 thousand kg lorries in 15 min. Another variation employs a large steel water tank with an outlet at one end which conveys fruit and water through a 23 cm plastic pipe to the elevator. The water is returned for recirculation. Pears contain less intercellular gas and so are denser than water and cannot be moved satisfactorily by flotation; movement in sodium sulphate solution, as used in pear-processing plants, would be expensive for making a lower cost product such as perry.

Any system using water for transporting fruit suffers from effluent problems. Grass and leaves choke the elevators, necessitating frequent removal of debris. The water rapidly becomes charged with silt, mud and ground-up fruit tissue from soft apples. The Biochemical Oxygen Demand of the water rises to very high levels due to admixture with the juice from broken tissue. With the enforcement in Great Britain of the Clean Water Act, measures have had to be taken to remove the solid particles on self-cleaning screens, to chlorinate as well as to give a constant input from sprays of fresh water mounted by the elevator. Even so, the outflowing water, as well as the recirculated water at the end of the shift, must now go together with any other effluent of similar Biochemical Oxygen Demand to settling tanks. In more and more areas, the outlet from these tanks must be passed through the company's treatment plant or, if accepted in the local sewerage system, a heavy charge is made depending on the load of organic matter. Hence, there is interest in an all-dry system of fruit handling in order to remove this financial burden, which means collecting the crop before it reaches the ground.

B. Juice Production

Apples and pears are milled to a fine pulp in a grater or hammer mill. Several patterns exist, and the choice is usually made on output and mechanical reliability. Chipping and vibration have been claimed (Flaumenbaum and Sejtpaeva, 1965; Körmendy, 1965a) to give an 8–10% greater yield on pressing than the equivalent chopped or milled fruit. The method has not yet been adopted commercially, neither has the system of electroplasmolysis using high electrical voltages (Lazarenko *et al.*, 1969). The size of the pulp particles is important, the smaller they are the higher the yield, but there is a limit since homogenized pulp is impossible to press (Wucherpfennig *et al.*, 1973b). The optimum pulp-particle size has not been determined since the mills tend to give a broad range of sizes around a mean, the value of which varies with the setting of the blades.

Pulp from true cider apples rarely contains a high proportion of soluble pectin, since the phenolic components in the fruit inhibit the action of the pectolytic enzymes that convert protopectin to soluble pectin (Pollard *et al.*, 1958; Williams, 1963; Goldstein and Swain, 1965). This occurs readily in stored dessert apples because their phenolic content is much lower. Loss of pectin from the cell walls causes loss of the rigidity needed in pressing (Pollard and Timberlake, 1971). The pulp of culinary apple varieties, for example Bramley's Seedling, Granny Smith, and Sturmer's, although having a low phenolic content, is also low in soluble pectin, because the enzymes are less active at low pH values. Hence, while the pulp of cider, culinary and under-ripe dessert apples can be pressed immediately after milling, it is becoming usual to treat the pulp of over-ripe dessert apples with pectin-destroying enzymes beforehand.

Under-ripe dessert pears can be milled and pressed without difficulty, whereas the pulp from ripe fruit needs the addition of cellulose or rice hulls, or admixture with culinary apples. True perry pears can contain a considerable amount of colloidal leuco-anthocyanins. Prolonged milling in the old stone mills or holding the pulp for some hours before pressing caused it to coagulate in the pulp. The expressed juice was free from the astringent effect on the lining of the mouth and a precipitate was not formed in the perry. Nowadays, with milling and pressing following one another, there can be haze or deposit formation during storage or in bottle (Pollard and Beech, 1963). Chilling the perry or treating it with gelatin prior to bottling are used as preventative measures.

Extraction of juice from the pulp, by whatever means, is a major operation in cidermaking. The machines employed must work throughout the season with dependable mechanical efficiency, have the necessary hourly throughput to handle the peak supply of fruit, give a good juice yield, be economical in operation and be capable of being cleaned and sterilized, otherwise they become the principal foci of infection in the factories.

It is not intended that this section of the chapter should give a detailed account of the necessary plant and associated equipment. Instead some indication will be given of the factors involved in extracting juice, and, because there is no one perfect press, the reasons for using different juice-extraction systems.

1. Factors Controlling Juice Yield

Considering how many years apples and pears have been pressed, it is surprising to find that only recently has there been any serious investigation on the basic factors underlying juice extraction (B. L. Flaumenbaum via Schaller and Blazejovsky, 1960).

According to Körmendy (1964, 1965b, 1972) the pressing time required to achieve the same percentage yield of press liquid is proportional to the square of the initial thickness of the material being pressed. In other words, the thinner the layer of pulp the more efficient the juice extraction. He developed theoretical equations to cover different conditions of pressing and laboratory machines for determining most of the constants in his equations. He showed that both the two-stage pressing process (three-bed pack press) and continual increase in pressure could be used to minimize pressure time appreciably. While this was a theoretical exercise to develop a small continuous press with higher yields, the problem became of practical importance with the need to process the increasing surplus of late-stored Golden Delicious apples in Holland. These develop a texture like porridge, and it is practically impossible to express juice from them. The problem was investigated by Pilnik and de Vos and their associates (Verspuy et al., 1970; Pilnik and de Vos, 1970a, b; de Vos, 1971; Beltman et al., 1971; de Vos and Pilnik, 1973), and more recently by Wucherpfennig et al. (1973b) and Wucherpfennig (1974) whose results can be summarized as follows.

The yield of juice obtained from apple pulp is governed by the following factors: the applied pressure, degree of size reduction, duration of pressing, the distance the juice has to flow, breaking up of the solid material during pressing, rate of increase of pressure applied, and the temperature of the pulp.

Pilnik and de Vos (1970a, b) were influenced by the current European practice of heating the more pectinous soft-fruit pulps (Ménoret, 1970) and were anxious to avoid yeast growth during the long holding periods used in their initial tests. Consequently they heated the pulp to 40°C since, above that temperature, the flavour of the juice expressed was adversely affected. There was a relationship between particle size, the pressure applied and the rate of increase in applied pressure. Juice yield from coarsely ground pulp of a hard-textured apple was strongly dependent on the degree of pressure applied, but the rate of increase in pressure had no effect. With finely ground pulp, the yield was independent of maximum pressure and distinctly greater. High pressures were unnecessary with pre-enzymed pulp (0.02%, 20 h at 40°C), since juice yield increased asymptotically and was constant and independent of pressure at time infinity. Also, as stated previously, by Körmendy's equation the times of pressing were proportional to the square of the thickness of the pulp. The effect of enzyme treatment on difficult-to-press soft apples with their unfavourable pulp structure is illustrated as follows:

No enzyme treatment   Rapid press rate → 40% (w/w) juice yield and turbid juice

                                    Very slow press rate → 80% (w/w) juice yield and clear juice

Enzyme treatment   Rapid press rate → 40% free run juice, 75% total yield

Similarly, nearly half of the juice ran freely from enzyme-treated pulp of hard-textured apples, and the total yield increased from 75 to 80% compared with pulp not treated with enzyme.

Subsequent experiments were designed to decrease the long period of enzyme treatment which was caused by inhibition of the added enzyme by phenolics in the pulp. Oxidation of the pulp by slow mixing, first for two hours and, in later experiments, for 15 min, caused a decrease in enzyme-treating time from 21 h to 20–30 min. The extracted juice became completely depectinized by holding for a few hours after pressing. Although the pulp was dark brown with precipitated phenolics, the juice was coloured pale yellow and there was very little adverse effect on flavour. A similar lowering of the time required for enzyme treatment can be obtained by removal of the phenolics using polyvinyl pyrolidone or gelatin. Pilnik and de Vos (1970a, b) continue to use a temperature of 40°C for the treatment and 0.04% enzyme (Ultrazyme 100, or any good commercial pectin-destroying enzyme, but not pectin lyase alone). However, as shown by Wucherpfennig *et al.* (1973b) working with similar fruit, while 0.04% w/w was the optimal amount of enzyme at 40°C for 1 h, the yield was only slightly greater than one hour at room temperature, and was actually less than after three hours at room temperature. Hence the duration of treatment was more important than temperature. Burroughs *et al.* (1973) achieved similar results using long stored Cox's Orange Pippin. Wucherpfennig *et al.* (1973b) also advanced an alternative explanation for the effect of phenolics, namely, that the monomeric and oligomeric polyphenols combine with pectins and the compounds formed are only degraded by the enzyme with difficulty.

Treating the pulp with enzyme causes a small increase in the Brix value and the acidity of the juice, but the reasons for this are not known at present. More importantly, the process gives rise to higher concentrations of methanol since there is much more pectin in the pulp than in juice. Hence juice from enzyme-treated pulp contains 300–400 mg methanol/l compared with 30–100 mg/l in enzyme-treated juice (Pilnik, 1973). The methanol is removed in juice concentration but not in aroma stripping. Little is known of the subacute toxicity of methanol but some consumer groups are concerned at the presence of methanol at any concentration in beverages for human consumption. Treating pulp with enzyme is economical whether combined with warming, oxidation or gelatin addition. It cannot be used with true cider apples (and, in any case, would be unnecessary with these) nor with non-cider varieties whose pomace is required for extraction of pectin.

In the U.S.A. and Canada, enzyme treatment is used to some extent, but is not as successful with the screw presses which are used there so extensively. Instead, cellulose pulp is added prior to pressing to create drainage channels within the pulp mass, and rice hulls to keep the holes clear in the retaining sieve. Some details are given in Greenwood *et al.* (1970). This treatment is uneconomic in Europe because of the cost of purified cellulose, but kieselguhr, Perlite and similar materials have been used to assist in the pressing of pulp from over-ripe apples and pears (Beech, 1963b; Eid and Holfelder, 1974).

The juice yield referred to so far has been measured under laboratory conditions but, in practice, it is necessary to monitor the efficiency of a press while it is running. It is almost impossible to obtain an accurate estimate simply by measuring the weight of the fruit input and the volume of juice expressed. Not only are there inevitable losses, but the moisture content of the expressed pomace can vary with pressing conditions. Two methods are available for measuring the juice yield of commercial machines while they are in operation and independent of physical measurement of the volume of juice. In the first (Greenwood et al., 1970), the insoluble solids of the pulp and pomace are determined after methanol and acetone extraction followed by drying the residue for 15 min. The yield is calculated from these values and the specific gravity of the juice with the following formula:

$$\text{Juice yield (litres/}10^3 \text{ kg)} = \frac{\left(10^3 \times 1 - \dfrac{\text{Pulp-insoluble solids}}{\text{Pomace-insoluble solids}}\right)}{\text{Specific gravity of juice (g/ml) at } 20°\text{C}}$$

The method described by Burroughs (1970a, 1971) required no analytical manipulation except for measuring the specific gravity of the juice and drying samples of pulp and pomace in a vacuum oven overnight. Hence it was meant to be an historical record of press performance rather than a means of adjusting operating efficiency while running. Both methods are of equal precision.

Most hydraulic presses operating on cider apples give 780–800 litres of juice to the tonne. Prolonging the pressing time and adding a small quantity of water yields 900 litres per tonne. Yields for cooking apples and enzyme-treated dessert apples are slightly less. Yields from over-ripe dessert apples are difficult to predict. Band and screw presses give slightly lower yields than hydraulic presses. Centrifugal separators rarely exceed 625 litres per tonne; this can drop to 560 litres with late-season fruit.

2. Machines for Juice Extraction

A number of papers have appeared over the last decade describing equipment suitable for extracting fruit juice (Schaller, 1965; Swindells and Robbins, 1966; Robbins, 1970; Crowe, 1970; Dupaigne, 1972; Bielig and Werner, 1972; Koch, 1972; Wucherpfennig et al., 1973b). In general they have been confined to data such as technical descriptions and costs, since it is extremely difficult to carry out a series of tests on a number of machines using samples taken from a uniform batch of fruit. References in which such comparisons have been made between a limited number of machines are Beech (1962, 1963a), Coffelt and Berg (1965), Daepp (1965) and de Vos (1972). Instead, Wucherpfennig *et al.* (1973b) designed a small press which could be used as a reference machine for comparing commercial equipment.

Machines that are being used at present or are in prototype form, can be classified as follows:

PRESSURE TYPE: Batch or semi-continuous
                Horizontal cage press
                Vertical pack press
                Semi-continuous or continuous
                    operating
                Screw (cage) press
                Band press

NON-PRESSURE MACHINES: Continuous operating
                         Strainers
                         Vacuum filters
                         Centrifuges
                         Diffusion systems

a. *Horizontal cage presses* are used mainly for processing berry fruits but they have been used for apples. The Willmes machine consists of a perforated stainless-steel cylinder with a movable piston, having several hundred strands of loosely plaited plastic cords between the fixed and movable heads. The cylinder is charged with pulp and the piston operated. The cords act as juice channels on the inward stroke, and break up the pomace on the outward. In another type, the cylindrical sieve contains a pneumatically inflatable bellow and the pulp is squeezed between this and the sieve. A cloth is normally interposed between pulp and sieve when pressing apples. Yields are good, but pressing times are prolonged and the juice has a high content of solids. In the Bucher H.P. press (Lüthi, 1969), used in many countries, the cords are thicker, grooved and each is covered with a nylon sleeve. Pulp is pumped into the press chamber through the fixed head, forcing the piston head back and causing juice to flow. The piston is then operated several times, more pulp pumped, and the process repeated until the press chamber is 70–80% full.

The outer casing is withdrawn, the piston retracted, and the whole cylinder rotated to discharge the pomace. The machine gives an excellent yield of juice with a low content of suspended solids but it is expensive and needs a considerable amount of power to operate.

b. *Vertical pack or rack and cloth presses.* A 'cheese' is made up consisting of alternate layers of pulp, enclosed in woven or knitted terylene or polypropylene cloth, and slatted racks made of ash or acacia wood. Hydraulic pressure is applied via a ram at the base and the structure is compressed against the fixed head of the press. Single bed, swinging double and triple-bed presses, with automatic pulp dispensers, have all been used. They are technically excellent machines, giving high yields of juice, but are now going out of use in large installations since they require a lot of labour, which is no longer available, to operate them. Fully automated versions are available (I.K.W. and Lambert) but they have not been adopted very widely.

c. *Screw cage presses* are used very extensively in the U.S.A. and to some extent in France. Both vertical (Jones, F.M.C.) and horizontal (Rietz; the Speichim, used widely in Northern France, is no longer being produced) models are available. The latter is more common. The vertical type has a screw with an increasing internal cross section and a decreasing thread pitch, operating in a sieve case with fixed pins. Pressure is exerted on the pulp at the outlet orifice by a stem cone. The second consists of two co-axial screws of contrary pitch, rotating in opposite directions, mounted one behind the other on the same shaft. Again the outlet has a cone on which the pressure can be varied. The cost is reasonable, the output is large and they can be operated automatically and continuously. The juice is turbid and needs to be passed through a vibrating screen or band filter. Soft-textured fruit requires enzyme treatment or the use of cellulose pulp and rice hulls.

d. *Band press.* A large number of types of band press have been invented and used, but the model favoured at present is the Ensink belt press. It has two endless belts made of plastic fibre interwoven with stainless steel wire. Pulp is sucked between them as they pass through rollers which are in sets of three, one large operating above two of smaller diameter. The pressure adjusts automatically to the thickness of the pulp layer. The machine gives a high yield of juice on normal fruit pulp and is economical in capital outlay and running costs. Enzyme-treated pulp of soft-textured apples can also be processed without loss of yield (Wucherpfennig, 1974). A vertical model is also available produced under licence by the Manor Engineering Company of Burton-upon-Trent, England.

e. *Strainers*. Vibrating screens have been used for separating free-run juice from pulp prior to pressing (Körmendy, 1965a; Flaumenbaum and Sejtpaeva, 1965). They are more common for grape, tomato and berry processing, but enzyme-treated apple pulp can yield up to 40% of its juice on suitable machines (White *et al.*, 1971). This would help to increase the throughput of the press to which the pulp was subsequently passed. Juice from screw or sieve cage presses needs to be passed through such strainers and the residue returned to the press for repressing.

f. *Centrifuges*. A number of companies make apple juice by passing pulp through a screening centrifuge. The Mercone and the Conjector have been used. The yield is low (580–625 litres per tonne), and screens have to be replaced at 10–14 day intervals. A basket centrifuge is more robust (Greenwood *et al.*, 1970). The attraction is the modest capital cost, and it is favoured in areas where fruit costs are low and labour scarce or expensive. The juice is usually passed through a rotary vacuum precoat filter (Sawler, 1961). In one process (White *et al.*, 1971) enzyme-treated pulp is passed directly to a similar filter.

g. *Diffusion*. Even the most efficient machine leaves a percentage of juice in the residue or pomace. In France it has been common practice to extract this material with water after the first pressing, reminiscent of the method of making ciderkin in the 17th Century. At least one large English cider factory had a similar system into the 1930s (Anon., 1931; Charley and Kieser, 1941). Originally eight square chambers were filled with pomace which was extracted counter-current with successive charges of water. The extract, virtually at full strength, was drawn off at one end and exhausted pomace at the opposite. This is now being replaced in France by the Speichim continuous and automatic band diffuser (Richard, 1973). Once pressed, pomace is broken up and spread automatically over a wide continuous wire mesh belt. Water is sprayed on at the opposite end and the weak extract collected from a trough underneath. From here it is pumped forward to the next spray and collection trough and so on along the length of the machine. In this way, a shallow layer of pomace receives up to 15 successive washings with water. In the U.S.A. and Canada, apple and grape juice residues from the vacuum filter are passed through a succession of simple screw presses with water being passed counter-current through the system (Tressler and Joslyn, 1971). An experimental stirred-tank system has also been developed (Berg *et al.*, 1968). The washings are concentrated afterwards and used in the manufacture of drinks rather than juices.

The increasing cost of apples has stimulated research into the total removal of soluble solids from pulp with water, pressing being confined to dewatering the residue prior to drying and subsequent pectin extraction. For this, two continuous systems have been developed, both of which are used extensively in sugar factories. One tried by Ott (1965) for apples (Ott *et al.*, 1960) has a J-shaped vessel through which passes a continuous chain of shallow buckets. He obtained 90–94% of the soluble solids at 60–65°C. When corrected for density, it compared very favourably with press juice made from the same fruit.

In the D.D.S.-diffusion process (Brunische-Olsen, 1969), the coarsely grated fruit passes up an inclined cylinder counter-current to downward-flowing water. The cylinder contains two slowly rotating internal longitudinal screw conveyors which are intermeshing and contrarotating. Spent material is discharged at the upper end with perforated scoops. The temperature of the incoming water is 85°C which gives a highest temperature of 70°C in the pulp at the discharge; a yield of 95–97% based on soluble solids is claimed. Recently an apple-juice factory in South Africa began using one of these machines, processing 762 thousand kg of apples per 24 hours. The extract was converted into a three-fold concentrate with aroma recovery.

To summarize: in England the fruit for cidermaking is processed as follows. (a) Double pressing on a rotatable pack-press, being changed soon to an Ensink/Bucher Guyer H.P. combination; (b) Single pressing on a Bucher Guyer H.P.; (c) Speichim screw press followed by a three-bed rack and cloth press. The pomace is fed to cattle direct, ensiled or, if the insoluble pectin content is sufficient, it is dried to 10% moisture and used in the manufacture of pectin (Lockwood, 1972).

In France the process is more standardized. The first stage involves use of a Bucher Guyer H.P., or a Speichim or a double or triple pack press, the second static or continuous diffusion, followed by dewatering in two continuous screw presses, drying in a horizontal rotary dryer, and discharge to silos for cattle food or pectin. Two men could manage the complete installation from fruit reception onwards and process 9.5–13.75 tonnes per hour.

In the U.S.A. and Canada the first pressing is usually a Rietz or Bucher Guyer H.P. press followed by addition of water and passage through a second Rietz. Centrifugal separation of juice is also practised as it is in Australia. There, hydraulic pack and Bucher H.P. presses are to be found.

3. By-Products

The by-products of apple processing and cidermaking can be utilized. From the first come peels and cores which, in England and Ireland, tend to be discarded in pits or on waste ground. They represent from 35 to 50% of the weight of the apples although, in the U.S.A., this can be as low as 30% with automatic spinning-knife mechanical peelers (Powers, 1973). The wastage with non-automatic machines and Bramley's Seedling is higher, namely 55% (Lawson and Arthey, 1974). Not only is a significant part of the crop wasted, but transport and labour charges are levied to remove it and there is always a danger of creating an effluent or fly problem. In Australia and U.S.A., it is more usual to use this waste material for the preparation of juice, or to concentrate it for use in making drinks, home-made wines, or vinegar. This economical use of the raw material is seen not only in large integrated fruit processing plants, but even in small family units where a canned apple-slice line is run alongside a small milling and pressing plant making juice under contract. It has been shown by Guadagni et al. (1971a, b) that apple peels can be used as a source of apple aroma. 'Held at ambient temperature (19–23°C) for 24 hours . . . an aroma solution could be recovered from them with 2–7 times more flavouring capacity than no-delay peels, without significant sacrifice in quality' (Guadagni et al., 1971b; Pilnik, 1973a). Bomben et al. (1974) also developed an apple-flavoured thickener by macerating the 24 hour-stored peel through a fine sieve, mixing it with milled cores, pressing hydraulically and drum drying the press cake. Production of aroma concentrates is discussed further in Section III.C.1 (p. 238).

Unless the pomace has been subjected previously to a diffusion process (Section III.B.2.g, p. 232), it still contains some juice sugars which are not utilized. Its uses were described by Barker and Gimingham (1915) and Barker (1933). It is often fed directly to store cattle or dairy cows, and is an excellent source of carbohydrate and fibre (Roten, 1948). It must be fresh, not mouldy or acetified and, if high in phenolics, it should be introduced gradually into the diet to avoid scouring. Some 9–14 kg per animal per day can be incorporated in the diet of cows and store cattle. For sheep and pigs, 0.9 and 1.8 kg per day are used, respectively. The material also ensiles easily, being low in pH value and high in carbohydrates. The fresh-press cake needs remilling then packing down hard in a suitable acid-resistant container and protection from rain and water seepage. Under these anaerobic conditions, it undergoes a slow alcoholic fermentation. The preparation of apple-pomace silage, and the composition of apple pomace and the ensiled material, have been described by Warcollier (Charley, 1949; Charley and Harrison, 1939; Smith, 1950). Pectin-extracted pomace can also be used as a cattle food, fresh or ensiled. Table 28 summarizes some of the data given in the last two publications (see also Smock and Neubert, 1950). The feeding value of average, well made, apple-pomace silage is equal to that of sugar beet pulp and about twice that of mangolds (Charley *et al.*, 1943; Smith, 1950). The feeding value of the pectin-extracted pomace is, of course, less by reason of the removal of some of the carbohydrate.

Pomace, which in its fresh state can soon spoil through the rapid action of yeasts and acid-tolerant bacteria, is quite stable when dried to 10–12% moisture content. Usually, drying is carried out in a horizontal rotary drier, either heated directly by furnace gases or by being tossed mechanically over pipes carrying steam at 5.3 Bar. The temperature of the pomace should not exceed 70°C. This process is profitable for pomace from which pectin of a good jelly grade can be extracted. However, the greatly increased cost of fuel oil may have now changed the position unless the price of pectin is increased commensurately. Certainly, in the Pacific North West, supplies of natural gas have become too expensive and are in too short supply to justify pomace drying.

Production of pectin from dried pomace consists essentially in the removal of soluble material by leaching with water followed by

Table 28

Composition of apple pomace and its silage. Values are given as percentages (w/v)

Material	pH value	Moisture	Crude protein	Crude fibre	Ether extract	Total mineral matter	Carbohydrate
						Content of	
(1) Fresh pomace[a]	3.5	69.6	2.0	7.4	0.4	0.7	19.9
Pomace silage	3.8	77.3	1.8	5.7	0.8	1.0	13.4
(2) Fresh pomace	2.8	64.5	2.3	8.1	0.9	0.7	23.6
Pectin-extracted pomace	2.6	79.2	2.0	7.0	0.8	0.5	10.7
Pectin-extracted pomace silage	3.1	80.1	2.2	7.0	0.8	0.4	9.6
Fresh pomace[b]		76.1	1.5	4.4	1.1	0.7	16.2
Wet brewer's grain		76.2	5.1	5.1	1.7	1.2	10.6
Mangolds (medium quality)		88.0	1.2	0.9	0.1	1.1	8.7

[a] From Smith (1950). Centres (1) and (2).
[b] From Charley and Harrison (1939).

boiling with acidified water. The extract is treated with amylase to remove starch, decolourized with charcoal, filtered and concentrated under vacuum. A range of pectins are now produced in powdered and liquid form and of high and low methoxyl or amide contents. Their manufacture is confined to a handful of companies only who sell World-wide. Apples are the main raw material in Europe and citrus, especially lemon, peels in the U.S.A. (Ben-Gera and Kramer, 1969). Details about manufacture, composition, grading, and content of pectic enzymes have been given by Baker (1934), Kertesz (1951), Jakovliv (1947), Smock and Neubert (1950), Charley (1951), Hottenroth (1951), Joslyn (1962), Joslyn and Deuel (1963), Potter (1966), Bulmer (1967), Voragen and Pilnik (1970), Gierschner (1970), Pilnik and Voragen (1970), Pilnik (1970), Tressler and Joslyn (1971), and Lockwood (1972).

Dried pomace, with or without removal of pectin, has been used in cattle food in the past as a filler with more concentrated nutrients in cakes or cubes. Its feeding value has been compared to that of dried beet pulp or corn meal. Details are given in Charley and Harrison (1939). It is doubtful whether the use of dried pomace for cattle food would be economic now in view of higher fuel costs.

C. Juice Treatment

Apart from the older process of maceration and défécation or keeving (Section I.C, p. 154), juice used to receive no further treatment, being allowed to ferment naturally with the organisms derived from the fruit or the processing equipment (Section II.A.2, p. 179). Subsequently, the spoilage microflora and oxidation were controlled by addition of sulphur dioxide (Steuart, 1935; Beech, 1953). Surpluses of fruit, instead of being pressed and fermented immediately, were concentrated and used or sold in years of poor crops. More recently, it is becoming common to base part, if not the whole, of a factory's output of cider and perry on the use of concentrated juice. The minimization in volumetric capacity required for their storage and their great resistance to spoilage by all but osmophilic yeasts more than compensate for the cost of concentration.

1. *Concentration*

Normally the process of concentration is carried out in two stages, first separation and concentration of the aroma fraction, and second concentration of the stripped juice.

Some 10–15% of the volume of the juice is removed by heating it to 95°C and flashing off the vapour in an expansion chamber. Sometimes the process is carried out under vacuum, but this entails a more complicated system for removing entrained aroma components from the outlet of the vacuum pump (Bomben *et al.*, 1969). In the original Kestner process (Charley and Reavell, 1939; Reavell and Goodwin, 1958), the vapour was condensed to give a weak aroma fraction which was added to the juice immediately after concentration. Following the work of Milleville and Eskew (1944), it is now more usual to fractionate the 10 times-concentrated aroma either directly or after condensing and feeding to a smaller fractionating column. The final concentrate is 150 times stronger than in the original juice (Büchi and Walker, 1962). It can be stored quite satisfactorily at 0°C for at least two years. The aroma concentrate is returned to the reconstituted juice concentrate for making apple juice (Brunner and Senn, 1962; Wucherpfennig and Bretthauer, 1970) but this is unnecessary for making cider, the aroma of which is largely derived from the products of yeast metabolism. Aroma concentrate surplus to requirements is sold internationally. It must have been made from clean, sound fruit originally, or its quality would have been spoiled by the presence of excess alcohol and acetic acid produced by the action of micro-organisms in the rotting fruit. Alternatively, the method can be used to remove excess methanol from juice prepared from enzyme-treated pulp. More recently, the original work of Bomben *et al.* (1969), in which a 1,000-fold or more aroma concentrate was produced, has been extended by a patented process for producing apple-aroma powders. This is done by mixing a 30,000-fold concentrate with sugars, modified starches or sugar esters, to make a paste which is then dried under vacuum giving a powder with a 200-fold concentration (Sugisawa *et al.*, 1970). It could have a considerably wider range of application for mixing with such materials as dehydrated ingredients than the liquid concentrate (Anon., 1970a, 1973b). A process has also been developed for preparing very strong aroma concentrates by the use of liquid carbon dioxide as a selective solvent (Schultz and Randall, 1970; Randall *et al.*, 1971) but so far no commercial plant has been manufactured using this process. Methods of aroma recovery and retention were reviewed by Bomben *et al.* (1974). There have been a number of publications on the composition of apple-aroma concentrates, for example Kevei *et al.* (1973).

The aroma-stripped juice can be concentrated four-fold under vacuum at 45–55°C without any difficulty. It is liable to microbial spoilage so it must be cooled to 0–5°C, injected with carbon dioxide (3.5 Bar) and stored under those conditions (Pollard and Beech, 1966a). Flash pasteurization prior to chilling may be necessary to avoid development of cold-tolerant lactic acid bacteria (Lüthi and Steiner, 1957; Pollard and Beech, 1966b). Apple juice is also made in South Africa from this type of concentrate, by redilution followed by pasteurization in the factory. Alternatively, the chilled, degassed concentrate may be sold to dairy companies who redilute it and sell it as a product with a three-day shelf life. For a fully stable product, the juice must be concentrated six- to seven-fold to a minimum total soluble solids content of 70% (w/v). To avoid gel formation at this degree of concentration of sugar, acid and soluble pectin, the juice from the aroma stripper must be cooled to 40°C, treated with a commercial preparation of pectin-destroying enzyme and left, usually 1–2 hours, until the soluble pectin has been converted to galacturonic acid or simple uronides. Juice from unripe fruit will also contain starch, and needs the addition of an amylase (Krebs, 1971). Thereafter, the enzyme-treated juice is filtered (or, more suitable for cidermaking, the juice is left unfiltered with any suspended solid material) and concentrated under vacuum at 45°C, until the required concentration of soluble solids has been achieved. It must then be cooled immediately and, preferably, stored below 5°C under conditions which prevent condensate falling on to its surface from the roof of the vessel.

Several systems exist for concentrating fruit juices, no one of which is satisfactory for all applications. Briefly, they can be divided into several types such as climbing and/or falling film, centrifugal, freeze concentration and reverse osmosis. Of these, the first is most common. Low temperature and long processing times have been supplemented by high-temperature, short-time systems. Freeze concentrators are still not economic, although improvements continue to be made (Grenco), sometimes based on experience gained with desalination systems. Reverse osmosis (Harrison, 1970a, b) also suffers from technical problems, but it can be used for preparing demineralized water when this is required for dilution of concentrates (Neubert, 1974). Descriptions of the different types of concentrators have been given in numerous publications of which the following are a selection: Gane (1948), Emch (1958), Royo-Iranzo (1958), Schneider (1958), Pollard and Beech (1966b), Armerding (1966), Casimir and Kefford (1968), Thijssen (1970), Sharples (1970), Harrison (1970a, b), Wiegand (1971), Shinn (1971), Robbins and Gresswell (1971), Thijssen (1971), Clarke (1971), Bedford (1972), Jansen (1972), Beech (1972a), Daepp (1974), Pilnik (1974). The process of concentration can be monitored in-line using a critical-angle refractometer (Basker, 1969; Carlson, 1972).

Concentrates produced by freeze concentration soon lose their initial superior quality (Charley, 1936) unless they are kept frozen. This is because the juice enzymes are not destroyed as in heat concentration, leading to the formation of hexanol and hexene-2-ol-1 by phenoloxidase or phenolase (catechol oxidase) derived from the fruit acting on linolenic and linoleic acids. Alternatively, the juice can be flash pasteurized prior to freezing (sulphur dioxide also prevents these changes, hence its value in making apple wine for example, Section III.C.2, p. 243). Even concentrates without active fruit enzymes can deteriorate for a number of reasons. If it is not chilled to around 5°C as soon as it leaves the concentrator, or it contains iron or copper, the colour darkens and the product acquires a stale character (Kern, 1962). The concentrate can undergo further chemical changes during storage which are time-temperature dependent (Beech et al., 1964a; Weiss et al., 1973). These changes are characterized by inversion of sucrose (Büchi, 1958), destruction of amino acids and B-group vitamins (Lüthi, 1958) and the formation of dihydroxyacetone, hydroxymethyl furfural and melanoidins (Vasatko and Príbela, 1965). Prolonged storage at unfavourable temperatures leads to severe darkening and precipitation of protein-phenolic complexes (Grob, 1958; Swain, 1965; van Buren et al., 1965; van Buren, 1971; Haslam, 1974). The concentrate may have to be stored for two or even three years, so it is clear that the temperature should be kept as near 0°C as is possible, that oxygen should be excluded, and oxidizing enzymes inhibited (by preheating the juice and/or adding vitamin C or sulphur dioxide). Alternatively, changes in chemical composition can be diminished by lowering the available water content, the ultimate being apple powder (Dupaigne, 1968). Apple powders are being produced both neutral (Powers, 1973) and flavoured (Bomben *et al.*, 1971) but it is doubtful if their use would be economical in cidermaking. A new and possibly more feasible method of lengthening the processing season is the storage of sterile fruit pulps in up to 1,800 hl lots (Lawler, 1973). Similarly, storage of sterile juice under an atmosphere of nitrogen at ambient temperature has not yet been used in cidermaking (Ménoret and Gautheret, 1962; Pollard and Beech, 1966a; Robbins, 1967).

Decreasing the amount of available water (Acker, 1969) also restricts microbiological spoilage to all but the most osmophilic yeasts and moulds (Zelenskaya and Tsvetkova, 1967). Spores of heat-resistant moulds can also survive heating of the juice during concentration (Lüthi and Vetsch, 1955) and cause problems in reconstituted juices. They are not normally a problem in cidermaking unless uncarbonated cider is flash pasteurized and cooled before filling into containers. The microbiology of fruit-juice concentrates has been described recently by Sand (1974) and Windisch (1974). Tests for the specific detection of osmophilic yeasts have been given by de Whalley and Scarr (1947), Scarr (1951, 1959), Devillers (1957), Ingram (1959), Mossel and Bax (1967). These organisms rise to the surface of the concentrates and grow in the thin film of slightly diluted sugars formed when water, condensing on the under-surface of the roof of the tank, falls onto the concentrate (Ingram, 1958b). Similar conditions occur with the ingress of moist air. To sum up, concentrate should be free of osmophilic yeasts so it is essential, if no aroma-stripping takes place, that the juice is flash pasteurized after enzyme treatment and prior to concentration. This is particularly important when using concentration equipment operating below 45°C where viable organisms could pass through. There should be a rigid sanitation programme in the juice treatment, concentration and storage rooms as spillages of concentrate act as enrichment media for these organisms. The concentrate should be cooled as soon as it emerges from the concentrator, which must be made of suitable grades of stainless steel, particularly if sulphur dioxide is added to the juice. Storage temperatures should be as low as possible, and condensate must be prevented from falling onto the surface of the stored material. A surface blanket of nitrogen, carbon dioxide, or a 70:30 mixture of the two, helps to prevent development of micro-organisms (Beech *et al.*, 1964b; Zelenskaya and Tsvetkova, 1967). The same considerations apply to storage of syrups, whether made from invert, sucrose or glucose.

At one time, problems were experienced in the fermentation of diluted concentrates (Pollard, 1958) until it was realized that these were caused by high storage temperatures destroying amino acids and producing yeast inhibitors (Pollard, 1958; Ingram, 1958a; Lüthi, 1958). Employing storage conditions such as those described in the previous paragraph should give diluted concentrates with essentially the same degree of fermentability as the juices from which they were made.

Table 29

Composition of certain differentiating components of apple, pear and grape juices

	Juice		
	Apple	Pear	Grape
Tartaric acid	nil	nil	high
Proline	low	high	high
Arginine	nil	nil	high
Sorbitol	low	high	nil

Reproduced by permission of L. F. Burroughs.

At intervals, cases occur involving adulteration of concentrated juices, usually apple with grape or grape with invert sugar (Mülhberger, 1960), especially when there is a considerable difference in the selling prices of the two constituents. Methods have now been evolved for detecting adulteration of apple with grape or the mixing of pear with apple juices (Tanner and Sandoz, 1973). Briefly, this involves the quantitative estimation of tartaric acid, proline and arginine. The concentrations of these components in different concentrates are given in Table 29. Confirmatory tests can be carried out by measuring the concentrations of calcium, potassium, sodium and magnesium. Such tests are now routine in the laboratories of the larger English cider companies. Methods are also available for detecting fruit juices made from concentrates (Reinhard, 1968; Bricout, 1973; Hess, 1974; Ménoret and Bricout, 1974).

2. *Control of Juice Microflora*

There are probably six methods of preparing juice for cidermaking; these range from no treatment to complete elimination of the microflora and its substitution by chosen strains of yeast and, possibly, bacteria.

A complete absence of control treatment was widely advocated for many years, as described in Section I.C (p. 147). It is still used by some farm cidermakers but, in most commercial productions, some microbial control is exercised. In Northern France, the juice is centrifuged or fined with gelatin and tannin, and filtered to give a slow rate of fermentation, with or without lowering of fermentation temperature or further centrifugation. Elsewhere the juice is treated with pectin-destroying enzymes and filtered before addition of yeast. In such methods there is always a danger of bacterial spoilage.

In Switzerland four-fold concentrated juice is diluted to a specific gravity of 1.050, treated with 35 to 40 p.p.m. sulphur dioxide and pitched with yeast two days later. In any factory where the seven-fold concentrates are used for whole or part of the production, a similar system is employed. These concentrates should be sterile. However, a small quantity of sulphur dioxide, ranging from 30 to 100 p.p.m., depending on the pH value of the juice, is added to restrict development of oxidized flavours, whether or not formed enzymically. The same is true if juice is flash-pasteurized prior to heating. Fifty p.p.m. of sulphur dioxide added to the juice immediately after sterilization gives a cider free from the caramel taste found in similar juices not sulphited. Sterile juices, or rediluted concentrates, with low concentrations of sulphur dioxide or none at all need to be kept in sterile equipment as they are readily infected by spoilage organisms.

The most common treatment of juice prior to fermentation is undoubtedly addition of sulphur dioxide. Its effects have long been utilized so that a cider that was fermenting too rapidly would be syphoned into a barrel in which sulphur had been burnt. From this stage, it became common to add an antiseptic (sulphur dioxide or salicylic acid) so that in 1909, when there were no preservative regulations, Durham (1909) found ciders containing between 0–600 p.p.m. sulphur dioxide. It was also added to the naturally sweet cider to prevent further fermentation, or to the fully fermented cider to prevent development of oiliness, acetification or film yeasts. Its use as a means of controlling the juice microflora had been considered by Jacquemin in 1902 (Barker, 1922) followed by addition of a sulphite-trained culture yeast. The method was not favoured because of the excessive flavour of sulphur dioxide and because it did not prevent growth of the 'sickness organism' (*Zymomonas anaerobia*). Barker (1922) reported the results of adding sulphur dioxide to different juices. There was a delay in the onset of fermentation, the length of which depended on the amount added and the natural rate of fermentation of the juice (presumably its yeast count and nutrient status). When fermentation started, the rate of fermentation was substantially the same as that of the non-sulphited control. The conclusion was that sulphur dioxide merely delayed the onset of fermentation, with the implication that sulphiting juice had no value in practical cidermaking. Unfortunately these empirical experiments were not accompanied by any examination of the microflora, nor was any comparison made between the flavours of treated and untreated ciders in spite of experiments reported earlier with more favourable results (Barker, 1912; Barker and Ettle, 1912).

The Food and Drugs Act and the Preservatives in Food Regulations (S.R.O. (1925) 775 England) limited the amount of sulphur dioxide in cider to a maximum of 200 p.p.m. In 1935, Steuart spoke of juice from bittersweet apples being 'slightly sulphured and then undergoing a biological defecation', but further details were not given. Almost certainly it was used mainly for preserving natural sweetness (Charley, 1940) or for preventing disorders in cider sent out for sale (Barker and Grove, 1927). Thus, the extensive experience gained in Switzerland, where sulphur dioxide had been used for controlling fruit-juice fermentations since 1914 (Müller-Thurgau and Osterwalder, 1914), was largely ignored. As far as cider is concerned, a concerted examination of its effects did not begin until the early 1950s (Beech et al., 1952; Beech, 1953). It was found that juice sulphiting did offer a means of removing the majority of the non-fermenting yeasts and spoilage bacteria, and that added yeast cultures could dominate the fermentation and impose their own flavour characteristics. At first, however, sulphiting alone was adopted in the factories, the fermentation being carried out by fermenting yeasts derived mainly from the pressing equipment. Subsequently, with the development of effective standards of cleanliness, there was often insufficient yeast to carry out the fermentations. It is now routine to add yeast grown in a pure-culture plant.

The effect of sulphur dioxide on the microflora has been described in Section II.A.2 (p. 179). The active form of sulphur dioxide was said to be undissociated sulphurous acid, H_2SO_3 (Ingram, 1948, 1958c; Vas, 1949; Vas and Ingram, 1949) but this could not be detected chemically (Falk and Giguère, 1958). It has now been confirmed that the active agent is dissolved or molecular sulphur dioxide, whose entry into the cell of *Saccharomyces cerevisiae* is probably controlled by a mediated-transport mechanism (Macris and Markakis, 1974).

In view of the concern that has been expressed over the amounts of sulphur dioxide used in foods and beverages (Anon., 1962b; Roberts and McWeeney, 1972), it is essential that only the minimum effective quantity should be used. The amount required depends on the pH value of the juice (Ingram, 1958c) and the concentrations of the sulphite-binding compounds present. The combined forms exist in equilibrium with aldehydes or ketones, and the values of the apparent equilibrium and velocity constants are also a function of the pH value. Since the active form of sulphur dioxide is the dissolved or 'free' sulphur dioxide, it is essential to keep the pH value and concentration of binding compounds as low as practicable. A summary of the binding compounds in apple juices and ciders has been given by Beech (1972a). More recently, Burroughs and Sparks (1973) have given a detailed account of sulphite-binding powers of wines and ciders. There is unfortunately very little information in the literature on the precise concentration of dissolved sulphur dioxide required to kill a particular yeast. Beech (1961) attempted to correlate the pH value and sulphur dioxide concentration required to kill 50% of cultures of a number of yeasts in six hours. The LD_{50} values for undissociated H_2SO_3 were one p.p.m. for *Saccharomyces uvarum* and 0.33 p.p.m. for *Sacch. cerevisiae*; *Saccharomycodes ludwigii* could not be inhibited within the permitted limits of 200 p.p.m. total sulphur dioxide. However, all processes inhibiting micro-organisms are also governed by both time and concentration. In this connection, Macris and Markakis (1974) have given such values for decimal reduction times for *Sacch. cerevisiae* as:

3.0×10^{-5} M molecular sulphur dioxide D = 19 min

2.0×10^{-5} M molecular sulphur dioxide D = 25 min

1.0×10^{-5} M molecular sulphur dioxide D = 83 min

From data of this kind it is possible to calculate the amount of free sulphur dioxide needed for any decrease in yeast count within a specified time period. Undoubtedly a considerable amount of quantitative information is required, not only on the amount of sulphur dioxide required to inhibit a specified population of *Saccharomyces cerevisiae* in unit time, but also on those organisms that cause spoilage or flavour problems in cider, for example *Kloeckera apiculata*, *Saccharomycodes ludwigii* and *Brettanomyces* spp. Recent work on the sensitivity of lactic acid bacteria to sulphur dioxide (Carr *et al.*, 1974) has given indications that a proportion of the inoculum could withstand quite high concentrations of sulphur dioxide. Perhaps it is for this reason that virtually all ciders, whether made from sulphited juices or not, eventually undergo a natural malo-lactic fermentation.

Until these data are available, the system developed at Long Ashton Research Station in England (Beech, 1972b; Burroughs, 1973a) is proving satisfactory under practical conditions. An addition of sulphur dioxide, usually in the form of a solution of sodium metabisulphite, is made to the juice, the precise amount being governed by its pH value. The concentrations required in the juice are: pH 3.0–3.3, 75 p.p.m.; pH 3.3–3.5, 100 p.p.m.; pH 3.5–3.8, 150 p.p.m. Experience has shown that juices of pH value greater than 3.8 cannot be treated satisfactorily within the legal maximum of 200 p.p.m. Fruit giving juices with pH values greater than 3.8 are blended with more acid fruit, or rediluted concentrate of acid fruit, or synthetic DL-malic acid is added before sulphiting. The juice is then left to equilibrate for at least six hours or even overnight (although a laboratory method taking only 30 min is available for checking if sufficient free sulphur dioxide is present; Burroughs, 1973a). Next morning the free sulphur dioxide concentration is determined (Burroughs and Sparks, 1964a) and the value should lie between the two curves given in Figure 12 where the effect of pH value is clearly demonstrated. Values below the lower curve

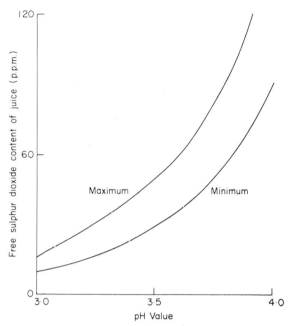

Fig. 12. Minimum and maximum values for the contents of free sulphur dioxide required to be present in an apple juice 12 hours after addition of sulphur dioxide, as influenced by the pH value of the juice. Reproduced from Beech (1972b) and Burroughs (1973a).

indicate the presence of excessive quantities of sulphite-binding compounds (Burroughs, 1964a; Burroughs and Sparks, 1964b), probably due to the use of some rotten fruit (Beech, 1963a). Patulin, an antibiotic, is found in apples rotted extensively by *Penicillium expansum*. The LD_{50} value for mice is 15 mg/kg. Concentrations of 0.5–1 p.p.m. have been found in a few Canadian and French apple juices, presumably where fruit sorting prior to pressing was ineffective. The antibiotic disappears rapidly during fermentation of sulphited juices (Drilleau and Bohuon, 1973). Acetic acid bacteria, mainly *Acetomonas* spp. (Shimwell, 1959; Shimwell and Carr, 1959; Burroughs and Sparks, 1963), growing in the rotten tissue, produce oxo-acids (Carr *et al.*, 1963; Burroughs and Sparks, 1963) which bind strongly with sulphur dioxide. Glucose, xylose, L-xylosone, arabinose and galacturonic acid normally present in apples or apple juice bind only weakly (Burroughs and Whiting, 1961a; Burroughs and Sparks, 1963). Ineffective concentrations do not inhibit *Kloeckera apiculata* and other aerobic yeasts completely, giving ciders without the fresh, clean palate of those made from correctly sulphited juices

(Beech, 1953; Beech and Davenport, 1970). Excessive quantities of free sulphur dioxide, i.e. values above the upper curve of Figure 12, cause undue delays in the onset of fermentation by the added yeast (Beech, 1958b).

Problems can arise in countries such as Australia, where the permitted maximum concentration in cider is 100 p.p.m. total sulphur dioxide. Careful attention to the fruit quality, plant hygiene and pH control are necessary in such circumstances. For greater safety, the use of stripped or flash-pasteurized juices would be advisable, confining the use of sulphur dioxide to that of an inhibitor of oxidizing enzymes. Perry-pear juices need an extra 50 p.p.m. of sulphur dioxide compared with apple juices of the same pH value. This is due to their natural acetaldehyde content (36–150 p.p.m. compared with 5 p.p.m. for apple and dessert-pear juices) and acetoin (Sparks and Burroughs, 1973).

It must be emphasized that 200 p.p.m. total sulphur dioxide is insufficient to inhibit *Saccharomycodes ludwigii* (Kroemer and Heinrich, 1922) and *Zymomonas anaerobia*. Both of these microbes enter the factory afresh each year (Beech and Davenport, 1970; Carr and Passmore, 1971b) and the only protection against them are, in the case of the first, the rigid maintenance of cleaning and sterilizing programmes in the bottling and kegging rooms. All ciders must be fermented, stored free from sugar, and kept below pH 3.8 to avoid problems with *Zymomonas* (Millis, 1956).

When making apple wines or ciders from dessert fruit where a vinous character is desired, it is better to add the sulphite to the apples as they are milled. The anti-oxidant action of sulphur dioxide gives a very stable pale product. Inhibition of browning by phenolase (Radler and Torokfalvy, 1973), more correctly catechol oxidase, is brought about partly by inactivation of the enzyme and partly by combination with the *o*-quinones previously formed by the enzyme (Embs and Markakis, 1965; Mathew and Parpia, 1971). Sulphite can also inhibit non-enzymic browning by combination with inter-mediate carbonyl compounds (Burton *et al.*, 1963). Vitamin C, used in the preparation of pale apple wines, combines directly with dissolved oxygen and reduces quinones already formed. It has no antimicrobial effect, so a limited addition of sulphur dioxide is also necessary. Some free sulphur dioxide must be present or the problem is worsened by the formation of hydrogen peroxide. Eventually sulphur dioxide and ascorbic acid react to form L-xylosone, a minor sulphite-binding compound. Prevention of oxidation by the sole use of inert gases (carbon dioxide, nitrogen) in the mill is ineffective (Daepp, 1964).

3. *Addition of Yeast*

Although two-thirds at least of the cider produced in the World is made by adding a yeast culture, there is still a nostalgic tradition that the best ciders were produced with the natural yeast flora. Unfortunately the desirable components of this flora can be accompanied by undesirable yeasts and bacteria able to spoil the flavour or appearance of the final product. In France which, up till now, has never practised yeast addition, the onset of spoilage is minimized by low-temperature fermentation and closed metal tanks in which an atmosphere of carbon dioxide can be maintained. Wooden vats, a potent source of infection, are rarely used there in commercial cidermaking.

In England, it has been traditional to use wooden vessels whether casks or large vats; hence sulphite control of the natural flora, whether derived from the juice or the vessels, was readily accepted. Sometimes the first juices of the season would be slow to begin fermentation and blocks of baker's yeast might be added to initiate fermentation. In one factory it was customary to dribble a yeast culture into the mill as apples were being crushed to ensure a prompt start to fermentation. From 1958 onwards, production of concentrated apple juice in France was begun in quantity and imported into England. The importation of Swiss pear concentrate also began about the same time. There was not a long tradition of using them although some importations of Canadian apple concentrate had been made previously. Consequently, problems were experienced in fermenting the juices in a satisfactory manner. Mixing diluted concentrate with dry cider, one of the methods tried, often lead to bacterial spoilage since much of the yeast left in the cider was dead. To remedy this, yeast cultures were grown up in flasks, jars and small tanks for initiating fermentation. Steadily the systems were made suitable for routine production of yeast under aseptic conditions. These culture plants (Olsen, 1956; Curtis, 1971), using sterilized diluted concentrate and nutrients, are to be found in all large cider factories, and yeast is used to inoculate all juices and diluted concentrates after sulphiting. Systems using even a limited degree of aeration give greater yeast crops of higher nitrogen content and faster rates of fermentation (Curtis and Clark, 1960). Similar systems are to be found in Germany and Switzerland (Schopfer, 1966) where cultures for winemaking have been available from the beginning of the century (Radler, 1973). Both culture plants and commercially produced dried-yeast cultures are used in Australia and North America for cider- and wine-making (Knappstein and Rankine, 1970). The dried culture is first added to small quantities of heat-sterilized juice and, when this is fermenting rapidly, its volume is increased with juice that has been adequately sulphited the previous day. Once this begins to ferment, it is pumped into the fermentation tank and its volume rapidly increased with successive additions of presulphited juice or diluted concentrate (Thoukis et al., 1963; Thoukis and Bouthilet, 1963; Reed and Peppler, 1973). The advantages to be gained from using yeast cultures have only been realized now that vessels with inert easily cleanable surfaces are becoming the rule in cider factories.

There are a large number of properties that could be considered desirable in a yeast for fermenting cider (Jokantaile, 1972) and wine. It is not proposed to make a complete listing since few, if any, yeasts would possess them all. These are described in reviews such as those of Rankine (1968a), Cook (1969), Harada et al. (1972), Stevens (1972), Radler (1973) and Richards (1973). Probably the most important properties required in yeasts for cidermaking (Beech, 1969a) are: fermentation to completion (the brewer's degree of attenuation); a rapid rate of fermentation; sedimentation (flocculation) at the end of fermentation; alcohol and sulphite tolerance; a predictable pattern of fusel oil (higher alcohol) formation; lack of formation of hydrogen sulphide, organic sulphides and diacetyl; stability against mutation; production or dissimilation of organic acids; a limited degree of autolysis or cell breakdown and a known effect on malo-lactic bacteria. The first three, together with head and deposit formation, are most conveniently tested using the tall-tube method with E.B.C. two-litre fermentors (Dixon, 1967). It has also been used by Ferguson et al. (1972) for investigating a wider range of yeast properties, and by Walkley and Kirsop (1969) for typing all strains of Saccharomyces cerevisiae in the National Collection of

Yeast Cultures in Great Britain. Alcohol tolerance is determined in a sterile apple-juice yeast extract medium (Beech and Davenport, 1969) to which increasing quantities of ethanol are added, care being taken to avoid dilution of nutrients. Sulphite tolerance can be determined by the method described by Carr et al. (1972, 1974) and Zambonelli et al. (1972). Establishing the pattern of fusel oil production (Rankine, 1967a; Äyräpää, 1968; Rankine and Pocock, 1969a) requires standardized fermentation conditions, whether these are in one-litre flasks or in experimental tanks (Beech et al., 1974) and simple g.l.c. analysis either of the distillate or head-space gases. A yeast liable to produce hydrogen sulphide in a large-scale fermentation will do so in a simple laboratory fermentation in the presence of finely powdered sulphur (Rankine, 1964; Beech, 1970; Acree et al., 1972). Free diacetyl and 2,3-pentanedione can be tasted in experimental ciders or can be detected in the headspace vapour using a gas-liquid chromatograph fitted with an electron-capture detector (Maule, 1967; Wainwright, 1973). The minor characteristics of some yeasts change with continued industrial use, particularly changes in flocculation characteristics (Hough, 1957) or, for a spoilage yeast, increased resistance to preservatives. The method of Stevens (1966), based on the flocculation pattern of a random selection of cells, is a valuable indication of the stability of the culture in practice.

Yeasts can produce a variety of organic acids during cider fermentations, especially of sulphited juices. Of these malic (Drawert et al., 1965), succinic, gluconic and lactic (Peynaud et al., 1967) acids merely increase the acidity. However, some yeasts produce α-oxoglutaric acid (Rankine, 1968b) and pyruvic acid (Rankine, 1967b) which bind sulphur dioxide strongly (Rankine and Pocock, 1969b). This is not of importance during fermentation since the sulphite is already bound to acetaldehyde produced during glycolysis. However, if sulphur dioxide is added at bottling, it will be bound by these oxo-acids. A single procedure for measuring the sulphur dioxide-binding power of ciders was described by Sparks (1972). Laboratory methods for testing acid production by yeasts in apple-juice fermentations were given by Coggins et al. (1974). Some yeasts also produce small quantities of acetic acid which is undesirable from the point of view of flavour (Whiting, 1973). Towards the end of a fermentation, particular strains of yeast can liberate aromatic amino acids, peptides and nucleotides (Steward et al.,

1974), which can support subsequent growth of malo-lactic bacteria. Changes in concentrations of soluble nitrogen during the different stages of cider fermentation have been examined for a number of yeasts by Burroughs (1974) and also for certain of the B-group vitamins by Goverd (1973b). Some work has also been done on the effect of yeast cultures on malo-lactic fermentation which again appears to depend on the strain of yeast used in the fermentation (Carr *et al.*, 1972; Rankine, 1973).

Technologically, it is important that the yeast should produce polygalacturonase and so be capable of degrading de-esterified pectin to galacturonic acid (Demain and Phaff, 1957; Pollard and Kieser, 1959; Malan, 1961; Jayasankar and Graham, 1970). Otherwise the cider will fail to clarify at the end of the fermentation (Charley, 1935a, b).

With so many factors to consider, it is not surprising that the main criteria chosen by the cider manufacturer are reliability in growth and fermentation behaviour and the production of ciders free from obvious undesirable flavour characteristics. The first such yeast to be found is usually adopted with very little attempt to find one with improved characteristics, although it is now realized that flavour can be markedly influenced by the strain of yeast used (Pollard *et al.*, 1966; Suomalainen, 1971). Not many cultures are in fact employed. In England it is either A.W.Y. 350R (from the Australian Wine Research Institute), *Saccharomyces uvarum*, or Champagne strains from the Institute for Microbiology and Biochemistry at Geisenheim. In Australia, the dried wine yeast is called Pinnacle (No. 729 Australian Wine Research Institute) and in the U.S.A. either the Montrachet (U.C.D. 522) or Champagne A.D.Y. available from Universal Foods Corporation is used. Originally the last two of these were produced as a frozen yeast cake, a method also employed by Adams (1962a, b). Both powder and press cake avoid the need for running a yeast-culture plant with technically trained personnel, and a culture is always available. The behaviour of most of these yeasts when used for making experimental ciders can be found in Beech and Davenport (1970), Beech (1972a) and the Annual Reports of Long Ashton Research Station from 1966 onwards.

When culture yeasts are used, it is necessary to examine the yeast crops to ensure they are free from infection and in an active condition. Not all of the tests need to be carried out on each batch but a number of routine tests are necessary (Beech and Davenport,

1969; Hough, 1973). Some information can be gained by simple microscopic examination (at a magnification of x400-500). The cells should be uniform in appearance and characteristic of the strain, for example circular, ovoid or elongated. The cells should be plump and the cytoplasm clear and almost transparent; granulations and shrinking away from the cell walls indicates poor nutrition. Suspending the cells in methylene blue on a Thoma haemocytometer slide (Anon., 1962a; Pierce, 1970b) gives a rapid routine method for counting the percentage of living cells (colourless), as well as enabling the calculation to be made of the required amount of culture to be added to the sulphited juice. Usually 3-7 million cells per ml are recommended in the juice after addition of yeast (Knappstein and Rankine, 1970). More accurate measures of yeast viability are obtained with the slide-culture technique (Pierce, 1970b) and a measure of quantity may be obtained using a turbidimetric method routinely or a gravimetric method for a reference standard (Rainbow, 1968).

The culture may be contaminated by other yeasts, moulds or bacteria (Green and Gray, 1950). Contaminants are usually only visible under the microscope if present in such large numbers that the presence would have been indicated already by changes in growth or fermentation behaviour. Wild yeasts can be detected by growth in lysine-containing medium (Walters and Thistleton, 1953; Fowell, 1965) or in the presence of actidione (cycloheximide; Gilliland, 1971) on Wallerstein Laboratories nutrient (W.L.N.) agar. The appearance of the culture yeast on these media should be examined carefully when it is first obtained since some *Saccharomyces* species, other than *Sacch. cerevisiae*, can show growth. The medium giving the clearest differentiation or inhibition of the culture yeast should be chosen. At intervals, a diluted sample of the culture should be grown on malt-wort agar at 30°C for two days so that small isolated colonies are formed (Hough, 1960; Pierce, 1970a). These should be examined for consistency of shape and appearance; the size is liable to vary depending on the proximity of other colonies and whether they are at the centre or edges of the plate. Any colonies of doubtful appearance can be tested using the very simple serological techniques of Campbell (1972). There is also a fluorescent-antibody method for detecting very low concentrations of cells of *Saccharomyces* species other than the culture in use (Richards, 1969; Richards and Cowland, 1967, 1968). This does require a source of ultraviolet radiation and a suitable microscope, so that it could only be used in the largest laboratories. 'Petite colonie' or respiratory-deficient yeasts can be detected by the use of 2,3,5-triphenyltetrazolium chloride in the medium (Nagai, 1963). The respiratory-deficient colonies, which tend to produce more diacetyl than cells of normal colonies, remain colourless. Bacteria can be detected by streaking a sample on apple-juice yeast extract or malt-extract medium containing actidione and 8-hydroxyquinoline (Beech and Carr, 1955, 1958, 1960).

At intervals, the fermenting and flocculating ability of the yeast should be tested under standardized conditions. For both of these, the E.B.C. two-litre fermentor (Cook, 1963; Dixon, 1967) can be used. Flocculation can be tested separately using the Burns sedimentation test (Burns, 1941; Helm *et al.*, 1953), Gilliland's (1951, 1957) method or Hough's technique (1957) using buffered calcium chloride solution. All three are simple and rapid, and up to 50 colonies taken at random from an incubated spread plate can be examined at one time. While the flavour produced by the yeast can be determined using small-scale fermentations, it is best monitored by comparing flavours of ciders from different production tanks.

4. Additives

Juice from the press or centrifuge, treated with sulphite or not, usually has other additions made to it. Probably most commonly the sugar content is adjusted to a standard specific gravity, while there may also be some adjustment to the juice solids. Excessive acidity is decreased by dilution, while deficiencies of acidity can be made up by addition of citric or malic acids. Pectin-destroying enzymes may also need adding if the pulp or juice has had any form of heat treatment.

The amounts and composition of these additives are usually governed by national legislation. In England, acids, bases and sequestrants would be covered by Proposed Miscellaneous Additives in Food Regulations, 1973 (see Section III.E.3, p. 285, for legislation on preservatives, antioxidants, colouring matter and artificial sweeteners).

Adjustment of the content of juice sugars has always been a tradition in cidermaking, partly to make lighter flavoured ciders but mainly to lower the final alcohol concentration. In brewing, this is readily achieved by varying the proportion of malt or water. Acceptance of the natural sugar content of the apple would show annual variations and ciders with alcohol contents greater than 5% v/v. Excessive consumption at these levels would soon lead to intoxication. Hence, in commercial cidermaking, a proportion of water is usually added, the amount depending on the quality and price of the final product. In France, diffusion juice, or 'petit jus' can be added to pure juice to give a mixture with a potential alcohol content of 5%, v/v, if it is to be used for cider or 4% of gravity if meant for calvados or eaux-de-vie (if 'petit jus' is fermented alone it must be distilled for industrial alcohol). It also has the advantage of decreasing excessive acidity of juices from culinary apples. For the same reason, addition of water and sugar to grape juices is authorized in New York State, Canada and, for certain grades of wine, in Germany. Standardization of the final alcohol content can also be brought about by the addition of sucrose in dry or syrup form, invert sugar syrup, glucose syrups or chips (Spence, 1971). Concentrated apple juice may be used in conjunction with fresh juice or in its place.

As described in Section III.C.2 (p. 243), low-acid juices, or more correctly those with a pH value greater than 3.8, are almost certain to undergo some form of bacterial spoilage even if the juice is treated with 200 p.p.m. total sulphur dioxide. It is now quite general in England to add sufficient synthetic DL-malic acid or citric acid for any necessary increase in acidity. The standard of purity for malic acid is specified in Food Chemicals Codex 1972, p. 484; that for citric acid is given in the Appendix to the Miscellaneous Additives Order.

The pectin-destroying enzymes are usually of fungal origin; the more recent are most often available in powdered form, with sucrose or kieselguhr as a filler. They contain a mixture of enzymes including pectin esterase (Mayorga and Rolz, 1971) and polygalacturonase which convert the pectins to di-, tri- and higher oligogalacturonic acid units (Martínez et al., 1958). The action is complete within two hours at 40°C, but an overnight hold is necessary at 15°C (pectin transeliminase has been proposed to avoid the formation of methanol; Ishii and Yokotsuka, 1971, 1972). However, unless a cider with a low content of fusel oils is required, any depectinization, and/or filtration (Mouchet, 1973) should be delayed until the end of fermentation. Removal of fine apple tissue causes yeasts to produce much less of these compounds (Beech *et al.*, 1968; Wucherpfennig and Bretthauer, 1968; Beech, 1972a, b). The reasons for this effect are not known but a similar observation has been made in wine-making (Cromwell and Guymon, 1963; Rankine, 1968a). If a low concentration of fusels is required, for example in order to have a cider with a more pronounced fruity flavour, then filtration of juice increases the effectiveness of any added sulphite (Beech *et al.*, 1952), while sterile filtration after depectinization ensures dominance of the added low-fusel-producing yeast culture, provided all equipment coming into contact with juice and cider subsequently is adequately sterilized. Apple starch is only a problem if the juice from under-ripe fruit is heated, for example during aroma stripping. On such occasions, the enzyme mixture should contain an acid-tolerant amylase. Otherwise the starch, representing a loss of sugar, remains in the yeast lees after fermentation.

D. Fermentation and Storage

1. *Factors Controlling Yeast Growth and Rate of Fermentation*

With an untreated juice, the heterogeneous microflora (see Section II.A.2, p. 179) soon gives way to a succession that usually begins with *Kloeckera apiculata* (Challinor, 1955) soon to be accompanied by a *Saccharomyces* species derived almost certainly from the pressing equipment. As the fermentation proceeds, the first yeast slowly dies out. The main part of the fermentation is carried out by the *Saccharomyces* strains which also diminish in numbers towards the end of fermentation (Beech, 1957). The precise shape of its growth curve is determined by the concentration of soluble nitro-genous compounds, thiamin and oxygen (Burroughs, 1958). Towards the end of the fermentation, a second, but haploid, *Saccharomyces* species often appears (Barker, 1951; Beech, 1958a), accompanied by growth of bacteria. If the cider is left on its lees exposed to air during fermentation, it ultimately develops a surface film, either of acetic acid bacteria or of yeasts such as *Pichia* or *Candida* spp. Usually its malic acid will be converted to lactic acid and carbon dioxide by lactic-acid bacteria.

The object of good cidermaking is to control these changes. Hence aerobic spoilage during storage was prevented by exclusion of air from the vats. However, with the use of sulphiting, it became possible to prevent development of all but fermenting yeasts (Beech, 1959). Correct sulphiting is marked by the absence of *Kloeckera apiculata* (Beech, 1972b), film yeasts and acetic bacteria from the juice. The presence of any *Saccharomyces* spp. is largely determined by the cleanliness of the plant (Beech, 1958b; Bowen and Beech, 1964, 1967). Correctly sulphited juice (Section III.C.2, p. 243) from properly cleaned pressing equipment is often difficult to ferment for lack of yeast. This enables a yeast culture with the required characteristics (Section III.C.3, p. 249) to be added instead of using the adventitious culture with unknown properties. If, however, cleaning procedures are not fully maintained, a high level of 'wild' yeast cells can soon develop, particularly where the press utilizes non-metallic material (see Table 18, p. 182) and the infecting yeast overgrows the added culture. Alternatively, a modest level of contamination with a yeast capable of very vigorous growth can have the same effect. This means that any strain of yeast used in a cider factory must have the ability to dominate a fermentation when present with another strain. Unfortunately, no one so far has devised a suitable test for measuring a yeast's ability to dominate the fermentation (Radler, 1973). Until the advent of the serological test of Campbell (1972), the great difficulty was to distinguish between strains of *Saccharomyces* spp. when present in a mixture. Beech *et al.* (1952) and Beech (1953) examined yeasts isolated during and after fermentation of a series of pretreated juices that had been pitched with yeast. Using the appearance of giant colonies, alcohol tolerance, growth in the presence of actidione, and vitamin requirements, it was found possible to assess the degree of dominance of the added yeast cultures. They were found in seven of the ten dry ciders examined but were only the major part of the microflora when the natural flora had been suppressed by sulphiting, flash pasteurization and sterile filtration. In all other cases, the concentration of added viable yeasts had been totally inadequate. Rankine and Lloyd (1963) carried out a similar investigation on Australian grape juices pitched with yeast in the presence and absence of the skins. Under hygienic working conditions, 2% by volume of active starter was necessary to dominate the experimental fermentations. Under factory conditions, they considered 3% would be necessary, a conclusion also reached by Gomes *et al.* (1962). Later (Knappstein and Rankine, 1970) a final concentration of 5×10^6 cells/ml was recommended for white wines and 10×10^6/ml for grapes fermented on the skins (compare this with a natural yeast count of 1×10^6/ml in fresh grape juice; Winkler, 1962). These concentrations have ensured suppression of hydrogen-sulphide forming yeasts derived from the grape which used to be a problem in some Australian wineries. This was taken further by Thoukis *et al.* (1963) who used a mass-pitching technique (1 kg of pressed yeast cake per 1,000 litres or 26×10^6 cells/ml final concentration) and claimed a rapid onset of fermentation, completion in six days, diminution of yeast growth and greater efficiency in conversion of sugar to alcohol. These high levels of inocula have not been used as yet in cidermaking, but they should be tried to discover whether the added yeast would overgrow the sulphite-resistant *Saccharomycodes ludwigii*, a notorious pest in cider factories (Beech and Davenport, 1970).

Large inocula help to overcome the initial lag before fermentation commences, which occurs in juices containing excessive quantities of free sulphur dioxide (see Fig. 12, p. 247), otherwise the length of the lag phase is related directly to the amount of sulphite added (Beech, 1958a). Concentrating the juice followed by redilution and addition of yeast also delays the onset of fermentation compared with untreated juice. Conversely, heating the juice or sulphiting before heating shortens the lag phase. The reasons why juice treatments have these effects is not known. Some yeasts, for example strain A.W.Y. 350R, also tend to have a longer lag phase than other strains added in the same amount to batches of the same juice.

When considering the intermediate stage of the fermentation, it is surprising how little is known about the factors that control its rate. Most of the earlier work, using untreated juice with a natural microflora, was concerned with attempting to arrest fermentation prematurely or, later when this had been abandoned, how to cure 'stuck' or incomplete fermentations. The researches of Burroughs (Challinor and Burroughs, 1949; Burroughs and Challinor, 1949, 1950, 1951; Burroughs, 1952, 1953) demonstrated that, during the lag phase, there was a marked uptake of soluble nitrogenous components from the juice as a result of yeast growth. During fermentation, the content of soluble nitrogen continued to fall until other nutrient factors became limiting. Uptake of soluble nitrogenous compounds then ceased and the amount of yeast in suspension began to diminish. This usually occurred about halfway through the fermentation. During the last 10 to 15 degrees loss of gravity, there was an increase in soluble nitrogen content due to excretion by the yeast. The amount of nitrogen excreted was proportional to the amount absorbed previously by the yeast (Volbrecht and Radler, 1973). This excretion, which consists of aromatic amino acids, peptides and nucleotides (Burroughs, 1970b; Burroughs and Sparks, 1972), is not necessarily the same as autolysis (Hough and Maddox, 1970). A similar phenomenon is also found in brewing (Clapperton, 1971).

The factor that causes uptake of nitrogenous compounds to cease was found to be thiamin. In a summary of the earlier work (Burroughs and Pollard, 1954) the importance of sufficient oxygen in maintaining growth during fermentation was also described.

In work with a pure culture of *Saccharomyces uvarum* and sulphited juice (Goverd, 1973b) the changes in the soluble nitrogen both high- and low-nitrogen juices were similar to those observed in the earlier experiments. From simultaneous assays of the B-group vitamins, a similar loss and excretion of thiamin (see also Okuda and Tanase, 1958) and, to a lesser extent, nicotinic acid, was also observed. Parallel tests on the yeast's vitamin requirements for growth under aerobic conditions disclosed no requirements for these vitamins, which suggests a different pattern of assimilation during fermentation. Not enough information is available on the vitamin requirements of yeast strains during fermentation. Riboflavin and pantothenic acid were produced by this yeast. The latter vitamin is sometimes added (Stewart *et al.*, 1962) with methionine (Wilson *et al.*, 1961) to suppress formation of hydrogen sulphide (Wainwright, 1970).

Rate of fermentation is also influenced by juice treatment. Sulphited juices fermented faster, and heated juices slower, than the corresponding untreated juices. Heating may in fact lower the thiamin content. The yeast strain also has a marked influence. Usually, but not always, non-flocculent yeasts ferment faster than flocculent, since, from the work of Burroughs, the yeast in the lees takes an active part in the fermentation. Yeast strains also vary in their fermentation efficiency which, according to Thorne (1954,

1961), is measured by the velocity divided by the nitrogen content of the yeast cell at the time of the test. This explains why an aerobically grown yeast ferments faster than one grown anaerobically (Hudson, 1968) since the former has higher cell-nitrogen and ergosterol contents (David and Kirsop, 1973). The permease systems and enzymic make-up of each yeast strain regulate its rate of uptake of sugars and therefore its specific fermentation velocity. Yeasts which require thiamin for growth also show an enhanced rate of fermentation when the medium is supplemented with thiamin.

A growing problem is the increasing concentrations of soluble nitrogen compounds in cider apple juices. Values of 5-10 mg N/100 ml are rising up to 40-50 mg as fruit from the old standard orchards gives way to that from new intensive orchards (Section III.A.1, p. 217) where high levels of fertilizer are used. If fermented without any attention to the size of the yeast crop, the final ciders would contain 20-30 mg N instead of 2-3 as previously. Burroughs (1970b) investigated the effect of oxygen and thiamin on uptake of soluble nitrogenous compounds in a juice with 20 mg N/100 ml (above this concentration, thiamin is known to be limiting; Burroughs and Pollard, 1954). Addition of thiamin led to a significant increase in the rate of fermentation whereas oxygen did not. The nitrogen level dropped to less than 3 mg/100 ml but doubled when the cider was left in contact with the yeast lees for more than a week. The pasteurized clarified cider, sweetened to a specific gravity of 1.020, was re-inoculated and allowed to referment. Addition of thiamin had no effect but aeration shortened the lag phase. The nitrogen content of all of the ciders was again decreased to less than 3 mg/100 ml. These ciders would also referment, particularly if 2 mg N/100 ml in the form of an amino-acid mixture was added. In further work, using a juice of still higher nitrogen content (35 mg/100 ml), Burroughs (1974a) found that none of the five yeasts tested was able to lower the nitrogen content below 10 mg/100 ml and excretion again took place, the amount varying with the strain. However, addition of glucose and thiamin to fermentations with *Sacch. uvarum* caused a further lowering in nitrogen concentration to 2.7 mg/100 ml but not with the other yeasts tested.

Reference has been made to earlier work on the effect of aeration on rate of fermentation. In a recent experiment, one of two batches of the same juice was aerated for one hour after addition of yeast, and fermented completely in seven days compared with 14 days for the non-aerated control and had a lower residual nitrogen content. Undoubtedly these effects can be explained by the work of David and Kirsop (1973). They showed that some yeast strains grown and fermented anaerobically would cease to ferment prematurely, whereas the same culture, pre-aerated, fermented completely. The oxygen demand of the first group could be overcome by addition of 10 p.p.m. ergosterol, which is formed in aerobically but not anaerobically-grown yeasts (David, 1974). Differences in rate of fermentation and rate of uptake of soluble nitrogenous compounds can also be found in fermentation vessels with different surface-to-volume ratios (Nilov, 1969; Mändl, 1970).

If ciders with such low contents of nitrogen can referment, it is perhaps questionable whether there is any need to attempt to lower the content in juices with high concentrations of nitrogen. Furthermore, it is theoretically possible with modern techniques for any cider, irrespective of its degree of fermentability, to be packaged without fear of subsequent yeast growth. However, not every cider factory is so well equipped, and exact knowledge of the mechanisms controlling rate of fermentation would be invaluable for any cidermaker since he could then schedule all of his fermentations. Until then, some fermentations will be unduly prolonged and even cease prematurely (stuck fermentations). To restart such fermentations, the temperature should be in the working range of 12–13°C with some fermentable sugar remaining, not solely sorbitol, glycerol and other non-fermentable carbohydrates (Whiting, 1961). At least 10^4 of the culture yeast cells/ml should still be capable of growth, otherwise a new inoculum must be added. Nutrient deficiencies, such as nitrogen and thiamin (50 mg $(NH_4)_2 SO_4$ and 0.2 mg thiamin/litre for each 10° of specific gravity remaining to be fermented), or those special to a particular strain (Shimada et al., 1972), can be corrected. Aeration can restore the yeast to activity in ciders containing adequate concentrations of nutrients, but which are still failing to ferment completely (Burroughs and Pollard, 1954; Rankine, 1955; Lüthi, 1957; White and Ough, 1973), as seen by the re-appearance of budding cells; alternatively it should be fully aerated before use. The role of ergosterol in ciders also needs to be investigated. Even so, the yeast may still not respond for several reasons. Concentrates stored at high temperatures may fail to ferment satisfactorily due to the presence of inhibitors and loss of nutrients. Treatment with charcoal, aeration and the addition of the above-mentioned nutrients with a strongly fermenting inoculum will ensure a satisfactory fermentation (Lüthi, 1958). Assuming the culture yeast has dominated the first part of the fermentation and is tolerant of the concentration of alcohol, it may have been killed by a toxin produced by acetic-acid bacteria either alone (Gilliland and Lacey, 1966; Kaneko and Yamamoto, 1966) or in conjunction with products from wooden staves (Comrie, 1951). Infection with certain strains of lactic-acid bacteria has been known to cause inhibition of fermentation (Boidron, 1969a, b) or to retard its rate by causing a yeast to flocculate prematurely. There has been at least one instance of an infecting yeast having 'killed' the culture yeast in a brewery (Maule and Thomas, 1973). It is due to a mutation of the brewery yeast which then possesses a double-stranded ribonucleic acid as a genetic element, enabling the yeast cell to excrete a toxic factor which is a thermostable protein, to which they themselves are immune (Woods *et al.*, 1974). The 'killer' cells produce almost exclusively non-killer cells when heated to 37–40°C, presumably due to loss of at least part of the non-chromosomal killer genome (Wickner, 1974). Finally there have been reports of residues of the fungicide Captan left on grapes, which prevent the start of fermentation of juice (Kasza, 1956; Sudario, 1958). Pasteurization of the juice accelerated decomposition of the Captan which also occurred naturally in time. Similar effects have been reported for the systemic fungicide Benomyl (Beuchat, 1973). This would not have been a problem in juices from fruit grown in the older type of orchard. However, in order to maintain high yields, fungicidal sprays are used in the modern intensive cider-apple orchards so that fermentation problems may be experienced in the future. Adams (1968) has reviewed the effect of biocidal residues in winemaking.

2. Changes Occurring During Fermentation

The effect of sulphur dioxide on the juice microflora has been described in Sections II.B and III.C.2 (pp. 183 and 243). Some of the free sulphur dioxide becomes bound by juice constituents such as acetaldehyde and glucose (mainly) within the first two hours. Thereafter, further small and similar losses of both free and total sulphur dioxide occur slowly, possibly due to oxidation to sulphate (Amerine, 1958; Paul, 1958) or combination with carbonyl compounds. When fermentation sets in, free sulphur dioxide rapidly becomes completely bound by acetaldehyde produced as an intermediate during alcoholic fermentation. Ciders made from sulphited juices contain more total acetaldehyde than those made from the corresponding non-sulphited controls (Veselov *et al.*, 1963; Schanderl and Staudenmayer, 1964). Sulphur dioxide is not lost in the stream of carbon dioxide evolved. Losses of total sulphur dioxide during clarification of the cider are minor but are greater during pasteurization and prolonged storage in the bottle (Burroughs, 1959), as found by Mills and Wiegand (1942) for stored wines.

Soluble pectin is present in juices that have not been treated with commercial pectin-destroying enzymes. Providing they have not been heated, the pectin methylesterase of the fruit initiates demethylation of the soluble pectin (Kieser *et al.*, 1949). Apple cultivars vary in the amount of the enzyme they contain and those of low pH value, for example Bramley's Seedling, and Granny Smith, show restricted activity. The yeast must also possess polygalacturonase which produces a range of lower galacturonides from the partially de-esterified pectin. Yeasts such as *Saccharomyces fragilis* and *Sacch. willianus* possess this enzyme in considerable quantities (Luh and Phaff, 1951). Most yeasts used in fermentation of wines and ciders possess it in sufficient amounts for there to be no pectin left in the fully fermented cider (Pollard and Kieser, 1959). There are reports of fermenting yeasts without the enzyme (Braverman and Lifshitz, 1957) when filtration problems are experienced. Ciders prepared with these yeasts, as well as those produced by any other yeast from heated juices, must be treated with a commercial pectin-destroying enzyme. As will be explained later in this section (p. 268), there are circumstances when the enzyme is better added to the final cider rather than the juice.

During fermentation there are changes in the amino-acid and B-group vitamin contents of the juice (Sections II.B.1.c and III.D.1, pp. 190 and 256). Very little information exists on the uptake of particular amino acids in cider or on the excretory products of the different yeast strains. Ascorbic acid, in the presence of sulphur dioxide, is converted to L-xylosone (Whiting and Coggins, 1960a) which is capable of binding some of the sulphur dioxide added subsequently. This is a factor to be considered in maintaining the free sulphur dioxide content prior to bottling of ciders made from juices rich in vitamin C (Kieser and Pollard, 1947a, b). Again there is very little information (Jacquin and Tavernier, 1952) on the rate of disappearance of juice sugars, some 80% of which are the hexoses fructose and glucose, mainly the former, with a quantity of sucrose. During fermentation, the last sugar is hydrolysed to glucose and fructose, and dry ciders normally contain traces of fructose and glucose (Warcollier and Le Moal, 1935; Challinor, 1955), sorbitol (Tutin, 1926) and traces of pentoses (Steuart and Duncan, 1954).

Besides the obvious products of fermentation, ethanol and carbon dioxide, fermenting yeasts are known to produce organic acids, higher (or fusel) alcohols, esters and aldehyde. Hydrogen sulphide and diacetyl can also be present as a result of yeast action (Section III.C.3, p. 240). While there is a considerable literature on the factors affecting formation of these compounds in brewing and winemaking, data are only just appearing for cidermaking.

In studies on formation of organic acids by a number of *Saccharomyces* spp., Coggins *et al.* (1974) showed that *Sacch. uvarum* was most active in this respect. It formed pyruvate in the earlier stages of fermentation, reaching a maximum when half of the sugar had been fermented. In other species, maximum pyruvate formation was delayed until later, in some cultures to the end of the fermentation. An interaction (Beech *et al.*, 1971) between the soluble nitrogenous compounds and pH value was confirmed. At constant pH value, pyruvate excretion increased with addition of increasing amounts of asparagine but only a small amount was derived directly from the amino acid. In high-nitrogen juices, decreasing the pH value from 4.0 to 3.0 caused a 50% decrease in excretion of pyruvate. Earlier, Beech *et al.* (1971) also found that the higher the pH value the greater the amount of pyruvate produced. Generally speaking, increasing the temperature from 15° to 35°C increases pyruvate excretion, the precise quantity being characteristic of the yeast strain. Pyruvate excretion, particularly by yeasts prone to producing it in large amounts, can be decreased by addition of thiamin (Trevelyan and Harrison, 1956). Similarly, prior growth of non- or poorly-fermenting yeasts (for example *Candida, Torulopsis, Hansenula* spp.) can also depress pyruvate formation (Beech *et al.*, 1972). Wines that have undergone a malo-lactic fermentation are lower in pyruvic acid than those in which it has not taken place (Rankine, 1965).

Fermenting yeasts also produce another sulphite-binding organic acid, α-oxoglutaric, which can also increase considerably in concentration during fermentation (Whiting and Coggins, 1960a). Its production tends to decrease with decreasing pH value (Coggins *et al.*, 1974). Hence, adjusting the pH value of juices to about 3.5 prior to fermentation by blending apple varieties or addition of malic acid would decrease formation of sulphite-binding compounds in the cider. Care in the choice of the yeast strain is of obvious importance.

During the fermentation of apple juice, yeasts can form acids which do not bind sulphite. These include malic, succinic (Carr and Whiting, 1956; Beech, 1959; Whiting and Coggins, 1960b) and, with some yeasts, lactic acid. Traces of volatile acids are to be found even in pure-culture fermentations (Whiting, 1973).

Production of malic acid is particularly noticeable in the fermentation of sulphited juices (Whiting and Coggins, 1960b). It is formed from glucose and a source of nitrogen (Drawert *et al.*, 1965); again acidity interacts with nitrogenous compounds in determining the amount of malate formed (Coggins *et al.*, 1974). *Saccharomyces uvarum* in a low-nitrogen juice of high pH value (4.0) produced large amounts of malate with even greater increases at 25°C compared with 15°C. Decreasing the pH value or increasing the nitrogen content decreased malate formation with all yeasts. Extensive decomposition of malate by yeasts has not been observed in ciders, as it has in wines (Rankine, 1968a). So far, yeasts such as *Schizosaccharomyces* spp. capable of this activity, have been isolated only very rarely from ciders.

All yeasts tested by Coggins *et al.* (1974) formed some D-lactate and trace amounts (0.01 mmol/100 ml) of L-lactate. *Saccharomyces veronae* is noted for the relatively large amounts it can produce of the latter isomer (Peynaud *et al.*, 1967). *Saccharomyces uvarum* is also capable of forming sizeable quantities of D-lactate; addition of aspartate to a juice with a high pH value trebled the amount excreted by this yeast to 0.46 mmol/100 ml.

a. *Fusel alcohols.* Apple juices contain only small concentrations of fusel or higher alcohols (Section II.A.2, p. 179); of these *n*-hexanol is lost during aroma stripping and *n*-butanol during concentration of the stripped juice under vacuum (Reinhard, 1968; Beech and Davenport, 1970). Absence of these two components from a cider is indicative that it was produced from a diluted concentrate. Virtually all of the other fusels and, therefore, the characteristic flavour of much of the World's cider and perry, are formed by the fermenting yeast. The conditions which govern formation of these metabolites are still only known very incompletely (Beech, 1969b) and can be summarized as follows.

i. Yeast strain. The strain of yeast used in the fermentation is probably the principal factor in determining the amount of fusel alcohols formed. Values ranging from 80 to 800 p.p.m. of total fusels have been reported for pure-culture fermentations in different batches of the same juice. It cannot be emphasized too strongly that this effect will only be observed with certainty when the added strain has dominated the fermentation. This means, as stated in Section III.C.2 (p. 243), cleanliness of all equipment, sound fruit, adequate control of pH value and free sulphur dioxide in the juice, a large yeast inoculum and fermenting vessels with impervious, sterilizable surfaces. Under these conditions, yeasts can be used according to whether a high- or low-fusel cider is required (Table 30).

ii. Juice composition. The amount of fusels produced during fermentation varies directly with the amount of sugars in the juice (Engan, 1972). They are not derived from de-amination of amino acids but via formation of oxo-acids (Äyräpää, 1963, 1965). In general terms, isobutanol increases in concentration with juice nitrogen up to 30 mg/100 ml, while isopentanol and 2-phenethanol concentrations decrease. The precise relationship between nitrogen content of apple juices and fusel alcohol production remains to be determined. It is complicated since other factors are involved. Beech et al. (1971) found there was an interaction between juice nitrogen content and pH value; even here the effect varied, to some extent, with the yeast strain. For the high-fusel producer *Sacch. uvarum*, concentrations of fusel alcohols are high at all combinations of levels of pH value and nitrogen except for low pH-high nitrogen conditions where fusel production is severely depressed. With a moderate producer (*Sacch. cerevisiae* N.C.Y.C. 1119), high pH-high nitrogen conditions gave lower fusel concentrations and low pH-low nitrogen conditions higher values than for other combinations of pH value and nitrogen content.

iii. Juice treatment. Most yeasts tested in sterile apple juice show maximum production of fusel alcohols in fermentations carried out between 15° and 25°C with decreases on either side of these temperatures (Pollard et al., 1966). The shape of the temperature-

Table 30

Contents of higher alcohols in pure-culture fermentations produced by different strains of yeast in batches of the same apple juice. From Beech et al. (1972)

Yeast strain	Strain	Content (p.p.m.) of			
		Isobutanol	Isopentanol	2-Phenethanol	Total fusel oils
Saccharomyces cerevisiae	A.W.Y. 350R	10	95	15	140
Saccharomyces cerevisiae var. ellipsoideus	Burgundy	20	145	65	260
Saccharomyces cerevisiae	N.C.Y.C. 1119	50	245	30	370
Saccharomyces uvarum	G.E.I.	35	235	135	425
Saccharomyces cerevisiae	N.C.Y.C. 1026	35	230	145	440
	Taranto	40	290	215	565

response curve varies with yeast strain (Otsuka *et al.*, 1963; Äyräpää, 1970; Webb, 1973).

The most marked effect is brought about by the presence or absence of finely divided apple-pulp particles in the juice. With any yeast strain at a constant temperature, any treatment that decreases the solids content, for example centrifuging or filtering, diminishes the fusel content of the cider. Addition of pulp particles enhances production, whereas flash pasteurization, sulphiting, aroma stripping, pectic enzyming (unfiltered) of the juice or enzyme-treatment of the dry cider give fusel concentrations equal to that of the untreated control (Beech and Davenport, 1970). The reason for this effect is not known. It has been suggested (Crowell and Guymon, 1963; Rankine, 1968a) that oxygen trapped within the pulp particles or in added kieselguhr was responsible. Experiments with apple juice have not given conclusive results (Burroughs, 1974b). Aeration during fermentation can have a marked effect on the pattern of fusel-oil formation. This was particularly noticeable in one study (Beech, 1967a) where aeration during continuous (homogenous) culture caused a severe decrease in the content of all fusel alcohols. However, in aerated stirred batch cultures, not only were the concentrations higher, but the yeast's (A.W.Y. 350R) characteristic pattern of alcohols produced was altered, *n*-propanol being lower and isopentanol greatly increased in content. In contrast, batch and continuous fermentations, both non-aerated, gave the normal pattern. Similar effects have been found in stirred wine (Crowell and Guymon, 1963) and in aerated continuous beer production (Ault *et al.*, 1969).

In all probability, production of fusel oils may well be conditioned by one factor, the extent of yeast growth (Anderson and Kirsop, 1974), although there is some conflict of evidence for this hypothesis (Lie and Haukeli, 1973).

3. Fermentation Systems

a. *Equipment.* Continuous fermentation of cider using stirred and tower (heterogenous) systems has been examined briefly (Beech, 1967a; Hough, 1969) but it is doubtful whether there is any one cider being produced at present in sufficient quantity to justify the capital outlay and degree of technical control required. Some beers are being produced by these two methods (Ault *et al.*, 1969; Royston, 1971; Portno, 1973a) but many brewers are now in favour of the cylindro-conical batch fermenter (Shardlow and Thompson, 1971; Anon., 1972) which offers the advantage of rapid fermentations, ease of yeast control and freedom from infection.

While wooden fermentation vessels are being abandoned by the English cider industry, the metal tanks that are replacing them do not have the sophisticated system of fermentation available in the cylindro-conical tank. Instead, the first cider tanks were simple horizontal glass-lined vessels. Even the vertical tanks now being installed, whether made of lined or stainless steel, have at most temperature and level indication, carbon-dioxide venting and blanketing systems. So far equipment for controlling temperature and yeast growth during fermentation is not employed in Britain, whereas it is available in most continental European cider factories.

Production of champagne or naturally conditioned cider or perry has been mentioned. In some countries, it is still made by a primary fermentation in tanks, followed by blending, sweetening, addition of yeast, fermenting in the bottle, disgorging of the yeast deposit, and recorking. Although the complete contents of the bottle can be extracted through a crown cork with the transfer process, followed by filtration and bottling under pressure, it is more usual to use the pressure tank or Charmat process (Tschenn, 1934; Tressler *et al.*, 1941). The method is used extensively in winemaking; its use for making sparkling apple wine has been described by Atkinson *et al.* (1959). The suitability of a number of varieties of dessert apples for making wines by this process was described by Bowen *et al.* (1959).

b. *Yeast lees.* Disposal of the yeast deposit or lees left at the end of the fermentation is a considerable problem to a cidermaker (Peden, 1974). Sometimes it is diluted with effluent from the fruit-transport system or bottle- or cask-washing equipment and sprayed on to land well away from natural waterways. Opportunities for such a cheap disposal system are becoming increasingly rare. The most direct method is to centrifuge or powder-filter the complete contents of the vat at the end of fermentation but prior to total settlement of the yeast in suspension. This entails considerable investment in clarification equipment in order to have sufficient capacity to empty very large vats in a reasonable time. More usually, the ciders are either left at the end of fermentation for the yeast to settle or, they are fined with gelatin and tannin. Afterwards the clarified ciders are 'racked', i.e. syphoned off from the yeast lees into a storage vat. The deposits from several vats are pumped to a small vat where further settling takes place. Even when the supernatant cider has been drawn off, there is still an appreciable amount of cider remaining in the lees. It is extremely difficult to remove this cider since the lees do not filter as well as wine lees, and the cost of vacuum filtration is not compensated by the sale of yeast cake for cattle feed. It is doubtful whether any one factory has sufficient material to justify the installation of a drying plant as has occurred in some Scottish distilleries. Unfortunately, the number of sites on which it can be dumped without causing a nuisance is extremely limited. If pure-culture methods became the rule, then the methods used by the brewer for waste-yeast treatment could be envisaged (Wysocki and Glöckner, 1972).

4. Storage and Stabilization

The cider racked, fined or mechanically clarified usually contains malic acid and traces of assimilable sugars so that it is susceptible to a malo-lactic fermentation. So far no method has been found of preventing this fermentation unless the cider is extremely acid or is kept cold (Grove, 1931). This fermentation occasions a financial loss, in the sense that synthetic DL-malic acid has to be added to restore any deficiency. In perry containing citric acid, bacteria produce acetic acid anaerobically (Carr and Whiting, 1971). For ciders containing quinic acid esters there is also the possibility of traces of acetic acid, 4-ethyl catechol and 4-ethyl guaiacol being produced, which cause an unwelcome loss of freshness in the flavour. These changes usually take place when the tank contents reach $15°C$ (Section II.B.2.b, p. 201). Without facilities for refrigeration, it is usual to maintain a concentration of free sulphur dioxide appropriate to the pH value (Section III.C.2, p. 243), and to sell the ciders after very short storage periods.

Some strains of lactic-acid bacteria also produce an extracellular polysaccharide, giving an oily consistency to the product. It is never observed in ciders made from sulphited juices. Treatment of oily cider involves addition of 100 p.p.m. sulphur dioxide and breaking up the mucilage by agitation or centrifugation. Any equipment coming into contact with the cider prior to sulphiting must be sterilized with chlorinated or sulphited and acidified water.

A second bacterial disorder, sickness, described in Section II.C.1 (p. 204) is never encountered in English ciders and perries, because they are always stored in the unsweetened state, or in similar beverages made from table fruit, the pH values of which are below 3.8. It does occur in naturally sweet French ciders stored without refrigeration. Where it does occur, the bacterial fermentation is allowed to go to completion, the cider is fined with gelatin, and racked and stored at least six months to allow the organism to die. Even then it has an indifferent flavour and has to be blended with sound cider prior to stabilization and packaging.

Tanks containing cider or perry must be kept completely full or under a blanket of carbon dioxide (Jenny, 1940; Kern, 1962), nitrogen (Peynaud, 1969), or a mixture of the two gases (Cant, 1960; Jaulmes and Hamelle, 1969), otherwise in the presence of air any acetic-acid bacteria present will produce acetic taints, including phenylacetic acid. Film yeasts will also develop and produce volatile acids (Windisch, 1958). The use of very large tanks with impervious surfaces, kept completely full (Anon., 1973a), together with the correct juice treatment, makes acetification a rare event in commercial cidermaking.

A problem of growing importance is the development of a 'mousy' taint in ciders (Tucknott and Williams, 1973), particularly those made without sulphur dioxide. The nature of the compound responsible for this taint has not yet been ascertained, but it is known to be produced in ciders made from juices with a high pH value which have been exposed to air unduly during fermentation. The causal organism can either be a yeast or a combination of a yeast and a lactic-acid bacterium. The preventive measures are those given earlier in Sections II.C.1.d (p. 212) and III.C.2 (p. 243) for production of clean sound ciders (Tucknott, 1974).

Hydrogen sulphide production is a characteristic of specific yeast strains (Anderson et al., 1972). Ensuring the dominance of a low hydrogen sulphide-producer during fermentation is the best preventive remedy. If it is found to be present in young wines, it must be removed promptly as it gives rise to the even more objectionable compound ethanethiol (Rankine, 1963). Aeration (Thoukis and Stern, 1962) or addition of sufficient sulphur dioxide to leave some free followed by filtration, are suitable remedial measures. Diacetyl is known to occur in ciders and, in theory, it could be removed by heat exchanging and passing through a yeast plug (Baker and Kirsop, 1973) as has been done in practice for diacetyl in beer.

In addition to safeguarding the cider against microbiological hazards, it is also essential to ensure it is free from non-biological hazes (Mouchet, 1973). Ciders sweetened with stored juice or diluted concentrate or made from heat-treated juice may contain undegraded pectin. One measured volume of each of such juices should be treated with two volumes of acetone in a test tube to give 66% concentration of acetone in the mixture. Formation of jelly-like particles is an indication of the need to add pectin-destroying enzymes. A general haze or no reaction indicates that the material has already been broken down to galacturonides.

Juices suspected of having a protein haze should be submitted to the tannin-heat test of Pocock and Rankine (1973). The procedure is: add 0.5 g B.P. tannic acid/l., membrane-filter, hold 100 ml at 60°C overnight and cool. If a haze forms in the test tube, it indicates the presence of protein in the cider which should be treated with acid-tolerant commercial protease, tannin (hydrolysable type) or bentonite (Somers and Ziemelis, 1973). The amount required can be determined by laboratory tests. Ciders made from nonsulphited juices are prone to turn opalescent and eventually develop a protein-tannin haze (Monties and Barret, 1965); the presence of copper accelerates its formation (Kieser et al., 1957). They should be treated with ascorbic acid, if sulphur dioxide is not to be used, and fined with gelatin or treated with polyvinyl polypyrolidone. Laboratory tests are necessary to determine the optimum concentrations. Gelatin (5% aqueous solution of acid-hydrolysed material of low Bloom grade, grade A), held five hours, and then injected into the cider as a thin jet under pressure) gives best results (Wucherpfennig et al., 1972, 1973a; Wucherpfennig and Possmann, 1972). Perries made from true perry pears, in which the leucoanthocyanins are still present, are liable to become hazy or form a deposit, especially on chilling. Treatment with gelatin has been used traditionally for preventing the change taking place after bottling.

It is now rare to find ciders subject to darkening on exposure to air due to the presence of excessive quantities of phenolase or iron. Enzymic darkening is prevented by addition of sulphur dioxide while iron can be chelated with citric acid or removed with bran or potassium ferrocyanide (Pollard and Beech, 1957). Prevention, by avoiding overripe fruit and contact with iron or mild steel, is better than cure.

These stabilization treatments may be carried out on individual vats of ciders or perries, but they are more usually made after blends have been produced based on the alcohol, sugar and acid contents of the brand names under which they are to be bottled. At present, chemical analysis alone is insufficient to determine the flavour of the product, although research is being carried out on this topic. Hence it is usual for sample trial blends, based on chemical analyses, to be tasted and compared with samples of previous bottlings. Any necessary adjustments are then made, followed by addition of sulphur dioxide (according to the pH value) and permitted colouring matters (Presgrave, 1971; S.I. 1973, No. 1340). Naturally the flavour of a blend must change due to the varying nature of the raw materials but such changes are minimized by blending old and new ciders or of concentrates of different years prior to fermentation. Blended ciders are then filtered using sheet or kieselguhr systems (Wyllie, 1971; Fox, 1972; Osgood, 1972) and pumped to reserve tanks in the bottling and kegging rooms.

5. Packaging

Cider and perry can be sold still (uncarbonated) or sparkling, the degree of carbonation varying from saturation for ciders in jars, to 2-2.5 volumes of carbon dioxide in most bottled ciders, with up to five volumes in champagne cider. The sweetness can vary from completely dry (sugar-free) through varying degrees of sweetness to excessively sweet. The sweetening may be from retained juice sugars, added juice, diluted concentrate, sucrose, invert sugar, glucose and/or saccharin. Colours vary from water-white (some perries) through pale straw to deep brown. Clarity also can range from distinctly turbid, although this type of cider is now confined to a few districts, to lightly hazy for some ciders, to brilliantly clear, the last being more usual in commercial ciders. Crown corks, roll-on external seals and plastic corks have largely replaced bark corks and screw stoppers, although these are still common in France or for champagne cider elsewhere. An excellent review on the treatment of corks has been written by Peres (1972).

a. *Uncarbonated ciders*. For generations, cider was sold in wooden casks which engendered innumerable problems of chemical and microbial stability. During the early 1960s the cost of repairing casks increased so much, while the sale of cider in such containers decreased to such a level, that they became uneconomic. The use of casks, whether hogsheads or pipes, is now usually confined to farm cidermaking.

Instead, the cider is sold in large bottles, glass or pottery jars (Anon., 1970c). If sold locally, dry cider may not necessarily be sterile and, in this condition, it will usually last two or three weeks without becoming noticeably acetic. More usually it is given a sterilizing treatment which includes sterile filtration (Portno, 1968) or one of the following heat treatments: pasteurization in the container at 68°C for 20–30 min; heating to 82°C, holding 30 sec (Brumstead and Glenister, 1963), regeneratively cooling to 63°C and filling at that temperature; or heating to 82°C, and cooling to 10–15°C before filling. The last method is only suitable in commercial practice since heat-resistant mould spores will develop in the container if the cider has not been saturated with carbon dioxide prior to heating and filling (Splittstoesser *et al.*, 1971).

When cider in jars was first produced, considerable trouble was experienced with darkening and haze formation. This was overcome by ensuring that the iron content of the cider was less than seven p.p.m., that it contained free sulphur dioxide, was saturated with carbon dioxide, or had been purged with a stream of nitrogen gas, and that the seal was airtight. When used in the home there is a greater danger of development of yeast contamination than in containers fitted with taps, since the cider is well aerated every time it is tipped to dispense a glassful. In this respect, plastic containers which deform when cider is withdrawn via the tap or are fitted with a small carbon dioxide dispensing capsule on the top, are more satisfactory.

b. *Carbonated ciders*. Cider or perry, whether carbonated artificially or by tank fermentation, is usually given a fine filtration via EK-sheets irrespective of its final stabilizing treatment (Beech, 1955). This can include a further filtration through EK or EKS-sheets, possibly followed by filtration through membranes or pleated cartridges made from sheets of plastic material (Kozulis *et al.*, 1971). The pore size of the membrane is usually 0.45 μm, but cocci able to pass through these are retained by the 0.2 μm grade. So far, growth of these organisms has not occurred in carbonated ciders. Alternatively carbonated cider is flash pasteurized under pressure at 82°C, held 30 sec and cooled to 10°C. Both methods require sterile equipment from the outlet of the filter or heat exchanger onwards. Modern bottle washing and bottling machinery are capable of producing bottles free from yeasts and bacteria without introducing infection. However, yeast growth can occur from time to time (Brightwell, 1972) due to infection retained in pressure gauges on the sterile side, non-return valves lifting, thereby allowing ingress of non-sterile cider. The chief bugbear in English cider factories since the use of juice sulphiting was introduced has been *Saccharomycodes ludwigii* which forms a flaky deposit in infected bottles, even when the original infection is of the order of one or two cells per litre. Carbonated cider, sold in kegs, is also sterilized by filtration or preferably by flash pasteurization. It is important to ensure that all components coming into contact with the cider are made of metals resistant to cider (Section I.B.1, p. 146); not all beer kegs are in fact suitable in this respect. Efficient keg washing, sterilizing and filling systems are now available. The top pressure of carbon dioxide maintained during dispensing prevents growth of aerobic contaminants and *Saccharomycodes ludwigii*, if present, remains on the bottom of the container.

Cider pasteurized in bottle requires only clean rather than sterile bottles and equipment. Because of higher costs and greater space requirements, cider pasteurized in bottle is not much used in England but is used quite extensively abroad. It is advisable to keep the cooling water chlorinated to prevent ingress of infection, through minute leaks, while the product is in the cooling bath.

6. Quality Control

In the commercial production of cider and perry, it is essential to ensure that the quality of the product is maintained throughout processing. Some of the essential factors have been described already; in this subsection the checks that should be carried out in the laboratory are outlined. It should be read in conjunction with Section III.E (p. 278).

Apples	Samples from selected deliveries should be examined to ensure they contain less than 10% rots and, where appropriate, that they contain the selected varieties ordered (Williams and Child, 1962, 1963, 1964, 1965, 1966; Smith, 1971; Luckwill and Pollard, 1963; national fruit registers and pomonas). Apples and pears ready for pressing should be free of starch.
Pulp and pomace	The juice yield from the press can be determined from the moisture content of the pulp and of the press residue or pomace (Section III.B.1, p. 226).
Juice—freshly pressed	Specific gravity (hydrometer or refractometer); titratable acidity (Burroughs, 1947); pH value; total sulphur dioxide (Burroughs and Sparks, 1973); Kjeldahl nitrogen (Burroughs, 1960); tannin (Burroughs and Whiting, 1961b).
Six to 18 h after sulphiting	Free sulphur dioxide (Burroughs and Sparks, 1964a); count of viable yeasts (Beech and Davenport, 1969, 1971) and acid-tolerant bacteria (Carr, 1968a, b) can be made to determine the combined efficiency of plant hygiene and the sulphiting procedure.
Yeast culture	Concentration of viable cells (Anon., 1970e).
Fermenting juice	Specific gravity and temperature at intervals of time suitable for determining the rate of fermentation. For cider in pressure tanks, a record of the pressures developed is also needed.
Cider—fully fermented	Total and free sulphur dioxide; alcohol; titratable and volatile acidities (Pilone *et al.*, 1972).
At intervals during storage	Malic acid (Mayer and Busch, 1963); titratable and volatile acids; flavour (Williams and Tucknott, 1973).
At blending	Freedom from chemical and biological problems (Sections II.C and III.D.4, pp. 183 and 270).
At bottling	Specific gravity; titratable and volatile acidities; total and free sulphur dioxide; alcohol; carbon dioxide (Howard, 1971); tannin; sugar-free extract

	(Burroughs, 1964b, 1973b). Optional tests would include those for permitted colours, and contents of Fe, Cu, Pb, Cd, As (Bradfield and Osbourne, 1966).
Bottled	Sterility (Beech, 1967b; Portno, 1973b); shelf life; consistency of flavour (Wren, 1972; Williams and Moorhouse, 1974; Clapperton, 1973).
Concentrated juice or syrups	Specific gravity or degrees Brix; total sulphur dioxide; freedom from adulteration (Section III.C.1, p. 238); alcohol; presence of pectin (acetone test); freedom from osmophilic yeasts (Beech and Davenport, 1971).

A valuable discussion on the interpretation of results obtained on fruit products has been given by Kefford (1969).

Methods are also available for determining size and frequency of sampling and presentation of results as Quality-Control Charts (Willox, 1967; Porter, 1970; Cranston, 1971, 1973). Similarly, tests for detergent concentration, efficiency of biocides (Perkins and Mossel, 1971), B.O.D. (for example Hoch B.O.D. apparatus) or C.O.D. of effluents and quality-control tests on packages and containers would be routine as in any large beverage plant.

Apart from the flavour of the product, probably its most important characteristic is a low concentration of sulphite-binding compounds (Burroughs and Whiting, 1961a). This reflects not only the quality of the fruit but also the choice of yeast and the effectiveness of the conditions chosen for fermentation and storage. A simple procedure for comparing this property in ciders was devised by Sparks (1972) in which the amount of bound sulphur dioxide in a cider, previously adjusted to 200 p.p.m., is measured after equilibration. In commercial ciders the concentrations of bound sulphur dioxide vary from 50 to 150 p.p.m.; those with the lower concentrations have been produced with the best cidermaking techniques. Apart from canned cider, where it is detrimental to the lining, concentrations of 70–100 p.p.m. free sulphur dioxide are now common in well-made commercial ciders as a result of elucidation of the factors controlling sulphite binding.

With high-speed bottling lines, it is becoming increasingly important to develop methods capable of detecting the presence of viable yeasts at levels of less than five per litre and, preferably, immediately after bottling. All of the existing methods involve membrane filtration of the complete contents of a bottle, sometimes with incubation for a short period on a nutrient-soaked pad, followed by staining and examination of the membrane under the microscope (Richards, 1970). The result is not always unequivocal, since some 500 cells need to be present to be certain of detection, and a large number of samples need to be examined daily in order to represent the very large number of bottles being filled. For want of an automatic method, not dependent on observation through a microscope, all cider factories (as indeed do most beverage bottlers) hold the filled goods for a 'quarantine' period in the warehouse until routine microbiological testing has been completed. However, the recently published method of Paton and Jones (1975) offers a means of detecting very low levels of viable yeasts in a few minutes using incident fluorescence microscopy.

E. The Final Cider

1. General Composition

The original juice components are changed by the micro-organisms and also by manipulations of the manufacturers. At a certain point, it is decided to sell to the public some cider under a branded name. What then can the customer expect to find in a bottle which bears on its label the word cider? Most of the figures are taken from some 15 commercial ciders, many of which are available today.

a. *Acidity and sweetness.* A glance at Table 31 shows that, amongst the ciders examined, there was quite a range of acidity. At

Table 31

Analyses of 15 commercial ciders

	Acidity (%, malic acid)	Sweetness (%, w/v sugar)	Alcohol (%, v/v)	Tannins (%, w/v)	Total sulphur dioxide (p.p.m.)
Range	0.40–0.69	1.56–5.58	3.2–6.6	0.028–0.171	64–189
Mean	0.55	2.80	4.71	0.10	130

the lower end it would be tolerably acid whilst at the upper end very sharp. This particular flavour cannot be divorced from sweetness which, although it does not in any way neutralize acid in the chemical sense, has the power to make the imbiber think that sour is less sour. The balance of sweet and sour is, therefore, of great importance. For example, the cider with the highest acidity (0.69%) contained 2.18% sugar and was described as sweet. Another with an acidity only a fraction lower at 0.63% contained 5.58% of sugar, and it might be thought that this would be extremely sweet. It seems probable that the second manufacturer had used all sugar whereas the first probably added a quantity of saccharin to boost sweetness.

b. *Alcohol.* There is no legal requirement to state alcoholic strength on a bottle of cider. As Table 31 shows, commercial ciders can range from 3.2 to 6.6% (v/v) and there are ciders and related beverages on the market with alcohol concentrations of up to 8.4%. This could raise a difficulty for, while a couple of glasses of cider with an alcoholic strength of 3.0% (v/v) might not be intoxicating, a similar volume with twice the amount of alcohol could have an effect. There does seem to be a case for displaying alcoholic strength on the container of this and other alcoholic beverages.

c. *Sulphur dioxide.* There is a remarkable variation in the total sulphur dioxide present in the 15 ciders surveyed. At the bottom is 64 p.p.m., which is quite low, whereas at the top is 189 p.p.m., which is close to the legal limit of 200 p.p.m. It is not the total amount of sulphur dioxide, however, that is important, since it is the free form that prevents microbial growth. It is not necessarily the cider containing the greatest total sulphur dioxide that has most free. For example, the cider containing 64 p.p.m. had 17 p.p.m. free, which is 27%. In contrast, one with 149 p.p.m. total sulphur dioxide had only 9 p.p.m. free, representing 6%. This indicates the poor quality of the original fruit, which contained a large number of sulphur dioxide-binding compounds. These factors will contribute to the amount of sulphur dioxide that is bound and the amount that stays free and active against undesirable micro-organisms.

d. *Tannins.* More properly these should be referred to as the phenolic compounds. It is not known whether these are changed during fermentation and preparation. What is known, however, is the fact that they can be divided into several categories, and that some of these compounds affect flavour while others do not. They can be divided into three major categories: phenolic acids, phloretin derivatives, catechins, and procyanidins which make up respectively 20, 7 and 73% of the total phenols. The largest category can be further subdivided into the following: monomers which have a slight flavour and constitute 9% of the whole; dimers and trimers which are slightly to moderately bitter and form 24% of the total; polymeric procyanidins which are very bitter and astringent and form 21% of the phenolics; and highly polymerized procyanidins which have little taste but produce the brown colour.

e. *Nitrogenous compounds and B-group vitamins.* Table 32 shows the range of nitrogenous compounds found in commercial ciders. Those with lower residual nitrogen are generally less susceptible to re-infection and growth of contaminants in bottles and other con-

Table 32

Concentrations of nitrogenous compounds and B-group vitamins in
15 commercial ciders

	Total nitrogen (p.p.m.)	Thiamin (μg/ml)	Nicotinic acid (μg/ml)	Pantothenate (μg/ml)	Riboflavin (μg/ml)
Range	18–63	all $<$ 0.005	0.03–0.33	0.10–0.80	0.41–4.7
Mean	42	$<$ 0.005	0.16	0.38	1.35

tainers. The very low thiamin concentrations mean that only those organisms without a requirement for this vitamin will be able to grow in a fully fermented cider. It has been noted by Goverd and Carr (1974) that the concentration of pantothenate and nitrogen seems to show a direct correlation.

f. *Volatile aroma compounds.* Williams and Tucknott (1971) listed a series of 66 volatile compounds that they report as present in dry cider. Of these, 43 were identified with certainty while the remainder were only tentatively reported as being true cider volatiles. In a more limited survey, some of the volatiles of 15 commercial ciders are shown in Table 33. It shows that all of these compounds can occur over quite a wide range, which means that their possible combinations in a series of ciders is infinite. Apart from acidity, sweetness and bitterness, they give ciders their individuality. Indeed it is these volatile compounds that indicate to the consumer that the product they are drinking is derived from the apple.

Table 33

Concentrations of some volatile compounds of 15 commercial ciders

	n-Propyl alcohol	Isobutyl alcohol	n-Butyl alcohol	2- and 3-Methyl butyl alcohols	n-Hexyl alcohol	2-Phenethanol
Range (p.p.m.)	4–27	24–82	3–6	113–176	2–29	51–160
Mean (p.p.m.)	12	45	5	150	10	79

Table 34

Mineral contents of 15 commercial ciders

	Mg^{2+}	Cl^-	PO_4^{3-}	SO_4^{2-}	Na^+	K^+	Fe^{3+}	Co^{2+}	Zn^{2+}
Range (p.p.m.)	8–41	33–146	20–195	120–380	30–275	415–1,420	0.95–6.73	0.10–1.05	0.21–1.77
Mean (p.p.m.)	27	112	100	227	123	722	3.7	0.42	0.56

g. *Mineral salts*. Table 34 shows the average mineral salts contents of the same 15 ciders. It may be noted that sulphate is present in fairly large quantities. This probably stems from the fact that ammonium sulphate is often used as a source of nitrogen in those ciders which are low in this element. As the ammonium ion is taken up and removed in the form of yeast cellular material, the residual sulphate is left in the cider.

2. Additives

The substances classified under this heading are used in the manufacture of cider from the time it comes into the factory as fruit until it is sold as the finished product. A fairly comprehensive list of these appears in Table 35.

Table 35

Additives used in the manufacture of cider

Functions	Substances
Antioxidants	Ascorbic acid (Vitamin C)
	Sulphur dioxide, nitrogen
Microbial nutrients	
B-group vitamins	Thiamin, pantothenate, biotin
Nitrogenous compounds	$(NH_4)_2SO_4$, $(NH_4)_2HPO_4$, $(NH_4)_2CO_3$
	Yeast extract
Acidifiers	DL-malic, lactic and citric acids
Sweeteners	Glucose, sucrose, invert sugars, saccharin
Filter aids	Cellulose, asbestos, kieselguhr
Fining aids	Tannin, gelatin, bentonite
Decolorizers	Charcoal
Preservatives	Sulphur dioxide
Clarifying enzymes	Pectolytic enzymes, dextranase
Carbonation	Carbon dioxide
Colourings	Tartrazine, indigo carmine, amaranth, green S, sunset yellow, carmoisine, ponceau 4R, caramel

a. *Antioxidants*. These prevent oxidative darkening of ciders. The phenolic substances mentioned in Section II.A.1.e (p. 172) and II.B.1.d (p. 193) darken if allowed to oxidize and, if this process is allowed to continue, in some juices the darkening is excessive.

b. *Microbial nutrients*. Some juices are very low in nitrogenous compounds and B vitamins and, if allowed to go untreated, ferment very slowly indeed and may even get 'stuck'. To avoid such slow fermentation nutrients may be added.

c. *Acidifiers*. These are acids added to ciders that have lost some acidity due to the malo-lactic fermentation. If DL-malic is added, it is only the L-isomer that will disappear due to bacterial activity. It therefore means that the D-isomer together with half of the acidity of the L-form is retained. Citric acid has been used in the past, but it is vulnerable to bacterial decomposition not only to lactic acid but to acetic acid and diacetyl. Lactic acid, a product of the lactic-acid bacteria, is very stable.

d. *Sweeteners*. Glucose, sucrose or invert sugars may be added for the purpose of increasing sweetness in a 'dry' cider but they may also be added for the purpose of acting as an energy source for the yeasts, thereby increasing the alcohol content. Saccharin can be used only to sweeten. It has the disadvantage that, if used in excessive amounts, it can impart an additional lingering bitter flavour. It also fails to give a feeling of 'body' to the drink.

e. *Filter aids*. Cellulose acetate is used nowadays in the form of membrane filters to remove micro-organisms. Cellulose may be combined with asbestos to form filter pads that can be made sufficiently fine to sterilize cider. The diatomaceous earth kieselguhr is sometimes used to filter cloudy cider, but generally on a first filtration to remove the majority of suspended matter.

f. *Fining aids.* Sometimes a haze may be removed by use of compounds with opposite electrical charges, and it is on this principal that they work. Tannin and gelatin will sometimes remove fine hazes that normally pass through filters. Bentonite is a clay which forms a colloidal suspension in water and is used to remove protein. Polyvinylpyrolidone removes phenolics specifically.

g. *Decolorizers*. The main substance used for this is charcoal. Since perries are traditionally water-white, it is essential to remove any brown discoloration that may have arisen due to oxidation or other causes.

h. *Preservatives*. Only one preservative is permitted in cider, namely sulphur dioxide at a maximum level of 200 p.p.m. Sorbic acid is also permitted as it is in some countries for sweet white wines.

i. *Clarifying enzymes*. Pectolytic or cellulolytic enzymes are often used in the early part of the processing to aid removal of juice from the fruit and sometimes to eradicate pectin hazes at a later stage. Dextranase is also used to get rid of a non-filterable haze caused by the presence of the long-chain polysaccharide dextran which arises from the activities of certain lactic-acid bacteria.

j. *Carbonation*. Carbon dioxide is dissolved in chilled cider to give that sparkle associated with bottled cider. In drinks made by the champagne process, the carbon dioxide is derived directly from the fermentation and is retained in the liquid.

k. *Colourings*. The list of colourings in Table 35 might seem to be very long. It is, however, just a list of permitted colours from which a cidermaker may choose two or three. They are mainly yellows, reds and brown. They need to be used because many apple juices are very pale and variable in colour. To overcome this variation, the manufacturer will colour a particular brand of cider to the same shade for each batch. The list shown in Table 35 is not exhaustive, but serves to show what a large number of substances are involved in producing the final cider. They all have to be approved and will be found in the lists of the Codex Alimentarius Commission (1973).

3. Statutory Requirements

In Great Britain, the legal requirements for cider have been framed both by H.M. Customs and Excise and by the Ministry of Agriculture, Fisheries and Food. Since the Treaty of Accession to the European Economic Commission (E.E.C.), reports and recommendations on all aspects of food composition are being prepared by the M.A.F.F. Committees on Food Standards, and Food Additives and Contaminants. These are used in discussions with the other E.E.C. partners, and finally a Directive is issued under Section 4, Schedule 4B of the European Committees Act 1972, which provides for the administration of E.E.C. legislation, and is incorporated as amendments to Food and Drugs Act 1955 and the Trade Descriptions Act.

a. *Legal definition of cider*. Cider is an intoxicating liquor which does not require a wholesale or excise licence for its sale (Table 36). It does not pay excise duty provided it contains less than 15° proof spirit (8.7%, v/v) alcohol or was derived solely from the fermentation of a natural juice of greater equivalent original gravity (1.065). Otherwise it is treated as a British wine and charged the current rate of duty, as it does also if flavoured or coloured in such a way as not

Table 36

Definitions relevant to cider as presently enacted in the U.K.

S.I. 1972 No. 1510.   The Labelling of Food (Amendment) Regulations 1972.
   'Intoxicating liquor' means spirits, wine, beer, cider, perry, British wine and
   any other fermented, distilled or spirituous liquor, but (apart from cider
   and perry) does not include any liquor for the sale of which by wholesale
   no excise licence is required.

H.M. Customs and Excise Notice No. 200 (April 1956).
   Cider or perry of 15 degrees of proof (8.7% v/v) or greater strength shall on
   or after 18th April, 1956, be treated as sweets (British Wine) unless it has
   undergone no other process than a single process of fermentation, was
   made from apple or pear juice which at the beginning of that process was
   in its natural state, and contains no ethyl alcohol derived from other
   materials.

H.M. Customs and Excise Notice No. 155 (June 1962).
   When cider or perry of any strength is used as a base or ingredient in the
   preparation of another beverage (e.g. when flavouring essences are added
   to it or it is mixed with fruit juices) in such a way as to mask the characteristics of the cider or perry so that the beverage is no longer recognizable
   as commercial cider or perry, the beverage is regarded as British wines . . .
   and duty is chargeable on the whole quantity of the beverage sent out for
   home use.

S.I. 1970 No. 400.   The Labelling of Food Regulations 1970.
   Provided that in the case of cider, the word 'vintage' may be used in or in
   conjunction with the expression 'made from vintage cider apples'.
   No person shall—in the case of cider and perry which has not been subject to
   a process of secondary fermentation, bear [on the label] or include any
   statement, name or words indicating either directly or indirectly that the
   liquor resembles, or is a substitute for or has the character of or is in any
   way connected with champagne.
   The term shandy is defined as a mixture of cider with lemonade containing a
   minimum of 1.5° proof spirit.
   No declaration of ingredients is necessary for intoxicating liquor.

---

to be recognizable as commercial cider (hence Section IV in Table 2).
Since the April 1974 Budget, Value Added Tax has also been levied
on cider and its containers. The current rate is 8%.

The word 'vintage' has been used for many years to describe the
best quality cider although little if any attempt was made to give the
date of the vintage when the cider was first fermented. Although the
term can be used in connection with the type of fruit employed, it is
still not clear whether this applies to those cultivars that were
selected as a result of the vintage trials held many years ago at the
Long Ashton Research Station (Annual Reports for 1909–1915,

Table 37

The composition of cider and cider vinegar as presently enacted in the U.K.

Component	Maximum level permitted	
Cider		
Alcohol	8.5% v/v (actual)	H.M. Customs and Excise Notice No. 162 (1976).
Copper	7 p.p.m.	Recommended in Food Standards Committee Report on Copper 1956.
Zinc	5 p.p.m. in beverages	Recommended in Food Standards Metallic Contamination Sub-Committee's Report, 1953.
Arsenic	0.2 p.p.m.	(S.I. 1959. No. 831) Arsenic Food Regulations 1959.
		(S.I. 1973. No. 1052) Arsenic in Food (Amendment) Regulations 1973.
Lead	0.5 p.p.m.	(S.I. 1961. No. 1931) Lead in Food Regulations 1961.
		(S.I. 1973. No. 1053) Lead in Food (Amendment) Regulations 1973.
Sulphur dioxide* or	200 p.p.m.	(S.I. 1962. No. 1532) Preservative in Food Regulations 1962.
sorbic acid	250 p.p.m.	(S.I. 1975. No. 1487) Preservatives in Food Regulations 1975.
Artificial sweeteners	Saccharin only	(S.I. 1967. No. 1119) Artificial Sweeteners in Food Order.
		(S.I. 1969. No. 1817) Artificial Sweeteners in Food (Amendment) Order 1969.
Colouring matter	See Table 35 (p. 283)	(S.I. 1975. No. 1488) Colouring Matter in Food (Amendment) Regulation 1975
		(S.I. 1973. No. 1340) Colouring matter in Food Regulation 1973.
Cider vinegar		
Description	Must be preceded by a word describing its origin	(FSC/REP/58). Food Standards Committee Report on Vinegars Jan. 1972.
Acetic acid	Minimum 4% (w/v)	

* When used together, the total shall not exceed 200 p.p.m.

1922, 1943, 1945, 1954) or merely that the trees from which the fruit was harvested were of a venerable age (unspecified). By the second interpretation, cider made from old dessert and culinary apple orchards could equally bear the description, while that made from the new cider apple orchards would not.

As a result of a court case in May, 1975, use of the terms 'champagne cider' and 'champagne perry' in Britain are now forbidden but an appeal is pending.

b. *Standards for composition.* The components of cider and the Statutory Instruments in which they are specified are given in Table 37. The maximum alcohol content is specified in terms of the amount actually present in the cider. This is unlike the French regulation which specifies the sum of actual-plus-potential alcohol (i.e. the theoretical equivalent of any sugar present).

F. Ancillary Products

1. *Vinegar*

In England, the amount of apple-cider vinegar made is small in comparison with the quantities produced in the U.S.A. Here some is used as a condiment but a considerable proportion is sold as a dietary supplement for humans and cattle. The medical and veterinary basis for this latter use has yet to be determined scientifically. Nevertheless, those who drink it diluted with hot water and those who add it to animal diets are convinced benefits are derived from its consumption.

The composition of English malt vinegar was established by a legal case (Kat v. Diment, 1950, 1KB34) which stated that it was produced by double fermentations, alcoholic and acetous. By agreement with the Vinegar Brewers' Federation (1952), the minimum content was 4% (w/v) acetic acid. Recommendations for future legislation on vinegars were published by the Food Standards Committee (1971). At present, the maximum legal limit for sulphur dioxide in Great Britain is 70 p.p.m. (S.I. 1962, No. 1532) but it is recommended (Food Additives and Contaminants Committee, 1972) that, in future legislation, this shall be raised to 200 p.p.m. Vinegar quality, legal and commercial standards, methods of analyses and analytical parameters have been described by White (1971, 1972).

Basically, cider or perry vinegar is made by leaving cider or perry in partially filled wooden barrels and allowing it to acetify by the action on any acetic-acid bacteria naturally present (Grove, 1918) or after deliberate addition of a quarter of its volume of non-sterilized cider vinegar. Initially, it might be necessary to use malt vinegar to start the process. Subsequently, a portion of the acetified product is drawn off and replaced with fresh cider. Various devices are available for maintaining the bacterial jelly-like surface film by use of floating wooden racks or of taps and long necked funnels, which allow changes in the volume of the liquid to take place. A very detailed account of this method has been given by Cruess and Joslyn (1943).

Commercial production of cider vinegar (Vaughn, 1942) is now carried out in towers, the upper part of which is packed with beech-wood shavings or bundles of birch twigs (see Schierbeck, 1951, for a complete account). The cider, acidified with a previous charge of vinegar, is pumped over the packing and percolates back into the base of the tower. The bacteria become established on the packing material and, as the process starts, air is drawn in from below, thereby accelerating the rate of acetification. The rate is regulated by control of temperature, rate of pumping and access of air. Normally, the mixture of organisms in the packing becomes established naturally but methods for isolating very active cultures for use as inocula are available (Vandecaveye, 1927; Schainskaja, 1953). It was usual to make the towers in the factory (Llanguno, 1971), but commercial deep-culture models are now more commonly used in which the operation is controlled automatically. More recently, these have been converted to continuous production and a tower-type model has also been brought into use (White, 1966, 1970; Joslyn, 1970; Green-shields, 1974). Interruption of the air supply in the continuous process, even for a few seconds, leads to complete cessation of acetification followed by a very slow regeneration when aeration is restarted.

The main problem with cider vinegar is the prevention of haze and deposit formation after bottling. The vinegar must have a low content of iron and copper, but the main cause of the precipitate is a protein-tannin complex, similar to that formed in non-sulphited apple juice. Formerly it was removed by prolonged storage in contact with beech wood chips. Treatment with sulphur dioxide and E.K.-sheet filtration is found to be more satisfactory. Alternatively, where the presence of sulphur dioxide is not permitted, treatment with P.V.P.P. prior to E.K.-filtration also gives a product that remains clear in bottle.

2. Distilled Spirits

a. *Brandies.* For hundreds of years, cider brandy or Calvados was produced by the peasants of Normandy and Brittany. Written records go back to 1553 (Charley, 1949). In the 17th Century, distillation of cider was not unknown in England (Haines, 1684). The product, Cyder-Royal, was made by distilling the contents of one cider barrel and condensing the alcohol fraction in another barrel of cider. With the difficulty of determining the correct 'cut' in the different fractions, it is not surprising that it was more notorious for its stupefying effect than for any appreciation of its flavour. Probably for this reason it was never manufactured commercially, and no equivalent to Calvados ever appears to have been made in England. In addition to Calvados, which at present is enjoying a revival of interest in France, there is also a considerable sale of Williams-pear liqueur made from the pear Williams Bon Chretien, or Bartlett as it is known in the U.S.A.

In France, only discontinuous stills may be used for the distillation of eaux-de-vie known as Calvados (Margerand and Theiller, 1946). By a series of ministerial decrees promulgated between 1942 and 1963, three categories of Calvados and cider brandies were defined, based on their area of production:

Appellation contrôlée, Calvados. Calvados of the Pays d'Auge.
Appellation réglementée, Calvados. Calvados of Avranchin, Calvados, Contentin, Domfrontais, Mortanais, Pays du Bray, Pays de Merlerault, Perche, Pays de la Risle and the Valley of the Orne.
Appellation réglementées, Brandies. Eaux-de-vie made from cider in Britanny, Normandy and Maine.

In all cases, the apples must be picked and the ciders produced and distilled within the defined areas. The apples must be crushed and pressed and the juice allowed to ferment naturally. The cider before distillation must be fit for drinking. The method of distillation varies with the type of appellation. For appellation contrôlée, Calvados, the cider must be distilled twice in a pot still (Charentais) fitted with taps allowing the alcohol fraction to be separated from the first and last running. For the lower grade of Calvados, the pot still must also be heated over a fire but is of a larger capacity. Appellation réglementée brandies can be made in steam-heated distillation columns. Not only is the whole process of fermenting and distilling carefully controlled, but a sample of the spirit must be submitted within one year and approved by the Tasting Committee belonging to the French Institut National des Appellation d'Origine. A description of the manufacture of Calvados and cider brandy has been given by Charley (1949).

Calvados can either be sold relatively young at 40% (v/v) alcohol, or it is stored in oak casks for many years at 68–72% at a temperature of 12–14°C. Alcohol is lost by evaporation during ageing and its concentration falls to 55–60%. Finally it is blended with similar Calvados from the same district and diluted to 44–45% before filtration and sale (Anon., 1970d).

b. *Liqueurs*. Brandies have been made elsewhere from dried, cull and surplus apples (Cruess, 1958) and apple pomace (Amemiya *et al.*, 1964). Williams pear, the most widely known, is made by storing the fruit until it is fully ripe before milling and pressing. The pH value of the juice is reduced to about 2.8 by addition of phosphoric acid which prevents growth of spoilage bacteria that otherwise would produce unpleasant volatile components during fermentation. It has the added advantage of not requiring separation of sulphur dioxide vapours in the still, or the need for specially resistant grades of stainless steel in the vapour head of the still to resist corrosive action of the gas. Nutrients are added with the yeast to achieve a rapid fermentation. The distillation is designed so as to retain the more volatile fruit aromas and less of the fusel alcohols, and the water-white product is not aged before sale.

A similar product was made some years ago at the Long Ashton Research Station from Cox's Orange Pippin, under supervision by the Customs and Excise authority. Fully ripened apples were milled and pressed and the 10% of the volume of the juice removed in an aroma separator. This was subsequently concentrated to give an aroma concentrate. The pH value of the stripped liquid was lowered to 2.8, it was pitched with a low fusel, non-hydrogen sulphide-producing yeast and the nutritional status of the juice and the temperature of the fermentation were adjusted to give minimum fusel-oil concentration. At the end of fermentation, the liquid was centrifuged and again passed through the aroma separator until all the alcohol was removed. Finally a liqueur was produced from a blend of the aroma concentrate, alcohol, glyccrine and sugar syrup. It had a very pleasant aroma and flavour of Cox's Orange Pippin. There is no reason why the same process should not be used for other fruit liqueurs.

IV. ACKNOWLEDGEMENTS

We wish to acknowledge that the Official Statistics quoted in Sections I.D and the Statutory Orders and Instruments in Section I.A and III.E.3 are used with the permission of the Controller of H.M.S.O. of Great Britain.

We are also grateful to the following individuals and organizations who very kindly supplied information on cidermaking in their own countries:

Australia	The Victorian Chamber of Manufacturers, Research Dept. Victoria
Austria	Fachverband der Nahrungs- und Gemussmittel-industrie, Zaunergasse 1-3, A-1030 Vienna
Brazil	Federação das Indústrias do Estado do Rio Grande do Sul, Caixa Postal 845, Porto Alegre, RS
Canada	R. E. Simard, Université Laval, Faculté d'Agriculture, Quebec 10e
	R. Stark, Food Technology Section, A.C.R.S., Kentville, Nova Scotia
	J. F. Bowen, A.C.R.S., Summerland, British Columbia
Denmark	M. Munch, Royal Danish Embassy, 29 Pont Street, London
Finland	R. Nyman, Viini ja Likooritehdas Marli, SF-20100 Turku 10
France	Comité des Fruits à Cidre et des Productions Agricoles, 75001, Paris
	J. R. Drilleau, Station de Recherches Cidricoles, Domaine de La Motte, 35650, Le Rheu

Germany (W)	R. Possmann, Institut für Weinchemie und Getranke-forschung, 6222 Geisenheim/Rh.
Norway	The Export Council of Norway, 20 Pall Mall, London
Spain	S. Alvarez R., Diputacion Provincial de Asturias, Estacion Pomologica de Villaviciosa, Villaviciosa
Sweden	Federation of Swedish Farmers' Associations—LRF, Klara Östia Kyrkogata 12, S-105 33 Stockholm
Switzerland	Schweizerischer Obstverband, Baarerstrasse 88, 6300 Zug.
United States of America	U.S. Dept. Agriculture, Office of Agriculture Attaché, American Embassy, Grosvenor Square, London
United Kingdom	Economics and Statistics Division, Dept. Trade and Industry
	Statistical Office, H.M. Customs and Excise
	Statistics Division, Ministry of Agriculture, Fishcries and Food
	National Association of Cidermakers, Dorchester, Dorset
	G. B. Nelson, H. P. Bulmer Ltd., Hereford
	C. F. M. Roberts, The Taunton Cider Co. Ltd., Norton Fitzwarren, Somerset
	W. R. Kinnersley, 38 Queens Square, Bristol

Lastly we are indebted to our colleagues (L. F. Burroughs, C. F. Timberlake, G. C. Whiting, A. A. Williams and R. R. Williams) who patiently answered our many questions and to Mrs I. M. Craddy who paid meticulous attention to the typing of the final manuscript.

REFERENCES

Acree, T. E., Sonoff, E. P. and Splittstoesser, D. F. (1972). *American Journal of Enology and Viticulture* 23, 6.

Acker, L. (1969). *DECHEMA Monograph* 63, 203.

Adams, A. M. (1961). 'Report of the Horticultural Experiment Station and Products Laboratory Vineland for 1959-60', p. 79.

Adams, A. M. (1962a). *In* 'Developments in Industrial Microbiology', Vol. 3, p. 341. Plenum Press, New York.

Adams, A. M. (1962b). 'Report of the Horticultural Experiment Station and Products Laboratory Vineland for 1961', p. 116.

Adams, A. M. (1968). *In* 'Biodeterioration of Materials' (A. H. Walters and J. S. Elphick, eds.), p. 685. Elsevier Publishing Co. Ltd., Barking, Essex.

Allcott, E. S. (1968). *Brewers' Guild Journal* 54, 416.

Alwood, W. B. (1903). *Bulletin Bureau Chemistry United States Department of Agriculture* No. 71.

Amemiya, S., Morozumi, S., Noritaka, S. and Hiroyuki, M. (1964). *Journal of Fermentation Technology, Japan* 42, 388.

Amerine, M. A. (1958). *Advances in Food Research* 8, 133.

Anderson, R. G. and Kirsop, B. H. (1974). *Journal of the Institute of Brewing* 80, 48.

Anderson, R. J., Howard, G. A. and Hough, J. S. (1972). 'Proceedings of the European Brewery Convention Congress Estoril', p. 253. Elsevier, London.

Anon. (1931). 'Statutory Rules and Orders 1931' No. 168. H.M.S.O., London.

Anon. (1957). 'Annual Report of the Agricultural and Horticultural Research Station, Long Ashton for 1956', p. 44.

Anon. (1962a). *Journal of the Institute of Brewing* 68, 14.

Anon. (1962b). 'F.A.O./W.H.O. Technical Report Series' No. 228. H.M.S.O., London.

Anon. (1962c). 'Consultative Assembly of the Council of Europe, Strasbourg', AS/Agr/V.Sp. (14).

Anon. (1970a). *Food Manufacture* 45, 79.

Anon. (1970b). *Food Processing Industries* 39, 9.

Anon. (1970c). *Food Manufacture* 45, 81.

Anon. (1970d). *La Revue Vinicole Internationale* No. 154, 53.

Anon. (1970e). *Journal of the Institute of Brewing* 76, 442.

Anon. (1970f). 'Standards for Cider and Perry'. National Association of Cidermakers, England.

Anon. (1972). *Journal of the Institute of Brewing* 78, 288.

Anon. (1973a). *International Bottler and Packer* 47, 14.

Anon. (1973b). *Food Technology, Champaign* 27, 34.

Armerding, G. D. (1966). *Advances in Food Research* 15, 305.

Atkinson, F. E., Bowen, J. F. and Macgregor, D. R. (1959). *Food Technology, Champaign* 13, 673.

Auclair, H. (1957). *Industries Alimentaires et Agricoles* 74, 465.

Ault, R. G., Hampton, A. N., Newton, R. and Roberts, R. H. (1969). *Journal of the Institute of Brewing* 75, 260.

Äyräpää, T. (1963). 'Proceedings of the European Brewery Convention Congress, Brussels', p. 276. Elsevier, London.

Äyräpää, T. (1965). *Brauwissenschaft* 18, 161.

Äyräpää, T. (1968). *Journal of the Institute of Brewing* 74, 169.

Äyräpää, T. (1970). *Brauwissenschaft* 23, 48.

Ayres, A. and Fallows, P. (1951). *Journal of the Science of Food and Agriculture* 2, 488.

Baker, D. A. and Kirsop, B. H. (1973). *Journal of the Institute of Brewing* 79, 487.

Baker, G. L. (1934). *Fruit Products Journal and American Vinegar Industry* 14, 10.

Barker, B. T. P. (1907). 'Report of the National Fruit and Cider Institute, Long Ashton, for 1906', p. 10.

Barker, B. T. P. (1908). 'Report of the National Fruit and Cider Institute, Long Ashton, for 1907', p. 31.

Barker, B. T. P. (1911). *Journal of the Institute of Brewing* 17, 425.

Barker, B. T. P. (1912). 'Report of the National Fruit and Cider Institute, Long Ashton, for 1911', p. 11.

Barker, B. T. P. (1913). 'Report of the National Fruit and Cider Institute, Long Ashton, for 1912', p. 29.

Barker, B. T. P. (1920). 'Annual Report of the Agricultural and Horticultural Research Station, Long Ashton, for 1919', p. 110.

Barker, B. T. P. (1922). *Journal of the Institute of Brewing* 28, 517.

Barker, B. T. P. (1933). *Journal of the Ministry of Agriculture* 40, 710.

Barker, B. T. P. (1946). 'Annual Report of the Agricultural and Horticultural Research Station, Long Ashton, for 1945', p. 192.

Barker, B. T. P. (1949). 'Annual Report of the Agricultural and Horticultural Research Station, Long Ashton, for 1948', p. 174.

Barker, B. T. P. (1951). 'Annual Report of the Agricultural and Horticultural Research Station, Long Ashton, for 1950', p. 178.

Barker, B. T. P. (1952). 'Annual Report of the Agricultural and Horticultural Research Station, Long Ashton, for 1951', p. 164.

Barker, B. T. P. (1953). *In* 'Science and Fruit' (T. Wallace and R. W. Marsh, eds.), p. 29. University of Bristol.

Barker, B. T. P. and Ettle, J. (1912). 'Appendix to Report of the National Fruit and Cider Institute, Long Ashton, for 1911', p. 22.

Barker, B. T. P. and Gimingham, C. T. (1915). *Journal of the Board of Agriculture* 22, 851.

Barker, B. T. P. and Grove, O. (1927). 'Annual Report of the Agricultural and Horticultural Research Station, Long Ashton, for 1926', p. 98.

Barker, B. T. P. and Hillier, V. F. (1912). *Journal of Agricultural Science* 5, 67.

Barker, B. T. P., Hewitt, E. J. and Nicholas, D. J. D. (1950). 'Annual Report of the Agricultural and Horticultural Research Station, Long Ashton, for 1949', p. 145.

Barker, B. T. P., Nicholas, D. J. D. and Plant, W. (1952). 'Annual Report of the Agricultural and Horticultural Research Station, Long Ashton, for 1951', p. 176.

Barker, S. A., Bourne, E. J., Salt, E. and Stacey, M. (1958). *Journal of the Chemical Society*, 2736.

Basker, H. B. (1969). *The Analyst* 94, 410.

Beale, J. (1664). General advertisements concerning cider, 32. *In* 'Pomona'. J. Evelyn, J. Martyn and J. Allestry, London.

Bedford, B. P. (1972). *Food Manufacture* 47, 24.

Beech, F. W. (1953). 'Annual Report of the Agricultural and Horticultural Research Station, Long Ashton, for 1952', p. 125.

Beech, F. W. (1955). 'Annual Report of the Agricultural and Horticultural Research Station, Long Ashton, for 1954', p. 179.

Beech, F. W. (1957). Ph.D. Thesis: University of Bristol.

Beech, F. W. (1958a). *Society of Chemical Industry Monograph* No. 3, 37.

Beech, F. W. (1958b). *Journal of Applied Bacteriology* 21, 257.

Beech, F. W. (1959). 'Annual Report of the Agricultural and Horticultural Research Station, Long Ashton, for 1958', p. 154.

Beech, F. W. (1961). 'Annual Report of the Agricultural and Horticultural Research Station, Long Ashton, for 1960', p. 40.

Beech, F. W. (1962). 'Annual Report of the Agricultural and Horticultural Research Station, Long Ashton, for 1961', p. 176.

Beech, F. W. (1963a). 'Annual Report Long Ashton Agricultural and Horticultural Research Station for 1962', p. 157.

Beech, F. W. (1963b). 'Annual Report Long Ashton Agricultural and Horticultural Research Station for 1962', p. 168.

Beech, F. W. (1967a). 'Annual Report Long Ashton Agricultural and Horticultural Research Station for 1966', p. 227.

Beech, F. W. (1967b). 'Annual Report Long Ashton Agricultural and Horticultural Research Station for 1966', p. 239.

Beech, F. W. (1969a). 'Report Long Ashton Research Station for 1968', p. 103.

Beech, F. W. (1969b). *Antonie van Leeuwenhoek* 35S, F11.

Beech, F. W. (1970). 'Report Long Ashton Research Station for 1969', p. 126.

Beech, F. W. (1972a). *In* 'Progress in Industrial Microbiology' (D. J. D. Hockenhull, ed.), p. 133. Churchill Livingstone, London.

Beech, F. W. (1972b). *Journal of the Institute of Brewing* 78, 477.

Beech, F. W. and Carr, J. G. (1955). *Journal of General Microbiology* 12, 85.

Beech, F. W. and Carr, J. G. (1958). *Chemical Products* 21, 285.

Beech, F. W. and Carr, J. G. (1960). *Journal of the Science of Food and Agriculture* 11, 38.

Beech, F. W. and Challinor, S. W. (1951). 'Annual Report of the Agricultural and Horticultural Research Station, Long Ashton, for 1950', p. 143.

Beech, F. W. and Davenport, R. R. (1969). *In* 'Isolation Methods for Microbiologists' (D. A. Shapton and G. W. Gould, eds.), p. 71. Academic Press, London.

Beech, F. W. and Davenport, R. R. (1970). *In* 'The Yeasts' (A. H. Rose and J. S. Harrison, eds.), Vol. 3, p. 73. Academic Press, London.

Beech, F. W. and Davenport, R. R. (1971). *In* 'Methods in Microbiology' (C. Booth, ed.), Vol. 4, p. 153. Academic Press, London.

Beech, F. W., Burroughs, L. F. and Codner, R. C. (1952). 'Annual Report of the Agricultural and Horticultural Research Station, Long Ashton, for 1951', p. 149.

Beech, F. W., Kieser, M. E. and Pollard, A. (1964a). 'Annual Report Long Ashton Agricultural and Horticultural Research Station for 1963', p. 139.

Beech, F. W., Kieser, M. E. and Pollard, A. (1964b). 'Annual Report Long Ashton Agricultural and Horticultural Research Station for 1963', p. 147.

Beech, F. W., Llewellyn, J. H. H. and Williams, J. G. (1974). 'Report Long Ashton Research Station for 1973', p. 173.

Beech, F. W., Pollard, A. and Williams, A. A. (1968). 'Report Long Ashton Research Station for 1967', p. 72.

Beech, F. W., Williams, A. A. and Whiting, G. C. (1971). 'Report Long Ashton Research Station for 1970', p. 138.

Beech, F. W., Williams, A. A. and Whiting, G. C. (1972). 'Report Long Ashton Research Station for 1971', p. 188.

Beltman, H., Pilnik, W. and De Vos, L. (1971). *Confructa* 16, 4.

Ben-Gera, I. and Kramer, A. (1969). *Advances in Food Research* 17, 77.

Berg, H. W., Coffelt, R. J. and Cooke, G. M. (1968). *American Journal of Enology and Viticulture* 19, 108.

Beuchat, L. R. (1973). *American Journal of Enology and Viticulture* 24, 110.

Bielig, H. J. and Werner, J. (1972). 'Agricultural Services Bulletin', No. 13. FAO, Rome.

Boidron, A. M. (1969a). *Compte rendu hebdomadaire des séances de l'Académie des Sciences, Paris, Series D* 269, 922.

Boidron, A. M. (1969b). *Connaissance de La Vigne et du Vin* No. 4, 315.

Bomben, J. L., Guadagni, D. G. and Harris, J. G. (1969). *Food Technology, Champaign* 23, 83.

Bomben, J. L., Guadagni, D. C. and Harris, J. G. (1971). *Food Technology, Champaign* 25, 1108.

Bomben, J. L., Bruin, S., Thijssen, H. A. G. and Merson, R. L. (1974). *Advances in Food Research* 20, 2.

Bowen, J. F. (1962). Ph.D. Thesis: University of Bristol.

Bowen, J. F. and Beech, F. W. (1964). *Journal of Applied Bacteriology* 27, 333.

Bowen, J. F. and Beech, F. W. (1967). *Journal of Applied Bacteriology* 30, 475.

Bowen, J. F., MacGregor, D. R. and Atkinson, F. E. (1959). *Food Technology, Champaign* 13, 676.

Bradfield, E. G. and Osborne, M. (1966). 'Annual Report Long Ashton Agricultural and Horticultural Research Station for 1965', p. 157.

Braverman, J. B. S. and Lifshitz, A. (1957). *Food Technology, Champaign* 11, 356.

Brewers' Society (1973). 'Statistical Handbook', Table C10. Brewing Publications Ltd., London.

Bricout, J. (1973). *Journal of the Association of Official Agricultural Chemists* 56, 739.

Brightwell, R. W. (1972). 'Proceedings of the Twelfth Convention of the Australia and New Zealand Section of the Institute of Brewing', p. 209.

British Plastics Federation (1974). *International Bottler and Packer* 48, 74.

Brooke-Hunt, A. E. (1904). *Journal of the Bath and West and Southern Counties Society* 14, 105.

Brumstead, D. D. and Glenister, P. R. (1963). *Brewers' Digest* 38, 49.

Brunner, H. and Senn, G. (1962). *Proceedings of the Scientific and Technical Commission of the International Federation of Fruit Juice Producers* 4, 409.

Brunische-Olsen, H. (1969). *Proceedings of the Scientific and Technical Commission of the International Federation of Fruit Juice Producers* 9, 243.

Bryan, J. M. (1948). 'D.S.I.R. Food Investigation Special Report' No. 50. H.M.S.O., London.

Büchi, W. (1958). *Proceedings of the Scientific and Technical Commission of the International Federation of Fruit Juice Procucers* 1, 125.

Büchi, W. and Walker, L. H. (1962). *Proceedings of the Scientific and Technical Commission of the International Federation of Fruit Juice Producers* 4, 103.

Bulmer, H. P. (1967). *Food Manufacture* 42, 37.

Burgess, Mrs (1897). *In* 'Bygone Somerset' (C. Walters, ed.), p. 122. William Andrews and Co., London.

Burns, J. A. (1941). *Journal of the Institute of Brewing* 47, 10.

Burroughs, L. F. (1947). 'Annual Report of the Agricultural and Horticultural Research Station, Long Ashton, for 1946', p. 127.

Burroughs, L. F. (1952). 'Annual Report of the Agricultural and Horticultural Research Station, Long Ashton, for 1951', p. 138.

Burroughs, L. F. (1953). 'Annual Report of the Agricultural and Horticultural Research Station, Long Ashton, for 1952', p. 110.

Burroughs, L. F. (1957a). *Journal of the Science of Food and Agriculture* 8, 122.

Burroughs, L. F. (1957b). *Nature, London* 179, 360.

Burroughs, L. F. (1958). Ph.D. Thesis: University of Bristol.

Burroughs, L. F. (1959). 'Annual Report of the Agricultural and Horticultural Research Station, Long Ashton, for 1958', p. 164.

Burroughs, L. F. (1960). *Journal of the Science of Food and Agriculture* 11, 14.
Burroughs, L. F. (1964a). *In* 'Microbial Inhibitors in Food' (N. Molin, ed.), p. 133. Almqvist and Wiksell, Stockholm.
Burroughs, L. F. (1964b). 'Annual Report Long Ashton Agricultural and Horticultural Research Station for 1963', p. 150.
Burroughs, L. F. (1970a). 'Report Long Ashton Research Station for 1969', p. 125.
Burroughs, L. F. (1970b). 'Report Long Ashton Research Station for 1969', p. 114.
Burroughs, L. F. (1971). 'Report Long Ashton Research Station for 1970', p. 141.
Burroughs, L. F. (1973a). 'Report Long Ashton Research Station for 1972', p. 164.
Burroughs, L. F. (1973b). 'Report Long Ashton Research Station for 1972', p. 165.
Burroughs, L. F. (1974a). 'Report Long Ashton Research Station for 1973', p. 167.
Burroughs, L. F. (1974b). 'Report Long Ashton Research Station for 1973', p. 173.
Burroughs, L. F. and Carr, J. G. (1957). 'Annual Report of the Agricultural and Horticultural Research Station, Long Ashton, for 1956', p. 162.
Burroughs, L. F. and Challinor, S. W. (1949). 'Annual Report of the Agricultural and Horticultural Research Station, Long Ashton, for 1948', p. 207.
Burroughs, L. F. and Challinor, S. W. (1950). 'Annual Report of the Agricultural and Horticultural Research Station, Long Ashton, for 1949', p. 115.
Burroughs, L. F. and Challinor, S. W. (1951). 'Annual Report of the Agricultural and Horticultural Research Station, Long Ashton, for 1950', p. 161.
Burroughs, L. F. and Pollard, A. (1954). 'Annual Report of the Agricultural and Horticultural Research Station, Long Ashton, for 1953', p. 184.
Burroughs, L. F. and Sparks, A. H. (1963). 'Annual Report Long Ashton Agricultural and Horticultural Research Station for 1962', p. 151.
Burroughs, L. F. and Sparks, A. H. (1964a). *The Analyst* 89, 55.
Burroughs, L. F. and Sparks, A. H. (1964b). *Journal of the Science of Food and Agriculture* 15, 176.
Burroughs, L. F. and Sparks, A. H. (1972). 'Report Long Ashton Research Station for 1971', p. 177.
Burroughs, L. F. and Sparks, A. H. (1973). *Journal of the Science of Food and Agriculture* 24, 187.
Burroughs, L. F. and Whiting, G. C. (1961a). 'Annual Report of the Agricultural and Horticultural Research Station for 1960', p. 144.
Burroughs, L. F. and Whiting, G. C. (1961b). 'Annual Report of the Agricultural and Horticultural Research Station for 1960', p. 140.
Burroughs, L. F., Beech, F. W. and Llewellyn, J. H. H. (1973). 'Report Long Ashton Research Station for 1972', p. 163.
Burton, H. S., McWeeney, D. J. and Biltcliffe, D. O. (1963). *Journal of the Science of Food and Agriculture* 14, 911.
Business Monitor. (1973 *et seq.*). 'Quarterly Statistics' PQ 239.2. H.M.S.O., London.
Campbell, I. (1972). *Journal of the Institute of Brewing* 78, 225.
Cant, R. R. (1960). *American Journal of Enology and Viticulture* 11, 164.

Cargill, B. F. and Rossmiller, G. E. (eds.) (1969-70). 'R.M.C. Reports' Nos. 16, 17 and 18. Michigan State University.

Carlson, D. R. (1972). *Food Technology, Champaign* 26, 84.

Carr, J. G. (1956). Ph.D. Thesis: University of Bristol.

Carr, J. G. (1957). *Journal of the Institute of Brewing* 63, 436.

Carr, J. G. (1958). *Antonie van Leeuwenhoek* 24, 63.

Carr, J. G. (1959a). *Proceedings of the Scientific and Technical Commission of the International Federation of Fruit Juice Producers,* 383.

Carr, J. G. (1959b). 'Annual Report of the Agricultural and Horticultural Research Station, Long Ashton, for 1958', p. 160.

Carr, J. G. (1959c). *Journal of Applied Bacteriology* 21, 267.

Carr, J. G. (1964a). *Brewers' Journal* 100, 244, 324 and 390.

Carr, J. G. (1964b). 'Annual Report Long Ashton Agricultural and Horticultural Research Station for 1963', p. 167.

Carr, J. G. (1968a). 'Biological Principles in Fermentation'. Heinemann Educational Books Ltd., London.

Carr, J. G. (1968b). *In* 'Identification Methods for Microbiologists' (B. M. Gibbs and D. A. Shapton, eds.), Part B, p. 1. Academic Press, London.

Carr, J. G. (1970a). 'Modern Methods of Cidermaking'. National Association of Cidermakers.

Carr, J. G. (1970b). 'Report Long Ashton Research Station for 1969', p. 118.

Carr, J. G. (1970c). *Journal of Applied Bacteriology* 33, 371.

Carr, J. G. and Davies, P. A. (1970). *Journal of Applied Bacteriology* 33, 768.

Carr, J. G. and Davies, P. A. (1972). *Journal of Applied Bacteriology* 35, 463.

Carr, J. G. and Davies, P. A. (1974). *Journal of Applied Bacteriology* 37, 471.

Carr, J. G. and Passmore, S. M. (1971a). 'Report Long Ashton Research Station for 1970', p. 133.

Carr, J. G. and Passmore, S. M. (1971b). *Journal of the Institute of Brewing* 77, 462.

Carr, J. G. and Whiting, G. C. (1956). 'Annual Report of the Agricultural and Horticultural Research Station, Long Ashton, for 1955', p. 163.

Carr, J. G. and Whiting, G. C. (1971). *Journal of Applied Bacteriology* 34, 81.

Carr, J. G., Coggins, R. A. and Whiting, G. C. (1963). *Chemistry and Industry,* 1279.

Carr, J. G., Davies, P. A. and Sparks, A. H. (1972). 'Report Long Ashton Research Station for 1971', p. 189.

Carr, J. G., Davies, P. A. and Sparks, A. H. (1974). 'Report Long Ashton Research Station for 1973', p. 171.

Carr, J. G., Coggins, R. A., Davies, P. A. and Whiting, G. C. (1972). 'Report Long Ashton Research Station for 1971', p. 184.

Carr, J. G., Pollard, A., Whiting, G. C. and Williams, A. H. (1957). *Biochemical Journal* 66, 283.

Casimir, D. J. and Kefford, J. F. (1968). *Food Preservation Quarterly* 28, 20.

Challinor, S. W. (1955). *Journal of Applied Bacteriology* 18, 212.

Challinor, S. W. and Burroughs, L. F. (1949). 'Annual Report of the Agricultural and Horticultural Research Station, Long Ashton, for 1948', p. 182.

Charley, V. L. S. (1934). 'Annual Report of the Agricultural and Horticultural Research Station, Long Ashton, for 1933', p. 152.

Charley, V. L. S. (1935a). 'Annual Report of the Agricultural and Horticultural Research Station, Long Ashton, for 1934', p. 227.

Charley, V. L. S. (1935b). 'Annual Report of the Agricultural and Horticultural Research Station, Long Ashton, for 1934', p. 246.

Charley, V. L. S. (1936). 'Annual Report of the Agricultural and Horticultural Research Station, Long Ashton, for 1935', p. 150.

Charley, V. L. S. (1940). 'Annual Report of the Agricultural and Horticultural Research Station, Long Ashton, for 1939', p. 109.

Charley, V. L. S. (1949). In 'The Principles and Practice of Cidermaking'. Leonard Hill Ltd., London.

Charley, V. L. S. (1951). Chemistry and Industry, 394.

Charley, V. L. S. and Harrison, T. H. J. (1939). 'Fruit Juices and Related Products'. First Edition. Technical communication No. 11. Imperial Bureau of Horticulture and Plantation Crops, East Malling, Kent.

Charley, V. L. S. and Kieser, M. E. (1941). 'Annual Report of the Agricultural and Horticultural Research Station, Long Ashton, for 1940', p. 89.

Charley, V. L. S. and Reavell, B. (1939). Food, August, 19.

Charley, V. L. S., Ling, A. W. and Smith, E. L. (1943). 'Annual Report of the Agricultural and Horticultural Research Station, Long Ashton, for 1942', p. 101.

Charley, V. L. S., Mumford, P. M. and Martin, E. J. (1953). 'The Cider Factory: Plant and Layout'. Leonard Hill Ltd., London.

Chatt, E. M. (1968). 'Scientific and Technical Surveys' No. 45. British Food Manufacturing Industries Research Association, Leatherhead.

Clapperton, J. F. (1971). Journal of the Institute of Brewing 77, 36.

Clapperton, J. F. (1973). Journal of the Institute of Brewing 79, 495.

Clarke, R. J. (1971). Journal of Applied Chemistry and Biotechnology 21, 349.

Codex Alimentarius Commission. (1973). 'C.A.C./F.A.L. 1–1973. F.A.O./W.H.O.' H.M.S.O., London.

Codex Alimentarius Commission. (1974a). 'Recommended International Standards for Apple Juice Preserved Exclusively by Physical Means.' H.M.S.O., London.

Codex Alimentarius Commission. (1974b). 'Recommended International Standards for Concentrated Apple Juice Preserved Exclusively by Physical Means.' H.M.S.O., London.

Coffelt, R. J. and Berg, H. W. (1965). Wines and Vines 46, 68.

Coggins, R. A., Passey, R. F. and Whiting, G. C. (1974). 'Report Long Ashton Research Station for 1973', p. 169.

Commonwealth Secretariat. (1925 et seq.). 'Fruit: a Review.' London.

Comrie, A. A. D. (1951). 'Proceedings of the European Brewery Convention Congress, Brighton', p. 168. Elsevier, London.

Cook, A. H. (1963). 'Proceedings of the European Brewery Convention Congress, Brussels', p. 477. Elsevier, London.

Cook, A. H. (1969). 'Proceedings of the European Brewery Convention Congress, Interlaken', p. 225. Elsevier, London.

Coulson, H. J. W. (1898). Journal of the Bath and West and Southern Counties Society 8, 92.

Cranston, P. M. (1971). Food Technology in Australia 23, 340.

Cranston, P. M. (1973). Food Technology in Australia 25, 180.

Crowe, D. S. (1970). Food Technology in Australia 22, 556.

Crowell, E. A. and Guyman, J. F. (1963). American Journal of Enology and Viticulture 14, 214.

Cruess, W. V. (1958). *In* 'Commercial Fruit and Vegetable Products', Chapter 23. McGraw Hill, New York.

Cruess, W. V. and Joslyn, M. A. (1943). Circular 332. University of California, Berkeley.

Curtis, N. S. (1971). *Brewers' Guardian* 100, 95.

Curtis, N. S. and Clark, A. G. (1960). *Journal of the Institute of Brewing* 66, 287.

Dadds, M. J. S., Martin, P. A. and Carr, J. G. (1973). *Journal of Applied Bacteriology* 36, 531.

Daepp, H. U. (1964). *Report of the Scientific and Technical Commission of the International Federation of Fruit Juice Producers* 5, 69.

Daepp, H. U. (1965). *Schweizerische Zeitschrift für Obstbau und Weinbau* 101, 509.

Daepp, H. U. (1974). *Report of the Scientific and Technical Commission of the International Federation of Fruit Juice Producers for 1973* 13, 43.

Daepp, H. U. and Verde, C. (1968). *Schweizerische Zeitschrift für Obstbau und Weinbau* 104, 528.

Daepp, H. U. and Verde, C. (1970). *Schweizerische Zeitschrift für Obstbau und Weinbau* 106, 545.

Davenport, R. R. (1968). Membership Thesis: Institute of Biology, London.

David, M. H. (1974). *Journal of the Institute of Brewing* 80, 80.

David. M. H. and Kirsop, B. H. (1973). *Journal of the Institute of Brewing* 79, 20.

Davis, E. G. (1968). *Food Preservation Quarterly* 28, 8.

De Leiris, J. P. (1970). *Industries alimentaires et agricoles* 87, 561.

Demain, A. L. and Phaff, H. J. (1957). *Journal of Agricultural and Food Chemistry* 5, 60.

Devillers, P. (1957). *Industries alimentaires et agricoles* 74, 269.

De Vos, L. (1971). *Voedingsmiddelentechnologie* 2, 7.

De Vos, L. (1972). *Report of the Scientific and Technical Commission of the International Federation of Fruit Juice Producers* 10, 191.

De Vos L. and Pilnik, W. (1973). *Process Biochemistry* 8, 18.

De Whalley, H. C. S. and Scarr, M. P. (1947). *Chemistry and Industry*, 351.

Dixon, I. J. (1967). *Journal of the Institute of Brewing* 73, 488.

Drawert, F., Rapp, A. and Ulbrich, W. (1965). *Vitis* 5, 20.

Drilleau, J. F. and Bohuon, G. (1973). 'Académie d'Agriculture de France. Extrait du procès—verbal de la Séance du 10 Octobre', p. 1031.

Dupaigne, P. (1968). 'Report of the Seventh International Fruit Juice Congress', p. 131.

Dupaigne, P. (1972). *Report of the Scientific and Technical Commission of the International Federation of Fruit Juice Producers* 11, 125.

Durham, H. E. (1909). *Journal of Hygiene* 9, 17.

Eid, K. and Holfelder, E. (1974). *Flüssiges Obst* 41, 88.

Embs, R. J. and Markakis, P. (1965). *Journal of Food Science* 30, 753.

Emch, F. (1958). *Report of the Scientific and Technical Commission of the International Federation of Fruit Juice Producers* 1, 87.

Engan, S. (1972). *Journal of the Institute of Brewing* 78, 169.

Evelyn, J. (1664). 'Pomona.' John Martyn and James Allestry, London.

Falk, M. and Giguère, P. A. (1958). *Canadian Journal of Chemistry* 36, 1121.

Ferguson, B., Richards, M. and Rainbow, C. (1972). 'Proceedings of the Twelfth Convention of the Australia and New Zealand Section of the Institute of Brewing', p. 169.

Field, G. (1789). 'A Treatise on the Improved Method of Making Cider.' R. Marchbank, Dublin.

Findlay, W. P. K. (1959). *Journal of the Institute of Brewing* 65, 405.

Flaumenbaum, B. L. and Sejtpaeva, S. K. (1965). *Fruchtsaft-Industrie* 10, 149.

Food Additives and Contaminants Committee (1972). 'Report on the Review of the Preservatives in Food Regulations 1962.' H.M.S.O., London.

Food Standards Committee. (1971). 'Report on Vinegars.' H.M.S.O., London.

Fowell, R. R. (1965). *Journal of Applied Bacteriology* 28, 373.

Fox, J. A. D. (1972). *Brewers' Guardian* 101, 31.

Gagnon, M. (1971). 'Directive pour Fabrication de Cidre.' Laboratoire de Chimie Alimentaire, Ministry of Agriculture, Quebec.

Gane, R. (1948). *Food Manufacture* 23, 282.

Gaunt, R. C. (1939). 'A History of Worcestershire Agriculture and Rural Evolution.' Littlebury and Co. Ltd., Worcester.

Gierschner, K. (1970). *Food Manufacture* 45, 96.

Gilliland, R. B. (1951). 'Proceedings of the European Brewery Convention Congress, Brighton', p. 35. Elsevier, London.

Gilliland, R. B. (1957). *Wallerstein Laboratories Communications* 20, 41.

Gilliland, R. B. (1971). *Journal of the Institute of Brewing* 77, 276.

Gilliland, R. B. and Lacey, J. P. (1966). *Journal of the Institute of Brewing* 72, 291.

Goldstein, J. L. and Swain, T. (1965). *Phytochemistry* 4, 185.

Gomes, J. V. M., Babo, M. F. da S. and Guimaraes, A. F. (1962). *Estudos, Notas e Relatorios* No. 5, 11.

Goverd, K. A. (1973a). M.Sc. Thesis: University of Bristol.

Goverd, K. A. (1973b). 'Report Long Ashton Research Station for 1972', p. 157.

Goverd, K. A. and Carr, J. G. (1974). *Journal of the Science of Food and Agriculture* 25, 1185.

Green, S. R. and Gray, P. P. (1950). *Wallerstein Laboratories Communications* 13, 357.

Greenshields, R. N. (1974). 'Institute of Food Science and Technology 10th Anniversary Symposium. Fermentation and Biotechnology', p. 10.

Greenwood, I. F., Coltart, M. L. and Paton, D. (1970). *Report of the Scientific and Technical Commission of the International Federation of Fruit Juice Producers* 10, 173.

Grob, A. (1958). *Report of the Scientific and Technical Commission of the International Federation of Fruit Juice Producers* 1, 361.

Grove, O. (1915). 'Annual Report of the Agricultural and Horticultural Research Station, Long Ashton, for 1914', p. 22.

Grove, O. (1917). 'Annual Report of the Agricultural and Horticultural Research Station, Long Ashton, for 1916', p. 18.

Grove, O. (1918). 'Annual Report of the Agricultural and Horticultural Research Station, Long Ashton, for 1917', p. 18.

Grove, O. (1924). 'Annual Report of the Agricultural and Horticultural Research Station, Long Ashton, for 1923', p. 106.

Grove, O. (1931). 'Annual Report of the Agricultural and Horticultural Research Station, Long Ashton, for 1930', p. 195.

Guadagni, D. G., Bomben, J. L. and Hudson, J. S. (1971a). *Journal of the Science of Food and Agriculture* 22, 110.

Guadagni, D. G., Bomben, J. L. and Harris, J. G. (1971b). *Journal of the Science of Food and Agriculture* 22, 115.

Haines, R. (1684). 'A Supplement to the Treatise Entitled Aphorisms upon the New Way of Improving Cyder, or Making Cyder-Royal etc.' Tho. James, London.

Ham, J. (1827). 'The Manufacture of Cider and Perry Reduced to Rules.' Longman and Co., London.

Harada, T., Nakagawa, A. and Amaha, M. (1972). 'Proceedings of the Twelfth Convention of the Australia and New Zealand Section of the Institute of Brewing', p. 39.

Harrison, P. S. (1970a). *Chemistry and Industry*, 325.

Harrison, P. S. (1970b). *Food Trade Revue* 40, 33.

Haslam, E. (1974). *Biochemical Journal* 139, 285.

Helm, E., Nøhr, B. and Thorne, R. S. W. (1953). *Wallerstein Laboratories Communications* 16, 315.

Henry, P., Blouin, J., Fourton, S., Guimberteau, G. and Peynaud, E. (1972). *Connaissance de la Vigne et du Vin* No. 2, 177.

Hess, D. (1974). *Flüssiges Obst* 41, 235.

Hogg, R. and Bull, H. G. (1876–1885). 'The Herefordshire Pomona', 2 Volumes. Jakeman and Carver, London.

Hottenroth, B. (1951). Die Pektine und Ihre Verwendung.' Verlag R. Oldenbourg, Munich.

Hough, J. S. (1957). *Journal of the Institute of Brewing* 63, 483.

Hough, J. S. (1960). *Journal of the Institute of Brewing* 66, 475.

Hough, J. S. (1969). *Dechema Monograph* 63, 255.

Hough, J. S. (1973). *The Brewer* 59, 69.

Hough, J. S. and Maddox, I. S. (1970). *Process Biochemistry* 5, 50.

Howard, G. (1971). *Journal of the Institute of Brewing* 77, 216.

Hudson, J. R. (1968). 'Proceedings of the European Brewery Convention Congress, Madrid', p. 187. Elsevier, London.

Ingram, M. (1948). *Journal of the Society of Chemistry and Industry* 67, 18.

Ingram, M. (1958a). *Report of the Scientific and Technical Commission of the International Federation of Fruit Juice Producers* 1, 187.

Ingram, M. (1958b). *Report of the Scientific and Technical Commission of the International Federation of Fruit Juice Producers* 1, 361.

Ingram, M. (1958c). *Revue de la fermentations et des industries alimentaires* 13, 179.

Ingram, M. (1959). *Journal of Applied Bacteriology* 22, 234.

Ishii, S. and Yokotsuka, T. (1971). *Journal of Agricultural and Food Chemistry* 19, 958.

Ishii, S. and Yokotsuka, T. (1972). *Journal of Agricultural and Food Chemistry* 20, 787.

Jacquin, P. (1955). *Bulletin de la Société Scientifique D'Hygiene Alimentaire* 43, Nos. 7, 8 and 9.

Jacquin, P. (1958a). *Annales de l'Institut national de la recherche agronomique. Serie E* 7, 229.

Jacquin, P. (1958b). *Annales de l'Institut national de la recherche agronomique. Serie E* 7, 259.

Jacquin, P. and Tavernier, J. (1952). *Industries agricoles et alimentaires* 69, 115.

Jacquin, P. and Tavernier, J. (1953). 'Academie d'Agriculture de France. Extrait du procès–verbal de la Séance du 1 juillet', p. 1.
Jakovliv, G. (1947). *Industries agricoles et alimentaires* **64**, 389.
James, D. P. (1948). 'Annual Report of the Agricultural and Horticultural Research Station, Long Ashton, for 1947', p. 192.
Jansen, V. (1972). *Food Manufacture* **47**, 33.
Jaulmes, P. and Hamelle, G. (1969). *Annales de falsifications et de l'expertise chimique* **62**, 20.
Jayasankar, N. P. and Graham, P. H. (1970). *Canadian Journal of Microbiology* **16**, 1023.
Jenny, J. (1940). *Landwirtschaftliches Jahrbuch der Schweiz* **54**, 739.
Johnson, G., Donnelly, B. J. and Johnson, D. K. (1968). *Journal of Food Science* **33**, 254.
Jokantaile, T. (1972). *Leituvos TSR Mokslu Akademijos darbai. Series C.* (3), 23.
Joslyn, M. A. (1962). *Advances in Food Research* **22**, 1.
Joslyn, M. A. (1970). 'Kirk-Othmer Encyclopaedia of Chemical Technology', 2nd edition, Vol. 21, p. 307. J. Wiley & Sons Inc., New York.
Joslyn, M. A. and Deuel, H. (1963). *Journal of Food Science* **28**, 65.
Kaneko, T. and Yamamoto, Y. (1966). *Report Research Laboratories of the Kirin Brewery Co. Ltd.*, No. 9, 37.
Kasza, D. S. (1956). *New Zealand Journal of Agriculture* **93**, 561.
Kefford, J. F. (1969). *Food Preservation Quarterly* **29**, 65.
Kern, A. (1962). *Schweizerische Zeitschrift für Obst- und Weinbau* **71**, 190.
Kertesz, Z. I. (1951). 'The Pectic Substances.' Interscience, New York and London.
Kevei, E., Kozma, E. and Lendvai, I. (1973). *Confructa* **18**, 267.
Kieser, M. E. and Pollard, A. (1947a). *Nature, London* **159**, 65.
Kieser, M. E. and Pollard, A. (1947b). 'Annual Report of the Agricultural and Horticultural Research Station, Long Ashton, for 1946', p. 132.
Kieser, M. E. and Pollard, A. (1952). 'Annual Report of the Agricultural and Horticultural Research Station, Long Ashton, for 1951', p. 188.
Kieser, M. E., Pollard, A. and Stone, A. M. (1949). 'Annual Report of the Agricultural and Horticultural Research Station, Long Ashton, for 1948', p. 228.
Kieser, M. E., Pollard, A. and Timberlake, C. F. (1957). *Journal of the Science of Food and Agriculture* **8**, 151.
Kluyver, A. J. and Hoppenbrouwers, W. J. (1931). *Archiv für Mikrobiologie* **2**, 245.
Kluyver, A. J. and Van Niel, C. B. (1936). *Zentralblatt für Bakteriologie. Abt II* **94**, 369.
Knappstein, A. T. and Rankine, B. C. (1970). *Australian Wine, Brewing and Spirit Review* **89**, 52.
Knight, T. A. (1809). 'A Treatise on the Culture of the Apple and Pear and on the Manufacture of Cider and Perry', 3rd edition. H. Procter, Ludlow.
Koch, J. (1972). *Flüssiges Obst* **39**, 7.
Körmendy, I. (1964). *Journal of Food Science* **29**, 631.
Körmendy, I. (1965a). *Fruchtsaft-Industrie* **10**, 145.
Körmendy, I. (1965b). *Fruchtsaft-Industrie* **10**, 247.
Körmendy, I. (1972). *Acta Alimentaire* **1**, 315.

Kozulis, J. A., Bayne, P. D. and Cuzner, J. (1971). 'Proceedings of the American Society of Brewing Chemists', p. 105.

Krebs, J. (1971). *Flüssiges Obst* 38, 137.

Kroemer, K. and Heinrich, F. (1922). *Deutsche Weinzeitung Mainz*, 258.

La Belle, R. L. (1973). *New York State Horticultural Society Newsletter* 30, 1.

Lavollay, J., Sevestre, J. and Dussy, J. (1944). *Compte rendu hebdomadaire des séances de l'Académie des sciences* 218, 82.

Lawler, F. K. (1973). *Food Engineering* 45, 100.

Lawson, N. and Arthey, V. D. (1973). 'The Processing Market for Bramley's Seedling Apples.' The Campden Food Preservation Research Association.

Lazarenko, B. R., Reset'ko, J. V. and Ivananko, V. L. (1969). *Flüssiges Obst* 36, 513.

Lea, A. G. H. (1974). M.Sc. Thesis: University of Bristol.

Lea, A. G. H. and Timberlake, C. F. (1974). *Journal of the Science of Food and Agriculture* 25, 1537.

Le Couteur, F. (1813). *In* 'General View of the Agriculture of the County of Worcester' (W. Pitt, ed.), p. 331. Sherwood, Neely and Jones, London.

Le Rouzic, J., Warcollier, G. and Leroy-Moulin, M. (1916). 'Le Cidre et les Industries Cidricoles en Angleterre.' Ministry of Agriculture, Paris.

Lethbridge, R. (1900). *Transactions of the Devonshire Association for the Advancement of Science, Literature and Art* 32, 142.

Lie, S. and Haukeli, A. D. (1973). 'Proceedings of the European Brewery Convention Congress, Salzburg', p. 285. Elsevier, London.

Lindner, P. (1928). *Bericht des Westpreussischen Botanisch-Zoologischen Vereins* 50 (Jubiläum No.), 253.

Llanguno, C. (1971). *Process Biochemistry* 6, 27.

Lloyd, F. J. (1897). *Journal of the Bath and West and Southern Counties Society* 7, 108.

Lloyd, F. J. (1903). 'Report on the Results of Investigations into Cidermaking carried out on behalf of the Bath and West and Southern Counties Society in the years 1893–1902.' H.M.S.O., London.

Lockwood, B. (1972). *Food Processing Industry* 41, 47.

Luce, W. (1973). 'The Goodfruit Grower', October 1, 4.

Luckwill, L. C. and Pollard, A. (eds.) (1963). 'Perry Pears.' N.F.C.I. and University of Bristol.

Luh, B. S. and Phaff, H. J. (1951). *Archives of Biochemistry and Biophysics* 33, 212.

Lüthi, H. (1957). *Mitteilungen aus dem Gebiet der Lebensmitteluntersuchung und- Hygiene* 48, 201.

Lüthi, H. (1958). *Report of the Scientific and Technical Commission of the International Federation of Fruit Juice Producers* 1, 391.

Lüthi, H. (1969). *Flüssiges Obst* 36, 190.

Lüthi, H. and Steiner, K. (1957). *Schweizerische Zeitschrift für Obst- und Weinbau* 66, 269.

Lüthi, H. and Vetsch, U. (1955). *Schweizerische Zeitschrift für Obst- und Weinbau* 64, 404.

Macris, B. J. and Markakis, R. (1974). *Journal of the Science of Food and Agriculture* 25, 21.

MAF (1949). 'Economic Series' No. 50. H.M.S.O., London.

Malan, C. E. (1961). *Atti. Accademia italiana della vite e del vino siena* 12, 201.

Mändl, B. (1970). *Brauereibesitzer Braumeister* No. 22, 509.

Margerand and Theiller (1946). *Revue de Viticulture*, November.

Markham, G. (1631). 'The Whole Art of Husbandry.' R. More, London.

Marshall, C. R. and Walkley, V. T. (1951). *Food Research* 16, 448.

Marshall, W. (1789). 'The Rural Economy of Gloucestershire', 2 volumes. G. Nicol, London.

Marshall, W. (1796). 'The Rural Economy of the West of England including Devonshire and Parts of Somersetshire, Dorsetshire and Cornwall', G. Nicol, London.

Martínez, D. V., Cortés, I. M. and Márquez, J. G. (1958). *Revista de ciencia aplicada Madrid* 12, 299.

Mathew, A. G. and Parpia, H. A. B. (1971). *Advances in Food Research* 19, 75.

Maule, D. R. (1967). *Journal of the Institute of Brewing* 73, 351.

Maule, A. P. and Thomas, P. D. (1973). *Journal of the Institute of Brewing* 79, 137.

Mayer, K. and Busch, I. (1963). *Mitteilungen aus dem Gebiet der Lebensmitteluntersuchung und- Hygiene* 54, 60.

Mayorga, H. and Rolz, C. (1971). *Journal of Agriculture and Food Chemistry* 19, 179.

Ménoret, Y. (1970). *Industries alimentaires et agricoles* No. 5, 511.

Ménoret, Y. and Bricout, J. (1974). *Report of the Scientific and Technical Commission of the International Federation of Fruit Juice Producers for 1973* 13, 253.

Ménoret, Y. and Gautheret, R. J. (1962). *Industries alimentaires et agricoles* 79, 419.

Miller, J. J. and Webb, N. S. (1954). *Soil Science* 77, 197.

Milleville, H. P. and Eskew, R. K. (1944). 'A1C-63, U.S.D.A.' U.S. Department of Agriculture, Bureau of Agricultural and Industrial Chemistry.

Millis, N. F. (1951). Ph.D. Thesis: University of Bristol.

Millis, N. F. (1956). *Journal of General Microbiology* 15, 521.

Mills, D. R. and Wiegand, E. H. (1942). *Fruit Products Journal and American Vinegar Industry* 22, 5.

Monties, B. and Barret, B. (1965). *Annales de Technologie agricole* 14, 167.

Mossel, D. A. A. and Bax, A. W. (1967). *Mitteilungen aus dem Gebiet der Lebensmitteluntersuchung und- Hygiene* 58, 154.

Mouchet, R. M. (1973). *Industries agricoles et alimentaires* 90, 767.

Mühlberger, F. H. (1960). *Zeitschrift für Lebensmitteluntersuchung und- forschung* 113, 265.

Müller-Thurgau, H. and Osterwalder, A. (1913). *Centralblatt für Bakteriologie Parasitenkunde und Infektionskrankheiten II* 36, 129.

Müller-Thurgau, H. and Osterwalder, A. (1914). *Landwirtschaftliches Jahrbuch der Schweiz* 28, 480.

Nagai, S. (1963). *Journal of Bacteriology* 86, 299.

Neubert, S. (1974). *Report of the Scientific and Technical Commission of the International Federation of Fruit Juice Producers for 1973* 13, 147.

Niedt, G. S. (1970). *Technical Quarterly of the Master Brewers Association of America* 7, 246.

Nilov, V. V. (1969). *Sadovodstvo, vinogradarstvo i vinodelie Moldavii* 24, 31.

Okuda, K. and Tanase, O. (1958). *Report of the Research Laboratories of the Kirin Brewing Co. Ltd.*, No. 1, 7.

Olsen, V. B. (1956). *Brewers' Digest*, **50**.

Osgood, G. (1972). *Brewers' Guardian* **101**, 34.

Otsuka, K., Hara, S. and Imai, S. (1963). *Nippon Jozo Kyokai Zasshi* 58, 631.

Ott, J. (1965). *Fruchtsaft-Industrie* 10, 79.

Ott, J., Gaál, F. and Peák, L. (1960). *Konzervés Paprikaipar* 8, 156.

Passmore, S. M. (1972). 'Report Long Ashton Research Station for 1971', p. 179.

Passmore, S. M. (1973). Ph.D. Thesis: University of Bristol.

Paton, A. M. and Jones, S. M. (1975). *Journal of Applied Bacteriology* 38, 199.

Paul, F. (1958). *Mitteilungen (Klosterneuburg) Rebe und Wein, Obstbau und Fruchtverwertung* 8, 123.

Peden, D. H. (1974). *Filtration and Separation* 11, 131.

Peres. (1972). *Australian Wine, Brewing and Spirit Review* 90, 50.

Perkins, F. T. and Mossel, D. A. A. (1971). *Alimenta* 10(2), 67.

Peynaud, E. (1969). *Compte rendu hebdomadaire des Séances de l'Académie d'agriculture de France* 55, 1213.

Peynaud, E., Lafon-Lafourcade, S. and Guimberteau, G. (1967). *Antonie van Leeuwenhoek* 22, 49.

Phillips, J. (1708). 'Cyder. A Poem in Two Books.' Jacob Touson, London.

Phillips, J. D., Pollard, A. and Whiting, G. C. (1956). *Journal of the Science of Food and Agriculture* 7, 31.

Pierce, J. S. (1970a). *Journal of the Institute of Brewing* 76, 441.

Pierce, J. S. (1970b). *Journal of the Institute of Brewing* 76, 442.

Pilnik, W. (1970). *Gordian* 70, 343.

Pilnik, W. (1973). *Flüssiges Obst* 40, 442.

Pilnik, W. (1974). *Report of the Scientific and Technical Commission of the International Federation of Fruit Juice Producers for 1973* 13, 19.

Pilnik, W. and de Vos, L. (1970a). *Report of the Scientific and Technical Commission of the International Federation of Fruit Juice Procuders* 10, 191.

Pilnik, W. and de Vos, L. (1970b). *Flüssiges Obst* 37, 430.

Pilnik, W. and Voragen, A. G. J. (1970). *In* 'The Biochemistry of Fruits and Their Products' (A. C. Hulme, ed.), Vol. 1, p. 5. Academic Press, London.

Pilone, G. J., Rankine, B. C. and Hatcher, C. J. (1972). *Australian Wine, Brewing and Spirit Review* 90, 64.

Pocock, K. F. and Rankine, B. C. (1973). *Australian Wine, Brewing and Spirit Review* 91(5), 42.

Pollard, A. (1956). 'Cider Fruit Production Pamphlet', No. 24. Bath and West and Southern Counties Society.

Pollard, A. (1958). *Report of the Scientific and Technical Commission of the International Federation of Fruit Juice Producers* 1, 351.

Pollard, A. and Beech, F. W. (1957). 'Cidermaking.' Rupert Hart-Davis, London.

Pollard, A. and Beech, F. W. (1963). *In* 'Perry Pears.' (L. C. Luckwill and A. Pollard, eds.), p. 195. University of Bristol.

Pollard, A. and Beech, F. W. (1966a). 'Annual Report Long Ashton Agricultural and Horticultural Research Station for 1965', p. 259.

Pollard, A. and Beech, F. W. (1966b). *Process Biochemistry* 1, 229.

Pollard, A. and Kieser, M. E. (1959). *Journal of the Science of Food and Agriculture* 10, 253.

Pollard, A. and Timberlake, C. F. (1971). *In* 'The Biochemistry of Fruits and Their Products' (A. C. Hulme, ed.), Vol. 2, p. 573. Academic Press, London.

Pollard, A., Kieser, M. E. and Bryan, J. D. (1946). 'Annual Report of the Agricultural and Horticultural Research Station, Long Ashton, for 1945', p. 200.

Pollard, A., Kieser, M. E. and Beech, F. W. (1966). *Journal of Applied Bacteriology* 29, 253.

Pollard, A., Kieser, M. E. and Sissons, D. J. (1958). *Chemistry and Industry*, 952.

Porter, A. M. (1970). *Brewers' Guild Journal*, **407**.

Portno, A. D. (1968). *Journal of the Institute of Brewing* 74, 291.

Portno, A. D. (1973a). *Brewers' Guardian* 102, 33.

Portno, A. D. (1973b). *Brewers' Guardian* 102, 25.

Potter, R. S. (1966). *Proceedings of the Biochemical Society, Calcutta*, 378.

Powers, M. J. (1973). *Food Research Quarterly* 33, 29.

Presgrave, J. E. (1971). *Processing Biochemistry* 6, 29.

Radcliffe Cooke, C. W. (1898). 'A Book about Cider and Perry.' Horace Cox, London.

Radler, F. (1973). *Weinberg und Keller* 20, 339.

Radler, F. and Torokfalvy, E. (1973). *Zeitschrift für Lebensmitteluntersuchung und- forschung* 152, 38.

Rainbow, C. (1968). *Journal of the Institute of Brewing* 74, 427.

Randall, J. M., Schultz, W. G. and Morgan, Jr. A. I. (1971). *Confructa* 16, 10.

Rankine, B. C. (1955). *Australian Journal of Applied Science* 6, 421.

Rankine, B. C. (1963). *Journal of the Science of Food and Agriculture* 14, 79.

Rankine, B. C. (1964). *Journal of the Science of Food and Agriculture* 15, 872.

Rankine, B. C. (1965). *Journal of the Science of Food and Agriculture* 16, 394.

Rankine, B. C. (1967a). *Journal of the Science of Food and Agriculture* 18, 583.

Rankine, B. C. (1967b). *Journal of the Science of Food and Agriculture* 18, 41.

Rankine, B. C. (1968a). *Vitis* 7, 22.

Rankine, B. C. (1968b). *Journal of the Science of Food and Agriculture* 19, 624.

Rankine, B. C. (1973). *American Journal of Enology and Viticulture* 23, 152.

Rankine, B. C. and Lloyd, B. (1963). *Journal of the Science of Food and Agriculture* 14, 793.

Rankine, B. C. and Pocock, K. F. (1969a). *Vitis* 8, 23.

Rankine, B. C. and Pocock, K. F. (1969b). *Journal of the Science of Food and Agriculture* 20, 104.

Reavell, B. N. and Goodwin, G. A. (1958). *Chemistry and Industry*, 1450.

Reed, G. and Peppler, H. J. (1973). *In* 'Yeast Technology', p. 92. The AVI Publishing Co. Inc., Westport, Connecticut.

Reinhard, C. (1968). *Deutsche Lebensmittel-Rundschau* 64, 251.

Rentschler, H. and Tanner, H. (1954a). *Mitteilung Lebensmittel und Hygiene Berne* 45, 142.

Rentschler, H. and Tanner, H. (1954b). *Mitteilung Lebensmittel und Hygiene Berne* 45, 305.

Retail Business. (1974). 'The Market for Cider.' Special Report No. 2. Retail Business 195 May, 33.

Rich, F. W. (1897). *Journal of the Bath and West and Southern Counties Society* 7, 105.

Richard, J.-P. (1973). *Industries alimentaires et agricoles* No. 6, June.

Richards, M. (1969). *Journal of the Institute of Brewing* 75, 476.

Richards, M. (1970). *Wallerstein Laboratories Communications* 33, 97.

Richards, M. (1973). *Brewers' Digest* 48, 48.

Richards, M. and Corbey, D. A. (1974). *Journal of the Institute of Brewing* **80**, 24.

Richards, M. and Cowland, T. W. (1967). *Journal of the Institute of Brewing* **73**, 552.

Richards, M. and Cowland, T. W. (1968). *Journal of the Institute of Brewing* **74**, 457.

Ricketts, R. W. and Stott, J. (1965). *Brewers' Guild Journal* **51**, 13.

Robbins, R. H. (1967). *Process Biochemistry* **2**(6), 47.

Robbins, R. H. (1970). *Food Manufacture* **45**, 65.

Robbins, R. H. and Gresswell, D. M. (1971). *Journal of Applied Chemistry and Biotechnology* **21**, 363.

Roberts, J. (1974). *Brewers' Guardian* **103**, 27.

Roberts, A. C. and McWeeney, D. J. (1972). *Journal of Food Technology* **7**, 221.

Roten, E. (1948). *Revue romande d'Agriculture, de viticulture et d'Arboriculture* **4**, 57.

Royo-Iranzo, J. (1958). *Report of the Scientific and Technical Commission of the International Federation of Fruit Juice Producers* **1**, 13.

Royston, M. G. (1971). *Chemistry and Industry*, 170.

Rudkin, T. H., Languno, R. D. and Halter, A. N. (1973). 'Special Report' No. 381. Agricultural Experiment Station, Oregon State University.

Sand, F. E. M. J. (1974). *Report of the Scientific and Technical Commission of the International Federation of Fruit Juice Producers for 1973* **13**, 185.

Sawler, F. K. (1961). *Food Engineering* **33**, 71.

Scarr, M. P. (1951). *Journal of General Microbiology* **5**, 704.

Scarr, M. P. (1959). *Journal of the Science of Food and Agriculture* **10**, 678.

Schainskaja, I. M. (1953). *Mitteilungen der Versuchsstation für das Gärungsgewerbe in Wein* **7**, 115.

Schaller, A. (1965). *Fruchtsaft-Industrie* **10**, 263.

Schaller, A. and Blazejovsky, W. (1960). *Fruchtsaft-Industrie* **5**, 99.

Schanderl, H. and Staudenmayer, T. (1964). *Mitteilungen der Höheren Bundeslehr- und Versuchsanstalten für Wein, Obst- und Gartenbau, Wien- Klosterneuberg Ser. A* **14**, 267.

Schierbeck, J. (1951). 'Technical Information Service Report' No. 17. National Research Council, Ottawa.

Schopfer, J.-F. (1966). *Agriculture Romande* **5**, 85.

Schneider, C. (1958). *Report of the Scientific and Technical Commission of the International Federation of Fruit Juice Producers* **1**, 113.

Schultz, W. G. and Randall, J. M. (1970). *Food Technology* **24**, 1282.

Shardlow, P. J. and Thompson, C. C. (1971). *Brewers' Digest* **46**, 76.

Sharples, A. (1970). *Chemistry and Industry*, 322.

Shimada, S., Kuraishi, H. and Aida, K. (1972). *Journal of General and Applied Microbiology* **18**, 383.

Shimwell, J. L. (1937). *Journal of the Institute of Brewing* **43**, 507.

Shimwell, J. L. (1950). *Journal of the Institute of Brewing* **56**, 179.

Shimwell, J. L. (1959). *Antonie van Leeuwenhoek* **25**, 49.

Shimwell, J. L. and Carr, J. G. (1959). *Antonie van Leeuwenhoek* **25**, 353.

Shinn, B. E. (1971). *Journal of Applied Chemistry and Biotechnology* **21**, 366.

Singleton, V. L. (1972). 'Report of the 3rd International Enological Symposium, Cape Town,' Part 9.

Smith, E. L. (1950). *Agriculture* **57**(7), 328.

Smith, M. W. G. (1971). 'National Apple Register.' M.A.F.F., London.
Smock, R. M. and Neubert, A. M. (1950). 'Apples and Apple Products.' Interscience Publishers, London.
Somers, T. C. and Ziemelis, G. (1973). *American Journal of Enology and Viticulture* 24, 51.
Sparks, A. H. (1972). 'Report Long Ashton Research Station for 1971', p. 193.
Sparks, A. H. and Burroughs, L. F. (1973). 'Report Long Ashton Research Station for 1972', p. 161.
Spence, J. A. (1971). *Brewer* 57, 402.
Spiers, C. W. (1915). 'Annual Report of the Agricultural and Horticultural Research Station, Long Ashton, for 1914', p. 56.
Splittstoesser, D. F., Kuss, F. R., Harrison, W. and Prest, D. B. (1971). *Applied Microbiology* 21, 335.
Steuart, D. W. (1935). *Journal of the Society of Chemical Industry* 54, 879.
Steuart, D. W. and Duncan, J. A. B. (1954). *Chemistry and Industry*, 634.
Stevens, T. J. (1966). *Journal of the Institute of Brewing* 72, 369.
Stevens, T. J. (1972). *Brewers' Guardian* 63, 91.
Steward, S. R., Smith, J. L., Kavanagh, T. E., Hildebrand, R. D. and Clarke, B. J. (1974). *Journal of the Institute of Brewing* 80, 34.
Stewart, E. D., Hinz, C. and Brenner, H. W. (1962). *Proceedings of the American Society of Brewing Chemists*, 40.
Sudario, E. (1958). *Rivista di viti coltura e di enologia* 11, 61.
Sudraud, P. and Cassignard, R. (1963). *Génie Chimique* 89, 162.
Sugisawa, H., Kitson, J. A. and Moyls, A. W. (1970). *Confructa* 15, 280.
Suomalainen, H. (1971). *Journal of the Institute of Brewing* 77, 164.
Swain, T. (1965). *Report of the Scientific and Technical Commission of the International Federation of Fruit Juice Producers* 6, 221.
Swindells, R. and Robbins, R. H. (1966). *Process Biochemistry* 1, 457.
Tanner, H. and Sandoz, M. (1973). *Flüssiges Obst* 40, 402.
Tavernier, J. (1952). 'Guide Practique de Cidrerie Fermière.' Groupement National Interprofessional des Fruits à Cidre et Dérivés.
Tavernier, J. (1958). *Revue Fermentations et des Industries Alimentaires* 13, 254.
Tavernier, J. (1960). *Revue des Fermentations et des Industries Alimentaires* 15, 53.
Tavernier, J. and Jacquin, P. (1946). *Chimie et Industrie* 56, 104.
Tavernier, J., Causeret, J. and Hugot, D. (1955). *L'Alimentation et la Vie* 43, 8.
Tennes, B. R., Levin, J. H. and Whittenberger, R. T. (1971). 'A.R.S. 42–180.' United States Department of Agriculture, A.R.S., Washington.
Thijssen, H. A. C. (1970). *Journal of Food Technology* 5, 211.
Thijssen, H. A. C. (1971). *Journal of Applied Chemistry and Biotechnology* 21, 372.
Thorne, R. S. W. (1954). *Brygmesteren* 11, 97.
Thorne, R. S. W. (1961). *Brewers' Digest* 36, 38.
Thoukis, G. and Bouthilet, R. J. (1963). *Wines and Vines* 44, 25.
Thoukis, G. and Stern, L. A. (1962). *American Journal of Enology and Viticulture* 13, 133.
Thoukis, G., Reed, G. and Bouthilet, R. J. (1963). *American Journal of Enology and Viticulture* 14, 148.
Timberlake, C. F. (1971). 'Report Long Ashton Research Station for 1970', p. 168.

Timberlake, C. F. (1972). 'Report Long Ashton Research Station for 1971', p. 145.

Tressler, D. K. and Joslyn, M. A. (1971). 'Fruit and Vegetable Juice Processing Technology.' AVI Publishing Co., Westport, Connecticut.

Tressler, D. K., Celmer, R. F. and Beavens, E. A. (1941). *Journal of Industrial and Engineering Chemistry* 33, 1027.

Trevelyan, W. E. and Harrison, J. S. (1956). *Biochemical Journal* 62, 183.

Tschenn, C. (1934). *Fruit Products Journal and American Vinegar Industry*, December, 111.

Tucknott, O. G. (1974). 'Report Long Ashton Research Station for 1973', p. 159.

Tucknott, O. G. and Williams, A. A. (1973). 'Report Long Ashton Research Station for 1972', p. 150.

Tutin, F. (1926). 'Annual Report of the Agricultural and Horticultural Research Station for 1925', p. 117.

U.S.D.A. (1965). 'ARS 51-4.' U.S.D.A., Market Quality Research Division, Washington.

Van Buren, J. P. (1971). *Report of the Scientific and Technical Commission of the International Federation of Fruit Juice Producers* 11, 101.

Van Buren, J. P., Senn, G. and Neukom, H. (1965). *Report of the Scientific and Technical Commission of the International Federation of Fruit Juice Producers* 6, 245.

Vandecaveye, S. C. (1927). *Journal of Bacteriology* 14, 1.

Vas, K. (1949). *Journal of the Society of Chemical Industry* 68, 340.

Vas, K. and Ingram, M. (1949). *Food Manufacture* 24, 414.

Vasatko, J. and Príbela, A. A. (1965). *Izvestiya Vysshikh uchebnykh Zavedenii Tekhnologija* 6, 17.

Vaughn, R. H. (1942). *Wallerstein Laboratories Communications* 5, 5

Verspuy, A., Pilnik, W. and De Vos, L. (1970). *Flüssiges Obst* 37, 518.

Veselov, I. Y., Kann, A. G. and Gracheva, I. M. (1963). *Mikrobiologiya* 32, 610.

Vinegar Brewers' Federation. (1952). 'The Legal History of Vinegar.' V.B.F., London.

Volbrecht, D. and Radler, F. (1973). *Archives of Microbiology* 94, 351.

Voragen, A. G. J. and Pilnik, W. (1970). *Zeitschrift für Lebensmitteluntersuchung und- forschung* 142, 346.

Wainwright, T. (1970). *Journal of General Microbiology* 61, 107.

Wainwright, T. (1973). *Journal of the Institute of Brewing* 79, 451.

Walkley, R. J. and Kirsop, B. H. (1969). *Journal of the Institute of Brewing* 75, 393.

Wallace, T. and Barker, B. T. P. (1953). *In* 'Science and Fruit' (Wallace, T. and Marsh, R. W., eds.), p. 11. University of Bristol.

Wallace, T. and Marsh, R. W. (1953). 'Science and Fruit.' University of Bristol.

Walters, L. S. and Thistleton, M. R. (1953). *Journal of the Institute of Brewing* 59, 401.

Warcollier, G. and Le Moal, A. (1935). *Annales des falsifications et des fraudes* 28, 517.

Webb, A. D. (1973). 'Proceedings of the 3rd International Special Symposium on Yeasts, Helsinki', Part 2, p. 297.

Weiss, J., Sāmann, H. and Jasenek, R. (1973). *Mitteilungen Rebe und Wein Obstbau und Fruchteverwertung* 23, 367.

White, B. B. and Ough, C. S. (1973). *American Journal of Enology and Viticulture* 24, 148.

White, J. (1966). *Process Biochemistry* 1, 139.

White, J. (1970). *Process Biochemistry* 5, 54.

White, J. (1971). *Process Biochemistry* 6, 21.

White, J. (1972). *In* 'Quality Control in the Food Industry' (S. M. Herschdoerfer, ed.), Vol. 3, p. 81. Academic Press, London.

White, J. E., Westberg, M. and Robe, K. (1971). *Food Processing* 32(6), 43.

Whiting, G. C. (1961). 'Annual Report of the Agricultural and Horticultural Research Station, Long Ashton, for 1960', p. 135.

Whiting, G. C. (1973). *Journal of the Institute of Brewing* 79, 218.

Whiting, G. C. and Carr, J. G. (1957). *Nature, London* 180, 1479.

Whiting, G. C. and Carr, J. G. (1959). *Nature, London* 184, 1427.

Whiting, G. C. and Coggins, R. A. (1960a). *Nature, London* 185, 843.

Whiting, G. C. and Coggins, R. A. (1960b). *Journal of the Science of Food and Agriculture* 11, 705.

Whiting, G. C. and Coggins, R. A. (1960c). *Journal of the Science of Food anu Agriculture* 11, 337.

Whiting, G. C. and Coggins, R. A. (1964). 'Annual Report Long Ashton Agricultural and Horticultural Research Station for 1963', p. 157.

Whiting, G. C. and Coggins, R. A. (1969). *Biochemical Journal* 115, 60P.

Whiting, G. C. and Coggins, R. A. (1971). *Antonie van Leeuwenhoek* 37, 33.

Whiting, G. C. and Coggins, R. A. (1974). *Biochemical Journal* 141, 35.

Wickner, R. B. (1974). *Journal of Bacteriology* 117, 1356.

Wiegand, J. (1971). *Journal of Applied Chemistry and Biotechnology* 21, 351.

Williams, A. A. and Moorhouse, K. (1974). 'Report Long Ashton Research Station for 1973', p. 162.

Williams, A. A. and Tucknott, O. G. (1971). *Journal of the Science of Food and Agriculture* 22, 264.

Williams, A. A. and Tucknott, O. G. (1973). 'Report Long Ashton Research Station for 1972', p. 153.

Williams, A. H. (1953). 'Annual Report of the Agricultural and Horticultural Research Station, Long Ashton, for 1952', p. 219.

Williams, A. H. (1963). *In* 'Enzyme Chemistry of Phenolic Compounds' (J. B. Pridham, ed.), p. 87. Pergamon Press, London.

Williams, R. R. (1961). *Agriculture* 68, 304.

Williams, R. R. (1963). *In* 'Perry Pears' (L. C. Luckwill and A. Pollard, eds.), p. 19. University of Bristol.

Williams, R. R. (1966). 'Annual Report Long Ashton Agricultural and Horticultural Research Station for 1965', p. 90.

Williams, R. R. (1972). *The Grower*, January 29, 262.

Williams, R. R. (1974). *The Grower*, January 12, 78.

Williams, R. R. and Child, R. D. (1962). 'Annual Report Long Ashton Agricultural and Horticultural Research Station for 1961', p. 77.

Williams, R. R. and Child, R. D. (1963). 'Annual Report Long Ashton Agricultural and Horticultural Research Station for 1962', p. 46.

Williams, R. R. and Child, R. D. (1964). 'Annual Report Long Ashton Agricultural and Horticultural Research Station for 1963', p. 55.

Williams, R. R. and Child, R. D. (1965). 'Annual Report Long Ashton Agricultural and Horticultural Research Station for 1964', p. 57.

Williams, R. R. and Child, R. D. (1966). 'Annual Report Long Ashton Agricultural and Horticultural Research Station for 1965', p. 71.

Willox, I. C. (1967). *Master Brewers' Association of America* 4, 145.

Wilson, L. G., Asaki, T. and Bandurski, R. S. (1961). *Journal of Biological Chemistry* 236, 1822.

Windisch, S. (1958). *Branntweinwirtschaft* 80, 21.

Windisch, S. (1974). *Report of the Scientific and Technical Commission of the International Federation of Fruit Juice Producers for 1973* 13, 217.

Winkler, A. J. (1962). 'General Viticulture.' University of California Press, Berkeley.

Woods, D. R., Ross, I. W. and Hendry, D. A. (1974). *Journal of General Microbiology* 81, 285

Worlidge, J. (1678). 'Vinetum Brittanicum: or a Treatise on Cider.' T. Dring and T. Burrel, London.

Wren, J. J. (1972). *Journal of the Institute of Brewing* 78, 69.

Wucherpfennig, K. (1974). *Flüssiges Obst* 41, 107.

Wucherpfennig, K. and Bretthauer, G. (1968). *Deutsche Lebensmittel-Rundschau* 64, 63.

Wucherpfennig, K. and Bretthauer, G. (1970). *Confructa* 15, 21.

Wucherpfennig, K. and Possmann, P. (1972). *Flüssiges Obst* 39, 46.

Wucherpfennig, K., Possmann, P. and Kettern, W. (1972). *Flüssiges Obst* 39, 388.

Wucherpfennig, K., Possmann, P. and Bassa, K. (1973a). *Flüssiges Obst* 40, 488.

Wucherpfennig, K., Possmann, P. and Hamacher, A. (1973b). *Flüssiges Obst* 40, 266.

Wyllie, D. M. (1971). *Process Biochemistry* 6(9), 53.

Wysocki, G. and Glöckner, H. (1972). *Brewing Review* 87, 161.

Zambonelli, C., Anerzoni, M. E. and Nanni, M. (1972). *Rivista di Viticoltura e di Enologia* 25, 170.

Zelenskaya, M. I. and Tsvetkova, L. M. (1967). *Trudȳ Nauchno-issledovatel' skogo instituta pischchevoĭ promȳshlennosti* 7, 86.

4. Table Wines

RALPH E. KUNKEE AND ROBIN W. GOSWELL

Department of Viticulture and Enology,
University of California,
Davis, California, U.S.A.
and *John Harvey and Sons, Ltd.,*
Bristol, England.

I. INTRODUCTION

It has been said that water separates the people of the World, but wine unites them (Gates, 1971). We hope so. It is certainly true that the industrial, scientific and social revolutions have brought with them an internationalization of wine usage and democratization of regard for wine. As Jobé puts it (Lausanne, 1970): 'The luxury of a private cellar is no longer the prerogative of lords spiritual or temporal'. Nevertheless, along with many ways of dividing the World, there is also a division between the wine World and the non-wine

315

World. Wine culture—that is, grape-wine culture—has generally spread along the same paths as western civilization, and perhaps only now is being accepted and appreciated in far Eastern and middle-African countries. Furthermore, in the wine World itself, one can see divisions, especially when viewed through economists' eyes. In much of Europe, the customs or laws are such that the wine trade (except for interruptions by wars) has been held mostly static. Fluctuations in wine fortunes more generally reflect the total economy rather than surges of expansions or contractions in vineyard areas or winery capacities. In other parts of the wine World, wine is doing well in capturing the imagination of the public, as one says, and 'expansion' is the managerial watchword. Table 1 shows the changes in gross

Table 1

Gross wine production of selected areas (1962–1973)

	Average production (in hectolitres $\times 10^{-3}$)			Fractional ten-year increase
	1962–63	1967–71	1972–73	
Europe	204,144	226,620	257,543	1.26
Americas	35,600	37,829	41,782	1.17
California	6,061	7,708	10,358	1.71
World Total	262,198	284,561	318,148	1.21

Data taken from *Bulletins de l'Office International de la Vigne et du Vin* (Anon., 1964a, 1974a) and *Wines and Vines* (Anon., 1964b, 1974b).

wine production in some selected parts of the world over a recent decade. Great differences can be seen between various regions—a 71% increase in California while Europe's increase was similar to that of the World as a whole (26% and 21% increase, respectively). These figures are somewhat difficult to interpret because of the large fluctuations from year to year (Anon., 1973a, 1974a) even though averages for two or more years were taken. In Table 2 are given *per capita* consumption data. One can see that, in countries with large *per capita* wine consumption, say greater than 50 litres (11 imperial gallons, 13.2 U.S. gallons) per person, consumption has changed little during this Century, or has decreased; in some of the lesser wine-consuming regions, the increases have been dramatic (Table 2). We

Table 2

Per capita consumption of wine by regions

	Consumption (litres per inhabitant) in				
	1900–14	1928–38	1950–60	1961–63	1973
France	145	156	136	127	106
Italy	118	115	97	113	109
Spain	95	74	53	60	75
Portugal	80	89	98	77	88
Argentina	45	49	63	80	73
U.S.A.	2	1.5	3.3	3.4	6.3
Great Britain	1.3	1.3	1.2	1.8	5.2
Germany	0.7	5	9	12.7	21.7

Data taken from *Bulletins de l'Office International de la Vigne et du Vin* (Anon., 1964a, 1974a).

have tried to keep both of these parts of the wine World in mind in this discussion of the economic aspects of wine making.

We have not had to worry about such a division when considering the microbiological aspects; here there seems to be only one World. We will see that the microflora seems to be generally the same in all vineyards, even when they are far removed from their wine-growing neighbours. Whether the common quality of the microbial flora of vineyards comes from movements of people, or from transport of grape plants, or just naturally, is hard to say. But it is a comforting thought, and it goes well with the opening quotation to this Introduction.

II. SOME ECONOMIC ASPECTS OF THE HISTORY OF WINE MAKING

When one considers microbiological processes of economic impor-tance, wine production comes immediately to mind. Many historical examples of wine as an instrument of commerce are familiar. Although the origin of wine making is obscured in prehistory, it is clear that, by the time of man's first recordings in both Egypt and Mesopotamia, full-scale wine industries had developed. In his history of wine, Younger (1966) comments that wine-making pursuits in these areas made use of knowledge of irrigation and pruning for large-scale vineyard management. The oenological practices included techniques for pressing, racking, a sort of primitive filtration, storing and even labelling. Also, in these early times, there were wine merchants and some transportation of wine, giving further indication of its early commercial importance.

These early wines were made by natural fermentation. They were what we call 'table wines', containing generally less than 14% (v/v) alcohol, in contrast to fortified wines, wines which contain a higher concentration of alcohol (see Chapter 7, p. 478). The latter wines could have been made only much later, after the discovery of distillation. In this chapter we will confine our discussion to table wines, and to wine made from grapes.

Although shipment of wine occurred earlier, large-scale transportation came with the classic period. The Athenian Greeks emerged as experts in producing wine on a commercial scale. As they became more and more colonial, they carried wine to settlements where vineyards did not exist. As early as 500 B.C., this trade apparently extended from Greece to southern France and the upper Rhône Valley (Langenbach, 1951). Shipments were also made northward to the Black Sea area and southward to Egypt. Accompanying this economic development of wine making and wine trade was the growth of competitive vineyards and, by the third Century B.C., protective tariffs (Younger, 1966). We have acquired considerable information concerning the wine trade from archaeological diggings showing the distribution of Greek amphoras, the wine jars used at this time. The large amphoras might hold 40 litres of wine, and would seem unwieldy except for wholesale transport and trade. Much has been written concerning these amphoras, particularly about their construction and beauty; but in the perspective of our discussion, the amphoras themselves can be considered a part of the commerce of wine making and there must have been a sizeable industry for their manufacture.

Under Roman domination, wine trade continued to spread throughout Europe and North Africa and even to the Far East. Again, knowledge of grape culture and wine production slowly followed the wine trade and, by the fourth Century A.D., wine was made in nearly every locale of the Roman world where weather permitted, including Britain. On the Italian peninsula, the expansion of viticulture was dramatic during the first Century of the Empire. Not only were the vineyards profitable, but soil which was no longer good for grain could be used for grapevines. The quality of wine improved. The Romans developed such a taste for wine that by the second Century A.D. perhaps half of their wine was imported— mostly from Spain (Frank, 1959). It is even claimed that a wine type was produced especially for the Roman market (Younger, 1966). Not to be neglected is another aspect of wine economics, namely the development of the wine room, where wines, usually of local origin, could be consumed. No less than now, these inns, bars, taverns, or other drinking establishments, were extremely popular in Roman imperial times (Carcopino, 1968).

The invention of wooden casks for transport of wine, and especially for ageing of wine, was a very important event for wine commercialization. This occurred during Roman times. Apparently some glass bottles were also used but, as we shall see, the common use of glass and of tight-fitting corks for stoppers came much later, towards the end of the 17th Century.

The Middle Ages are characterized in part by the decline of economic conditions in Western Europe. Nevertheless, the setback to what is called civilization seems to have had less effect on wine production than one might think. Sometimes the monastic movement is credited with taking agricultural sciences, including viticulture, to the barbarians, yet even under barbarian domination vineyard areas were tended and even expanded. Church ritual is also often given as an important part of viticultural history. It is said that the Church carried over and maintained the required expertise from the Romans until better days, and that the monastic movement was greatly responsible for the continued expansion of vineyard areas. Younger (1966) suggests a more commercial basis. He writes 'Wine-growing was brought over the Dark Ages by private enterprise, and the traditions of viticulture were continued through the memories of lay *vignerons* rather than through the manuscripts of monastic libraries'. On the one hand, it was common for churches with small staffs to accept donations of wine for sacramental purposes, rather than produce their own. On the other hand, where religious foundations were large enough to support vineyards and wine making, the main purpose of these endeavours was commercial not theological. Still, the monastic system probably was able to provide a positive influence toward upgrading the quality of mediaeval wine, which from all indications was generally rather unpalatable. An especially successful monastery was Eberbach Abbey (*Kloster Eberbach*) founded in the Rheingau in 1131 A.D. by the Cistercian Order. These Burgundians brought with them a mastery in the art of reclaiming barren and waste areas, of clearing woods and draining marshes and turning them into fertile fields and vineyards. They cultivated the land which the Archbishop of Mainz had given them, and to which he added as the order flourished. Eventually the Cistercians cleared and terraced even the steep northern slopes of the Rhine. Langenbach (1962) says that, by the 16th Century except for Johannisberg, there was hardly a place in the Rheingau not planted by Eberbach converts. Their wine-storage capacity was approximately 300,000 litres—with one vat holding about 80,000 litres. This would seem to be more than required for celebration of the Mass!

Although international trade was never at a standstill during the Middle Ages, it blossomed forth as the economy of Europe re-awakened. With it came the availability of regional wines. Renaissance wines were probably of poor quality but, with revival of prosperity and sophistication came a restoration of connoisseurship, practically missing since the fall of Rome. The wines of Bordeaux (clarets), of southern Spain (sack) and of middle Germany (Rhenish wines) were recognized and appreciated. But, with time, the new international trade routes became selective—based on politics as well as economics. Later sections of this chapter describe the importance of such factors as climate, grape variety, fermentation temperature and other viticultural and oenological factors on wine quality, but the assessment of quality is also influenced by the customs and habits of the consumer, which are often established by economics and politics. As an example, the anti-French policies of England, through William and Mary and the Methuen Treaty (in 1703), which favoured importation of Portuguese wines into England, radically, if reluctantly, changed the wine-drinking habits of the English (Allen, 1961). The effect was two-fold. First of all, a new type of wine was developed in Portugal's Douro Valley. This port wine (which is discussed in more detail in the chapter on Fortified Wines, p. 500) is made by addition of brandy to partly fermented red must. The second effect was a revival of the recognition of the importance of ageing of wines to enhance their complexity. The use of amphoras for storing wine had been abandoned after classic Greek and Roman times. Thus the practice of allowing wines to mature, which had given some of the wines of the ancient times their high repute, had been lost. However, by the middle of the 18th Century, port-wine bottles were being made with cylindrical sides (Allen, 1961) which permitted them to be laid down, or binned, and allowed for ageing of the contents. This enhancement of flavour quality was fortuitous for port wines' best customers, namely the English, since their choice of wine markets was so curtailed. This advancement in wine art was readily discerned, appreciated and praised. By the end of the 18th Century, the practice of intentional storage of wine in bottles for ageing purposes had spread to other parts of Europe. The restoration of international trade accelerated the appreciation of this practice. Ageing of wines in bottles became especially valued with Bordeaux wines; wine historians are unanimous in their praise of clarets of the Victorian era. The fame of the wine of Burgundy did not fare as well because of difficulty of transporting these wines out of the region. It is well to point out in this discussion of some economic aspects that the accessibility of a wine location to easy routes of transport can be as important a factor as any in the wine's notability. This was true for both the Bordeaux and Douro regions. Indeed, because of access of these regions to coastal waters, in spite of the embargo on French wines, some clarets, disguised as Portuguese wine, reached England from Bordeaux via Oporto (Younger, 1966).

Another new type of wine was developed, or accidentally discovered, toward the end of the 18th Century. This had to do with *Botrytis cinerea*, a potent fungus which can infect the grapevine and have a disastrous effect on the harvest if it is uncontrolled before the fruit ripens. Infection of the stem can so weaken it that the weight of the ripening grapes is sufficient to cause breakage of the stem, and also of the heart of the grower to see most of the harvest prematurely taken from the vine and fallen to the ground. However, when the infection comes later at about the time of harvest, as it often does in cool and damp regions such as in the wine areas of the Rhine and Moselle rivers and in Sauternes, it can play an exceedingly interesting role in the ripening process. Although the appearance of the bunches bearing this infection is anything but attractive, the experienced winegrower knows this infection by the name *pourriture noble* or 'noble rot'. The effect of the mould is to cause dehydration of the berries and a subsequent increase in sugar concentration. The dehydration does not, however, bring about a corresponding increase in acidity. It does seem to add some characteristic flavour to the grapes or to the fermented product. The resulting wines, named Sauternes in France and in Germany given special picking-designations such as Beerenauslese, are highly prized. These delicious wines are sweet and contain enough alcohol to make them micro-biologically stable. We know of at least two stories concerned with the discovery of this type of wine (Shand, 1929): The year 1775 was apparently a terrible vintage year in the Rheingau because of a devastating attack of *Botrytis*. In Hochheim, nearly all of the grapes dropped before ripening and were rotting on the ground. There was some salvage collection for making rough 'peasant wine'. Later it was realized that this was the finest wine made there in 50 years. The other story is also romantic. At Schloss Johannisberg, in the same year, the absentee landlord, the Bishop of Fulda, forgot to send to the castle a very necessary document, namely the picking authoriz-ation. The harvest time passed by. In desperation, a messenger was sent to the Bishop who then gave the belated authorization. In the meantime, the noble rot (or *Edelfäule,* as it is commonly known in Germany) had done its magic and it was the best vintage in years. An appropriate monument to the worthy messenger is standing at the winery.

When the appreciation of aged clarets and other vintage wines was reaching a high point in the 19th Century, a new economic disaster fell. Diseases of the new world had come to old-world vineyards; first came two mildew fungi and then the root louse. None of these had any benevolent side effects as was described for *Botrytis cinerea*. Eventually control was gained over powdery mildew and downy mildew by the use of sulphur and copper dusts and sprays. The devastation of vineyards by the root louse, *Phylloxera*, which Allen (1961) calls 'an Attila from the New World, the Scourge of the Wine God', is now a familiar story. The destructive effect of *Phylloxera* sp. was first noticed in the 1860s. During the next 20 years, the infestation spread to virtually all European vineyards and finally even back to America, to the newly established California vineyards. The control was, and is, the expensive practice of removing old vines and replanting new vines grafted onto native American grape rootstocks. There were several outstanding vintage years in the 1800s preceding the phylloxera devastation. The opinion, more sensational than factual, is sometimes given that these pre-phylloxera years made up the golden age of vintage wines and that they never have been repeated. However, the damage was not irreversible. Recovery came slowly, but recovery came, and with it something new. The great advantage of the times since the recovery was the availability of new information from the rise of scientific viticulture and the beginnings of microbiology. Although application of the sciences was slowed in the first part of the present Century by the interruptions by two World wars, progress continued. Modern miracles of distribution and of technology, which we will be discussing in this chapter, have made more wine—good, better and best—produced and made available to more people than ever before. Surely, the contemporary era is more aptly called the golden age of wine.

We had only a brief look at some of the commercial aspects of the history of the wine industry. Perhaps the most important historical economic aspect is also a microbiological one, namely the discovery of ways of preventing microbiological spoilage. With regard to oxidative bacterial spoilage (formation of acetic acid and ethyl acetate by acetic-acid bacteria or *Acetobacter* spp.), the ancients had empirical knowledge that tightly-sealed amphoras would delay spoilage. As we have seen, this idea seems to have been lost until the development in the late 18th Century of bottles which could be stored on their sides (which was the beginning of bottle ageing), thus preventing the drying of corks and entrance of air (Allen, 1961). Before that, in the Middle Ages, the Germans understood that large storage tanks (consequently having small surface area-to-volume ratios), when kept full, would help to preserve wine from acetic-acid bacterial attack. Spoilage control using sulphur dioxide, or fumes from burning elemental sulphur, was known in early times, but apparently it was not used much for wine preservation until the late Middle Ages. Sulphur dioxide is now widely used for stabilizing all wines and, when used wisely as discussed below, it might be classified as an ideal chemical additive (see Section VII.B, p. 375).

Scientific control of wine spoilage came only after Pasteur's discoveries of the causes of wine spoilage. At a time when as much as one-quarter of France's wine production could be classified as spoiled wine, Napoleon III asked Pasteur for his help (Porter, 1972). In his characteristic thoroughness, Pasteur studied the problem of wine 'diseases', provided a solution, and gave us the beautiful drawings of wine microflora in his wonderfully illustrated 'Études sur le Vin' (Pasteur, 1866, 1873). This was not Pasteur's first encounter with wine. As a matter of fact, his basic discovery and subsequent proof that fermentation is a living process had much to do with wine. His thesis presented to the University of Paris was concerned with crystallography, especially of tartaric acid. By separating crystals of the natural acid [L(+)-tartaric acid of grapes] from the unnatural or chemically synthesized form [D(−)-tartaric acid], he came to the conclusion that naturally occurring optically active isomers are the results of some biological process (Dubos, 1960). Later he was asked to examine the problem of a spoiled production in a commercial distillery, where alcohol was produced by fermentation of sugar beets. We can imagine his excitement when he detected optical activity (from 2-methylbutanol, one of the fusel-oil components) in the product. He reasoned that the spoilage and then the alcoholic fermentation must be biological processes, and he set out to prove this hypothesis. By boiling grape juice in specially constructed flasks to prevent recontamination from air, he showed the boiled product to be stable until deliberately contaminated. Another proof involved the use of grape berries. He collected fruit which had been covered since the time of berry-set in such a way as to prevent contact of the grape skins with microbes. After collection and crushing of the fruit under sterile conditions, he showed that fermentation would not take place unless the juice was deliberately inoculated.

Pasteur's discovery of the microbiological basis of alcoholic fermentation, and of wine spoilage, had far-reaching effects. An immediately applicable solution to the spoilage problem was the use of small amounts of heat, enough to kill most of the organisms without too much damage to the product. Thus 'pasteurization' became a common practice. Pasteur was of the opinion that careful heating of wine would not only prevent future spoilage, but would also be a technique for quick ageing and a practical means of improvement of even the best wines (Vallery-Radot, 1924). It is now believed that some loss of quality accompanies pasteurization of wine, and other methods for preventing spoilage are preferred (see Section VII, B., p. 368). Nevertheless, cleaning and sterilizing procedures stemming from his discoveries of the true basis of microbiological spoilage are so commonly utilized that spoiled wines should now never reach the consumer, and seldom do.

Pasteur insisted on his ideas concerning the true basis of fermentation, and this marked the beginning of microbiological science. Strangely enough, although his discoveries were made largely in connection with wine fermentation, the great strides which followed in the discoveries of the metabolic pathways of sugar fermentation came mainly with the use of animal tissue and bacteria. We feel that, when more attention is given to basic physiology of wine yeast and bacteria under the unusual conditions of wine making, the economic and technical impact could be as great as that which resulted from the discovery of methods for prevention of microbiological wine spoilage.

III. GRAPES

More than 50 specics are recognized in the grape genus, *Vitis*, most of them native to North America and the Far East (Winkler *et al.*, 1974). However, nearly all of the World's wine is made from only one species, namely *Vitis vinifera*. This species is native to the area south of the Caucasus Mountains and the Caspian Sea. Species other than *V. vinifera* have some desirable features, such as resistance to disease and cold, which are important for the grape breeder in the development of new and more vigorous varieties. However, it is *V. vinifera* which is ideally suited for wine production. We have seen that, over the many centuries of wine making, few changes in technology occurred. It remains true that, even with our present sophistication, the most important element for production of wine of high quality is the starting material: the fruit of this unique species. Some of the reasons why the juice of *V. vinifera* is a perfect medium for wine production, as compared to other species, include: (1) the juice of the wine grape usually contains high concentrations of nutrients, making it a luxurious medium for the growth of wine yeast; (2) the natural acidity of the juice is high enough to inhibit growth of undesirable and dangerous microbes during and after the fermentation, but not so high as to be unpalatable; (3) fermentation of the high concentration of sugar in the wine grape gives a high concentration of ethanol which assists in the inhibition of microbial activity in the product; and (4) the aromas and flavours from the grapes, when carried directly over into the wine or modified during fermentation, are organoleptically pleasing.

With *Vitis vinifera* as the starting material, the most important considerations for production of good wine are the variety of this species selected, the weather of the growing region to match the variety, and the time of harvest, which is also particular for the variety. We will see that these factors influence the concentration of sugars and acids in the berry; the wine quality can be largely foretold on the basis of these values and on the ratio of these values. The importance of these elements cannot be overemphasized, but we must not overlook the important role of the viticulturist. In order to obtain a successful harvest, financially and aesthetically, the vineyard manager must also consider the kinds of pruning and thinning operations, pest controls and sometimes the need for frost protection and irrigation. In established vineyards, the decisions taken by the winemaker and viticulturalist have come about more or less empirically. In the major wine-producing countries, there has been little change in the extent of wine production in the last 10 years (Anon., 1973a), where the development of new vineyards is often forbidden or highly restricted. However, wine production has dramatically increased in some localities; in California it has almost doubled in the last decade (see Table 1, p. 316). For new vineyards, the grower is faced with decisions involving all of the above-mentioned factors and more. These include the climate of the region, the type of grape variety, the kind of resistant rootstock needed, soil type and soil nutrients, need for soil fumigation, kinds of spacing and trellising and systems of training-pruning, need for irrigation, methods of pest and frost control, control of bird and other animal depreditors, and availability of labour and marketability of the product. We shall go on to discuss some of these considerations in more detail, but we will begin with a brief look at some aspects of the physiology of the grapevine. For additional information, the reader is directed to Winkler *et al.* (1974).

Vitis vinifera is a member of the vine family (Vitaceae) and is a perennial plant with an effective tendril system. In the untrained plant, the growth will spread to amazingly high and distant reaches wherever there is support. Under good growing conditions, the plant is a prolific producer of fruit. Husmann (1905) and Winkler *et al.* (1974) reproduce photographs of an old grapevine of the Mission variety in Carpinteria, California, U.S.A., which at that time was considered to be the largest grapevine in the world. The trunk had a circumference of some 2.3 metres and in its fifty-third year it bore about 10 tons of fruit. Destined to vie for the reputation of this giant, or at least to serve as a fascinating educational exhibit, is the 'Winkler' vine on the Davis campus of the University of California. This vine, which is also of the Mission variety, has received tender, loving and expert care by Emeritus Professor Winkler. He has limited its spread to about 160 square metres (0.04 acre), but it produced the equivalent of about 40 tons of fruit per hectare (16 tons per acre) in 1973, when it was eight years old.

In the natural condition, the grapevine tends to overcrop, that is, produce more fruit than can ripen to the degree needed for wine. Good vineyard practices include thinning or removal of flower clusters or immature berry clusters to prevent delay of fruiting-bud development and delay in fruit maturity. Vegetative growth of the vine must also be restrained by pruning in order to give proper development of fruit. The grapevine has a winter dormancy period that is necessary for vine longevity, but this adds to the complexity of the pruning operations. The fruit for the next season's crop arises from buds formed during the previous growing season. These buds must be left intact by the pruner in order to have a harvest the next year. Too severe pruning results in rank growth and lower yields, and severe overcropping can stress the vine enough to restrict growth and delay maturity of the fruit. Pruning operations also give form to the vines, anticipating the desired future shape. The desired shape also depends upon the kinds of trellising and spacing of the vines being used. The viticulturist must therefore be experienced in pruning, trellising and thinning techniques to be able to control the vine for adequate vigour and for production of consistently good yields of high quality fruit.

For the winemaker, an outstanding attribute of *V. vinifera* is its capability of storing enormous quantities of sugar in its berries. The physiology of this (Winkler *et al.*, 1974) is interesting. During the winter dormant period, there is little catabolism of the carbohydrate stores of the woody plant. With springtime and the return of warm weather, the dormant period is broken. There is rapid shoot elongation and utilization of the stored reserves. During the spring, following budbreak, there comes the development of flower parts. By bloom time, the leaves are mature, photosynthesis is rapid, and carbohydrates accumulate in the shoots, primarily as starch. In the early stages of berry development the berry size increases, but the sugar concentration inside stays low. Suddenly, when the berries are about one-half of their mature size, the photosynthetic product from the leaves is directed to the developing fruit. The increase in sugar content of the berries, now represented by glucose and fructose, is extremely rapid, rising from about 4% to 20% (w/w) in the span of a month or so. At the same time, there is an interesting change in the organic-acid content of the berry. Indeed, recent biochemical studies on L(−)malic acid, one of the important grape organic acids, modify the classic description of sugar development in the berry. Ruffner *et al.* (1974) have shown that some of the sugar can come from metabolism of malic acid inside the berry itself.

Besides malic acid, L(+)tartaric acid is the other important organic acid of grapes. During the early stage of berry development, there is an increase in the contents of both malic acid and tartaric acid. It is not completely clear if this increase is due to synthesis of the two acids in the berry or translocation of them from the leaves or both (Kliewer, 1966; Kliewer *et al.*, 1967). When rapid accumulation of sugars commences, there is also a change in the acidity of the fruit; the value drops from about 20–30 g/l to 10 or below. This is caused by dilution resulting from the increase in the berry size, the decrease in activity of enzymes synthesizing organic acids, and also from respiration of the organic acids by the berry tissue. The respiration rates are affected by temperature. The final composition of the berry with respect to its acidity varies widely, depending on the climate. In cooler regions, such as northern Europe, the concentration of malic acid in the berry at harvest is often higher than that of tartaric acid. In warmer areas, such as California, malic acid usually accounts for less than one-third of the total acid content.

The root system of the grape plant is as sensitive and, for some, as fascinating to study as the above-ground counterparts. We have mentioned the terrible vineyard destruction which can be brought about by phylloxera (now named *Dactylosphaera vitifoliae*). As the common name, root louse, indicates, the pest effects its damage below ground by feeding on rootlets and at the same time poisoning the roots with its saliva. Phylloxera usually thrives on roots planted in heavy soils; in lighter soils the damage may come from other pests, including several kinds of nematodes. Nematodes, depending on the species, do their damage by causing toxic disfigurements or lesions of the roots, or by serving as grape-virus vectors. In California, another root depredator is the oak-root fungus (*Armillaria mellea*) which slowly saps the vigour of the plants by destruction of the roots, sometimes actually girdling the large roots. Some rootstocks, notably Riparia Gloire, are rather resistant (Ribéreau-Gayon and Peynaud, 1971). The only effective control of oak-root fungus and of some species of nematodes is pretreatment of the soil by fumigation. This is an expensive process and one which is sometimes frowned upon by environmentalists. Control of some nematodes can be obtained by grafting of the scion onto resistant rootstocks, which is, of course, the usual means of control of phylloxera. In some soils, phylloxera can be controlled by flooding the vineyard for 40 to 60 days during the autumn. Selection of non-*vinifera* varieties of rootstocks for use in control of phylloxera and nematodes is far more complicated than merely assessing resistance and making the graft. Intensive long-range applied research has been required to find rootstocks which will be most suitable in the partnership with the desired *V. vinifera* scion. There must be compatibility to ensure a high probability of success in the grafting process, and the union should also be without negative influences either on the yield of fruit or on the wine quality. The rootstock is chosen by taking into account its resistance to drought, to excess humidity, excess salinity, or excess acidity in the soil, and the possible presence of harmful nematodes or root rot. In addition, rootstocks very in vigour and some match certain scion varieties better than others. It is also possible to advance or retard maturation of the scion slightly by the appropriate choice of rootstock (Foulonneau, 1971). Lider (1958) has given a short history of the research on development and selection of rootstocks.

In Europe, where vineyard plantings are renewed at rather short time intervals (often every 15–20 years in Germany), the need for grafted stock-scions is great. A rather large industry has arisen for the production of benchgrafted plants (graftings made indoors, 'at the bench', and then established in greenhouses (Alley, 1974), as opposed to graftings made in the field on the rootstocks already established there). C. J. Alley (personal communication) estimates 40–50 million benchgrafts are prepared in Europe per year.

In spite of its sensitivity to various ground-borne diseases, the grape-root system has some special positive features which allow the grapevine to function in otherwise adverse conditions. Depending on the soil structure, the grape roots reach down at least two metres, but penetration of the earth much more deeply to six metres is not uncommon in very sandy deep soils. Obviously this extended root development has a good influence on the plant; water and nutrients become more readily available. The access to water is especially worthwhile. With a well developed and deep root system, the mature grape plant can survive in very dry regions without irrigation, this being an important characteristic in Mediterranean climates with long dry summers. The effect of this one attribute of the grapevine on the development of western civilization cannot be underrated when one remembers that the economic well-being of Ancient Greece, with this type of climate, was greatly dependent on its viticulture.

Naturally, several years are required before extremely deep root systems are established. For young plantings, special watering regimens must be provided for up to three years in dry-farmed regions. The expense of this irrigation is deemed worthwhile, since the plants may then survive without supplemental watering attention for scores of years. Where water stress occurs, not only may vegetative growth be severely restricted, but berry size and crop yield may be greatly decreased. If the stress is not severe enough to cause defoliation, fruit maturity of a lesser crop is usually enhanced. Kasimatis (1971) gives some guide lines for the amounts of irrigation water to bring to vines, depending on the annual and summer rainfalls and soil depths.

Historically, water has been added to the soil by surface flooding, especially by flooding of furrows made alongside the planted rows. Overhead sprinklers are now becoming a popular method of supplying water. These have an added advantage in that they can also be used as a frost-protection device, if designed for this purpose and a large enough supply of water is available. Frost protection is especially important in vineyard areas where springtime arrives early enough to break winter dormancy and while there is still a chance of late season frosts, which have a deadly effect on the young greening shoots. Often this occurs where vineyards are situated in the lower reaches of valleys and where they receive cold-air drainage from the surrounding slopes. Use of sprinklers, as well as some other methods for frost protection, are described in a pamphlet by Burlingame *et al.* (1971). Also given in this pamphlet are cost analyses of the various systems (based on 1971 cost estimates).

Increased irrigation efficiency, and perhaps increased effectiveness with relation to vine growth, have come from the relatively new method of drip irrigation. This method was first used commercially with grapes in Israel in 1958, but it had its origins a decade earlier in greenhouse culture in England. For this method, small amounts of water are continually, or intermittently, dripped, or trickled, into the soil from emitters located near each plant. The emitters can be placed at each vine along the water delivery lines. In California, delivery lines are often made of flexible tubing, placed in the vineyard temporarily to be moved to new areas when no longer needed in the matured vineyard. Permanent sub-surface pipelines are also used. Nutrients as well as water can be delivered directly to the plants by drip irrigation. At a recent international conference on drip irrigation (Anon., 1974c), even the use of sewage effluent in the trickle system was described. Some of the problems with the drip system mentioned at this conference were the clogging of emitters by particulate material and nutrients and by algal growth.

Because of the highly developed root system of the grapevine, the need for addition of nutrients is generally minimal. Soils are fairly often deficient in nitrogenous compounds and, in some areas notably in California, this element is supplied in the form of nitrates. Requirements for nitrogenous compounds are quite variable and methods have been developed to measure nitrogen deficiency before harm has come to the plant. Petiole-nitrate levels or levels of arginine in grape vines and fruit can serve as indicators of the nitrogenous status of vineyards (Cook and Kishaba, 1957; Kliewer and Cook, 1974). In some parts of Spain and France, the vines suffer from lack of iron, giving rise to chlorosis. This is because the vines cannot take up sufficient iron from the soils which are rich in calcium and have a high pH value. Attempts are made to correct this condition by treating the soil with iron salts, with or without the addition of a sequestering agent; but the most satisfactory method is the choice of an appropriate calcium-resistant rootstock. Other common deficiencies are those of phosphorus, zinc and boron. In California, boron toxicity is more common than boron deficiency. This malady can only be corrected by flushing away the mineral with irrigation water with a low boron content (Winkler et al., 1974).

In casual observation of vineyards in different World-wide locations, one of the great surprises is the variation in arrangement of the vineyards, particularly in the spacing and trellising of the plants. In

Figures 1, 2 and 3 are shown typical vine plantings in France, Germany and California, U.S.A. Tradition probably plays a big role in deciding the style of vineyards. There is a need for more data to indicate which of the systems of spacing and trellising, for particular varieties, is best in terms of crop yields and, more importantly, in terms of the quality for wine production. The machine age has, of course, had a great influence on the form of new plantings. Wherever practical, wide spacings are needed for mechanical cultivation and

Fig. 1. Pomerol (Bordeaux) vineyard in late spring.

pesticide control and, nowadays, for mechanical harvesting. Winkler (1959) discusses the effects of spacing on yields, and Gagnon (1973) gives the effects of spacing on cash flow in the development of vineyards.

Considering mechanical harvesting, the use of machines to harvest grapes has had qualified success in some wine-growing areas. The economic advantages of mechanical harvesting are obvious. Besides the cost factors, another appeal is the better control which the winemaker has over the precise time of the harvest. Many fewer persons are involved in the picking; two to four people may handle the harvesting machine and the collection vehicles, doing the work

Fig. 2. Harvest time in the Rheingau near Rüdesheim, West Germany.

Fig. 3. Mechanical harvesting in Salinas Valley, California, U.S.A.

carried out previously by approximately 65 people (Mendall, 1975). Thus the logistics for arranging the time of the harvest are simpler. At present, there are several systems of harvesting by machine in operation, and several opinions as to their relative worth. Perhaps surprisingly, there are differences of opinion as to the value of mechanical harvesting at all, by any of these systems. In other words, mechanical harvesting has not met overall acceptance because of problems with unsuitable terrain and trellising, difficulties of removing berries from some wine-grape varieties, problems of collection of other plant parts besides berries (leaves and stems), browning and prefermentation of the exposed juice, large capital outlay for single annual usage, and sociological problems arising from the decreased demand for hand labour. Some of these factors, and others, have been reviewed by Amerine and Ough (1972). In spite of these shortcomings, mechanical harvesting has had a definite impact and many of the difficulties listed above are expected to be resolved in the near future. Figure 3 (p. 333) shows a harvesting machine in operation.

The European vine is subject to numerous fungal infections (Ribéreau-Gayon and Peynaud, 1971). Two infections were especially troublesome during the last Century, namely, powdery mildew, caused by the ascomycete *Uncinula necator* (better known under the name of the imperfect form *Oïdium tuckeri*), and downy mildew, caused by the phycomycete *Plasmopara viticola*. Other significant infections are black rot, caused by the ascomycete *Guignardia bidwellii*; grey rot, caused by the ascomycete *Botryotinia fuckeliana* (more often known under the name of the imperfect form *Botrytis cinerea*); and black spot (anthracnose) caused by an imperfect fungus *Sphaceloma ampelinum* (or *Elsinoë ampelina*). This is not a comprehensive list. Hewitt (1974) discusses the characteristics and control of fungus infection of grape berries in California.

Historically it is of interest that a number of these pests were introduced into Europe from resistant vines imported from America. First to arrive was *Oïdium* in 1845. This was followed in 1868 by the root louse *Phylloxera* and by *Plasmopara* in 1878. All three of these invasions caused great devastations to European vines and many vineyards were abandoned. In 1885 black rot also arrived but, by that time, the treatment of fungal infections was better understood and it did not cause such widespread damage.

Infection with *Oïdium* remains widespread. This mould attacks all green parts of the vine. If allowed to persist, the berries split so that the seeds are visible and the surface is covered with a grey powder. Traditionally the vines are treated with finely divided sulphur early in the season, and this probably is still the most effective treatment available.

Plasmopara viticola is a most serious disease of the vine in areas where the humidity remains high in the summer. In such regions, spraying is a routine procedure until at least June if the vineyard is in the northern hemisphere. Traditionally copper sulphate, precipitated either with calcium hydroxide or sodium carbonate, was used, the object being to bring copper into contact with the under surfaces of the leaves in such a form that it would not be washed off by the first shower of rain.

Treatment with copper, in the form of Bordeaux or Burgundy mixture, was at one time the most usual method of combating all fungus diseases except *Oïdium*; but it has been demonstrated that copper in this form has certain phytotoxic effects (Boubals *et al.*, 1957), and its use is becoming obsolete. Some organic fungicides are effective, notably captan, phaltan, zineb and maneb. The spectrum of diseases against which each is active varies. All are good against downy mildew, black rot and anthracnose. Various combinations of copper and organic fungicides are also in use to combine the advantages of both (Anon, 1973b).

Botrytis cinerea, or the noble rot, can have severe damaging effects on the grape plant if the infection comes before ripening of the fruit. Although this kind of damage is rare in California, it can be of disastrous proportions in more humid regions. The damage is nowadays usually controlled by application of the chemical Benomyl, otherwise known as Benlate. We have seen (Section II, p. 321) that this infection of white grapes is not necessarily a negative quality factor. In the Sauternes and Barsac districts of France, the white grapes are attacked by *Botrytis cinerea*, especially when the weather is warm and humid. The mould on the skin allows the berry to lose moisture. It shrivels and the percentage of sugar in the juice increases. These berries, especially if the shrivelled ones can be kept separate at the vintage, produce a juice with a strength of up to about 30° Brix (see Chapter 1, p. 35). The wine is partially fermented and sold sweet. The mould gives it a special flavour; the glycerol and volatile acid contents tend to be high. The Auslese wines, produced from Riesling grapes in the Rhine wine areas, are somewhat similar, although the infection occurs at lower temperatures so that picking must be very late.

The grapevine can also be host for a variety of virus infections. These infections are systemically associated with the vine, and will be carried in all new plantings made from cuttings of the diseased vine. Grapevine viruses can be soil-borne or spread naturally by leafhoppers and nematodes of the genera *Xiphinema* and *Longidorus* (Raski *et al.*, 1973; Winkler *et al.*, 1974). Virus-free stock can be obtained by heat treatment of the dormant wood, and great efforts are being made in California to make new plantings only of virus-free stock. In Europe, the research interest concerning virus disease seems to be more with the breeding of virus-resistant stock. Vineyards of virus-free vines are being viewed with great interest by viticulturists and winemakers alike, since it is expected that the disease-free vines will show substantially better patterns of maturity for the wine harvest; see Hewitt (1970) for a discussion of the virus diseases of the grapevine.

The above-mentioned considerations for proper grape cultivation are of little benefit to the winemaker if the variety of grape selected for planting is not suited to the climatic region. This was exemplified in the early wine industry in California. For decades, varieties of grapes were widely planted in the wrong locations because of the easy availability of the variety or because the winemaker was familiar with it in its original European setting. What was needed, first of all, was a system for describing or delimiting the various climatic regions of the State. The use of heat summation data ('degree days') to define the climate of a region (Amerine and Winkler, 1944; Winkler *et al.*, 1974) is now widely used as the best guide for varietal plantings in new regions. By this method, the average amount of 'heat' received per year (during the growing season from April to October) is calculated. To calculate this value, the average temperatures on each day above $10°C$ are summed. No significant growth of the vine, depending on variety, is noted below a temperature of $10°C$. While this method is only a first approximation, it is an important one, and its application has been of inestimable value to the Californian wine industry and undoubtedly in many other new wine-industry regions of the World.

Once the climatic region has been delimited, then the proper varieties for that region need to be defined. These selections are determined empirically and the decisions are complicated. Data collection over many years must be made. These data should include evaluations of crop yield and of the quality of wine produced therefrom. To be of worth, the information collected from various regions for a particular variety should be standardized as to rootstock, kind of soil and need for irrigation. A sufficient number of different pickings should be made to obtain wine from grapes harvested at the optimal maturity. Plantings from the same clone of variety should be made, and only 'indexed' stock (that free from diseases) should be used. In spite of all of these complications, recommendations for varietal selections for defined regions are available (Amerine and Winkler, 1963; Rankine et al., 1971). Nevertheless, some short-sighted vineyard managers would rather plant varieties with the most renowned names rather than those more properly suited to the locale. In well-established winegrowing countries, there are lists of recommended varieties for each area. Often these varieties must be used if the name of the area appears on the label. France has a very complete system (Loustaunau-Deguilhem, 1946).

Varietal planting selections have also been based on other systems. A method widely used in Europe involves a comparison of the harvest time of the variety in question with the harvest time of a single standard variety, in this case Chasselas doré. Pulliat (1888) listed the harvest times of a thousand varieties and compared them with Chasselas du Doubs (Chasselas doré).

Fitting existing varieties of grapevines to the proper climatic region is one thing, but to 'make' new varieties for these regions is something else. And that is exactly what plant breeders and geneticists are doing. We have already mentioned the development of new varieties for pest and disease resistance. But now we refer to new varieties for production of quality table wines in regions which had hitherto been considered unsuitable. Two important examples are the development and selection of the varieties Emerald Riesling and Ruby Cabernet by Professor Olmo at the University of California at Davis. Plantings of these two varieties in California now exceed eight thousand hectares (twenty thousand acres; Anon., 1974d).

Once the well equipped and knowledgeable winemaker has control over obtaining the best grown grapes of the best variety for the region, all that is needed is control over the harvest time. In cold or cool regions, one can more or less equate the optimum harvest time with the sweetness of the fruit, that is with the concentration of sugar here expressed as Brix percent (w/w) soluble solids. In California, it is common to hear the term 'sugar point' used, indicating the maturity of the harvested fruit and the price for the crop. In Germany, the legal definition of wine quality is in terms of the amount of sugar (or the potential amount of alcohol) at harvest; increasing quality corresponds to later or selected harvests of more mature and sweeter fruit (Hieke *et al.*, 1971). There is the further advantage for the grower in cool regions to wait for later harvesting, weather permitting, since ripening will also increase the weight of the crop. In warmer regions, the concentration of acid as well as that of sugar ought to be considered. Classification of wine varieties by the Brix:acid ratios of the must for regions was suggested by Amerine and Winkler (1940). Brix:acid ratios are calculated from the number of degrees Brix and from titratable acidity expressed as percent (w/v) tartaric acid. The practice of using Brix:acid ratios of the must has been applied as a criterion for maturity of grapes (Ough and Singleton, 1968; Ough and Alley, 1970). In cooler regions, the quality of wine obtained increased with the Brix:acid ratio at harvest. In warmer areas, the highest quality wine came from grapes at some optimal Brix:acid ratio around 30; the optimal ratios were dependent upon the variety and the region. In these investigations, the quality of the wine was determined by sensory evaluation by an expert taste panel, and the significance of the results subjected to statistical analysis. Brix:acid ratios have had some commercial application for measurement of crop maturity; in some instances in California, growers are penalized in payment for their crop if the ratio does not fall within specified limits. In the German co-operative at Gau-Bickelheim, the member farmers receive less payment when their grapes are too high in acid and have too low Brix:acid (Oechsle:acid) ratios (R. E. Kunkee, personal observation).

In the beginning of this section of the chapter, we mentioned the importance of non-*vinifera* grape varieties, native to North America, which are more disease- and cold-resistant than the *vinifera* varieties. These varieties are used in breeding programmes for the development of more resistant grape vines and for use as *Phylloxera*-resistant rootstocks. Because of their cold tolerance, some of them, especially varieties of the species *V. labrusca*, are used for wine making in regions too cold for *V. vinifera*. There are many production problems with the use of these 'Concord-type' grapes. They are generally low in sugar, high in acid, have 'slip skins' which make them difficult to crush, and contain methyl anthranilate, a compound which gives the wine a peculiar 'foxy' flavour. Over sixty thousand tons of grapes are crushed annually in New York State (U.S.A.) for wine production (about 8% of the total U.S.A. production), although some of these grapes are 'French hybrids' (hybrids of European and American species). Further economic considerations of vineyard practices, including some cost estimates, are given in the appendices of Winkler *et al.* (1974).

IV. MUST TREATMENT

Grape juice is naturally conducive to a clean alcoholic fermentation. We have seen that, except for addition of sulphur dioxide, little improvement in must-handling technology was deemed necessary from ancient until near-modern times. Mere exposure of the juice to the endogenous yeast in the environment was the necessary starting point. For red-wine fermentation, the stems, skins and seeds remain in contact with the fermenting must until the end of the alcoholic fermentation, when the wine is separated from them by draining and pressing. For white-wine fermentation, it was discovered at sometime in the past that early separation of the juice from the stems, skins and seeds decreases the astringency and brownness of the wine. In recent years, other important innovations of these time-tested methods of must handling have been adopted; we discuss some of these in this section of the chapter.

Grape musts (and wines) are subject to oxidative browning. This is especially noticeable in white-wine fermentation, but must also be heeded in fermentation of red wines. The oxidation reactions are inhibited by use of anaerobic conditions or by removal of particulate material (Amerine and Ough, 1972). Sulphur dioxide is a very effective inhibitor of the browning reactions, and it is usually added (in the form of solid potassium metabisulphite) to the grapes before they are crushed. Alternatively, grapes which have been crushed in the field can have a concomitant addition of sulphur dioxide. Field

crushing is sometimes used where the grapes are harvested mechanically, or in very northern regions such as the Rhine Valley, where the
temperature of the grapes and of the air is generally low during the
harvest time. We have found wines made from field-crushed grapes,
with immediate addition of sulphur dioxide at crushing, to be of high
quality. (The use of sulphur dioxide is discussed further in Section
VIII, p. 375). Another way of inhibiting oxidative reactions is the
use of equipment to maintain anaerobic conditions in the must. This
is done by the maintenance of a blanket of carbon dioxide continually over the grapes before, during and after crushing. It is
claimed that not only is the finished (white) wine lighter in colour,
but that it also retains more fruitiness and freshness (Rankine, 1974).
On the other hand, van Wyk (1973) has demonstrated that, if
oxidation of Riesling, Steen and Palomino juices occurs before
fermentation, phenols are precipitated and the wine produced is
more resistant to subsequent oxidation. There seemed to be no
correlation between the degree of oxidation of the must and the
tasters' rating of the quality of the wine produced.

Again for white wines, settling, centrifugation or vacuum filtration
of the must are effective means of removing the particulate browning
enzymes. Pretreatment of the juice with pectic enzymes can facilitate
these operations. Centrifugation will also aid in the removal of
elemental sulphur which might be present on grapes which had
recently been dusted or sprayed. Thus centrifugation is also a means
of preventing formation of hydrogen sulphide in the making of white
wines. White and Ough (1973) have shown that the polyphenol
oxidase activities (or the oxygen-uptake capabilities) of the must are
greatly dependent upon the variety of grape from which the juice
was taken. Of the 24 varieties tested, White Riesling had a moderate
capacity for oxygen uptake, while there was little uptake in Merlot
or Flora musts. Pinot blanc variety had by far the fastest rate of
uptake, it being twice that of its nearest competitor, Grenache. Any
of these treatments for inhibiting browning add expense to the
wine-making operation. The judicious winemaker should therefore
apply these treatments as dictated by experience with respect to each
grape variety.

In red-wine production, the skins are left in contact with the
fermenting wine must in order to allow ethanolic extraction of the

pigments which are located in the grape skin tissue. At some point during or at the end of the fermentation, depending upon the degree of colour extraction sought, the skins are removed with the aid of a press. Handling of the material before the time of pressing is expensive since the skins, which tend to float, should be held in contact with the liquid as much as possible. Many attempts, usually involving heat, to remove pigments from the skins before the beginning of the fermentation at first met with limited success (Amerine *et al.*, 1972). One of these techniques, referred to as thermovinification, has now become widespread. One of us (R.W.G.) has seen it in commercial use in Australia, in France in the Midi as well as in Bordeaux, and in Germany in Baden-Württemberg. The equipment is manufactured in Italy and in France. There are two main variants, one in which all of the must is heated by steam in a rotary heat exchanger, the other in which the free-run juice is separated, heated in a heat exchanger and then used to extract the pigment from the pomace which is moved through the hot liquid by means of an archimedean screw. Both methods have been successful, but proper control of temperature, sulphur dioxide content and time of maceration is essential. The wine produced differs in style from that prepared in a more orthodox way, but often scores as high for quality (da Rosa, 1972; Wagner, 1972; Milisavljevic, 1972; Coulon, 1971; Nègre *et al.*, 1971; Troost, 1971).

Modernizations of vinification practices for production of red wine in the premium regions of western France are reviewed by Amerine and Ough (1972). These changes include shortening the time of fermentation 'on the skins' before pressing to decrease the amount of astringency and to shorten the time for ageing. Continuous operations are generally more economic than batch processes. Equipment for continuous stemming, crushing and pressing operations (Amerine *et al.*, 1972; Amerine and Ough, 1972) are now evident in many wineries. Discussions of other recent developments in must handling and in other winery operations can be found in reviews by Rankine (1971a, 1973) and by Amerine and Ough (1972). Descriptions of modern equipment for stemming, crushing and pressing can be found in oenological source books such as Amerine *et al.* (1972), Amerine and Joslyn (1970) and Troost (1972).

V. ALCOHOLIC FERMENTATION

The juice within the intact healthy grape berry is sterile, and the inoculum from a natural or 'spontaneous' fermentation—in contrast to a fermentation initiated by inoculation with a yeast starter culture—comes from the grape skin. The distribution of yeast on grape skins has been elegantly shown with the use of the scanning electron microscope (Belin, 1972; Belin and Henry, 1972, 1973). The yeasts are not distributed evenly over the skin and appear to be in a slowly reproducing state except where there are breaks in the skin which might allow escape of some juice. The predominant yeasts present on the skins, at least in warm climates, are those with lower tolerance to ethanol, generally apiculate yeasts (Kunkee and Amerine, 1970). These yeasts may survive the alcoholic fermentation (Malan and Cano Marotta, 1959; Castelli, 1969; Carisetti and Kunkee, 1975). Nevertheless, their activities are suppressed by ethanol and they are soon overwhelmed by more ethanol-tolerant faster-growing yeasts. These latter yeasts are also found on the grape skin, but in smaller numbers (Domercq, 1957; Castelli, 1969). The succession of yeast types in a spontaneous wine fermentation is often given as: *Kloeckera* spp., *Hansenula* spp., *Saccharomyces cerevisiae* and *Sacch. bayanus,* using the appellations recommended by Lodder (1970) (Kunkee and Amerine, 1970). In warmer regions, *Kloeckera* spp. are replaced by their perfect forms, namely *Hanseniaspora* spp. There seem to be several important varieties of *Sacch. bayanus.* The varieties previously classified in the species *Sacch. oviformis* are the types referred to here. It is worth mentioning that the revised classification of the wine yeasts (Lodder, 1970) has not been universally accepted (Castelli and Rossi, 1974).

In newer wine-growing areas, such as California, South Africa and Australia, where the establishment of a persistent and desirable microflora in the vineyards may not be so certain, winemakers prefer to use yeast starter cultures. A detailed description of the distribution of yeast in a new vineyard, in an area with very few grapes (south west England), shows how rarely good-fermenting yeasts occur in these conditions (Davenport, 1973). Descriptions of the large-scale production of yeast starter cultures have been given by De Soto (1955) and Knappstein and Rankine (1970). The availability of wine-yeast strains and commercial yeast-starter cultures has been given by Kunkee and Amerine (1970). Generally, an inoculum of 2 to 10% is used. Inoculation with a starter culture has the advantage of shortening the lag time for the yeast population to develop and to assure a fermentation with a yeast strain of known characteristics. There is a legitimate disagreement, however, over the relative merits of the two kinds of inoculation, namely the use of starter cultures *versus* spontaneous fermentation. Some oenologists (Renaud, 1939–40; Sisani, 1948; and others, referred to in Kunkee and Amerine, 1970) believe that mixed cultures, especially the succession of organisms, provide flavourful end products which the 'pure strains' cannot duplicate. Other winemakers find that spontaneous fermentation allows for wild, non-wine yeast development which can result in some off-flavours such as that produced by hydrogen sulphide. For a further discussion of the relative merits of mixed yeast fermentations, as compared with the use of pure strains, see Kunkee and Amerine (1970), Knappstein and Rankine (1970) and Rankine (1972). Obviously more data are needed. Most wine yeasts are more tolerant to sulphur dioxide than non-wine yeasts, or they will adapt more easily to sulphur dioxide. Future controls on the use of sulphur dioxide, restricting the amounts that can be added to must (see Section VIII, p. 375), will tend to encourage the practice of using yeast starter cultures. With lower concentrations of sulphur dioxide, the winemaker will be reluctant to depend on the natural wine yeasts for a spontaneous fermentation because of the competition from non-wine yeasts, which would no longer be inhibited.

Yeasts are defined as fungi whose predominant growth form is unicellular (Lodder, 1970). A list of yeasts found on grapes, in musts, in wines (both table and fortified) and in wineries, has been given by Kunkee and Amerine (1970). Table 3 is based on this listing, but has been revised to include new information already given in this chapter and in a review article by Amerine and Ough (1972). Also included are yeasts which have recently been found associated with wine in the Cognac area (Park, 1974). Nomenclature of the yeasts listed in Table 3 has been updated to conform with the taxonomy of Lodder (1970). On healthy berries, moulds (non-yeast fungi) which might also be present, are of little consequence since

Table 3

Yeasts reported on grapes, in musts and in wines
Yeasts marked [a] are species or varieties accepted by Lodder (1970)

Genus and species	Notes or where reported
Brettanomyces	
[a] *bruxellensis*	In musts and wines
bruxellensis var. *lentus* (see *Br. bruxellensis*)	Differs in rate of growth
bruxellensis var. *nonmembranae-faciens* (see *Br. bruxellensis*)	In a must
[a] *claussenii*	
[a] *custersii*	In musts and wines
[a] *intermedius*	In South African wines
italicus (see *Torulopsis bacillaris*)	
[a] *lambicus*	In musts and wines
patavinus (now *Br. intermedius*)	In musts and wines
schanderlii (now *Br. intermedius*)	In South African wines
vini (now *Br. intermedius*)	In wines
Candida	
[a] *albicans*	
[a] *boidinii*	
[a] *brumptii*	In wines, rare
[a] *catenulata*	From the sherry district of Spain
[a] *guilliermondii*	In a dry table wine and in winery
guilliermondii var. *membranae-faciens* (now *Pichia ohmeri*)	
[a] *ingens*	
intermedia var. *ethanophila*	
[a] *krusei*	Common in musts and in wines
[a] *lipolytica*	
[a] *melinii*	In musts and wines, but rare in Greek and South African musts
mycoderma (now *C. valida* or *C. vini*)	Very common
[a] *parapsilosis*	In a cloudy wine and in winery, in South African and Czechoslovakian musts and wines
pulcherrima (now *Metschnikowia pulcherrima*)	Common in musts and wines; on grapes
reukaufii (now *M. reukaufii*)	
[a] *rugosa*	In a California wine; rare
[a] *sake*	Formerly included in *C. vanriji*
scottii (now *Leucosporidium scottii*)	In Czechoslovakia; on green grapes from New Zealand
[a] *solani*	In Greek musts
[a] *sorbosa*	

[a] *stellatoidea*	In South African musts; on grape flowers
[a] *tropicalis*	Isolated from a film on grape juice, in Greek musts
[a] *utilis*	In Spanish musts; in a cork stopper
[a] *valida* (see *C. vini*)	Formerly included in *C. mycoderma*
vanriji (now *C. sake*)	In grape juice
[a] *veronae*	Formerly *Trichosporon veronae*
vinaria (now *C. zeylanoides*)	In Czechoslovakia
[a] *vini* (see *C. valida*)	Formerly included in *C. mycoderma*
[a] *zeylanoides*	

Citeromyces
[a] *matritensis*	Formerly included in *T. globosa*

Cryptococcus
[a] *albidus*	In wine, rare
[a] *albidus* var. *albidus*	Formerly *T. pseudaeria*
[a] *albidus* var. *diffluens*	Formerly *Cr. diffluens*
diffluens (now *Cr. albidus* var. *diffluens*)	On green grapes in New Zealand
[a] *laurentii*	In wine, including a fortified wine, but rare
[a] *luteolus*	In a table wine

Debaryomyces
dekkeri (now *Saccharomyces fermentati*)	
globosus (now *Sacch. kloeckerianus*)	On grapes and in grape juice
[a] *hansenii*	In a must, rare
kloeckeri (now *Deb. hansenii*)	Very rare; reported once in California
kursanovi	In German musts
nicotianae (now *Deb. hansenii*)	In musts
[a] *phaffii*	On grapes in Cognac region
vini (see *Pi. vini*)	In a spoiled wine

Dekkera
[a] *bruxellensis*	Perfect form of *Br. bruxellensis*
[a] *intermedia*	Perfect form of *Br. intermedius*

Endomyces   In musts

Endomycopsis
lindneri (see *E. vini*)	On grapes and in must in Brazil
[a] *vini*	Isolated in Brazil

Hanseniaspora
apuliensis (now *H'spora uvarum*)	In Italian musts; in wine
guilliermondii (now *H'spora uvarum* or *H'spora valbyensis*)	

Table 3—*continued*

Genus and species	Notes or where reported
Hanseniaspora—continued	
[a] *osmophila*	Formerly included in *H'spora vineae*
[a] *uvarum*	
[a] *valbyensis*	In wine, especially in warm countries
vineae (see *H'spora osmophila*)	From vineyard soil
Hansenula	
[a] *anomala*	Common
[a] *saturnus*	In wine made from late-harvested grapes
schneggii (see *H. anomola*)	In wine
suaveolens (see *H. saturnus*)	In wine
[a] *subpelliculosa*	In Spanish musts
subpelliculosa var. *jerezana*	From the sherry district of Spain
Hyalodendron	In cellars
Issatchenkia	
orientalis (now *Pi. kudriavzevii*)	
Kloeckera	
[a] *africana*	Fairly common on grapes and in musts and wine
[a] *apiculata*	Very common
[a] *corticis*	In musts and wines; rare
[a] *javanica* var. *javanica*	Formerly included in *Kl. jensenii*
[a] *javanica* var. *lafarii*	Formerly included in *Kl. lafarii*
jensenii (now *Kl. javanica* var. *javancia*)	In musts in Sardinia
lafarii (now *Kl. javanica* var. *lafarii*)	
magna (see *Kl. corticis*)	In musts in Italy
Kluyveromyces	
[a] *lactis*	In the sherry district of Spain; in sparkling wine
[a] *marxianus*	Formerly included in *Sacch. marxianus*
[a] *vanudenii*	Formerly included in *Sacch. vanudenii*
[a] *veronae*	Formerly included in *Sacch. veronae*
Leucosporidium	
[a] *capsuligenum* (see *T. capsuligenus*)	
[a] *scotti*	

Metschnikowia
   [a]*pulcherrima*   Formerly included in *C. pulcherrima*
   [a]*reukaufii*   Formerly included in *C. reukaufii*

Nadsonia
   [a]*elongata*   In musts from the Cognac region

Pichia
   alcoholophila (now *Pi. membranae-*
      faciens)
   [a]*etchellsii*
   [a]*farinosa*   In wine
   [a]*fermentans*   On grapes, and in musts and wine
   [a]*kluyveri*   In wine from Cognac
   [a]*kudriavzevii*   Formerly included in *Issatchenkia*
                                     orientalis
   [a]*membranaefaciens*   Relatively common in musts at start
                                   of fermentation or in films or in
                                   wine
   [a]*ohmeri*   Italian musts, formerly included in
                                   C. guilliermondii var. *membranae-*
                                   faciens
   [a]*polymorpha*
   [a]*vini*   Formerly included in *Deb. vini*

Rhodotorula
   [a]*aurantiaca*   Very rare
   [a]*glutinis*   Rarely reported on grapes, musts or
                                   wines
   [a]*minuta*   From green grapes in New Zealand
   mucilaginosa (now *Rh. rubra*)   In dry and sweet table wines; in
                                   Greek must
   [a]*pallida*   From southern Italy
   [a]*rubra*   From northern Italy
   vini   From wine, rare

Saccharomyces
   [a]*aceti*   In Spanish wine
   acidifaciens (now a variety of   In spoiled wines and on grapes;
      Sacch. bailii)   resistant to sulphur dioxide (a
                                   fructophile)
   [a]*bailii*   In South African and Italian dry
                                     table wine
   [a]*bailii* var. *bailii*   Grape juice concentrate
   [a]*bayanus* (now includes *Sacch.*   On grapes and in musts and wines;
      oviformis)   common but low frequency; in
                                   sparkling wines
   beticus (now *Sacch. capensis, bayanus*   Flor yeast
      or *fermentati*)
   [a]*bisporus*   On grapes; low alcohol yield
   [a]*capensis*

Table 3—*continued*

Genus and species	Notes or where reported
Saccharomyces—continued	
carlsbergensis (now *Sacch. uvarum*)	On grapes and less often in wine (used for lager beer fermentation)
[a] *cerevisiae*	The classical wine yeast, and possibly the most widely distributed
cerevisiae var. *ellipsoideus* (now *Sacch. cerevisiae*)	
[a] *chevalieri*	In wines in Africa and Italy and on grapes in Czechoslovakia
chodati (now *Sacch. italicus*)	On Georgian (U.S.S.R.) grapes
[a] *cidri*	In musts from the Cognac region
cordubensis	Flor yeast
[a] *coreanus*	Rare, from grapes
coreanus var. *armeniensis*	In Russian wine
delbrueckii	In beer and wine
[a] *delbrueckii* var. *mongolicus*	In must and wine
[a] *diastaticus*	
elegans (now *Sacch. bailii* var. *bailii*)	On grapes and in wine (a fructophile)
elegans var. *intermedia* (now *Sacch. bailii* var. *bailii*)	On grapes in Brazil
[a] *eupagycus*	
[a] *exiguus*	Originally found in pressed yeast, later in grape juice and wine
[a] *fermentati*	Formerly included in *Sacch. beticus*; flor yeast
[a] *florentinus*	In musts and rarely in wines
fructuum	In musts and in grape juice
gaditensis	Flor yeast
[a] *globosus*	On grapes and grape juice and wine, rare
[a] *heterogenicus*	On grapes, in musts, and in grape juice, but rarely
hispanica (now *Sacch. prostoserdovii*)	In Spanish wines
[a]*inconspicuus*	In grape juice
[a] *italicus*	On grapes and in grape juice from warm climates
[a]*kloeckerianus*	
[a] *kluyveri*	In Greek musts and wines
lactis (see *K. lactis*)	
marxianus (now *K. marxianus*)	
mellis (now *Sacch. bisporus*)	In Japanese wine and wineries; from the sherry district of Spain; originally from honey

[a]*microellipsoides*	In Greek musts and wines
montuliensis	
oviformis (now *Sacch. bayanus*)	On grapes, in musts, grape juice and wines; common
oxidans (now *Sacch. capensis*)	In Spanish wines
pastorianus (now *Sacch. bayanus*)	In grapes, in musts and frequently in Loire fermentations
[a]*pretoriensis*	In musts from the Cognac region
[a]*prostoserdovii*	Flor yeast
[a]*rosei*	Common on grapes and in wines
[a]*rouxii*	From overripe grapes
rouxii var. *jerezana*	From the sherry district of Spain
rouxii var. *polymorphus* (see *Sacch. rouxii*)	In musts
steineri (now *Sacch. italicus*)	In wine and on grapes
[a]*transvaalensis*	In Greek musts
[a]*unisporus*	
[a]*uvarum* (now includes *Sacch. carlsbergensis*)	In musts and frequently in wines
vanudenii (now *K. vanudenii*)	
veronae (now *K. veronae*)	In *Drosophila* spp. and in wines
vini (now *Sacch. cerevisiae*)	
willianus (now *Sacch. cerevisiae*)	Found more in beer than in wine
Saccharomycodes	
bisporus (now *S'codes ludwigii*)	In Italian wine
[a]*ludwigii*	From grape juice and wine; common, resistant to sulphur dioxide
Schizosaccharomyces	
acidodevoratus (now *Schiz. pombe*)	
[a]*japonicus* var. *versatilis* (see *Schiz. versatilis*)	
[a]*octosporus*	Originally found in a must from sulphited currants
[a]*pombe*	Utilizes malic acid
pombe var. *acidodevoratus* (see *Schiz. pombe*)	
pombe var. *liquefaciens*	
versatilis (now *Schiz. japonicus* var. *versatilis*)	Originally isolated from home-canned grape juice
Sphaerulina	
intermixta	
Sporobolomyces	In a cork stopper; in a film on ageing wine

Table 3—*continued*

Genus and species	Notes or where reported
Torulopsis	
anomala (now *T. versatilis*)	In Czechoslovakian musts and wines
arnaudii	Sardinian must
bacillaris (now *T. stellata*)	On grapes and in wine (a fructophile)
behrendi	In Greek musts
burgeffiana (now *M. pulcherrima*)	From grapes and in musts
[a] *candida*	In sweet table wine
[a] *cantarellii*	From grape musts
capsuligenus (now *Leu. capsuligenum*)	From a winery culture
[a] *colliculosa*	In wine
[a] *domercgii*	
[a] *etchellsii*	In musts from the Cognac region
famata (now *T. candida*)	In musts and wines
[a] *glabrata*	In musts and wines
globosa (now *Citeromyces* *matritensis*)	In a bottle storage room
[a] *inconspicua*	In winery; in musts and wine
[a] *lactis-condensi*	In musts from the Cognac region
[a] *norvegica*	Formerly included in *T. vanzylii*
pseudaeria (now *Cr. albidus* var. *albidus*)	From a vineyard soil
pulcherrima (now *M. pulcherrima*)	
[a] *stellata* (now includes *T. bacillaris*)	
vanzylii (now *T. norvegica*)	From a refrigerated cellar floor
[a] *versatilis*	In Czechoslovakian musts and wines
Trichosporon	
[a] *cutaneum*	In musts in Brazil
[a] *fermentans*	In musts or on diseased grapes
hellenicum	In Greek musts
intermedium	In musts
[a] *pullulans*	In musts
veronae (now *C. veronae*)	In musts

they are aerobes and are inhibited by the anaerobic conditions of, and the alcohol in, the fermenting wine-must, both of which develop soon after the beginning of alcoholic fermentation. With mould-damaged grapes, the situation is at least disagreeable. Breakage of the berry skins by moulds and subsequent exposure of the juice to premature initiation of fermentation by endogenous yeasts also bring about the possibility of oxidative formation of acetic acid from ethanol by acetic-acid bacteria. The situation might even be dangerous if there were a large-scale infestation by mycotoxin-producing strains of *Aspergillus flavus*. However, Drawert and Barton (1974) tested many wines which had been made from grapes infected with noble rot (in the Rhine and Palatinate areas of Germany) and failed to find traces of aflatoxin, a carcinogenic mycotoxin which is produced by *A. flavus*.

In California, there is a self-imposed limitation. Grapes used for table-wine production must contain less than 15% (w/w) mouldy material. The Howard Mold Count method has been applied to grapes as a microscopic technique for determining the mould level of mechanically harvested grapes (Traverso-Rueda *et al.*, 1973).

Grape juice is an excellent nutrient medium. Once it has been inoculated, either by yeasts from the grape skin or by addition of a yeast starter, the yeasts multiply rapidly. The Montrachet strain (referred to as U.C.D. Enology 522) of *Sacch. cerevisiae*, which is widely used in Californian wineries, has a generation time in grape juice of one to three hours at room temperature. Most wine yeasts will multiply in grape juice until a population of about 1 to 2×10^8 cells/ml is reached. Figure 4 shows the course of fermentation (Singh, 1975) of a synthetic medium designed to simulate grape juice. The increase in optical density, due to yeast growth, and the decrease in degrees Brix, due to fermentation of sugar, are shown. Concomitant with yeast growth, glucose and fructose are converted to ethanol and carbon dioxide by the yeast enzymes of the Embden–Meyerhof–Parnas pathway (see Chapter 1, p. 21). The overall yield of sugar to ethanol is about 50%, depending especially on the temperature of the fermentation. Variability in yield measurements under practical wine-making conditions can come from inaccuracies in the initial sugar measurement because of the presence of undissolved sugar within raisined berries.

The number of compounds found in wine has been given as at least 400 (Rankine, 1971b), and this is probably a low estimate. The compounds of greatest interest are those which are sensorially detectable—those with low sensory thresholds, either on the nose or on the palate. To be odoriferous, the compounds must not only have a low threshold level but must also be volatile. Thus, the odour of wine consists mainly of alcohols, esters, fatty acids and carbonyl compounds. Before referring to some of the important members in

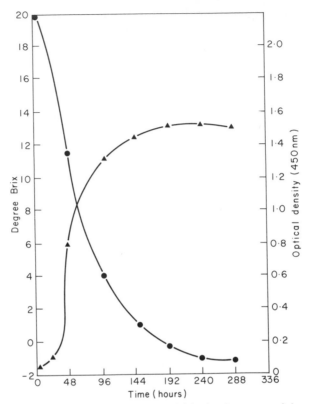

Fig. 4. Fermentation of a synthetic medium which simulates grape juice. The medium contained 20% glucose, phosphoric and organic acids, vitamins and minerals (final pH value 3.5). The medium was sterilized by being autoclaved. The fermentation was carried out at room temperature by the Montrachet strain (U.C.D. Enology 522) of *Saccharomyces cerevisiae*. ▲ indicates optical density; ●, degrees Brix. Figure taken from Singh (1975). See Chapter 1, p. 35 for a definition of degrees Brix.

each of these classes of compounds, we wish to point out that the yeast and the fermentation process seem to play the most important role in producing the odour components of wine, and indeed of all alcoholic beverages. Suomalainen and Nykänen (1966) and Ronkainen *et al.* (1967) showed that the product of baker's yeast fermentation of synthetic medium contained a great number of the flavour components we shall mention.

Besides the compounds produced by the yeast, there are some compounds found in wine which are related to the starting material—the variety of grape. These are either carried over directly into the wine or are transformed by the yeast during the fermentation.

Although in this section of the chapter we are discussing alcoholic fermentation, it might be well to mention the identification of some wine aromas with certain grape varieties. The intense and easily recognizable flavour of the muscat varieties of *V. vinifera* is attributed to the terpene alcohols, linaloöl and geraniol (Webb, 1970). The 'foxy' flavour of the American *V. lubrusca* varieties and some of their hybrids is from methyl anthranilate. No other varieties have been shown to contain a single component or group of compounds which are totally responsible for their character aromas, although White Riesling, which often has a muscat note in its aroma, does contain a small amount of linaloöl (van Wyk *et al.*, 1967a). Further efforts are being made to characterize varietal distinctiveness with the chemistry of the product. For example, Muller *et al.* (1971) identified 4-ethoxy-4-hydroxybutyric acid-γ-lactone as at least one important aroma component of Cabernet-Sauvignon and Ruby Cabernet wines.

Besides compounds coming from the grape and the fermentation, compounds are formed during ageing processes by: (1) bacteria during the malo-lactic fermentation; (2) interaction with wood and air during storage in wooden cooperage; and (3) interaction of the wine components during bottle storage, that is, in the development of 'bottle bouquet'. One can appreciate the complex nature of the studies on the biochemical and organochemical pathways of the formation and conversion of these compounds. However, there are difficulties enough in the detection and identification of these components. Some of them are present in extremely low concentrations. Certainly gas-liquid chromatography, especially when coupled with mass spectrometry, as a means of detection and identification of the separated compounds has been the most important tool in the advancement of our knowledge of the composition of wine. Sometimes, however, the human nose has been used in connection with gas chromatography as the most sensitive detector of compounds, qualitatively and quantitatively! Further difficulties come from attempts to associate the various components found with the property which we call 'wine flavour'. Some of the components have extremely low sensory threshold levels, and minute concentrations, nearly undetectable by present physicochemical means, may make important flavour and aroma contributions to the wine. Secondly, these compounds are often extremely volatile. This latter quality can be appreciated by the experienced wine taster who is aware of the change (for good or ill) which often occurs when one allows a wine to 'breathe' after it has been unstoppered. Thus, even with the benefits of gas chromatography and associated techniques, many important components of wine are probably being missed. There are further difficulties. The human perception of the quality of a flavour or odour component can vary greatly with the concentration of the component. For example, even the obnoxious odour of hydrogen sulphide has been found to be pleasant at thresholds of detection (MacRostie, 1974). Not enough is known about the interrelationships between various components, and how much one component might interfere with the qualitative estimation of another component. And at least one more difficulty should be mentioned; preparation of the wines for analyses may bring about alteration in some compounds, although precautions are naturally taken to prevent this kind of change. Distillations are carried out under vacuum to avoid the use of high temperatures; acidic portions are separated from alcoholic ones to prevent esterification, and inert solvents are used for extractions. The 'headspace' analytical method (Kepner *et al.*, 1963, 1964) would seem to be the method of choice to prevent artifactual changes, although by this method only the most volatile components are detected.

Before giving a list of types of compounds which have been detected in wines, we must mention the higher-alcohol components—the fusel oil fraction (Webb and Ingraham, 1963). This fraction is composed mainly of 2- and 3-methylbutanols and isobutanol. Sometimes *n*-propanol is also included. These compounds are not formed in large amounts, but they are flavourful enough to be of considerable interest. This is especially true in wines which are going to be used for distillation, when this fraction becomes more concentrated. Pathways for the formation of these alcohols have been worked out (Webb and Ingraham, 1963). They are derived mainly from carbohydrate substrates, although their formation from amino acids by the Ehrlich reaction also takes place during the exponential growth phase of yeast (Vollbrecht and Radler, 1973). In the Ehrlich reaction, a branched-chain amino acid is transaminated to the corresponding α-oxo acid, which is then decarboxylated and reduced to the alcohol; for example, valine is converted to α-oxo-isovalerate and then to isovaleraldehyde and finally isobutanol. The type reaction is the same as from alanine to pyruvate to acetaldehyde to ethanol, but the pathways leading to higher alcohols are under separate control mechanisms compared with those leading to ethanol (Kunkee and Singh, 1975). The strain of yeast seems to have an influence on the formation of these flavour components, but the importance of the yeast strain in comparison with other factors such as pH value, temperature and composition of the grape juice is not clear. The presence of branched-chain amino acids, which are also formed in part by the same metabolic pathways (for example, valine to isobutanol), has some controlling effect in wine yeast, but not a large one (Kunkee et al., 1972). Multiple forms of alcohol dehydrogenase, the final enzyme on the pathways for formation of the higher alcohols, have been found by varying the growth conditions of the yeast (Kunkee et al., 1966; Schimpfessel, 1966, 1967, 1968; Kunkee and Singh, 1975). Only the constitutive form of these isozymes is involved in the last step in the formation of higher alcohols, but the level of activity of the constitutive isozyme was found to be under metabolic control (Singh, 1975).

Webb (1970) has given a check list of the volatile compounds which have been detected in wine. All of the saturated straight-chain aliphatic acids from acetic acid (C_1) to pelargonic acid (C_9) and the even-numbered to palmitic acid (C_{16}) have been found. The odd-numbered acids are found in lower concentrations. The saturated C_4, C_5 and C_6 iso-acids are also present. A few unsaturated acids are found, including 9-decenoic, oleic, linoleic and palmitoleic acids, as well as some phenolic acids such as cinnamic acid. Webb (1970) mentions that the ethyl esters of tartaric, malic and succinic acids are known to occur, but these have high sensory threshold levels. Carbonyl compounds with low threshold levels are found, and they include saturated straight-chain aldehydes from formaldehyde to hexanal, and also C_4 and C_5 iso-aldehydes, cis-2-hexenal, vanillin, cinnamaldehyde and benzaldehyde. Several ketones are present, notably acetone, 2-butanone, 2-pentanone, 2,3-butanedione and 2,3-pentanedione. Of these ketones, 2,3-butanedione (or diacetyl) is of special importance. This compound can be formed by yeast, but it is of greater significance when formed by the malo-lactic fermentation (see Section VII.A, p. 366). Of the alcohols, all of the saturated straight-chain alcohols from methanol to decyl alcohol and the C_3, C_4 and C_5 iso-alcohols are found. We have mentioned some of these, namely, iso-, 2- and 3-methylbutanols, as fusel-oil components. In addition, benzyl alcohol, 2-phenethanol and the isomers of 2,3-butanediol are present. 2-Phenethanol is not usually classified as a component of fusel oil because of its low volatility. It has a strong rose-like odour and is found in wine at concentrations as high as 50 mg/l (Äyräpää, 1962; Usseglio-Tomasset, 1967). The mechanism of 2-phenethanol formation is analogous to that of the branched-chain higher alcohols (Äyräpää, 1963; see p. 354). Nearly all of the possible combinations of esters from the above acids and alcohols have been found, amounting to at least 100 individual compounds. To complete this check list of components of table wine, Webb (1970) adds: diethyl acetal; acetamide with ethyl, iso-amyl or 2-phenethyl groups substituting for one of the protons on the N atom; ethyl pyroglutamate; and some lactones. At least seven lactones have been identified in table wines which had not received wood storage: these are γ-butyrolactone, the physiological effect of which has been studied (see p. 357); 4-ethoxy-4-hydroxybutyric acid-γ-lactone, the lactone found in Ruby Cabernet wine; 6-methyl-dihydro-2,5(3H)-pyrandione, also found in Ruby Cabernet wine; solerone, 5-acetyldihydro-2(3H)-furanone; two reduction products of solerone, the two isomers of 4,5-dihydroxyhexanoic acid-γ-lactone; and pantolactone (Webb, 1970; Augustyn et al., 1971; Muller et al., 1969, 1971, 1972, 1973). Muller et al. (1973) indicate that many other gamma and delta lactones, which could arise during fermentation and which would be expected to contribute to the total wine aroma, so far remain undetected. Some are likely to be present in extremely low concentrations and others may be decomposed during gas chromatographic analyses.

Solerone was discovered in wine which matured under a sherry film-yeast in a solera, but since then has been found in table wine (Augustyn et al., 1971; Sakato, 1974). It is considered of special importance because it has a pronounced wine-like aroma, as does one of the isomers of its reduced form, namely 4,5-dihydroxyhexanoic acid-γ-lactone. These two compounds may even contribute to 'bottle bouquet' (Muller et al., 1973; A. D. Webb, personal communication).

Gamma-Butyrolactone was also first discovered in flor sherry (Webb and Kepner, 1962) and then in White Riesling table wine (van Wyk et al., 1967b). Since then it has been found in practically all fermented products (Muller et al., 1973). It has an anaesthetic effect on man (Blaise, 1963) and other animals (Rubin and Giarman, 1947). Since the intoxicating effect of ethanol on the human system is not well understood, one might speculate that γ-butyrolactone might be contributing to this effect, even though it is present in table wines at low concentration—5 mg/l or less (Ribéreau-Gayon and Sapis, 1965). However, studies by Eriksson and Webb (1970) showed this not to be the case. Open-field tests of the behaviour of rats receiving intraperitoneal injections of the lactone at relatively high concentrations (0.1% to 1%, in ethanol) revealed no change in behaviour compared with the control rats. Behaviour studies with the two isomers of 4,5-dihydroxyhexanoic acid-γ-lactone (Webb et al., 1972) showed some changes, but these were small. The ethoxy-lactone, 5-ethoxydihydro-2(3H)-furanone, was found to change behaviour significantly in tests with intraperitoneal injections, but there was no effect when it was administered by the gastro-intestinal route. This result is believed to indicate breakdown of the compound by the high acidity of the stomach.

Several factors influence the rate of yeast growth and fermentation. The most important of these are yeast strain, temperature, pH value, initial sugar concentration, and the nature of nutrients (Kunkee and Amerine, 1970). By defining these variables, Ough and Kunkee (1968) accounted for 84% of the factors which influence the fermentation rate in grape juice. While the winemaker is interested in the speed of fermentation, of more importance is the quality enhancement which results from temperature control, that is, cooling the fermenting juice and slowing the rate of fermentation. This is especially true for white-wine fermentation but also true for red wine in warm regions. Cooling is now standard technique in many wine areas (see p. 359). Without cooling, it is not uncommon in hot regions for the temperature of the fermenting juice to reach over 38°C, resulting in death of some yeast and 'stuck fermentations'.

The role of oxygen in alcoholic fermentation is fascinating. It has been known for nearly a century that aeration of a fermentation will increase the growth and fermentation capabilities of the yeast (Cochin, 1880; Ergang, 1899; Buchner and Rapp, 1903; Brown, 1905). Knappstein and Rankine (1970) found that aeration increased the final yeast count in grape juice by about 167%. Several oxygen-inducing mechanisms are known which could account for these stimulations. Oxygen could: (1) induce synthesis of enzymes on pathways leading to formation of essential unsaturated fatty acid and sterols (Andreasen and Stier, 1953, 1954; Babij *et al.*, 1969; Bréchot *et al.*, 1971; Gordon and Stewart, 1972; David and Kirsop, 1973; David, 1974); (2) allow induction of functional mitochondria and respiratory enzymes (Tustanoff and Bartley, 1962, 1964; Polakis *et al.*, 1965; Rogers and Stewart, 1973; Cartledge and Lloyd, 1973; Rogers *et al.*, 1974); (3) induce synthesis of citric-acid cycle enzymes for production of substrates for vitamin and amino-acid formation (Sols *et al.*, 1971); and (4) 'switch-on' the Pasteur effect (Pasteur, 1876; Meyerhof, 1925) which decreases the rate of catabolism of carbohydrate substrates and brings about their more efficient utilization.

However, because of the high glucose and fructose concentrations in grape juices, the Crabtree effect, or catabolic repression mechanism (Crabtree, 1929; De Deken, 1966; Paigen and Williams, 1970), should prevent any of the above-mentioned oxygen-induced reactions from taking place. Furthermore, the high concentration of nutrients present in grape juice should dampen any need for oxygen-induction of metabolite formation. The nutrients present in grape juice include oleanolic acid, a sterol found on the waxy coating of grapes (Radler, 1965). This sterol is needed for growth of *Sacch. cerevisiae* under anaerobic conditions (Bréchot *et al.*, 1971).

Nevertheless, in spite of all of these theoretical arguments which predict that oxygen should have no effect, an *immediate* stimulation of growth of anaerobically-grown wine yeast has been found by aeration in complete medium or in grape juice (Traverso-Rueda and Kunkee, 1974). This stimulation was found in growth of both wine yeast and a respiratory-deficient mutant derived from it. Thus oxygen, and perhaps other electron acceptors, act to stimulate growth in some way other than involving the well-known processes described above.

As mentioned in the beginning of this chapter (p. 325), it is interesting that so much of our present knowledge of microbiology began with a study of wine and fermentation. Yet there is still very little known about the physiology of wine yeast under practical wine-making conditions; that is, low pH value, initially high concentrations of sugar, long fermentation time at low temperatures ending with a high concentration of ethanol, and extremely anaerobic conditions.

The high concentration of sugars (glucose and fructose) in the grape juice have another effect besides bringing about catabolite repression. Perhaps because of the osmotic effect, the sugars slow down the rate of yeast growth and fermentation (Ough, 1964). This inhibitory effect, along with the inhibitory effect of ethanol, can be used as a means of preventing yeast fermentation of sweet wine. This effect, first described by Delle (1911), has been applied to wine making with Californian musts (Amerine and Kunkee, 1965; Kunkee and Amerine, 1968). The principle could also be used for storage of grape juice to be used later as sweetening agent. If the grape juice is to be conserved by the addition of high-proof spirits, a final ethanol concentration of 13% (v/v) would be sufficient, rather than 17% which is ordinarily used.

We have said that the practice of inoculation with starter cultures is certainly one of the important recent advances in the technology of wine making. Perhaps more important than this is the intro-duction of cooling systems to lower and to control the temperature of the fermentation, especially in warm wine-producing regions. It is generally agreed that, for high-quality wine production, fermen-tations for white wine should be held to 7–16°C, while red wines should be fermented at a somewhat higher temperature, around 24–29°C. Ough and Amerine (1966) and Amerine et al. (1972) should be consulted for more extensive discussion of the effects of temperature on yeast growth and fermentation, on wine quality, and equipment used for cooling.

Another new technique enjoying some success is the use of continuous fermentation to produce red wine. Here 'continuous' means continuous or semi-continuous fermentation during the vint-age, rather than continuously all year round. The economic advan-tages of continuous fermentation are well known. They include no 'down-time' for emptying, cleaning and refilling of containers, no 'lag phase' before build up of yeast population, smaller container space required, and, most importantly, susceptibility of the system to automatic control.

A number of installations have been constructed, notably in southern France, for the continuous maceration and fermentation of grape juice to produce red table wines (Peynaud, 1967; Fages-Bonner, 1967; Flanzy et al., 1968). The first installation of this type was constructed in 1948 by Gremaschi, an Argentine engineer, using an open fermentor. Most subsequent installations have used closed fermentors which give greater protection against accidental acetification. Two systems are used in France. In the first, known as the Vico system, a closed vertical fermentor of about 500×10^3 kg capacity, constructed in lined steel, receives the crushed, destemmed grapes, 160×10^3 kg being added during each working day. The skins float to the surface forming a cap. A corresponding amount of wine is drawn off each day once the fermentor is filled. An appropriate amount of skins is extracted mechanically from the cap each day and pressed immediately. The average residence time of wine in the fermentor is about three days. The lower part of the fermentor is conical in shape to facilitate removal of the seeds. The second system, widely used in France, is the Ladousse system, which is similar, except that the fermentor is divided into two sections by a concentrically placed grid. The space outside the grid receives crushed grapes which are not destemmed, and it is here that the fermentation begins and the maceration is carried out. Fermentation of the wine is completed in the centre section in the absence of the skins.

When these fermentors were first tried, very low concentrations of sulphur dioxide were used, but this led to a continuously increasing bacterial population and, ultimately, to the production of very poor wine. Now, control of the sulphur dioxide levels is carefully maintained between 80 and 100 mg/l, which in turn controls the bacterial population. By the time the volatile acidity begins to rise measurably (an indication of bacterial spoilage), it is already too late for easy correction. Therefore, it has been found necessary to estimate the levels of bacterial contamination by direct microscopic observation or by analysing the wine for L(+) lactic acid. It has been found advantageous to use a large inoculation of yeast when the fermentor is brought into operation, even in areas where cultured yeasts are not normally used.

Temperature control is very important in this type of operation. Similar temperatures to those used in the batch fermentation of red wines are required, namely 26°C to 28°C. Fermentors of lined steel are cooled with an external film of water. This system is impossible with concrete fermentors, which have become less popular.

There are about 100 continuous fermentors in use in the Midi district of France; comparatively few have been constructed recently. The main advantage of the system is that considerably less labour is required for its operation. A slight increase in the alcohol strength of the wine, of the order of 0.1%, is claimed. The main disadvantage of this type of fermentor is that it cannot easily be scaled down, so that it is only suitable where at least 40,000 hectolitres of must of uniform constitution are available during a single vintage. A skilled technician is required to operate the system (Nègre et al., 1971; Fages-Bonnery, 1967).

In Italy, a number of special fermentors have been developed which are described as continuous fermentors but which, in practice, seem to be operated on a batch basis. In these fermentors, maceration of the skins takes place, the seeds are separated and fermentation begins. Mechanical means are provided to ensure extraction of pigment from the skins by the juice and for mechanical discharge of the skins. Red wines with a normal depth of colour are produced with 16 to 20 hours' maceration. Very intensely coloured red wines, for which there seems to be demand in Italy, can be produced with 24 to 48 hours' maceration. As with the French fermentors, there is a considerable saving in labour because of the mechanical handling of the skins. The fermentors are of rather smaller capacity, being between 600 and 800 hectolitres. As they are operated more or less on a batch basis, they do not suffer from the limitation of over-capacity inherent in the French design. Most are made of stainless steel or are steel lined. Various designs are produced by Padovan, Gainnaza, Da Dalt and L.A.I. They vary mainly in the equipment used to extract the skins from the cap (da Rosa, 1972; Coulon, 1971).

The Italian fermentors should not be confused with the Auto-vinificateur of Ducellier-Isman, widely used in Algeria. Some are also used in Portugal and Australia. In this system, a closed fermentor, usually in concrete, is fitted with valves arranged so that the pressure developed by the production of carbon dioxide during fermentation is used to force some of the fermenting liquid up into a subsidiary container situated on top of the fermentor. The fermenting liquid can be cooled during this transfer if required. A hydraulic valve releases the carbon dioxide from the interior of the fermentor at intervals, allowing the liquid from the subsidiary container to fall back spraying over the surface of the cap. A high colour extraction is achieved. It should be emphasized that, in these fermentors, discharge of the skins is not automatic (Brémond, 1957).

Another interesting recent development is the Roto tank. The fermentation vessel consists of a horizontal cylinder, with an inner cylinder or vanes which can be rotated mechanically. It can be used either for juice extraction from grape pomace or for red-wine fermentation. It can produce red wine of a good colour and tannin content in 24 hours. With a longer period of extraction, it can produce more deeply coloured wines. Considerable control of the maceration process can be achieved by controlling the temperature and by using a suitable schedule for rotation of the inner cylinders or vanes. As a fermentor, the device is expensive, but it has considerable potential when fine red wines are to be produced. Machines are in use in Austria, South Africa, Portugal and the U.S.A. (Haushofer, 1972).

Before leaving this discussion of alcoholic fermentation, we want to mention how some red wines are being made in parts of France by a special process called 'carbonic maceration' (Flanzy, 1972; Hiaring, 1974b; McCorkle, 1974). The wines are light and fruity and are made to be drunk fresh and early, traditionally, by the fifteenth of November *of the year of the vintage.* In the carbonic maceration procedure, the grapes are not crushed but placed whole in the fermentation tank and blanketed with carbon dioxide—and then sometimes heated to as much as 37°C. Fermentation apparently occurs *either* as an anaerobic fermentation inside the intact grapes, *or* the carbon dioxide, which was added originally or which developed during the anaerobic fermentation, destroys the integrity of the grape-skin cells and allows seepage of grape juice. The heating process would aid the latter process. An intriguing aspect of this process is that the malo-lactic fermentation is said to accompany the alcoholic fermentation, and thus the wine is stabilized, even at the time of early bottling. It is not clear whether the malic acid formed is lost by bacterial malo-lactic fermentation (see Section VII, A., p. 366) because of the low concentration of alcohol present, or because of the low concentration of sulphur dioxide used, or by anaerobic fermentation of the acid by grape-tissue enzymes. Virtually no microbiological studies have been made on this process. Beelman and McArdle (1974) found experimental wines made by this method to have a different sensory quality compared with the control; one they described as spicy. Their wines were lower in acid and more susceptible to malo-lactic fermentation. Other experimental wines have been made by this process (Amerine and Ough, 1968, 1969; Amerine and Fong, 1974).

VI. POST-FERMENTATION OPERATIONS

At the end of the alcoholic fermentation, the new wine is vulnerable to spoilage. It is important at this stage, when the degrees Brix reading is less than zero or when the concentration of residual sugar is only a few tenths of a percent, to rack the wine off of the lees, add sulphur dioxide and store at a cooler temperature (13–18°C) under anaerobic conditions. This is done in preparation for later clarification and stabilization operations. Sulphur dioxide is added as solid or gas to prevent oxidative browning, to complex with free acetaldehyde produced during the alcoholic fermentation, and to inhibit bacterial growth. Sulphur dioxide should not be added, however, and the wine should not be stored at such a cool temperature, if a malo-lactic fermentation is expected and desired (see Section VII.A, p. 366). The anaerobic conditions are extremely important to prevent spoilage by acetic acid bacteria. This subject is discussed further in Section VII.B (p. 368). The early racking off of the lees tends to inhibit later formation of hydrogen sulphide, which might occur if the particulate matter of the lees contained some elemental sulphur (Rankine, 1963).

The subject of prevention of hydrogen sulphide formation is an important one, but not one which we find easy to understand (Shimwell, 1947; Thoukis and Stern, 1962; Rankine, 1963; Wainwright, 1971; Acree et al., 1972). Hydrogen sulphide, which has a very unpleasant odour, is extremely volatile. Nevertheless, it is our experience that aeration of new wine to remove or prevent formation of hydrogen sulphide must be done only after the wine has been clarified of all yeast. Furthermore, this operation should not be carried out if any hydrogen sulphide has been transformed into a mercaptan (for example ethyl sulphide; Rankine, 1963). Aeration under these conditions would oxidize the monomercaptan to a disulphide, for example diethyl disulphide, which is also obnoxious. Addition of sulphur dioxide can be used to oxidize hydrogen sulphide to elemental sulphur, which then must be removed. However, we are not sure of the duration of time required for this reaction nor if the elemental sulphur then formed can always be easily removed. Where it is legal, addition of a minimum amount of cupric ions can be used to remove hydrogen sulphide and monomercaptans. This treatment is not effective for removal of disulphides. Use of cultured strains of wine yeast, strains which produce only small amounts of hydrogen sulphide from sulphur, is desirable (Rankine, 1964). The ideal solution, already mentioned, is to avoid the presence of elemental sulphur in the must in the first place.

Premium quality wines should receive additional ageing treatments. Only a brief description of some of the cellar operations will be given here, and details can be found elsewhere (Amerine and Joslyn, 1970; Amerine *et al.*, 1972; Amerine and Ough, 1972; Troost, 1972).

Premium white wines of the Rhine type (for example White Riesling and Sylvaner) often receive only a short ageing time in wood, sometimes only for storage convenience. The fruitiness of these wines can be overwhelmed by too long a contact with wood. Other premium white wines of the Burgundy type (for example Chardonnay) may be aged in wood in order to impart some of the woody character to the wine. These latter wines usually undergo a malo-lactic fermentation (see Section VII.A, p. 366) during this storage period. Premium red wines (for example Pinot noir and Cabernet-Sauvignon) should always receive some wood ageing, from six months to as long as two years being the usual period of storage. Often new barrels of one of several types of French oak are used, which contributes significantly to the expense of the wine. For further discussion of some practical and theoretical aspects of barrels and barrel ageing, see Graff and Tchelistcheff (1969) and Singleton (1972, 1973). Premium red wines nearly always undergo malo-lactic fermentation during storage. While the wine is stored, it is imperative that the barrels or the holding tanks be faithfully attended to prevent head-space development, and thus oxidation, and to maintain a significant concentration of free sulphur dioxide, unless malo-lactic fermentation has not yet occurred. At the time of bottling, or before, unless the wine is naturally brilliant from storage and racking procedures it is generally clarified with fining agents. A variety of absorptive materials, such as bentonite, egg white or gelatin are used. After being fined, the wines often receive a final clarification by filtration. This has generally been done with depth filters (filter pads) made of asbestos and coated with filter aid. Some winemakers are now using filter pads made from materials other than asbestos; cellulose or modified cellulose are among materials often used. The performance of the new pads is said to match nearly the old ones (Robe, 1974). Often membrane- or screen filters are used after the wine has received a preliminary filtration with the depth filters. The depth filters have the advantage of greater filtration capacity before becoming clogged; the membrane filters have the advantage of removing all material of a specified particle size. Sterile or aseptic filtration is discussed in Section VII.B (p. 373).

With high-quality wines, storage is continued after bottling to bring about bottle ageing, or the development of special flavours and odours known as 'bottle bouquet'. Some work has been done on the role of oxygen in this development and on methods to make it proceed faster (Singleton *et al.*, 1964; Wildenradt and Singleton, 1974).

Ageing operations are costly. Not only is the extra handling expensive, but the maintenance of the storage facilities, which often require cooling, is also expensive. In some regions the wines are sold even before the cellar treatments are finished to help defray these final costs.

Less expensive wines, which make up the bulk of the World's wines, are bottled earlier, within the same year of production—often on market demand. Even though inexpensive, these wines, both red and white, when well made, have a charm of their own. They have a fresh and fruity character, rather than being woody and aged. One problem with this type of wine is its susceptibility to malo-lactic fermentation, which often would be expected to occur at about the time the winemaker wishes to bottle the wine. Microbiological stabilization of wines against malo-lactic fermentation and against secondary yeast fermentation in semi-dry wines is discussed in Section VII (p. 366). The young, fresh wines nearly always need clarification before being bottled. Centrifugation can be used to remove yeast and other sediment before the final fining and filtration procedures.

Other required cellar treatments, which again add expense to the production of wine, are stabilizations against chemical precipitations. Potassium bitartrate is rather insoluble in alcoholic solutions and will precipitate out when wine is chilled. To prevent this from occurring in the bottle, wine is usually stored at freezing temperatures and then filtered cold to remove the precipitate. This procedure can also occur naturally in very cold cellars. Berg and Keefer (1958, 1959) have outlined conditions and methods of analysis which can be used to test for tartrate stability. Protein stabilization is also necessary in some wines to prevent cloudiness. This stabilization is done by bentonite treatment, but heating is also used (Amerine *et al.*, 1972).

VII. MICROBIOLOGICAL STABILIZATION

A. Malo-Lactic Fermentation

Some lactic-acid bacteria are surprisingly 'at home' in wine. In spite of the low pH value, high concentration of ethanol, low storage temperature, and added sulphur dioxide, strains of *Leuconostoc*, *Lactobacillus* and *Pediococcus* will grow in wine, albeit slowly. During this growth, synthesis of enzymes is induced which allow the bacteria to carry out the malo-lactic reaction, which involves decarboxylation of malic acid to lactic acid. There are three important aspects to the malo-lactic fermentation: (1) loss of acidity due to the decarboxylation; (2) change in the flavour of the wine resulting from the end products of bacterial fermentation; and (3) microbiological stability following growth of the organisms.

In moderate climates, where the wines are not too acid to begin with, the stability following the fermentation is probably the most important consideration. If a wine is susceptible to malo-lactic fermentation, the winemaker will not be content until the fermentation has occurred, since it is disagreeable to have it take place in the wine after it is bottled. The fermentation can be encouraged by delayed racking from the yeast lees, by elevated temperatures, or by avoiding addition of acid or sulphur dioxide. Practical information on how to induce the malo-lactic fermentation, including inoculation with *Leuconostoc oenos* ML 34, is given in two review articles by Kunkee (1967, 1974). After the malo-lactic fermentation has taken place, the wine should be aerated, sulphited and filtered (A. Tchelistcheff, personal communication).

Alternatively, if the wine is unlikely to undergo a malo-lactic fermentation because of a very low pH value or very high content of ethanol, the winemaker may wish to inhibit the fermentation by using the opposite techniques (Kunkee, 1974). Where legal, fumaric acid has also been used to inhibit the malo-lactic fermentation (Cofran and Meyer, 1970; Tchelistcheff *et al.*, 1971; Pilone *et al.*, 1974; Ough and Kunkee, 1974; Pilone, 1975).

In the very cool wine-producing regions, de-acidification brought about by the malo-lactic fermentation is its main value. This is especially true in central and northern Europe, where, even in the best years, the wines might benefit from the loss of acid coming from this fermentation. In the warmer regions, the de-acidification is not important and may even be undesirable. There, acid additions are often made.

Malo-lactic bacteria may add complexity of flavour to the wine by formation of end products, some at very low concentrations (Pilone *et al.*, 1966). Of course, there is a flavour change brought about by the de-acidification, but any further change or improvement in flavour by increasing the complexity of compounds present (Singleton and Ough, 1962) is much talked about, but hard to establish, since the differences are small (Rankine, 1972; Pilone and Kunkee, 1965). One of the end products easily detected is diacetyl. At low concentrations, diacetyl probably brings about a flavour enhancement, but at high concentrations it would have to be considered a spoilage factor (Rankine *et al.*, 1969). A discussion of the malo-lactic fermentation as a spoilage reaction is presented below.

Recent biochemical studies have furnished answers to some interesting questions concerning the intermediary metabolism of malo-lactic bacteria. *Leuconostoc oenos* ML 34 is not able to utilize malic acid as an energy source, and malic acid does not increase the $Y_{glucose}$ value (Pilone, 1971; Kunkee, 1974). Nevertheless, malic acid has a profound effect on the metabolism of this malo-lactic organism. In the presence of malic acid, there is an increase in the formation of D($-$)-lactic acid not derived from L($-$)-malic acid, and there is a striking stimulation of growth rate, especially at wine pH values (Pilone, 1971; Kunkee, 1974). These effects do not result from the increase in pH value which accompanies the malo-lactic fermentation. Enzymic studies reveal that most of the conversion of malic acid to lactic acid is a direct decarboxylation by a malate carboxyl lyase with NAD^+ acting as a coenzyme (Schütz and Radler, 1973). However, a small proportion of the malic acid is released from the enzyme as pyruvic acid and, along with it, NADH (Morenzoni, 1973, 1974; Kunkee, 1975). The second reaction has been confirmed by isotope experiments (Alizade and Simon, 1973). Pyruvic acid, or derivatives of it such as acetyl phosphate, could act as hydrogen acceptors, which would stimulate early growth of the organism, but which would not provide for any net energy to allow for an increase in cell yield (Morenzoni, 1974). Kunkee (1974) should be consulted as a source of additional literature on basic and applied information on the malo-lactic fermentation. Further descriptions of the malo-lactic fermentation are given in articles by Peynaud and Domercq (1961), Radler (1966), Kunkee (1967) and Gandini (1969).

B. Microbiological Spoilage

1. Bacterial Spoilage

Pasteur (1866) noted that wine is the most hygienic of all beverages. For reasons already given, we can say that wine is a difficult environment for microbes. The very few spoilage organisms which can survive in wine may be unpleasant but not unhealthy. With the safeguard of the wine itself, winemakers in the past have not had to be too conscious of winery hygiene. With the consumers' demands for more cleanliness and with the advances in sanitary engineering, which made cleanliness relatively easy, wineries are now appearing more and more hygienic, much the way breweries and dairies have had to present themselves (Amerine, 1972). Happily, more often than not, winery owners are also artistic enough to combine aesthetic appeal with antisepsis in new winery planning.

Lactic-acid bacteria are the only bacteria which will grow in properly stored table wine, that is, table wine kept under anaerobic conditions and with a measurable concentration of free sulphur dioxide. We have noted the beneficial aspects of growth of lactic-acid bacteria (see p. 366). However, some of the malo-lactic organisms can produce end products which are undesirable and persistent. The fermentation would then have to be considered to be a spoilage reaction which occurred in basically sound wine where a clean malo-lactic fermentation had been desired (Pilone et al., 1965). For this reason, it is recommended to winemakers with some microbiological expertise to use bacterial inoculation with a known, 'good' strain of a malo-lactic organism to encourage the malo-lactic fermentation (Kunkee, 1974). Ough and Kunkee (1974) have shown that, with wines having very low concentrations of acid, quality was improved by bacterial inoculation with *L. oenos* ML 34 as compared with the same wine in which there was a spontaneous malo-lactic fermentation.

The 'cottony mould' or 'hair bacillus' (*Lactobacillus trichodes*) is a spoilage organism of fortified and aperitif wines (see Chapter 7, p. 532). One wonders why the occurrence of this type of spoilage is seldom, if ever, reported in table wines. Possibly table wines which are in a condition to be susceptible to infection become spoiled first by some faster-growing spoilage organisms, organisms which would never present a problem in fortified wines with their high concentration of ethanol.

Spoilage by acetic-acid bacteria will not occur in anaerobically stored wine, that is wine in bottles with tight, wet corks or screw caps, or in tanks regularly topped to prevent accumulation of air in the head space, or in tanks blanketed with an inert gas such as carbon dioxide or nitrogen. With today's technology there should be no excuse for a consumer receiving a vinegary bottle of wine, and indeed it is a very rare occurrence. Winemakers need more than best intentions, however. They need to be constantly alert to maintain proper cellar treatment, especially during the hectic times of the vintage, and particularly during vintages with high production.

2. Yeast Spoilage

a. *Spoilage of bulk wine.* Yeasts can cause spoilage of wine. A well-known example of yeast spoilage of bulk wine is the surface appearance of species of *Candida*, still sometimes referred to by the appellation given by Pasteur, namely *Mycoderma vini*. These films, which occasionally appear on new wine in storage tanks, are unsightly, but apparently have little effect on the flavour of the wine. The film can be removed by skimming and by raising the sulphur dioxide concentration. This is sometimes done by carefully laying wine with a high concentration of sulphur dioxide on top of the stored wine. The *Mycoderma vini* films should not be confused with *Mycoderma aceti*, the old name for film-forming acetic-acid bacteria. Strains of *Pichia* have also been reported as surface contaminants of stored wine.

Another example of a yeast spoilage is that caused by *Brettanomyces* spp. Problems with this organism seldom occur, but the astute winemaker should be familiar with its appearance, effect and control (van der Walt and van Kerken, 1958, 1961; van Zyl, 1962). The spoilage can often be noticed by a metallic character imparted to the flavour of the wine. The organisms are easily diagnosed by their microscopic appearance; they have multilateral budding, similar to *Saccharomyces* spp., but they are smaller and a large proportion of the cells have an ogive shape. They are also distinguished from most species of *Saccharomyces* by being resistant to cycloheximide (Lodder, 1970). In California, there was a recent occurrence in some wineries of spoilage by *Dekkera* spp. which are the sporogenous forms of *Brettanomyces* spp. (R. E. Kunkee, personal observation). The focal points of the infections were quickly discovered, and corrected by filtration or centrifugation of the affected wine, followed by addition of sulphur dioxide. The contaminated equipment and vessels received thorough cleansing and were sterilized where possible.

Perhaps the most serious yeast infection of bulk wine would be that by *Saccharomycodes ludwigii*, since this organism has been found in wines made from highly sulphited musts (Amerine and Kunkee, 1968). Widespread contamination of a winery by any micro-organism with a high resistance to sulphur dioxide could spell disaster for the winery.

b. *Spoilage of bottled wine.* i. Dry wine: In bottled wine, the most common type of yeast spoilage is that of refermentation of any residual sugar by wine yeast or other contaminating yeast. However, bottled wine normally classed as completely dry sometimes may become contaminated with visible yeast growth. Rankine and Pilone (1974) reported on contaminated wine which contained only non-fermentable pentoses. Some of the yeast species which have been said to cause this kind of spoilage in dry table wines are *Candida rugosa, Pichia membranaefaciens, Saccharomyces acidifaciens, Sacch. bayanus, Sacch. cerevisiae, Sacch. chevalieri* and *Sacch. uvarum* (Scheffer and Mrak, 1951; van der Walt and van Kerken, 1958). *Brettanomyces* spp., already mentioned in connection with spoilage of bulk wine, have sometimes been the causative agent of bottled-wine spoilage (van der Walt and van Kerken, 1958).

ii. Semi-dry wine: Economic loss by spoilage of bottled wine is more likely to occur in semi-dry wines which have not received proper preventative treatment at the time of bottling. The wines themselves are usually those which have been fermented to dryness, stored as dry wine and then sweetened by addition of conserved grape juice at the time of bottling. Several methods of conserving the grape juice may be employed; they include aseptic filtration (to remove yeast) followed by aseptic storage, addition of distilled spirits, or addition of very high concentrations of sulphur dioxide. In all instances, it is usual to store this sweetening agent at near 0°C. A more difficult method of preparing semi-dry wine is to interrupt the fermentation when the desired residual sugar is obtained, either by centrifugation or by chilling, and then to store this semi-dry wine under conditions which will prevent refermentation until the time of bottling.

The types of yeast which causes refermentation in bottled semi-dry wine are generally the same as those involved in the primary fermentation, namely *Sacch. cerevisiae* or *Sacch. bayanus*. But other yeasts which are also resistant to high concentrations of ethanol, and which might be present, could also cause spoilage. *Brettanomyces* spp., *Candida* spp., *Pichia membranaefaciens*, several species of *Saccharomyces* including *bailii* var. *bailii, bisporus* and *capensis, Saccharomycodes ludwigii* and *Torulopsis stellata* have all been reported (Amerine and Kunkee, 1968; Rankine and Pilone, 1974). It has been demonstrated (Campbell and Thompson, 1970) that as few as four viable yeast cells in a bottle of wine may be sufficient to cause spoilage.

Refermentation in the bottle results in yeast growth and carbon dioxide formation so that the wine becomes cloudy and gassy. Sometimes so much gas is evolved that the cork is ejected. Often the wine also acquires a very poor flavour and is unsaleable. In this case, it is rarely worthwhile to attempt to recondition the wine. At other times, the wine may contain so little sugar that the fermenting yeast is unable to produce perceptible amounts of gas, or it may be infected with a yeast which assimilates the sugar without fermenting it. In such instances, the yeast produces an unsightly deposit, but frequently the flavour does not suffer. When this happens, it is often possible to recondition the wine by sterile filtration, although this is not always economically feasible. The wines most susceptible to this type of refermentation are semi-dry white wines, which contain less than 11% alcohol by volume, but red wines and also fortified white wines with alcoholic strengths up to 17% by volume are occasionally infected.

The three most common methods used to prevent refermentation of semi-dry wine after bottling are: (1) hot bottling; (2) addition of sorbic acid; and (3) sterile filtration and sterile bottling. The last method is the most desirable system as it is likely to have the least effect on the flavour and character of the wine being processed.

Hot bottling is relatively easy and certain. The wine is heated by a heat exchanger and then is usually cooled by ambient air. The temperatures required vary with pH value and alcoholic strength of the wines. It has been shown (Müller-Späth, 1973) that, under ideal conditions with the presence of some sulphur dioxide, temperatures of 40°C are sufficient to inactivate yeast and 45°C to inactivate bacteria. To achieve sterility under the most unfavourable conditions, 57°C may be required but, in practice, temperatures between 45-50°C are usually found to be adequate. It has been said that this procedure brings about some deterioration of wine quality, especially in white wines. The wine should be properly protected from air contact with an inert gas during bottling.

Sorbic acid addition: In most countries, sulphur dioxide and sorbic acid are the only legally permitted preservatives for wine. At the maximum permitted concentration, which is usually around 300 mg/l, sulphur dioxide has little inhibitory action on many yeasts. Sorbic acid, which is usually permitted up to 200 mg/l, is more effective. The minimum concentration to be used must be determined empirically and is dependent on the concentration of ethanol, sulphur dioxide, nutrients and the number of yeast cells themselves (Ough and Ingraham, 1960). Sorbic acid is not very soluble in wines and is usually used in the form of potassium sorbate. In either form it is difficult to store, and old samples of the compound sometimes develop an inferior flavour. Even fresh sorbic acid in good condition has a flavour perceptible to many tasters when used at the maximum permitted concentration. Certain tasters are particularly sensitive to this compound and can detect it, and dislike it, in all wines, even when it is used at quite moderate concentrations. Another disadvantage of sorbic acid is that wines treated with it sometimes develop a very strong odour resembling the odour of geraniums ('geranium tone'), which is obnoxious in wine.

Wines which contain sorbic acid should be handled as hygienically as possible, since some yeasts are able to grow in its presence at the maximum permitted concentration. Sulphur dioxide must be used in combination with sorbic acid, since sorbic acid has little inhibitory action against bacteria. Some lactic-acid bacteria may metabolize sorbic acid and give rise to undesirable odours such as the 'geranium tone'.

Sterile filtration and sterile bottling: It is possible to remove all yeasts from wine by a suitable filtration procedure. For convenience we are calling this procedure *sterile filtration* although, strictly speaking, this is an inaccurate term unless all micro-organisms, including bacteria, are also removed. After the filtration, to avoid subsequent spoilage by yeast the wine must come into contact only with sterile equipment. In practice, a bottling line consisting of the sterilizing filter, pipework, intercepting tanks and fillers, is assembled and the whole is sterilized with live steam or hot water. In addition, sterile bottles and sterile corks or other closures must be used.

Sterile filtration can be achieved either with asbestos- or cellulose-containing filter pads of a suitable type; those graded as type EK ('Entkeimung', i.e. 'degerming') are recommended, or alternatively a membrane filter may be used. If EK filter sheets are used, it is important that the wine supplied to the filter should not be grossly contaminated. The wine should be prefiltered with a coarse filter so that it is free from visible material in suspension and contains less than 500 yeast cells/ml. The filter holder should be properly designed so that there are no crevices, which are difficult to sterilize, and it should be fitted with inlet and outlet pressure gauges. Manufacturers themselves indicate the maximum differential pressure which should exist across the sheets, and this recommendation should be rigidly followed. Sudden surges of pressure must not be permitted, and a suitable automatic pressure relief valve should be fitted so that these surges do not occur. Failure to observe these precautions may result in sterility failures which will not be immediately apparent. Generally, the filter sheet is not the source of re-infection if this occurs. More often, unsuitable filters or defective fittings, such as pressure gauge diaphragms, are responsible.

Membrane filters have rather different properties from depth filters. If a suitable grade is chosen, they give complete protection against yeast contamination even with some unsuitable pressures or when some surges of pressure are permitted. However, they have a very small capacity for removing contaminating material from the wine. Therefore, a thorough prefiltration system must be employed if their use is to be economic. One significant advantage of some membrane filters is their capability of being examined *in situ* by the 'bubble-point' test for integrity and proper installation.

A difficulty with sterile bottling is that one cannot immediately discern whether sterile conditions have actually been achieved. A number of methods are used to judge the efficiency of sterile bottling. Some operators take bottles from the lines, centrifuge the wine and examine the deposit microscopically. This will only serve to reveal gross filtration failures. In addition to such a direct microscopic test, most operators use a biological test which may take a variety of forms. Earlier, the tests involved the use of a few millilitres of wine, either spread directly onto a nutrient-agar surface or mixed with molten nutrient agar for making a 'pour plate'. The samples were then incubated for several days to determine if any colonies would appear. These tests were comparatively insensitive since only a small sample of wine was examined. It has now become more usual to pass the contents of a whole bottle through a membrane filter which retains all of the contaminating micro-organisms, and to incubate this filter in contact with a suitable nutrient medium. After two to three days' incubation, the filters are examined for colony formation. One difficulty has been that there are some wine-contaminating yeasts which grow little, if at all, on the surface of solid media. Therefore, tests in liquid media should be used in addition to this standard test. The test described by Campbell and Thompson (1970) is ideal.

These biological tests suffer from the disadvantage that the results are not obtainable until two or three days after bottling. Therefore, attempts have been made to devise an immediate test whereby the yeast from bottles of wine are concentrated, usually on a membrane filter of small diameter, and the filter examined microscopically. It is, however, difficult to distinguish between living and dead yeast in this situation. Three methods to detect viability have recently been proposed. One method, already in use in several wineries (Neradt and Kunkee, 1973; Kunkee and Neradt, 1974) involves the use of a methylene-blue stain and microscopical examination with incident light. This is followed by staining with red Ponceau S solution and re-examination. The difference between the number of blue (dead) and red (total) yeast cells gives the number of viable yeast in the sample.

A second quick method (Anon., 1975) is similar to the first method, except that a single staining procedure, with a proprietary stain, is used to obtain two colours of yeast, one colour for live yeasts and another for dead yeasts. In this test, Nucleopore membrane filters are used which are transparent enough to allow the use of transmitted light during microscopic examination. With a third method (Paton and Jones, 1975), filtration is carried out on brown or black membrane filters, which are then treated with an optical whitener, such as CH3558, and stained with fluorescein diacetate. The membrane is examined with a suitable microscope using ultraviolet radiation. Only living cells fluoresce.

For more information concerning bacterial and yeast spoilages of wine, and for historical interest too, the reader is directed to review articles by Vaughn (1955), Lüthi (1957, 1959) and, of course, to the first or second edition of Pasteur's text, 'Études sur le Vin' (1866, 1873).

VIII. SULPHUR DIOXIDE ADDITION

We have mentioned the need for sulphur dioxide to prevent browning reactions in juice and wine, in inhibition of wild yeast in must, and in the prevention of growth of spoilage organisms in wine. Organoleptically, there is no objection to the use of sulphur dioxide at low concentrations provided that free sulphur dioxide is not detected on the nose or that bound sulphur dioxide is not detected on the palate. Clearly, at high concentrations of sulphur dioxide, health hazards might be present. However, studies with animals would indicate that at low concentrations sulphur dioxide has low toxicity when administered either with or without acetaldehyde (Lanteaume et al., 1969). Lüthi (1972a) discussed the question of safety of sulphur dioxide, especially in the light of recommendations of the F.A.O.-W.H.O. Toxicology committees of the International Codex Alimentarium. This body concluded that the maximum daily intake per person should not exceed 20 to 30 mg (Lüthi, 1972a). At the Third International Oenological Symposium held at Cape Town,

Lüthi (1972a) suggested that oenologists should volunteer to take 'the inevitable step' to lower the concentration of sulphur dioxide in wine as much as possible and as soon as possible. Can wine be made with little or no added sulphur dioxide? A qualified 'yes' seems to be the answer (Lüthi, 1972a, b). First, it needs to be stressed that sulphur dioxide is a natural product and wine yeasts, in the absence of added sulphur dioxide, can produce as much as 80 mg of this compound/l during alcoholic fermentation (Würdig and Schlotter, 1971; Eschenbruch, 1972; Minárik, 1972; Dittrich et al., 1973). There would be some difficulties in making wine without added sulphur dioxide, and the winery operations would certainly be more expensive, although the procedure is possible. With white-grape must, careful use of high temperature–short time (HTST) heating would kill the wild yeasts and inactivate browning enzymes. When this is done carefully, there is apparently no deteriorative effect on the subsequent wine quality. A much more difficult situation is encountered with crushed grapes for red-wine production. It would not be feasible to apply HTST treatment to this bulky material. The skins could be removed after pigment extraction in order to allow this treatment, but the best thermovinification procedure (see Section IV, p. 341) also requires addition of sulphur dioxide. Other methods of extraction might be developed, or perhaps a greater maceration of the skins could be used to allow for a suspension which could receive HTST treatment. After fermentation, browning of the wine could be inhibited by strict anaerobic conditions. The use of ascorbic acid has been suggested, but this compound seems to cause unusual flavours in some red table-wine. Preventing spoilage of wine without the use of sulphur dioxide could be done by sterile filtration and continual storage under sterile conditions, followed by sterile bottling. Centrifugation could be used to prepare the new wine for this sterile filtration. The procedure for maintaining sterile storage conditions is technically possible but would be difficult to put into practice. It would require an extensive indoctrination programme for winery personnel to make them aware of the problems in this kind of operation. This may be an expensive programme, but not an impossible one. We have seen positive changes in attitude towards sterilization requirements by production personnel in wineries which have converted to sterile bottling of semi-dry wine.

Sulphur dioxide is sometimes added at the end of the alcoholic fermentation to bind any excess acetaldehyde present. This is necessary in white wine for taste purposes. In red wine, if acetaldehyde is not bound, it tends to react with pigments, inducing premature ageing, undesirable flavours and the deposition of complexed pigments. However, if sulphur dioxide were not added to begin with, formation of acetaldehyde would be minimized, or the small amount formed would be bound with the natural sulphur dioxide formed by the yeast.

IX. ECONOMIC FUTURE

We feel that we can make one prediction about the outlook for the future, as far as table wines are concerned. With advanced technology, the average wines, the *vins ordinaires*, will become of higher and higher quality, and probably less expensive. To predict whether the savings gained from modern technology will really keep up with increased costs from inflation and scarcity of resources, we will leave to the professional economists. Perhaps we should also leave to them any predictions about the volume of consumption and production of wine in the years to come. In order to make this kind of assessment, it might be helpful again to consider our 'wine world' in two parts, as we did in the Introduction to this chapter. We saw that there has been a striking increase in production and consumption of wine in traditionally low wine-consuming regions, such as in the United States of America. Should we be optimistic and expect this increase in production to continue steadily? A look at the history of some of the 'new' wine regions shows that these expansions have often led to over-production and to economic disasters for the wine grower. So would it be wiser to be pessimistic? A survey of a few years ago is of interest here. Thirty American wine merchandisers (representing over half of the American wine sales) were asked in 1969 to predict what the table-wine consumption in the United States would be ten years hence (Marcus, 1969). They seemed to be very optimistic; they gave an average estimate of 191 million U.S. gallons (723 million litres) for 1979, over four times the consumption in 1969. Amazingly enough, that 191 million gallons is precisely the figure for the sale of table wine in the United States in 1973 (Anon., 1974b), only five years later.

We would venture the opinion that future prosperity for wine producers on a World-wide basis is, however, more realistically grounded on increased efficiency rather than increased wine consumption. We can present some suggestions for advanced technology which have come out of informal discussions on this subject with colleagues. These include the use of solid support enzymes rather than bacteria for the malo-lactic fermentation, storage of raw material in such a way that fermentation can be conducted throughout the year instead of only at vintage time, and use of continuous fermentation with multi-stage fermentors of varying dilution rates to correspond to fermentation rates of various yeasts to give a product with more complex flavour.

Cream of tartar (potassium bitartrate), grape seed oil and dried pomace (as fodder adjunct or mulch) are traditional by-products of the wine industry (Amerine *et al.*, 1972). The economic feasibility of collecting and distributing each of these products has been extremely variable with respect to time and place, and largely dependent upon competition with other products. More efficient recovery methods of these by-products or more accurate assessment of markets should be a means of improving the economics of wine production. For example, except for cost, tartaric acid is probably the best of the organic acids for use as an acidulating agent (Kunkee, 1974). Tartrates make up a substantial portion of the waste material of wineries. Yet at present, World production of tartaric acid is low and the supply is extremely limited.

We end on an encouraging note. Whether the fortunes of the wine growers and wine makers of the world are destined for unparalleled prosperity or not—because of new efficiencies of production, increased markets and better use of by-products—we reject the notion that their lot will much deteriorate. In addition to the economic value, the wine craftsman is able to take satisfaction in the intrinsic value of the product. We have mentioned that for so long, and so far and wide, wine has been the beverage of choice amongst much of the World's population. This choice continues into many parts of the modern World, in spite of the competition with other beverages. It must be gratifying for the wine maker who realizes that, with people of moderation, wine drinking is ever being rediscovered as an enriching experience. All of this has been said more poetically (Fitzgerald, 1942): 'I wonder what the Vinters buy One half so precious as the stuff they sell.'

REFERENCES

Acree, T. C., Sonoff, E. P. and Splittstoesser, D. G. (1972). *American Journal of Enology and Viticulture* 23, 6.

Alizade, M. A. and Simon, H. (1973). *Hoppe-Seyler's Zeitschrift für Physiologische Chemie* 354, 163.

Allen, H. W. (1961). 'A History of Wine'. Horizon Press, New York.

Alley, C. J. (1974). *Wines and Vines* 55 (2), 34.

Amerine, M. A. (1972). *Journal of Milk and Food Technology* 35, 373.

Amerine, M. A. and Fong, D. (1974). *American Journal of Enology and Viticulture* 25, 1.

Amerine, M. A. and Joslyn, M. A. (1970). 'Table Wines'. 2nd edition. University of California Press, Berkeley, California.

Amerine, M. A. and Kunkee, R. E. (1965). *Vitis* 5, 187.

Amerine, M. A. and Kunkee, R. E. (1968). *Annual Review of Microbiology* 22, 323.

Amerine, M. A. and Ough, C. S. (1968). *American Journal of Enology and Viticulture* 19, 139.

Amerine, M. A. and Ough, C. S. (1969). *American Journal of Enology and Viticulture* 20, 251.

Amerine, M. A. and Ough, C. S. (1972). *Critical Reviews in Food Technology* 2, 407.

Amerine, M. A. and Winkler, A. J. (1940). *Proceedings of the American Society for Horticultural Science* 38, 379.

Amerine, M. A. and Winkler, A. J. (1944). *Hilgardia* 15, 493.

Amerine, M. A. and Winkler, A. J. (1963). 'California Wine Grapes'. California Agricultural Experiment Station Bulletin 794. University of California Division of Agricultural Sciences, Richmond, California.

Amerine, M. A., Berg, H. W. and Cruess, W. V. (1972). 'Technology of Wine Making'. 3rd edition. Avi Publishing Co., Westport, Connecticut.

Andreasen, A. A. and Stier, T. J. B. (1953). *Journal of Cellular and Comparative Physiology* 43, 23.

Andreasen, A. A. and Stier, T. J. B. (1954). *Journal of Cellular and Comparative Physiology* 43, 271.

Anon. (1964a). *Bulletin de l'Office International de la Vigne et du Vin* 37, No. 403, pp. 935, 965.

Anon. (1964b). *Wines and Vines* 45 (4), 39.

Anon. (1973a). 'California Wine Outlook'. Bank of America NT & SA Brochure, p. 12, San Francisco, California. Data compiled from *Bulletin de l'Office International de la Vigne et du Vin*.

Anon. (1973b). '1973 Pest and Disease Control Program for Grapes'. University of California Agricultural Extension pamphlet R898LKB. University of California Division of Agricultural Sciences, Richmond, California.

Anon. (1974a). *Bulletin de l'Office International de la Vigne et du Vin* 47, No. 525, pp. 934, 938, 939, 949.

Anon. (1974b). *Wines and Vines* 55 (4), 32.

Anon. (1974c). *Wines and Vines* 55 (8), 33.

Anon. (1974d). 'California Grape Acreage 1974'. California Crop and Livestock Reporting Service, Sacramento, California.

Anon. (1975). 'Differential Yeast Counts'. Johns-Manville, Denver, Colorado.

Augustyn, O. P. H., van Wyk, C. J., Muller, C. J., Kepner, R. E. and Webb, A. D. (1971). *Agricultural and Food Chemistry* 19, 1128.

Äyräpää, T. (1962). *Nature, London* 194, 472.

Äyräpää, T. (1963). *Proceedings of the European Brewery Convention*, Vienna 276.

Babij, T., Moss, F. J. and Ralph, B. J. (1969). *Biotechnology and Bioengineering* 11, 593.

Beelman, R. B. and McArdle, F. J. (1974). *American Journal of Enology and Viticulture* 25, 219.

Belin, J.-M. (1972). *Vitis* 11, 135.

Belin, J.-M. and Henry, P. (1972). *Comptes Rendus Hebdomadaire des Séances de l'Academie des Sciences, Paris* 274D, 2318.

Belin, J.-M. and Henry, P. (1973). *Comptes Rendus Hebdomadaire des Séances de l'Academie des Sciences, Paris* 277D, 1885.

Berg, H. W. and Keefer, R. M. (1958). *American Journal of Enology* 9, 180.

Berg, H. W. and Keefer, R. M. (1959). *American Journal of Enology* 10, 105.

Blaise, J. (1964). *Anesthesie, Analgesie, Reanimation, Paris* 21, 677.

Boubals, D., Agulhon, R., Amphoux, M. and Vergnes, A. (1957). *Progrès Agricole et Viticole* 147, 251.

Bréchot, P., Chauvet, J., Dupuy, P., Croson, M. and Rabatu, A. (1971). *Annales de Technologie Agricole* 20, 103.

Brémond, E. (1957). 'Techniques Modernes de Vinification'. La Maison Rustique, Paris.

Brown, A. D. (1905). *Annales de la Brasserie et de la Distillerie* 8, 457.

Buchner, H. and Rapp, R. (1903). *Annales de la Brasserie et de la Distillerie* 6, 121.

Burlingame, B. B., Kasimatis, A. N., Bearden, B. E., Lider, J. V., Sisson, R. L. and Parsons, R. A. (1971). 'Frost Protection Costs for North Coast Vineyards'. University of California Agricultural Extension pamphlet AXT-267. University of California Division of Agricultural Sciences, Richmond, California.

Campbell, I. and Thompson, J. W. (1970). *Journal of the Institute of Brewing* 76, 465.

Carcopino, J. (1968). 'Daily Life in Ancient Rome'. Yale University Press, New Haven, Connecticut.

Carisetti, D. A. and Kunkee, R. E. (1975). Program of the 26th Annual Meeting of the American Society of Enologists p. 32.

Cartledge, T. G. and Lloyd, D. (1973). *Biochemical Journal* 132, 609.

Castelli, T. (1969). 'Il Vino al Microscopio', p. 156, Luigi Scialpi, Rome.

Castelli, T. and Rossi, J. (1974). *Vignes et Vins*, March, 19.

Cochin, D. (1880). *Annales Chimie et de Physique* 21, 551.

Cofran, D. R. and Meyer, J. (1970). *American Journal of Enology and Viticulture* 21, 189.

Cook, J. A. and Kishaba, T. (1956). *Proceedings of the American Society for Horticultural Science* 68, 131.

Coulon, P. (1971). *Bulletin de l'Office International de la Vigne et du Vin* 44, 680.

Crabtree, H. G. (1929). *Biochemical Journal* 23, 536.

da Rosa, T. (1972). *Bulletin de l'Office International de la Vigne et du Vin* 45, 44.

Davenport, R. (1973). *Society for Applied Bacteriology, London Technical Series* No. 7, p. 143.

David, M. H. (1974). *Journal of the Institute of Brewing* 80, 80.

David, M. H. and Kirsop, B. H. (1973). *Journal of General Microbiology* 77, 520; 79, 20.

De Deken, R. H. (1966). *Journal of General Microbiology* 44, 157.

De Soto, R. T. (1955). *American Journal of Enology* 6 (3), 26.

Delle, P. N. (1911). *Odessa, Otchet" Vinodiel'cheskoi stantsii russkikh" vinogradarei i vinodielov* za 1908 i 1909g., 118–160.

Dittrich, H. H., Staudenmayer, T. and Sponholz, W. R. (1973). *Die Wein-Wissenschaft* 28, 84.

Domercq, S. (1957). *Annales de Technologie Agricole* 6, 5, 139.

Drawert, F. and Barton, H. (1974). *Zeitschrift für Lebensmittel-Untersuchung und -Forschung* 154, 223.

Dubos, R. (1960). 'Pasteur and Modern Science'. 159 pp. Anchor Books, Garden City, New York.

Ergang, A. (1899). *Annales de la Brasserie et de la Distillerie* 2, 101.

Eriksson, K. and Webb, A. D. (1970). *Annales Medicinae Experimentalis et Biologiae Fenniae* 48, 273.

Eschenbruch, R. (1972). *Die Wein-Wissenschaft* 27, 40.

Fages-Bonnery, A. (1967). 'Fermentations et Vinifications', p. 553. Institut National de la Recherche Agronomique, Paris.

Fitzgerald, E. (1942). In 'A Treasury of Great Poems' (L. Untermeyer, ed.), p. 851. Simon and Shuster, New York.

Flanzy, C. (1972). *Revue Française d'Oenologie* No. 45, p. 42.

Flanzy, M., Poux, C., Dubois, P. and Dupuy, P. (1968). *Annales de Technologie Agricole* 17, 207.

Foulonneau, C. (1971). 'Guide de la Plantation des Vignes'. Institut Technique du Vin, Paris.

Frank, T. (1959). 'An Economic Survey of Ancient Rome'. 445 pp. Vol. 5. Pageant Books, Inc., Paterson, New Jersey.

Gagnon, A. J. (1973). *Wines and Vines* 54 (12), 32.

Gandini, A. (1969). *Vini d'Italia* 11, 125, 227.

Gates, N. E. (1971). Slogan for 'Universal Order of the Knights of the Vine of California', Sacramento, California.

Gordon, P. A. and Stewart, P. R. (1972). *Journal of General Microbiology* 72, 231.

Graff, R. H. and Tchelistcheff, A. (1969). *Wines and Vines* 50 (5), 30.

Haushofer, H. (1972). In 'Third International Oenological Symposium', Cape of Good Hope, paper 8. Cape Wine and Spirit Institute, Stellenbosch.

Hewitt, W. B. (1970). In 'Virus Diseases of Small Fruits and Grapevines' (N. W. Frazier, ed.). University of California Division of Agricultural Sciences, Richmond, California.

Hewitt, W. B. (1974). 'Rots and Bunch Rots of Grapes'. California Agricultural Experiment Station Bulletin 868. University of California Division of Agricultural Sciences, Richmond, California.

Hiaring, P. (1974a). *Wines and Vines* 55 (8), 39.

Hiaring, S. (1974b). *Wines and Vines* 55 (4), 65.

Hieke, E., Järgen, H. and Sebastian, R. (1971). 'Wegwiser durch das neue Weinrecht'. Rhein-Hahe-Druckerei Raupach, Bingen.

Husmann, G. C. (1905). 'Yearbook of the United States Department of Agriculture 1904' (G. W. Hill, ed.), p. 363. Washington, D.C.

Kasimatis, A. N. (1971). 'Vineyard Irrigation'. University of California Agricultural Extension pamphlet AXT-199. University of California Division of Agricultural Sciences, Richmond, California.

Kepner, R. E., Strating, J. and Weurman, C. (1963). *Journal of the Institute of Brewing* 69, 399.

Kepner, R. E., Maarse, H. and Strating, J. (1964). *Analytical Chemistry* 36, 77.

Kliewer, W. M. (1966). *Plant Physiology* 41, 923.

Kliewer, W. M. and Cook, J. A. (1974). *American Journal of Enology and Viticulture* 25, 111.

Kliewer, W. M., Howarth, L. and Omori, M. (1967). *American Journal of Enology and Viticulture* 18, 42.

Knappstein, A. T. and Rankine, B. C. (1970). *Australian Wine, Brewing and Spirit Review* 89 (3), 52, 54.

Kunkee, R. E. (1967). *Advances in Applied Microbiology* 9, 235.

Kunkee, R. E. (1974). *In* 'Chemistry of Winemaking' (A. D. Webb, ed.), Advances in Chemistry Series, No. 137, p. 137. American Chemical Society, Washington.

Kunkee, R. E. (1975). *In* 'Lactic Acid Bacteria in Beverages and Foods' (J. G. Carr, C. V. Cutting and G. C. Whiting, eds.), pp. 29–42. Academic Press, London.

Kunkee, R. E. and Amerine, M. A. (1968). *Applied Microbiology* 16, 1067.

Kunkee, R. E. and Amerine, M. A. (1970). *In* 'The Yeasts' (A. H. Rose and J. S. Harrison, eds.), Vol. 3, pp. 5–71. Academic Press, London.

Kunkee, R. E. and Neradt, F. (1974). *Wines and Vines* 55 (12), 36.

Kunkee, R. E. and Singh, R. (1975). *Journal of the Institute of Brewing* 81, 214.

Kunkee, R. E., Guymon, J. F. and Crowell, E. A. (1966). *Journal of the Institute of Brewing* 72, 530.

Kunkee, R. E., Guymon, J. F. and Crowell, E. A. (1972). *In* 'Yeasts Models in Science and Technics' (A. Kockova and E. Minárik, eds.), p. 531. Bratislava, Czechoslovakia.

Langenbach, A. (1951). 'The Wines of Germany'. Harper & Co., London.

Langenbach, A. (1962). 'German Wines and Vines'. Vista Books, London.

Lanteaume, M. T., Ramel, P., Jaulmes, R. and Manin, D. (1969). *Annales des Falsifications et de l'Expertise Chimique* 62, 231.

Lausanne, E. (1970). 'The Great Book of Wine'. Galahad Books, New York.

Lider, L. A. (1958). *Hilgardia* 27, 287.

Lodder, J. (1970). 'The Yeasts, A Taxonomic Study'. North-Holland Publishing Co., Amsterdam.

Loustaunau-Deguilhem, J. (1946). 'La Vigne et le Vin'. Montsouris, Paris.

Lüthi, H. (1957). *American Journal of Enology* 8, 176.

Lüthi, H. (1959). *Advances in Food Research* 9, 221.

Lüthi, H. (1972a). *In* 'Third International Oenological Symposium', Cape of Good Hope, paper 16. Cape Wine and Spirit Institute, Stellenbosch.

Lüthi, H. (1972b). *Schweizerische Zeitschrift für Obstbau und Weinbau* 108, 477.

MacRostie, S. W. (1974). M.S. Thesis: University of California, Davis.

Malan, C. E. and Cano Marotta, C. (1959). *Atti della Accademie Italiana della Vite e del Vino, Siena* **XI**, 405.

Marcus, I. H. (1969). *Wines and Vines* **50** (11), 35.

McCorkle, K. (1974). *Wines and Vines* **55** (4), 62.

Mendall, S. C. (1975). *Wines and Vines* **56** (2), 24.

Meyerhof, O. (1925). *Biochemische Zeitschrift* 162, 43.

Milisavljevic, D. (1972). *Bulletin de l'Office International de la Vigne et du Vin* 45, 57.

Minárik, E. (1972). *Mitteilungen Rebe und Wein, Obstbau und Früchteverwertung* 22, 245.

Morenzoni, R. A. (1973). Ph.D. Thesis: University of California, Davis.

Morenzoni, R. (1974). *In* 'Chemistry of Winemaking' (A. D. Webb, ed.), Advances in Chemistry Series, No. 137, p. 151. American Chemical Society, Washington.

Muller, C. J., Maggiora, L., Kepner, R. E. and Webb, A. D. (1969). *Agricultural and Food Chemistry* 17, 1373.

Muller, C. J., Kepner, R. E. and Webb, A. D. (1971). *American Journal of Enology and Viticulture* 22, 156.

Muller, C. J., Kepner, R. E. and Webb, A. D. (1972). *Agricultural and Food Chemistry* 20, 193.

Muller, C. J., Kepner, R. E. and Webb, A. D. (1973). *American Journal of Enology and Viticulture* 24, 5.

Müller-Späth, H. (1973). *Allgemeine Deutsche Weinfachzeitung* 109, 838.

Nègre, E., Robert, J. and Martem, G. (1971). *Bulletin de l'Office International de la Vigne et du Vin* **44**, 827.

Neradt, F. and Kunkee, R. E. (1973). *Weinberg und Keller* 20, 469.

Ough, C. S. (1964). *American Journal of Enology and Viticulture* 15, 167.

Ough, C. S. and Alley, C. J. (1970). *American Journal of Enology and Viticulture* 21, 78.

Ough, C. S. and Amerine, M. A. (1966). 'Effects of Temperature on Wine Making', California Agricultural Experiment Station Bulletin 827. University of California Division of Agricultural Sciences, Richmond, California.

Ough, C. S. and Ingraham, J. L. (1960). *American Journal of Enology and Viticulture* 11, 117.

Ough, C. S. and Kunkee, R. E. (1968). *Applied Microbiology* 16, 572.

Ough, C. S. and Kunkee, R. E. (1974). *American Journal of Enology and Viticulture* 25, 188.

Ough, C. S. and Singleton, V. L. (1968). *American Journal of Enology and Viticulture* 19, 129.

Paigen, K. and Williams, B. (1970). *Advances in Microbial Physiology* 4, 252.

Park, Y. H. (1974). *Connaissance de la Vigne et du Vin* 8, 253.

Pasteur, L. (1866). 'Études sur le Vin'. 1st edition. Masson, Paris.

Pasteur, L. (1873). 'Études sur le Vin'. 2nd edition. F. Savy, Paris.

Pasteur, L. (1876). 'Études sur la Bière', p. 241. Gauthier-Vallars, Paris.

Paton, A. M. and Jones, S. M. (1975). *Journal of Applied Bacteriology* 38, 199.

Peynaud, E. (1967). *Process Biochemistry*, December, 44.

Peynaud, E. and Domercq, S. (1961). *Annales de Technologie Agricole* 10, 43.

Pilone, G. J. (1971). Ph.D. Thesis: University of California, Davis.

Pilone, G. J. (1975). *In* 'Lactic Acid Bacteria in Beverages and Foods' (J. G. Carr, C. V. Cutting and G. C. Whiting, eds.), p. 121. Academic Press, London.

Pilone, G. J. and Kunkee, R. E. (1965). *American Journal of Enology and Viticulture* 16, 224.

Pilone, G. J., Kunkee, R. E. and Webb, A. D. (1966). *Applied Microbiology* 14, 608.

Pilone, G. J., Rankine, B. C. and Pilone, D. A. (1974). *American Journal of Enology and Viticulture* 25, 99.

Polakis, E. S., Bartley, W. and Meek, G. A. (1965). *Biochemical Journal* 97, 298.

Porter, J. R. (1972). *Science, New York* 178, 1249.

Pulliat, V. (1888). 'Mille Variétés de Vignes'. 3rd edition. Camille Coulet, Montpellier.

Radler, F. (1965). *American Journal of Enology and Viticulture* 16, 159.

Radler, F. (1966). *Zentralblatt für Bakteriologie Parasitenkunde und Infektionskrankheiten, Abteil II* 120, 237.

Rankine, B. C. (1963). *Journal of the Science of Food and Agriculture* 14, 79.

Rankine, B. C. (1964). *Journal of the Science of Food and Agriculture* 15, 872.

Rankine, B. C. (1971a). *Australian Wine, Brewing and Spirit Review* 90 (1), 52; (2), 40.

Rankine, B. C. (1971b). *Food Technology in Australia* 23, 246.

Rankine, B. C. (1972). *American Journal of Enology and Viticulture* 23, 152.

Rankine, B. C. (1974). *Australian Wine, Brewing and Spirit Review* 92 (8), 30.

Rankine, B. C. and Pilone, D. A. (1974). *Australian Wine, Brewing and Spirit Review* 92 (11), 36.

Rankine, B. C., Fornachon, J. C. M. and Bridson, D. A. (1969). *Vitis* 8, 129.

Rankine, B. C., Fornachon, J. C. M., Boehm, E. W. and Cellier, K. M. (1971). *Vitis* 10, 33.

Raski, D. J., Hart, W. H. and Kasimatis, A. N. (1973). 'Nematodes and their Control in Vineyards', California Agricultural Experiment Station Circular 533, University of California Division of Agricultural Sciences, Richmond, California.

Renaud, J. (1939–40). *Annales des Fermentations* 5, 410.

Ribéreau-Gayon, R. and Sapis, J.-C. (1965). *Comptes Rendus Hebdomadaire des Séances de l'Academie des Sciences, Paris* 261, 1915.

Ribéreau-Gayon, J. and Peynaud, E. (1971). 'Science et Techniques de la Vigne', Vol. 2. Dunod, Paris.

Robe, K. (1974). *Food Processing* August, 32.

Rogers, P. J. and Stewart, P. R. (1973). *Journal of General Microbiology* 79, 205.

Rogers, P. J., Yue, S. B. and Stewart, P. R. (1974). *Journal of Bacteriology* 118, 523.

Rubin, B. A. and Giarman, N. J. (1947). *Yale Journal of Biology and Medicine* 19, 1017.

Ruffner, H. P., Koblet, W. and Rast, D. (1974). *Vitis* 13, 319.

Sakato, K. H. (1974). M.S. Thesis: University of California, Davis.

Scheffer, W. R. and Mrak, E. M. (1951). *Mycopathologia et Mycologia Applicata* 5, 236.

Schimpfessel, L. (1966). *Revue des Fermentations et des Industries Alimentaires* 21, 117, 161, 201.

Schimpfessel, L. (1967). *Revue des Fermentations et des Industries Alimentaires* 22, 31, 67, 69, 145.

Schimpfessel, L. (1968). *Biochimica et Biophysica Acta* 151, 317.

Schütz, M. and Radler, F. (1973). *Archiv für Mikrobiologie* 91, 183.

Shand, P. M. (1929). 'A Book of Other Wines—than French'. Alfred A. Knopf, Ltd., London.

Shimwell, J. L. (1947). *American Brewer*, May, 21, 56.

Singh, R. (1975). Ph.D. Thesis: University of California, Davis.

Singh, R. and Kunkee, R. E. (1975). Annual Meeting of the American Society for Microbiology, p. 197.

Singleton, V. L. (1972). *In* 'Third International Oenological Symposium', Cape of Good Hope, paper 9. Cape Wine and Spirit Institute, Stellenbosch.

Singleton, V. L. (1973). *Wines and Vines* 54 (5), 26; (6), 70.

Singleton, V. L. and Ough, C. S. (1962). *Journal of Food Science* 27, 189.

Singleton, V. L., Ough, C. S. and Amerine, M. A. (1964). *American Journal of Enology and Viticulture* 15, 134.

Sisani, L. (1948). *Rivista di Viticoltura e di Enologia* 1, 142.

Sols, A., Gancedo, C. and dela Fuente, G. (1971). *In* 'The Yeasts' (A. H. Rose and J. S. Harrison, eds.), Vol. 2, pp. 271–307. Academic Press, London.

Suomalainen, H. and Nykänen, L. (1966). *Suomen Kemistilehti B* 39, 252.

Tchelistcheff, A., Peterson, R. G. and van Gelderen, M. (1971). *American Journal of Enology and Viticulture* 22, 1.

Thoukis, G. and Stern, L. A. (1962). *American Journal of Enology and Viticulture* 13, 113.

Traverso-Rueda, S. and Kunkee, R. E. (1974). Programme of the 25th Annual Meeting of the American Society of Enologists, p. 26.

Traverso-Rueda, S., Kunkee, R. E. and Nelson, K. E. (1973). *American Journal of Enology and Viticulture* 24, 72.

Troost, G. (1971). *Bulletin de l'Office International de la Vigne et du Vin* 44, 1149.

Troost, G. (1972). 'Technologie des Weines'. E. Ulmer, Stuttgart.

Tustanoff, E. R. and Bartley, W. (1962). *Biochemical Journal* 84, 40P.

Tustanoff, E. R. and Bartley, W. (1964). *Canadian Journal of Biochemistry* 42, 651.

Usseglio-Tomasset, L. (1967). *Rivista di Viticoltura e di Enologia* 20, 10.

Vallery-Radot, P. (1924). 'Oeuvres de Pasteur'. Vol. 3, p. 411. Masson, Paris.

van der Walt, J. P. and van Kerken, A. E. (1958). *Antonie van Leeuwenhoek* 24, 239.

van der Walt, J. P. and van Kerken, A. E. (1961). *Antonie van Leeuwenhoek* 27, 81.

van Wyk, C. J. (1973). *Die Wynboer* No. 507, 36.

van Wyk, C. J., Webb, A. D. and Kepner, R. E. (1967a). *Journal of Food Science* 32, 660.

van Wyk, C. J., Kepner, R. E. and Webb, A. D. (1967b). *Journal of Food Science* 32, 669.

van Zyl, J. A. (1962). 'Turbidity in South Africa Dry Wines Caused by the Development of the Brettanomyces Yeasts', Science Bulletin No. 381. Department of Agricultural Technical Services, Pretoria.

Vaughn, R. H. (1955). *Advances in Food Research* 6, 67.

Vollbrecht, D. and Radler, F. (1973). *Archiv für Mikrobiologie* 94, 351.

Wagner, G. (1972). *Bulletin de l'Office International de la Vigne et du Vin* 45, 54.

Wainwright, T. (1971). *Journal of Applied Bacteriology* 34, 161.

Webb, A. D. (1970). *Die Wynboer* No. 468, 62.

Webb, A. D. and Ingraham, J. L. (1963). *Advances in Applied Microbiology* 5, 317.

Webb, A. D. and Kepner, R. E. (1962). *American Journal of Enology and Viticulture* 13, 1.

Webb, A. D., Muller, C. J., Kepner, R. E., Eriksson, K. and Närhi, M. (1972). *American Journal of Enology and Viticulture* 23, 121.

White, B. B. and Ough, C. S. (1973). *American Journal of Enology and Viticulture* 24, 148.

Wildenradt, H. L. and Singleton, V. L. (1974). *American Journal of Enology and Viticulture* 25, 119.

Winkler, A. J. (1959). *American Journal of Enology and Viticulture* 10, 39.

Winkler, A. J., Cook, J. A., Kliewer, W. M. and Lider, L. A. (1974). 'General Viticulture', 2nd edition. University of California Press, Berkeley, California.

Würdig, G. and Schlotter, H. A. (1971). *Deutsche Lebensmittel-Rundschau* 67, 86.

Younger, W. (1966). 'Gods, Men, and Wine'. World Publishing Co., Cleveland, Ohio.

5. Fruit and Honey Wines

ANDRZEJ JARCZYK AND WIESLAW WZOREK

Department of Food Technology,
Agricultural University of Warsaw, Warsaw, Poland

I. INTRODUCTION

Fruit wines have for many years now been an important product obtained from fruit processing. Like the term 'grape wine' or 'wine', the oenological product obtained from fruits is designated 'fruit wine'. Production of fruit wines has gained a foothold in many countries, particularly those characterized by a rougher climate in which cultivation of the grape vine cannot be developed.

The term 'fruit wines' is hard to define, particularly as regards distinguishing it from fermented grape musts with a content of several per cent alcohol, and from cider and perry, all products with a long standing tradition (Warcollier, 1928; Charley, 1954). Considering that legal rules covering fruit wines, as enforced in many countries at the present time, recognize as a fruit wine any fermented fruit must with at least 8–9% alcohol content by volume, the authors have decided not to deal in this chapter with the production of cider, perry or other fruit beverages with an alcohol content below 8–9%. Moreover no further consideration has been given herein to the relatively limited production of wines of pineapples, oranges, grapefruits (Amerine and Cruess, 1960), or to those derived from other tropical fruits like dates or figs.

The authors have discussed wines made from fruits typically originating from regions with climatic conditions most close to those of Central Europe. Such fruits include mainly apples, currants (and other berry fruits) as well as certain stone-fruits, such as plums or cherries.

Production of fruit wines differs essentially from that of grape wines, particularly with regard to the highly differentiated raw material, the need for sweetening and dilution of fruit musts, and the resulting differences as regards the process of fermentation and mellowing.

II. GENERAL INFORMATION

Fruit wines are beverages obtained by alcoholic fermentation of fruits (with the exception of vine grapes) or of juices thereof, with an alcohol content amounting to between approximately 8-9 and 18% (v/v), and sometimes even more. Fruit wines are made mainly out of pome fruits, berry fruits and stone fruits, and less frequently out of citrus and other fruits.

The above definition does not include alcoholic fruit—beverages like cider or perry, since these have a lower alcohol content than fruit wines, of the order of 5-7% (v/v) because sucrose is not added to the juice. The desired strength of fruit wines is obtained by sweetening prepared fruit juices with sugar.

Many criteria have been adopted as valid in connection with the classification of fruit wines. Firstly they are divided, depending on the colouring, into white and red wines, usually with no distinction being made to pink (or rosé) wines (Wzorek, 1973). The basic components which affect the properties of wine are the sugar and the alcohol contents. Detailed wine classification is based upon a differentiation in the contents of the above components. In Poland, for example, a distinction is drawn between dry wines, containing between 0 and 10 g sugar/l and 9–11% alcohol by volume; semi-dry wines, containing from 20 to 30 g sugar/l and 10–12% alcohol by volume; slightly sweet wines, containing 45 to 65 g sugar/l and 11–13% alcohol by volume; sweet wines, containing 80 to 110 g sugar/l and 12–14% alcohol by volume; and very sweet wines with a sugar content in excess of 120 g sugar/l and an alcohol content of the order of 13–18% by volume. Dry and semi-dry wines are designated also as table wines, while those slightly sweet, sweet or very sweet are known as dessert wines. A similar classification is adopted, furthermore, in other countries which is specified by the pertaining standards (GOST 17292-71—Vina plodovo-jagodnye, 1971; GOST 5400-70—Vina plodovo-jagodnye naturalnye, 1970; ČSN 567810—Ovocne vina, PN-71/A-79121 Wino owocowe, 1971); Tables 1 and 2. A distinction is also made for carbonated fruit wines, following a mechanical saturation with carbon dioxide, and sparkling wines containing carbon dioxide obtained by alcoholic fermentation. A separate group is represented by herb wines (including vermouths) with certain added herb and spice ingredients. As far as the commercial turnover is concerned, a distinction is made between ordinary and fine wines, the latter being marked by constant properties and by a higher quality. Dry and semi-dry fruit wines are made in only limited quantities. Also wines produced out of a single brand of fruits are rather scarce.

The chemical composition of typical fruit wines produced at present in Poland is shown in Table 3. Table 4 lists the chemical composition of certain fruit wines made in the U.S.S.R. The chemical composition of wines produced in the German Federal Republic is listed by Wucherpfennig (1969, 1971).

Certain of the chemical components listed in Tables 3 and 4 have an influence upon the quality of fruit wines. Such components include the non-sugar soluble extract, ash and volatile acids.

Table 1

Standards for analytical data for some fruit wines produced in U.S.S.R.
(Norma GOST 17292-71—Vina plodovo-jagodnye)

Wine	Alcohol (% by volume)	Total sugars (g/100 ml)
Sparkling wines	11.5	5
Carbonated white wines	11	7
Carbonated rosé wines	10–11	10
Table dry wines	10–13.5	0.3
Table white wines with sugar content up to 1% (w/v)	12	1.0
Table slightly sweet wines	10–13	5–8
Sweet unfortified wines	13–14.5	10–16
Liqueur-type unfortified wines	14	25
Fortified strong wines	16–18	7–10
Fortified sweet wines	14–16	10–18
Liqueur-type fortified wines	13–16	20–30
Sweet honey wines	12–16	16–20
Liqueur-type honey wines	14	30
Aromatized strong wines	16–18	8–10
Aromatized sweet wines	16	13–16
Liqueur type aromatized wines	16	20

Table 2

Analytical data for some fruit wines produced in Czechoslovakia
(CSN Standard 567810—Ovocná vina)

Wine	Alcohol (% by volume)	Total sugars (g/100 ml)
Table wines	10	2.0 (max)
Slightly sweet wines	12	3.0–8.0
Sweet wines	14	10.0

Standardization of non-sugar soluble extracts and ash content is aimed at preventing excessive wine dilution. The chemical component that is related to the quality of the raw material used and of the hygiene in the technological process involved is the volatile acidity. With general technological and sanitary requirements being adhered to, and with the correct fermentation course, the volatile acid (expressed as acetic acid) does not usually exceed 1.2 g/l for white and 1.6 g/l for red wines.

Table 3

Composition of some Polish fruit wines. From data supplied by the Warsaw Institute of Fermentation Industry (1974)

Type of wine	Alcohol (% by volume)	Total sugars	Non-sugar soluble	Acid (as malic acid)	Volatile acidity	Ash
				(g/l of wine)		
White slightly sweet	12.3	64.7	19.1	5.1	0.87	1.9
Red slightly sweet	12.6	66.9	22.2	6.6	0.9	2.2
White sweet	12.9	103.1	23.2	5.6	0.82	2.0
Red sweet	13.0	104.0	30.3	7.3	0.95	2.9
White very sweet	14.1	135.3	22.9	6.7	0.65	2.2
Red very sweet	13.5	131.8	25.9	7.0	0.75	2.7
Single fruit wines						
Apple, slightly sweet	12.4	62.0	18.0	6.2	1.10	1.8
Apple, sweet	13.0	101.8	23.7	5.4	0.85	2.0
Red current, slightly sweet	12.4	72.2	22.1	6.9	0.90	2.0

Table 4

Composition of some fruit wines produced in U.S.S.R. (Mitjukov *et al.*, 1965)

Wine	Alcohol (% by volume)	Acidity (g/l)	Total sugars (g/l)	Non-sugar solubles (g/l)
White dry	12.3	7.4	15.6	22.0
Red semi-dry	12.7	8.5	33.7	30.1
White slightly sweet	12.8	7.3	65.7	25.0
Red slightly sweet	13.1	8.4	59.3	31.5
White sweet	13.3	7.6	104.9	30.6
Red sweet	13.6	8.7	97.9	35.1

The concentration (in g/100 l) of non-sugar solubles is calculated using the formula:

$$E_t - [S_r + (S_t - S_r) \cdot 0.95]$$

in which E_t is the value for the concentration (g/100 ml) of soluble solids, S_r of reducing sugars (g/100 ml), and S_t of total sugars (g/100 ml).

The U.S.S.R. and Poland are ranked among the two World leading fruit-wine makers. Annual output of fruit wines amounted in the U.S.S.R. in 1968 to 323 million litres, with plans for 1975 providing for 480 million litres (Trofimenko, 1969) and, in Poland, to 160 million litres in 1972 (Rocznik Statystyczny, 1973). Other European countries are producing smaller quantities of fruit wines (cider not included). For example, the German Federal Republic produces approximately 15 million litres (Korth, 1973; Skibe, 1969). Large-scale wineries in operation at the present time are offering a production capacity of up to 10 million litres of fruit wine annually.

III. RAW MATERIALS

Basic raw materials for production of fruit wines are fruits of different varieties. Used most frequently are fruits typical of countries with a moderate climate (Golomštok and Šapiro, 1962). Apart from the fruit classifications as adopted in the wine-making industry, namely into stone, berry and pome fruits, fruits can also be divided, for practical reasons, into cultivated fruits (for example apples, currants, strawberries) and those growing in the wild (for example bilberries, blackberries, bog bilberries, elderberries, rose hips, bird

Table 5

Chemical composition of edible parts of several fruits used in wine making. From Pijanowski et al. (1973)

Fruit	Content (per cent weight of)											
	Water	Dry matter	Insoluble substances	Total sugars	Sucrose	Inverted sugar	Nitrogenous compounds (N × 6.25)	Acid (as malic acid)	Cellulose	Pectin (as calcium pectate)	Tannins	Ash
Apples (Pirus malus)	85.0	15.0	2.0	10.0	2.5	7.6	0.3	0.6	1.3	0.6	0.07	0.3
Apricots (Armeniaca vulgaris Lam.)	86.0	14.0	2.5	6.7	3.6	2.9	0.8	1.3	0.8	0.9	0.07	0.7
Bilberries (Vaccinium myrtillus)	86.5	13.5	3.7	6.6	0.2	6.4	0.8	0.8	2.3	0.6	0.22	0.3
Blackberries (Rubus fruticosus)	85.0	15.0	6.2	5.5	0.5	4.9	1.3	0.9	4.0	0.7	0.29	0.6
Black currant (Ribes nigrum)	80.3	19.7	6.0	7.0	1.8	5.0	1.7	3.0	4.0	1.1	0.39	0.8
Cherries (Prunus cerasus)	83.1	16.9	2.2	9.7	0.5	9.2	1.0	1.3	0.3	0.25	0.14	0.5
Cowberries (Vaccinium vitis idaea L.)	83.6	16.4	4.1	8.7	0.5	8.2	0.7	2.0	1.8	–	0.25	0.3
Currant (Ribes rubrum)	83.8	16.2	7.2	5.3	0.2	5.1	0.5	2.4	4.5	0.6	0.21	0.7
Gooseberry (Ribes grossularia)	85.5	14.5	4.7	6.1	0.5	5.6	0.5	1.9	2.7	0.8	0.09	0.5
Peaches (Persica vulgaris Mill)	84.5	15.5	3.0	7.8	4.3	3.3	0.7	0.8	1.0	0.7	0.10	0.6
Pears (Pirus communis)	83.5	16.5	3.0	9.5	1.3	8.2	0.4	0.3	2.6	0.5	0.03	0.4
Plums (Prunis domestica)—and others	82.0	18.0	2.4	9.3	1.8	7.3	0.7	1.2	0.6	0.8	0.07	0.5
Raspberries (Rubus idaeus)	84.0	16.0	9.1	4.7	0.2	4.5	1.4	1.6	5.7	0.55	0.26	0.6
Rose hips (Rosa canina L.)	70.0	30.0	8.0	7.0	–	–	1.5	2.0	–	–	–	1.6
Strawberries (Fragaria vesca, F. virginiana)	88.5	11.5	2.2	6.5	0.6	5.9	0.7	1.0	1.8	0.55	0.20	0.7

cherries; Kulešova 1959). The chemical composition of certain fruits used for the making of wine is presented in Table 5.

Certain of the cultivated fruits may grow wildly (for example apples), added to which certain wild fruits (such as rose hips) may be grown on plantations. Fruits grown in the wild are noted for a higher content of acid, of vegetable tannins, and by a stronger aroma, and present for the above reasons a valuable raw material for production of wine. Dried fruits can be used for the production of wine (Amerine and Cruess, 1960).

The next basic raw material, indispensable for the production of practically all types of wine, is sugar. Used usually for this purpose is sucrose obtained from sugar beet or from sugar cane.

Water used for diluting must in the making of certain fruit-wine brands must meet the requirements demanded generally of drinking water. Furthermore, wine production from only slightly sour fruits involves an after-acidification with edible organic acids, like citric acid, tartaric acid and lactic acid. Auxiliary agents used in the production of fruit wines include: pure yeast cultures, carbon dioxide, sulphur dioxide, sulphites, filter aids (asbestos, cellulose, diatomaceous earth), clarifying agents (bentonites, egg white, tannin, gelatin, silica gel, activated carbon), ascorbic acid, nitrogen, pectolytic preparations, and other substances (Jakob, 1971).

IV. TECHNOLOGICAL PROCESSING

A. Pressing

Fruits are delivered to the winery in cases, chip baskets, or sometimes in bulk by lorries or railway cars. The raw material is sorted out on conveyor belts, and washed in washers of various types. Primary washing of a raw material, such as apples, is sometimes commenced while in the flumes when water handling is used in the process.

With an increased must yield in mind, fruits are disintegrated prior to pressing, using disintegrating equipment of various types. In some cases, parts of the fruit that can cause a deterioration in the flavour and aroma of ready must (shanks) are removed prior to disintegration. For many years soft, mainly berry, fruits have been crushed with the use of crusher equipment, while hard fruits (such as apples and pears) have required the use of hammer mills. The present practice provides for an even more frequent application of disintegrators, mostly of the Rietz type.

Most commonly in use for pressing the majority of fruits are the hydraulic rack-and-cloth presses in which pulp is filled into cloths which are then ploughed in by press racks made of wood, aluminium or plastics. The pressure obtained inside rack-and-cloth presses, within the layers of the pulp subjected to pressing, is of the order of up to 30 kg/cm^2. Despite the labour involved in loading the pulp and offloading the pomace, the rack-and-cloth press finds a ready application, with a high pressing output that amounts in the case of apples to approximately 75% of the total available. Basket presses find a limited application with fruit pressing, because of the low output of must. Useful, on the other hand, for pressing of fruit of various varieties, have been the Bücher–Guyer modified basket presses incorporating a draining system for rendering the pulp fluffy in the course of the pressing action, and a mechanized attachment for feeding pulp and offloading pomace (Fig. 1). The processing capacity of a Bücher–Guyer type HP-5000 press amounts to 5,000–6,000 kg for apples, and up to 34,000 kg for black currants per hour, with the volume capacity of the basket of 6 m^3 (Mrożewski and Chwiej, 1969).

Presses offering a continuous action, namely screw, band, band-and-roller presses, as well as those operated on the principle of continuous vacuum filters, find a limited application with fruit pressing, because of their low working output, and particularly in the case of worm presses, of a considerable content of slurry in the juice obtained.

Pomace pressing in order to increase the yield of must is seldom applied because of a low profitability. The pressing yield can, on the other hand, be boosted effectively by adding pectolytic preparations in doses of 0.1–0.5% (Rzędowski, 1956; Pijanowski et al., 1964; Daškevič and Vol, 1966), as well as by pressing a primarily fermented pulp.

An ever more frequently applied practice involves pressing the pulp following a previous warming up to a temperature of approximately 80–85°C, with simultaneous addition of pectolytic prepa-

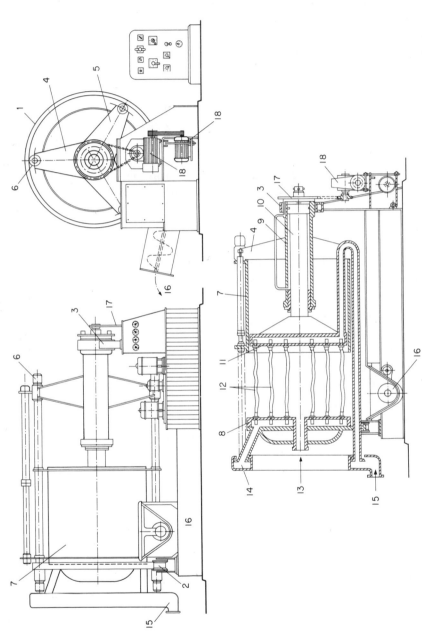

Fig. 1. Diagram of a Bücher-Guyer type HP-5000 press (Mroźewski and Chwiej, 1969). 1, indicates a horizontal rotary basket; 2, rolls; 3, ball bearing; 4 and 5, resistance blocks; 6, turnbuckles; 7, pressure-resisting shell; 8, pressure plate; 9, cylinder; 10, piston; 11, pressing plate; 12, draining system; 13, feeding; 14, juice collector; 15, juice outlet; 16, pomace worm; 17, drive of basket; and 18, electric motor.

rations following a partial cooling off. These measures are taken in order to boost the pressing output, and at the same time to obtain a more intensely coloured must.

B. Conservation and Storage of Fruit Must

Not all of the must obtained by pressing is used directly for production of prepared wine juices. Part of the must is reserved for storage, to be used as required for the making of prepared wine juices.

Must earmarked for storage is purified primarily by straining, centrifuging, sometimes by filtration, frequently by pasteurization (thereby giving the possibility of an aseptic storage), then fixed by adding a preserving agent. The dose of preservative, mostly sulphur dioxide, must be selected so as to protect must against the effects of micro-organisms over the period of foreseen storage.

Doses of sulphur dioxide applied on an industrial scale vary considerably, and oscillate within the limits of 400 to 1200 mg/l, depending on the storage period scheduled. Sulphur dioxide is mostly administered in a gaseous form, with the use of a continuous-action batching (sulphitating) equipment. Dosing can also be effected in the form of, say, a 6% aqueous solution of sulphur dioxide, as well as of sulphites, the most handy of which is the potassium pyro-sulphite $(K_2S_2O_5)$. Preserved must is stored in metal, concrete or wooden tanks, properly protected, for a period of several months. A trend is noted, at the present time, towards a limitation in the use of sulphur dioxide for preserving fruit musts for wine-making purposes.

Preserving fruit must for wine-making purposes with the use of carbon dioxide under pressure is at present seldom used. Fruit musts for the production of wine are, on the other hand, concentrated some 7-fold in volume following the removal of pectic substances and filtration, and then stored in the form of a concentrate at a temperature of 5–7°C. Prior to the processing of must into prepared wine juice, the concentrate is diluted with water as required, and sometimes mixed with non-concentrated must (Popova, 1960). While diluting concentrated juices, an additive is sometimes used, usually during the final stage of fermentation, made up of a condensate of previously separated aromatic substances, and this is, in certain countries, legally required. Addition of chemical preservative agents is made superfluous owing to the concentration of the must, and this permits also a decrease in the storage-volume capacity. Masior *et al.* (1972a) recommend adding bentonites to prepared juices of concentrated musts.

Application of sorbic acid for the preservation of fruit musts used for making prepared wine juices has found little application in the wine industry (Burkhardt, 1973), largely because of difficulties encountered in removing it from preserved must.

C. Preparation of Fruit Must for Fermentation

1. *Desulphiting*

Operating a winery fermentation with continuously prepared juices from preserved fruit musts necessitates removal of sulphur dioxide. Desulphiting of must involves cleaving bonds between carbohydrates and sulphurous acid which results in the greater part of the sulphur dioxide escaping from the preserved must. The process used most commonly and effectively in order to lower the concentration of sulphur dioxide in must is aeration usually following a preliminary warm-up. Owing to the high volatility of sulphur dioxide, and also to partial oxidation to give sulphurous acid, the sulphur-dioxide content of must decreases. Lowering the concentration of sulphur dioxide may also be obtained by passing neutral gases through the must. Nitrogen gas is often used, but carbon dioxide is seldom used on an industrial scale. Excess sulphur dioxide can furthermore be removed by warming *in vacuo*. Desulphiting by warming has the effect of losing aroma and alcohol (in partially incipient fermented musts), and produces an off-flavour that accompanies boiling.

Oxidation of sulphur dioxide with hydrogen peroxide, to give sulphur trioxide, is not recommended, as desulphiting effected by this method deteriorates the flavour and aroma of the must.

Installations to facilitate desulphitation of musts include desulphitators in which the separation of sulphur dioxide is performed in a continuous way, without losses of aromatic substances and alcohol. All methods of desulphiting are fairly difficult to perform.

2. Adjustment of Acidity

Fruit musts contain various quantities of organic acids, usually amounting to 0.3 to 3% (w/v). Ensuring that a correct course is taken during alcoholic fermentation, with the possibilities being minimized of infecting the prepared juice with a contaminant microflora and of ensuring the correct organoleptic features in the wine, necessitates raising the acidity of the prepared juice usually to 6–8 g malic acid equivalent/l. This requires the acidity of certain musts to be lowered, and rarely necessitates an addition of edible organic acids.

Lowering the acidity is most frequently effected by diluting must with water, thereby offering the chemical and microbiological features of good drinking water. Water-must, obtained as a result of secondary fruit pressing, may be used instead of water for this purpose. An effective and purposeful procedure to control the acidity of musts involves blending sour-must brands with those with a lower acidity. A certain lowering of acidity is obtainable, furthermore, by sweetening must with sucrose.

An excessive dilution of must is prevented by neutralization with calcium carbonate. Removal of oxalic acid from, say, rhubarb must by treating with calcium carbonate facilitates, to a high degree, the growth of yeast and the course taken by the alcoholic fermentation (Pijanowski and Wasilewski, 1955). Ion exchangers are known to be used on a limited scale, both for lowering (Begunovova and Zacharinova, 1960) and increasing the acidity of must (Agabal'janc and Drboglav, 1960).

Used mainly for increasing the acidity of must are citric, tartaric and lactic acids. It is sometimes necessary to acidify must during fermentation because of the excessive growth of *Schizosaccharomyces pombe* and a considerable drop in the malic-acid content (Čalenko and Korsakova, 1960). When the fruit-must fermentation is operated correctly, its acidity should not need to be lowered (Zacharina and Fridman, 1967).

3. Addition of Sucrose

A process typical of the production of fruit wines, unlike that of grape wines, is sweetening must prior to, and sometimes during, the fermentation. Sweetening is necessary because of the low content of sugar in the majority of fruits, particularly of those grown in rougher climate zones. Addition of sugar enables the fermentation to take its proper course, and ensures greater stability of the wine, due to the higher alcohol concentration. Sucrose is added in a dose amounting mainly to between 150 and 300 g/l of must.

Sugar to produce the final sweetness in ready wine should be added on completion of fermentation. Addition of 100 g of simple sugar (hexose) yields practically 44–47 g of ethanol (Pijanowski and Wasilewski, 1955). Sucrose may be added to must directly, or in the form of syrup which causes the prepared juice to become additionally diluted. With a high rate of addition of sucrose, and the concentration in must exceeding 25%, difficulties may be experienced in prepared wine-juice fermentation. It is for this reason incorrect, in connection with strong and sweet wines that require a sugar dose of the order of 300 g per litre of must to give some unfermented sugar, to add the entire sugar batch at once. Sugar is instead in such cases added in two to three portions (Pijanowski and Wasilewski, 1955). Fermentation of must containing a high concentration of sugar would cause most frequently an excessive increase of volatile acidity. Sugar is dissolved in separate tanks, with the use of manual or mechanical agitation action.

4. Preparation of Nitrogenous Yeast Food

Must of fruits, particularly of currants, strawberries and of hedge rose, and especially following a strong dilution, contain an excessively low concentration of nitrogenous compounds which are indispensable for the propagation of yeast. Even an undiluted apple must frequently contains an insufficient concentration of nitrogenous compounds, while musts of bilberries suffer a permanent shortage in this respect.

Ammonium salts, like dibasic ammonium phosphate $((NH_4)_2HPO_4)$ are used as nutrients, the latter compound offering at the same time the main source of phosphate that plays an important part in alcoholic fermentation. Also used are ammonium chloride, ammonium sulphate and ammonium carbonate. The dose of dibasic ammonium phosphate used usually amounts to approximately 0.1–0.3 g/l of must. Sometimes, hydrolysates of rye are used as a source of nutrient (Masior and Czyżycki, 1959), particularly with currant and rhubarb must, as well as yeast autolysates (Masior and Czyżycki, 1965).

5. Preparation of Pure Yeast Starter

The purpose of inoculating a prepared wine juice with a pure culture of wine yeast is the rapid production of alcohol to a concentration of more than 4% by volume, which decreases growth of any undesirable microflora, while ensuring a correct course of alcoholic fermentation. Use of suitable cultures enables favourable organoleptic features of the ready wine to be obtained. For this purpose, it is necessary to add, to every litre of must, approximately 100 million yeast cells (Wasilewski, 1958). An optimum content of dry matter of yeast in a yeast starter is 12.5 g/l (Hronček and Malik, 1973).

Preparation of a yeast starter requires the use of thoroughly pasteurized fruit must, sweetened with sugar to approximately 15% (w/v), a yeast culture in the form of an agar culture and special pastes. Yeasts are grown mainly in small volumes of must, amounting to 1–5% of the volume of the portion to be inoculated, and are added to some scores or some hundreds of litres of pasteurized and sweetened must, for a further propagation at 22–25°C. Thus, the yeast starter is the only material to be added to properly prepared wine juices. The two-stage preparation of a yeast culture lasts for four to six days. Yeast starter is usually prepared in premises reserved for this purpose, inside glass balloons, wooden vats, and in some plants, in special installations called propagators. A correctly fermenting prepared must may be used instead of a yeast starter. It is possible to use strains of *Saccharomyces oviformis* (Lipiec, 1966) for fermentation of fruit musts.

6. Inoculation

The dose of propagated yeast amounts to between 1% and 10% of the volume of fruit must, depending on the kind of must. Sometimes even smaller batches are deemed sufficient. Wasilewski (1958) recommends doses of yeast starter for various musts as indicated in Table 6.

Adding pure cultures in uncontrolled quantities may cause a highly turbulent fermentation of prepared juice, including frothing.

Table 6

Doses of yeast starter culture used for various musts. From Wasilewski
(1958)

Must	Dose of yeast starter culture (l/hl)
Apple	1–2
Pear	2–3
Fruit musts containing an excessive concentration of sulphur dioxide	2–5 or larger
Berry musts	1–2
Cherry pulp	2

It is recommended, when adding yeast starter to prepared juice, to add sulphur dioxide simultaneously, in quantities of 30 to 150 mg/l, in order to suppress growth of any undesirable microflora. These doses of sulphurous acid would inhibit most effectively propagation of bacteria in fruit musts, particularly of acetic-acid bacteria, as well as growth of wild yeasts, especially those of the apiculate type.

Selection of the correct species of yeasts depends on the variety of the fruit, acidity of the must, and its sugar, tannin, and sulphur dioxide contents, as well as on the brand of wine. Production of strong wines requires the use of yeasts that tolerate a higher concentration of alcohol. With bilberry wine, fermentation in pulp means that consideration must be given to the resistance of yeasts to tannins. Propagation or starter yeast culture is mixed with must prepared previously, at a temperature usually higher than 12°C but not exceeding 20°C.

D. Fermentation

1. Classical Fermentation

Fruit must prepared as required is subjected to fermentation in containers made of various types of material including plastic, metal and concrete, or in casks (Matheis, 1973). The fermentation may be conducted in a continuous manner (Usov, 1964). Prepared wine juice is subjected to incipient fermentation (which lasts several days), effervescent fermentation, and after-fermentation, which lasts altogether for approximately 5 to 6 weeks. After-fermentation of strong wines lasts usually for a longer time, because of an inhibition of yeast activity due to the higher alcohol concentration. With the process being characterized by production of abundant froth, some one-fifth of the volume of the fermentation tank should be left empty. One more fermentation stage is singled out distinctly, namely the silent or secondary fermentation during which a lowering of acidity in young wines occurs due to the malo-lactic fermentation by bacteria.

The fermentation should be commenced at a temperature of 12–15°C which prevents the fermenting prepared juice from attaining an excessively high temperature that could weaken or even annihilate the wine yeast. One kilogram of sugar produces, during fermentation, approximately 133 kcal. A normally fermenting prepared juice should attain, during the period of peak fermentation intensity, a temperature of 20–25°C, and not higher than 28°C. When the alcohol content has increased by a few percent and when the fermentation rate has diminished, the temperature may drop below 20°C. The higher the fermentation temperature, the lower in general the ultimate alcohol concentration in the wine.

Problems in the fermentation process often result from using too low an initial temperature with the prepared wine juice, too high a concentration of sulphur dioxide, an insufficient nutrient content, and too low a yeast content (Wasilewski, 1958).

On completion of fermentation, young wine must be drawn off from the lees. Keeping wine on the lees would cause unpleasant off-flavours to develop, and increase the susceptibility to diseases. Drawing wine off the lees at a suitable time is particularly important with wines with a low concentration of alcohol and fermented at high temperatures.

2. Cold Fermentation

Fermentation of processed juice may be conducted at lower temperatures than those used in the classical fermentation (Masior *et al.*, 1972b). Lowering the fermentation temperature to 5–10°C requires the use of special cultures of wine yeast (cryophilic yeasts). Using cryophilic yeasts allows wine juices to be fermented even at

unfavourable temperatures, without the need to heat the fermentation premises, or even in the open. Using cryophilic yeasts permits,
furthermore, the possibility of obtaining a higher content of alcohol
in the wine, while helping to preserve more effectively the volatile
components of the fruit aroma. It also cuts down alcohol losses.
Wines fermented at low temperatures are noted for better qualities of
flavour and aroma. Cold fermentation lowers furthermore the rate
of yeast autolysis.

Disadvantages of low-temperature fermentation include a slower
rate of fermentation and a greater possibility of infection of the
prepared juice, a more difficult clarification of the wine thus
obtained and, sometimes, the occurrence of a yeast off-taste. Cold
fermentation is not much used with fruit-pulp fermenting.

3. Fermentation in Pulp

For a more effective extraction of pigments contained in the peel of
fruits like bilberries, black currants, cherries, blackberries, strawberries and elderberries, the pulp is subjected to fermentation prior
to pressing. Fermentation in the pulp facilitates furthermore the
extraction of must from the majority of fruits, particularly of plums
and strawberries (Schanderl and Koch, 1972), and subsequent wine
clarification.

What with the relatively large number of micro-organisms on the
surfaces of fruits, which with apples may amount to several hundred
thousand mould spores and several million yeast cells per 1 cm^2
(Wasilewski, 1958), it is necessary to inoculate the pulp with a pure
culture of wine yeast. Fermenting pulp is to a certain degree thus
isolated from the environment by the evolving carbon dioxide which
offers favourable circumstances for the alcoholic fermentation
(Taguena, 1972; Žukov et al., 1968).

In order to minimize contact of the fermenting pulp with
atmospheric oxygen, it is recommended that special tanks be used
holding solid parts of fruits underneath the surface of fermenting
liquid. Wine yeasts find in fruit pulp an environment considerably
more rich in nutrients as compared with musts; thus fermentation is
in such an environment more intense. Fermented pulp is subjected to
pressing, and the 'must' thus obtained is sweetened immediately
and fermented further.

A recent development involves a heat treatment of pulp in order to extract pigment out of intensely coloured fruits more effectively (Nègre *et al.*, 1971; François, 1972), instead of fermentation in the pulp which has already been mentioned in the section on 'Pressing' (see p. 394).

E. Mellowing

1. Natural and Accelerated Mellowing

A young wine, on completion of fermentation, is characterized by the absence of a definite bouquet, with flavour and aroma undefinable, clarity and stability insufficient, and organoleptic qualities short of the standard required. These quality features are first obtained during the mellowing process, as well as a result of stabilization operations, and when methods of accelerated ripening are applied.

Mellowing of fruit wines is effected usually at a temperature of 7-15°C, inside metal, concrete or wooden tanks filled completely (by frequent replenishing) with racking performed at regular intervals. The first racking is usually effected one month after the drawing of wine from the lees, the next racking, on elapse of the successive two months as from that date. The successive operations are performed during the first year of mellowing, once every quarter, then once every half year during the following years. The purpose of racking from the lees is not solely to separate the wine from yeast cells and lees. It also serves to introduce into the cuve a certain amount of oxygen on which a correct mellowing process depends, and which is of particular importance in the case of tanks made of metal, concrete, or of plastics where there is not any diffusion across the tank walls.

Mellowing is usually accompanied by a further decrease in the acid content which involves bacterial transformation of malic acid into lactic acid and carbon dioxide, as well as of citric acid into citromalic acid with evolution of carbon dioxide (Carles *et al.*, 1958). Micro-organisms which effect these transformations are *Bacterium gracile* and *Micrococcus malolacticus*. The process of biological de-acidification cannot proceed too far in a grape wine that contains, apart from malic acid, tartaric acid. Apple wine, on the other hand, containing mainly malic acid, may acquire, as a result of an excessive malo-lactic fermentation, a too mild, hollow flavour (Pijanowski and Wasilewski, 1955).

Mellowing is the process in the course of which the bouquet is forming. Components that contribute to the bouquet include alcohols, aldehydes, acetals, ketones and esters. Production of these compounds may occur as a result of decarboxylation and deamination reactions. Alternatively, they may arise by purely chemical means as a result of oxidation and esterification. The components of the bouquet are formed early during the fermentation, whereas it is, for example the breed of yeasts and the content of amino acids that play an important part in the process (Wucherpfennig and Bretthauer, 1968a, b; Pisarnicki and Goliševa, 1971). The content of amino acids depends, in turn, for example, on the nature of the raw material and, in the case of fruits with a low content of nitrogenous compounds (bilberries, apples, currants following dilution), on the content of nitrogenous nutrients (Flanzy, 1965) and on the time during which the wine stays in contact with the yeast lees.

A significant part is played in the mellowing process by oxygen that diffuses across the staves of the casks, or is absorbed in the course of racking or other technological operations. A moderate access of oxygen is very essential throughout the initial period of mellowing (oxido-reduction processes).

Mellowing of dessert wines is effected without the application of sulphur dioxide. Wines with a flat aroma (including those from apples, white and red currants) display better organoleptic properties when there is an access of oxygen (for example during the initial stage of mellowing) which results in an off-taste of 'rawness' growing milder and the bouquet being more strongly pronounced. In the case of wines obtained from fruits noted for a strong aroma (for example black currants), it is advisable to ensure a minimum access of oxygen which for one thing allows preservation of the appreciated aroma, while, on the other hand, smoothing the excessively sharp shades thereof.

Mellowing dessert wines, while maintaining a slight content of free sulphur dioxide in order to preserve the aroma more effectively, seems of no avail, as the organoleptic properties thus obtained are inferior to those that follow mellowing with a slight access of oxygen

(Kurek, 1973). In the case of dry wines and semi-dry wines, it is sometimes a matter of routine to maintain a slight content of sulphur dioxide, usually of the order of 20–25 mg/l, in a free state in order to prevent undesirable oxidation processes.

The process of mellowing is accompanied furthermore by a decrease in turbidity caused by a precipitation of yeast and bacterial cells, pectic substances, unstable pigment–tannin fractions (possibly in combinations with iron), as well as of gums and slimes. Precipitation of tartaric acid-containing sludges is not observed in the case of fruit wines, and the occurrence of protein sludges is noted extremely rarely. The mellowing period does not exceed usually one year, with low-priced popular wines mellowing for 1–3 months (in Poland a minimum of two months), and fine wines for a much longer time (in Poland for a minimum of four months).

An accelerated fruit-wine mellowing process is also in use, and this mainly involves exposure to oxygen and warming-up, less frequently also with alternate cooling or subjecting wine to an accelerated sherryzation (see below; Pijanowski and Wasilewski, 1955).

Fruit wines present, generally speaking, an advantageous product for madeirizing (Eliasz, 1959, 1960). The madeirizing process is based on warming of wine at temperatures of 40–65°C, for 2–3 months, with some access of oxygen. It is advisable, for economic reasons, to warm up wines obtained from popular fruits like apples, plums or white and red currants, as the strong, characteristic bouquet so produced masks the aroma of the raw material. It is also desirable to enrich the wine in nitrogenous compounds in the form of an addition of wine-yeast lees to a concentration of 2.5% (Lewkowicz, 1973), since such wines have better organoleptic properties. In the case of raw materials with a slight tannin content, and of madeirization performed for example in metal tanks, it is a known practice to add oak wood shavings or wine tannin. Warming is effected usually with access of oxygen at a temperature of 55–65°C for 6–12 weeks, while it seems sufficient to maintain warming at temperature of 55°C for a period of six weeks.

Certain types of fruit wines are suitable for sherryzation. Schanderl and Koch (1972) recommend an accelerated sherryzation method for fruit wines, in which the bouquet is obtained within several weeks, under the action of wine yeasts in the oxidative phase. The yeast-cell lees (produced prior to filling in) gathers on the inner walls of the cask above the wine, or may also be maintained directly underneath the liquid level on an absorbant paper or other porous surface. Yeast films, owing to their limited contact with the liquid surface, stay slightly moistened, thus promoting an intense oxidation of alcohol and aromatization of wine. Most suited for this purpose are sherry yeasts (see p. 502). Other strains of wine yeasts may, however, also pass over to the oxidative phase. Control of temperature within the limits of 13–28°C, and of the duration of the process, permit various kinds and intensities of bouquet to be obtained. Good results are offered by sherryzation of heavy wines made from gooseberries, strawberries and rhubarb, although this process is not recommended for table wines made from apples, pears or cherries.

2. Final Procedure

The process of mellowing involves blending, flavouring, as well as other measures taken in order to ensure correct stability and clarity in the final product.

Blending improves the flavour and aroma of wine by mixing together wine brands of mutually complementary qualities, as well as ensuring standard properties in the final product. Wines with a flat aroma and other less advantageous features, such as in those made of rhubarb or apples, are usually subjected to blending with wines offering a strong aroma and highly appreciated organoleptic properties. Particularly suitable for blending are wines made from, for example, hedge rose, black currant, bilberry, cranberry and elderberry. Notwithstanding, a notion is prevalent (Pijanowski and Wasilewski, 1955) that blending of wines made from various fruit varieties should be limited in favour of a trend towards production of specific single-fruit wines.

Flavouring has the aim of improving the quality of wines, and correcting various physical and chemical properties, in compliance with the requirements as listed in the standard specifications. The most commonly applied operation is sweetening with sugar (sucrose). The sugar may be cold-diluted in wine, or warm-diluted in water reserved for this purpose. In the case of low acid content, the practice provides for adding a required amount of an edible organic acid, mainly citric acid and less frequently tartaric or lactic acid, and it is to be noted that the legislation of many countries restricts the maximum amount of acid added to 1–3 g/l. A correct acidity in the wine is usually obtained by skilled blending, and subsequent acidification is effected mainly when there is an undesirable excessive biological de-acidification.

It is frequently necessary, in the course of production of fruit wines, to increase the alcohol content, a process which is effected by adding rectified spirit. The alcohol thus added 'harmonizes' with wine slowly, and its presence is then distinctly perceptible by organoleptic evaluation. It is for this reason desirable to carry out wine fortification towards the end of the fermentation process or directly following this process. Very good results are obtained as a result of diffusive fortification. Wine fortification was until recently the rule in all republics of the Soviet Union which practise fruit-wine production. Musts fermented down to 5–8% alcohol were fortified to 12–16%, and sweetened afterwards (Mitjukov et al., 1968; Sosina et al., 1968).

A frequently applied measure, particularly with dessert wines, is cross-dyeing, with the amber-brownish tinge being obtained mostly by addition of caramel, i.e. a product obtained by roasting sucrose or technical glucose at a temperature of approximately 210°C. An improvement in the colour of red wines is obtained frequently by the use of musts of intensely coloured fruits, for example elderberry and bilberry. The correct colour of wines is, however, ensured by competent blending. It is to be stressed at this point that legislation in the majority of countries does not permit the use of synthetic dyes for the colouring of wines.

A different process is the widely used technique of aromatization of fruit wines, mainly in the form of adding herb or spice extracts (vermouths). Most commonly used are alcoholic extracts obtained by repeated (usually three times) extraction with an alcohol solution at a concentration of 45–70% (v/v). A good base for herb wines are apple wines which are decoloured if necessary prior to addition of herb extracts with the use of activated carbon (Madejska, 1972).

Wines with high sugar and alcohol contents are sometimes aromatized with muscatel essences (Anon., 1960) or of essential oils, so as to comply with local organoleptic preferences (Pijanowski and Wasilewski, 1955).

Wines, including blended and flavoured fruit-wine brands, are subjected to clarification and stabilization processes. Industrial production methods involve most frequently clarification with gelatin or tannin with added gelatin, in doses of up to 10 g/hl of each of these reagents. Clarification is usually carried out with the use of potassium ferrocyanide or of salts of phytic acid (in cases of an excess of iron) with further treatment with pectolytic preparations in the cold, in quantities of 50–300 g/hl, with wine tending towards the precipitation of pectin compounds.

Another phenomenon is likely to occur in wines mellowing for a longer time. This is the production of complexes of iron with organic acids, and particularly with oxalic acid (Krug, 1964a). When wine is clarified with potassium ferrocyanide, it is frequently not possible to remove sufficient quantities of iron. This is so because of the occurrence, noted as early as during the initial tests, of an excess of potasium ferrocyanide along with considerable quantities of iron being left over (iron contained in complex compounds with organic acids is not removable by potassium ferrocyanide). Where iron occurs in complex compounds, and in the presence of oxalic acid, Krug (1964b) recommends precipitation of that acid by addition of calcium carbonate at 50–70 mg Ca/l.

Good results are also obtained by a two-stage clarification. The first stage involves precipitation of iron in the ionic state, followed by the gradual dissociation of complexes in order to remove the released iron (Nilov and Skurychin, 1967). The presence of cyanides in wine is not permissible.

Kljačko et al. (1969) report on clarification of wine with bentonite, with the complementary addition of powdered polyacrylamide for accelerating sedimentation of the lees, while Masior et al. (1972a) describe attempts at adding bentonite to fruit musts prior to fermentation. Wucherpfennig and Possmann (1972) describe a combined clarification with the use of gelatin and silica gel.

Masior and Czyżycki (1969) discuss the stabilizing of fruit wines by cooling, while ascertaining that, apart from hedge-rose wine, they have not noted the need to apply this kind of treatment to any other type of fruit wines. Small-scale winery plants use traditional clarification agents, such as egg white, albumin, skimmed milk, casein, and the bladder of sturgeon or sheatfish.

Sedimentation of clarification agents is usually followed by drawing wine off from above the lees, combined with filtration through a layer of kieselguhr, or through cellulose and asbestos filtering plates. A particularly thorough filtration is required following clarification with ferrocyanide. Small-scale winery plants use filtration through an asbestos mass, with an occasional use of bag filters. It is also possible to stabilize wines by pasteurization at a temperature of 65–68°C, with holding times of up to 30 seconds.

3. Wine Defects and Diseases

The term 'wine defect' implies changes in the properties thereof (clarity, colour, flavour, aroma) resulting in a deterioration of the quality, and caused as a result of chemical, biochemical or physico-chemical changes. Defects mostly frequently noted in fruit wines are as follows:

(i) Black casse (wine blackening) is caused by the occurrence and precipitation of iron–tannin compounds. The defect is manifested by a loss of glaze, appearance of turbidity, and by the precipitation of a black coloured sediment.

(ii) Opalescent cloud (white casse) occurs as a result of precipitation of ferric phosphate. A specific feature of this defect is the occurrence of a whitish-blue turbidity, followed by precipitation of a whitish-blue sediment.

(iii) Wine browning (oxidation turbidity) is caused by oxidation of tannins and pigments catalysed by oxidases and oxygen contained in the air. The wines tend to brown in contact with the air, become turbid, and the taste and aroma of the wines change. A strong off-taste of 'aeration' becomes discernible.

Defects also arise as a result of turbidity due to pectins or copper (for example CuS, Cu_2S connected with protein), an odour of hydrogen sulphide, and an off-taste of yeasts or of mildew.

Also recognized as wine diseases are abnormal changes caused by growth of micro-organisms, and resulting in a deterioration of the quality of the product. Two basic groups of wine diseases are distinguished, namely those caused by growth of aerobic bacteria, and those caused by growth of anaerobic or relatively anaerobic bacteria. Microbial infection can be manifested in several forms. There may arise a 'coating' on the surface, caused by the propagation of yeasts (*Candida mycoderma, Hansenula* spp., *Pichia* spp. and *Torulopsis* spp). Wine acetation can be attributed to propagation of acetic-acid bacteria including *Acetobacter kutzingianum, Aceto-bacter xylinum, Acetobacter pasteurianum* and *Acetobacter aceti.* Diseases caused by growth of anaerobes or relatively anaerobic bacteria include mannite fermentation, lactic fermentation, sliming, bittering of the wine and 'mouse' off-taste. Such diseases are caused by complexes of micro-organisms including *Micrococcus acidovorax, Micrococcus variococcus, Bacterium mannitopeum, Bacterium inter-medium* and *Bacterium gracile.* One or other disease process develops depending on the composition of the wine, temperature, acid content and on other conditions. Curing methods in use for micro-bial diseases include, pasteurization, sterile filtration, sulphitation, acidification of wines with an insufficient acid content, and clarifi-cation with the use of tannin and gelatin.

F. Filling-up

Filling-up of wine is effected in bottling machines of various types, either by a non-sterile or by a sterile method. Sterile methods include basically two bottling systems, namely hot bottling at a temperature of 50–55°C, and bottling combined with running wine through microbiological filter plates (of type EK).

G. Sparkling and Carbonated Wines

The Soviet Union, the Federal Republic of Germany and other countries are known for production of sparkling fruit wines, made mainly from apples. Mitjukov *et al.* (1963) supply a description of the technology of production of sparkling apple wines as developed by the White Ruthenian Institute of the Food Processing Industry in Minsk (Soviet Union). Apple juice is sweetened prior to fermen-tation, up to a sugar content of approximately 19% (w/v), and this is followed by fermentation usually for a period of about 14 days. The wine juice thus obtained is sweetened with syrup, and carbonated in an acratophore (pressure tank), with the pressure of carbon dioxide towards the end of fermentation at a value of 4–5 kg/cm^2. On completion of the carbonation process, the wine is cooled to a temperature of 5°C. After 48 hours, the wine is filtered and bottled in an isobaric bottling machine.

An important process in the production of sparkling fruit wines is the selection of a correct breed of yeasts (Mitjukov et al., 1963), while the duration of the mellowing period for the wine seems to have no great impact on the quality of the final product (Jurčenko et al., 1972).

Carbonated fruit wines (mostly made from apples) are manufactured furthermore in many countries. Wines with an alcohol content of 10–12% (v/v) are sweetened with syrup, saturated with carbon dioxide in saturation equipment under a pressure of approximately 6 kg/cm², and filled into bottles in isobaric bottling machines (Pijanowski and Wasilewski, 1955).

V. HONEY WINE (MEAD)

A. Definition and Classification

Mead is an alcoholic beverage obtained as a result of fermentation of honey obtained from bee honey by suitable dilution with water or with fruit juice. Meads are divided in Poland into the following classes, depending on the relation by volume of honey to water added: (i) 'póltorak' (poowtorack) which contains half a volume of water per volume unit of honey; (ii) 'dwójniak' (dvooyniack) containing an equal volume of water and honey by volume; (iii) 'trójniak' (truiniack) with a 1 : 2 relation, by volume, of honey and water; and (iv) 'czwórniak' (tschvoorniack) with a 1 : 3 relation, by volume, of honey and water. Certain legislations permit a part of the honey to be replaced by sugar.

A further distinction is made between; natural meads which have no addition of herb and spice ingredients, and no fruit juices; aromatized meads which receive an addition of extracts of herbs or spices; and fruit meads in which some of the water (usually at least 30%) is replaced by fruit juice. Table 7 lists certain basic analytical data covering Polish meads.

Wojcieszak and Witkowski (1953) have published the following chemical composition for Polish 'trójniak' meads: alcohol, 14.23% by volume; total sugars, 110.2 g/l; non-sugar solubles, 37.6 g/l; total

Table 7

Some analytical data for Polish meads
(Polska Norma, PN-64/A-79123. Miody pitne—Honey wines)

Components	Type of mead		
	'Czwórniak' (1:3)	'Trójniak' (1:2)	'Dwójniak' (1:1)
Alcohol (% by volume)	9–12	more than 12–15	more than 15–18
Total sugars (g/l)	35–90	65–120	175–230
Factors (alcohol x 18 + total sugars)	250 ± 10	333 ± 10	500 ± 10
Non-sugar solubles not less than (g/l)	15	20	25
and for grape- and fruit mead	20	25	30
Acids as malic (g/l)	3.5–7	4–8	5–9
Volatile acids (as acetic acid, not more than, g/l)	1.6	1.6	1.6

acid content, 5.08 g/l as tartaric acid; volatile acidity, 1.09 g/l as acetic acid. Patschky and Schöne (1970) suggest standardizing the components as chlorides, sulphates, phosphates.

B. Honey as a Raw Material

Natural honey is produced by bees out of floral nectar or honey dew. In this connection, a distinction is drawn between three types of honey, namely nectar honey, honeydew honey, and nectar-honeydew honey. A further distinction is drawn among nectar honies, depending on the kind of plant from which the nectar is obtained, and they are thus subdivided into the individual varieties, namely acacia, buckwheat, lime tree, clover, heather, and others differing from one another by organoleptic qualities and by chemical composition.

The average chemical composition of natural honey of various origins is presented in Table 8. Any kind of honey may be used for production of meads. Notwithstanding this fact, highly appreciated are those honies noted for a strong aroma, and obtained from

Table 8

Chemical composition of honey. From Pijanowski *et al.* (1973)

Component (g/100 g)	Average	Variations	Normal
Water	17.7	13.9–21.4	<20
Inverted sugar	72.4	66.4–77.0	>70
Sucrose	2.0	0.2–7.6	<3.0
Other carbohydrates and 'non-sugars'	7.3	2.0–15.0	>2.0
Nitrogenous compounds (N x 6.25)	0.4	0.25–0.64	>0.3
Ash	0.2	0.07–0.75	>0.1
Acids (as millilitres of N base per 100 g)	2.0	0.9–3.3	>1.0

buckwheat, lime trees, heather and of multi-flower combinations. Jojrys (1966) states that the so-called 'express' honey brands, produced in the Soviet Union, are obtained by feeding fruit (containing sugar) or vitamin syrups to bees. This method proves to be highly economical. Meads produced from express-honey brands differ greatly from beverages obtained from natural honey, the former having a delicate flavour with the fragrance of mead, but slightly marked.

C. Technological Processing

1. *Preparation for Fermentation*

A distinction is drawn between unboiled and boiled meads, depending on the procedure used to prepare the mead wort. Wort for unboiled meads is prepared by cold-mixing honey with water. This procedure, despite its many advantages which include preservation of aroma, vitamins and enzymes (Popova, 1961), is not advocated because it is accompanied by a weaker fermentation, a more difficult clarification, and an off-taste of wax and raw honey in the final product. The procedure is recommended for preparing a beverage from bee honey brands of high quality.

Mead boiling, which is widely used on an industrial scale, involves cooking honey diluted with water, with a possible addition of herb and spice ingredients. Boiling results in a complete 'skimming', i.e.

separation of the resulting froth. The boiling procedure favours an accelerated and more correct fermentation (including volatilization of a part of the formic acid), a better clarification (coagulation of proteins), and contributes to a certain degree to an improvement in the flavour of the beverage thus obtained (Majewski, 1959; Morquin, 1962). Aroma losses occur, however, at the same time. As far as production of boiled fruit meads is concerned, this involves addition

Table 9

Some recipes for production of meads. From Ciesielski (1925) and Tokarz (1927)

| Type of mead | Ratio of honey to water (by volume) | Spices | | Time of ageing (years) |
		Kind	Amount (per 100 litres of honey wort)	
Bernardyński	1:2	Hop	50 g	1
		Root of violet	20 g	
		Rose attar	2 drops	
Kasztelański	1:0.5	Hop	100 g	5–10
		Vanilla	3 pods	
		Leafs of celery (fresh)	250 g	
Królewski	1:0.5	Hop	350 g	5–10
Litewski	1:0.5	Fruits of juniper	150 g	4–6
	1:1	Flowers of elder	100 g	

of freshly obtained or pasteurized fruit must on completion of boiling and cooling off, in order to avoid a compote type off-flavour. Examples of constituents for making typical meads, selected on the basis of recipes collected and checked by Ciesielski (1925) and Tokarz (1927), are presented in Table 9.

Honey earmarked for obtaining alcohol is added to mead wort at once ('czwórniak', 'trójniak' brands), or in two or three separate portions (for heavier and strong meads). When a part of the honey is replaced by sugar (usually no more than 20%, w/v), the sugar is added when the wort is prepared and not reserved for later sweetening.

Bee honey has a relatively low content of nitrogenous substances, and this necessitates the addition of nitrogenous nutrients, usually diammonium phosphate in the quantity of 0.3–0.5 g/l. Application of autolysates of wine yeast (in quantities of up to 5 ml/l) as a nitrogenous nutrient greatly accelerates the rate of fermentation, and permits an improvement in fermentation of the product (Masior and Czyżycki, 1965; Wzorek and Chruszczyk, 1972). When wort is prepared by addition of fruit juices with a high content of nitrogenous compounds (from grapes, raspberries, cherries), addition of a nitrogenous nutrient would be to no avail (Popova, 1961). With the low content of organic acids in honey, wort is frequently after-acidified with citric or tartaric acids. The prepared mead wort is inoculated with a yeast starter prepared from highly fermenting wine yeasts, the inoculum usually being 3–10% by volume of the prepared juice.

2. Fermentation

The optimum fermentation temperature is 15–25°C (Ciesielski, 1925; Morquin, 1962; Maugenet, 1964), and the duration of the process is up to 6–8 weeks. The brand of bee honey used is of decisive importance for the course of fermentation. Dark-coloured honey of the heather type ferments quicker than light-coloured ones (Morquin, 1962), while worts made from nectar honey derived from fruit-tree flowers ferment more intensely than those from the lime tree and from various grass varieties (Popova, 1961). Racking from above the lees is carried out three weeks after effervescence of the fermentation has ended, whereas the first drawing-off is carried out sooner if the fermentation temperature is higher and the brand of mead is lighter.

3. Ageing

Ageing is effected usually in oaken casks at a temperature of 10–15°C (Morquin, 1962). A temperature of 15–30°C is also permissible, but a higher temperature shortens the ageing time, and also leads to loss of volume (Eliasz, 1959).

Raising the ageing temperature to 55°C, with a moderate access of oxygen, allows the period of ageing to be decreased (approximately six weeks at an increased temperature), while an addition of lees of wine yeasts during that process (1.5%) and of tannins (0.4 g/l) results in an improvement of organoleptic qualities (Wzorek and Chruszczyk, 1972; Wzorek and Lisak, 1973). The course of the ageing process depends furthermore on the kind of mead, the variety of bee honey used, the type of tanks, and on the kind of fruit juice added, if any. An addition of fruit juice obtained from bilberries retards the ageing process, while that from raspberries, on the other hand, helps to adjust the organoleptic qualities of the final product (Popova, 1961).

The duration of ageing of the mead increases as the concentration of honey in the wort is increased. The 'trójniak' brand is ripe after one year from completion of fermentation; the 'dwójniak' brands require a period of at least two years, while some of them are aged for up to ten years (Tokarz, 1927).

The time reserved for effecting the ageing process is used also to adjust the chemical composition of the meads. Obtaining a correct total acidity is effected by addition of citric or tartaric acids, with better flavour effects being obtained from the use of citric acid (Maugenet, 1963, 1964). Fortification with rectified spirit is sometimes used in the production of meads with a high alcohol content, although increasing the mead strength by addition of alcohol is permissible in Poland only when the alcohol content is raised above 13% by volume. Sweetening with bee honey to a required degree of sweetness is effected by adding dilute honey in water, made by a cold or a hot process. Sweetening with cold diluted honey permits a more effective preservation of aroma, while at the same time causing an addition to the beverage of proteins which may cause a turbidity and protein precipitation in the form of lees. Only high quality honey, with a strong, appreciated aroma, should be used for sweetening.

Racking is performed periodically throughout the time of ageing, and this is accompanied by measures taken to obtain stability and clarity (pasteurization, clarification by the use of various methods, and filtrations). Filling up is effected into stoneware or glass bottles styled exclusively for this purpose.

REFERENCES

Agabal'janc, G. G. and Drboglav, S. (1960). *Vinodelĭe i Vinogradarstvo S.S.S.R.* 20(6), 4.

Amerine, M. A. and Cruess, W. V. (1960). 'The Technology of Wine Making'. The AVI Publishing Company, Inc., Westport, Connecticut, U.S.A.

Anon. (1960). *Vinařstvi* 53(10), 160a.

Begunovova, R. D. and Zacharinova, O. S. (1960). *Vinařstvi* 53(2), 25.

Burkhardt, R. (1973). *Der Deutsche Weinbau* 28(19), 713.

Carles, J., Lamazou-Bedbeder, M. and Pech, R. (1958). *Comptes Rendus Hebdomadaires des Séances de l'Acadèmie des Sciences, Paris* 246(14), 2160.

Charley, V. L. S. (1954). 'Principles and Practices of Cider Making'. Leonard Hill, London.

Ciesielski, T. (1925). 'Miodosytnictwo'. Wydawnictwo Księgarni Gubrynowicza, Lwów.

Čalenko, D. K. and Korsakova, T. F. (1960). *Vinodelie i Vinogradarstvo S.S.S.R.* 20(8), 12.

Daškevič, T. N. and Vol, Ž. I. (1966). *Vinodelie i Vinogradarstvo S.S.S.R.* 26(7), 27.

Eliasz, K. (1959). *Przemysł Fermentacyjny* 3(6), 235.

Eliasz, K. (1960). *Przemysł Fermentacyjny* 4(2), 63.

Flanzy, C. (1965). *Weinberg und Keller* 12(11), 539.

François, M. (1972). *Vignes et Vins* 210, 37.

Golomštok, M. M. and Šapiro, D. K. (1962). *Vinodelie i Vinogradarstvo S.S.S.R.* 22(8), 21.

Hronček, J. and Malik, F. (1973). *Vinohrad* 11(6), 139.

Jakob, L. (1971). *Der Deutsche Weinbau* 26(31), 1034.

Jojryš, N. P. (1966). 'Pčely i Medicina'. Medicina, Taskent.

Jurčenko, L. A., Vasilkevič, S. I., Brilevskij, O. A. and Romanovec, E. S. (1972). *Vinodelie i Vinogradarstvo S.S.S.R.* 32(2), 30.

Kljačko, Ju. A., Vejcer, Ju. I. and Ivannikova, E. I. (1969). *Vinodelie i Vinogradarstvo S.S.S.R.* 29(8), 16.

Korth, A. (1973). *Flüssiges Obst* 40(8), 317.

Krug, K. (1964a). *Die Industrielle Obst- und Gemüseverwertung* 49(18), 531.

Krug, K. (1964b). *Weinberg und Keller* 11(12), 589.

Kulešova, E. S. (1959). *Vinodelie i Vinogradarstvo S.S.S.R.* 19(5), 22.

Kurek, Z. (1973). Thesis: Agricultural University of Warsaw, Poland.

Lewkowicz, D. (1973). Thesis: Agricultural University of Warsaw, Poland.

Lipiec, M. (1969). *Przemysł Fermentacyjny i Rolny* 13(11), 13.

Madejska, H. (1972). Thesis: Technological University of Lodz, Poland.

Majewski, T. (1959). 'Miód Pszczeli'. Wydawnictwo Przemysłu Lekkiego i Spożywczego, Warszawa.

Masior, S. and Czyżycki, A. (1959). *Roczniki Technologii i Chemii Żywności* 4, 29.

Masior, S. and Czyżycki, A. (1965). *Przemysł Fermentacyjny i Rolny* 8(8-9), 292.

Masior, S. and Czyżycki, A. (1969). *Przemysł Fermentacyjny i Rolny* 13(9), 13.

Masior, S., Czyżycki, A. and Adamów, M. (1972a). *Przemysł Fermentacyjny i Rolny* 16(1), 4.

Masior, S., Czyżycki, A. and Adamów, M. (1972b). *Przemysł Fermentacyjny i Rolny* 16(10), 1.

Matheis, H. (1973). *Der Deutsche Weinbau* 28(10), 344.

Maugenet, J. (1963). *La Revue Française, d'Apiculture* 10(205), 382.

Maugenet, J. (1964). *Annales de L'Abeille* 7(3), 165.

Mitjukov, A. D., Daskevič, T. N., Nesterovskaja, T. V. and Tuz, T. A. (1965). *Vinodelie i Vinogradarstvo S.S.S.R.* 25(7), 17.

Mitjukov, A. D., Filippovič, Z. S. and Kačanovskaja, Z. I. (1963). *Vinodelie i Vinogradarstvo S.S.S.R.* 23(4), 17.

Mitjukov, A. D., Majonova, Z. M., Kalinina, E. S. and Simanovskaja, G. B. (1968). *Vinodelie i Vinogradarstvo S.S.S.R.* 28(8), 15.

Morquin, M. (1962). *L'Apiculteur* 106(7-8), 147.

Mrożewski, S. and Chwiej, M. (1969). 'Urządzenia i Aparaty w Przemyśle Owocowo-warzywnym.' Wydawnictwa Naukowo- Techniczne, Warszawa.

Nègre, E., Roubert, J. and Marteau, G. (1971). *Bulletin de l'O.I.V.* 44(487), 827.

Nilov, V. I. and Skurychin, I. M. (1967). 'Chimia Vinodelia'. Piščevaja Promyšlennost, Moskva.

Patschky, A. and Schöne, H. J. (1970). *Deutsche Lebensmittel-Rundschau* 66(5), 150.

Pijanowski, E. and Mrożewski, S. (1964). 'Technologia Produktów Owocowych i Warzywnych', Vol. II. Państwowe Wydawnictwa Rolnicze i Leśne, Warszawa.

Pijanowski, E., Mrożewski, S., Horubała, A. and Jarczyk, A. (1973). 'Technologia Produktów Owocowych i Warzywnych', Vol. I. Państwowe Wydawnictwa Rolnicze i Leśne, Warszawa.

Pijanowski, E. and Wasilewski, Z. (1955). 'Zarys Technologii Winiarstwa'. Wydawnictwo Przemysłu Lekkiego i Spożywczego, Warszawa.

Pisarnicki, A. F. and Goliseva, T. N. (1971). *Vinodelie i Vinogradarstvo S.S.S.R.* 31(3), 24.

Popova, E. E. (1960). *Vinodelie i Vinogradarstvo S.S.S.R.* 20(1), 13.

Popova, E. E. (1961). 'Medovye Vina'. Piščepromizdat, Moskva. 'Rocznik Statystyczny' (1973) 33. Główny Urząd Statystyczny, Warszawa.

Rzędowski, W. (1956). 'Klarowanie Win i Soków Pitnych'. Wydawnictwo Przemysłu Lekkiego i Spożywczego, Warszawa.

Schanderl, H. and Koch, J. (1972). 'Die Fruchtweinbereitung'. Eugen Ulmer, Stuttgart.

Skibe, H. (1969). *Die Industrielle Obst- und Gemüseverwertung* 54(24), 729.

Sosina, S., Kačanovskaja, Z. I. and Simanovskaja, G. B. (1968). *Vinodelie i Vinogradarstvo S.S.S.R.* 28(8), 18.

Taguena, M. X. (1972). *Bulletin de l'O.I.V.* 45(496), 497.

Tokarz, W. (1927). 'Wyrób Win i Miodów'. Polska Księgarnia, Lwów i Warszawa.

Trofimenko, A. V. (1969). *Vinodelie i Vinogradarstvo S.S.S.R.* 29(3), 8.

Usov, V. M. (1964). *Vinodelie i Vinogradarstvo S.S.S.R.* 24(2), 57.

Warcollier, G. (1928). 'La Cidrevie'. J. B. Braillière et Fils, Paris.

Wasilewski, Z. (1958). *In* 'Poradnik Mikrobiologa w Przemyśle Fermentacyjnym i Owocowo-warzywnym' Zbiorowo. Wydawnictwo Przemyslu Lekkiego i Spożywczego, Warszawa.

Wojcieszak, P. and Witkowski, T. (1953). *Przemysł Rolny i Spożywczy* 7(12), 419.

Wucherpfennig, K. (1969). *Flüssiges Obst* 36(8), 322.

Wucherpfennig, K. (1971). *Flüssiges Obst* 38(3), 98.

Wucherpfennig, K. and Bretthauer, G. (1968a). *Die Industrielle Obst- und Gemüseverwertung* 53(1), 1.

Wucherpfennig, K. and Bretthauer, G. (1968b). *Deutsche Lebensmittel-Rundschau* 64(3), 63.

Wucherpfennig, K. and Possmann, Ph. (1972). *Flüssiges Obst* 39(2), 46.

Wzorek, W. (1973). *Przeglad Gastronomiczny* 28(4), 19.

Wzorek, W. and Chruszczyk, A. (1972). *Przemysł Fermentacyjny i Rolny* 16(12), 11.

Wzorek, W. and Lisak, M. (1973). Report to the VI Scientific Session of the Committee for Foodstuffs Technology and Chemical Engineering of the Polish Academy of Science, Lublin.

Zacharina, O. S. and Fridman, S. G. (1967). *Vinodelie i Vinogradarstvo* 27(4), 26.

Żukov, A. M., Vodorez, G. D. and Fialkovskij, V. I. (1968). *Vinodelie i Vinogradarstvo S.S.S.R.* 28(4), 40.

6. Saké

K. KODAMA AND K. YOSHIZAWA

Kodama Brewing Co., Ltd., Iitagawa, Akita Prefecture, Japan, and
The National Research Institute of Brewing, Tokyo, Japan

I. OUTLINE OF SAKÉ BREWING

Saké is the traditional alcoholic beverage in Japan and still one of the most popular drinks for Japanese. The raw materials used in *saké* brewing are rice and water. Characteristic features of *saké* brewing are the use of *koji*, a culture of *Aspergillus oryzae* on steamed rice, and parallel fermentation. *Koji*, which is comparable to malts used for beer brewing, is used for saccharification of starch and decomposition of protein contained in the raw material, rice grains. Whereas fermentation takes place after filtration of the mash in beer brewing, in the *saké* mash, which is called *moromi*, sugars liberated from rice grains are fermented successively by yeast. Parallel fermentation means the combination of progressive decomposition of starch and

423

of other substances, and slow fermentation at a low temperature. These contribute to the high ethanol production which can be up to 20% (v/v) in the *moromi* mash. The first step in the procedure is the preparation of polished rice (the polishing ratio is 70 to 75% in general) and its steaming. The second is the preparation of *koji*; the third is the preparation of *moto*-mash, which is a starter for *saké* yeast, and is prepared by mashing steamed rice, *koji* and water followed by inoculation of a pure yeast culture. To avoid growth of harmful bacterial contaminants and help growth of the inoculated yeast, 0.5% lactic acid is added at an early stage in the preparation of *moto*-mash.

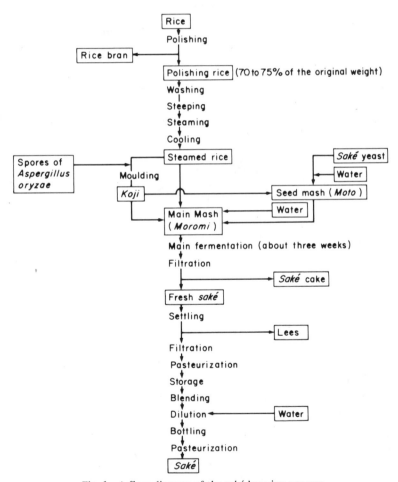

Fig. 1. A flow diagram of the *saké* brewing process.

About 5 to 9% of the total amount of polished rice is used for preparing the *moto*-mash. The fourth step involves the preparation of *moromi*-mash, the main fermentation mash, which is made by mixing a larger amount of residual steamed rice, *koji*, water and *moto*-mash in a large fermentation vessel. The additions are divided successively into three batches. The fermentation takes 20 to 25 days after addition of the final batch. Contrary to the situation in beer brewing, the mash is dense and mushy. These solids are considered to help to retain large numbers of yeast cells in suspension during the fermentation, which is one of the reasons why *saké* contains as much as 20% (v/v) ethanol without resorting to distillation. The final step is aging and bottling of *saké*. While *saké* is stored, it matures and develops a smooth taste and colour. After storage, *saké* is finally blended, adjusted to the appropriate ethanol content by adding water, treated with activated carbon followed by filtration, bottled and pasteurized. Figure 1 shows a flow diagram of the *saké* brewing process.

II. HISTORY OF SAKÉ BREWING

Saké has been favoured by the Japanese for thousands of years. According to Volume 30 of the 'Romance of the Three Kingdoms', one of the most famous mediaeval novels in China, the ancestors of Japan, drank *saké* because it was their nature to appreciate *saké*. Even during the period of mourning, the visitors gathered from here and there to perform a memorial service for the dead by singing, dancing and drinking *saké*. Thus, from ancient times, Japanese people already had *saké* for their own consumption, and they made it any time and any place according to their need. This can be termed '*saké* by the general public'.

In olden times when they did not use mould for *saké* brewing, *saké* was supposedly brewed by chewing water, soaked or steamed rice so that amylases of the saliva decomposed rice starch like the mould. We find this primitive method in our old literatures as well as in some festivals in local districts of Japan. It is generally assumed that the technique of using mould for *saké* brewing originated in China, but a comparison of processes for producing *saké* with those used for producing Chinese alcoholic beverages shows remarkable differences, especially with respect to the micro-organisms concerned and the physical condition of the raw materials. In Japan, since prehistoric times, rice has been consumed as a daily food, and Japanese ate rice after roasting, boiling down into gruel or pounding it into cake, and these rice foods could easily become covered by mould. Thus, for the ancient Japanese who had succeeded in choosing suitable varieties of rice, it might have been easy to select *koji* mould and to devise a unique *koji*-making method in which steamed rice grains were prepared in a loose heap. On the other hand, in producing Chinese alcoholic beverages, various moulds such as species of *Rhizopus, Mucor* and yeasts are grown spontaneously on wheat flour or other materials, most of which are prepared like a compact brick or a dumpling and known as *Kyokushi*. It is likely that the techniques for making Chinese alcoholic beverages, including *Kyokushi*, were introduced into Japan in the beginning of the 5th Century A.D., and made a great contribution to improving the Japanese traditional skill in *saké* brewing which had already been established.

After the beginning of the 5th Century A.D., the Imperial Household and the government were the strong driving force for culture and industry, and they established large-scale factories and employed many technicians and workmen in various fields to furnish them with all kinds of supplies, all of which were monopolized, *saké* brewing being no exception. Meanwhile, there appeared a group of *saké* brewers authorized by the government to form a guild system. Thus, *saké* brewing from the 5th to the 9th Centuries A.D. can be referred to as '*saké* by the court' in contrast to '*saké* by the general public'. After the 8th Century, buddhists and shinto priests gradually began to brew *saké* and, from the end of the 12th Century, they granted authorization for *saké* brewing to several specialists who were required either to offer *saké* or to pay tax in return for it. From the end of the 10th Century, *saké* came on to the commercial market. This meant that *saké* had to endure long storage as a commodity unlike the one brewed before. Thus, taking the place of '*saké* by the court', '*saké* by the professional brewers made its appearance. As to the know-how on *saké* brewing in the Middle Ages, the following two documents reveal that it was based on almost the same principles as those of today. According to the '*Goshu no Nikki*' in the beginning of the Muromachi period, *saké* brewing was already carried out through a process in which rice-*koji* and steamed rice and water were mashed successively in two steps. This document further describes both application of a spontaneous lactic-acid fermentation (which protects the mash from bacterial contamination and allows dominant growth only of *saké* yeast during *moto* preparation) and activation of enzymes and promotion of microbial growth by elevation of the mash temperature. At the *Tamon-in* monastery in the *Kofukuji* temple in Nara City, there is the '*Tamon-in Diary*' which had been written for about 100 years in the late Muromachi age (second half of the 16th Century). Various parts of this document indicate that *saké* was brewed at a number of small temples belonging to the *Kofukuji* temple. It is noteworthy that this diary describes in detail a heating method to kill the germs that had already been established in this Century. This is almost identical with the process invented in Europe by Louis Pasteur in 1865 for low-temperature pasteurization of wine and milk. This knowledge laid the foundation for *saké* brewing of today. During the Edo period, under the tightly closed circumstances of national isolation, the *saké* brewing skills and methods which had been handed down from the Middle Ages led to the setting up of thousands of *saké* brewing schools. The brewing seasons extended from the autumnal equinox to the vernal equinox and afterwards, producing respectively equinox *saké*, winter *saké*, interval *saké* and before-winter *saké*. But, after many trials and failures, they settled on '*kanzukuri*', that is, brewing in midwinter based on the techniques of those brewers in the Ikeda, Itami and Nada districts (Osaka City and Hyogo Prefecture) who held the leadership in *saké* brewing at that time. Besides these specialized breweries in the main producing districts, there emerged great numbers of small breweries run by landowners and rice traders. Until the Genroku period (at the end of the 17th Century), the total number of breweries was reported to be more than 27,000.

In the Meiji Era, under the influence of the new brewing technology based on European science, there occurred a drastic change in the method of *saké* brewing, and many attempts to improve *saké* brewing were made by directly applying the European beer-brewing method. But they all ended in failure because, in *saké* brewing, many special techniques of mould culture not required in beer brewing are employed. But not until the end of the Meiji Era did the Japanese brewers note that *saké* brewing could be carried out in no other way than by using the old traditional techniques.

Plate 1. Photograph of a traditional *saké* cup and jug, the property of the Japanese Society of Brewing, Japan.

However, it was notable that the old know-how regarding *saké* brewing, which had been devised and handed down from generation to generation, was rationalized and placed on a theoretical basis through the incursion of European science. Plate 1 shows a photograph of an old *saké* cup and jug.

III. TAXATION AND CLASSIFICATION OF SAKÉ

Saké is a valuable factor in the Japanese national economy because of its importance as a source of indirect tax revenue. At the beginning of this century, the revenue from indirect tax on alcoholic beverages, in which *saké* was the main constituent, was about one third of the total national revenue. Thereafter the ratio of the revenue from indirect tax on alcoholic beverages to the total national revenue has decreased gradually to about 7.5% in 1971 as shown in Table 1. The revenue from indirect tax on alcoholic beverages in 1971 consisted of 215×10^9 yen from *saké* and 328×10^9 yen from beer.

Table 1
Changes in the national revenue in Japan from indirect tax on *saké*

Year	Saké	Alcoholic beverages	Percentage ratio of revenue from saké to that from all alcoholic beverages	Percentage ratio of revenue from all beverages to the total national revenue
1955		161		17.1
1960	100	249	40.2	13.8
1965	126	353	35.7	10.8
1971	215	609	35.3	7.5

Revenue values are in yen $\times 10^{-9}$.

Saké is classified by the law in Japan on alcoholic beverages into three classes, namely special, first and second classes as shown in Table 2, on the basis of the results of organoleptic evaluation by experts mainly belonging to the Tax Administration Bureau in Japan. A *saké* brewery must submit a sample of each lot which it wishes to sell in either the special or first class for accepting evaluation. The rate of indirect tax on each class differs according to its ethanol content. The standard rates are shown in Table 2. Besides these duties, *ad valorem* taxes are applied on the special class sold at a higher price.

Table 2
Classification of *saké*

Class	Standard ethanol content (%, v/v)	Tax (yen/kl)
Special	16.0	285,400
First	15.5	174,300
Second	15.0	85,800

The law also regulates raw materials as well as many additives such as activated carbon and minerals. Rice is the only cereal used in *saké* brewing. Ethanol, glucose, millet-jelly, sodium glutamate, lactic acid and succinic acid can be used in restricted amounts.

IV. PRODUCTION AND CONSUMPTION

Saké has for a long time been the main alcoholic beverage in Japan, and it is still one of the main alcoholic beverages along with beer. Since *saké* is consumed within one year after it is produced, production of *saké* has generally kept pace with its consumption, as with beer brewing. Table 3 shows the changes in *saké* production, the amount of rice used in *saké* brewing, and the numbers of *saké* breweries in Japan, over a period of 45 years. In 1926, 929,000 kl of *saké* were produced. During the Second World War, production decreased remarkably and, in 1947, only 91,000 kl were produced. Thereafter production was restored gradually and reached 1,384,000 kl in 1971. Recently there has been little increase in production.

In general, 280 kl of *saké* is made from 150 tons of brown rice. During the Second World War, a shortage of rice resulted in an increase in the amount of *saké* made by adding ethanol, water and sugars to fermented *moromi*-mash. At present, these methods have been improved and applied so widely that they play an important role in providing *saké* with a mild and smooth taste, besides increasing the amount of *saké* produced. Table 4 shows changes in

Table 3

Changes in Japan in the amount of *saké* produced, the amount of rice used in *saké* manufacture, and the number of *saké* breweries, over a period of 45 years

Year	*Saké* production ($\times 10^{-3}$ kl)	Rice used for *saké* production ($\times 10^{-3}$ ton)	Number of breweries
1926	929	509	9,587
1931	635	354	8,481
1936	771	435	7,499
1941	373	204	—
1946	154	80	—
1951	251	87	—
1956	481	195	4,073
1961	797	352	3,978
1966	1,121	468	3,862
1971	1,384	593	3,433

The amount of rice used is expressed as the weight of the polished rice for the period 1926-1951, and as the weight of the brown rice for the period 1956-1971.

the consumption of various alcoholic beverages in Japan in a recent decade. In 1961, 2,627,000 kl of alcoholic beverages were consumed, including 830,000 kl of *saké* and 1,284,000 kl of beer. Consumption has increased steadily and, in 1971, reached 5,153,000 kl, including 1,588,000 kl of *saké* and 3,090,000 kl of beer. While consumption of beer increased rapidly and doubled in amount in this period, the rate

Table 4

Changes in consumption of various alcoholic beverages in Japan over the period 1961-1971

		Consumption ($\times 10^{-3}$ kl) in			
		1961	1964	1967	1971
Saké	Special class	12	59	56	84
	First class	85	270	379	692
	Second class	733	951	858	812
	Total	830	1,280	1,293	1,588
Beer		1,285	1,992	2,462	3,090
Whisky			55	113	145
Shochu (a Japanese domestic spirit)		267	219	221	195
Total		2,627	3,688	4,226	5,153

of increase in consumption of *saké* has retarded. Since 1958, *saké* consumption has decreased from 36% to 31% of the total consumption in 1971. This is mainly due to decreased sales of the second class of *saké*.

Whereas consumption of second class *saké* increased only from 562,000 kl in 1958 to 812,000 in 1971, consumption of the special and first classes of *saké* increased from 9,000 to 84,000 kl and from 60,000 kl to 692,000 kl, respectively. As a result, consumption of second class *saké* decreased from 88% to 51% of the total consumed. These facts are of great advantage to the large breweries, because the majority of special and first classes of *saké* are being produced by them.

Table 5

Data on production and shipment of *saké* in Japan in 1973

Amount of *saké* produced (kl)	Number of breweries	Percentage of total *saké* production (%)	Percentage of total shipment (%)
Less than 300	2,367(71.1%)	28.4	16.5
300 to 1,000	767(23.1%)	29.7	19.2
1,000 to 3,000	158(4.8%)	20.7	20.0
3,000 to 5,000	15(0.4%)	4.3	5.8
Over 5,000	19(0.6%)	16.9	38.5

In 1971, there were about 3,400 *saké* breweries scattered all over Japan; however, the number is decreasing. The most famous districts for *saké* production are the 'Nada' area in Hyogo Prefecture and the 'Hushimi' area in Kyoto City followed by Akita and Hiroshima Prefectures. The first two areas contributed about 20% of the *saké* produced in Japan in 1971. About 70% of all of the breweries produce less than 300 kl of *saké* per year (Table 5). Moreover, about 50 large breweries, producing over 3,000 kl of *saké* per year, half of this being in the 'Nada' and 'Hushimi' areas, ship nearly 50% of the total *saké* production, including over 70% of the special and first-class *saké* produced in Japan. Besides *saké* brewing, many small breweries carry on various businesses (such as management of liquor-shops, restaurants afforestation) to get a sufficient income.

Since fermentation proceeds in an open vessel usually at below

15°C, *saké* is generally produced only in the winter. Recently, development of production techniques, including refrigeration and sanitation as well as brewing, has enabled *saké* production to be continued throughout the four seasons. Many large breweries build modern factories equipped with air conditioning and various facilities, and thus increase the scale of production, and also decrease labour costs, which have become one of the most serious problems in *saké* brewing. On the other hand, for most of the small breweries who have been manufacturing *saké* in the old fashioned factories, it may be difficult to build modern factories due to financial circumstances in spite of their ardent desire, unless they establish a joint concern or organize a co-operative association. Thus, the differences in profits between large and small breweries may increase unless the latter produce a unique, refined, and therefore valuable *saké* by using their elaborate and manual techniques. Economical and technical rationalization of the *saké* brewing industry, including combination and co-operation between breweries, is now on the way.

V. INDUSTRIAL PRODUCTION OF SAKÉ

A. Raw Materials

1. *Water*

Water, one of the most important raw materials in *saké* brewing, accounts for about 80% (v/v) of *saké*. It is not only used as a raw material but also in many other procedures such as washing and steeping of rice, bottle-washing, and for boiling. In general, about 25 kl of water is necessary for one ton of rice used for *saké* brewing. The water for *saké* brewing needs to be colourless, tasteless and odourless; neutral or weakly alkaline; and to contain only traces of iron, ammonia, nitrate and organic substances, and no harmful micro-organisms. Several ions, especially potassium ions, existing in water in minor concentrations have been reported to affect fermentation and *koji* making (Kano, 1961; Noshiro and Aoki, 1957; Noshiro and Nakagawa, 1957; Yoshizawa *et al.*, 1973b).

Iron is injurious to *saké* because it gives an intense colour and leads to deterioration (Eda *et al.*, 1929; Yoshizawa, 1958; Yoshizawa and Makino, 1960; Kobayashi and Akiyama, 1961; Takase *et al.*, 1963; Nishi *et al.*, 1966; Takeda and Tsukahara, 1963; Tadenuma and Sato, 1967). Appropriate treatments, such as aeration, successive filtration, adsorption and flocculation, adsorption on activated carbon or ion-exchange resins and flocculation with reagents such as alum, are generally employed to remove iron in brewing water (Totsuka *et al.*, 1971).

2. Rice

Rice is the principal raw material of *saké*, and its quality largely affects *saké* brewing, but details of this are not clearly elucidated. Many studies on the nature of the rice used in *saké* brewing have been carried out. Japonica short-grain varieties, produced in Japan, have been found to be most suitable, and some other short-grain varieties, such as Korean and Taiwanese, may also be used, though the quality of the *saké* produced from them is sometimes inferior to that from domestic rice (Eda, 1922; Kawasaki *et al.*, 1967a, b; Kumagai *et al.*, 1968; Nunokawa, 1968; Nunokawa *et al.*, 1968, 1969; Tadenuma and Sato, 1965). Among the many domestic Japanese varieties, some are considered to be especially suitable for *saké* brewing and are sold at a higher price. As a guide to rice selection, many physiochemical properties are considered, the following being of particular importance.

a. *Size of grain.* Large grains are considered desirable. The size of the grain is generally expressed by the weight of 1,000 kernels; a weight of 25.03 g has been quoted as a mean value of 101 selected varieties, and 23.05 g as a mean value of 24 ordinary varieties (Sato and Yamada, 1925). Many kernels in selected varieties have a white spot in the centre known as 'Shinpaku'. Small-grain varieties scarcely contain any 'Shinpaku'.

b. *Chemical constituents.* Most rice varieties contain 72 to 73% carbohydrate, 7 to 9% crude protein, 1.3 to 2.0% crude fat, and 1.0 to 1.5% ash, with 12 to 15% of water. It has been shown that there exist close correlations among the weight of 1,000 kernels, the crude protein content, the speed of adsorption of water during steeping, and formation of sugars by saccharification of rice with amylases

(Yoshizawa *et al.*, 1973c; Akai, 1963; Uchida, 1966; Yonezaki, 1962).

3. Polishing

In contrast to the use of malt and corn in brewing and spirits production, in *saké* brewing rice is polished before it is used. The main purpose of polishing is to remove proteins, lipids and minerals which are present in excess in the germ and surface layers of the rice grain, and which are considered undesirable in *saké* brewing.

The ratio (percentage by weight) of cleaned rice (after polishing) to the original brown rice is defined as the polishing ratio. Changes in the amounts of some constituents of the processed grain with various polishing ratios are shown in Table 6 (Research Institute of Brewing,

Table 6

Changes in the contents of some components of rice grains as a result of polishing

Content (% weight) of		Polishing ratio (%)					
		100	90	80	70	60	50
Moisture	A	13.5	13.5	13.3	13.0	11.0	10.5
	B	13.3	13.3	12.9	11.8	11.0	11.0
Crude protein	A	6.55	5.66	5.12	4.41	4.06	3.80
	B	7.95	7.24	6.36	5.83	5.47	5.12
Crude fat	A	2.28	0.67	0.11	0.10	0.07	0.05
	B	1.90	0.55	0.11	0.08	0.05	0.04
Ash	A	1.00	0.38	0.25	0.19	0.20	0.15
	B	1.06	0.39	0.25	0.20	0.18	0.19
Starch	A	70.9	73.5	74.3	76.1	76.3	77.6
	B	69.6	72.8	74.6	75.8	76.9	78.3

The data for A are for *Yamadanishiki* rice harvested in Hyogo Prefecture; for B, an ordinary rice harvested in Chiba Prefecture in Japan.

Japan, 1964). Crude fat and ash contents decrease most rapidly, while the protein content decreases gradually until the polishing ratio reaches 50%, after which it remains practically constant. In contrast to changes in the crude fat content, the content of lipids (by hydrolysis) does not change with an increase in the polishing ratio (Mori and Watanabe, 1953; Yoshizawa *et al.*, 1973a). In general, cleaned rice of 75–70% polishing ratio is used for *saké* brewing.

A type of roller mill is used for polishing the rice as shown in

Figure 2. The roller, made of carborundum and feldspar, rotates around a vertical axis and scrapes the surface of grains. Rice grains fed from the hopper, are polished in the polishing chamber, and fall to the bottom of the basket conveyer through the sieve where the rice bran is removed. The basket conveyer carries rice grains to the hopper. Thus the operation continues until the grains are polished to the required ratio. The polishing efficiency and the shape of the

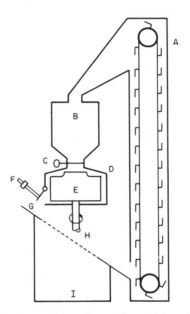

Fig. 2. Diagram of a vertical type rice mill used in *saké* brewing. A indicates the basket conveyor, B the rice hopper, C the rice flow adjusting bulb, D the polishing chamber, E the roller, F a resistance, G the exit, H the sieve, and I the bran reservoir.

polished kernels are influenced by rotation speeds, resistance, and the particle size of carborundum in the roller. The speed of polishing decreases gradually when the ratio decreases. The nature of the rice also affects the speed at which the grain is polished as well as the polishing efficiency (Sakamoto *et al.*, 1966; Furuhashi and Ishikawa, 1967, 1968; Yoshizawa *et al.*, 1973a). With a mill having a roller 40 cm in diameter, average times for polishing are 6 to 8 h for 89%, 7 to 10 h for 75%, 10 to 13 h for 70%, and 16 to 20 h for 60% polishing ratio, respectively.

4. Washing and Steeping

Rice is washed and steeped in water before steaming. During washing, the grains are subjected to a kind of polishing caused mainly from collision of rice grains in the water. This process removes some of the surface parts of the grains (1 to 3% of the total grain weight), which make up most of the suspended solids and account for most of the biochemical oxygen demand in the waste water discharged from saké breweries (Yoshizawa et el., 1972a). To eliminate these contributions to suspended solids and biochemical oxygen demand, steeping of rice without washing is adopted in a few saké breweries.

During washing, the grains absorb water up to 9 to 17% of their weights. Various pieces of washing equipment, including that which transports rice grains in water in continuous washing, are also used.

Washed rice grains are passed into a vat and immediately steeped in water. During the washing and steeping procedures, the grains absorb water to about 25 to 30% of their original weight, which promotes penetration of heat into the grains during steaming, and accelerates modification of the starch granules in the grains. Absorption of the appropriate amounts of water is a very important process in preparing properly steamed rice, and controlling koji making and fermentation. The absorption velocity differs with the variety of rice and polishing ratio (Kawamata et al., 1958; Uchida, 1966; Uchida et al., 1968; Saijo et al., 1968; Akai, 1963; Yoshizawa et al., 1973a, c). Rice grains are steeped in water for 1–20 h according to the rate of water absorption. Soft rice absorbs water within 1 to 3 h. Highly polished rice absorbs water more rapidly.

During washing and steeping, some minerals, such as potassium ions, as well as sugars are eluted from the grains (Noshiro and Aoki, 1957; Kano, 1962; Yoshizawa et al., 1973b), whereas calcium and iron ions are absorbed onto the grains (Horie et al., 1965; Takase and Murakami, 1965; Muto and Takahashi, 1957). After steeping, excess water is drained off from the grains for about 4 to 8 h before steaming.

5. Steaming

During steaming, starch is changed to the α-form, and protein is denatured and becomes susceptible to enzyme action by koji.

Moreover, the grains are sterilized by steaming. To obtain completely steamed rice, the grains are usually steamed for 30 to 60 min, though it has been reported that steaming for as little as 15 to 20 min is sufficient to modify the starch and protein of rice produced in Japan (Akiyama and Takase, 1958; Akiyama and Yamamoto, 1963; Oana and Mizuno, 1933; Yamada *et al.*, 1945). During steaming, the grains absorb water to the extent of 7 to 12% of the weight of the starting rice grains, thus resulting in a total water gain of about 35 to 40% from the beginning of the brewing process.

In small breweries, steam is usually generated from water in a large pot, but boilers are often used in many larger breweries for steaming. Steeped rice grains are heaped up in an insulated shallow tub with a

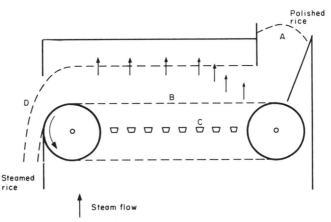

Fig. 3. Diagram of a belt conveyor type apparatus for steaming rice. A indicates the entry port for the rice, B the wire mesh belt conveyor, C steam nozzles, and D the exit port for the steamed rice.

special jet in the centre of the base through which steam is blown. This is placed on top of a large kettle filled with water, and steamed for about a half to one hour under atmospheric pressure.

The tub is about 160 to 190 cm in diameter and 50 to 90 cm in height. In modern procedures, two types of continuous steaming apparatus are often used, namely a belt-conveyor system (Imayasu *et al.*, 1963) and a cylinder system. In the former system (Fig. 3), steeped grains are carried on the screened conveyer, and are steamed for about 20 to 30 min with the pressure-controlled steam jetting out from steam nozzles. In the latter system (Fig. 4), steeped grains pass down from the hopper into the cylindrical vessel and are steamed from jets from the lower part of the cylinder. At the bottom of the cylinder, there are two plates which open and close the bottom. By opening the upper plate and closing the lower one, steamed grains, accumulated between the two plates, fall down and, by closing the upper one and opening the lower one, the grains are then removed from the system. These movements are carried out continuously. The flow of grain is adjusted to take about 20 min from the top to the bottom. After steaming, the kernel is slightly sticky, somewhat translucent, and strongly resistant to crushing between the fingers. The steamed rice is cooled to nearly 40°C for *koji* making, and to about 10°C when used for preparing *moto* and *moromi*-mash.

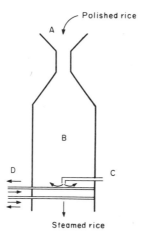

Fig. 4. Diagram of a cylinder type apparatus for steaming rice. A indicates the rice hopper, B the steaming chamber, C the steam inlet, and D rice cutters which move reciprocally.

Breweries usually use machines which cool the steamed rice by employing a draught of air as it moves on the screened belt. A pneumatic conveyer system is often used to transfer steamed rice.

B. Preparation of *koji*

Koji is a culture of the *koji* mould, *Aspergillus oryzae*, grown on and within steamed rice grains, and which accumulates various enzymes involved in *saké* production. For the preparation of *koji*, seed-moulds, termed *tane-koji*, are used in all breweries. The *Aspergillus oryzae* strains are cultured in steamed rice (the polishing ratio is 98 to 99%) at 34 to 36°C for 5 to 6 days during production of *tane-koji*. This process results in abundant spore formation.

The scientific name for the Japanese *koji* mould, *Aspergillus oryzae*, dates back to Ahlburg and Matsubara (1878) and Cohn (1883), but it was not until the work of Wehmer (1895) was published that *A. oryzae* was described in detail. Later, mycological studies on *koji* mould revealed that *A. flavus-oryzae* is a large group, including innumerable strains among which there are slight graded variations in morphological and physiological properties (Takahashi, 1912; Thom and Church, 1926; Sakaguchi, 1933; Saito, 1950; Nehira and Nomi, 1956). However, Murakami *et al.* (1968) claimed that most of the *koji* mould strains used for *saké* brewing belong to the species *A. oryzae* and not to *A. flavus*. The latter species is clearly distinguishable from the former on the basis of the mycological characteristics of the authentic type cultures of the two species and various industrial strains (Murakami, 1972; Murakami and Makino, 1968). It is worth noting that aflatoxin-producing strains have not been found among the Japanese industrial strains of *koji* mould (Yokotsuka *et al.*, 1967; Murakami *et al.*, 1967; Kurata, 1968). Strains of *A. oryzae* can be grouped according to their physiological characteristics into three types, namely aerobic, anaerobic and intermediate. The aerobic strains most widely distributed in *tane-koji* used for *saké* brewing have been classified mainly in a group of *A. oryzae* having large intracellular vesicles (Murakami, 1958; Murakami and Kawai, 1958; Murakami and Takagi, 1959).

Though about 50 kinds of enzymes have been found in *koji*, the most important of these are amylases and proteases. *Alpha*-Amylase (liquefying amylase) and saccharifying amylase (amyloglucosidase) play the leading roles in the amylolytic action in *koji* (Shimada *et al.*, 1953; Tokuoka, 1941, 1942). Acid- and alkaline-proteases are found in *koji*. In *moto* and *moromi*, the former acts mainly to decompose protein to form amino acids and peptides at low pH values such as 3 to 4 (Kageyama and Sugita, 1955; Nunokawa, 1962; Nunokawa *et al.*, 1963; Suzuki *et al.*, 1958).

Cultural conditions influence the formation of enzymes. In general, the higher the cultivation temperatures (~42°C), the greater the activities of amylases; lower temperatures (~30°C) favour the development of protease activities. As cultivation times become longer, more enzymic activities appear in the *koji* (Suzuki *et al.*, 1956). The moisture content of the rice kernels is important; nitrogenous substances and acids are accumulated more in *koji* which has been prepared from steamed rice of higher moisture content (Nunokawa *et al.*, 1962). These substances are considered to be related to the flavours and tastes of *saké*. Protein turbidity, which occurs in *saké* after pasteurization and bottling and cannot be removed by simple filtration, is caused by enzyme proteins, such as saccharifying amylase, which have been produced in *koji* and rendered insoluble by pasteurization (Akiyama, 1962a, b; Sugita and Kageyama, 1957, 1958; Suzuki *et al.*, 1958). Blackening *saké* cake sometimes appears during storage of the sheet-formed *saké* cake, and this is attributed to the action of enzymes in *koji* which react with phenolic substances such as tyrosine to develop a black colour (Oba *et al.*, 1969).

The following account is an example of conventional *koji* manufacture. After the steamed rice has been cooled to about 35°C by passing through a cooling apparatus, it is transferred into the *koji-muro*, a large incubation room in which the temperature (26-28°C) and humidity are controlled at suitable levels for growth of the mould. After inoculation of *tane-koji* in the proportion of 60-100 g/1,000 kg of rice, the mixture is left heaped in the centre of the floor. At this stage, the temperature of the material is 31-32°C. As the spores germinate and mycelia develop, the rice begins to smell mouldy. After incubation for 10-12 h, the heap of rice grains is mixed in order to maintain uniformity of growth, temperature and moisture content. After another 10-12 h, when growth of the mould mycelia on the grains can be distinctly seen as small white spots, and the temperature of the material has risen to 32-34°C, it is dispensed into wooden boxes, each of which contains 15-45 kg of mouldy grain. To control the rise in temperature and the moisture content in the mass of grain, the bottom of the box is made of wooden lattice or wire mesh.

Temperature and moisture content are also controlled by the thickness of the grain layer heaped in the box (usually 8 cm at the beginning, 6 cm at the first mixing, and 4 cm at the second mixing) and by the cloth covering the grain mass. Thereafter, at intervals of 6-8 h, the material is mixed and heaped again in the box. During the latter stages, special caution must be taken to prevent over-heating of the material caused by respiration of the mould. After incubation for about 40 h, the temperature of the material rises to 40–42°C, white mycelium develops to cover and penetrate the grains, and the grains contain sufficient enzymes, vitamins and various nutritive substances for mashing and growth of *saké* yeast, and *koji*-fragrance is formed. Then the *koji* is taken out of the room and spread on a clean cloth to be cooled until it is used for mashing.

In order to save labour, and to prepare *koji* of as uniform a quality as possible, the conventional method is continually being improved, and automatic methods are being devised for commercial application. Various types of *koji*-making machines have been devised, and are

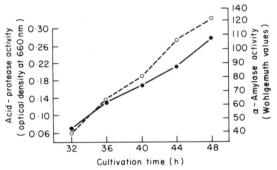

Fig. 5. Development of α-amylase (o) and acid protease (•) activities in *koji* during cultivation. *Alpha*-Amylase activity is expressed as Wohlgemuth values (D at 40°C for 30 min). Acid protease activity is expressed as the optical density at 660 nm of a casein solution reacted with the phenol reagent after incubating with 1 ml of enzyme solution at pH 3.0 at 38°C for 6 min.

used for preparing large amounts in many breweries. In these machines, a large quantity of steamed rice is heaped thickly on a wire mesh or perforated metal plates fixed in a closed box, and clean air from an air conditioner passes through the layer of heaped material at an appropriate humidity and temperature, automatic adjustment being applied according to the progress of the culture. By adequate control of the temperature and moisture content of the material by the conditioned air flow, *koji* with almost the same quality as that prepared by the conventional method can be obtained, thus saving labour and shortening the time needed for *koji* making by about 6–8 h.

During *koji* making, various changes take place in the rice grains. Hydrolytic enzymes, B-group vitamins, sugars, peptides, and amino acids accumulate with various components and precursors of the flavour and taste of *saké*. Figure 5 shows the development of α-amylase and acid-protease activities during *koji* making (Hara, 1970). Carbohydrates are decomposed finally to water and carbon dioxide, which leads to the production of energy for growth of the mould. Table 7 shows changes in the contents of moisture and of carbohydrates during *koji* making (Toyosawa and Yonezaki, 1953, 1954).

Table 7

Changes in the content of some carbohydrates during koji cultivation

Operations	Moisture	Starch	Dextrins	Direct reducing sugars	Glucose	Maltose
Inoculation	34.4	90.4	5.0	0.2	—	—
Mori	32.8	90.7	2.1	1.7	—	—
1st Mixing	31.7	88.0	2.7	4.2	1.9	2.5
2nd Mixing	30.3	79.2	2.4	13.1	7.5	7.8
Finishing	25.7	69.9	2.7	21.4	14.7	14.3

Data are shown as percent dry matter, except for moisture content. *Mori* is a heap of mouldy grains dispensed in wooden boxes.

C. Preparation of *moto* (yeast starter)

1. Yeast and Fermentation

In *saké* brewing, *koji* and steamed rice are mixed with water to make a yeast starter, called *moto*, for the main fermentation mash which in turn is called *moromi*. *Moto* is classified into two types according to the procedure by which it is prepared, *Ki-moto* and *yamahai-moto* are acidified by naturally occurring lactic-acid bacteria, whereas in *sokujo-moto* lactic acid is added at the beginning of the process. In *ki-moto* and *yamahai-moto*, various aerobic bacteria, wild yeasts, lactic-acid bacteria and *saké* yeasts grow successively in that order, while, in the *sukujo-moto*, *saké* yeast inoculated in pure culture is almost the only micro-organism present. There is an accumulation of a large amount of sugar (over 20%) at an early stage in both *moto* processes. This, together with the acidification produced either microbiologically or by the addition of acid, facilitates the predominant growth of *saké* yeast in the later stages. In the *moromi* process, however, the presence of a high concentration of yeast cells used as inoculum (10^7–10^8/g), and the acidity of the mash originating from the added *moto*, permit enhanced growth of the *saké* yeast. The high initial yeast cell count is characteristically obtained by the stepwise addition of *koji*, rice and water at definite time intervals. As the volume is increased in this way, there is a gradual increase in the population of *saké* yeast. In particular, the high concentration (40–45%) of steamed rice used in the preparation of *moto* and *moromi* contributes to sound brewing practice. *Saké* yeast has a high resistance to unfavourable and violently changing conditions. High viscosity, and high concentrations of sugar, acid and alcohol in the mash, are all undesirable for growth of *saké* yeast itself, but these conditions prevent the mash from being invaded by contaminating micro-organisms. Furthermore, by overcoming many of the above-mentioned difficulties, *saké* yeast gives the mash a good flavour and taste as well as a high alcohol concentration. On the basis of these characteristics, authentic strains of yeast suitable for *saké* brewing have been selected. The Society of Brewing in Japan, with the collaboration of the National Research Institute of Brewing, has long been engaged in the selection of yeast strains and distribution of these strains to *saké* breweries, designating them by *Kyokai* numbers, of which Nos. 6, 7, 8 and 9 (Fig. 6) are the most popular. They are used not only for commercial production of *saké* but also for studies on *saké* yeast.

Saké yeast is taxonomically classified as a member of the *Saccharomyces cerevisiae* group (Kodama, 1970). However, from a practical and ecological point of view, *saké* yeast can be differentiated from other strains of *Sacch. cerevisiae* by additional properties. The properties include vitamin requirements (Takahashi, 1954, 1956; Fukui *et al.*, 1955; Sugama *et al.*, 1965; Takeda and Tsukahara, 1965a; Furukawa and Akiyama, 1962), sugar and acid tolerance, osmophilic character, adaptability to anaerobic conditions and dominant growth in the culture fluids of *koji* mould (Takeda and Tsukahara, 1965b). These characteristics of *saké* yeast may be evaluated by a consideration of its dominancy over the other micro-organisms, including wild yeasts, in the *saké* brewing process carried out in the open and under non-sterile conditions.

Generally, a large amount of foam is formed during the *moromi-*mash fermentation. Since approximately one-third of the capacity of the fermentation vessel is occupied by foam in the usual *moromi* fermentation, preventing foam formation would be of great advantage to the brewery, saving the space occupied by the foam and scaling up the amount of *moromi* produced. Foam formation was

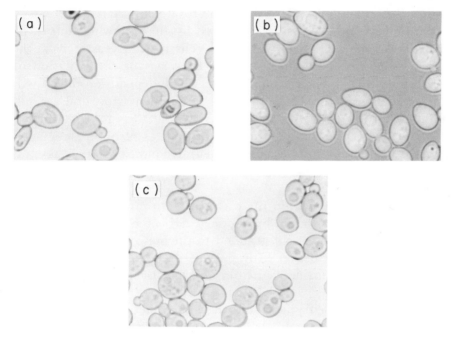

Fig. 6. Photomicrographs of cells of *saké* yeast strains *Kyokai* number 6 (micrograph a), 7 (micrograph b) and 8 (micrograph c). The cells were grown on rice *koji*-extract medium. Magnification x 1,000.

found to depend on the nature of the yeast cells, and many foam-less mutants, which have the same characters as the parent yeast except foam-formation, have been obtained (Ouchi and Akiyama, 1971; Nunokawa and Ouchi, 1971). A foam-less mutant of *Kyokai* No. 7, a favourite strain of *Saccharomyces cerevisiae*, has become available in *saké* brewing (Ishido *et al.*, 1971). Some large molecular-weight compounds which arise from steamed rice grains are also considered to take part in foam formation.

2. Preparation of Moto

In *saké* brewing, *moto* plays an important role as a starter of the yeast culture in carrying out fermentation of *moromi*. *Moto* is required to provide a pure and abundant yeast crop, and to supply sufficient lactic acid to prevent multiplication of harmful wild micro-organisms during the preparation of *moto* and in the early stages of *moromi* fermentation. The purity of *moto*, measured as the ratio of the cultured yeast cells to the total yeast cells at the end of *moto* preparation process, is influenced by the following factors: (i) the ratio of inoculated cultured yeast cells to wild yeast cells at the commencement of mashing; (ii) the time lag for the initiation of yeast growth at the given temperature which depends on the growth characteristics of the yeast; (iii) the requirements for, and assimilability of, nutrients by the yeast; (iv) tolerance for the various components of the fermentation mash such as alcohol, lactic acid, nitrite and sugar, and for environmental conditions such as temperature, viscosity and osmotic pressure of the mash; (v) the nature of the oxygen supply.

As already mentioned, in the classical *moto* procedure, lactic acid is produced in the mash by lactic-acid bacteria whereas, in the modern method, lactic acid is added to the mash at the beginning of *moto* preparation, so that little growth of lactic-acid bacteria and other micro-organisms derived from *koji* and the water supply takes place.

Lately, compressed yeast, cultivated by a method similar to that used in the preparation of baker's yeast, has become available, and in some breweries *moromi* are fermented safely with this yeast instead of *moto*. Addition of sufficient lactic acid and yeast crop ensures the safety of the fermentation. The amount of rice used for *moto* preparation is usually 7% of the total rice used for the entire *saké* mash.

a. *Yamahai-moto*. *Ki-moto* is a representative example of classical *moto* and, though it has been handed down from generation to generation since olden times, its practice is still significant from the viewpoint of modern ecology of micro-organisms. A modified method of *ki-moto*, devised by Kagi *et al.* (1909) and called *yamahai-moto*, is based on the same microbiological principle as *ki-moto*, and has practically replaced *ki-moto* because the procedure is simpler.

The following is an example of the conventional method for preparing *yamahai-moto* (Kodama *et al.*, 1956; Kodama, 1963). Steamed rice (120 kg) is mixed with 60 kg of *koji* and 200 litres of water in a vessel at an initial temperature of 13–14°C, and kept for three to four days with intermittent stirring and agitation. During this period, the rice grains are partially degraded and saccharified, and the temperature gradually falls to 7–8°C. The mash is then warmed at a rate of 0.5–1.0°C/day by an electrical heater placed under the bottom of the vessel, or by placing a wooden or metal cask filled with hot water in the mash and, after warming for a further 10–15 days, the temperature reaches 14–15°C. This completes the first half of *moto* preparation. During this stage, successive changes in the wild microflora occur because mashing starts at a near neutral pH value, and groups of organisms which require few nutrients are gradually replaced by others which have complex requirements as compounds are dissolved from *koji* and steamed rice.

In the early stages, nitrate-reducing bacteria such as *Achromobacter, Flavobacterium, Pseudomonas* or *Micrococcus* spp. (derived from *koji* and water) appear, followed by lactic-acid bacteria including *Leuconostoc mesenteroides* var. *saké* and *Lactobacillus saké* (derived from *koji*). These bacteria multiply to reach a maximum count of about 10^7–10^8/g, but successively disappear before fermentation by *saké* yeast begins, due to the accumulation of a high concentration of sugar and acidification resulting from the growth of lactic-acid bacteria (Katagiri and Kitahara, 1934; Saito and Oda, 1932; Oda, 1935; Saito, 1950; Kodama, 1959; Kitahara, 1960; Kodama *et al.*, 1960; Ashizawa, 1961; Ashizawa and Saito, 1965).

During this stage, changes in the numbers of wild yeasts present also occur. Over the first few days, various wild yeasts appear. Most of them are derived from *koji* (Saito and Oda, 1934; Kodama *et al.*, 1957; Kodama and Kyono, 1963; Kodama, 1966; Akiyama and Sugano, 1967). They disappear within the first two weeks as a result of the toxic effect of nitrite, produced by nitrate-reducing bacteria from nitrate contained in or added to the water (Hanaoka, 1918; Zenda, 1920; Kanai and Iida, 1932; Ashizawa, 1961, 1962, 1963). Yeasts of the *Hansenula anomala* group are resistant to nitrite but, since they cannot survive under anaerobic conditions in the viscous mash (Saito, 1950; Kodama, 1960), they disappear as fermentation proceeds. When wild yeasts have almost disappeared, and the temperature of the mash reaches about 15°C, the pure culture of *saké* yeast is added to give a count of 10^5-10^6/g. The composition of the mash at this stage is as follows: density, 16.0-16.5 degrees Baumé; reducing sugars, 26-28%; amino acids (as glycine), 0.5-0.8%; total acids (as lactic acid), 0.30-0.40%, w/w. After 2-3 days, when the temperature has risen to 17-19°C and increased acidity (0.5-0.6%) has caused the removal of nitrite, the inoculated yeast grows fully and fermentation begins. When the yeast cell count has reached about 10^8/g, vigorous fermentation takes place, accompanied by a temperature rise to 20-23°C. A few days later, the mash is gradually cooled to prevent the yeast from dying or being weakened by the high concentrations of alcohol and acids. After resting for a further 5-7 days, *moto* is used for the main fermentation of *moromi*. The final *moto* has the following composition: density, 4-6 degrees Baumé; alcohol, 12-15%, v/v; amino acids (as glycine), 0.45-0.65%; total acids, 0.9-1.0%, w/w.

It is noteworthy that the amounts of amino acids contained in *moto* of this classical type are two or three times higher than that in the modern type, *sokujo-moto* (Oana, 1931). Regarding the cause of the difference between the two types of *moto* with respect to the amounts of amino acids present, it has long been thought that, in the former, sufficient breakdown of rice protein by *koji* proteases is attained under conditions in which the pH values change slowly from almost neutral to slightly acid due to the growth of lactic-acid bacteria; whereas in the latter, strongly acidic conditions, caused by the initial addition of lactic acid, inhibit the activity of *koji* proteases (Sugiyama and Nagahashi, 1932). However, it was found that *koji* proteases consist mainly of an acid protease by the action of which rice protein in *moto* is broken down to soluble compounds, but is not fully decomposed to amino acids under the strongly acidic conditions, as in the case of *sokujo-moto* (Kageyama, 1955). Akiyama (1957, 1958) assumed that, in the early stages of *yamahai-moto* preparation when the pH value of the mash is almost neutral, the rice protein is degraded to an intermediate substance which is acid-soluble but insoluble in water and trichloroacetic acid, easily decomposed into amino acids under the acidic conditions, and therefore presumably a precursor of amino acids. Further, by adding lactic acid to *moto* in small concentrations at intervals during the first stage of *moto* preparation, in order gradually to lower the pH value, the content of amino acids could be increased to almost the same as in *yamahai-moto* (Akiyama, 1959). On the other hand, Takeuchi and Shimada (1965) and Takeuchi *et al.* (1967, 1969) pointed out that, in *moto* solubilization, non-specific physico-chemical interactions between protein and starch gel might occur as observed between some of the cereal proteins and starch gel under acidic aqueous conditions, or that enzymic hydrolysis of protein over a wide range of pH values may be affected by the co-existence of protein and starch gel. However, no interference with rice protein solubilization by starch gel, observed under acidic conditions, occurs at the neutral pH values existing in the early stages of *moto* of the classical type. This phenomenon may be explained if protein and starch combine by electrostatic forces. Further, enzymic hydrolysis of protein adsorbed on the starch gel is presumably inhibited by Van der Waals' forces.

To avoid interference with the hydrolysis of protein, it is necessary to remove the mash of gelatinized starch, which causes pastiness, as soon as possible by hydrolysing it to glucose. The procedure for hardening steamed rice (by cooling it to a low temperature before mashing) and kneading or braying the hardened rice (procedures which have been practised since olden times) are effective, not only for saccharification of the degraded starch, but also for solubilization of the rice protein with resultant abundant formation of amino acids. Both of the suggestions provide strong clues regarding the mechanism of the proteolysis that occurs during the preparation of *ki-moto* or *yamahai-moto*. The kneading procedure also helps to dissolve the nutrients contained in the *koji* and steamed rice, and provides semi-anaerobic conditions in the mash which promote growth of lactic-acid bacteria in the early stages (Kodama, 1960). An example of the changes in temperature and in composition during *yamahai-moto* preparation is shown in Table 8 (Kodama, 1963).

b. *Sokujo-moto*. *Sokujo-moto*, which was devised by Eda (1909), is very popular in modern *saké* brewing. It is based on the principle

Table 8

Changes in temperature and composition during *yamahai-moto* preparation

Day	Operation	Temperature of mash (°C)	Density (° Baumé)	Reducing sugars (%, w/v)	Acids (as lactic acid, w/v)	Amino acids (as glycine, %, w/v)	Ph value	Alcohol (%, v/v)
1	Mashing	13						
2		10						
3		8.5						
4	Warming	7.0–10.0	15.0	19.8	0.027	0.09	6.5	
5	Warming	8.0–11.0						
6	Warming	9.0–12.0	15.5	20.9	0.03	0.11	5.0	
7	Warming	10.0–13.0						
8	Warming	10.0–13.0	15.7	23.3	0.12	0.16	4.2	
9	Warming	11.0–14.0						
10	Warming	11.0–14.0	16.1	25.8	0.25	0.28	4.0	
11	Warming	12.0–15.0	16.2	26.5				
12	Inoculation of yeast	13.0–16.0						
13		14.0–17.0	16.6	26.8	0.38	0.45	3.8	
14		15.0–18.0						
15		15.0–18.0	16.7	27.9	0.45	0.55	3.7	
16		16.0–19.0						
17	*Wakitsuki*	17.0–20.0	15.2		0.62	0.52	3.6	
18		22.5						
19	Cooling	22.5	11.0		0.78	0.50	3.5	6.0
20	Cooling	17.0						
21	Cooling	14.0	7.5		0.90	0.48	3.5	9.0
22	Cooling	11.0						
23	Cooling	10.5						
24	Cooling	10.0	4.5		0.95	0.47	3.5	12.5
25		9.5						
26	Usage	9.5	4.0		0.96	0.47	3.5	14.5

which it means that vigorous fermentation is taking place

that addition of lactic acid to *moto* prevents contamination by wild micro-organisms. It can be prepared in a relatively short time (7–15 days), since the time required for lactic-acid formation by naturally occurring lactic-acid bacteria is saved, and solubilization and saccharification of the mash proceed more quickly with the high initial mashing temperature (18–22°C). In this method, commercial lactic acid (75%; sp. gr. 1.21) is added to the mash (650–700 ml/100 l water) to lower the pH value to 3.6–3.8.

Although pure culture yeast is used as the inoculum, wild yeasts as well as pure-culture yeast can develop during the *moto* process, and sometimes the latter finally predominates (Akiyama and Sugano, 1967). This may be ascribed to the fact that the high mashing temperature and acidic conditions are close to the optimum for multiplication of both culture and wild yeasts. In addition, as opposed to the behaviour in the classical process, no natural selection of wild yeasts by the toxic effect of nitrite occurs, because nitrate-reducing bacteria are inhibited by the presence of lactic acid. To prepare *moto* containing a high proportion of culture yeast, it is necessary to inoculate the yeast at a high concentration (10^5–10^6/g) at as early a stage as possible (Tsukahara, 1954). Also, in contrast to the classical method, gentle mixing rather than kneading should be used under the strongly acidic conditions that exist during the early stage of the preparation, to produce a mash which is less pasty, and rich in sugar and other nutrients necessary for growth of *saké* yeast.

An example of the preparation of *sokujo-moto* is as follows: *koji* (60 kg) is mixed with 200 l of water and 140 ml of lactic acid (75%). A pure culture of *saké* yeast is added to the mixture to give a count of 10^5 to 10^6/g. The temperature of the mixture is about 12°C. Steamed rice (140 kg) is added to the mixture, cooling it sufficiently to give a temperature of about 18 to 20°C. After keeping the mash for one to two days with intermittent stirring and agitation, it is warmed gradually, in the same way as *yamahai-moto*, by increasing the temperature at a rate of 1.0 to 1.5°C/day. As the temperature rises to about 15°C, growth of the inoculated yeast reaches its peak and fermentation begins. The cultivation period can be further shortened by starting the mashing at 25°C and keeping the temperature of *moto* over 18°C. A typical example of the temperature and composition changes during *sokujo-moto* preparation is shown in Table 9 (Tanaka, 1970).

Table 9

Changes in temperature and composition during *sokujo-moto* preparation

Days elapsed	Operation	Temperature of mash (°C)	Density (°Baumé)	Reducing sugars (%, w/v)	Acids (as lactic acid) (%, w/v)	Amino acids (as glycine) (%, w/v)	Alcohol (%, v/v)
1	Mashing	20	–	–	–	–	–
2	Mashing	13	15.0	18.0	0.27	0.18	–
3	Warming	8–11	–	–	–	–	–
4	Warming	10–13	16.0	24.8	–	–	–
5	Warming	11–14	16.5	25.8	0.32	0.20	–
6	*Wakitsuki*	14–17	15.5	–	0.36	–	–
7		17–20	13.0	17.1	0.47	0.16	–
8		20	10.5	–	–	–	–
9	Cooling	20	8.0	–	0.63	–	10.0
14	Usage	7	6.0	8.5	0.63	0.16	12.5

Wakitsuki means that vigorous fermentation is taking place.

c. *Koontoka-moto* (Hot-mashed *moto*).. This is a variety of *sokujo-moto*, in which mashing is carried out at 56–60°C in several hours, followed by inoculation of pure cultured *saké* yeast. To prevent excessive accumulation of sugars and the development of a high viscosity, the ratio of water to rice used is raised to 150–160 l/100 kg.

The following example is typical. To 220 l of water (out of a total of 270 l) warmed to 60°C, a mixture of 120 kg of steamed rice, cooled to about 55°C, and 60 kg of *koji* are added. After incubation at about 58°C for around 6 h, the mash is cooled by adding ice blocks equivalent to the remaining water (50 l), and lactic acid is added at a temperature below 50°C. The filtrate thus obtained has the following composition: density, 16.0–16.5 degrees Baumé; reducing sugars, 24.5–25.5%, w/v; amino acids, 0.16–0.20%, w/v; total acids, 0.30–0.35%, w/v. The mash is further cooled to about 20°C, and transferred to another vessel for inoculation with a pure culture yeast. From this stage on, the procedure is almost the same as that for *sokujo-moto*.

d. *Utilization of pure culture yeast in large quantity*. An attempt to use culture yeast in place of *moto* was made by Takahashi (1907). Later Yamada *et al.* (1939) showed that an experimental brewing could safely be carried out using the *saké* yeast crop from a culture in Carlsberg vessels as a substitute for conventional *moto*. Recently, based on the same principle, a new procedure which may be called 'the compressed yeast method' has been devised by Shimoide *et al.* (1964, 1965b). By this procedure, compressed *saké* yeast, harvested from an aerobic propagation, is used.

The following is an example of this method. One hundred litres of medium, composed of molasses, salts and 0.5% (w/v) lactic acid with nitrogenous compounds, are placed in a closed vessel of 180 l capacity equipped with coils for sterilization and cooling, an agitator, a compressor and an air filter. After the seed culture has been added, propagation is continued for about 48 h at 28°C with an aeration rate of 90–120 l/min and agitation at 250 rev/min. The yeast crop is harvested by centrifugation and washing, and then put through a filter press. In this way, 3.5–4.0 kg of fresh yeast, with a water content of about 70%, is obtained from 100 l of culture. Instead of *moto*, about 300–500 g of compressed yeast is added to the first stage of *moromi*, for each ton of polished rice used for mashing, with a lactic acid content equivalent to that contained in *moto*.

When this method is used for *saké* brewing, nutrients for the yeast, such as B-group vitamins and amino acids that are transferred from *moto*, are considered to be deficient in the early stage of *moromi* fermentation process. However, the cells obtained by this method have a high respiratory activity and grow sufficiently well for fermentation to proceed normally (Fukui *et al.*, 1966). A comparison of *saké* brewed by using conventional *moto* with that produced with compressed yeast failed to reveal differences in the amino-acid content or in organoleptic quality (Shimoide *et al.*, 1965a).

D. Preparation of *moromi*

The main mash, called *moromi*, is fermented in a large open vessel with a capacity ranging from 6 to 20 kl without special sterilization. The weight of polished rice used for mashing one lot has long been standardized at 1.5 tons, but, recently, in some breweries 3 to 7 tons and sometimes over 10 tons have become accepted in correspondingly larger vessels. The *moromi* is composed of steamed rice, *koji* and water. Table 10 shows an example of the proportions of the various raw materials used for a typical *moromi*. Stepwise mashing, covering three steps, is one of the characteristics of *moromi* production. First, steamed rice, *koji* and water are added to the *moto*, the amounts of the materials added being almost the same as that to *moto*. Thus, the total acid and yeast population in *moto* are diluted to about a half, but there is still an inhibitory effect against wild micro-organisms. The temperature of the first mash is about $12°C$, and the yeast propagates gradually. After two days, the yeast count having reached about $10^8/g$ which is the same order as in *moto*, a second addition of materials is made by adding an amount nearly twice as much as the first addition. Since the yeast population and total acids are diluted by about half, thereby decreasing the inhibitory activity against contaminations, the temperature of the second addition is lowered to 9 to $10°C$. A third addition of materials is made on the next day at 7 to $8°C$, by adding a larger amount of them.

Table 10
Proportions of raw materials used in a typical *moromi*

	Total rice (kg)	Steamed rice (kg)	*Rice-koji* (kg)	Water (litres)
Moto mash	140	95	45	155
1st Addition	280	200	80	250
2nd Addition	530	405	125	635
3rd Addition	890	715	175	1,260
4th Addition	160	160		160
Total	2,000	1,575	425	2,460

The weights of steamed rice and *koji*-rice quoted are based on the weight of the original white rice.

This stepwise addition of material, (accompanied by stepwise dilution of the dense population of proliferated *saké* yeast and concentration of lactic acid in the *moto* used) plays an important role for suppressing the invasion of wild contaminants, together with lowering the mashing temperature in each addition. It should be noted that, in *saké* brewing and especially in *moromi* fermentation, temperature control is very important for balancing saccharification and fermentation, both of which occur simultaneously in *moromi*. While being released in small quantities from steamed rice and *koji*, sugars are fermented gradually by *saké* yeast until the alcohol content reaches nearly 20% (v/v). For a concentration of about 20% (v/v) of alcohol accumulated in the mash, about 40% (w/v) sugars are needed; if such a high concentration of sugars is supplied at once, *saké* yeast would not ferment it.

Fermentation of *moromi* carried out at a low temperature (below 15 to 18°C) is also a characteristic of *saké* brewing which gives the mash a balanced flavour and taste as well as a high alcohol concentration. The existence of suspended materials such as steamed rice and *koji* is also considered to promote the production of high concentrations of alcohol in the mash.

After the third addition of materials, the mash is agitated, usually twice daily. Three to four days later, the density of the mash reaches a maximum. The composition of a filtrate of the mash at this stage is: density, 7–8 degrees Baumé; alcohol concentration, 3–4% (v/v); total acids (as succinic acid) 0.06–0.07% (w/v). A foam resembling soap suds gradually spreads over the surface, and subsequently increases to form a thick layer. A fresh fruit-like aroma at this stage indicates a healthy fermentation. The fermentation gradually becomes more vigorous with a rise in mash temperature, and a rather viscous foam rises to form *taka-awa* (deep layer of foam) which reaches to the brim of the vessel as shown in Fig. 7, and is broken down with a small electric agitator. At this stage, the yeast cell count reaches a maximum of about $2.5 \times 10^8/g$ (Noshiro, 1959). As the alcohol and acid concentrations increase, the foam becomes less dense, and is easily dispersed. Later, when the density of the mash

Fig. 7. Photograph of a manhole on a *moromi* fermentation vessel, showing a deep layer of foam and an electric agitator which prevents the foam from overflowing.

falls, the froth begins to recede, displaying numerous beautiful hemispheres, followed by various features including a wrinkled scum, a smooth thick or thin covering, or no covering on the surface of the mash, according to the type of *saké* yeast and the physical and nutritional conditions in the mash (Tsukahara *et al.*, 1964; Saito, 1965).

The temperature of the mash reaches a maximum of 13–18°C by the sixth to ninth day, and this temperature is maintained for another 5–7 days, after which time it decreases as fermentation subsides. On the 20th to 25th day, when the alcohol concentration in the mash has reached 17.5 to 19.5% (v/v) and fermentation has almost ceased, pure alcohol (30–40%) is usually added to the mash to adjust the final concentration to about 20 to 22% (v/v). If necessary, an alcohol solution containing glucose, lactic acid, succinic acid, or sodium glutamate is added to the mash in amounts conforming to the official standards. This practice had been officially permitted in the 1940s to compensate for the fall in *saké* production due to the shortage of rice, and today, this practice is applied for the purpose of increasing the amount of *saké* to some extent and making the quality of *saké* uniform, clean and mild. To obtain the rich-bodied *saké*, this practice is omitted. Usually alcohol is not added to the mash for export-*saké* and so called 'none added *saké*'.

Quite often, in order to sweeten the mash, 7–10% of the total amount of steamed rice is added during the final stage of the *moromi* process. By this means a certain amount of glucose produced from starch by the saccharifying action of rice-*koji* accumulates in the mash, because of the weakened fermentative activity of the yeast in the presence of over 15% alcohol.

Table 11 gives an example of the changes with time in various mash components during the *moromi* fermentation process. There

Table 11

Changes with time in the mash components during *moromi* mash fermentation, without the fourth addition

Days from the 3rd addition	Density (° Baumé)	Reducing sugar (%, w/v)	Alcohol (%, v/v)	Acid (as succinic acid) (%, w/v)
3–4	7–8	7–8	3–4	0.06–0.07
6	5–6	6–7	6–7	0.08–0.09
9	4–5	6–7	9–10	0.09–0.10
12	3–4	5–6	11–12	0.10–0.11
15	2–2.5	4–5	15–16	0.11–0.15
18	1–1.5	3–4	17.5–18.5	0.14–0.16
21	0–0.5	2–3	18.5–19.5	0.14–0.16

would be more contamination by wild yeast in the *moromi* than in the *moto* process. If wild *saké* yeast predominates over the *saké* culture yeast in the *moto* process, this effect is further accentuated in the *moromi* process where a greater bulk of material is mashed, and the culture yeast may be completely overgrown by the contamination. It is important, therefore, to suppress wild yeast in the *moto* process as much as possible; its proportion should not exceed 10% of the total yeasts in *moto* (Akiyama and Sugano, 1967).

Deterioration due to contamination by *Lactobacillus* sp. rarely occurs during *moromi* fermentation. If growth of *saké* yeast is extremely retarded during the early stages of *moromi* process, by use of over-aged *moto* in which the majority of yeast cells are weakened or dead, lactic-acid bacteria derived from *koji* predominate over the yeast, and acid damage occurs when the viable cell count of the bacteria reaches more than $10^7/g$ (Momose *et al.*, 1965). Under these circumstances, fermentation declines rapidly and may cease entirely, while accumulation of lactic acid and sugar continues progressively, resulting in an excessively sweet and acid-damaged *mash* containing less alcohol. Competition between *saké* yeast and lactic-acid bacteria for the uptake of nutrients may be the basic cause (Itoh and Uemura, 1957).

E. Filtration, pasteurization, storage and bottling

1. Filtration

One or two days after the addition of alcohol to the *moromi*-mash, the mash is divided into *saké* and solids by filtration. The mash is poured into bags of about five-litre capacity made of synthetic fibre, which are laid in a rectangular box and the pale yellow liquid, *saké*, is squeezed out under hydraulic pressure. After complete filtration, the solids pressed in a sheet are stripped out of the bags. Recently several automatic filter presses for filtering *moromi*-mash have been used. The cake, called 'saké-kasu', contains starch, protein, yeast cells and various enzymes, and is used for making foodstuffs such as pickles and soup.

In general, about 3 kilolitres of *saké* containing 20% ethanol and 200–250 kg of *saké-kasu* are obtained from one ton of polished rice. The slightly turbid *saké* is clarified to separate lees by placing it undisturbed in a vessel for 5 to 10 days at a low temperature. During this process, the fresh *saké* is gradually aged, probably because of continuing enzymic activity in the *saké*. To maintain a low temperature for suitable periods is important in order to avoid over-ripening of the *saké* and autolysis of the yeast, which result in a deterioration in quality. After settling, the supernatant is filtered with activated carbon, asbestos and cotton. The clarified *saké* is blended in order to ensure uniform quality.

2. Pasteurization

After settling the clarified *saké* for a further 30 to 40 days, it is pasteurized to kill yeasts and harmful micro-organisms if present, and to destroy enzymes and adjust the rate of maturation. The *saké* is then heated to 55–65°C by passing it through a tube-type heat exchanger for a short time. Recently multitube or plate-type heat exchangers with a high efficiency of heat transfer have become available.

As mentioned in Section II (p. 425) of this chapter, the history of pasteurization of *saké* began in the 16th Century, before Pasteur's discoveries. Since the middle of this century, pasteurization has been used to sterilize *saké* produced during the warm seasons. Immediately after pasteurization, *saké* is transferred to sealed vessels for storage with or without addition of activated carbon. Pasteurization and the high content of alcohol in *saké* (usually 20%) prevent microbial infection.

3. Storage (Ageing) and Bottling

During storage, *saké* is gradually matured. The maturation process is probably due to oxidation reactions and to physicochemical changes. The storage temperature should be carefully kept at 13 to 18°C, consideration being paid to the rate of maturation and the time of bottling. Since *saké* may vary in flavour and taste in each batch during storage, blending is necessary to provide a uniform quality. The blended *saké* is diluted with water to the appropriate alcohol content, usually 15.0 to 16.5% (v/v) and is filtered through activated carbon to improve the flavour and taste and to adjust the colour and clarity. In modern procedures, filtration through activated carbon is followed by filtration through the membranes or sheets having numerous pores of micrometre size, thus removing minute particles including micro-organisms if any are present. This procedure enables the *saké* producer to omit pasteurization in the bottling procedure and thus to prevent deterioration of quality caused by heating *saké*.

The amount of activated carbon used for *saké* brewing has increased recently to 0.3 kg to 1.5 kg per 1 kl of *saké*. Table 12 shows an average analysis for several components of *saké* (Hayashida *et al.*, 1968).

Table 12

Composition of an average *saké*

Component	Content
Total sugar as glucose (%, w/v)	4.20
Direct fermentable sugar as glucose (%, w/v)	3.46
Acidity (meq/100 ml)	1.52
Total organic acid (mg/100 ml)	115.22
Glutamic acid (mg/100 ml)	20.23
Total nitrogen (%, w/v)	0.0726
Formol nitrogen (%, w/v)	0.0288
Alcohol (%, v/v)	15.0

Clarity is one of the important properties of *saké*. It was found that the main tubidity-forming compounds formed in *saké* are enzyme proteins especially saccharifying amylases from *koji* (Yamada *et al.*, 1957; Sugita and Kageyama, 1957, 1958; Suzuki *et al.*, 1958; Akiyama, 1962a), which decrease in solubility by heating and become suspended in *saké*. These compounds react with bacterial and fungal proteinases to aggregate and settle down (Akiyama, 1962b). Insoluble compounds are also deposited by constituents reacting with tannin from persimmon, followed by addition of protein such as zelatin and egg-white to complete the reaction (Akiyama *et al.*, 1969; Miyai, 1957; Yoshizawa and Uchiyama, 1971; Mena and Nunokawa, 1971; Nunokawa and Mena, 1971, 1972; Nakabayashi, 1968). These substances are prepared commercially for the purpose of clarifying *saké*.

Concerning the mechanism of browning of *saké* during storage, amino-carbonyl reactions may account for about 10% of the total browning reactions, but the major factors are still unknown, although manganese and nitrogenous compounds are found to participate (Takahashi *et al.*, 1971). During ageing, some compounds such as 2-deoxyglucosone are found to increase in concentration in *saké* (Oka *et al.*, 1965).

Saké is usually sold in a pale blue bottle of 1.8 l capacity, which is pervious to the short and medium wavelengths in sunlight. Since *saké* is very sensitive to exposure to sunlight, bottled *saké* increases its colour intensity and this is accompanied by a deterioration in quality if it is exposed to sunlight during transportation or window display. Brown and emerald bottles, which are impervious to most wavelengths in sunlight, effectively prevent colour development caused by exposure to sunlight.

As to the mechanisms of colour development, two photo-oxidation reactions are presumed to take place. In one reaction, deferriferrichrysin participates, while in the other, tyrosine or tryptophan, kynurenic acid or flavin participate, respectively, as the precursors of colourants (Nakamura *et al.*, 1970, 1971a). Concerning the colour of *saké*, flavin and melanoidin have long been considered to be the main components. Whereas the former is considered to make little contribution (Ueno *et al.*, 1966), the latter compound may contribute about 40 to 80% (Sato and Tadenuma, 1967). Many investigations have been done on the colouring compounds of *saké*, recently ferrichrysin, one of the ferrichromes (Neilands, 1967), was found to be one of the main iron-containing colouring compounds in *saké* (Tadenuma and Sato, 1967). *Aspergillus oryzae* produces the colourless compound deferriferrichrysin, the iron-free form of ferrichrysin, during the *koji*-making procedure. This compound develops a colour by combining with the iron originating from rice grains, water and various other contaminants in the *saké*-brewing process. Contrary to the ease with which malanoidin and riboflavin can be removed, it is difficult to remove ferrichrysin from *saké*. Breweries therefore take care to prevent contamination by iron in the *saké*-brewing procedure. To remove iron from the water used in brewing, appropriate treatments are employed according to its form and content in the water.

During storage and after bottling, spoilage of *saké* is sometimes encountered, causing turbidity and disagreeable off-flavours and tastes which are attributed mainly to the formation of diacetyl (Tomiyasu, 1933) and acetic acid when the *saké* is infected by the so-called *hiochi* bacteria. These are now known to be lactic-acid bacteria (Kitahara *et al.*, 1957; Momose and Noshiro, 1970). Most of these bacteria require peptides, amino acids, vitamins and other growth factors such as mevalonic acid (Tamura, 1958; Tamura and Suzuki,

1958; Teramoto *et al.*, 1954; Teramoto and Hashimoto, 1957). Moreover, they have a preference to 4 to 8% alcohol, as well as a tolerance of 16 to 20% of alcohol (Momose and Noshiro, 1971; Momose *et al.*, 1971). Treatment of *saké* with an excess of activated carbon prevents growth of these contaminating bacteria because of the removal of vitamins, such as riboflavin, which are essential for their growth.

4. Biochemical Changes During Fermentation

During fermentation, various biochemical changes occur in the *moromi*-mash. Firstly starch, changed to the α-form by steaming of the rice grains, is saccharified by *koji* amylases to glucose and other sugars as seen in Table 13 (Aso *et al.*, 1954; Fukinbara and

Table 13

Sugar composition of *saké*

| Sugar | Content (%, w/v) reported by: | | |
	Aso *et al.* (1954)	Fukinbara and Muramatsu (1952)	Masuda *et al.* (1965)
Total	4.53		3.76
Directly fermentable	3.77		2.38
Glucose	3.69	2.31	2.28
Sakebiose	0.08		
Kojibiose	0.08	0.18	
Isomaltose	0.33	0.54	0.48
Panose	0.08	0.21	
Isomaltotriose	0.08		0.23
Other oligosaccharides	0.28	0.32	

Sakebiose (nigerose) is 3-0-α-D-glucopyranosyl-D-glucose.
Kojibiose is 2-0-α-D-glucopyranosyl-D-glucose.

Muramatsu, 1952; Masuda *et al.*, 1965). *Koji* amylases are relatively stable and continue to act in the *moromi*-mash throughout fermentation. Secondly, glucose is fermented by the yeast to form ethanol and carbon dioxide. Lactic, succinic and other organic acids are produced at the same time. In general, the first two acids, being nearly equal in concentration, account for about 80% of the total organic acids as shown in Table 14 (Matsui and Sato, 1966; Muto *et*

Table 14

Organic acid composition of *saké*

Acid	Content (mg/100 ml) reported by:			
	Otaka and Yamanouchi (1955)	Ueda *et al.* (1960)	Matsui and Sato (1966)	Muto *et al.* (1964)
Acetic		3.5–11.9	7.8–12.0	7.2–23.4
Propionic		0.5–0.6		
Oxalic	trace		0–2.7	
Malonic			0–7.3	
Succinic	54.0	49.4–61.5	73.2	28.3–44.9
Fumaric	1.0	1.7–3.4	18.6–33.7	
Aconitic		2.0–7.8		
Glycolic		4.7–6.4	7.6–13.7	
Lactic	55.0	37.1–52.1	34.2	13.5–36.9
Malic	19.0	19.4–39.0	22.8–44.2	9.4–32.2
α-Hydroxyglutaric				trace–1.5
Citric	12.0	3.5–5.4	17.3–48.0	trace–7.1
Pyruvic	1.0	0.5	0–6.2	
α-Oxoglutaric	trace	0.3–1.2	0–17.5	
Pyroglutamic	18.0		12.9–23.2	

al., 1964; Otaka and Yamanouchi, 1955; Toyozawa *et al.*, 1960; Ueda *et al.*, 1960). Protein in the rice grains is then decomposed by *koji* proteases to peptides and amino acids, some of which are assimilated successively by *saké* yeast. Eighteen different amino acids have been found in *saké* as shown in Table 15 (Tamura *et al.*, 1952; Omachi and Kawano, 1957). These compounds may contribute, with various other substances, to the smoothness and balance in the taste of *saké*.

Higher alcohols and esters, which are characteristic of individual *saké*, are produced by *saké* yeast (Koizumi, 1968; Yoshizawa *et al.*, 1961). Higher alcohols are formed from glucose and partly from amino acids (Yoshizawa, 1966a, b). Formation of higher alcohols and esters keeps pace with alcohol formation. When the velocity of alcoholic fermentation decreases, the concentrations of some of these higher alcohols and esters decrease in the *moromi*-mash as shown in Figures 8 and 9 (Yoshizawa, 1966b, c). *Saké* contains fairly large concentrations of various higher alcohols and esters as shown in Tables 16 and 17 (Komoda *et al.*, 1966; Yoshizawa, 1966c), some of

Table 15

Amino-acid composition of *saké*

Amino acid	Content (mg/100 ml) reported by:	
	Tamura *et al.* (1952)	Omachi and Kawano (1965)
Alanine		38
Arginine	48	46
Aspartic acid	45	26
Cystine	3	trace
Glutamic acid	75	47
Glycine	36	30
Histidine	17	21
Isoleucine	21	
Leucine	53	105
Valine	50	
Lysine	19	18
Methionine	9	trace
Phenylalanine	37	29
Proline	40	27
Serine	51	22
Threonine	22	18
Tryptophan	3	trace
Tyrosine	39	12
Total	538	349

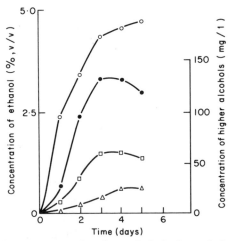

Fig. 8. Changes in the amounts of various alcohols formed during a *moromi* mash fermentation. ○ indicates changes in the concentration of ethanol; ●, of isoamyl alcohol; □, of isobutanol; and △, of 2-phenethanol.

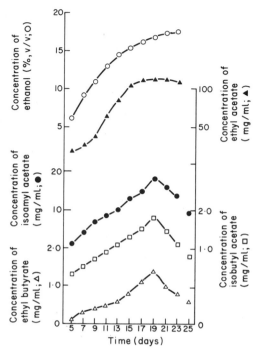

Fig. 9. Changes in the amounts of various esters formed during a *moromi* mash fermentation. ▲, indicates changes in the concentration of ethyl acetate; ●, of isoamyl acetate; and
□, of isobutyl acetate. For comparison, changes in the concentrations of ethanol (○) and of
ethyl butyrate (△) are also indicated.

Table 16

Contents of the principal higher alcohols in *saké*

Alcohol	Mean value (mg /l)	Standard deviation
n-Propanol	120	46
Isobutanol	64	21
Isoamyl alcohol	170	47
2-Phenethanol	75	

The value quoted for isoamyl alcohol includes active amyl alcohol.

which make a major contribution to the aroma of *saké* (Komoda and
Yamada, 1966; Yamamoto, 1961; Yoshikawa *et al.*, 1963;
Yoshizawa *et al.*, 1966). Formation of these compounds may depend
on the concentration of amino acids in the *moromi*-mash, the
fermentation temperature, and the yeast strain used.

As shown in Table 17 'ginjoshu', one of the most refined saké, contains high concentrations of esters such as ethyl acetate, ethyl caproate, ethyl caprylate, ethyl caprate and isoamyl acetate. 'Ginjoshu'

Table 17

Ester contents of saké

Ester	Content (mg/l) in:		
	Ginjoshu	Good saké	Ordinary saké
Ethyl acetate	120	50	20–30
Isobutyl acetate	1.0–1.5	0.5	0.2–0.5
Ethyl butyrate	2.0–5.0	1.5	0.5
Isoamyl acetate	10	5	2
Ethyl caproate	10	3	2
Ethyl caprylate	10	5	5
Ethyl caprate	10	10	10
Ethyl pelargonate	5		3
Ethyl laurate	11	5	2
Ethyl lactate	5	2	2
Phenethyl acetate	7	5	8

is brewed by elaborate, skilful and manual techniques of veteran workers using highly polished rice (polishing ratio of 40–50% containing little protein) at an extremely low temperature (9–11°C) taking longer periods (25–30 days) of slow fermentation. Thus, in ginjoshu, the high concentrations of esters and rather low concentrations of nitrogenous compounds, organic acids and sugars, all combine to provide the special flavour and taste.

F. Treatment of waste water

Water pollution has become a serious problem which needs to be solved immediately. From 1972, saké breweries have been requested to decrease the suspended solids (S.S.) content and the biochemical oxygen demand (B.O.D.) of the discharged waste water, and to adjust its pH value to one approved by the Japanese governmental ordinance. About 25 kl of the waste water, containing 500 to 1,000 p.p.m. of S.S. and B.O.D., respectively, are discharged per ton of rice used in *saké* brewing. Among *saké*-brewing procedures, the bottle-washing process discharges about 40% of the total amount of waste water. This waste water contains little S.S. and B.O.D., but its pH value should be adjusted by adding a solution of mineral acid. The rice-washing procedure, followed by the rice-steeping procedure, accounts for 10 to 25% of the total amount of waste water, which contains most of the S.S. and 80 to 90% of the total amount of the B.O.D. (Noshiro *et al.*, 1971). Therefore, it is important to treat the waste water discharged from the rice-washing procedure in order to lower effectively the S.S. and the B.O.D. of the total waste water. Judging from the fact that most breweries produce *saké* on only a small scale, and only in winter, without any expert who is skilled in treating waste water, the coagulation method for treating waste water would seem to be most suitable for them. Among many studies on the treatment of waste water from *saké* breweries (Naito, 1971; Hayashi and Kosaka, 1972; Nakamura *et al.*, 1971b; Tokado and Sono, 1972), two coagulation methods using, respectively, poly-aluminum chloride and ferric chloride, with high molecular-weight coagulating reagents such as polyacrylamide, were most effective and simple in lowering the S.S. content and the B.O.D. of the waste water discharged from the rice-washing procedure (Yoshizawa *et al.*, 1972b, c).

Using one of these methods, the majority of the S.S. and over 95% of the B.O.D. are removed. Some large factories adopt a combination of a coagulation method and a microbiological treatment, which can lower the B.O.D. in the discharged water to below 20 p.p.m. Some breweries steep rice grains without washing them, by which procedure about 80% of the B.O.D. generated in the usual procedure can be avoided (Itoh, 1972; Noshiro *et al.*, 1971). Besides, in some districts, larger breweries are requested to use fuel containing less sulphur to minimize the sulphur dioxide content of exhaust gases.

VI. CONCLUSION

The characteristic difference between procedures used in *saké* pro-duction and those used in the production of the Western alcoholic beverages is the use of *koji* in place of malt, and the complicated procedures, such as parallel fermentation, which brings *saké* its own flavour and taste. For example, *saké* contains a large amount of *n*-propanol, 2-phenethanol and ethyl esters of C_6 to C_{14} fatty acids (Yoshizawa, 1966a, d). Advances in our understanding of the physiology, biochemistry, organic chemistry and ecology of the micro-organisms participating in *saké* brewing enable us not only to confirm the fundamental soundness of many traditional techniques of *saké* brewing but also to improve the technology by eliminating certain irrational procedures and introducing various new items of equipment such as those for continuous steaming, micro-filtration, automatic *koji* preparation and yeast cultivation. These advances, together with the application of saccharifying enzyme preparations in place of *koji*, and semi-continuous fermentation, will bring about revolutionary changes in the technology of *saké* brewing, and will compel breweries to use large-scale processing. On the other hand, refined *saké*, having the individual character, will continue to be made in small breweries by relatively elaborate and luxurious manual techniques, and using the traditional procedures. These refined *saké* will continue to be highly appreciated by connoisseurs, just as are the 'chateaux' wines in European countries.

REFERENCES

Ahlburg, H. and Matsubara, S. (1878). *Tokyo Ijishinshi* 24, 6.

Akai, Y. (1963). *Journal of the Society of Brewing, Japan* 58, 1106.

Akiyama, H. (1957). *Journal of the Agricultural Chemical Society of Japan* 31, 913.

Akiyama, H. (1958). *Journal of the Agricultural Chemical Society of Japan* 32, 355, 526.

Akiyama, H. (1959). *Journal of the Agricultural Chemical Society of Japan* 33, 1.

Akiyama, H. (1962a). *Journal of the Agricultural Chemical Society of Japan* 36, 825.

Akiyama, H. (1962b). *Journal of the Agricultural Chemical Society of Japan* 36, 903.

Akiyama, H. and Sugano, N. (1967). *Journal of Fermentation Technology* 45, 1093.

Akiyama, H. and Takase, S. (1958). *Journal of the Society of Brewing, Japan* 53, 434.

Akiyama, H. and Yamamoto, T. (1963). *Journal of the Society of Brewing, Japan* 58, 319.

Akiyama, H., Uchiyama, K., Koide, I., Himeno, K. and Noda, Y. (1969). *Journal of the Society of Brewing, Japan* 64, 889.

Ashizawa, H. (1961). *Journal of the Society of Brewing, Japan* 56, 1135.

Ashizawa, H. (1962). *Journal of the Society of Brewing, Japan* 57, 422.

Ashizawa, H. (1963). *Journal of the Society of Brewing, Japan* **58**, 543.
Ashizawa, H. and Saito, Y. (1965). *Journal of the Society of Brewing, Japan* **60**, 803.
Aso, K., Shibasaki, K. and Yamauchi, F. (1954). *Journal of Fermentation Technology* **32**, 47.
Cohn, F. (1883). *Jahreb. Schles. Gesellschaft Culture*, Breslau 226.
Eda, K. (1909). *Journal of the Society of Brewing, Japan* **25**, 22.
Eda, K. (1922). *Journal of the Society of Brewing, Japan* **17**(9), 54.
Eda, K., Oana, F. and Arimatsu, K. (1929). *Journal of the Society of Brewing, Japan* **103**, 1.
Fukinbara, T. and Muramatsu, K. (1952). *Journal of the Agricultural Chemical Society of Japan* **26**, 583.
Fukui, S., Tani, Y. and Kishibe, T. (1955). *Journal of Fermentation Technology* **33**, 1.
Fukui, S., Tani, Y. and Shimoide, M. (1966). *Journal of Fermentation Technology* **44**, 610.
Furuhashi, M. and Ishikawa, M. (1967). *Reports of the Shizuoka Prefectural Industrial Research Institute* **11**, 63.
Furuhashi, M. and Ishikawa, M. (1968). *Reports of the Shizuoka Prefectural Industrial Research Insitute* **12**, 62.
Furukawa, T. and Akiyama, H. (1962). *Journal of the Agricultural Chemical Society of Japan* **36**, 354.
Hanaoka, M. (1918). *Journal of the Society of Brewing, Japan* **13**, 1.
Hara, S. (1970). In 'Shin Shuzo Gijutsu', p. 40. Society of Brewing, Japan, Tokyo.
Hayashi, Y. and Kosaka, T. (1972). *Journal of the Society of Brewing, Japan* **67**, 649.
Hayashida, M., Ueda, R. and Teramoto, S. (1968). *Journal of Fermentation Technology* **46**, 77.
Horie, S., Kawakami, H. and Nagashima, T. (1965). *Journal of the Society of Brewing, Japan* **60**, 1120.
Imayasu, S., Kuriyama, K. and Ando, N. (1963). *Journal of Fermentation Technology* **41**, 254.
Ishido, T., Ouchi, K., Akiyama, H., Kasahara, H. and Nunokawa, Y. (1971). *Journal of the Society of Brewing, Japan* **66**, 1170.
Itoh, K. (1972). *Journal of the Society of Brewing, Japan* **67**, 582.
Itoh, Y. and Uemura, T. (1957). *Journal of the Agricultural Chemical Society of Japan* **31**, 783.
Kageyama, K. (1955). *Journal of Fermentation Technology* **33**, 53.
Kageyama, K. and Sugita, O. (1955). *Journal of Fermentation Technology* **33**, 109.
Kagi, K., Otake, I., Moriyama, Y., Ando, F., Eda, K. and Yamamoto, T. (1909). *Reports of the Research Institute of Brewing, Japan* **29**, 1.
Kanai, H. and Iida, S. (1932). *Reports of the Research Institute of Brewing, Japan* **114**, 184.
Kano, S. (1961). *Journal of the Agricultural Chemical Society of Japan* **35**, 1304.
Kano, S. (1962). *Journal of the Agricultural Chemical Society of Japan*, **36**, 379, 484.
Katagiri, H. and Kitahara, K. (1934). *Journal of the Agricultural Chemical Society of Japan* **10**, 942.

Kawamata, S., Takahashi, N. and Shimada, S. (1958). *Journal of the Society of Brewing, Japan* 53, 790.

Kawasaki, W., Aso, N., Noshiro, K. and Momiya, N. (1967a) *Journal of the Society of Brewing, Japan* 62, 68.

Kawasaki, W., Sugama, S., Ouchi, K., Aso, N. and Kato, K. (1967b). *Journal of the Society of Brewing, Japan* 62, 1453.

Kitahara, K. (1960). In *'Ecology of Micro-organisms'*, Symposium of the Institute of Applied Microbiology, Japan 11, 42.

Kitahara, K., Kaneko, T. and Goto, O. (1957). *Journal of the Agricultural Chemical Society of Japan* 31, 556.

Kobayashi, I. and Akiyama, H. (1961). *Journal of the Society of Brewing, Japan* 56, 171.

Kodama, K. (1959). *Journal of the Society of Brewing, Japan* 54, 138, 770.

Kodama, K. (1960). In *'Ecology of Micro-organisms'*, Symposium of the Institute of Applied Microbiology, Japan 11, 54.

Kodama, K. (1963). *Annals of the Brewing Association of Japan* 18, 64.

Kodama, K. (1966). *Journal of the Society of Brewing, Japan* 61, 677.

Kodama, K. (1970). *In* 'The Yeasts', (A. H. Rose and J. S. Harrison, eds.), volume 3, pp. 225–282. Academic Press, London.

Kodama, K. and Kyono, T. (1963). *Journal of Fermentation Technology* 41, 113.

Kodama, K., Kyono, T. and Kodama, S. (1956). *Reports of the Synthetic Saké Corporation, Japan* 11, 329.

Kodama, K., Kyono, T. and Kodama, S. (1957). *Reports of the Synthetic Saké Corporation, Japan* 14, 554.

Kodama, K., Kyono, T. and Kodama, S. (1960). *Reports of the Synthetic Saké Corporation, Japan* 20, 919.

Koizumi, T. (1968). *Journal of the Society of Brewing, Japan* 63, 446.

Komoda, H. and Yamada, M. (1966). *Journal of the Agricultural Chemical Society of Japan* 40, 173.

Komoda, H., Mano, F. and Yamada, M. (1966). *Journal of the Agricultural Chemical Society of Japan* 40, 127.

Kumagai, E., Omachi, T., Kinuyama, Y., Kuruma, K. and Akasaka, K. (1968). *Journal of the Society of Brewing, Japan* 63, 478.

Kurata, H. (1968). *Journal of Food Hygiene Society, Japan* 9, 23.

Masuda, Y., Yamashita, K., Sasaki, S., Hattori, K. and Itoh, Y. (1965). *Journal of the Society of Brewing, Japan* 60, 1114.

Matsui, H. and Sato, S. (1966). *Journal of Fermentation Technology* 44, 14.

Mena, E. and Nunokawa, Y. (1971). *Journal of the Society of Brewing, Japan* 66, 620.

Miyai, K. (1957). *Journal of the Society of Brewing, Japan* 52, 39.

Momose, H. and Noshiro, K. (1970). *Journal of the Society of Brewing, Japan* 65, 999, 1108.

Momose, H. and Noshiro, K. (1971). *Journal of the Society of Brewing, Japan* 66, 271.

Momose, H., Kobayashi, N., Koizumi, T. and Tonoike, R. (1965). *Journal of the Society of Brewing, Japan* 60, 539.

Momose, H., Adachi, K., Sato, Y. and Akiyama, H. (1971). *Journal of the Society of Brewing, Japan* 66, 1190.

Mori, T. and Watanabe, K. (1953). *Journal of Fermentation Technology* 31, 213.

Murakami, H. (1958). *Journal of the Agricultural Chemical Society of Japan* 32, 91.

Murakami, H. (1972). *Reports of the Research Institute of Brewing, Japan* 144, 20.

Murakami, H. and Kawai, M. (1958). *Journal of the Agricultural Chemical Society of Japan* 32, 96.

Murakami, H. and Makino, M. (1968). *Reports of the Research Institute of Brewing, Japan* 140, 4.

Murakami, H. and Takagi, K. (1959). *Journal of the Agricultural Chemical Society of Japan* 33, 905.

Murakami, H., Takase, S. and Ishii, T. (1967). *Journal of General and Applied Microbiology, Tokyo* 13, 323.

Murakami, H., Sagawa, H. and Takase, S. (1968). *Journal of General and Applied Microbiology, Tokyo* 14, 251.

Muto, H. and Takahashi, S. (1957). *Journal of the Society of Brewing, Japan* 52, 460.

Muto, H., Tadenuma, M. and Furuichi, A. (1964). *Reports of the Research Institute of Brewing, Japan* 136, 1.

Naito, S. (1971). *Journal of the Society of Brewing, Japan* 66, 910.

Nakabayashi, T. (1968). *Journal of the Society of Brewing, Japan* 63, 1149.

Nakamura, K., Sato, S. and Tadenuma, M. (1970). *Journal of the Society of Brewing, Japan* 65, 1120.

Nakamura, K., Sato, S., Tadenuma, M., Hamachi, M. and Koseki, T. (1971a). *Journal of the Society of Brewing, Japan* 66, 62.

Nakamura, K., Ishikawa, T., Sano, E., Den, S. and Noshiro, K. (1971b). *Journal of the Society of Brewing, Japan* 66, 783.

Nehira, T. and Nomi, R. (1956). *Journal of Fermentation Technology* 34, 391, 423.

Neilands, J. B. (1967). *Science, New York* 156, 1443.

Nishi, K., Tadenuma, M. and Sato, S. (1966). *Journal of the Society of Brewing, Japan* 61, 551.

Noshiro, K. (1959). *Journal of the Society of Brewing, Japan* 54, 658.

Noshiro, K. and Aoki, M. (1957). *Journal of the Society of Brewing, Japan* 52, 1008, 1012.

Noshiro, K. and Nakagawa, K. (1957). *Journal of the Society of Brewing, Japan* 52, 897.

Noshiro, K., Nakamura, K., Ishikawa, T., Sano, E. and Yamashita, S. (1971). *Journal of the Society of Brewing, Japan* 66, 779.

Nunokawa, Y. (1962). *Journal of the Agricultural Chemical Society of Japan* 36, 884.

Nunokawa, Y. (1968). *Journal of the Society of Brewing, Japan* 63, 259.

Nunokawa, Y. and Mena, E. (1971). *Journal of the Society of Brewing, Japan* 66, 1077.

Nunokawa, Y. and Mena, E. (1972). *Journal of the Society of Brewing, Japan* 67, 258, 801.

Nunokawa, Y. and Ouchi, K. (1971). *Journal of the Society of Brewing, Japan* 66, 512.

Nunokawa, Y., Kutsukake, T., Takahashi, K. and Suzuki, M. (1962). *Journal of the Society of Brewing, Japan* 57, 813.

Nunokawa, Y., Namba, Y. and Kinuyama, Y. (1963). *Journal of the Society of Brewing, Japan* 58, 305.

Nunokawa, Y., Kanamori, T. and Kobuyama, Y. (1968). *Journal of the Society of Brewing, Japan* 63, 678, 874.

Nunokawa, Y., Totsuka, A., Namba, Y. and Kobuyama, Y. (1969). *Journal of Fermentation Technology* 47, 408.

Oana, F. (1931). *Reports of the Research Institute of Brewing, Japan* 111, 124.

Oana, F. and Mizuno, S. (1933). *Reports of the Research Institute of Brewing, Japan* 117, 101.

Oba, T., Murakami, H. and Hara, S. (1969). *Journal of the Society of Brewing, Japan* 64, 1074.

Oda, M. (1935). *Journal of Fermentation Technology* 13, 629.

Oka, S., Ide, H., Shimizu, K. and Sakai, M. (1965). *Journal of the Agricultural Chemical Society of Japan* 39, 415.

Omachi, H. and Kawano, Y. (1957). *Reports of the Synthetic Saké Corporation, Japan* 14, 528.

Otaka, Y. and Yamanouchi, A. (1955). *Journal of the Agricultural Chemical Society of Japan* 29, 880.

Ouchi, K. and Akiyama, H. (1971). *Agricultural and Biological Chemistry, Tokyo* 35, 1024.

Research Institute of Brewing, Japan (1964). *Reports of the Research Institute of Brewing, Japan* 136, 26.

Saijo, T., Uchida, T., Furuhashi, M. and Kawamura, O. (1968). *Reports of Shizuoka Prefectural Industrial Research Institute* 12, 70.

Saito, K. (1950). In 'The Mycology of Saké Brewing'. pg. 94. Osaka.

Saito, K. and Oda, M. (1932). *Journal of Fermentation Technology* 10, 787.

Saito, K. and Oda, M. (1934). *Journal of Fermentation Technology* 12, 159.

Saito, T. (1965). *Journal of the Society of Brewing, Japan* 60, 898.

Sakaguchi, K. (1933). *Annals of the Brewing Association of Japan* 3, 247.

Sakamoto, M., Ishikawa, M. and Saijo, T. (1966). *Reports of the Shizuoka Prefectural Industrial Research Institute* 10, 72.

Sato, S. and Tadenuma, M. (1967). *Journal of the Society of Brewing, Japan* 62, 1279.

Sato, J. and Yamada, M. (1925). *Reports of the Research Institute of Brewing, Japan* 93, 585.

Shimada, S., Sugita, O. and Mizumoto, K. (1953). *Journal of Fermentation Technology* 31, 498.

Shimoide, M., Tani, Y. and Fukui, S. (1964). *Journal of the Society of Brewing, Japan* 59, 996.

Shimoide, M., Tani, Y. and Fukui, S. (1965a). *Journal of the Society of Brewing, Japan* 60, 801.

Shimoide, M., Tani, Y., Sumino, K., Yamashiro, K. and Fukui, S. (1965b). *Journal of the Society of Brewing, Japan* 60, 443.

Sugama, S., Saheki, H. and Noshiro, K. (1965). *Journal of the Society of Brewing, Japan* 60, 362.

Sugita, O. and Kageyama, K. (1957). *Journal of Fermentation Technology* 35, 347.

Sugita, O. and Kageyama, K. (1958). *Journal of Fermentation Technology* 36, 63, 157.

Sugiyama, S. and Nagahashi, K. (1932). *Reports of the Research Institute of Brewing, Japan* 115, 99.

Suzuki, M., Nunokawa, Y., Imajuku, I., Teruuchi, Y. and Uruma, M. (1956). *Journal of the Society of Brewing, Japan* 51, 318.

Suzuki, M., Nunokawa, Y. and Baba, K. (1958). *Journal of the Society of Brewing, Japan* 53, 431.

Suzuki, M., Nunokawa, Y., Hara, S., Baba, K. and Itoh, Y. (1958). *Journal of the Society of Brewing, Japan* 53, 603.

Tadenuma, M. and Sato, S. (1965). *Journal of the Society of Brewing, Japan* 60, 818.

Tadenuma, M. and Sato, S. (1967). *Agricultural and Biological Chemistry, Tokyo* 31, 1482.

Takahashi, T. (1907). *Journal of the Society of Brewing, Japan* 1, 20.

Takahashi, T. (1912). *Reports of the Research Institute of Brewing, Japan* 42, 361.

Takahashi, M. (1954). *Journal of the Agricultural Chemical Society of Japan* 28, 395.

Takahashi, M. (1956). *Journal of the Agricultural Chemical Society of Japan* 30, 140.

Takahashi, Y., Sato, S., Nakamura, K. and Tadenuma, M. (1971). *Journal of the Society of Brewing, Japan* 66, 611, 723.

Takase, S. and Murakami, H. (1965). *Journal of the Society of Brewing, Japan* 60, 624.

Takase, S., Sahara, T., Tamaru, F., Sakamoto, M., Kono, K. and Sugahara, S. (1963). *Journal of the Society of Brewing, Japan* 58, 1086.

Takeda, M. and Tsukahara, T. (1963). *Journal of the Society of Brewing, Japan* 58, 174.

Takeda, M. and Tsukahara, T. (1965a). *Journal of the Fermentation Association of Japan* 23, 352.

Takeda, M. and Tsukahara, T. (1965b). *Journal of the Fermentation Association of Japan* 23, 453.

Takeuchi, I. and Shimada, K. (1965). *Journal of the Agricultural Chemical Society of Japan* 39, 83, 89.

Takeuchi, I., Shimada, K. and Nakamura, S. (1967). *Journal of the Agricultural Chemical Society of Japan* 41, 260.

Takeuchi, I., Shimada, K. and Nakamura, S. (1969). *Journal of Fermentation Technology* 47, 102.

Tamura, G. (1958). *Journal of the Agricultural Chemical Society of Japan* 32, 701, 707, 783.

Tamura, G. and Suzuki, Y. (1958). *Journal of the Agricultural Chemical Society of Japan* 32, 778.

Tamura, G., Tsunoda, T., Kirimura, J. and Miyazawa, E. (1952). *Journal of the Agricultural Chemical Society of Japan* 26, 480.

Tanaka, T. (1970). In '*Shin Shuzo Gijutsu*', pg. 57. Society of Brewing, Japan Tokyo.

Teramoto, S., Hashimoto, W. and Yasuda, E. (1954). *Journal of Fermentation Technology* 32, 366.

Teramoto, S. and Hashimoto, W. (1957). *Journal of Fermentation Technology* 35, 242.

Thom, C. and Church, M. (1926). '*The Aspergilli*', pp. 198–207. Williams and Wilkins, Baltimore.

Tokado, S. and Sono, K. (1972). *Journal of the Society of Brewing, Japan* 67, 376.

Tokuoka, U. (1941). *Journal of Fermentation Technology* 19, 791, 925.
Tokuoka, U. (1942). *Journal of Fermentation Technology* 20, 14, 219.
Tomiyasu, S. (1933). *Journal of Fermentation Technology* 10, 515.
Totsuka, A., Sumikawa, T., Ogino, H., Namba, Y. and Kobuyama, Y. (1971). *Journal of the Society of Brewing, Japan* 66, 495.
Toyozawa, M. and Yonezaki, H. (1953). *Journal of Fermentation Technology* 31, 412.
Toyozawa, M. and Yonezaki, H. (1954). *Journal of Fermentation Technology* 32, 321.
Toyozawa, M., Yonezaki, H., Ueda, R. and Hayashida, M. (1960). *Journal of Fermentation Technology* 38, 342.
Tsukahara, T. (1954). *Journal of the Agricultural Chemical Society of Japan* 28, 405.
Tsukahara, T., Sakai, T., Maeda, K. and Miyasaka, T. (1964). *Journal of the Society of Brewing, Japan* 59, 358.
Uchida, T. (1966). *Reports of the Shizuoka Prefectural Industrial Research Institute* 10, 64.
Uchida, T., Kawamura, D. and Saijo, T. (1968). *Reports of the Shizuoka Prefectural Industrial Research Institute* 12, 66.
Ueda, R., Hayashida, M. and Kitagawa, E. (1960). *Journal of Fermentation Technology* 38, 337.
Ueno, H., Yao, T., Tadenuma, M. and Sato, S. (1966). *Journal of the Society of Brewing, Japan* 61, 1169.
Wehmer, C. (1895). *Zentralblatt für Bakteriologie, Parasitenkunde, Infektionsükrankheiten und Hygiene (Abteilung II)* 1, 150.
Yamada, M., Matsui, H., Ishimaru, K. and Masui, S. (1939). *Reports of the Research Institute of Brewing, Japan* 128, 265.
Yamada, M., Kobuyama, Y., Yamasuga, K., Takagi, S. and Suzuki, D. (1945). *Journal of the Society of Brewing, Japan* 40, 44.
Yamada, M., Akiyama, H., Shimizu, A., Fujii, R. and Harada, M. (1957). *Journal of the Agricultural Chemical Society of Japan* 31, 127.
Yamada, K., Minoda, Y., Kodama, T. and Kotera, U. (1969). *In* 'Fermentation Advances', (D. Perlman, ed.). pg. 541. Academic Press, New York.
Yamada, K., Furukawa, T. and Nakahara, T. (1970). *Agricultural and Biological Chemical, Tokyo* 34, 670.
Yamada, K., Minoda, Y., Kodama, T. and Kotera, U. (1971). United States Patent 3,585,109.
Yamamoto, A. (1961). *Journal of the Agricultural Chemical Society of Japan* 35, 616, 711, 715, 819, 824, 1082.
Yokotsuka, T., Sasaki, M., Kikuchi, T., Asao, Y. and Nobehara, A. (1967). *Journal of the Agricultural Chemical Society of Japan* 41, 32.
Yonezaki, H. (1962). *Journal of the Society of Brewing, Japan* 57, 976.
Yoshikawa, K. Okumura, U. and Teramoto, S. (1963). *Journal of Fermentation Technology* 41, 357.
Yoshizawa, K. (1958). *Journal of the Society of Brewing, Japan* 53, 771.
Yoshizawa, K. (1966a). *Agricultural and Biological Chemistry, Tokyo* 30, 634.
Yoshizawa, K. (1966b). *Journal of the Society of Brewing, Japan* 61, 952.
Yoshizawa, K. (1966c). *Journal of the Society of Brewing, Japan* 61, 629.
Yoshizawa, K. (1966d). *Journal of the Society of Brewing, Japan* 61, 481.
Yoshizawa, K. and Makino, R. (1960). *Journal of the Society of Brewing, Japan* 55, 54-59, 734.

Yoshizawa, K. and Uchiyama, K. (1971). *Journal of the Society of Brewing, Japan* **66**, 624.

Yoshizawa, K., Furukawa, T., Tadenuma, M. and Yamada, M. (1961). *Bulletin of the Agricultural Chemistry Society of Japan* **25**, 326.

Yoshizawa, K., Koshiba, M. and Otsuka, K. (1966). *Journal of the Society of Brewing, Japan* **61**, 824.

Yoshizawa, K., Ishikawa, T., Unemoto, F., Sato, H., Noshiro, K. (1972a). *Journal of the Society of Brewing, Japan* **67**, 645.

Yoshizawa, K., Ishikawa, T., Unemoto, F., Kato, S. and Noshiro, K. (1972b). *Journal of the Society of Brewing, Japan* **67**, 457.

Yoshizawa, K., Ishikawa, T., Suzuki, T., Tezuka, M. and Noshiro, K. (1972c). *Journal of the Society of Brewing, Japan* **67**, 1059.

Yoshizawa, K., Ishikawa, T. and Noshiro, K. (1973a). *Journal of the Society of Brewing, Japan* **68**, 614.

Yoshizawa, K., Ishikawa, T., Unemoto, F. and Noshiro, K. (1973b). *Journal of the Society of Brewing, Japan* **68**, 705.

Yoshizawa, K., Ishikawa, T. and Hamada, Y. (1973c). *Journal of the Society of Brewing, Japan* **68**, 767.

Yuill, J. L. (1948). *Nature*, London **161**, 397.

Zadrodski, S. and Krzysztofik, W. (1953). *Acta Microbiologica Polonica* **2**, 209.

Zahorski, B. (1913). United States Patent 1,066,353.

Zenda, N. (1920). *Journal of the Society of Brewing, Japan* **15**, 1.

7. Fortified Wines

ROBIN W. GOSWELL AND RALPH E. KUNKEE

John Harvey and Sons Limited,
Harvey House, Whitchurch Lane, Bristol, England
and *Department of Viticulture and Enology,*
University of California, Davis, California, U.S.A.

I. DEFINITIONS

In this review we define fortified wines as beverages in which some of the alcohol is derived from the yeast fermentation of grapes and some from the addition of distilled spirits. We are only considering those wines where the intention is to use the addition of distilled spirits as a means of preparing a wine largely different in character and style from an unfortified wine; we are ignoring those rare cases where fortification is used to conceal the deficiencies of an ostensibly unfortified table wine.

Fortified wines, which are also known as dessert wines in some countries, are of two main types, namely, those which consist of, and owe their characteristic flavour to, wholly or partially fermented grapes and distilled spirits; and those which in addition contain, and owe part of their flavour to, non-grape products. In the first class fall the products most usually sold under such names as port, sherry and madeira. In the second class we have the vermouths, aperitif wines and some, but not all, of those wines which are flavoured with fruits other than the grape. For simplicity of exposition in this article, we will refer to the first class simply as fortified wines and to the second class as flavoured fortified wines.

II. NOMENCLATURE

While the production of table wines is a process of considerable antiquity and the techniques for its production have become very widely diffused, production of fortified wines only became possible after methods for the distillation of alcohol became available. It is believed that fortification was adopted in an attempt to use the preservative properties of alcohol rather than to take advantage of the special flavour and characters so produced. Although fortification came into commercial use in Europe early in the 17th Century, fortified wines are much less widely prepared than table wines. However, a number of regions in Southern Europe, notably Jerez de la Frontera in Spain, the Douro Valley in Portugal and the island of

Madeira, specialize in the production of such wines, most of the product being exported to the cooler regions of the world. The characteristic processes used in each of these areas are not identical and lead to the manufacture of those rather different styles of wine known respectively as sherry, port and madeira. Most of the fortified wines from other areas are made by methods based upon one or other of these three processes, or a combination of them. The products so made are frequently marketed under the name of one of these wines qualified by that of the producing area; for example, Australian sherry, South African port. It also may happen that these names are misleadingly applied; for example, California (baked) sherry might be more appropriately referred to as a California madeira.

There seem to us to be three basic methods for producing (unflavoured) fortified wines which we will call the sherry processes, the port processes and the madeira processes, respectively, and a description of these three forms an adequate basis for the understanding of any of the currently available commercial fortified wines (Table 1). Even such an excellent and traditional product as Marsala, as prepared in Sicily, can be interpreted in terms of a combination of the sherry and madeira processes. We feel that there will be little to be gained in a publication concerned with microbiology in describing the production of a whole series of flavoured wines with different added flavours, and we have therefore restricted ourselves to describing the manufacture of vermouth and American Special Natural (flavoured) Wines (Amerine et al., 1967).

III. THE BASIC PROCESSES

In theory, fortified wines could be prepared by adding any sort of potable spirit to any type of table wine. In practice, it has been found that the resultant products are not always attractive to the consumer and that some procedures give products with a balance, style and character of their own. The style of these products is distinct and cannot be regarded simply as an average of the flavours of the constituent spirits and unfortified wines. In one group of processes, fortification with spirit does not take place until the alcoholic fermentation of the base wine is complete. If this type of

Table 1. A slightly simplified flow sheet showing the main processes involved in the manufacture of fortified wines

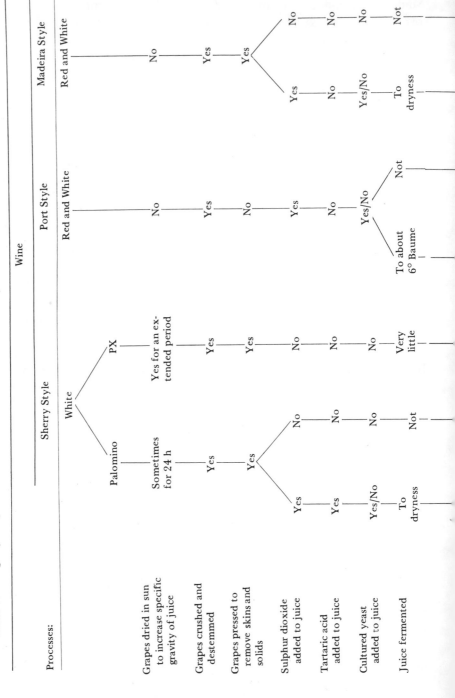

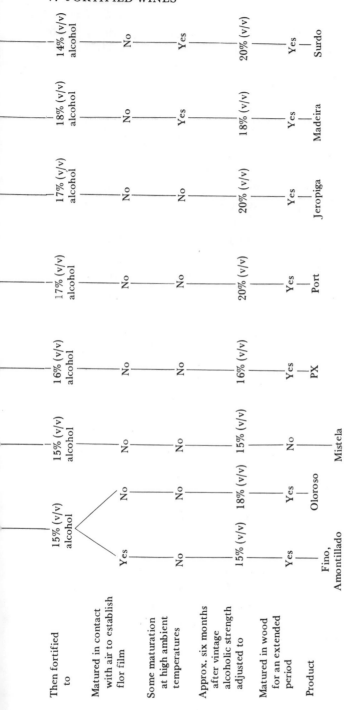

Then fortified to	15% (v/v) alcohol	15% (v/v) alcohol	16% (v/v) alcohol	17% (v/v) alcohol	17% (v/v) alcohol	18% (v/v) alcohol	14% (v/v) alcohol
Matured in contact with air to establish flor film	Yes / No	No	No	No	No	No	No
Some maturation at high ambient temperatures	No / No	No	No	No	No	Yes	Yes
Approx. six months after vintage alcoholic strength adjusted to	15% (v/v) / 18% (v/v)	15% (v/v)	16% (v/v)	20% (v/v)	20% (v/v)	18% (v/v)	20% (v/v)
Matured in wood for an extended period	Yes / Yes	No	Yes	Yes	Yes	Yes	Yes
Product	Fino, Amontillado / Oloroso	Mistela	PX	Port	Jeropiga	Madeira	Surdo

wine is to be sweetened, this process is carried out by the addition of largely unfermented sweetening materials usually at a comparatively late stage in its maturation process. These wines are almost always made from white grapes. When fermented they are normally fairly neutral in character, and they owe their distinction to the maturation techniques employed. This method is characteristic of the wines of Jerez de la Frontera in Spain. There are a number of related variants of the basic process. We will deal with these as a group and describe these as 'the Sherry processes' (Berg, 1960a; Goswell, 1968).

The second group of wines are fortified with spirit when they have fermented to the appropriate sweetness. They owe much of their character to the flavours of the red and white grapes employed. Maturation procedures vary slightly, producing different modifications to these primary grape flavours. This method is characteristic of the wines of the Douro Valley in Portugal, and we will refer to this method as 'the Port process' (Goswell, 1972; Twight and Amerine, 1938).

The third group of wines are usually fortified with spirit when they have been fermented to the desired sweetness, although they may be allowed to ferment dry and be sweetened subsequently. Red or white grapes may be used. The time of fortification is less important since the wines are subsequently heated over a period of some weeks to temperatures up to 58°C. This confers a strong characteristic flavour on the wine which is only slightly modified by variations in flavour of the grapes used and by variations in the time at which fortification is carried out. This method is characteristic of wines of the island of Madeira and we refer to it as 'the Madeira process'.

The fourth group of wines, which includes the vermouths and bitter aperitif wines, are those produced by the addition of non-grape flavours to a fortified base wine. The flavours are not added until fermentation has been carried out as far as is desired and at least some of the spirit has been added. Usually, but not invariably, there is some period of maturation before the flavours are added and a further period of maturation afterward. For convenience we will refer to this as 'the Vermouth process', although it must be understood that vermouth only results if suitable flavouring materials are chosen, and that non-vermouth fortified wines are an important part of the market.

In the interests of clarity we have elected to describe the manufacture of fortified wines by describing in detail the way in which each of the four processes is carried out in one specific area. The areas we have selected are: for the Sherry process, the Jerez de la Frontera part of Southern Spain; for the Port process, the Douro Valley and the Entreposto of Gaia in Portugal; for the Madeira process, the characteristic wines of the island of Madeira; and for Vermouth the production of Italian vermouth. Since interest in the production of Vermouth lies almost entirely in the methods used for incorporating flavours in the previously prepared wine, it is not convenient to describe this process in parallel with the other three methods. We have therefore relegated all references to Vermouth and other flavoured wines to a separate section at the end of this review.

We have chosen as far as possible the areas in which each particular style of fortified wine was first developed. The methods used were devised empirically by persons who were craftsmen rather than scientifically trained technologists. Many of the techniques they devised were peculiar to their own area, and helped to give the wine for that area its own individual characteristics. Economics have forced the wine makers to modify the original methods, but, in so doing, they have attempted to retain the flavours which were originated by the traditional techniques. The reputation for quality possessed by wines from these areas enables the present-day producers to use methods which, while cheaper than the original methods, would be uneconomic without the price advantage conferred by the product's reputation.

It is of interest to see how wine makers producing similar wines in other parts of the world have been forced to modify their techniques to lower costs. The modified techniques practised in countries such as Australia, South Africa and California are discussed in a final section of the review.

IV. PRODUCTION OF SHERRY, PORT AND MADEIRA

A. Areas of Production

Almost all serious wine-producing areas have taken some steps to give legal protection to the producers of their own wines so that wines made by inadequate means or from outside the designated area cannot be labelled in such a way that it can be passed off as the product of the area concerned. There is very considerable variation in the degree of protection given to different fortified wines in different areas. Almost invariably, however, there is some geographical limitation on the area of production of the grapes which may be used, and if this limitation is not total a restriction on the proportion of grapes from outside the area, which may be incorporated in the wine without its right to the geographical description being lost (Jeffs, 1970).

The rules for Spanish sherry are complex. Spanish sherry is made in a restricted area close to the town of Jerez de la Frontera in Southern Spain. The materials and methods used in its manufacture, the vineyards where the grapes may be grown, and the places where it may be fermented and matured, are strictly controlled by a committee known as the Consejo Regulador de la Denominacion de Origen 'Jerez-Xeres-Sherry', appointed under Government authority (Jerez-Xeres-Sherry, 1964).

The area in which the grapes may be grown is carefully defined but, in the years when production is 'below normal', the Consejo may give permission for new wines of a similar type to be brought into the approved sherry area from suitable places outside the normal area. These wines must be matured in the approved sherry production area. The quantity of wine brought in in this way must not exceed 10% of that produced in the sherry area in the same year. As sufficient sweetening and colouring wines cannot be produced in the sherry-producing area, such wines may be bought from other areas where they have been traditionally produced, providing the Committee approve of the area chosen, and also providing that the total wine brought in does not exceed in quantity 14% of the total production of all sherry and ancillary sweetening wine in the official sherry-producing area. In present-day practice, much of the sweetening wine, known as PX, is brought into the sherry-producing area from Montilla-Moriles in the province of Cordoba. It should be noted that the wine, somewhat similar to Sherry, produced in Montilla-Moriles may not be called 'Sherry' by Spanish law.

Similarly, the rules for Port are complex (Bradford, 1969). Port is made in Portugal in an approved area surrounding the upper River Douro and its tributaries, and matured in the delimited area and in approved premises in Vila Nova de Gaia at the mouth of the Douro at Oporto. The viticulture of the area is controlled by an organization known as the Casa do Douro, a Guild of all farmers with a government-appointed directorate. The production and shipment of a wine is controlled by the Instituto do Vinho do Porto, which is also a government body which works in association with the Grémio of Guild of shippers and the Casa do Douro. These organizations are currently being modified by the new administration in Portugal. The grapes must be produced and the wine matured in the area known as the Região Demarcada do Douro. This follows the River Douro from the Spanish border near Barca d'Alval to about two kilometres past Mesão Frio. The vineyards extend from the river bank to the north and south for between two and five kilometres, or somewhat further in some places, especially in the west of the area, and also from the lower valleys of the main tributaries of the Douro wherever the soil and drainage are suitable (Villa Lobos Machado, 1950).

Madeira is less rigidly controlled. The grapes may be grown anywhere on the islands of Maderia; in practice they are all grown on the main island or on the neighbouring island of Porto Santo. Most of the better quality grapes are grown west of Funchal, surrounding and inland from the village of Camara de Lobos and Estreito de Camara de Lobos. A large number of grapes are also grown on the north of the island, but, owing to the less satisfactory climate and the poorer grape varieties planted, they are not much used for the better wines. Grapes grown on the island of Porto Santo are important in the industry because they normally become sweeter than those growing on the main island, and consequently they play an important part in production of the sweeter wines. This wine tends to be rather expensive as the alcohol must travel to Porto Santo from Funchal under Customs' guard, and heavy freight charges are made both on the empty and full casks (Johnson, 1971).

B. Influence of Climate and Soil

The choice of a suitable site for raising grapes for fortified wine production is a function of the overall climate of the area and the microclimate of the vineyard area which develops in response to such factors as slope, aspect and drainage.

The Sherry vineyards are situated in a diamond-shaped area with Jerez de la Frontera more or less at the centre, Lebrija at the northern apex, Chipiona at the western apex, Chiclana de la Frontera at the southern apex, and the eastern apex a few miles short of Arcos de la Frontera. The best vineyards are situated in the hills composed of a rather chalky soil known locally as *albariza*. In Jerez, great importance is attached to the chemical composition of the soil. Careful analyses are always carried out before any planting is done. The preferred soil is one containing from 30% to 80% (w/w) chalk, with the remainder consisting of sand, clay and humus. This soil is known as the 'albariza'. The advantages of this soil type seem to lie in its physical structure rather than its chemical composition. It has the virtue of retaining water from the winter rainfall throughout the very dry summer. Even after many weeks without any rainfall, it remains damp a few centimetres below the surface. Grapes are also produced on the more normal soils of the same general type, which contain less than 30% chalk. The soils known as 'barros' are said to produce rather coarser wines. The soils known as 'arenas', containing more than 80% sand and less than 10% chalk, are also used. These soils are said to be easy to work but to produce grapes of rather inferior quality.

Rainfall is moderate (about 60 cm per annum) but quite variable. Very little falls in the summer months from May until August. Rain during the vintage period, i.e. September, is not uncommon. The rainfall is predominantly from the end of November to February when it may be quite heavy and prolonged. Frost is not uncommon in winter, although it is not usually severe. It occurs while the vines are dormant, and frost damage to the growing vine is rare. There is very little cloud cover in the summer. August temperatures are usually highest, but July temperatures approach them. The maximum shade temperatures are about 40°C. The predominant winds are either south-westerlies, which are off the sea and cooling, or south-easterlies, which are dry and give rise to high temperatures. The south-easterlies, known locally as the 'levante', are not popular with the growers as they are said to diminish the yield from the vines.

In the Douro Valley the best quality must is produced on the slopes of the hills above the river. Unfortunately these are so steep that they must be extensively terraced to prevent soil from being washed away. The valley floor and lower slopes are often composed of alluvial sand, grapes from which give a rather light type of wine with a high production but a rather low grade must. Grapes from the hill top will give a 'green', i.e. an acid, sort of wine which is lower in alcohol. The preferred aspect is facing south-west. This, in general, is the north back of the River Douro. The advantage is that the grapes will be exposed to the sun from about 1000 h until late in the evening. On the south bank, where the sun shines for a shorter length of time, it is usual to remove some of the leaves. Farmers wishing to prepare a proportionally lower quality wine in greater quantity prefer vineyards in the shade as there is less tendency for the grapes to dry to form raisins. However, the sugar content will, in general, be lower, and suitable types of grapes must be selected.

In the Douro, the preferred soil is based on schistous rock which absorbs and holds moisture well. It is found on the lower slopes of the river valley. Between the schistous rock and the granite there is a 'transition' type of soil. Grapes grown upon the granite produce a wine low in alcohol and with little flavour. White grapes grow rather well on the 'transition', and even on granite, but red wines are less good and are thin and poor on granite.

Rainfall is fairly heavy in the period November to the end of February with a tendency for the rain to be heavy at the end of February. From February to April, there are frequent showers, while from May to September only odd showers are likely. Frost is common during January and February and is frequently severe. Snow sometimes falls, but it has no ill-effect upon the vine. Frost after growth of the grape begins is comparatively rare and infrequently troublesome. The mean maximum shade temperatures are likely to be between about 33°C at Tua and 30°C at Regua. A drying easterly wind sometimes blows, and is known as the 'Suão'. The wind is harmful if it occurs when the grapes are still small and green. The most desirable wine is produced in the northerly part of the region which maintains a cool balanced climate. A southerly wind frequently carries rain especially in the Baixo Corgo. Westerly winds also carry rain but it may not extend very far inland.

In Madeira, the average rainfall is about 75 cm, of which over 50 cm fall between October and March, 8 cm between April and June, and less than 3 cm in the period between July and September. However, the mountains at the centre of the island produce marked local variations in rainfall, and there is insufficient rainfall without irrigation for the proper development of grapes on the lower slopes of the wine-growing area. Frost and snow are very rare on the southern wine-growing areas, and are so transient if they occur that damage is not done to the vines. There is remarkably little variation in the average temperatures during the year. In January and February, the average temperature is 13°C with an average daily maximum of 18°C and a minimum of 9°C. Corresponding values for March and April are 13.5°, 19° and 12°; May and June, 18°, 21° and 10°; July and August, 23°, 24° and 19°; September and October, 19°, 14° and 18°, and November and December, 14°, 20° and 11°C. The prevailing winds are not harmful to the vines.

C. Layout of the Vineyard

In Jerez, most new vineyards are planted in rows about 2.3 metres apart with the vines about 1.1 metres apart in each row. The moderately wide spacing between each row permits the driving of small tractors between the rows, allowing a deep mechanical cultivation. It would also permit the use of small mechanical harvesters, although as yet (1974) none is in commercial use. Traditionally, vines are planted in rows 1.5 metres apart with 1.5 metres between each vine in a single row. The traditional systems suffer from the disadvantage that mechanical cultivation is difficult even with special equipment. More labour is required for operations such as planting and pruning, and more money is expended upon the purchase of rootstocks, yet the yield per hectare is no better. In fact, the fewer vines of the wide-spaced system benefit to such an extent from the more thorough cultivation in depth by the more powerful agricultural machinery that the yield is usually significantly improved.

In the Douro, where the land is flat and regular enough, it is common practice to plant the vines in parallel rows 1.5 metres apart and 1.5 metres between each vine. This spacing of the vines is usually somewhat irregular and no overall pattern is followed traditionally in the area, as almost always the ground is too irregular in contour to permit the use of the elaborate patterns sometimes utilized in other areas. In many places, especially in the better vineyards, the ground slopes steeply and it is necessary to terrace the vineyards. The vineyards are terraced so that several rows of vines are planted on a flat piece of ground which is then stepped down, the step being held in position by a retaining dry stone wall constructed of the local schistous rock.

Modern vineyards are often on wider terraces with about nine rows of vines. These can be formed by earth-moving machinery from terraces which have long been abandoned and have fallen into disrepair. Of necessity, design and layout of these terraces are somewhat irregular as the contours of the hill must be followed. Cultivation of the soil, which consists largely of single-furrow ploughing using a light plough drawn by a mule especially trained for the work, is carried out several times during the growing season to remove most of the weeds, and during the winter to open the soil for maximum absorption of the rain. In many places, the vines are interplanted with olive trees which, during the depression years of the twenties and thirties of this Century, were often thought to be a more reliable and rewarding crop. The roots of these olive trees are now having a deleterious effect upon the vines, and it is usual in vineyards so planted to see many gaps in the rows of vines. It is extremely difficult to plant fresh rootstocks under these conditions and, if possible and if the rootstock survives, an attempt is made to graft on a fresh scion.

In Madeira, the vineyards are planted in rows conforming to the terrain with the plants in each row usually about one metre apart and the rows 1 to 1.5 metres apart but, as the vines are apt to get quite tall, the spacing is to some extent governed by the training system adopted. Mechanical cultivation is not possible. In most of the vineyards, there is not room to permit the use of animals between the rows of vines. The method of training precludes it. In Madeira, there is a severe shortage of good agricultural land, so that catch crops, such as cabbage, are taken from the ground surrounding the vines in early Spring. This is almost never done in the Port and Sherry areas.

D. Grape Varieties

The wine grape, *Vitis vinifera* L., in its many varieties is used exclusively for quality wine production, except in areas where the winter climate is unsuitable, such as New York State, U.S.A., and Eastern Canada. All of the named varieties listed below are of this species.

In Jerez, there has been a steady simplification in the number of varieties used until, at present, the dry components of the wine are made almost exclusively from the Palomino grape. The Palomino grape seems to exist in two strains, namely, the *Palomino Fino* and the *Palomino de Jerez*. The former produces the heavier crops and is now used in almost all new vineyards. For some special sweetening wines, the *Pedro Ximenez* (PX) grape is used but is not much planted in the Jerez area as it grows better in the hotter Montilla district where most of the sweetening wines for sherry are made, as already explained.

This situation is in great contrast to the Douro Valley where over 50 varieties are grown. Some of these grapes are of excellent characteristic flavour, some quite poor, some produce high yields, some very little. Many older vineyards contain a very miscellaneous selection, including varieties which produce wine of poor flavour and low yield. Recently planted vineyards are likely to consist of a more rational selection including for red wine: *Touriga Nacional, Mourisco, Mourisco de Semente, Tinta Roriz, Tinto Cão* and *Tinta Francisco*; and for white wines: *Codega, Malvasia Fina* and *Rabigato*.

In Madeira, for cheaper wines the *Tinta Negra Mole* (a red grape) from the main island and the *Listrao* (white) and the *Negra* (red) from Porto Santo are used. The traditional varieties, the *Malvasia Candida* (very scarce), the *Sercial, Verdelho* and the *Bual de Madeira*, all in short supply, are used as far as possible for the better wines. New plantings of these varieties soon should ease the supply shortage. Many poor varieties exist, including hybrids between American vines and *Vitis vinifera*; these are avoided by reputable producers.

E. Rootstocks

In Jerez, the Douro and Madeira, the vines are almost always grafted, since the soil is contaminated with the root aphid, phylloxera. The rootstocks are hybrids between European vines and American species. The influence of American species is to confer some resistance to attacks by phylloxera and sometimes root eelworms.

The rootstock does not influence the flavour of the scion grafted on to it, but may influence the vigour of the plant. The hybrid name indicates in most cases the *V. vinifera* variety used, the American species used and the number applied to the cross by the hybridizer. The choice of rootstock is made after a soil analysis has been carried out, as not all resistant rootstocks are suitable for growing in soil with a high content of calcium carbonate. The following rootstocks are often used:

Riparia x Berlandieri 161/49, where the calcium content is very high;
Cabernet x Berlandieri 333EM;
Chasselas x Berlandieri 41B.

In the Douro, the rootstocks most commonly used are:

Rupestris du Lot;
Riparia x Rupestris 3309;
Aramon x Rupestris No. 9;
Cordifolia x Rupestris 4416-144.

It is possible to buy rootstocks from specialist nurserymen, but many growers raise their own by taking cuttings from rootstocks which have produced shoots after the European variety grafted into it has died, or from the heads of decapitated stock at the moment of grafting. A few *Vitis vinifera* vines are grown on their own roots as a curiosity, but they deteriorate after six to ten years.

Vines in Madeira were more severely damaged by the phylloxera infection which struck the island in 1872 than even the badly hit vines of the mainland of Europe. At one time, it was thought that cultivation of the vine would be completely abandoned but fortunately, as elsewhere, it has proved possible to graft the local varieties of vine on the American rootstocks. The local agriculture service has recommended the following rootstocks as suitable for use on the island with the variety specified:

Boal x Rupestris du Lot, 161-49, 110R;
Listrao x 99R, 420A, 41B;
Malvasia Candida x Rupestris du Lot, 34EM, 420A, 41B;
Sercial x 99R, 34EM, 41B;
Terrantez x 99R, 110R, 34EM;
Tinta Negra Mole x 99R, 4416-144, Rupestris du Lot;
Verdelho x 99R, 110R, 34EM, 41B.

Virus-free stock does not seem to be available in any of these areas. Single clones are not normally selected by nurserymen, but propagating is done from cuttings taken in the field from healthy looking vines.

F. Age of the Vines

In Jerez, it is found that, two or three years after grafting, the vines begin to produce a very small quantity of grapes of poor quality. The quantity and quality improve year by year. After six years, the vine gives a good commercial yield and, after about 25 years, the vineyard is giving fine quality wines at maximum production. From then on, the quantity of sherry gradually falls off while the quality continues to improve until, after 30 or 40 years, the yield has fallen to such an extent that the vine is no longer economic. When this happens, the vines are pulled up and the vineyard is put over to the production of sugar beet and leguminous crops for three or four years to enable the soil to recover.

In the Douro Valley, the vineyards are held in economic production for 40 or 50 years, after which they are replanted. When the vines are pulled up, new rootstock is planted immediately; a period of rest is seldom allowed, especially in the Baixo Corgo, nor are other crops planted to recondition the soil. In the Cima Corgo, fallow land is often available.

The age of the vines in Madeira is not accurately known in most cases, but it is generally believed that 25 years is about ideal, with the vines becoming too unproductive to be economic after about 35 years. Little statistical information is available, but there is no reason to think that the age will be very different from that appropriate in other areas.

G. Crop Sprays

In Jerez, during May and June, the vines are usually dusted several times with sulphur (to combat the spread of *Oidium* spp.). Bordeaux mixture or, more likely, a modern colloidal copper-containing preparation, is sprayed several times depending on the humidity, to prevent the spread of *Plasmopora viticola*. Spraying is usually done from manpacks. Some large vineyard owners have used spraying by helicopter.

In the Douro Valley, the vines are sprayed with a Bordeaux mixture of colloidal copper after the bunch is first formed and thereafter whenever humidity makes this necessary. Spraying may be necessary as much as ten times in a difficult year. The vines are dusted with sulphur when the first flowers appear, and possibly once more. Insecticides are not used in a systematic way but are employed if any particularly vigorous outbreaks of a specific insect pest are noticed.

Oidium spp. have been troublesome in Madeira since about 1852. Sulphur is dusted on the vines; usually about three dustings a year are necessary before June and a further two during this month. Diseases caused by *Plasmopora* spp. became troublesome in about 1912 and copper sprays, either as Bordeaux mixture or colloidal copper, are used extensively.

These intensive spraying programmes are expensive, and form a significant part of the cost of producing the grapes.

H. Fertilizers

In Jerez, horse and mule manure, which is in short supply, is applied to vineyards once every four years, but artificial fertilizers are used annually. A blend of super-phosphate, potassium sulphate and ammonium sulphate is recommended.

In the Douro Valley, horse and mule manure, which again is in short supply, is applied to the vineyards whenever it is available. Proprietary organic or chemical fertilizers have been widely used on an individual basis, but there seems to be no general policy, their use depending upon the prosperity and enthusiasm of the grower and the representatives of the supplier, although some soil analyses are carried out. In some areas, a genuine boron deficiency has been noted, and application of specific boron-containing materials has been very successful.

Lime is usually deficient in soils of Madeira but not in Porto Santo. There is little limestone on the island, although a small marble quarry exists. Guano is used extensively, although this is partly used to fertilize the crops growing between the vines rather than the vines themselves. Super-phosphate is used quite extensively as are bone-meal and compound fertilizers. Horse and mule manure are used when available.

I. Irrigation

In Jerez, irrigation is forbidden. Fortunately, the albariza soil has the remarkable property of retaining water tenaciously and does not dry out during the long hot summer. Very little irrigation is used in the Douro Valley, although a few growers use a system of irrigation canals. A very few use rotary sprayers. A system of water channels is used throughout the main agricultural districts of Madeira, the water being supplied from reservoirs situated at higher altitudes where rainfall is greater. Water is allocated to each farmer, either for a fee or sometimes as a right to the owners of several areas of land. Normally about two hours' supply of water are available in each two-week period. The water is directed from the irrigation channels along the rows of vines by a system of ridges and improvised dams. Irrigation should not be carried out after about six weeks before the grapes ripen.

J. The Vintage

The vintage in Jerez begins between September 1st and September 15th each year and lasts for about 15 days. The virtually exclusive use of a single grape variety presents economic problems in that all of the grapes must be processed over a very short period of time, so that a relatively high investment in plant is required, added to which this plant is only used for a short time during each year.

One-kilogram bunches of grapes, representative of the state of the whole crop, are selected. They are brought into the laboratory in paper bags and crushed in a small hand-screw press. A few operators prefer to cut the grapes with a small domestic blender equipped with a cutting blade, as the must so produced more closely resembles that produced by the large-scale presses. The specific gravity of the must is measured in degrees Baumé (see Chapter 1, p. 35) using a glass hydrometer. A value between 11.5 and 12.5 degrees Baumé is considered to be satisfactory (this is equivalent to a Balling value of 19–22.5). Total acidity is measured by a titration with standard alkali against phenolphthalein. A reading of 31.3 g per litre as sulphuric (0.51% as tartaric acid) is desirable, but readings as low as 2.1 (0.32) are common. In many years, the grapes are deficient in acidity, and the total acidity is adjusted in each butt to a value of 2.9 (0.45). Towards the time of the vintage, these measurements are made every three days or so until it is considered that the grapes will not improve further. In hot years, when the weather is dry with frequent easterly winds, the vintage is early and more *olorosos* are formed. A late vintage, often when conditions are more or less humid, may favour production of *finos*.

The grapes are traditionally cut with a clasp knife rather than with shears, and are gathered in wooden boxes holding between 12 and 14 kg of grapes, in wicker baskets made of olive branches, or increasingly into stackable plastic containers. Traditionally, the boxes or baskets are made of such a size that 60 of them will give approximately enough must to fill one sherry butt of about 108 gallons (490 litres). The boxes and baskets are scrubbed before use, and are exposed to the sun partially to sterilize them. The full baskets are often transported on special carriers, attached to the back of a mule, to the pressing house, but larger installations, which gather grapes from a greater area, of necessity use tipping lorries. The interior of a tipping lorry is commonly made of wood. The yields of must from vineyards were traditionally regarded as being approximately three butts of 108 gallons per aranzada (1.1 acres or 0.45 hectares) for albariza soil, 3.5 butts per aranzada for barro soil, and approximately four butts per aranzada for arena soil. But, with more modern and deeper methods of cultivation, yields much higher than these could be obtained. It would be possible to get between 8 and 12 butts of must per acre from albariza soil.

In the Douro Valley, the vintage usually begins between the 12th September and the 1st October, but, depending on the season, it has been known to begin as early as the 31st August or as late as the 15th October. The tendency is for earlier dates in hot areas well inland, and later dates for high ground and in the Baixo Corgo, the picking taking about three weeks in any one district. It would be desirable for some varieties to be picked rather earlier, but this does not normally happen as the varieties are not kept separate in the vineyards. The exact date of the vintage is normally determined by the purchaser of the crops in consultation with the grower. The decision is based on the aspect of the vineyard, the predicted weather and the facilities for crushing which are available, together with the colour and taste of the grapes. A few attempts have been made to assess the must for the vintage by squeezing a sample of the grapes through sack cloth and determining the refractive index of the juice. The method is not normally operated in any satisfactory statistical manner, and it has been found less reliable than a subjective judgment of the condition of the grapes.

The yield of must from the vineyards varies enormously depending upon the quality. The finest varieties might give one pipe, i.e. 118 gallons (536 litres) of must per 1,000 vines; more average varieties might yield three or four pipes per 1,000 vines, and very poor quality material up to seven or eight pipes per 1,000 vines. It is very doubtful if the production of port would be authorized from wines of such quality that only seven or eight pipes per 1,000 vines were produced. Because of the terracing and uneven nature of the ground, it is not very meaningful to discuss yields in gallons per acre. For purposes of comparison, it may be mentioned that, in a suitable place, vines might be planted at a density of 1,000 per hectare. As far as possible, grapes are crushed almost immediately after picking. When brought in from outlying vineyards to a central crushing station, they might remain for up to eight hours before crushing. They are weighed upon receipt and inspected for maturity and the presence of moulds.

In the south of Madeira, in an average year, the vintage begins about the 22nd August and continues until the first week in October, The vines on higher ground mature late, especially the Sercial variety. In the north, the vintage tends to begin in the first week in September and continues through until the last week in October. In the south, most of the better quality grapes are bought for crushing by the producer. The purchaser, who is usually an exporter or a middle-man specializing in the purchase of grapes and their fermentation, controls the time of the vintage, as he supplies the mechanical crusher. The price each year is fixed before the vintage by a committee formed by the purchasers (mostly exporters) and agents who represent the interests of the growers.

Grapes which should produce between 10 and 12.5% (v/v) alcohol are considered satisfactory for *Tinto Negra Mole, Sercial* and *Boal*, but the *Verdelho* may produce only 7 to 10%. In Porto Santo, theoretical yields of alcohol of between 13, 15 and exceptionally 18% may be obtained. Total acidities expressed as tartaric acid, would be typically 0.7% per litre for Tinta wine, 0.85% for Verdelho and 0.95% for Malvasia.

The grapes are cut and placed in baskets of a truncated cone shape holding about 60 kg. They are crushed and pressed as soon after as possible. Many, but not all, purchasers add between 50 and 100 mg of sulphur dioxide per litre during the crushing process. Yields may be as much as 750 litres per hectare with cheap high-yielding grapes, but the average for premium quality grapes is probably no more than half of this value.

K. Crushing and Pressing

In Jerez, the grapes were traditionally crushed by treading in a low wooden trough known as a lagar, but this method is now obsolete and is performed only on a small scale as a demonstration for tourists. In this method, the grapes were crushed by treading with nailed boots and pressing was carried out by heaping the pomace around a screw covered with bands made with esparto grass. The free-run juice and first pressing were mixed; this accounted for approximately 85% of the total. A second pressing gave a further 5%, and further pressings produced material only suitable for distillation or vinegar making (Jeffs, 1970). Calcium sulphate, in the form of gypsum, was sprinkled on the grapes to assist the pressing mechanically and to give some increase in the total acidity of the must (Carrasco, undated). The reaction is said to be as follows:

$$2HK(C_4H_6O_6) + CaSO_4 = K_2SO_4 + Ca(C_4H_4O_6) + (C_4H_6O_6)H_2$$

| potassium bitartrate | calcium sulphate | potassium sulphate | calcium tartrate (insoluble) | tartaric acid |

Currently, bunches of grapes are dumped into a trough and conveyed by a screw conveyor to a crusher-destemmer. The grapes have been harvested as complete bunches. These machines can be adjusted either simply to crush the berries, or alternatively and more usually, to crush the berries and remove the stems. This is done by a device which forces the crushed grapes through a perforated cylinder, which retains most of the stems. After destemming, the must is usually transported by a must pump to horizontal presses, usually the Vaslin or Wilmes horizontal mechanical type, although Wilmes pneumatic presses are also used fairly extensively. The use of continuous presses is envisaged. The first three operations of the press make a wine similar to the first press wine of the traditional method. The wine from the fourth and fifth operations is classed as second pressing wine but, owing to the smaller amount of oxidation with this operation, it is still useful for making 'raya' sherry—a sherry of inferior quality. Calcium sulphate is added to the must by most producers when the wine is pressed mechanically, but the quantity may be less than that used traditionally, being between 750 g and 1.5 kg per butt (600 litres) of wine. In some installations, a hydraulic pressing may follow a pressing with a horizontal press especially when the special sweetening wine known as PX is produced.

In the Douro Valley, crushing and pressing are rapidly being transformed from an essentially small-scale traditional operation to an industrial-scale mechanical process. If the work is to be done by the most traditional methods, which are still used by some farmers producing special high-quality wines, enough grapes are placed without preliminary crushing in the stone troughs or lagars to fill them to a depth of about 50 cm. These lagars, which are made of granite, are rectangular in shape, the sides being between 3 and 6 metres long and about 60 cm deep. They contain enough grapes to make from between 5 and 22 pipes of must. Between 100 and 300 mg of sulphur dioxide per litre is added to the lagar, the larger quantity being added in wet or very hot years when the grapes may be mouldy or the fermentations very vigorous. Treading is begun as soon as the lagar is full. It is desirable that there should be about one man for each two pipes of must to be prepared, but there is a shortage of persons willing to carry out this rather uncomfortable task so that, in most establishments, fewer people are used. In most of the larger installations, the grapes are no longer crushed by treading. Two types of mechanical crushers are used, namely the centrifugal type and the roller crushers. Centrifugal crushers are driven electrically or by an internal combustion engine when electricity is not available. The larger roller crushers are also driven by electricity or internal combustion engines but, for small installations, manually operated roller crushers are still manufactured.

The tendency is increasing for the shipper to buy uncrushed grapes from farms in the south of Madeira and to bring them into a central installation for crushing and pressing. A co-operative government-supervised crushing station also exists. Crushing in the purchaser's own plant permits him to have greater control of the type and quality of the grapes he is purchasing, and enables him to encourage the growers to plant the traditional low-yielding classic grapes of the island by paying a high premium price for this type.

In the north, difficulties of communication make it impossible to transport the grapes rapidly to the purchasers' installations on the south of the island and, therefore, most of the grapes are crushed on a small scale by the farm growers themselves. At least one middle-man has constructed a central crushing installation. Many of the grapes, in any case, are of poor quality, and even the better grapes are only suitable for use as blending wines. Most of the growers press the grapes in wooden or stone lagars. These are troughs, at the most 3 metres by 1.5 metres and not more than 0.75 metre in depth. The grapes are usually not crushed before placing in the lagar, but the whole process is carried out by treading. Four men are usually sufficient to work the grapes in a lagar of this size. Pressing may still be carried out by an ingenious manually-operated press built over the lagar. The press consists of a wooden beam with press boards situated close to the fulcrum, the pressure being exerted by suspending a stone at the end of the same beam and the whole being arranged so that there is probably ten times that of the weight of the stone which probably weighs about 500 kg. The expressed juice is strained through basket work.

In the south, use is made of small horizontal continuous presses. These are so adjusted that the pomace is only lightly pressed, so that excessive protein is not extracted. The final pressing of the uncom-pleted pomace is done either with a hydraulic press or a manual press of the type used in the north of the island.

L. Fermentation

In Jerez, most producers place the must in new oak butts for fermentation, although some larger concrete fermenters are used.

Butts are popular, partly because fermentation conditions the new oak wood so that it does not contribute too much flavour when later it is used to hold more mature wine. Also the temperature which prevails in the bodegas allows the fermentation to proceed in containers of this size without the need for ancillary heating or cooling. The casks to be used for shipping the wine have a capacity of 490 litres (108 gallons).

Most of the grapes are crushed and pressed by the grower, and the must is run into casks which are transported as rapidly as possible (within a few hours) to the premises of the bodega owner. It is desirable that these casks be taken into relatively cool premises before fermentation becomes active.

Characteristically, the specific gravity of the must will be between 1.085 and 1.095 (11.5-12.5° Baumé, 21-23° Balling) with a tannin content of 300 to 600 mg/litre, and a total acidity of 3.5-4.5 g/litre (expressed as tartaric acid). Butts are treated with about 100 mg of sulphur dioxide per litre; more is added if any mouldy grapes are present.

The temperature of the must when brought into the bodega will probably be about 21°C. There will be sufficient natural yeasts present for fermentation to be detectable within 24 hours, and the must will be in full fermentation within 48 hours. The temperature in the butt will rise to about 27°C, and most of the sugar will be removed in eight days. The wines will normally be completely dry by the end of October (after six weeks).

In the Douro Valley, the specific gravity of the must before fermentation begins is between 1.090 and 1.100 in the case of must for red port, and between 1.085 and 1.095 in the case of must for white port. In a year of average quality (not a vintage year), the total acidity, given as tartaric acid per 100 ml, would be between 0.39 and 0.60 grams. The pH value is between 3.3 and 3.7. The tannin content is between 400 and 600 mg/litre. There is remarkably little difference in the analysis of red and white musts in these respects. The fermentation is allowed to continue until the specific gravity is 1.045 (±0.005).

About 20% of port wine is still fermented in the traditional stone lagars. Treading will be carried out more or less all day every day until fermentation is complete. Three four-hour periods with three two-hour breaks for rest are considered acceptable. In most years, the grapes would be rather cold, probably at 15–16°C, when first placed in the lagar, so that, if the first fermentation of the season were being carried out, it might be anything from two to four days before fermentation commences. Fermentation is likely to take from two to thirty hours depending upon the temperature developed. There is an outlet at the side of the lagar through which the free-run juice is allowed to escape when the Baumé value, measured with a hydrometer, has fallen to about 6.5° (11.5° Balling). The lagars, or some of them, are equipped with a large vertical screwed rod around which a simple vertical manually-operated basket press can be erected. The pomace from the lagar is shovelled into the press, and the pressed wine so obtained is added to the appropriate batch of juice which is then fortified to arrest fermentation. Three pressings are made, but only the first is added to the free-run juice. Its volume represents about 20% of the free-run juice, and its Baumé value will have fallen to about 4°, i.e. 7° Balling. The second pressing, which will be at about 2° Baumé (3.5° Balling) or even lower, is used for table wine. The third pressing, if made, will be at 0° Baumé and will also make table wine. The dry pomace after distillation is used as a fertilizer on the vineyards. If not distilled it can be used or sold as cattle feed.

Many installations now use tanks of between 50 and 150 hecto-litres' capacity. They are open at the top and equipped with a manhole low down at the side, and suitable valves to allow the wine to be drawn off before the door in the manhole is opened to permit withdrawal of the pomace. The tanks are often lined with an epoxy coating. In such an installation, the grapes are crushed mechanically with a centrifugal or roller crusher, and the crushed fruit, including some stalks, fed by a must pump into the tank. Cultured yeast is used in only a few installations. Temperatures are controlled by pumping the must through an external cooler, probably a cascade cooler, deriving its cooling water from the River Douro with or without auxiliary refrigeration. Colour is extracted by spraying the wine over the skins floating on the surface in the orthodox way.

A number of installations make use of the autovinificators of the type perfected in Algeria. These devices utilize the pressure of gas produced during fermentation to circulate the must over the cap. A cooling coil through which water may be circulated is incorporated (Brémond, 1957). At least one producer has experimented with thermovinification (Pachedo de Azevedo and Pereira, 1967; Rankine, 1972) and also with Roto tanks (Haushofer, 1957).

If the must is analysed immediately before drawing off, there is shown to be remarkably little change in the composition, apart from the decrease in specific gravity and, in the case of red wines, a sharp deepening in colour. There is usually, but not invariably, an increase in the tannin content of about 60 mg/litre. There is little change in the pH value or total acid content. In spite of the relatively crude conditions in which fermentation is carried out, the content of volatile acids in the wine rarely rises above 0.035 g acetic acid equivalent per 100 ml. Apart from the sulphur dioxide added during crushing, it is unusual to supplement the must at this stage. At one time, the addition of citric acid was thought to be advantageous, but it seems to have achieved little and the practice has died out since it is no longer legal. Tartaric acid has also been added, and this is still permitted.

Small producers in Madeira may well allow the fermentation to proceed in wooden casks which, at the prevailing temperatures, are quite satisfactory for this purpose. Larger producers use cubical concrete tanks closed at the top but with a large manhole. These range in capacity from 20,000 to 28,000 litres. These tanks are lined with tartrate or with an epoxy resin. They have proved very satisfactory.

At the temperatures prevailing during the vintage, cooling is not necessary if a suitable position has been selected in which to site the fermentation tanks, providing the building has been well designed to provide good thermal insulation in the roof. The ambient temperature of a well designed installation is usually around 16–18°C, and the ambient temperature normally does not rise much above 22°C. The fermentation takes four to six weeks, and is usually regarded as complete when the specific gravity has fallen to 0.995.

M. Fermentation Yeasts

In Jerez, cultured yeast is rarely added to juice as the grapes have adequate amounts of suitable fermentative yeasts present on the skin. A few producers are beginning to experiment with cultured yeast, but it is too early to assess the results.

Inigo Leal *et al.* (1963) have studied the yeasts responsible for the fermentations in the Jerez area. As in many other areas, they found that the first phase of fermentation was dominated by *Kloeckera apiculata*, with *Metschnikowia pulcherrima* (*Candida pulcherrima*), *Saccharomyces cerevisiae* (*Saccharomyces ellipsoideus*), *Saccharomyces chevalieri* (*Saccharomyces mangini*), *Saccharomyces italicus*, *Saccharomyces rosei* (*Torulaspora rosei*) and *Hanseniaspora valbyensis* (*Hanseniaspora guilliermondii*) present in a significant proportion. As the alcohol concentration increased, the population of *Metschnikowia* spp. declined in size, and there was some increase in the proportion of *Sacch. chevalieri*. During the final phase of fermentation, *Sacch. cerevisiae*, *Sacch. chevalieri* and *Sacch. italicus* predominated.

The authors were able to show significant differences between the yeasts in musts taken from vineyards in different parts of the Jerez area during the early stage of fermentation but, in all cases, the final phase was dominated by *Sacch. cerevisiae, Sacch. chevalieri* and *Sacch. italicus*. One of us (R. W. Goswell) has made some studies on the flora of the unfermented must, and has identified *Hanseniaspora osmophila, Kloeckera africana. Debaryomyces hansenii, Hansenula anomala* var. *anomala, Candida guilliermondii, Pichia strasburgensis, Saccharomyces rosei, Saccharomyces uvarum, Saccharomyces chevalieri, Kluyveromyces marxianus, Metschnikowia pulcherrima,* and many moulds similar to *Mucor* spp. At least one producer is experimenting with the use of cultured yeast starters.

Cultured yeast is rarely needed in the Douro Valley as the grapes have adequate amounts of suitable fermentative yeasts on their skins. Some producers have used compressed yeast of the Montrachet strain with success. Marques Gomes (1962) has stated that *Saccharomyces italicus* (*Saccharomyces steineri*) is the dominant yeast in over 80% of the fermentations studied in the Douro. He has made a detailed study of the varieties of this organism and of their value in oenology. There is no comprehensive survey published of the yeasts active in this region but, in an earlier paper, Marques Gomes (1949) implies by his choice of organisms for a study of the progress of experimental fermentation that *Kloeckera apiculata* and *Metschnikowia pulcherrima* (*Candida pulcherrima*) are active at the beginning of the fermentation followed by *Saccharomyces cerevisiae* var. *ellipsoideus* and sometimes *Hansenula anomala* var. *anomala*.

Cultured yeasts are not required or used in Madeira. We know of no microbiological studies that have been carried out on the yeast flora of this wine.

V. DEVELOPMENT AND MATURATION OF THE WINES

Up to this point, the methods used to produce the three main types of fortified wine differ in many points of detail, but are designed to achieve the same overall objectives. For each wine, it is necessary to grow the grapes, to harvest them at the appropriate time, to carry out a complete or partial fermentation and then to add a certain amount of distilled spirit. Because these operations are essentially similar, it has been possible to describe and compare each part of the operation for wines of the three areas we have selected before going on to the next operation. However, once fortification with alcohol has been carried out, the production methods begin to diverge so widely that it is no longer advantageous to pursue this form of description. From now on, therefore, we will describe the maturation procedures of the three types of wine separately, after which we will make comparisons.

A. Sherry From the Jerez District of Spain

1. Treatment after Fermentation

Between December and March, Spanish sherry usually clarifies spontaneously. It is racked off the lees into washed casks which have been treated with sulphur dioxide, either by injecting the gas or by burning elemental sulphur. The alcohol concentration is increased to between 14.5 and 15.5% (v/v) by addition of between 12 and 36 litres of 95% alcohol per butt of neutral grape spirit. To obviate the heavy clouding which takes place when high-strength alcohol is mixed with new wine, the alcohol is premixed with an equal quantity of a suitable wine of the same type, and the cloud is allowed to settle; this takes about three days. The resultant mixture, known locally as *mitad y mitad* (half and half), is used for fortification. The casks of slightly fortified wine are only about 80% full so that a large air-to-wine surface is present in each cask. The casks remain in the bodegas and are racked a second time in July and August, a little more *mitad y mitad* being added if necessary to maintain the alcohol concentration between 14.5 and 15% (v/v). Soon it becomes increasingly apparent that the wines are developing in different ways (Casas-Lucas, 1967).

In some butts a thick film of yeast (known as the flor) will develop at the air–wine interface. These yeasts seem to be special strains of *Saccharomyces cerevisiae* and *capensis* (called *Saccharomyces beticus* in Spain) and special strains of *Saccharomyces bayanus* (called 'cheresiensis' in Spain). Growth of these yeasts influences the character of the wines which are said to be of the *fino* type. In other butts, which may be from the same part of a vineyard, comparatively little film yeast will grow. In general, wines made from grapes grown in warmer vineyards, from vineyards with a lower percentage of chalk in the soil, and those containing a percentage of press wine, are less likely to grow flor, although the result for any individual cask is unpredictable (Bobadilla, 1943, 1944; Castor and Archer, 1957; Chaffey, 1940; Feduchy, 1956; Feduchy and Sandoval, 1960; Freiberg and Cruess, 1955; Fornachon, 1953; Marcilla *et al.*, 1939; Cruess, 1948).

2. *Types of Dry Sherry*

By July, it is readily apparent that two fundamentally dissimilar products are being made in the sherry bodegas, which we may call 'dry sherry with much flor' and 'dry sherry with little flor'. The experienced producer would have a very good idea much earlier, probably in November or December, as to whether a given butt would develop a good or poor flor and, at an early stage, it is customary to chalk some indication on the cask of the type of sherry which is likely to be produced and the quality expected. This classification is subject to refinement and modification as the development progresses. Although it is not possible to predict the exact behaviour of any given butt of wine, the experienced producer has a good idea of the production of flor and non-flor wine which will be produced from a given vineyard in any one year. In general terms, grapes grown on soil with a very high percentage of calcium carbonate, and from vineyards with a westerly (cool) exposure, tend to produce more flor (*fino*) sherries. A year in which temperatures have been rather lower than average (usually because of predominantly westerly winds) tends to give rise to a higher percentage than usual of flor wines.

In local nomenclature, the characteristic sherry without much flor of good quality is described as an *oloroso* (Gonzalez-Gordon, 1972). These are rather dark wines of full-bodied type. A very small percentage of good-quality wine develops slightly differently and becomes lighter in both colour and body; this is classified as a *palo cortado*. This type of wine is prized locally, probably because of its scarcity value. The coarser wines of less quality are referred to as *rayas*. The young wines with a good flor film are all regarded as *finos* of varying quality.

Sherries are matured in tall, well-ventilated buildings, known as bodegas. These are not air-conditioned but are designed to remain as cool as practicable, particularly at ground level and up to about two metres above the ground. In the traditional bodegas, the ground is often not covered over part of the area, so that at least some of the soil is in contact with the air. This is said to lead to a desirable increase in humidity in the building.

The young *finos* of a single year are allowed to mature as unblended wine for a suitable period of time, usually about a year. Such a collection of butts of wine of a single year is referred to locally as an *añada*. The alcohol concentration is maintained at between 14.5 and 15.5% by volume, and the casks are filled to a little over 80% of their capacity so that the *flor* can develop freely on the air–wine interface. Care is taken to keep the wine in a cool position near the ground. The level of wine in the cask must not be allowed to fall too much by evaporation but, at the same time, the casks are subject to a minimum of disturbance both during filling and during storage (Kepner *et al.*, 1958).

The young *oloroso* sherries of a single year are fortified to between 18 and 19% by volume using *mitad y mitad*. They are also stored in an *añada* for one or more years. As the yeast film has been inactivated by fortification, the storage conditions are not quite so critical. The casks are kept at about 95% full, and topping up is not required so frequently as with *fino* sherry. Also the temperature of that part of the bodega in which they are stored may not be quite so cool and uniform.

Raya sherries are treated in a similar way to *olorosos*, but they are usually not stored for such a long time in the *añada*. Many producers store their *raya* wines out of doors in the sun which improves the maturation of this style of wine.

Dry sherries remain in an *añada* until they are required for blending. Since, as will be apparent from the earlier part of this chapter, the butts of sherry are essentially non-uniform in quality and character and their properties are rather unpredictable, an elaborate blending system is required, the more so as sherry is sold largely under brand names for which wine of consistent quality and character is required. To meet these requirements, a very elaborate fractional blending has been devised known as the 'solera system'.

3. The Solera System

The solera system may best be explained by describing the preparation of a fictitious wine. Suppose that it is desired to prepare 20 butts of a straight *fino* wine. The shipper has in his bodegas a collection of casks containing wine at different stages of maturity devoted to the preparation of this type of wine. The wine, which is mature and ready for use, is in a collection of butts known as the *solera*. If he is to withdraw 20 butts at once from the solera, he will need to have at least 50 butts of wine in the solera if the equilibrium of this system is not to be disturbed.

Let us suppose that he has 100 butts of wine in his solera and that they are kept 80% full, i.e. 80 butts of wine. He withdraws 20 butts for use. To keep the conditions uniform so that the character of his wine is not altered, he takes one-fifth of a butt (20%) of wine from each of the 100 butts, making 20 butts of wine in all. Each butt was 80% full, but is now only 60% full. This wine must be replaced almost at once, or not only will the stock of wine be depleted at each operation but the condition of the wine undergoing maturation in each cask will alter and the character of the wine will change. To supply this wine, the producer keeps a further stock of 100 butts of wine, also 80% full, which he calls his first *criadera*, and treats them in the same way, taking one-fifth of a butt of wine from each butt to make up 20 butts of wine, which he blends and uses to replace the wine in each cask in the solera. Evidently this operation will result in a deficiency of wine in the first *criadera*. This deficiency is rectified by taking wine from another collection, known as the second *criadera*, similar in every respect to the first *criadera* but being refreshed from yet another collection of butts known as the third *criadera*. In the case of a very high quality *fino* wine, there may be as many as six *criaderas* all operated in sequence. Even if there are as many as six *criaderas*, the question logically arises: 'how is the sixth *criadera* filled?'. The wine from the final *criadera* is obtained by selecting wines from suitable butts resting in the *añada* as already described. This wine is chosen from casks in the *añada* on their individual merits after a careful tasting and analysis. It will be evident that, in the case of a complex solera–*criadera* system, over 1,300 movements of wine are required to prepare 20 butts of the final product (Gonzalez-Gordon, 1948; Purser, 1968; Baker *et al.*, 1952).

The operation of a solera is not quite as simple in practice as it is described, for the wine does not mature at a steady rate and, to some extent, impresses its own rate upon the operation of the system. Wine must be drawn at suitable intervals from the system, whether it is required or not, or it will become over-mature and the character of the product will change. Furthermore, if too much wine is drawn off, the character will change again. Therefore, the producer must be in a position to anticipate demand for his product a long time in advance so that he can operate soleras of a suitable size. Further complications are caused by the fact that not all butts develop uniformly in spite of all of the precautions taken. Any exposure to slight draughts or currents of warmer air, or even vibration, will cause a variation, and butts will sometimes have to be over-, or under-drawn during the transfer operations. The wines from different seasons will not be uniform, and adjustments must be made when filling from the *criadera* with the highest number. Evaporation also takes place, so that the *criaderas* taking the younger wines would have slightly more butts than *criaderas* with the more mature product and the solera.

Once established, satisfactory solera–*criadera* systems are operated for many years. Some have been in operation for 60 years or more. To establish a new solera, it is necessary to obtain wine of various ages and to place in each *criadera* a wine of the degree of maturity it is expected will exist there when the new unit achieves equilibrium. This is extraordinarily difficult to do, so that it may be expected that wine drawn from a newly established solera will vary in character over a number of years until equilibrium is reached.

The solera–*criadera* system already described is typical of that producing a high quality *fino* which is still under flor. Similar soleras are also used for production of other types of sherry, but there are minor variations. A solera for *oloroso* sherry has fewer *criaderas*— probably three or four—since this type of sherry matures slowly. Obviously there is no flor, and the air space in each cask will be smaller. Due to the slow maturation, a smaller percentage of wine is involved at each operation and movements take place less often. In a *fino* solera of quality, a quarter of the wine might be moved every three months. In an *oloroso* solera, 15% might be moved every 12 months. Typically the behaviour of an *oloroso* solera is less uniform, and the operator must use considerable skill and judgment in deciding when and in what proportion to move the wine.

Raya sherries may be regarded as similar to *oloroso* sherries though of inferior quality. Although blended in a similar way, for economic reasons they obviously must be passed rather quickly through a solera of a few stages.

A further form of sherry which should be discussed here is the *amontillado*. This is a sherry which is first matured in a *fino* solera under flor and, when this maturation has been carried out, the wine has, either spontaneously or because of an extra fortification, lost its film of flor and been further aged in a second solera–*criadera* system. The original *fino* sherry rapidly loses its *fino* colour and character taking on a different colour and characteristic flavour quite distinct from that of an *oloroso* or a *fino*. It will be evident that genuine *amontillado* sherry must inevitably be a very expensive wine because of the very large amount of manipulation and time required for its production. A fine *amontillado* sherry may be passed through six *flor* criaderas and a *flor* solera, followed by six *amontillado criaderas* and an *amontillado* solera.

4. Sherry Flor

A detailed and comprehensive study of the sherry flor was carried out by Fornachon for the Australian Wine Board (Fornachon, 1953). This remains essential reading for anyone interested in the subject. He concluded that the base wine should be white, have little varietal character, and be fermented completely dry. The alcohol concentration should be adjusted to between 14.5% and 15.2% by volume. Its tannin content should be low and its pH value between 3.1 and

3.4. The sulphur dioxide content of the wine should be below 100 p.p.m. There should be a surface area for film growth of about 11 sq. inches per gallon wine (15 cm² per litre). The temperature should be between 15° and 20°C. The yeasts he used were apparently those classified by Spanish workers as *Saccharomyces beticus* (*Saccharomyces bayanus* or *Saccharomyces chevalieri*).

A similar but less detailed study was carried out by Cruess (1948), who recommended dry, white base wine of neutral flavour fortified to between 15% and 16% alcohol by volume. Other specifications listed by Cruess (1948) were: a sulphur dioxide content of 150 p.p.m., a pH value between 3.1 and 3.3, and a temperature between 18° and 24°C. He recommended that the process take place in 80% full oak casks of a capacity between 225 and 550 litres.

A related process, in which the yeast is distributed throughout the body of the base wine and air or oxygen is pumped in (the submerged flor process), is discussed in Section VI.D (p. 528), since this process is rarely, if ever, used commercially in the Jerez area of Spain.

5. *Sweetening and Blending*

All sherry is fermented dry, and is dry when it is matured in the *añada* and the solera, whether it be *fino*, *amontillado* or *oloroso*. *Fino* sherries are usually consumed dry or only very slightly sweetened but, outside the Jerez area, *amontillados, olorosos*, and particularly blends of more than one basic type, are usually sweetened. Some are made very sweet with Baumé values up to 6° (up to 10° Balling). Even in Jerez, the *olorosos* and *amontillados* are often slightly adjusted by the addition of a judicious amount of sweetening material. Traditionally, those wines made very sweet are also darkened in colour by the use of colouring wines.

All but the very cheapest sherries are sweetened by the use of speciality sweetening wines, either PX or Mistela. The PX wine has an alcohol concentration of about 9% (v/v) and a Baumé value of 22° (40° Balling). It has a full colour and a strong characteristic flavour of the variety of grape from which it is made. Mistela, which contains about 13.5% (v/v) alcohol, has a Baumé value of about 8° (14.5° Balling). This is a lighter material which has a less intense varietal flavour.

Colouring is adjusted with a wine which has been very intensely darkened with a caramelized grape must. It has a Baumé value of about 13° (22° Balling) and an alcohol concentration of about 15% (v/v); also it has a very characteristic odour.

i. *Preparation of PX.* This wine is made exclusively from Pedro Ximenez grapes. The juice from these grapes has a Baumé value of about 16° (29° Balling). The freshly picked grapes are dried on straw mats in the sun for 10 to 20 days, being covered at night, until the Baumé value rises to around 32° (59° Balling). These sun-raisined grapes develop a strong and characteristic colour and flavour which are not present to any extent in the fresh grapes.

The grapes are then pressed using firstly horizontal presses of the Vaslin type. Due to the drying, the pressing is very difficult to carry out and the yield is poor. Should the grapes become over-dried, fresh PX grapes are added to adjust the gravity and facilitate pressing. The expressed juice is fortified to about 9% (v/v) alcohol and, after a period of rest in cask or in concrete tanks, it is passed into a special solera for aging. As far as possible, such a solera is operated in the same way as one for producing the dry sherry but, owing to the considerable non-uniformity in the development of PX, every cask in each *criadera* must be considered separately and, when wine is drawn from the solera, it is taken more or less from each individual cask in each *criadera* in making the blend of PX for topping up the next stage in the system.

Insufficient PX grapes are grown in the Jerez district to meet the demands for sweetening material, so that much PX wine must be obtained from the Montilla-Moriles district in the province of Cordoba. It is permissible at the moment to draw upon this source, but it is the declared aim of the Consejo Regulador of Jerez and Sanlucar de Barrameda to forbid this traffic when sufficient PX vines are planted in Jerez. Personal observations suggest that it may be many years before this aim is achieved.

ii. *Preparation of Mistelas.* Palomino grapes are used in the preparation of Mistela wine. Many of the installations where Mistela is produced also make colour wine, and it is therefore convenient to take only the free-run juice and first pressing for Mistelas, and use the second-pressing juice for the preparation of colour. The juice is blended in a tank (often in the tankers used to collect the juice from the pressing station) to produce a product with about 15% (v/v) alcohol and a Baumé value of 9° (16° Balling). The material is allowed to fall bright, and is then pumped into casks, or more often into concrete storage tanks. The product is aged for one or more years, but no attempt is made to pass it through a solera system as with all of the other constituents of the average sherry.

iii. *Preparation of colour wine.* Second pressings from the Palomino grapes, moscatel juices and, if this is insufficient, free-run and first-pressings of Palomino juice, are boiled in a copper or stainless-steel (usually wood-fired) boiler, the scum being scooped off until the volume is decreased to about one-fifth of the original. This gives a sticky, highly caramelized liquid with a Baumé value of about 37° (69° Balling). Meanwhile about 320 litres of Palomino must are allowed to begin fermenting in a new butt made of American oak. When the fermentation begins, some of the concentrate is added which slows down the fermentation. By judicious fresh additions of the caramelized material, when fermentation begins again, it is possible to add in all about 160 litres of the 5 : 1 concentrate before fermentation finally stops, by which time the wine has a Baumé value of about 12° (21.5° Balling) and a strength of about 8% (v/v) alcohol. The wine is fortified to about 15% (v/v) alcohol and aged in a solera. As with PX wine, development of the colour is somewhat irregular and the casks receive individual attention.

iv. *Blending for shipment.* Good *fino* wines are often the unblended product of one solera. The wine is fortified to about 16.5% (v/v) alcohol to stop the development of flor, and is then racked, fined and possibly very slightly sweetened with Mistela to bring the sugar content from about 1.4 g/l to about 2.5 g/l. The wine is fortified further if the market demands it. Most countries take the wine at about 20% (v/v) alcohol but, in England, it is often consumed at about 17.5% and in Spain at 16.5%.

Amontillado wines are taken completely dry and then very slightly sweetened as for *fino* in Jerez but, if shipped abroad, they are usually blended with sufficient PX or Mistela to bring the sugar content to between 10 and 30 g/l. They contain about 18% (v/v) alcohol in the solera, and may be left at this strength or brought up to 20% by fortification.

Medium sherries may be blended from *fino*, genuine *amontillado, oloroso, raya*, PX, Mistela and colour wine. The strength and sweetness are as for the *amontillado* sherry. *Oloroso* sherries are consumed in Jerez almost dry, as are *amontillado* wines. For consumption abroad, they are usually sweetened to at least 30 g sugar/l with PX and the strength brought to 20% (v/v) alcohol. Brown sherries are proprietary wines containing a large quantity of colour wine. They are usually very sweet, containing 80 g or more of reducing sugar/l.

Milk and cream sherries are proprietary wines. In the milk type, the emphasis is on *oloroso* sherry, colour wine and a large quantity of PX. They often contain more than 100 g reducing sugar/l. In blending cream sherries, the emphasis is on aged components; old *oloroso* sherry and often genuine *amontillado* sherry are used with especially fine PX. The reducing sugar content is usually over 100 g/l. They contain less colour wine (Webb and Kepner, 1962; Webb et al., 1964, 1966a, b, 1967).

6. Clarification and Stabilization for Shipment

Although the individual dry-sherry components and the Mistelas often reach a high degree of stability in their passage through their *criaderas* and *soleras*, often becoming completely free from unstable colour matter and protein, blending of the wines disturbs the equilibrium profoundly and the wine almost inevitably becomes cloudy. This is especially so when large quantities of PX wine and colour wine are used, as the composition of these components is markedly different from the rest of the blend.

As in other wine-growing districts, proteinaceous finings are used to remove unstable colouring matter and other materials closely allied to tannins. Egg whites are the traditional fining material for this purpose, between 4 and 20 whites per butt being used, but processed albumen may be used if very large quantities are being fined. Gelatin may be better if a particularly vigorous tannin removal is required. Charcoal may be used if the colour is to be lightened. There follows a second fining to remove unstable protein matter, whether inherent in the wine or resulting from over-fining with proteinaceous material. Approximately 200 grams of Spanish earth (tierra de Lebrija) is used with each butt; its action is similar to, but less powerful than, that of Wyoming bentonite, which is also used. During maturation of the dry sherries, there is often a loss of acidity.

This is particularly so with flor sherries as malic acid disappears and lactic acid is formed during passage of wine through a solera growing flor. There is some evidence that this process is not a simple malolactic fermentation by lactic acid bacteria as might be supposed, but is the result of a large number of reactions taking place during metabolism of the flor yeast. Food-grade citric acid is often used to replace the lost acid when blending takes place, except for wines destined for Germany. German wine law does not permit the use of citric acid, and tartaric acid is used in spite of the deleterious effect that it has on the future tartrate stability of the wine (Saavedra Garcia and Garrido, 1962).

These treatments are fairly successful in stabilizing the colouring matter and protein in the lighter coloured sherry blends. The final sherry, however, in spite of storage in the soleras, is usually unstable in that precipitation of tartrate often occurs. PX wine in particular often contains four times the normal quantity of tartrate. If PX wine is used for sweetening, enough tartrate will be present in all of the sweeter sherries to destroy completely the tartrate stability of the blend. For this reason, many shippers use refrigeration plants to stabilize the blend. The wine is chilled very rapidly to about $-9°C$, and the wine is maintained at this temperature in insulated tanks for 5 to 10 days. This length of treatment has to be adopted because it has been found that potassium hydrogen tartrate and neutral calcium tartrate tend to form super-saturated solutions in wine at low temperatures. The shock treatment is to induce the formation of crystal nuclei, and the extended holding period is employed to permit growth of these crystals. After the holding period, the wine is filtered, still at the low temperature, using diatomaceous earth. In spite of the presence of calcium ions from the gypsum during fermentation, the crystals thrown out are usually predominantly of potassium hydrogen tartrate (Berg, 1960b; Berg and Keefer, 1958, 1959).

B. Port Wine from the Douro Valley

1. Fortification

Fortification of port wine must be carried out with special brandy supplied for the purpose by the Casa do Douro or the Junta Nacional dos Vinhos. It is supplied at the strength of approximately 75% (v/v) alcohol, and is added to the must either in the cask or in vats. If the must is in a vat, it is drawn off into a tub after fortification and pumped in again at the top of the vat to cool and mix it. If fortified in a cask, it is simply roused (mixed) with a stick. Eighty-six litres of brandy are added to the must at approximately 6° Baumé in a 600-litre pipe (cask); 125 litres of brandy per 600-litre pipe are used for Jeropigas, and 50 litres of brandy per 600-litre pipe are used for musts with a Baumé value of 2°. The brandy is by no means neutral in character, and it imparts a character to the finished wine different from that produced if neutral alcohol is used. In recent years, a number of experiments have been made with neutral grape alcohol and satisfactory, if rather light, wine has been produced. These experiments have been conducted at Quinta de Santa Barbara and in association with certain port-wine shippers.

2. Maturation Procedures

After the vintage, the wine is stored in the installation in the valley of the River Douro throughout the winter. It is stored in wooden vats with a capacity of up to about 27,000 litres, cement tanks treated internally with tartaric acid, cement tanks with proprietary plastic linings, or matured 600-litre casks. Second-pressing wine is often stored in new casks to condition them. These containers are kept as full as possible, aeration being avoided. It is very cold in the Douro during the winter but, as the weather permits, the first racking is carried out between November and March, and the wine is fortified to a minimum of 18% (v/v) alcohol; more usually it is fortified to between 19 and 20.5%. The wine is not filtered at this stage.

When practicable, a high proportion of red wine is shipped at this stage to Vila Nova de Gaia in Oporto, but white wine is usually left in the Douro Valley rather longer, perhaps for several years, as it matures better whether used as a white port or for blending purposes when making a tawny port. The schedule of shipments of red and white varies from firm to firm. The practice in Vila Nova de Gaia also varies with different companies. Some companies rack the wine every three months for the first three years, but others only half as frequently. A little brandy, between one and two litres per pipe, is added at each racking to bring the strength eventually to about 21%

(v/v) alcohol. Certain speciality wines are made where the wine is stored for long periods up the valley of the River Douro. If the red wine is stored under these conditions for twelve years or so, a very concentrated liqueur type of tawny wine is produced. A few producers prefer to mature a considerable percentage of their red wines under the hotter conditions of the Douro Valley. The wine then takes on a rather different character (Jurd, 1969).

3. Blending

A large shipper may have several hundred individual lots of wine at his disposal immediately after the vintage. It is impracticable and unnecessary to mature every one of these wines separately and, therefore, over the next two years the shipper will gradually blend these wines together to produce the comparatively few types of wine (perhaps no more than a dozen) which he needs to incorporate in his blend. If any of the wine is to be put on the market as vintage wine, this wine must be set aside for this purpose at an early stage.

The wines not destined to be marketed as vintage port are destined to be blended with wines of other years to make 'basic blending wines', which the shipper mixes to produce the styles of wine which he puts on the market. The shipper, for instance, probably produces a basic blending wine for medium-tawny port. This might be composed of two parts of a three-year-old red wine, four parts of a four-year-old red wine and one part of a four-year-old white wine. These wines are mixed with an equal quantity of a similar wine in 'reserve' blended the year before, half of the wine so produced being left in the reserve for the following year and the other half being used as current stock. The new blend might consist of 50% of a basic wine blended as described, perhaps 20% of another basic wine similar to the first but rather more intense in colour, 10% of white Jeropiga, 5% of sweet white port and 10% of a dry tawny wine. It might seem rather odd to add sweet and dry wines to balance a port which was nominally of the right sweetness from the time of its initial fortification but, in practice, it is found that such a procedure adds to the richness and complexity of flavour. Most shippers would try to have at least two lots of each proprietary wine available, so that the blended wine is allowed to mature in wooden vessels in its final state for some months before the final stabilization and export.

It will be evident that this blending system is, in effect, a partial fractional blending system serving much the same purpose as the solera system in Spain, except that the wine is not allowed to lie on the lees in the reserve and therefore does not mature so rapidly. Attempts to let the wine lie on its lees have not been successful as the wine deteriorates under these conditions. The degree of fractional blending and the average age of the wine depend upon the size of these reserves in proportion to the annual amount of wine used. Obviously the reserve is proportionately much larger with expensive wines.

4. Sweetening and Blending Wines

As the fermentation of port is stopped when the appropriate Baumé value is reached, it is not necessary to use large quantities of sweetening wine as is the case when sweet sherries arc required. Nevertheless, the Baumé value of a wine falls during racking and fortifying operation, and it is sometimes necessary to adjust the sweetness slightly when the final blends are being prepared. For this purpose, the very sweet wines, known as Jeropiga, are prepared. Alternatively, a certain amount of concentrated grape must is used. The quality of this concentrate are carefully supervised by the Instituto do Vino do Porto. Colouring material is not permitted unless it consists of wines made from grapes which contain a large concentration of pigment.

i. *Preparation of Jeropiga.* Jeropigas are essentially ports which are prepared by fortifying must as soon as enough carbon dioxide has been evolved to lift the skins to the suface. It is obviously desirable that the Baumé value of the must selected should be as high as possible, normally between 12.5 and 14°. The juice is fortified until the strength is at 20% (v/v) alcohol. Either white grapes (*Jeropiga Branca*) or red grapes (*Jeropiga Loira*) are used. Formerly, when a very deeply coloured Jeropiga was required, *Jeropiga Tinta*, made from elderberries, was added, but this is no longer permitted. At present, if specially coloured material is required, half of the lagar is run off and treading is begun again with skins in contact with the other half of the wine. This process is known as 'repisa'.

ii. *Concentrate.* A little material is produced by concentrating grape must under vacuum; the Baumé value should reach around 40°.

Caramelization should not take place during the concentration. The concentrate is not fortified. This concentrate, which is produced by a very few specialist manufacturers, must be approved by the officials of the Instituto do Vinho do Porto before it may be used.

iii. *Blending for shipment.* a. *Vintage wine.* This is a deep-red full wine of the best available quality of a year, chosen for its special character and virtue. It is a blend of wines from the same year and is kept in wood for two or three years. The Baumé value of the wine is adjusted according to the house style, which would normally be between 3 and 4.5°. It is fortified to between 20 and 21.5% (v/v) alcohol. It is not filtered before bottling. The bottles must be closed with very high quality corks which are coated with wax or fitted with heavy capsules. They are then laid down to mature in a cool cellar for a number of years. Maturation should take between 10 and 15 years, but the wine will be drinkable within seven years. It will, however, often benefit by considerably longer periods of maturation in bottle.

b. *Ruby ports.* These are either wines of the vintage type which have a longer aging in wood to soften them further, but not sufficient to turn them into *tawny ports*, or lighter wines aged for a shorter period in wood and probably blended with a little white port. The aim is to prepare a very fresh fruity wine. These lighter wines usually contain a blend of wines which have been aged for between two and five years in wood. The wines are fined and refrigerated and expected to remain bright in bottle.

c. *White ports.* These are mainly blends of wine two to six years old, but very old white port was once popular in Scandinavia and Russia. Excessive aging can give the wine a tawny colour. Some are sold fairly dry for use as aperitif wines, but they may be shipped in a sweet condition as the corresponding tawny wines. There is also a small demand for special Muscatel-flavoured white port and for an extremely sweet white port sold under the name of Lacrima Christi.

5. *Clarification and Stabilization for Shipment*

The usual fining for port is gelatin which is used not only to give the wine great clarity and brilliance but also to make adjustments to the body and depth of colour. The final blend is fined after between four weeks and six months, before bottling and shipment. There is a tendency for shippers nowadays to prefer the shorter period of fining. Fifty grams or so of tannin are usually added to the pipe (550 litres) before gelatin is added in the form of a hot aqueous solution.

Traditionally, egg white has been used to fine port, and sometimes it still is. It is believed to be a superior fining by some shippers, but it seems to have no real advantage over the rational use of gelatin. Isinglass, sometimes in the form of patent finings, was popular one or two decades ago, but its use seems to have little advantage other than the fact that it is more difficult to over-fine the wine by the injudicious use of excess isinglass.

Ruby wines and the young tawny ports are difficult wines to stabilize, and the growing demand that they should remain bright in bottle has led many companies to adopt stabilization by refrigeration. The temperature of the wine is lowered rapidly to about −10°C and the wine is stored in insulated tanks for two weeks or rather less. A very large quantity of condensed anthocyanin pigments with a little tartrate, pectin and proteinaceous material, is deposited. The wine is then filtered while still cold using diatomaceous earth (kieselguhr), possibly with the aid of a centrifuge. It is usual to bring the wine back to ambient temperatures using a plate-type heat exchanger which precools the next batch of wine. Excessive refrigeration can cause loss of colour and body, and careful control is necessary at all stages.

The use of gum arabic or gum acacia in the wine to act as a colloid protector, replacing the natural gums and mucilages of the wines which are lost during clarification, has often been used. The method suffers from the disadvantage that only a very limited quantity of the material can be used if its flavour is not to be apparent, and that most filtration processes remove the material from the wine so that it must be added immediately before bottling.

Between 50 and 100 mg sulphur dioxide/l has a marked stabilizing effect if added to a finished blend, preferably just before bottling. However, different blends of port differ in their susceptibility to this compound. The flavour of the wine may be impaired so that much discretion must be exercised before the procedure is adopted.

C. Madeira

1. Fortification

Fortification of madeira is carried out with pure neutral grape spirit containing 95% (v/v) ethyl alcohol. It is prepared under government supervision and added to the wine under the supervision of a Customs official. The spirit is of excellent quality and would be considered good enough to use in the manufacture of vodka without further rectification. It is sold at a standard price, and may be purchased only on proof that must has been purchased. The purchaser may only obtain a supply to the extent of 11% of the volume which he has purchased of clear wine, i.e. having first deducted 10% off for lees. Since a good deal of this alcohol is needed to fortify must in the production of *surdo*, which requires some 33% by volume, some discretion must be used in the fortification of dry wine. In the case of dry wines containing 10–11% (v/v) alcohol, 6–8% alcohol by volume is usually added in the form of spirit. The producer must pay the expenses of the Customs officer who supervises the fortification. After fortification the wine is clarified with Spanish earth to put it into a suitable condition for the Esteufagem treatment.

2. Heating—Esteufagem

As soon as possible after fermentation and fortification is complete, the process of heating or Esteufagem is begun. More than 90% of the wine used for export is treated in this way. Most is treated in cement-lined tanks with a capacity of about 20,000 to 28,000 litres similar to the fermentation tanks. A sample is taken by the government Customs official who, after approving the wine, seals the maximum thermometer on the tank so that he can see the maximum temperature reached during the process. The tank is also sealed so that wine cannot be withdrawn or added during the process. The temperature is gradually raised over about two weeks, and is then maintained at the process temperature for a period of about three months. The process temperature varies according to the practice of the operator. It must not exceed 45°C by Portuguese law, but most shippers prefer a temperature of about 41°C.

At the end of three months' treatment, the temperature of the wine is allowed to fall. As it takes several weeks for the temperature in the tanks to fall, some shippers find it more economical to cool with refrigerated water. Before the wine can be drawn off from the tank, the seals are removed by the Customs official and the sample taken for Customs' tasting and analysis. Occasionally, the Customs require that wine be given an additional heat treatment before cooling. After the heat treatment, at the discretion of the shipper, some wines are drawn off into wooden butts and stored on the floor of the warehouse immediately above the heating tanks for a period of up to six months. This, in effect, gives the wine a second milder heat treatment which may be advantageous for some wines.

Some of the better quality wines, which are not available in lots of 20,000 litres, are heated in wooden butts in warehouse rooms, the temperature of which is raised by steam pipes. There is apparently little difference in the quality of the wine produced by heating in butts rather than in concrete tanks.

3. Further Maturation

The wine requires considerable fining after the heating process is carried out. If too much colour has been acquired during the heating process, a fining with bone charcoal is usually carried out, but this should not be overdone as flavour may be lost. Spanish earth, bentonite and isinglass are also used at this stage.

Shipment is permitted 13 months after Esteufagem, but this would only be for wines shipped at minimum prices. Such wines are occasionally shipped to France for use in the preparation of Madeira sauce. Wines of superior quality, such as those shipped to England and Scandinavia, are matured for not less than five years (Roessler and Amerine, 1973).

4. Sweetening and Blending

Most Madeira wine is stored in single vintage lots for the first two years; usually the *surdo* is not added at this stage. After about two years, most shippers like to blend the wines of different ages together and gradually sweeten them to obtain the type of wine they carry as basic house styles.

i. *Surdo*. This wine is made by fortifying very sweet musts with alcohol. About 33% (v/v) alcohol is usually added and this produces a wine with about 20–23% (v/v) alcohol and a gravity ranging from 8 to 16° Balling. This sweetening wine is subject to the Esteufagem process as is the dry wine. It is usually heated separately, but sometimes wines are blended before heating. Occasionally a sweet wine is not heated, and this produces a surdo of rather fresher flavour which is useful in preparing some types of blend. As far as possible, surdo is prepared from Porto Santo grapes as, owing to the warmer climate, these grapes are sweeter and a material with a higher density can usually be prepared.

ii. *Colouring*. Colouring wine is not usually prepared on the island of Madeira, but a caramelized wine, which has been prepared by evaporating must without vacuum until the concentration is increased at least threefold, is imported from Portugal.

5. *Clarification before Shipment*

Most Madeira wines are fined with isinglass and Spanish earth before shipment. Filtration through asbestos cellulose pads is frequently used. Owing to the considerable age of most of the wines, little stabilization against tartrate deposition is usually necessary, and refrigeration is rarely used (Pato and Amerine, 1959).

VI. FORTIFIED WINES FROM OTHER WINE-GROWING AREAS

A. Sherry-Style Wines

Fortified white wines, intended for consumption in the same way as Spanish sherry and usually sold with a geographical description followed by the word 'Sherry', are produced in many countries outside Spain. The Spanish sherry producers resent strongly the way in which the name of their product, which they claim is a variant of the name of Jerez, the chief centre of production, has been appropriated by so many other products. Some of these products are clearly intended to resemble quite closely the Spanish wine; in others, no attempt is made to produce the same type of flavour.

South African Sherry (Niehaus, 1963) is of interest because the methods used in its production are very similar to those used in Spain. The climate in which the grapes are grown is quite similar to that of the Jerez district in Spain, although the soils are rather different. Most of the grapes for South African sherry are grown on soils containing predominantly sandstone, and the soil is not alkaline.

Sherry is made in South Africa either from the Stein or Palomino grape. The Palomino grape appears to be identical with that used in the Jerez district. The Stein is rather more difficult to identify; it is said to be a bud sport of a European grape, possibly the Chenin Blanc. Its desirable characteristic is that, grown under similar climatic conditions to the Palomino, it produces a wine which is neutral in character. The pomace is at least as rich in sugar as that of the Palomino grown under similar conditions, while the total acidity is up to 50% greater.

Most sherry in South Africa is produced by one of several large organizations, notably a very efficient farmers' co-operative known as K.W.V. (Co-operative Winegrowers Association of South Africa Limited). Grapes designated for sherry production are fermented by the growers using a special yeast supplied by the co-operative. This yeast has been chosen because it is not only a good fermentation yeast but also gives rise to an excellent flor film under aerobic conditions when the alcoholic fermentation has been completed. The farmers conduct the alcoholic fermentation as if they were making table wine, adding about 100 p.p.m. of sulphur dioxide to the must and conducting the fermentation between 22°C–25°C.

When the wine is almost dry, it is placed in containers which are completely filled so that flor will not readily develop, and then supplied to the co-operative. Grapes from the cooler districts are picked to give a juice at about 12° Baumé, and are destined for flor sherries known in South Africa as 'Bleak wine'; those from the warmer districts are picked at about 13.5° Baumé and are used for the heavier wines, which in South Africa are known as 'Bruin wines'.

When the wine intended for flor sherry is received, it is fortified to 15.5% (v/v) alcohol and, without settling, placed in French oak casks with a capacity of 500 litres, 90% full. The flor forms in about two months. The wine remains under these conditions nominally for two years, or in practice nearer four years. The whole contents are then transferred to a 'solera'. The solera consists of groups of a single 1,800-litre cask and two 1,800-litre *criadera* casks. Groups of three casks are operated as a separate solera. The wine is not fractionally divided between many casks in the same *criadera* or solera as in Spain. Wine is drawn from the solera in 450-litre batches, so that the whole contents of the *'añada'* cask (including the lees) can be added to the *criadera*. The wine acquires a further eight years' average age in the *criadera*–solera system. Evaporation during this aging ensures that the alcoholic strength in these butts is too high for survival of much flor, and the wine acquires an intermediate *fino-amontillado* character.

When wine not intended to be matured under flor is received, it is fortified to 17% (v/v) alcohol and stored for about ten years in filled 500-litre oak casks. A solera system is not used. The sweetening wines used are Stein or Palomino mistelas fortified to 17% (v/v) alcohol and aged for up to ten years in full 500-litre American oak casks. Concentrated wines of the PX type are not made. Colour wines are made by mixing heat-concentrated grape juice with young sherries, and maturing for about ten years in full 500-litre oak casks.

Due to the very long period of aging in the two *criadera* and the solera casks, the wine becomes too strong, and the flor used does not survive in sufficient quantity to maintain reducing conditions, so that the characteristic flavours of Spanish *fino* wines are not produced. The eventual flavour of the wine is somewhat similar, but not identical, with that of a Spanish *amontillado* wine. Many of the heavier wines, because of their extensive aging in wood, acquire a flavour not dissimilar from that of many *oloroso* wines but, due to the absence of aged sweetening wines of the special types produced in Spain, the sweetened wood-aged wines which eventually reach the market are rather dissimilar in character from the corresponding Spanish wines.

In Australia most wineries, rather than specializing in one particular type of wine, produce a whole range including fortified wines of the sherry type, as well as brandy. Because there is a considerable market for brandy, it is usually possible for manufacturers of fortified wines to use only free-run juice for their white-wine base. The grape varieties used are usually the Palomino Paulo (Lustau) for the better types of sherry (this is believed to be the same as the Palomino of Jerez) and the Doradillo. The juice is extracted by placing crushed grapes in stainless-steel draining tanks overnight. Fermentation is always conducted with a cultured yeast. Normally these yeasts would not be *flor* yeasts which, if used, would be inoculated at a later stage. Brandy is produced at 96% (v/v) alcohol, and it is very neutral in character. Flor is grown on all dry and medium-dry sherries for a period varying from a few months to two years, depending upon the manufacturer. Most manufacturers grow the flor on sherry stored in small oak casks with a capacity of 275 litres, but a few use lined concrete tanks of about 1,000 litres' capacity. *Criadera–solera* systems are not used, and the flavours produced by the flor under these conditions are very different from those produced in Spain. Further aging is almost always given to the flor sherry in small oakwood casks usually for a period of one to three years. A small proportion of much older wine of excellent quality is used for sweetening. So-called sweet sherries are often quite different, and are often made from Muscatel grapes fortified before the fermentation is complete, frequently with comparatively little aging. Such wines can probably be more appropriately regarded as White-Port types than as Sweet Sherries (Allan, 1939).

B. Port-Style Wines

In Australia, port-style wines are also an important part of the domestic market. Port-style wine, i.e. wine produced by adding alcohol to a fermenting must while considerable sugar remains, thus retaining much of the fruity character of the grape, has always presented a problem. This is because the colouring in most grapes is contained in the cells which are in contact with the skins, and it is not readily extractable from these cells until the alcohol content has risen sufficiently to permeate the cell membranes. Unfortunately, about the time that the alcohol content has risen sufficiently to facilitate this extraction, the sugar content has fallen to a level at which fortification takes place. It is normal practice to separate the skins from the fermenting must before fortifying. If this is not done, a considerable amount of expensive alcohol is lost with the skins when they are removed. This would normally result in wines of rather poor colour. In Portugal, and to some extent in California, this difficulty is overcome by using special grape varieties, such as the Tinta Cao, which have a very intense colour, and also by the intensive working of the must during the early stages of fermentation by treading or other means (Olmo and Koyama, 1962).

In other wine-growing areas, intensely coloured grapes of this type are not available, and it is uneconomic to tread the grapes or submit them to the intense manipulation which is normally carried on in the Douro. To overcome these difficulties, in many areas, alternative forms of colour extraction have been adopted. This colour extraction is normally achieved by some heating process which breaks down the cells near the skins to release the colouring matter. Primitive heating processes have been used in California for some years for production of a cheaper type of red wine (Berg, 1940). Recently, more sophisticated apparatus has been developed for colour extraction for red wines in Europe, and this type of apparatus, which is usually known as a thermovinification apparatus, has been adopted quite widely in Australia for production of port-style wines (Prass, 1974; Kolarovich, 1974). In addition, some experiments are being made with the same type of equipment in the Douro Valley, although it is believed that fully satisfactory Douro wines have not yet been produced by this method. Grapes used for preparing such wine include the Grenache, the Carignane and the Shiraz.

Several thermovinification systems have been tried. In one system, the grapes are destemmed and crushed, sulphur dioxide is added and the must pumped into a holding tank where the skins and juice are very thoroughly mixed to prevent separation. The must is then pumped through a special heater where its temperature is raised to 63°C, and it is then maintained in a tank with an agitator for a period of 30 minutes. The must is then run into a drainer. In a drainer, the juice is removed and the hot skins are pressed. The skins are treated in two continuous presses in series, the produce from the second continuous press being kept separate and used for distillation. The juice after thermovinification treatment is cooled to a temperature of 15°C–18°C, and the fermentation then begun. Port produced in this way has nearly as much colour as that produced by the conventional method. It is clean, and is said to show a mellow and round palate. However, it is not identical with port produced by the traditional system, although it is an acceptable product. Alternative thermovinification systems, in which the free-run juice is partially separated from the skins, then heated by a heat exchanger, poured back after heating over the skins and passed through a maturation tank, have also been tried, apparently with some success.

As well as thermovinificated port, wine produced by the more conventional process is also made in Australia in some quantity, and a smaller quantity from the finest grapes is aged for a considerable time in wood to produce a premium product. In South Africa some good-quality port has also been treated in a way similar to vintage port in the Douro Valley, being bottled after two years in wood. In California, for production of red port, there has been considerable interest in the use of new varieties of red grapes, specially developed to produce considerable quantities of pigment in the warmer grape-growing areas, such as Royalty and Rubired (Olmo and Koyama, 1962). In addition, there is some interest in producing white ports. These are produced from free-run juice of almost any white grapes, probably largely the Thompson Seedless, with about 100 p.p.m. sulphur dioxide being added and 2–3% (v/v) yeast starter. Sometimes, almost no fermentation is allowed before the must is fortified, when the wine is often referred to in California as 'angelica' wine. If fermentation continues to about 6° or 7° Baumé, as in the white ports of the Douro area, the wine is referred to as 'white port'. It is traditional either to decolorize this wine with charcoal or to store it in large inert tanks so that the wine picks up the minimum possible colour and is almost water-white when bottled.

Rather more interesting wines of this type are produced from Muscatel grapes, such as the Muscat Fontignon and the Muscat of Alexandria. These grapes produce rather large amounts of sugar; they are crushed and destemmed and about 100 p.p.m. of sulphur dioxide added as before, together with about 2% by volume of a pure yeast culture, but the skins are not separated for something like 24 hours to allow the maximum possible muscat flavour to be extracted from the grapes. Similar muscat wines are produced in many other wine-producing regions, and are often very popular.

C. Madeira-Style Wines

The Madeira process is less often imitated outside that island, with the notable exception of California where most of the wines sold under the name of sherry are produced by a similar heating process. These are known as California Baked Sherries, or simply as California Sherry (Amerine and Joslyn, 1964). The grape of preference for producing California sherry seems to be the Palomino, but the

Thompson Seedless, which is very readily available in California, is also often used, as are a number of grapes intended primarily for table use, such as the Malaga and the Emperor. The grapes are crushed and destemmed in a Garolla-type crusher, sulphur dioxide is added, and usually only the free-run juice is used. Fermentation is conducted in very large tanks, often of 227,500 litres' capacity or more, at temperatures of about 27°C. The wine is usually fermented to dryness. The wine is fortified to approximately 20% alcohol by volume with pure neutral grape spirit, settled, and prepared for the baking process. Before baking, sweetening material is added to bring the reducing sugar content to about 20 mg/litre. This usually takes place in tanks of about 227,500 litres' capacity. The temperatures used are somewhat variable, but are normally between 55°C–60°C, and the times of baking extend from about 6 to 20 weeks. The current tendency is for the temperature to be somewhat lower, even as low as 49°C. A few premium quality producers age the baked product in small oakwood casks; the majority give little further aging, and such aging as takes place is carried out in inert tanks (Brown and Nightingale, 1949; Mattick and Robinson, 1960a, b; Crawford, 1952; Ehlers, 1952).

D. Submerged Flor-Style Wines

An interesting development has been the tendency of a number of producers to modify the flavour of their baked sherry by incorporating a proportion, most often about 10% (v/v) but, in some cases, considerably more, of sherry made by the submerged flor process and subsequently aged in small oakwood. The intention presumably is to impart a more complex flavour to the finished blend.

Submerged flor sherry is produced by inoculating the base wine, which as in the case of base wine for the flor-film process should be a neutral flavoured, low tannin, dry white wine at a pH value of 3.1–3.4, with a suitable yeast, and then promoting growth of the yeast by injecting air or oxygen, usually under pressure and with vigorous agitation. Over a period of weeks, the flavour of the wine is modified and comes to resemble that of flor-film sherry. As with the flor process, acetaldehyde is produced, but the concentration achieved is usually much higher than in the film process. The earliest published experiments on this process were undertaken in Canada (Crowther and Truscott, 1955a, 1957).

The yeast originally used was of the *Saccharomyces bayanus* type and was isolated from flor-film in Spain. The wine was circulated with considerable violence, in one experiment for four minutes at 13-minute intervals for 21 days. Air was not introduced but the 180-litre containers were only half full (Castor and Archer, 1957). By 1960, commercial trials were being made in California using Palomino sherry material at 14.5% (v/v) alcohol. Production was in a 20,000-litre container with a 15% headspace, and the temperature 18°C. A 10% inoculation of *Saccharomyces beticus* was used and a pressure of 14.2 p.s.i. was maintained. The wine was agitated three times a day for 20 minutes over a period of 6 to 7 weeks. Experimental production continued (Ough and Amerine, 1958; Ough, 1961).

A special type of fermenter for the conversion was designed and patented in Spain (Cabezudo *et al.*, 1968) but seems not to have been used in Jerez except experimentally as a means of treating acid wines. It is not easy to obtain reliable information, but the submerged flor process seems not to have been used on an extensive commercial scale in the U.S.A. until about 1970. It is still probably not used in South Africa or Australia. It is however used in Russia and other wine-making countries in Eastern Europe (Kozub *et al.*, 1972). It is believed to have been in use in Great Britain for some years to produce a sherry-like beverage from imported grape must.

VII. FLAVOURED FORTIFIED WINES

A. Vermouth

Vermouth has been defined (Anon, 1974) as an 'aromatized wine which must incorporate aromatic substances and bitter plants from which it derives its specific qualities'. It is used largely as an aperitif, either straight or mixed with various potable spirits. Aromatized wines have been popular in Mediterranean countries since classical times. In the middle of the Nineteenth Century, the North of Italy, mainly around Turin, and the Chambery district of France, both areas close to mountains where suitable herbs may be found, became established centres of herb production for vermouth. The French vermouths are traditionally white, rather dry and with a fairly intense aromatic flavour derived from the botanical ingredients. Italian vermouths are more variable, red or white, sweet or dry, with a rather less intense aromatization. Nominally, similar products are prepared in most wine-producing areas. The essential requirements of the base wines are that they should be sound, neutral and cheap. For example, for Italian vermouths, wine from the Emilia district is popular. This is a fairly neutral wine with 10–11% (v/v) alcohol and a low acidity (as tartaric acid) of 0.5–0.6% v/v. It is prepared largely from the Ugni Blanc grape. Rather stronger wines with lower acidities are obtained from the Puglie district, and low-acid wines with 13–15% (v/v) alcohol from Alacamo in Sicily. This last wine is often somewhat oxidized, which gives it a characteristic flavour that is desirable in the finished vermouth. The Trebbiano and Apulia wines are very heavily fined with gelatin, bentonite or charcoal, to take away much of the characteristic flavour. Many Italian producers use refined beet sugar for preparation of the vermouth, although in France mistelas (fortified grape musts) are preferred. Caramel is an important constituent and is carefully prepared, often by relatively small-scale producers operating by traditional methods. The flavour must be extracted from the plant materials chosen, usually by a maceration process. The plant material is covered by a mixture of wine and alcohol in a tank for several weeks with occasional agitation. The liquid is drawn off, and the plant material pressed to recover further liquid. Details of the extraction processes differ among the various manufacturers, and in general they do not disclose their methods in full. Nor do they divulge the composition of the botanical ingredients they use. Some companies use a type of fractional blending system to maintain consistency in the composition of the botanical extract. It is believed that the more important botanical ingredients include common wormwood, coriander, cloves, chamomile, dittany of Crete, orris and quassia. After blending, the mixture undergoes a short aging period and either refrigeration or ion-exchange stabilization. About 100 p.p.m. of sulphur dioxide is added, and it may be flash pasteurized or hot-bottled (Rizzo, 195 ; Valaer, 1947b; Pilone, 1954; Anon, 1958; Anon, 1974).

B. California Natural Flavoured Wine

In addition to classical-type vermouths, a new style of flavoured high-alcohol wine was introduced in the United States of America in 1957. This natural type of proprietary wine is prepared from neutral-base wine without distinctive grape varietal aroma. The base wine is fortified with high-proof fractions of wine distillates which are themselves composed only of ethanol without other congeneric flavours and odours. The resulting neutral fortified wine is converted into dessert or aperitif wine by addition of defined (but often secret) natural flavours and then sweetened. These wines enjoy great popularity since they approximate some mixed drinks or cocktails. They can be purchased, somewhat inexpensively, because they are taxed as fortified wine rather than as distilled spirits. In the U.S.A., consumption of many products of this type has been spectacular, from practically zero to over 40 million litres per annum ten years later. Since 1967, sales have declined somewhat, probably because of the competition, also spectacular, from another new type of wine introduced at this time, namely, the special natural flavoured wines with low concentrations (9–10%) of alcohol.

VIII. TECHNOLOGY OF FORTIFIED WINES

A. Biological Spoilage of Fortified Wines

Generally, fortified and aperitif wines are immune from microbiological instability because of their high concentration of alcohol. Most wine yeasts lose any substantial fermentation capabilities at 14–15% (v/v) alcohol. Growth of acetic-acid bacteria is also inhibited in this range of alcohol concentrations. Above 16% (v/v) alcohol, it is very rare and difficult to obtain a secondary fermentation in sweetened wines, although a wine-maker probably should exercise caution and use sterile conditions at all alcohol concentrations lower than 18% (Phaff and Douglas, 1944; Rankine, 1966). *Fino* sherries, commonly bottled at 17% (v/v) alcohol, occasionally undergo fermentation in bottle. Most lactic-acid bacteria are also inhibited by high concentrations of alcohol, but several exceptions can be given. The most notorious of these is *Lactobacillus trichodes*, sometimes called the cottony mould or the hair bacillus (Fornachon *et al.*, 1949). These trivial appellations come not only from the appearance as a ball of cotton or hair in an infected fortified wine, but also from the microscopic appearance of the cells which appear as extremely long interwound rods. This organism is easily controlled by judicious use of sulphur dioxide. In all of the reported instances, whenever spoilage by the organism has occurred, it has also been found that some aspect of good winery practice has been neglected. A special situation has been noted in the U.S.A. where transportation of California port wine to the East Coast of the country is of long duration. With some delay in transport, there is a real possibility of loss of all free sulphur dioxide in the wine by the time it reaches its destination. With even further delays before the wine can receive proper prebottling attention, especially in warm weather, spoilage by *L. trichodes* has sometimes occurred. The wines which had remained properly stored in California retained their high quality. There is also a report of isolation of pediococci and bacilli from some high-alcohol wine (Gini and Vaughan, 1962), but we are not aware of any serious spoilage problems of this sort. Individual casks of sherry often show high concentrations of volatile acidity, but living bacteria usually cannot be isolated from such wines, and it is thought that the acetic acid must be derived from contaminated wood which is not always detectable when the casks are filled. Port wine, stored for too long in contact with fining lees, becomes infected with lactic-acid bacteria, which frequently produce a diacetyl flavour (Fornachon, 1943).

B. Fortifying Alcohol

Most dessert wines are fortified with grape alcohol, which has been distilled to about 96% by volume. This has been chosen as a comparatively cheap product, neutral in character, which increases the alcoholic content of the wine without contributing any strong flavour other than that of increased ethyl alcohol to the resultant beverage. In contrast, port wines are fortified with a grape spirit distilled to about 75%, which has a marked flavour of its own. One of us (R.W.G.) has, with the permission of the Portuguese authorities, tried the effect of using pure neutral grape-spirit in fortification of port wines. Initially the result was very pleasing, the experimental wine being lighter and more elegant than the control but, as the wine was matured in small wood, it was found that the wine fortified with 75% alcohol was becoming more characteristically port-like and complex in odour, whereas the experimental wine seemed thin and in comparison resembled slightly fortified table wine. This no doubt accounts for the legal requirement that port wine be fortified with 75% grape alcohol and that it be matured for three years before sale. Most wine-producing countries insist that the high-proof neutral spirits used for fortifying wines should be prepared from grapes. There seems to be no good reason for this since spirits distilled from cane, potatoes or molasses are often of equal quality (Berard *et al.*, 1958; Filipello, 1951; Guymon and Amerine, 1952; Webb, 1951; Caputi *et al.*, 1967; Pool and Heitz, 1950).

REFERENCES

Allan, H. M. (1939). *Australian Brewing and Wine Journal* 58, 31, 70.
Amerine, M. A. and Joslyn, M. A. (1964). 'Dessert, Appetizer and Related Flavoured Wines', University of California, U.S.A.
Amerine, M. A., Berg, H. W. and Cruess, W. V. (1967). 'The Technology of Wine Making', 799 pp. The Avi Publishing Co. Inc., Westport, U.S.A.
Anon (1958). *Wines and Vines* 39, 41.
Anon (1974). *Review Vinicole Internationale* 1, 32.
Baker, G. A., Amerine, M. A. and Roessler, E. B. (1952). *Hilgardia* 21, 389.
Berg, H. W. (1940). *The Wine Review* 8, 12.
Berg, H. W. (1960a). *Wines and Vines* 4, 16.
Berg, H. W. (1960b). *American Journal of Enology and Viticulture* 11, 123.
Berg, H. W. and Keefer, R. M. (1958). *American Journal of Enology and Viticulture* 9, 180.
Berg, H. W. and Keefer, R. M. (1959). *American Journal of Enology and Viticulture* 10, 105.
Bobadilla, G. S. de (1943). *Agricultura, Madrid* 12, 203.
Bobadilla, G. S. de (1944). *Agricultura, Madrid* 9, 358.
Bradford, S. (1969). 'The Englishman's Wine. The Story of Port', 208 pp. Macmillan, London.
Brémond, E. (1957). 'Techniques Modern de Vinification', 296 pp. La Maison Rustique, Paris.
Brown, E. M. and Nightingale, M. S. (1949). *Wines and Vines* 11, 17.
Cabezudo, M. D., Llanguno, C. and Garrido, J. M. (1968). *American Journal of Enology and Viticulture* 19, 63.
Caputi, A., Ueda, M. and Brown, T. (1967). *American Journal of Enology and Viticulture* 19, 60.
Carrasco, J. M. Q. (undated). El Xerez de Siempre il Unas Notas divulgadoras sobre el Empteo enologico de Yeso, Jerez.
Casas-Lucas, J. F. (1967). '2^e Symposium Internationale d'Oenologie', Vol. 2, p. 495. I.N.R.A., Paris.

Castor, J. C. B. and Archer, T. E. (1957). *Applied Microbiology* 15, 56.

Chaffey, W. B. (1940). *Australian Brewing and Wine Journal* 58 (9), 33; (10), 31; 11, 31.

Crawford, C. (1952). *Proceedings of the American Society of Enologists* 2, 76

Crowther, R. F. and Truscott, J. H. L. (1955a). *Report of the Horticultural Experiment Station and Products Laboratory, Vineland, Ontario*, 75.

Crowther, R. F. and Truscott, J. H. L. (1955b). *Canadian Journal of Agricultural Science* 35, 211.

Crowther, R. F. and Truscott, J. H. L. (1957). *American Journal of Enology and Viticulture* 7, 91.

Cruess, W. V. (1948). 'Investigations of the Flor Sherry Process', 38 pp. Bulletin 70, University of California.

Ehlers, H. (1951). *Proceedings of the American Society of Enologists* 2, 207.

Feduchy, M. E. (1956). *Boletin de Instituto Nacional de Investigaciones Agronomicas* 35, 211.

Feduchy, E. and Sandoval, J. A. (1960) Boletin de Instituto Nacional de Investigaciones 42, 960.

Filipello, T. (1951). *Proceedings of the American Society of Enologists* 1, 154.

Fornachon, J. C. M. (1943). 'Bacterial Spoilage of Fortified Wines', 126 pp. Adelaide, Australia.

Fornachon, J. C. M. (1953). 'Studies on the Sherry Flor', 139 pp. Adelaide, Australia.

Fornachon, J. C. M., Douglas, H. C. and Vaughan, R. H. (1949). *Hilgardia* 19, 129.

Freiberg, K. J. and Cruess, W. V. (1955). *Applied Microbiology* 3, 208.

Gini, B. and Vaughan, R. H. (1962). *American Journal of Enology and Viticulture* 13, 20.

Gonzalez-Gordon, M. (1948). 'Jerez-Xerez-Scheris', 605 pp. 2nd edition. Jerez, Spain.

Gonzalez-Gordon, M. (1972). 'Sherry, the Noble Wine', 237 pp. Cassell, London.

Goswell, R. W. (1968). *Process Biochemistry* 3 (2), 47.

Goswell, R. W. (1972). *Process Biochemistry* 7 (10), 27.

Guymon, J. F. and Amerine, M. A. (1952). *Wines and Vines* 39 (9), 19.

Inigo-Leal, B., Vazquez Martinez, D. and Arroyo Varela, V. (1963). *Revista Ciencia Aplicada* 93, 317.

Jeffs, J. (1970). 'Sherry', 268 pp. 2nd edition. Faber and Faber, London.

Jerez-Xerez-Sherry (1964). Regulations for the Denominations of Origin 'Jerez-Xerez-Sherry' and 'Manzanilla–Sanlucar de Barrameda' and the regulating Council.

Johnson, H. (1971). 'The World Atlas of Wine', 272 pp. Mitchell Beazley, London.

Jurd, L. (1969). *American Journal of Enology and Viticulture* 20, 191.

Kepner, R. E., Webb, A. D. and Maggiora, L. (1958). *American Journal of Enology and Viticulture* 19, 116.

Kolarovitch, G. (1973). *Second Wine Industry Technical Conference, Tanunda*, p. 47. Australian Wine Research Institute, Adelaide.

Kozub, G. I., Averbukh, B. Ya. and Koreisha, M. A. (1972). *Sadovod Vinograd Vinodel Mold* 27 (8), 26.

Marques Gomes, J. V. (1949). *Anais do Instituto do Vinho do Porto* 1, 51.

Marques Gomes, J. V. and Lourenco de Castro Reis, A. M. (1962). *Anais do Instituto do Vinho do Porto* 19, 7.

Marcilla, J., Alas G. and Feduchy, E. (1939). *Anal do Centro Investigacione do Vinicultura* 1, 1.

Mattick, L. R. and Robinson, W. R. (1960a). *Food Technology* 14, 30.

Mattick, L. R. and Robinson, W. R. (1960b). *American Journal of Enology and Viticulture* 11, 113.

Niehaus, C. J. G. (1963). *Harper's Wine and Spirit Gazette*, 26th April, p. 613.

Olmo, H. P. and Koyama, A. T. (1962). *The California Agricultural Experiment Station Bulletin*, No. 789, 1.

Ough, C. S. (1961). *Applied Microbiology* 9, 316.

Ough, C. S. and Amerine, M. A. (1958). *American Journal of Enology and Viticulture* 9, 111.

Pachedo de Azevedo, M. and Pereira, J. (1957). '2ᵉ Symposium Internationale d'Oenologie', Vol. 2, p. 481. I.N.R.A., Paris.

Pato, G. M. and Amerine, M. A. (1959). *American Journal of Enology and Viticulture* 10, 110.

Phaff, H. J. and Douglas, H. C. (1944). *Fruit Products Journal* 23, 332.

Pilone, F. J. (1954). *American Journal of Enology and Viticulture* 5, 30.

Pool, A. and Heitz, J. (1950). *Proceedings of the American Society of Enologists* 1, 101.

Prass, G. (1973). *Second Wine Industry Technical Conference, Tanunda*, p. 45. Australian Wine Research Institute.

Purser, R. E. (1968). *American Journal of Enology and Viticulture* 18, 175.

Rankine, B. C. (1966). *American Journal of Enology and Viticulture* 17, 82.

Rankine, B. C. (1972). *Australian Wine, Brewing and Spirit Review* 90 (11), 52.

Rizzo, F. (1955). 'La Fabricazione del Vermouth', 99 pp. Bologna, Italy.

Roessler, E. B. and Amerine, M. A. (1973). *American Journal of Enology and Viticulture* 24, 176.

Saavedra Garcia, I. and Garrido, J. (1960). *Agricultura, Madrid* 336, 1.

Twight, E. H. and Amerine, M. A. (1938). *Wines and Vines*, February, 5.

Valaer, D. (1947a), 'Sherry Wine, Methods of its Production and Analysis of Spanish and American Sherry Wine', 30 pp. U.S. Treasury Department Miscellaneous Publications.

Valaer, D. (1947b). 'Vermouth and Other Aperitif Wines', 12 pp. U.S. Treasury Department Miscellaneous Publications.

Villa Lobos Machado, C. D. (1950). 'Qu'est ce que le vin de Purto', 68 pp. Oporto, Portugal.

Webb, A. D. (1951). *Proceedings of the American Society of Enologists* 1, 148.

Webb, A. D. and Kepner, R. E. (1962). *American Journal of Enology and Viticulture* 13, 1.

Webb, A. D., Kepner, R. E. and Maggiora, L. (1964). *American Journal of Enology and Viticulture* 15, 1.

Webb, A. D., Kepner, R. E. and Galetto, W. G. (1966a). *American Journal of Enology and Viticulture* 17,1.

Webb, A. D., Kepner, R. E. and Maggiora, L. (1966b). *American Journal of Enology and Viticulture* 17, 247.

Webb, A. D., Kepner, R. E. and Maggiora, L. (1967). *American Journal of Enology and Viticulture* 18, 190.

8. Gin and Vodka

A. C. SIMPSON

Research and Development Department,
International Distillers and Vintners Limited,
Harlow, Essex, England

I. INTRODUCTION

Gin, vodka, and related spirits like aquavit, are distinguishable from whisky, rum and brandy, which themselves have a number of common characteristics. The most evident difference is in colour, with gin and vodka normally being colourless while whisky, rum and brandy vary in shade from straw-coloured to the deepest brown. This immediate difference is linked with distinguishing features of composition and flavour, which are reflected in the methods of production of the two groups of spirits.

The colour in whisky, rum and brandy owes its origin to the practice of ageing or maturing these spirits in wooden casks, which as containers have previously been used for transporting some compatible liquid such as sherry, wine or molasses. Residues of the previous contents, together with substances extracted from the wood itself, serve to give the maturing spirit a brown colour which, in the interest of standardization, is supplemented by the addition of caramel. The requirement for maturation in wood is now codified in long-standing distillery practice and, in many countries, has been absorbed into statute. But, in discovering and developing the ameliorating effects of storage in wood, our ancestral distillers were seeking ways to improve the flavour of newly distilled spirit which, doubtless, was harsher and more fiery than the new distillates of today. The gin and vodka group of spirits may be seen to have arisen from similar motivation. Instead of improvement by maturation in wood, gin spirit was improved or disguised by blending and redistillation with flavouring herbs, while vodka evolved through the technique of purification based upon treatment with charcoal. From this theory of common origin, the two principal distinguishing features of these two groups of spirits can be identified:

(1) Whisky and its related group are aged, generally in wood, after distillation, whereas gin and vodka may be made from new spirit which requires no ageing.

(2) Spirits for gin and vodka have no requirement for flavours derived from congenerics in the distillate, which originate in the raw material or are formed in processing and pass through the still. Such congenerics, however, make up an essential part of the flavour of whisky and its group of spirits.

There are clearly exceptions to these rules. Geneva, for example, owes its special flavour to a strongly congeneric flavoured spirit and, like the high-quality German grain spirits, undergoes some ageing after distillation. From the other spirit group, white rum overlaps in being very pale in colour, or colourless, like gin and vodka. Its flavour may be modified by processing through charcoal, and it is either aged in wood for a shorter period than classic rum or not at all, although it does, of course, have to meet a statutory age requirement in some markets.

As gin and vodka do not depend significantly on congeneric flavouring in the spirit, resulting from specific raw materials and methods of processing, manufacturers of gin and vodka are able to choose spirit on grounds of quality and economics rather than precedent. The spirit for gin and vodka can be regarded as a raw material in a way that has no counterpart in the congeneric or self-flavoured spirits where a fermentable starting material is traditional and the conditions of fermentation and distillation are prescribed. Spirit for gin has traditionally been of grain source, although molasses spirit can be used if it is sufficiently good in quality and neutrality. Vodka is made from spirit of various sources, though mainly of grain and potato, with the cost and availability of these raw materials being important factors. Resulting from this flexibility of choice and the requirement for a spirit of good quality and neutrality, gin and vodka manufacturers have been able to take advantage of recent advances in spirit technology, such as the introduction of fungal and bacterial enzymes to replace malt in the conversion of starch, and the use of multicolumn continuous stills. Innovations and developments such as these have been responsible for a great improvement in the quality, purity, and production yields of neutral spirits and, consequently, have had an important influence on the quality of gin and vodka.

Within this generalized grouping of gin and vodka, which in the commercial jargon is recognized and categorized as 'white spirits', it is possible to define the individual spirit types of gin, geneva, grain spirit, vodka and several others. The term 'gin', in the broadest context, can be applied to any spirit made from a relatively pure base alcohol of fermentation origin which bears the flavour of a number of plant materials or botanicals, the most important being juniper. Indeed, the significance of juniper to gin and geneva can be estimated by the derivation of these names from the French word for juniper, namely genièvre. The most important gins commercially are those described as 'London dry' and marketed as international brands by a number of London-based companies. The qualification 'London dry' does not necessarily mean that the gins are produced in or near London, although originally the distilleries were founded there and still produce a large proportion of the gin sold as 'London dry'. Several distillers have opened distilleries overseas where their gins are produced, under licence, from spirit and botanicals of equivalent quality and by a process which exactly reproduces the original. Gin produced in these distilleries has a common style based upon a uniform method of operation. The style of London dry gin can be attributed to a number of factors of which the quality of spirit, the selection and composition of botanicals, and the structure and operation of the still are the most important. In the past, when spirit distillation plant was simpler and knowledge of spirit making rudimentary, it was impossible to produce spirit which did not have a background flavour due to the presence of congenerics. The background of grain spirit was considered to be more compatible with the flavour of gin, but in London gin this was always secondary to the juniper and other added flavours (Simmonds, 1919). However, for traditional reasons, many distillers still choose a grain-based spirit for London dry gin. Apart from juniper, the other botanicals commonly used by distillers include coriander seeds, angelica root and orange peel, with lesser amounts of cassia or cinnamon bark, and many others.

Gin was first made in Holland, and the earliest reference is to Francisco de la Boe (Encyclopaedia Britannica, 1969) who distilled an 'essence de genième' for medicinal purposes in the Seventeenth Century. Gin was imported into England by soldiers returning from wars in the Low Countries, and popularized by the ascent to the throne of William of Orange in 1688. Since then gin has featured large in the history of English social life (Clutton, 1972). The accessibility of the spirit and the impossibility of controlling either its production or consumption over a period of two centuries led to excessive consumption and much misery, portraited in Rowlandson and Hogarth. Successive attempts at legislative control proved useless with the Gin Act of 1836, which caused a pamphleteer (Sabourn, 1738) to write 'Distillers as well as others subject to the survey of the Officers of Excise may truly be said in great measure to be deprived of their birthright', leading only to an increased illicit trade. The description of the gin of the period as a 'blue ruin' is suggested (Anon., 1974) to be due either to the cyanotic faces of the chronic alcoholic or to the poor quality of the product which, being oversaturated with essential oils, had a colloidal bluish tinge. In the latter half of the Nineteenth Century, Victorian sense of order and respectability succeeded in suppressing the excesses and abuses of earlier years, and gin came to be socially acceptable. This period coincided with the development of the London distilling houses which are well known today. Gin became exceedingly popular as a base for cocktails in the 1920s and, nowadays, is drunk with tonic water or mixed with vermouth as a martini.

Gins of the style—though not perhaps the quality—of London dry gin are made for local markets by a multitude of distillers. The methods of production approximate those of London dry gin in the better operations; however, much gin is produced locally by means of the addition of essential oils, obtained from an essence house, to the spirit.

Another distinctive type of gin of high repute, which if not of the same importance as London dry gin in international markets is known wherever the Dutch influence is strong, is geneva, sometimes referred to as Hollands gin or Schiedam gin because of its long-standing association with the Dutch town of Schiedam. Made according to methods and recipes which are as peculiar and traditional to the Dutch distilling trade as the formulae evolved across the North Sea are to London gin, geneva has many distinctive features not shared by other gins. These include a strongly flavoured base spirit and a flavour developed by maturation. With its stronger and more aromatic flavour, geneva is more properly consumed in the traditional way as a schnapps rather than as a cocktail base or a long drink.

Steinhäger and the German Korn and Doppelkorn form a bridge between the more flavoured London and Dutch gins and vodka, which is very low in any flavour except that of ethyl alcohol. Steinhäger is a traditional German spirit redistilled from a juniper-based distillate and neutral spirit. The juniper element in the flavour is very low compared with traditional gins. Similar products called Borovička are made in Hungary. Korn and Doppelkorn are good-quality grain spirits made in many small-scale distilleries in Germany by careful traditional methods. These products are not intended to be neutral spirits, and they retain a degree of self-flavouring resulting from batch and semi-continuous distillation systems. These grain spirit flavours, however, are agreeable and may be modified and improved by ageing.

Vodka, or Wodka, meaning little water in Russian, is recorded as being produced in Russia as early as the Fourteenth Century (Encyclopaedia Britannica, 1966). As produced today, it is intentionally a spirit where the predominant character is that of ethyl alcohol alone. To achieve this high standard of purity and flavour neutrality, only spirit of the highest quality is used to make vodka and, by additional processing, any residual substances are removed or decreased in quantity. In Poland and the U.S.S.R. there are several types of flavoured vodka such as Zubrovka which is flavoured with buffalo grass; Pertsovka, a hot chilli vodka; and Limonnaya and Vishnyovka, flavoured respectively with lemon and cherries (Latham, 1966). These are made by addition of these flavouring ingredients to the purified spirit. Some attention is given to the composition of water used to dilute the spirit to bottling strength, which is considered to be improved by the addition of sodium salts. In the West, vodka tends to be drunk like gin as a cocktail or long drink, whereas in Russia it is consumed like a schnapps.

Gin and vodka, like many food and beverage products, are subject to the national regulations which in the future are likely to be aligned with international legislation, for example, within the European Economic Community. In the United Kingdom, where spirits of the matured type are required to be certified for minimum age before sale, special provisions have been laid down for gin and vodka in the Customs and Excise Act of 1952. Under the terms of this Act, gin and vodka are classified as British compounded spirits, and can only be produced in registered premises under the supervision of Customs and Excise Officers; when removed from bonded premises for sale, they must have some identifiable quality to distinguish them from unlicensed immature spirit. For gin, this identity lies in the characteristic flavours acquired during the distillation, or in the official terminology 'rectification', to produce the gin. In the case of vodka, the problem of identification is less straightforward because vodka is unflavoured and therefore, in sensory terms, is insufficiently distinguishable from immature spirit. Vodka therefore, to be properly classified as a British compounded spirit, is compounded with some marker which has no effect on odour or taste but which is measurable analytically.

In the United States, standards of identity for distilled spirits are written into Federal legislation (Regulations under the Federal Alcohol Administration Act, Title 27, Code of Federal Regulations). Neutral spirits or alcohol is defined as distilled spirits distilled from any material at or above 190° U.S. proof (95% ethyl alcohol, by volume). Vodka is neutral spirit which, after reduction of strength to a specified range, is treated either with charcoal or in some other approved way so as to be without distinctive character, aroma or taste. Gin is classified as either distilled gin or compound gin and, for labelling purposes, may be further designated Dry gin, London dry gin, Hollands gin, Geneva gin or Old Tom, according to type. To qualify for the description 'distilled', a gin has to be 'a distillate obtained by original distillation from mash, or by the redistillation of distilled spirits over or with juniper berries and other aromatics customarily used in the production of gin, and deriving its main characteristic flavour from juniper berries'. A compound gin is obtained by mixing neutral spirits with distilled gin or gin essence or other flavouring materials customarily used to flavour in the production of gin, and drawing the main characteristic flavour from juniper berries.

Geneva and vodka are subject to definition in Germany (Begriffs-bestimmungen fur Spirituosen in der Fassung vom. 10, November 1956). Geneva is required to be made from grain saccharified with dried malt to which juniper berries are added before the final distillation, or alternatively by blending geneva distillates with spirit or grain spirit. The geneva distillate moreover is required to undergo some ageing. Vodka is a spirit made from alcohol which has been finely filtered or treated by some other special process. The resulting vodka must acquire a purity and mildness of flavour.

The total production of distilled spirits for consumption as alcoholic beverages was estimated for 1963 in the course of a World-wide survey of the fermentation industries by the International Union of Pure and Applied Chemistry (1966). The figure quoted in this report is eighteen million hectolitres, calculated as 100% ethyl alcohol. In compilation of these statistics, a difficulty was experienced in collating the reported figures as a result of differing national standards of volume and strength measurement. However, the global total is made up of the following production figures for individual countries, as millions of hectolitres of 100% ethyl alcohol: United Kingdom 3.6; United States 3.2; West Germany 1.6; France 0.5; and Japan more than 4.0. Figures for the production of distilled spirits in 1972 in the United Kingdom and the United States are available but, here again, transposition into common units is needed before comparisons can be made. These figures, with approximate conversion to the units of the International Union of Pure and Applied Chemistry survey, are: United Kingdom, 180.8 million proof gallons (4.6 million hectolitres) (Annual Abstracts of Statistics, Central Statistics Office, London, 1973); United States, 183.5 million tax gallons (5.4 million hectolitres) (Annual Statistical Review of Distilled Spirits Inst., Washington, D.C., 1972). World production of gin in 1972 is estimated at 31 million cases (approximately 1.2 million hectolitres on the scale of the International Union of Pure and Applied Chemistry), of which about half was produced in the U.S.A. Production of vodka outside the U.S.S.R. and Eastern Europe for 1972 is estimated to be 29 million cases (approximately 1.1 million hectolitres) with two-thirds being produced in the U.S.A. (International Distillers and Vintners Ltd., internal information). At best, rough estimates can be made of current vodka production in Poland (one million hectolitres) and the U.S.S.R. (about seven million hectolitres).

II. PRODUCTION OF SPIRIT FOR GIN AND VODKA

A. Raw Materials

The production of alcohol is not an intrinsic part of the process of manufacture of gin and vodka where a suitable high-quality spirit is selected and redistilled with flavouring materials or processed in some other way. The manufacturer of gin or vodka, therefore, may select a spirit to suit his purpose from a range of distilled neutral spirits. He may be motivated in his selection by a number of factors, among them the influence of any particular spirit-flavour quality on the ultimate quality of his product, or a marketing requirement to claim that his product is made from spirit from a particular origin, for example, grain. In general, however, it can be claimed that any fermentation-based spirit, correctly made and distilled in modern multicolumn stills, is likely to serve as a suitable base for the manufacture of the London dry style of gin, and for vodka.

Any material containing carbohydrate which can easily and economically be made available for fermentation can be considered as a suitable source material for spirit production. Such materials are generally rich in starch, which requires to be converted into a readily fermentable form, for example grain and potatoes, or in directly fermentable sugars, such as molasses. Other substrates for spirit production are important in particular regions; for example the waste sulphite liquors in the wood pulp industry (Suomalainen et al., 1968) while local limited production has been reported from such substrates as Jerusalem artichokes, pineapple juice and whey (Prescott and Dunn, 1940). A comparison of the content of fermentable carbohydrate in a variety of distillery raw materials and the weights required to produce one kilogram of pure alcohol are given in Table 1. The most important raw material of spirit for gin and vodka in the

Table 1

Comparative carbohydrate content of raw materials. After Suomalainen et al. (1968)

Raw material	Fermentable carbohydrate calculated as mono-saccharide			Quantity of raw material (kg) per kg alcohol (100%) produced	
	Percentage dry weight	Percentage whole weight	Percentage dry weight	Whole material	Dry weight
Beet molasses	80	50	63	4.2	3.4
Cane molasses	80	35	44	6.0	4.8
Potato	25	19	76	11.0	2.8
Barley	86	57	66	3.7	3.2
Rye	86	65	76	3.2	2.8
Wheat	86	66	77	3.2	2.8
Maize	87	67	77	3.1	2.7
Millet	88	67	76	3.1	2.7

United Kingdom and North America is maize, although potato spirit is widely used in Europe for aquavit, and in Poland and Russia for vodka. Many European distilleries are equipped to handle and ferment both grain and potatoes. The German grain spirits, Korn and Kornbranntwein, are made in specific distilleries in a traditional way, mainly from rye (Laatsch and Sattelberg, 1968). In the past, large quantities of industrial spirit were produced from fermentation alcohol, principally made from molasses and potatoes. Except in less developed countries, this source of industrial spirit has been largely superseded by synthesis from ethylene.

B. Production from Grain

The system of spirit production in a grain distillery encompasses a number of discrete stages, namely grain storage and handling, cooking and conversion, fermentation and, finally, distillation and by-product recovery. The efficiency of each stage in the system is important in contributing to the overall optimal performance of the distillery.

1. Cooking

Maize is delivered to the distillery in bulk and drawn out of the transportation container by suction or mechanical screw conveyor. It is sifted to remove fines and large particulate material and conveyed to silos for storage; provided the moisture content of the maize is below 14% it can be safely stored in silo. When required for mashing, the grain is drawn mechanically from the base of the silo in weighed quantities. In order to transform the starch granules of maize into a medium capable of being fermented by yeast, they require to be first disintegrated and then subjected to conversion into sugars, normally by enzymes. Several procedures exist to achieve these ends, among them being some important new developments in distillery technology. The first stage is effected by cooking the grain under conditions of temperature and pressure intended to bring about gelatinization of the starch granules. There are four distinct methods of cooking in operation in grain distilleries. These are: (i) boiling at atmospheric pressure; (ii) infusion at low temperature; (iii) high-pressure batch cooking; and (iv) continuous cooking. Boiling at atmospheric pressure, a simple but obsolete method of operation, suffers the disadvantage of incomplete gelatinization of the starch granules, with consequent lower yields of spirit. Infusion methods of grain softening and conversion are appropriate only where spirit is made from small grains, such as barley, rye and wheat, for example in Scotch malt whisky or German Kornbranntwein. For a specific type of distillery operation, infusion mashing gives excellent spirit yields although the temperatures used are not sufficiently high to sterilize the mash. The other two methods of cooking under high pressure are economically important. Until recently, all large maize spirit distillers operated a batch pressure-cooking process using cylindrical pressure vessels equipped with agitators and capable of withstanding about 7×10^5 Pascals (100 p.s.i.) but, in many distilleries, this system has now been superseded by continuous cooking. The batch cooker is normally charged with milled grain and about 1% of ground malt, called the pre-malt, which is added to bring about some early liquifaction of the starch and improve the handling characteristics of the cooked grain. Some distilleries prefer to operate with unmilled grain. Maximum pressures and temperatures vary with practice in individual distilleries, and have been reported to lie in the ranges 150°C to 135°C and 4×10^5-2.5×10^5 Pascals (4–2.5 atm) pressure. Overall batch cooking time is reported to be three hours (Suomalainen et al., 1968; Stark, 1954). These variations are the result of independent process optimization in different distilleries. In European distilleries, a conical design of pressure cooker with a vertical-axis paddle, called the Henze cooker, is commonly used. This cooker is designed for potatoes but will equally well handle grain. Stark (1954) reports that blowdown from the Henze cooker is so violent that the resultant disruption of the grain causes interference with by-product recovery. Continuous cooking has been in operation in some North American distilleries for more than two decades, and it is now becoming more widely adopted. In operation, milled grain, pre-malt and hot water are metered into a slurry tank for mixing and provision of a supply of mash for the process. The mash is pumped under pressure into a wide-bore stainless-steel tube constructed in serpentine form, injected with steam. The process is designed to hold the mash in the tube for a specified time under controlled conditions of temperature and pressure. Typical conditions in a continuous cooking process are: temperature 150°C, 4.5×10^5 Pascals pressure (65 p.s.i.) and a total holding time of 10 minutes. At the exit of the cooking tube, the cooked mash is brought down to a suitable conversion temperature by continuous vacuum cooling. Stark (1954) lists the advantages of the continuous cooking system as: uniform cooking, automatic control, even power requirement, lower wet steam consumption and a lowered capital investment in plant and buildings. Alcohol yields are equivalent to or better than batch cooking systems.

2. Conversion

At the termination of cooking, the gelatinized starch in suitable condition for conversion into fermentable sugars is cooled to a temperature favouring amylolytic enzyme activity and mixed with the enzyme medium in a suitable conversion vessel. The agent of starch conversion in the potable-spirit distillery has until recently been the enzymes of malted grain, usually barley, although enzymes from mould sources have historical interest in the Amylo process (Foth, 1929), and current importance in the manufacture of saké (Kodama, 1970). Barley malt in grain-spirit production is regarded simply as a vehicle for enzymes and, being a relatively expensive material compared with maize, its proportion in the mash is kept as low as possible consistent with efficient conversion. To this end, malt with a high content of enzymes is preferred, leading to the use of unkilned or green malt in grain-spirit distilleries. In the United Kingdom, production of grain spirit has, in the past, closely followed the pattern of Scotch grain whisky where cooked maize and malt are mixed in a large mash tun and clear worts are drawn by percolation through the bed of settled grain *via* the perforated floor of the mash tun (Pyke, 1965). In whisky production in North America, separation of wort from the grains does not take place after conversion, and the entire contents of the mash tun go forward to the fermenters and still. This 'in-grains' or 'thick mash' process is superior in terms of spirit yield because fermentable carbohydrate is not lost as a result of inefficient extraction in the mash tun. Furthermore, enzymic conversion of non-fermentable material continues in the fermenters, also leading to an improved attenuation and an enhancement of spirit yield. In distilleries using a continuous cooking process, it is logical to operate conversion on the same principle. After the cooked grain is cooled, a malt slurry is added and the mash thoroughly blended in an intermediate-slurry vessel before being fed into the conversion tube. A residence time of a few minutes is sufficient to achieve an amylolysis approaching equilibrium; the converted mash after passage through another tubular cooler is discharged direct into the fermenter. A line drawing of a continuous cooking and conversion process is shown in Figure 1.

The importance of spirit yield in distillery economics does not have to be underlined, and one of the most important factors governing yield is the correct functioning of enzymic conversion.

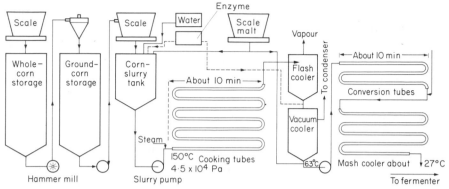

Fig. 1. A diagram of continuous cooking and conversion systems used in grain-spirit production.

This can be appreciated by examining the nature and activity of the malt amylases. The major starch-liquefying and saccharifying enzymes of malt are, respectively, α-amylase and β-amylase. The former rapidly cleaves the internal α-1,4 linkages in amylose and amylopectin, giving rise to both branched and straight-chain dextrins, while the latter enzyme simultaneously acts on the non-reducing ends of the dextrin chains, splitting off maltose. Conversion of the starch proceeds rapidly following the admission of malt enzymes, but slows and approaches equilibrium when the maltose content in the wort rises to 60–70%. The remaining carbohydrate fraction is mainly in the form of branched-chain dextrins with 4–8 glucose residues, the so-called limit dextrins, arising from incomplete breakdown of amylopectin. These limit dextrins are incapable of further significant hydrolysis by α- or β-amylase; but they are converted into fermentable sugars by secondary enzymes present in the malt which attack α-1,6-glucosidic linkages. The presence of enzymes with this capability in malt was first suggested by Myrbäck in 1943, and attempts were made to measure the potential of malts for limit dextrinase activity (Keen and Spoerl, 1948). Hopkins and Weiner (1955) confirmed the significance of limit dextrinase in distillery worts, and compared the activity to amylo-1,6-glucosidase found in muscle and a debranching enzyme found in broad beans. Manners and Yellowlees (1973) used pullulan as a substrate to measure specific limit dextrinase activity in malts. Degradation of limit dextrins proceeds slowly in the fermenters providing a release of sugars, which are available after the initial rapid fermentation. In order to promote the slow second stage conversion throughout mashing and fermentation, conditions of temperature and pH value which favour the dextrin-breaking enzymes have to be observed. While α-amylase has a high thermal resistance, particularly in the presence of calcium ions and starch hydrolysate, it has an optimal pH range of 4.7 to 5.4 (Fischer and Haselbach, 1951); β-amylase and the dextrin-cleaving enzyme can function at lower pH values but are relatively temperature sensitive. A high initial conversion temperature can seriously deplete these enzymes with a critical effect on the second-stage conversion. Conversion temperatures therefore should not rise above 65°C and the pH value during fermentation should not fall below 4.0.

Recent years have seen the widespread introduction of industrially produced enzymes into starch-conversion processes, for instance in the preparation of sugar syrups (Windish and Mhatre, 1965). Amylolytic enzymes are now displacing malt as the agent of conversion in grain and potato spirit distilleries (Aschengreen, 1969). It has been found necessary in distillery conversions to use two separate enzymes, namely an α-amylase prepared from cultures of *Bacillus subtilis*, and an amyloglucosidase produced from special strains of *Aspergillus niger*. The α-amylase has an improved heat stability particularly in the presence of calcium ions and starch hydrolysate, compared with the enzyme from malt, but it is more sensitive to pH values below 5. Amyloglucosidase attacks both long- and short-chain dextrins, and is able to split off glucose at the α-1,6-linkages of the branched chains in addition to the straight-chain α-1,4-links. These enzymes are available to the distiller in liquid form, and may be used as a direct replacement for malt in both batch and continuous systems of operation. The α-amylase may be substituted for pre-malt. Where conversion conditions are suitable, it is advantageous to add the two enzymes separately in order to improve enzyme efficiency. The α-amylase is added first at a temperature which favours rapid liquifaction of starch, and this is followed by a cooling to 60–55°C before addition of the amyloglucosidase. At this lower temperature, the stability of the saccharifying enzyme is safeguarded, leading to an effective utilization of all of the convertible and fermentable substrate in the mash. In view of the susceptibility of the α-amylase preparation to low pH values, the practice of returning a proportion of the thin stillage into the mash has to be delayed until after the major liquification activity is completed. In general, enzyme preparations have been accepted in the production of spirit from starch-containing substrates on the grounds of cost, convenience and an improvement in yield related to a more effective breakdown of dextrins during the later stages of fermentation.

3. Fermentation

Strains of *Saccharomyces cerevisiae*, suitable for distillery fermentation, are available from commercial yeast suppliers and are obtained from these sources by distillers with a moderate or small-scale operation. Large distilleries maintain their own selected yeast on culture medium, from which, by means of successive transfers to progressively larger sizes of inocula, the fermenter is finally set. Distiller's yeast strains are selected for an optimum performance under the specific conditions of distillery wort, to have a good fermentation vigour, and to be capable of a yield of alcohol approaching the theoretical maximum. A relatively low pitching rate is desirable, consistent with an adequate rate of fermentation, to avoid production of a large mass of yeast to the detriment of fermentation efficiency (Harrison and Graham, 1970). Suomalainen *et al.* (1968) recommended a rate of between 0.1 and 0.15 kg yeast dry weight per 1,000 litres of mash. Distillers growing up a yeast from culture medium pass it through a minimum of three inoculation stages in the laboratory before the first plant stage or dona (Stark, 1954). The medium used for the plant inocula is an enriched version of the fermentation wort, adjusted to a pH value below 4.0. Each stage is allowed to ferment for 12–18 hours, and is transferred to the next when the degrees Brix reading (see Chapter 1, p. 35) drops by 50%. There is a yeast multiplication of 10 to 20 times at each stage. The final stage may be used to pitch two fermenters and, to allow some flexibility, an inoculum can be stored for a short period by holding the temperature at 16–18.5°C, provided the degrees Brix reading is not lowered by more than 40%. The final inoculum represents about 2% of the fermentation mash, and is discharged into the fermenter when it is about a tenth full. Yeast may be propagated in the yeast plant continuously over a week or even a month without renewal from the culture source. Yeast plants are constructed of stainless steel, and the inoculation vessels are sterilized on being emptied. Infection in the yeast-propagation system is uncommon because, in addition to the sterilization programme, conditions in the inoculum (low pH value, high initial sugar and final alcohol contents) do not favour multiplication of bacteria.

Stark (1954) makes the telling point that problems in the fermentation, with the exception of the control of temperature, are due to factors arising from previous processing. Although special equipment for temperature control may not always be necessary in northern regions, where ambient temperatures are relatively low, many distillery fermenters situated in hotter climates require some cooling mechanisms. The simplest and most common cooling device is a water pipe circling the top of the fermenter with water running from it in a curtain over the vertical sides of the fermenter and cooling it through evaporation. In distilleries with higher capital investments, cooling by refrigeration may be applied, either by means of a refrigerant cycling through a jacket or internal coil, or by passing the fermenting wort through a heat exchanger. In the absence of supplementary temperature control, the setting temperature of the fermenter is capable of critical variation. Stark (1954) advises a setting temperature within the region 15-25°C and an eye on the weather forecast to prevent a rise in temperature during fermentation above 33°C. When temperature control is available, the fermenter may be set at 30°C without risk of rising above 33°C. The fermentation reaches a maximum rate within 12-30 hours of commencement, but may last for 40-60 hours with temperature control and 56-72 hours without. Suomalainen et al. (1968) quote a 48-96 hour duration period of fermentation for grain, compared with 24-50 hours for a molasses fermentation. The prolongation of a grain fermentation is due to incomplete but continuing conversion of dextrins which, after rapid consumption of the accumulated wort sugars by the yeast, becomes the rate-determining factor in the fermentation. The persistence of yeast vigour and activity throughout the latter stages of the fermentation is important in securing a good spirit yield; and this may be adversely affected by allowing the temperature to rise above 33°C during the early stages of fermentation. Stark (1954) indicates a loss in yield of 10-15% as a result of excessive temperature rise. Deckenbrock (1957), pointing to a possible danger in the higher concentrations of glucose in enzyme-converted worts compared with malt-converted worts, suggests that this could result in too rapid an early phase of fermentation and failure to sustain optimum conditions for conversion and fermentation in the last phase of the fermentation. At the end of the fermentation, a correctly fermented mash should have a specific gravity of less than 1.000 and an alcohol content, depending on the proportion of grain mashed, within the range 6–10% by volume.

The major biochemical transformation in a distillery fermentation is, in common with fermentation in other branches of the alcohol-producing industry, conversion of simple sugars into ethyl alcohol. This transformation is well documented in the literature (Baldwin, 1963; Wilkinson and Rose, 1963). Pyke (1965), in describing the manufacture of Scotch grain whisky, comments that the processes involved in fermentation of grain worts are complex. Suomalainen and Nykänen (1966) attribute many of the compositional characteristics of alcoholic beverages to the products of yeast metabolism in the fermentation. These metabolites are important in determining the flavour of fermented beverages (Suomalainen, 1971). But, in the case of neutral spirits, all except the most volatile substances present in the wash are eliminated in the course of distillation. A group of compounds generated in the fermentation and which have relatively low volatility, separate as a distinct liquid phase in the still, and are called the fusel oil These are mainly the higher alcohols, iso- and optically active amyl alcohols, isobutyl and n-propyl alcohols, with lesser amounts of n-hexanol, ethyl caprylate and many other compounds (Hirose, 1962). Hough and Stevens (1961) investigated the factors of yeast strain, temperature of fermentation, composition of the wort and method of fermentation on production of higher alcohols in brewing worts. For wine and cider, the presence of suspended solids in the fermentation has been found to lead to the formation of greater amounts of higher alcohols (Crowell and Guymon, 1963; Beech, 1972), and this factor is likely to be important in the fermentation of in-grains worts. Other more volatile compounds generated during fermentation will distil over and may be present in the final spirit. Among these, ethyl acetate, acetaldehyde and diacetyl have an important bearing on the quality of the spirit.

The slow final phase of a grain fermentation provides a suitable opportunity for the multiplication of infective bacteria, unless stringent precautions are taken for avoidance. These include attention to plant hygiene, control of pH value and temperature, and correct regulation of the process, for example in not storing the wash for long periods. Outbreaks of infection are frequently attributed by the distiller to bacterial contamination of the malt, but Adams *et al.* (1941) have demonstrated that high levels of contaminant in malt are effectively lowered at normal conversion temperatures during the mashing stage. Sources of infection therefore have to be sought elsewhere in the distilling process, for example in the yeast or as a persistent contaminant of the process plant. In a modern distillery equipped with systems of quality control, both of these sources of infection are monitored and the risks of significant and widespread infection are decreased to a minimum (Simpson, 1973). Plant hygiene in the distillery is well recognized as an essential contributor towards overall process efficiency, and methods of cleaning and sterilization using a 2% (w/v) solution of caustic soda and steam are generally adequate. Stark (1954) reported a fast-growing bacteria of short-rod or coccoidal form which was thermoduric and able to develop below pH 4.8. Pyke (1965) indicates the importance of lactobacilli and *Leuconostoc* spp. in Scotch grain fermentations, and Harrison and Graham (1970) draw attention to the importance of lactobacilli and other lactic acid-forming bacteria to distillers. In surveying the bacteria of malt whisky fermentations, Bryan Jones (1973) identified *Lactobacillus fermenti, L. brevis, L. delbreuckii, L. plantarum, L. casei* and a bacterium resembling *L. collinoides, Leuconostoc* spp., *Streptococcus lactic* and *Pediococcus cerevisiae.* Most of the bacteria isolated were able to ferment pentoses which represents an energy source in the wash not available to yeast. Bacteria isolated during the later stages of fermentation had similar growth rates at 30°C and 35°C and survived at pH 4.1.

Mackenzie and Kenny (1965) considered the change in the pH value of fermenting grain wort in relation to the buffering power of the wort and the production of lactic acid by bacterial infection. As the fermentation progressed, buffering power was weakened due to assimilation of amino nitrogen and phosphate and production of succinic acid by the yeast, and the pH value fell to 3.8 after 16 hours. Subsequent excretion of phosphate led to a recovery of buffering power and a rise in pH value to 4.2 but, in the latter stages of the fermentation, production of lactic acid by bacteria causes a lowering to pH 3.8. In order to secure an early decrease in pH value and to improve the buffering power of the wort in the range 4.4 to 4.1, a practice has grown up in North American distilleries of recycling liquid stillage into the next mash to make up about 20% of its volume. This stabilization of the pH value creates conditions early in the fermentation which discourage the growth of bacteria. Bacterial infection is additionally dangerous in generating compounds which are both odorous in low concentration and volatile. The likelihood of distilling these compounds risks a devaluation of the flavour quality of the spirit. Harrison and Graham (1970) give the example of bacterial metabolism of glycerol to β-hydroxypropionaldehyde which, on heating in the still, is converted to acrolein. Bacteria are responsible for formation of volatile sulphur compounds. Diacetyl, which is normally present in small but varying concentrations in fermented wash, is likely to be produced in higher concentrations by infective bacteria (Wainwright, 1973).

C. Production from Other Sources

Alcohol has long been made from molasses for industrial use (Hodge and Hildebrandt, 1954; Paturau, 1969), but molasses spirit has been considered less suitable in quality than spirit produced from grain for production of spirits like gin and vodka. With improvements in the operation and control of distilleries and the development of stills with a high potential for stripping out and separating volatiles, grades of molasses spirit with the high degree of purity and neutrality of odour required for gin and vodka have become available. Production of spirit from molasses is a simpler process than production from starch sources because the carbohydrate is present in forms readily fermentable by yeast, mainly as sucrose and invert sugar. The cooking and conversion stages in the grain distillery are consequently avoided. Molasses from both sugar cane and sugar beet are suitable raw materials. Beet molasses provides an important source of spirit in the European distilling industry; and, while cane molasses is used locally as a basis for manufacture of rum, it is transported from sugar cane-growing regions to industrial countries for production of neutral spirit. The form of molasses normally available for spirit production is blackstrap molasses which is the residue after crystallization of sucrose from evaporated cane juice. Blackstrap molasses contains

83-85% solids, which consists of 30-40% sucrose, 12-18% invert sugar, 7-10% ash and 20-25% non-fermentable organic substances (Hodge and Hildebrandt, 1954). Molasses has been available in the past as a high-test molasses, made by inverting evaporated cane juice with mineral acids. Molasses is so viscous that, in cooler climates, it has to be heated to facilitate pumping.

For fermentation, batches of molasses are weighed, diluted with water to 15-18° Brix, acidified to pH 4.5-4.7 to minimize bacterial activity, and pitched with yeast. The yeast inoculum is made up, as in a grain distillery, in progressive stages in diluted presterilized molasses or is recycled from a preceding fermentation under the system patented by Les Usines des Melle (Boinot, 1936, 1941). It is normal practice to supplement the molasses with ammonium salts in order to provide sufficient nutrients for the yeast. Fermentation proceeds more rapidly than with a starch-based fermentation and at slightly higher temperatures. The fully fermented wash has Brix readings in the range 5-7° as a result of the high concentrations of non-fermentable solids in the molasses. The method of molasses fermentation, which has become known as the Melle process and is suitable for the smaller scale operation, is based upon the re-addition of yeast to the next fermenter, after separation from a previously fermented mash by centrifugation. The addition of a relatively large inoculum of active yeast shortens the lag phase at the beginning of fermentation, thus increasing the overall rate of fermentation. It is also claimed to be more efficient in the production of alcohol in that the diversion of carbohydrate to form yeast mass is minimized. A fermentation efficiency of 95% of the theoretical yields assumed in the Gay-Lussac equation (see p. 21) is normally accepted as standard but, in the Melle process, the efficiency may be as high as 97% (Lagomasino, 1949). The continuity of the process depends on both the vigour and freedom from infection of the yeast. The first characteristic is ensured by rapid, successive fermentation and re-use, and the second by transferring the centrifuged yeast cream directly into an empty fermenter and mixing with water acidified to a low pH value. These conditions of operation effectively prevent the development of bacterial infection in the wash which is of great benefit to distillery hygiene and spirit yield. The alcohol content of fermented molasses wash lies in the region of 8-10% by volume, rising to as high as 12% in the Melle process.

Potatoes have formed an important carbohydrate raw material in Central and Eastern Europe for the production of both industrial and potable spirit (Kreipe, 1963). Being a starch source, potatoes require to be treated in a comparable manner to grain with a conversion step based upon green malt or, increasingly now, an enzyme preparation.

D. Distillation

The theory and practice of chemical engineering are relevant to the production of neutral spirits where the object is the separation and concentration of alcohol from the fermented wash without carry-over of significant quantities of congenerics. As a result, spirit stills have increased in design complexity and efficiency over the years, whereas the stills used to produce self-flavoured spirits like whisky and brandy—pot stills and early patent stills like the Coffey still—have with minor improvements, remained largely unchanged.

Separation and concentration of the components of liquid mixtures by distillation is possible as a result of differences in volatility between the components of the mixture. When a liquid mixture boils, the vapour generated is richer in the more volatile component and yields, on condensation, a liquid of enriched composition. By successive evaporation and condensation, a theoretical separation of the components of the mixture is possible. This is well illustrated in the equilibrium diagram for alcohol and water (Carey and Lewis, 1932) shown in Figure 2. Reference to this diagram demonstrates that, when a water–alcohol mixture of the composition of distillery wash boils, the proportion of alcohol rise from 8% (v/v) in the liquid to 47% (v/v) in the vapour. Condensation yields a liquid of the same composition as the vapour and, by successive evaporation and condensation, liquids of progressively higher alcohol content are obtained. In the case of alcohol–water mixtures, complete separation by successive evaporation and condensation is not possible as the diagram shows, because stepwise progression along the curve leads to a point at which this coincides with the diagonal line. At this point, the composition of the vapour and liquid phases are the same and a constant-boiling mixture or azeotrope is formed. This corresponds to an alcohol content of 95.58% (w/w). Separation of the alcohol from a distillery wash to a concentration at or approaching the azeotrope

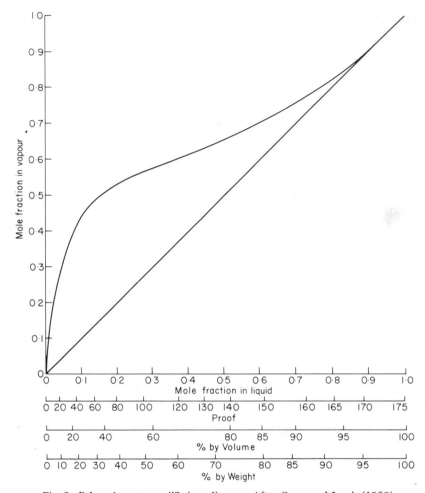

Fig. 2. Ethanol–water equilibrium diagram. After Carey and Lewis (1932).

is effected in the still by successive partial evaporation and condensation and by the separation of condensate falling under gravity from
the vapours rising through the still. The process of separating a
distillate, which is very different in composition from the original
liquid, is of great importance in producing a high-strength spirit from
distillery wash; this process is known as *rectification*. Stills for
rectification are designed to operate with maximum efficiency and
achieve a separation performance as close as possible to the equilibrium diagram. Two factors are important in optimum design,
namely multiple evaporation and condensation through maintenance

of contact between vapour and liquid, and the minimum disturbance to a balanced condition in the still by withdrawal of product at the head. The second condition is satisfied by returning to the still a part of the condensed vapour, called the reflux.

Distillation plant for spirit separation and purification has several features designed to assist rectification, in common with distillation plant for other liquid mixtures. In addition, the more complex stills are equipped with special sections for purification. Stills for neutral-spirit production are clearly distinguishable from self-flavoured spirit stills, which are normally simple pot stills, by their

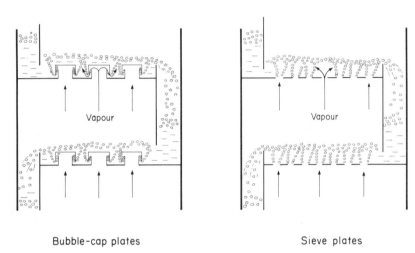

Bubble-cap plates   Sieve plates

Fig. 3. A diagram showing two types of distillation column plates used in distilleries. See text for an explanation.

columnar construction. These columns are tall, slim cylinders fitted internally with plates or trays with the purpose of causing the maximum intermixing of vapours rising and liquid falling in the column. Two types of plate in common usage are illustrated in Figure 3. Both plates support a depth of liquid which overflows the weirs and passes down to the plate below through the downcomer. The vapours rising in the column pass through apertures in the plates which, in the case of the sieve plate, are plain holes, but which in bubble-cap plates are topped by a short riser and cap intended to divide the vapour into small bubbles and promote mixing. Both types of plate are used in spirit distillation columns, the sieve plate being preferred where liquid passing through the still has a high content of solids. Suomalainen *et al.* (1968) claim that sieve plates are finding more general use in distillery columns as a result of their relative cheapness of construction.

Distillery separating and rectifying columns are designed for either batch or continuous operation. In batch distillation, the still resembles a pot still but has superposed on the boiler a rectifying column fitted with sieve or bubble-cap plates (see Figure 4). In

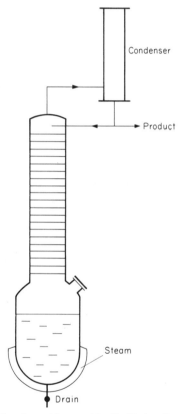

Fig. 4. Diagram of a batch rectifier used in distilleries. See text for explanation.

continuous distillation, which is advantageous in large-scale operations, the still consists of vertical columns served by a system of feed, steam and reflux supply, and condensate and stillage removal. Continuous distillation can be run in a single column still but, normally, a minimum of two columns is necessary to produce a distillate at or near the azeotrope, and of sufficient purity. In a two-column still, the first column is called the wash, or beer, or boiling column, and primarily separates alcohol from the fermented wash, while the second, the rectifying column, concentrates the alcohol to higher strength. The wash is normally preheated by vapour from the wash column, and fed into a point near the top of this column. Passing downwards, the wash is stripped of alcohol in the lower stripping section by ascending steam which is injected at the base of the column; in the upper section of the column, some rectification to an intermediate concentration of alcohol occurs depending on the number of plates in the section. Alcohol-free stillage is drawn continuously from the foot of the wash column. The condensate from the wash column passes to the rectifying column, entering at a point above a short stripping section. The upper section of the rectifying column, fitted with a large number of plates, ensures a high concentration of alcohol at the top of the column and an alcohol–water mixture at or close to the constant-boiling composition is drawn off at an upper plate. The fusel oils, which consist mainly of higher alcohols formed by the yeast, separate out on a series of plates just above the feed point, and are drawn off either direct to a decanter whence the oils, as the floating phase, may be drawn off, or are first concentrated in an extra column called the fusel oil column. Fusel oil is a source of commercial amyl alcohol. Volatile vapours consisting mainly of esters and aldehydes are condensed at the top of the rectifier as a heads fraction, and this is cycled back into the still.

It is well established in the distilling industry that, while spirit can be rectified in a two-column still to a high strength, the purity of the distillate falls short of the highest standards. For this reason, most distilleries producing high-quality spirit have three-column stills, while many have four and five columns to improve not only product quality but also the overall efficiency of the process. The important third column is called the *purifier*, and is set between the wash and rectifying columns. Condensate from the wash column enters about half-way up the purifier, while a supply of water is fed either into a plate near the top of the column or, alternatively, to coincide with the mainfeed point. Systems with water injection at the top of the purifying column are known as *hydroselection*. Alcohol is drawn from the foot of the purifying column at a strength below that of the feed, and the column is maintained in balance by a supply of steam.

Conditions in the purifier are intended to maximize the difference in volatility between alcohol and those volatile esters, aldehydes and other components which are less well separated in the rectifier. These volatile products are removed, together with some alcohol, as a heads fraction, and are fed into the fusel oil column which, as a supplementary rectifying column, produces a second grade of alcohol. The main alcohol fraction then passes to the rectifying column for rectification to high-strength spirit. A multicolumn continuous still is shown in line drawing in Figure 5. Heads fractions ultimately drawn

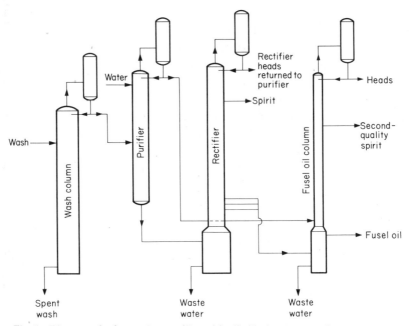

Fig. 5. Diagram of a four-column still used in distilleries. See text for explanation.

from a still may amount to 2–20% of the distilled product depending on the design and efficiency of the still (Guymon and Nakagiri, 1955). These authors suggested that, as a means of disposal, heads fractions can be added to the distillery fermenters and re-absorbed in actively fermenting wash (Guymon and Pool, 1957).

In many continuous processes, the wash column has to accept a liquid containing a high concentration of solids, for example with an in-grains wash in grain-spirit production. To avoid or minimize a build-up of solids, the wash column is normally fitted with sieve plates with enlarged apertures. In some distilleries, it is found advantageous to eliminate the downcomer and operate with fully flooded sieve plates; these columns have to be run with a throughput of within 10% of the rated capacity. In molasses distilleries, difficulty is frequently experienced with scaling in the columns. This is caused by the presence in the wash of calcium sulphate formed from calcium ions, occasionally present in molasses in high concentrations, and the sulphuric acid added to the wash for the adjustment of pH value. Several methods have been suggested to overcome or minimize scaling, among them being modification of the plates above the feed point to avoid a localized high concentration of alcohol (Ramana Rao, 1964) and treatment of the wash by a variety of chemical and physical methods including centrifugation (Samaniego and Srivastas, 1971). Still columns and condensers are normally made of copper, which historically has been the most suitable material available. In recent years, it has been the practice to build wash columns in stainless steel to overcome problems of corrosion; but construction of the entire still in stainless steel has not proved successful because chemical interaction between the liquid and vapour in the still and copper has a beneficial effect on spirit quality, for example by fixing volatile sulphur compounds.

E. By-Product Recovery

Spirit distillers are concerned with by-products for two reasons. Firstly, their recovery is producing an increasingly economic return and, secondly, legislative control is becoming stricter. In the past, it has been the practice to discharge distillery liquid waste into rivers or the sea, but anti-pollution regulations have limited the Biochemical Oxygen Demand of distillery effluents to values where effective pretreatment is necessary. The residue of wet grains, which represents 6–8% of stillage from grain distilleries, has been separated and supplied without additional treatment as an agricultural feedstuff. Recently, it has become economically attractive to recover most of the solids in grain-distillery effluent in a compact and consistent form, and many large spirit distilleries have been equipped with recovery plant for the production of distiller's dark grains. This material is rich in protein and yeast solids, is capable of being stored, and constitutes a valuable feed supplement for livestock. In the recovery of distiller's dark grains, the thick stillage is screened or centrifuged to separate the solid grain residue from the liquid stillage. The separated grains are then pressed in a conical screw press which lowers the moisture content to about 40%. The liquid from the press is combined with the liquid stillage separated at the previous stage, and the combined liquid is concentrated to a syrup of 40–50% (w/v) solids in a series of multiple-effect evaporators. This syrup is reblended with the pressed solids for final drying in hot-air driers. The final product has a moisture content of 10–12%, and is formed into pellets before filling into bags. The stillage of molasses distilleries is also recovered by evaporation and, as a syrup of 50% solids, is used as an alternative to molasses as a valuable animal-feed supplement. The recovery of solid by-product in the Scotch whisky distilling industry has been described by Rae (1966) and Gray and Moynihan (1968).

A second by-product of economic value is the carbon dioxide evolved during fermentation which, in weight, amounts to only slightly less than the alcohol produced. Collection of carbon dioxide is justified in larger distilleries where the capital cost of the plant may be quickly recovered in revenue from sales. The process of collection is simple. It involves scrubbing and drying the gas and then liquifying it by condensation under pressure. In the first stage, where the gas passes through overhead water sprays, all solids and most volatile materials are separated, and 0.5–1% of the alcohol produced in fermentation is recovered. In subsequent stages, the gas passes through activated alumina towers for drying, and through activated carbon towers for odour removal. It is finally liquified under pressures of 17.5–21×10^5 Pascals (250–300 p.s.i.), and passes by gravity into a bulk holding tank. Fermentation-generated carbon dioxide recovered in this way is disposed of mainly in the brewing and soft-drink industries. The economics of carbon dioxide recovery in brewery fermentations has recently been reviewed by Turvil (1974).

III. BOTANICALS

The principal agents of flavour in gin are the plant materials, known in the terminology of the trade as *botanicals*, with which the spirit is redistilled. A wide variety of botanicals noted for their richness in aromatic essential oils is known to be used in gin formulae (see Table 2). While juniper berries always constitute the major definitive ingredient, and coriander seeds and angelica root are also normally used in the distillation of London dry gin, the selection of other ingredients in any formula is generally limited. In the botanical formula, the proportions of ingredients normally remain constant. A

Table 2

List of gin botanicals used in gin manufacture

Common name	Botanical name
Juniper berries	*Juniperus communis*
Coriander seed	*Coriandrum sativum*
Angelica root	*Archangelica officinalis*
Sweet orange peel	*Citrus sinensis*
Bitter orange peel	*Citrus aurantium*
Lemon peel	*Citrus limon*
Cinnamon bark	*Cinnamomum zeylanicum*
Cassia bark	*Cinnamomum cassia*
Cardomom seeds	*Elettaria cardomomum*
Nutmeg	*Myristica fragrans*
Orris root	*Iris pallida*
Liquorice root	*Glycyrrhiza* spp.
Caraway seed	*Carum carvi*
Aniseed	*Pimpinella anisum*
Fennel seed	*Foeniculum vulgare*
Calamus root	*Acorus calamus*
Grains of paradise	*Afromomum melegueta*
Cubeb berries	*Piper cubeb*

Table 3

Typical standard for gin formula. After Wilkie *et al.* (1937)

Ingredient	kg	Ingredient	kg
Juniper berries	45.4	Angelica root	4.5
Coriander seeds	22.7	Lemon peel	0.45
Cinnamon bark	4.5	Cardamom	0.45

The weights are expressed as kilograms per charge of 113.5 hl at 50% (v/v) alcohol.

hypothetical gin formula has been published by Wilkie *et al.* (1937; see Table 3). In Dutch gin, caraway seed is an important ingredient in the botanical formula.

A. Juniper

The juniper berries used to make gin are the fruit of *Juniperus communis*, a tree or shrub growing to a height of at least 3 m, which is widely dispersed in Europe. The main source of juniper berries for gin is centred on the villages of San Donato, Pocchi Ponzi and Castellina in the Italian province of Tuscany (Guenther, 1952). Here the juniper flourishes on the hillsides at altitudes of between 600 and 1,200 metres. Juniper berries suitable for gin are also obtainable from Yugoslavia. Both Hungary and Czechoslovakia produce a crop of juniper, but much of this is used locally for production of Borovička, which is similar to the German Steinhäger. The juniper berry is a biennial crop and, when ripe, the berries are large and smooth skinned, deep purplish blue in colour with a slight surface bloom. The crop is gathered in a primitive but effective way. Sheets are placed on the ground surrounding the trees which are then shaken so that the ripe berries fall onto the sheets for collection. The green first-year berries remain attached to the trees. The crop is winnowed, or sifted, and spread out for partial drying. Storage of fresh juniper berries in sacks can lead to overheating and fermentation. The berries are sorted into grades, the best quality being sold for domestic use, while the second grade go for production of gin and other alcoholic beverages, and the third is distilled for recovery of the essential oil. At one time, juniper berries were subject to adulteration with the berries of *Juniperus oxycedrus* which are larger in size and reddish in colour. This practice has disappeared, apparently as much for the reason that it is no longer economic as for standards of control implemented at the shipping ports.

Juniper for gin production is selected on the basis of appearance, moisture content and the content and flavour of the distilled oil. The berries should be of uniform size, within a diameter range of 5–8 mm, smooth surfaced, of typical blue-black colour, and without a high proportion of wrinkled or brown berries. The odour of the berries should be clean and aromatic without any trace of mustiness.

The moisture content of juniper berries, measured by the method of Bidwell and Sterling (1925; Guenther, 1947) normally lies within the range 10–20%. Too high a moisture content brings about storage problems due to the danger of overheating, while too low a content is characteristic of old, dry berries. The oil contained in the berries is normally and conveniently collected for measurement after chopping or grinding the berries to break up the impervious epidermis and hypodermis which enclose the oil-bearing tissue, and then steam distilling in the apparatus designed by Clevenger (Langenau, 1947). The volume of collected oil, and its colour which should be a pale greenish-yellow, are important factors in the assessment and quality control of juniper supplies. Italian berries have an oil content within the range 1.0–1.5% (w/w); berries from other sources are either higher or lower in percentage oil content. Wilkie et al. (1937) examined the value of analytical measurements on the extracted oil as a means of quality control. They considered the acid number and refractive index, but found the first value to be unspecific and the second to depend on the method of distillation. They do, however, record a stringent specification for juniper berries intended for gin manufacture. These authors also draw attention to the change in composition which occurs during storage. They found a linear fall in both oil and moisture contents in juniper berries stored over a period of four years in an uncontrolled warehouse environment. In order to compensate for changes in the oil and moisture contents of juniper during storage, which may cause fluctuation in the flavour of the gin, they recommended that the gin formula be based upon a weight of oil contained in the botanicals rather than a fixed weight of the botanicals themselves. An alternative, but commercially simpler, method of ensuring consistency of quality is to maintain a standardized blend of juniper to which a proportion of selected new crop is added each year.

Juniper oil has been subject to analysis first by chemical methods and more recently by gas-liquid chromatography (g.l.c.). Luckner et al. (1965) described the distilled oil as consisting predominantly of mono- and sesquiterpenes, the most important being terpineol-4. Other components are α-pinene, camphene and δ-cadinene, and various terpene alcohols. Two groups of authors have analysed the oil of *Juniperus communis* and compared it with those of other species of *Juniperus*. Hirose et al. (1960) examined the oils of *Juniperus rigida*, a Japanese species, and *Juniperus communis* by fractionation *in vacuo*, gas-liquid chromatography, liquid chromatography and infrared spectroscopy. They found that, in addition to a number of common components, *Juniperus communis* oil contained sabinene,

Table 4

Composition of juniper oil

Peak no.	Component	Composition of oil (v/v) in:			
		Juniperus communis	*Juniperus communis*	*Juniperus phoenica*	*Juniperus macropoda*
—	α-Thujene	—	1.2	0.2	0.9
1	α-Pinene	38.9	26.5	70.4	38.4
2	Camphene	0.1	0.2	0.7	0.5
3	β-Pinene	1.2	1.7	2.3	1.5
4	Sabinene	6.6	8.8	0.3	0.6
5	Myrcene	11.5	9.0	3.4	11.5
—	α-Phellandrene	—	0.3	1.1	0.9
6	α-Terpinene	2.3	0.8	0.2	0.15
7	(+)-Limonene	4.0	3.8	8.3	
8	β-Phellandrene	0.5	—	—	9.0
9	γ-Terpinene	3.7	1.9	0.05	0.4
10	*p*-Cymene	1.9	2.4	0.5	0.65
11	Terpinolene	1.2	0.9	0.4	0.5
12–22	Unknown	1.1			
23	*p*-Terpinenol	11.9			
24	Caryophyllene	0.8			
25–27	Unknown	0.9			
28	α-Terpineol	2.8			
29–30	Unknown	1.15			
31	Decyl alcohol	2.4			
32–50	Unknown	7.5			

The peak numbers refer to the peaks in the chromatogram of juniper oil shown in Figure 6 (p. 569). The data for the more complete analysis of the oil from *Juniperus communis*, in which terpene hydrocarbons make up 72% of the total, were communicated by D. W. Clutton. All other data are from Klein and Farnow (1965).

camphene, α-terpinene, γ-terpinene, terpinolene, α-terpineol, ethyl caprylate and an unknown saturated hydrocarbon. Klein and Farnow (1965) isolated the monoterpene fraction of the oils of *Juniperus communis, Juniperus phoenica* and *Juniperus macropoda* by distillation through a packed column, and submitted the fractions to g.l.c. analysis. The results of these comparative analyses are given in Table

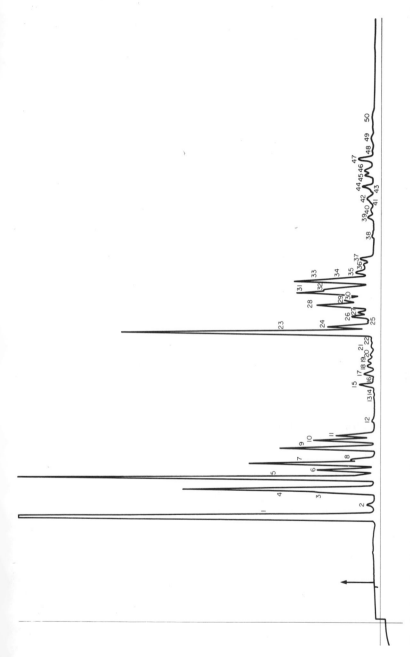

Fig. 6. A gas-liquid chromatogram of the volatile components of juniper berry oil. The analysis was conducted with a Pye 104/64 chromatograph, using flame-ionization detection. The column (internal diameter: 4 mm; length: 3 m), of 15% Carbowax (20M/AW D.C.M.S.) on Chromosorb W 80/100, was heated from 70°C to 220°C at the rate of 3°C/min, and the nitrogen gas flow rate was 40 ml/min. A 0.2 μl sample was injected onto the column, the sensitivity was 10⁴, the detector was held at 250°C, and the chart speed was 25 cm/h.

4. It is notable that the oil of *Juniperus communis* is lower in α-pinene than that of the other species; a strong pine-like character associated with high levels of α-pinene is undesirable in juniper for gin distillation. Figure 6 shows a gas-liquid chromatogram of the oil of *Juniperus communis* berries selected for gin production, prepared for analysis by steam distillation. Identification of several components is given in Table 4.

The selection and approval of juniper for gin rests largely on organoleptic assessment. Samples of the berries are distilled with alcohol, either alone or in combination with other botanicals, in laboratory stills to simulate distillation under production conditions. Reference samples are distilled in an exactly comparable way and the distillates, diluted to a correct alcoholic strength, are examined blind for odour and taste by expert tasters, preferably operating as a panel. Samples of juniper submitted for gin production, which have a harsh pine-like character or a fishy odour, are rejected, and preference is given to berries with a softer aromatic character associated with lower proportions of α-pinene. Organoleptic examination of juniper distilled in alcohol and by steam distillation followed by dilution with alcohol shows the distillates to be similar in odour quality.

B. Coriander

Coriander is an ingredient in both London dry and Dutch gin. The plant, an umbelliferous annual which grows to a height of 0.7 m, is cultivated in Eastern Europe, in Morocco and elsewhere (Guenther, 1950). Coriander for gin production generally comes from the first two sources, though traditionally it has been grown in England for gin distillation. The fruit is spherical, composed of two concavo-convex mericarps, and is subject to shattering when overripe. Harvesting must therefore begin as soon as the fruit changes colour from green to reddish or yellowish brown at the end of July or early August. Early harvesting of coriander is recommended because the central-order umbels carry fruit with a higher proportion of oxygenated terpenes, which is indicative of a higher quality seed (Tsvetkow, 1970). Traditionally the seed is harvested by hand and threshed but, in Eastern Europe, grain combine harvesters have been used.

As selected for gin production, coriander seed, which is how the

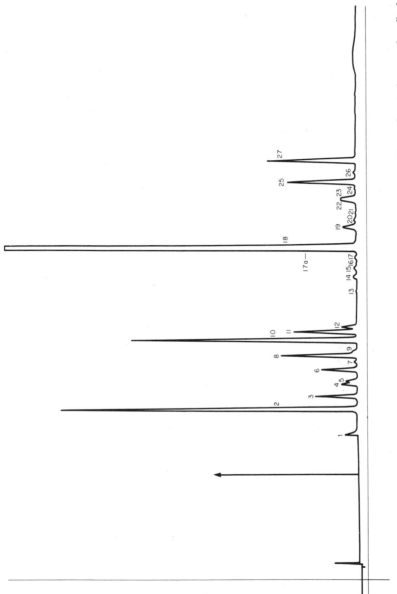

Fig. 7. A gas-liquid chromatogram of the volatile components of coriander seed oil. The conditions of analysis are as described in the caption to Figure 6.

fruit is described commercially, is tawny or reddish yellow in colour, 2–4 mm in diameter with 100–130 seeds to the gram; there should not be a large proportion of broken seed. Coriander has a mellow, spicy odour; seeds which remain green have a hard pine-like odour and are unsuitable for gin production. Coriander from Eastern Europe has an oil content of 0.5–1.0% (w/w); with seeds from other sources, the oil content tends to be lower. With a normal moisture content of 10–15%, the commercial seed can be stored in bulk bins without risk of high-temperature damage. The oil, which may be isolated by steam distillation for flavour assessment and analysis, should be colourless or pale yellow; it contains 64–72% linaloöl (Guenther, 1950). Gas-liquid chromatography has been applied by a number of workers to analysis of coriander oil. Ikeda *et al.* (1962) estimated the proportions of monoterpene components, finding

Table 5

Composition of coriander oil

Peak number	Component	Content (%, v/v)
1	α-Thujene	0.4
2	α-Pinene	6.9
3	Camphene	1.1
4	β-Pinene	0.4
5	Sabinene	0.1
6	Myrcene	0.8
7	α-Terpinene	—
8	(+)-Limonene	2.2
9	β-Phellandrene	0.03
10	γ-Terpinene	7.0
11	*p*-Cymene	1.3
12	Terpinolene	0.4
13–17	Unknown	—
17a	Camphor	4.3
18	Linaloöl	70.5
19	*p*-Terpinenol	0.3
20–21	Unknown	—
22⎫ 23⎭	α-Terpineol	0.7
24	Unknown	—
25	Geranyl acetate	2.2
26	Unknown	—
27	Geraniol	2.6

The numbers refer to peaks in the chromatogram of coriander oil in Figure 7 (p. 571). Terpene hydrocarbons amount to 20.6% of the total.

γ-terpinene, *p*-cymene, d-limonene and α-pinene to be the most quantitatively important, while Akimov and Voronin (1968) confirmed the presence of linaloöl, geraniol, camphor, geranyl acetate, borneol, nerol, decyl aldehyde and linalyl acetate. Figure 7 shows a gas-liquid chromatograph of oil from a sample of coriander approved for gin distillation, and several components are identified in Table 5.

C. Other Botanicals

Of the other botanicals commonly present in the formula of London dry gin, angelica root, cassia and cinnamon bark and orange peel are the most significant; caraway seed is used for flavouring Dutch gin. Angelica of a quality suitable for gin production is obtained from Belgium and the German province of Saxony. The thick fleshy tap roots, 12.5–25 cm long, with many rootlets, are harvested after three years and require immediate drying (Guenther, 1950). On storage, the roots develop a characteristic musk-like odour which can be isolated in the oil obtained by prolonged steam distillation. The oil is mobile and light brown, and has been subject to g.l.c. analysis by Klouwen and ter Heide (1965). These workers isolated and identified the high-boiling lactone, pentadecanolide, by infrared spectroscopy and comparative retention on four different stationary phases. This compound, which makes up 1–1.5% (w/w) of the root oil, has the characteristic musk odour of angelica root.

Cinnamon and cassia are related botanically, and have similar flavour characteristics. Cinnamon is the dried inner bark of a coppiced tree cultivated in Ceylon and increasingly in the Seychelles Islands. The outer bark of the tree is stripped, peeled and dried, and then rolled into quills. The bark has an essential oil content of 0.9–2.3% (w/w), of which 65–75% is cinnamic aldehyde. Other components are eugenol (4–10%), caryophyllene, β-phellandrene, *p*-cymene, α-pinene, linaloöl, furfural, methylamyl ketone, nonyl aldehyde, benzaldehyde, hydroxycinnamaldehyde and cumaldehyde (Heath, 1973). Cassia quills, the dried bark from trees grown in Viet Nam and Ceylon, are thicker owing to an adhesion of cork. The essential oil content is 1–2% (w/w) composed of 80–95% cinnamaldehyde, together with cinnamyl acetate, cinnamic acid, benzaldehyde, methyl salicylate, methyl *o*-coumaraldehyde, salicylaldehyde and coumarin (Heath, 1973).

The essential oil of orange peel contains about 90% d-limonene and 5% linaloöl, although both of these components are less important in flavour characterization than the aldehydes octanal, decanal and dodecanal present in much lower concentrations. The α,β unsaturated aldehyde, α-sinensal, found at about 0.1% in orange oil, has a low odour threshold and a sweet, pungent aroma (Kefford and Chandler, 1970).

Caraway is a bienniel, easily cultivated, umbelliferous plant, grown in many parts of the World but principally in Holland. The seeds contain 3–7% oil, of which the most important constituent in flavour and quantity (53–63%) is d-carvone (Anon. 1970). D-Carvone extracted from caraway seed is stable over a wide range of pH values and temperatures (Yusen Yin *et al.*, 1970). Caraway seed has a characteristic flavour which is the basis of the German liqueur, kümmel.

IV. PRODUCTION OF GIN AND VODKA

A. Gin and Juniper-Flavoured Spirits

From the starting point of a supply of spirit and botanicals of suitable quality, there is a great deal of variation in the methods used to distil gin. This variation has already been referred to for gins and related spirits of different national origins (London dry gin, geneva and Steinhäger); but, in considering distillation practice for London dry gin, there are within accepted limits some variations (Simpson, 1966).

1. *London Dry Gin*

In principle, the basic production methods for London dry gin are simple. Spirit and botanicals are charged into a pot still and a distillation is made in a controlled manner. However, points of difference between distilleries arise at each part of the process. Stills are traditionally and universally made of copper and, while it is widely believed that the copper still plays some part in regulating and conditioning gin flavour, there is evidence that the material of which the still is made is not critical. In shape and design, the pattern of still is well suited to the distillation of gin, and is an indispensable factor in the quality of London dry gin. Pot stills are frequently and graphically described as onion shape. The bulbous pot or boiler curves upwards into a tapering neck which, at the top of the still, turns gracefully over into the swan neck or lyne arm connecting the condenser (see Fig. 8). In large distilleries, lyne arms of several stills

Fig. 8. Photograph of a gin still.

placed round the still room generally converge to a battery of tubular condensers mounted vertically on the still room wall. To conserve condenser water, this is cycled through externally sited cooling towers. Stills vary in size, and a distiller making his gin in several distilleries of varying capacity scales his still design up or down in order to keep comparable distillation characteristics. Stills may be equipped with devices to increase rectification, for example, a water jacket on the column, or return pipe reconnecting the lyne arm to the boiler so that part of the distillate may be recycled. The degree of rectification, however, remains low and the alcoholic strength of the distillate seldom exceeds twice that of the spirit charge.

To begin a distillation, the still is charged with the ingredients to an established formula. The botanicals are weighed and placed in the still boiler and the charge is made up with spirit of approved quality and alcoholic strength. The quantity and strength of alcohol used in a gin formula has an important bearing in regulating the rate of distillation of the flavouring essential oils. After charging, the still boiler is half full of liquid and normally the still stands overnight for distillation on the following day. In many formulae, the botanicals are charged loose into the still, but some distillers place the botanicals into porous bags which are sealed up, thus preventing their dispersal in the boiling spirit. This method has the advantage that, at the end of the distillation, the exhausted botanicals may be easily removed from the still, but is likely, in the course of distillation, to cause some restriction in the maceration of botanicals and the release of essential oils which this action engenders. In order to avoid the effect of maceration altogether, some distillers place the botanicals in a tray suspended in the still above the level of the boiling spirit; this variation of technique has the effect of diminishing the amount and range of oils extracted and distilled, with consequent flavour modification in the gin distillate.

Gin stills were originally directly fired by means of furnaces set below the stills; but, today, they are steam heated, either by means of an internal steam coil, or through a hemispherical jacket covering the base. The temperature of the charge is raised from ambient to boiling point as quickly as is convenient but, as the boiling point is approached, the steam supply has to be shut off in order to avoid tumultuous boiling and the risk of entrainment. In order to promote even boiling throughout the distillation and avoid foaming and entrainment, antifoaming agents of the silicone type may be added to the still charge. The progress of the distillation is regulated by means of distillate flow, and this is normally controlled by reference to a weir-type flowmeter. The other controlling parameter is the alcoholic strength of the distillate, and measurements of this value, together with flow rate, can be taken by the still operator at the spirit safe, which is a sighting cabinet or cylinder into which the condensed distillate flows, first through the weir flowmeter and then into an alcohol hydrometer sample glass. Reference to these instruments enables the still operator to regulate steam pressure throughout the course of distillation. The distillate is fractionated by selection in order to give a gin of the correct flavour. The first runnings from the condenser at the beginning of a distillation are rejected as they are likely to be tainted with the heavier oils from the tail end of the previous distillation. The quantity of distillate rejected—termed 'heads'—is proportionately small and amounts to only a few gallons. Following separation of the heads fraction, gin is evenly collected over a period of several hours during which the distillate strength remains at a constant value. Finally, due to depletion of alcohol in the still, the strength of the distillate begins to fall and, at the same time, the temperature of the boiling liquid rises and continues to rise until all of the alcohol has distilled over. This rise in temperature in the still allows the distillation of higher boiling-point components in the botanical oils, many of which are undesirable in the distilled gin. At some point in the distillation, determined by alcoholic strength, collection of the distillate as gin is terminated; this point is known as the 'strike'. Distillation, however, is continued until substantially no alcohol remains in the still; the distillate collected after the strike, namely the 'tails', together with the heads fraction, is subsequently redistilled in a still of high rectification to recover the alcohol. This recovered alcohol is used up as a proportion of successive gin-still charges. The distillate collected as gin, after equalization by mixing, has an alcoholic strength in the range of 75–85% by volume, depending on the strength of the original spirit charge and the degree of rectification in the gin still. High-strength gin may be blended with other distillates to ensure a greater consistency of quality, and may be stored in a tank before dilution and processing prior to bottling.

The batch-distillation procedure described may be used either to produce a gin distillate which requires only a dilution to bottling strength or, alternatively, a concentrated gin. In the latter case, the still is charged with greater quantities of botanicals and the gin collected is several times richer in flavouring compounds than a standard-charge gin. The flavour level in the concentrated gin is corrected by blending with spirit before dilution and bottling. Gins produced by the standard- and high-charge methods from a proportionate combination of still and botanicals are not identical in flavour after blending and dilution. This is thought to be related to a less efficient extraction of the botanical oils in the high-level charge resulting in a lower level as well as a proportionate difference of flavouring in the blended gin. These differences, however, are not great and are unlikely to be commercially significant. The concentrate method of producing gin is more convenient, and is adaptable to the bottling of gin remote from the distillery, as for example, overseas.

2. Geneva

The manufacture of geneva is subject to a number of conditions and controls, but the procedures followed depend upon the style of geneva intended. There are two distinct types: oude (old) geneva which has a distinctive grain-spirit character combined with the flavour of the juniper and other herbal ingredients, and jonge (young) geneva which is lighter in flavour and closely resembles German Korn. Oude geneva, in its characteristic stoneware bottles, is more widely known outside Holland, where it is normally consumed as an aperitif, chilled and straight, that is, without dilution or mixing. The prominent grain-spirit character of geneva is the result of using in its production a traditional, strongly flavoured spirit, more akin to a malt whisky than the rectified spirit normally used to distil London dry gin. This spirit, called the *moutwijn*, is made by mashing approximately equal amounts of the malts of rye, barley and maize. After the addition of yeast, the mash is aerated and fermentation starts vigorously, producing a voluminous foam. This is skimmed off and the yeast is recovered in a press. Fermentation lasts two days, and the wash is then charged into a batch still and distilled without rectification to give a distillate of about 23% by volume alcohol. The stillage is allowed to stand and when, the solids have settled, the liquid is racked off and added to the next mash. By means of a second similar distillation, the strength of the moutwijn is raised to 46%, by volume, alcohol. Geneva was originally made by including the botanicals in the grain mash, but this technique has been superseded in favour of an additional distillation of moutwijn and botanicals or, more recently, by blending the moutwijn with a distillate made of the botanicals in neutral spirit. The botanicals commonly used for geneva are juniper, caraway, coriander and aniseed. Geneva is required to undergo a period of storage and ageing before it is available for bottling. Nowadays the production of moutwijn is undertaken in a few specialist distilleries from which it is available to the geneva manufacturers. In the production of jonge geneva, a much lower proportion of moutwijn is used, the balance being made up with neutral spirit. The comparative lightness and neutrality of flavour is due to the presence of smaller amounts of spirit congenerics in jonge geneva.

3. Steinhäger

Steinhäger is a distilled spirit flavoured with fermented juniper. Production of the fermented base for Steinhäger, the *Wacholder-lütter*, is in the hands of a few traditional specialized distillers who supply it for blending and redistillation into the final product. The fermentation substrate is entirely dried, crushed juniper berries, which contain 20-30% fermentable sugars. A mash is made in the ratio of 100 kg berries to 200 litres warm water, and 250-700 g of pressed or brewer's yeasts are added per 100 litres of mash; yeast nutrients in the form of ammonium phosphate or other salts are also added. The fermentation is slow and difficult, and the temperature has to be maintained at 25°C in order to achieve completion within 8-14 days. During this slow fermentation, there is a great risk of acetification and, to minimize this risk by preserving an atmosphere of carbon dioxide, the fermenters are kept covered. The entire fermented mash is run into a simple pot still, and the charge is distilled without removal of the heads-and-tails fractions. As the juniper berries contain about 1% essential oil, this distils over and separates as a floating phase on the distillate. The oil is removed and disposed of as commercial oil of juniper.

The juniper distillates have an alcoholic strength of up to 12% by volume depending on the condition of the juniper and the success of the fermentation. In the preparation of Steinhäger, the juniper distillate is used without pretreatment. It is mixed in a proportion of 2-10% with neutral spirit and redistilled, together with a small quantity of added dried berries, in a pot still. A distillate is collected with separation of heads and tails. The middle fraction is high-strength Steinhäger which is diluted with water for bottling. Matzik (1965) has studied the production of juniper distillate on a laboratory scale. A product comparable with Steinhäger, called *Borovička*, is made in Hungary.

B. Vodka

Just as there are various styles of gin with different flavour characteristics, so there are differences in vodka. The vodkas which have become accepted and now widely produced outside Russia and Eastern Europe are the flavourless type where high-purity spirit is chosen and further treated so that the product reaching the consumer has only the flavour of pure ethyl alcohol. Vodkas of this type are popular in the U.S.S.R. for, in analysing by g.l.c. a number of Western brands together with Russian-made vodka, Slavutskaya *et al.* (1969) claimed to find more volatile compounds in the former type. On the other hand, there are vodkas which are flavoured in manufacture either with fruit or herbs, and are sold with an intentionally flavoured character. Many flavoured vodkas are produced in Poland.

In the production of neutral vodkas, much depends on the selection of a suitable spirit, and the fermentation base of the spirit is less critical than the degree of rectification and purification achieved in distillation. In Russia, vodka is made from both grain and potato spirit; in the West, grain and molasses spirit are used. The selected spirits are diluted in alcoholic strength and subject to treatment with activated carbon. Two alternative methods are normally used: agitation of the spirit in a tank with powdered charcoal or passing the spirit through granular charcoal packed into a column. To improve contact and efficiency, several packed columns may be linked in series (see Fig. 9). Treatment of spirit with charcoal lowers the concentrations of congenerics by adsorption, with consequent improvement in flavour quality. The concentration of diacetyl in a spirit may be lowered ten-fold by treatment with charcoal (A. C. Simpson; unpublished data). Slavutskaya *et al.* (1969) have advocated using g.l.c. to optimize the time of contact between the spirit and charcoal. To maintain flavour standards, the water used to dilute the strength of vodka must be high in quality and purity. Several

Fig. 9. Photograph of a vodka charcoalation plant.

Russian authors have drawn attention to the importance of sodium ions in the water used to dilute vodka. Danillzo *et al.* (1972) have claimed that, following demineralization by ion-exchange, water intended for dilution of vodka is improved in quality by the presence of sodium and calcium ions. Some Russian vodkas claim mellowness as a result of the presence of sodium ions. The co-existence of flavoured vodkas has already been indicated. These vodkas are made from neutral spirit, and are blended with infusions and flavouring substances before bottling. A Ukrainian vodka is flavoured with honey.

V. COMPOSITION OF SPIRIT, GIN AND VODKA

A. Spirit

Some analytical standards have been set for high-quality spirit, such as those of the German Bundesmonopolverwaltung and the official Swiss standards. Spirit intended for production of gin and vodka should fall within these analytical standards. The specification and measurement of spirit congenerics in terms of functional group, e.g. esters, aldehydes and acids, is conventional in the industry and forms the basis of definitions and legal standards. These analytical methods are constantly being tested and revised with the introduction of techniques such as gas-liquid chromatography where this is appropriate (Anon., 1970, 1972). However, is has not yet been possible to quantify or specify the flavour quality of spirits in terms of analytical, gas-liquid chromatographic data. Of the tests quoted in the official specifications, the permanganate-time test is generally considered to provide a good empirical measure of spirit quality. The test is based upon the time taken for a standard solution of potassium permanganate to fade to a specified colour at a given temperature, and presupposes a relationship between the overall reducing capacity and the odour quality of a spirit (Ethyl Alcohol Handbook, National Distillers and Chemical Corporation, p. 112; Horak *et al.*, 1968). The response of the permanganate-time test (referred to as the P-test) to varying acidity in spirit has been studied by Horak and Lehman (1959), who found values for the test to decrease with increasing acidity, the extent of this decrease being greater for strong as compared with weak acids. Alfredsson and Losell (1965) studied the effect of addition of a number of congenerics to spirit on the value obtained for the P-test. They found that higher alcohols had little impact except at high concentrations, although this effect increased with increasing molecular weight. Saturated aldehydes, in low concentration, had a strong decolourizing effect, which was particularly rapid with iso-aldehydes. Aromatic compounds with fully saturated side chains had a small effect, but the presence of a double bond in the side chain brought about a strong decolourization. Unsaturated alcohols lowered the value obtained with the P-test. But the most rapid lowering in this value was obtained with unsaturated aldehydes. Ultraviolet absorption has also been considered as an instrumental basis for an assessment of spirit purity (De Vries, 1958).

  Several factors combine to call in question the value of published and accepted methods for assessment of spirit purity. Among these are the ability of modern distillers to produce spirit of much higher purity and flavour quality, the use of g.l.c. to separate and measure individual congenerics or contaminants, and the application of systematic sensory analysis. The odour thresholds of many spirit congenerics have been studied by Salo (1970) and, while the higher boiling-point components are not relevant to rectified spirit, information on the odour thresholds of volatile congenerics is important in assessing analytical data. For instance, iso-amyl alcohol and n-propyl alcohol have odour thresholds of 7.0 and more than 720 mg/litre, respectively; however, iso-amyl alcohol is unlikely to be found at this concentration and n-propyl alcohol, if present, would be well below the odour threshold. Of the other relevant congeners examined (Salo *et al.*, 1972), ethyl acetate, acetaldehyde and diacetyl have odour thresholds in ethyl alcohol of 17.0, 1.20 and 0.0025 mg/litre respectively. Sulphur-containing compounds are known to have an effect on the flavour of beer at low concentration levels (Brenner *et al.*, 1955; Thorne *et al.*, 1971). Fiero (1958) reports organoleptic detection of ethyl mercaptan in ethyl alcohol at two parts per billion, and a ten-fold higher concentration caused the product to be rejected. Austin and Boruff (1960) considered the potential of g.l.c. to identify and measure volatile congenerics in neutral-grain spirit. Such was the low concentration of the congenerics present that they found it necessary to concentrate in a preliminary step by stripping with helium, followed by condensation in a low-temperature trap. Using retention data they identified several components including acetaldehyde, acetal, acetone, ethyl formate, ethyl acetate, methyl alcohol and a group of hydrocarbons. In comparing a sample of spirit taken during the start-up period in the distillery, which was organoleptically unacceptable, with a sample of acceptable quality, they found several chromatographic differences, among them a higher concentration of acetaldehyde and two unidentified components in the unacceptable sample. Another rejected sample showed a higher ester content, and a compound thought to be diethylether. Diacetyl can be measured by g.l.c. using electron-capture detection (Wainwright, 1973). Direct injection of spirit onto the column enables diacetyl to be estimated down to concentrations of 0.05 mg/litre; the presence of diacetyl in spirit at 0.2 mg/litre has been associated with a pronounced buttery odour (Simpson, 1973). Use of a flame photometric detector to estimate the concentration of volatile sulphur compounds in spirit has been reported (Ronkainen *et al.*, 1973). Several spirit samples have been analysed by this technique, giving values of 2 to 33 parts per billion of dimethyl sulphide for spirit of poor and unacceptable quality, and less than two parts per billion in a good-quality sample (A. C. Simpson, unpublished data).

Austin and Boruff (1960) comment that the permanganate-time test does not correlate well with organoleptic assessments, and they conclude that the latter method must remain the final arbiter of quality. However, they point to the difficulty of selecting and storing samples of sufficiently high quality to serve as organoleptic standards. It does seem that, until more work has been undertaken on the odour contributions made by trace volatile congenerics remaining in high-grade spirit and on methods of analysis, odour panels will continue to play a dominant role in quality assessment, specification and control.

B. Gin and Vodka

Little has been published on the composition of gin but, as the constituents responsible for its flavour are originally introduced by distillation, their analysis by g.l.c. is a logical undertaking. Some chromatograms of gin are shown in Figures 10 and 11. Figure 10 shows chromatograms of three gins analysed by direct injection of the gin, without any preparation or preconcentration, onto the g.l.c. column. This is both possible and convenient for gin, because its components are, in varying degrees, all volatile. At this level of dilution, only a limited amount of information on the flavour constituents of gin can be discovered. But, nevertheless, the major components of the main botanical ingredients are recognizably present. Gins 1, 2 and 3 show peaks representing β-pinene, myrcene, d-limonene, γ-terpinene, linaloöl, *p*-terpinenol and a major unknown peak. Differences in the concentrations of these compounds represent differences in the botanical formulae of the gins. For example gin 3, with a high concentration of d-limonene, includes orange peel in the formula; and gin 2 with a small peak corresponding to cinnamic aldehyde is made with cassia or cinnamon bark. Gin 1 contains a relatively large concentration of linaloöl and, therefore, has a higher coriander–juniper ratio than gins 2 or 3; and gin 2, with a lower concentration of all components, was distilled from a small botanicals charge. Gin 2 might, in a commercial context, be described as 'dry', which is interpreted as a low degree of flavour. The presence of cinnamic aldehyde in gin 2, which is not well revealed on the chromatogram, is amply confirmed by ultraviolet absorption measurements on the gin, which show a definite absorption hump in the spectrum with a maximum at 289 nm. The other chromatograms in Figure 10, of geneva and Steinhäger, demonstrate the distinctiveness of these products compared with London dry gin. In geneva, the spirit constituents, namely isobutyl alcohol, iso-amyl alcohol, n-hexanol, furfural and β-phenyl ethanol, occur in much higher concentrations than the botanical constituents and, although this does not necessarily signify a greater contribution to flavour, all of these spirit congenerics are present in excess of their odour thresholds. Steinhäger, in contrast, shows an absence of spirit congenerics and only trace quantities of botanical constituents. These chromatograms, therefore, adequately reflect the flavour of these products and their different methods of manufacture.

To get more chromatographic data on gin, it is necessary to concentrate the flavouring substances by one of the established methods of extraction and concentration (Weurman, 1969). The chromatogram shown in Figure 11 was obtained using a sample prepared by extraction with Freon 11. The gin extracted for this analysis was the same as gin 1 in Figure 10, and the similarity of these two chromatograms is evident. Many of the component peaks in Figure 11 are identifiable with the constituents of juniper and coriander oils (see Figs. 6 and 7, pp. 569 and 571), but several peaks in the gin chromatogram have no counterparts in the botanicals. These peaks are only minor quantitative components of the gin flavour extract, but the major component represented by peak J31/C24 (Fig. 11) shows a large relative increase in peak height in the gin compared with individual botanical components. These changes in composition of the botanical flavouring substances are evidently related to their distillation with ethyl alcohol (D. W. Clutton, personal communication). The identity of these gin constituents has not yet been established. The gas-liquid chromatogram of vodka depicted in Figure 12, and obtained by direct injection, provides no evidence of any component other than ethyl alcohol.

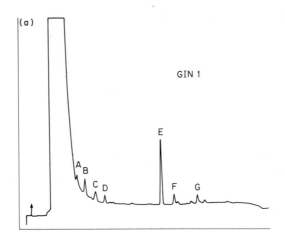

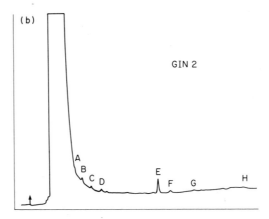

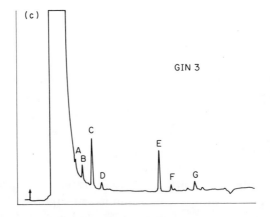

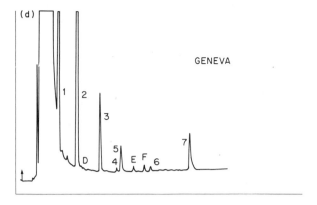

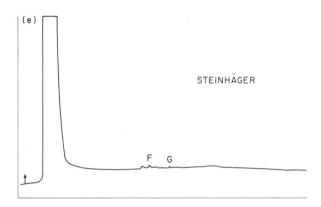

Fig. 10. Gas-liquid chromatograms of the volatile components of three gins, geneva and Steinhäger. The key to the compounds is: A, β-pinene; B, myrcene; C, d-limonene; D, γ-terpinene; E, linaloöl; F, p-terpinenol; G, unknown; H, cinnamaldehyde; I, isobutyl alcohol; 2, iso-amyl alcohol; 3, n-hexanol; 4, ethyl caprylate; 5, furfural; 6, ethyl caprate; 7, β-phenyl alcohol. The conditions for analysis were as described in the caption for Figure 6, except that 10 μl was injected onto the column, and the sensitivity was x 200.

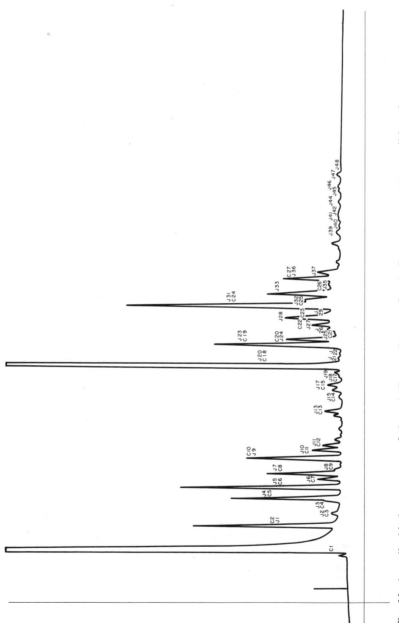

Fig. 11. A gas-liquid chromatogram of the volatile constituents of a gin-flavour extract. The conditions for analysis were as described in the caption for Figure 6.

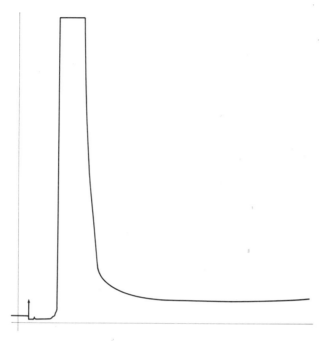

Fig. 12. A gas-liquid chromatogram of the volatile constituents of a vodka. The conditions for analysis were as described in the caption for Figure 10.

VI. FINISHING AND BOTTLING

Gin and vodka, being made from a rectified spirit which carries little or no congenerics, and in manufacture being flavoured or compounded with relatively small quantities of stable substances, are not subject to hazing or precipitation after packaging for sale. In this respect, these spirits differ from whisky and brandy which are rich in congenerics originating both from the still and from ageing in wooden casks. Gin and vodka, therefore, in preparation for bottling, are diluted in alcoholic strength and clarified without low-temperature conditioning. The quality and composition of the water used to dilute gin and vodka to bottling strength is important. Critical values for ion concentration in vodka were calculated by Zeltser (1959) to avoid precipitation after bottling. Using these data, standards could be set for the analytical quality of the dilution water. Warwicker (1963) undertook a similar study for gin. In modern distilleries and bottling plants, water quality is assured by softening, or preferably demineralizing by ion exchange, all water used for addition to spirits. As well as analytical purity, the flavour quality and suitability of water must remain under constant check. In most countries, statutory minimum levels have been set for the alcoholic strengths at which spirits can be sold, and this is normally in the region of 40% by volume.

Gin and vodka diluted to the correct strength for bottling, contain negligible concentrations of suspended solids, and are clarified by passage through filters such as a sheet-filter press, which give a high polishing brilliance. With both products, the avoidance of contact with any material in processing likely to transmit a contaminating odour is imperative; but this condition is particularly critical in the case of vodka when product quality is equated with the absence of any character other than that of pure ethyl alcohol. Vodka, once packaged, should retain its quality during subsequent storage. Gin, if exposed to the atmosphere for a period of time, e.g. in a half empty bottle, will alter in flavour due to oxidative changes in the terpenic constituents; these flavour changes, however, are not normally considered to be commercially significant.

VII. ACKNOWLEDGEMENTS

The author would like to thank the Directors of International Distillers and Vintners Limited for permission to contribute this chapter. He wishes to credit Mr D. W. Clutton with the gas-liquid chromatographic data on gin given in the chapter, which are to form part of a thesis to be submitted to the C.N.A.A. for a Ph.D. degree, and also to thank Gilbey Canada Limited for Figure 1, Dr K. J. Tarbuck for Figures 3, 4 and 5, and Mrs Irene Nicholson for typing the manuscript.

REFERENCES

Adams, S. L., Stark, W. H. and Kolachov, P. (1941). *Journal of Bacteriology* **42**, 292.
Akimov, Y. A. and Voronin, V. G. (1968). *Zhurnal Prikladnoi Khimii* **41**, 2561.
Alfredsson, M. and Losell, R. (1965). *Branntweinwirtschraft* **17**, 469.
Anon (1970). *The Flavour Industry* **1**, 524.
Anon (1974). *The Pharmaceutical Journal* **212**, 80.
Aschengreen, N. H. (1969). *Process Biochemistry* **4**, 23.

Austin, F. L. and Boruff, C. S. (1960). *Journal of the Association of Analytical Chemists* 43, 675.

Baldwin, E. (1963). 'Dynamic Aspects of Biochemistry', 4th edition. University Press, Cambridge.

Beech, F. W. (1972). *Progress in Industrial Microbiology* 11, 178.

Boinot, F. (1936). U.S. Patent 2,063,223.

Boinot, F. (1941). U.S. Patent 2,230,318.

Brenner, M. W., Owades, J. L. and Fazio, T. (1955). *Proceedings of the American Society of Brewing Chemists* p. 125.

Bryan-Jones, G. (1975). *In* 'Lactic Acid Bacteria in Beverages and Foods', Proceedings of Fourth Long Ashton Symposium (J. G. Carr, C. V. Cutting and G. C. Whiting, eds), pp. 165–175. Academic Press, London.

Carey, J. S. and Lewis, W. K. (1932). *Industrial and Engineering Chemistry* 24, 882.

Crowell, E. A. and Guymon, J. F. (1963). *American Journal of Enology and Viticulture* 14, 214.

Clutton, D. W. (1972). *The Flavour Industry* 3, 454.

Danilko, G. V., Danilyak, N. I., Egorov, A. S., Kaminskii, R. S., Nizkova, N. K., Tomashevich, G. S., Shaldenko, D. K., Lavirishcheva, T. N. and Savchenko, N. Y. (1972). *Otkrytiya Izobret., Proml Obraztsy, Tovarnye Znaki* 49, 79.

Deckenbrock, W. (1957). *Stärke* 9, 34.

De Vries, M. J. (1958). *South African Journal of Agricultural Science* 1, 195.

Encyclopaedia Britannica (1966). Vol. 10, pp. 421.

Fiero, G. W. (1958). *In* 'Flavour Research and Food Acceptance' (sponsored by Arthur D. Little, Inc.), pp. 241–248. Rheinhold Publishing Corporation, New York.

Fischer, E. H. and Haselbach, C. H. (1951). *Helvetica Chimica Acta* 4, 326.

Foth, G. (1929). 'Handbuch der Spiritusfabrikation', pp. 351–357. Paul Parey, Berlin.

Gray, R. M. and Moynihan, A. B. (1968). 'Symposium on Waste Disposal.' Institution of Chemical Engineers, London.

Guenther, E. (1950). 'The Essential Oils', Vol. 4. D. Van Nostrand Inc., New York.

Guenther, E. (1952). 'The Essential Oils', Vol. 6. D. Van Nostrand Inc., New York.

Guymon, J. F. and Nakagiri, J. A. (1955). *American Journal of Enology and Viticulture* 6, 12.

Guymon, J. F. and Pool, A. (1957). *American Journal of Enology and Viticulture* 8, 68.

Harris, G. (1962). *In* 'Barley and Malt' (A. H. Cook, ed.), pp. 581–694. Academic Press, London.

Harrison, J. S. and Graham, J. C. (1970). *In* 'The Yeasts' (A. H. Rose and J. S. Harrison, eds.), Vol. 3, pp. 283–348. Academic Press, London.

Heath, H. (1973). *The Flavour Industry* 3, 169.

Hirose, Y., Nishimura, K. and Sakai, T. (1960). *Nippon Kagaku Zasshi* 81, 1766.

Hirose, Y., Ogawa, M. and Kusuda, Y. (1962). *Agricultural and Biological Chemistry, Tokyo* 26, 526.

Hodge, H. M. and Hildebrandt, F. M. (1954). *In* 'Industrial Fermentations' (L. A. Underkofler and R. J. Hickey, eds.), Vol. 1, pp. 73–94. Chemical Publishing Company, New York.

Hopkins, R. H. and Wiener, S. (1955a). *Journal of the Institute of Brewing* 61, 488.

Hopkins, R. H. and Wiener, S. (1955b). *Journal of the Institute of Brewing* 61, 492.

Horak, W. and Lehman, H. (1969). *Alkohol-Industrie* 72, 235.

Horak, W., Frey, A. and Günther, G. (1968). *In* 'Handbuch der Lebensmittel-chemie', Band 7, Alcoholische Genussmittel (J. Schormuller, ed.), pp. 654–719. Springer-Verlag, Berlin.

Hough, J. S. and Stevens, R. (1961). *Journal of the Institute of Brewing* 67, 488.

Ikeda, R. M., Stanley, W. L., Vannier, S. H. and Spitler, E. M. (1962). *Journal of Food Science* 27, 455.

Kefford, J. F. and Chandler, B. V. (1970). 'The Chemical Constituents of Citrus Fruits.' Academic Press, New York.

Klein, E. and Farnow, H. (1965). *Dragoco Report* 12, 30.

Klouwen, M. H. and ter Heide, R. (1965). *Perfumery and Essential Oil Record* 56, 156.

Keen, E. and Spoerl, J. M. (1948). *Proceedings of the American Society of Brewing Chemists* p. 20.

Kodama, K. (1970). *In* 'The Yeasts' (A. H. Rose and J. S. Harrison, eds.), Vol. 3, pp. 225–282 Academic Press, London.

Kreipe, H. (1963). 'Technologie der Getreide und Kartoffelnbrennerei.' Hans Carl, Nuremberg.

Laatsch, H. U. and Sattelberg, K. (1968). *Process Biochemistry* 3, 28.

Lagomasino, J. M. (1949). *International Sugar Journal* 51, 338.

Langenau, E. E. (1947). *In* 'The Essential Oils' (E. Guenther, ed.), Vol. 1, pp. 227–348. D. Van Nostrand Corporation, Inc., Princeton, New Jersey.

Latham, P. (1966). 'Travel, Business, Study and Art in the U.S.S.R.' Blackie & Sons Limited, Glasgow.

Luckner, M., Bessler, O. and Schröder, P. (1965). *Pharmazie* 20, 77.

Mackenzie, K. G. and Kenny, M. C. (1965). *Journal of the Institute of Brewing* 71, 160.

Manners, D. J. and Yellowlees, D. (1973). *Journal of the Institute of Brewing* 79, 377.

Matzik, B. (1966). *Zeitschrift fur Lebensmittel Untersuchung und Forschung* 130, 345.

Myrbäck K. (1943). *Journal für Praktische Chemie* 162, 29.

Paturau, J. M. (1969). 'By-Products of the Cane Sugar Industry.' Elsevier, Amsterdam.

Prescott, S. C. and Dunn, C. G. (1959). 'Industrial Microbiology', 3rd edition. McGraw-Hill, New York.

Pyke, M. (1965). *Journal of the Institute of Brewing* 71, 209.

Rae, I. J. (1966). *Process Biochemistry* 1, 407.

Ramana Rao, B. V. (1964). *In* 'Ethyl Alcohol Production Technique', Symposium Report, p. 55. Noyes Development Corporation, New York.

Ronkainen, P., Denslow, J. and Leppänen O. (1973). *Journal of Chromatograph Science* 11, 384.

Sabourn, R. (1738). 'A Perfect View of the Gin Act.' Thorne, London.

Salo, P. (1970). *Journal of Food Science* 35, 95.

Salo, P., Nykänen. L. and Suomalainen, H. (1972). *Journal of Food Science* 37, 394.

Samaniego, R. and Srivastas, R. L. (1971). *Sugar News* 47, 301, 311.
Simmonds, C. (1919). 'Alcohol, its Production, Properties, Chemistry and Industrial Applications.' MacMillan, London.
Simpson, A. C. (1966). *Process Biochemistry* 1, 355.
Simpson, A. C. (1973). *Process Biochemistry* 8, 2.
Slavutskaya, N. I., Sal'nikova, G. M. and Yashin, Y. I. (1969). *Fermentnaya I Spirtovaya Promyshlennost* 35, 12.
Stark, W. H. (1954). *In* 'Industrial Fermentations' (L. A. Underkofler and R. J. Hickey, eds.), Vol. 1, pp. 17-72. Chemical Publishing Company, New York.
Suomalainen, H. and Nykänen, L. (1966). *Journal of the Institute of Brewing* 72, 469.
Suomalainen, H., Kauppila, O., Nykänen, L. and Peltonen, R. L. (1968). *In* 'Handbuch der Lebensmittelchemie', Band 7, Alcoholische Genussmittel (J. Schormüller, ed.), pp. 496–653. Springer-Verlag, Berlin.
Suomalainen, H. (1971). *Journal of the Institute of Brewing* 77, 164.
The Analysis of Potable Spirits (1970). First Report of the Research Committee on the Analysis of Potable Spirits: Estimation of Higher Alcohols. *Journal of the Association of Public Analysts* 8, 81.
The Analysis of Potable Spirits (1972). Second Report of the Research Committee on the Analysis of Potable Spirits: The Estimation of Methanol in Potable Spirits. *Journal of the Association of Public Analysts* 10, 49.
Thorne, R. S. W., Helm, E. and Svendsen, K. (1971). *Journal of the Institute of Brewing* 77, 148.
Tsvetkov, R. (1970). *Planta Medica* 4, 350.
Turvil, W. R. (1974). *Brewing and Distilling International* 4, 23.
Wainwright, T. (1973). *Journal of the Institute of Brewing* 79, 451.
Warwicker, L. A. (1963). *Journal of the Science of Food and Agriculture* 17, 371.
Weurman, C. (1969). *Journal of Agriculture and Food Chemistry* 17, 370.
Wilkie, H. F., Boruff, C. S. and Althausen, D. (1937). *Industrial and Engineering Chemistry* 29, 78.
Wilkinson, J. F. and Rose, A. H. (1963). *In* 'Biochemistry of Industrial Micro-organisms' (C. Rainbow and A. H. Rose, eds.), pp. 379–414. Academic Press, London.
Windish, W. W. and Mhatre, N. S. (1965). *Advances in Applied Microbiology* 7, 273.
Worldwide Survey of Fermentation Industries 1963 (1966). *Pure and Applied Chemistry* 13, 405.
Yusen Yin, Zarghami, N. and Heinz, D. E. (1970). *Journal of Food Science* 35, 531.
Zeltser, I. V. (1959). *Fermentnaya I Spirtovaya Promyshlennost* 25, 28.

9. Rum

M. LEHTONEN AND H. SUOMALAINEN

Research Laboratories of the State Alcohol Monopoly (Alko), Box 350, SF-00101 Helsinki 10, Finland

I. INTRODUCTION

Rum, the alcoholic beverage made from sugar cane, has been known for centuries. The origin of the name 'rum' is obscure. It may have been derived from the Latin for sugar, *Saccharum*. Another, and according to some sources more probable, origin of the word rum is the Devonshire dialect word *rum*, bullion (= rum), which British colonists took with them to the West Indies. Equally probable is a derivation from the Spanish 'ron' (= rum), for the Spaniards may well have had distilleries in the West Indies before the arrival of the British (Clutton, 1974).

Rum production is centred on the West Indies. The best known distilleries are situated in Jamaica, Martinique, Puerto Rico and Cuba, but Barbados, Trinidad, Haiti, Guadeloupe, the Virgin Islands, the Dominican Republic and Guyana (known as Demerara in the rum trade) all have old traditions of making rum. Rum is also produced in the U.S.A., Brazil, Peru, Mexico and parts of Asia and Africa. In general, rum is produced wherever the climate is suitable for the cultivation of sugar cane.

II. PRODUCTION OF RUM

A. Types of Rum and the Raw Materials Used

Rum is produced from cane sugar or sugar by-products, the most common raw material being cane juice, syrup or molasses. The raw material used largely determines the type of rum produced. Cane juice is best suited for the production of rum with a light aroma. Finely ground sugar-cane is pressed into a dry mass, and the cane juice so obtained is used as such or after concentration (Garnier-Laroche and Cottrell, 1975). Syrup, a thick, viscous liquid, is obtained by evaporating water from cane juice by vacuum distillation. Most rum is produced from molasses, which is especially suitable for the preparation of rums with very heavy aromas. Brown, syrupy molasses is a by-product in the production of sugar. It remains as the mother liquor when sugar is separated from cane juice by repeated crystallization. Depending on the sugar-cane variety, production methods and other factors such as climate, it contains some 50–60% sugar. The characteristics of two types of cane molasses are compared in Table 1.

Molasses also contains a number of compounds that can affect the aroma of rum. Yokota and Fagerson (1971) isolated 35 components from sugar-cane molasses, of which they identified 29 (Table 2). The compounds included aliphatic and aromatic esters, aldehydes, alcohols, furan derivatives and phenols. The 14 nucleic acid derivatives listed in Table 2 were identified by Hashizume et al. (1966). Other

Table 1

Analyses of two different types of cane molasses. From Burrows (1970)

	Type of molasses	
Constituent	Refiner's cane	Blackstrap cane
Total reducing sugar after inversion (wt %)	50–58	50–65
Total nitrogen (wt %)	0.1–0.6	0.4–1.5
α-Amino nitrogen (N, wt %)	0.03	0.05
Phosphorus (P_2O_5, wt %)	0.01–0.08	0.20–2.0
Calcium (CaO, wt %)	0.15–1.0	0.1–1.3
Magnesium (MgO, wt %)	0.25–0.8	0.3–1.0
Potassium (K_2O, wt %)	0.8–2.3	2.6–5.0
Zinc ($\mu g/g$)	5–20	10–20
Total carbon (wt %)	28–33	nd
Total ash (wt %)	3.5–7.5	7–11
Biotin ($\mu g/g$)	0.9–1.8	0.6–3.2
Calcium pantothenate ($\mu g/g$)	16	20–120
Inositol ($\mu g/g$)	2,500	6,000
Thiamin ($\mu g/g$)	nd	1.4–8.3
Pyridoxin ($\mu g/g$)	nd	6–7
Riboflavin ($\mu g/g$)	nd	2.5
Nicotinamide ($\mu g/g$)	nd	20–25
Folic acid ($\mu g/g$)	nd	0.04

nd indicates that the value was not determined.

compounds identified in cane molasses include sugar alcohols, amino acids and other organic acids (Binkley, 1966).

Some of the components in molasses can have adverse effects on various stages of the production process. Considerable amounts of hydroxymethylfurfural are often found in cane molasses that has been heated too much in the sugar factory. This compound has been found to retard yeast fermentation in anaerobic conditions at as low a concentration as 0.05% (Burrows, 1970). Some fatty acids have also been shown to retard fermentation (Dierssen et al., 1956); inhibition by acetic acid occurs even at a concentration of 0.75% (w/v). Of the higher acids, low concentrations of butyric and valeric acids can, depending on the pH value of the solution, adversely affect fermentation. Olbrich (1956) showed that even 0.1% (w/v) butyric acid completely inhibits fermentation.

Table 2

Compounds identified in sugar-cane molasses

Carbonyl compounds
Acetaldehyde[a]
Furfural[a]
5-Methylfurfural[a]
Acetyl benzaldehyde[a]*
o-Methoxybenzaldehyde[a]*
Furfuryl methyl ketone[a]
δ-Valerolactone[a]
(−)-2-Deceno-5-lactone[b]

Alcohols
Ethanol[a]
Propanol[a]
2-Methyl-1-propanol[a]
2-Methyl-2-butanol[a]
3-Methyl-1-butanol[a]
Furfuryl alcohol[a]
Melissyl alcohol[e]
Phenethyl alcohol[a]

Esters
Ethyl formate[a]
Ethyl acetate[a]
Isoamyl acetate[a]
Methyl benzoate[a]
Ethyl benzoate[a]
Benzyl formate[a]*
Phenethyl acetate[a]

Nitrogenous compounds
Acetyl pyrrole[a]
Alanine[e]
β-Alanine[e]
γ-Aminobutyric acid[e]
Asparagine[e]
Aspartic acid[e]
Cystine[e]
Glucosamine[e]
Glutamic acid[e]
Glutamine[e]
Glycine[e]
Histidine[e]
Homoserine[e]
Isoleucine[e]
Leucine[e]

Ethers
Anisole[a,c]
Phenetole[a,c]
Benzyl ethyl ether[a]
Furfuryl ethyl ether[a]*

Phenolic compounds
Phenol[c]
m-Cresol[c]
Guaiacol[a]
Salicylic acid[c]
Resorcinol[c]
Vanillic acid[c]
Syringic acid[c]
p-Coumaric acid[c]
Vanillin[c]

Acids
Formic acid[d,e]
Acetic acid[d,e]
Propionic acid[d,e]
n-Butyric acid[d,e]
n-Valeric acid[d]
Aconic acid[e]
Benzoic acid[c]
Citric acid[e]
Glycolic acid[e]
Lactic acid[e]
Malic acid[e]
Mesaconic acid[e]
Succinic acid[e]
Tricarballylic acid[e]

Nucleic acid derivatives
Adenine[f]
Adenosine[f]
Adenylic acid[f]
Cytidine[f]
Cytosine[f]*
Guanine[f]
Guanosine[f]
Guanylic acid[f]
Hypoxanthine[f]*
Inosine[f]
5′-Inosinic acid[f]
Thymine[f]*
Uridine[f]
Xanthine[f]*

Nitrogenous compounds—cont.

Lysine[e]	*Sugar alcohols*
Methionine[e]	D-Arabitol[e]
Phenylalanine[e]	D-Erythritol[e]
Pipecolic acid[e]	Myo-Inositol[e]
Proline[e]	D-Mannitol[e]
Serine[e]	
Threonine[e]	
Tryptophan[e]	*Miscellaneous*
Tyrosine[e]	2-Acetylfuran[a]
Valine[e]	4-Methyl-2-propyl furan[a]*

References: [a]Yokota and Fagerson (1971); [b]Hashizume *et al.* (1968); [c]Hashizume *et al.* (1967); [d]Dierssen *et al.* (1956); [e]Binkley (1966); and [f]Hashizume *et al.* (1966).
* Indicates that the compound was only tentatively identified.

The use of molasses in the production of rum does, however, offer some advantages over other possible raw materials. Being a natural by-product of the sugar industry, it is cheaper than, for example, cane juice. It keeps better than cane juice, so that its storage causes no problems.

B. Pretreatment of the Raw Materials

Depending on the quality, cane juice is fermented as it is or after heating and clarifying (Wollny, 1964). Pretreatment of molasses can be divided into several different stages. It must first be clarified to remove colloidal matter, especially calcium sulphate, which could otherwise block the column during distillation. Chemical clarification can be carried out by precipitation with alumina and calcium phosphate or by adding sulphuric acid. This, however, can lower the sugar content. Most of the remaining insoluble impurities can be removed by centrifugation, either cold or at higher temperatures. Micro-organisms, which could cause difficulties during the fermentation, are destroyed by pasteurization.

The final stage in the pretreatment of molasses is dilution with water, which lowers the viscosity and brings the total sugar content to 10–12 g/100 ml wash, which is a suitable concentration for fermentation. At the same time, it is usual to adjust the pH value of the solution to about 5.5 and to add ammonium sulphate or urea as yeast nutrients. The composition of a typical wash ready for fermentation is presented in Table 3.

Table 3

Typical properties of the wash after molasses pretreatment. From Paturau (1969)

Density (°Brix)	15–17
pH value	5.5–5.8
Total sugar content (g/100 ml)	10–12
Nitrogen content (g/100 ml)	2.0–2.5
Titratable acids (ml 0.1 N alkali/10 ml)	1.5–2.0
Phosphoric acid content (mg/100 ml)	600–750

C. Fermentation

The course of fermentation depends mainly on the fermentation temperature and time, the pH value of the solution and the kind of yeast present.

1. Fermentation Temperature

Various fermentation temperatures and times are used. According to I'Anson (1971), the temperature is held between 31°C and 32°C and the fermentation allowed to run for 36–48 hours. Puerto Rico rum distilleries use a temperature between 28°C and 33°C and a fermentation time of some 28–36 hours (Arroyo, 1949). Temperatures as high as 35–37°C have been reported (Kampen, 1967). According to Arroyo (1945) a temperature between 30°C and 33°C is usual but, when bacteria are used for fermentation, the temperature of the solution must not be allowed to exceed 30°C after addition of the bacteria.

2. pH Value

The pH value of the wash radically affects the course of fermentation and the metabolic products formed. Relatively high contents of alcohol can be obtained at lower pH values, but the optimum pH value for production of good aroma is probably in the region

5.5–5.8. Because bacteria lose their activity even at pH 4, the pH value must not be allowed to fall much below 5 when a combination of yeast and bacteria is used for fermentation.

3. Fermentation Time

The fermentation time depends on the amount and kind of yeast, the fermentation temperature, sugar concentration and quantity of yeast nutrients. A time of 30–48 hours is normally employed, but a period as long as 72 hours has been reported.

4. Yeasts

Fission-type top yeasts, such as *Schizosaccharomyces* strains, are best suited for the production of rums with a heavy aroma whereas, for the lighter rums, the quick-fermenting budding-type *Saccharomyces* yeasts are better (Paturau, 1969).

The best yeasts are from molasses. El-Tabey Shehata (1960) has isolated 26 yeasts from sugar cane and cane juice. Parfait and Sabin (1975) later isolated and identified mainly the same yeasts from molasses and cane juice. The yeasts are listed in Table 4. The rum yeasts must be able to produce a high content of alcohol, the correct aroma composition and, in order to minimize infection, a rapid fermentation.

Bacteria also play an important part in the production of rum. Arroyo (1945) has investigated the characteristics of *Clostridium saccharobutyricum* and its behaviour in fermentation. It was shown to accelerate the formation of alcohol during fermentation by yeast. He found that the best rum yield and aroma were obtained when the ratio of bacteria to yeasts was 1:5. The bacteria were added when the alcohol concentration was about 3.5–4.5 (v/v), and the sugar content at or below 6 g/100 ml wash. Oshmyan (1961) showed that pure cultures of the butyric acid bacterium, *Clostridium pasteurianum*, produced mainly butyric acid. Nemoto *et al.* (1975a) investigated the benefits of using a pure culture of a butyric-acid bacterium in the production of rum. While examining the tolerance of the butyric-acid bacterium to sugar and ethanol, they found that *Clostridium butyricum* A.T.C.C. 6015 produced mainly volatile acids. Production of acids was found to be most rapid when the sugar content was 5%

Table 4

Yeasts isolated from molasses or cane juice*

Candida guilliermondii[a]	*Saccharomyces carlsbergensis*
Candida intermedia	var. *alcoholophila* n. var.[a]
var. *ethanophila*[a]	*Saccharomyces cerevisiae*[a,b]
Candida krusei[a,b]	*Saccharomyces chevalieri*[a,b]
Candida mycoderma[a]	*Saccharomyces delbrucki*[b]
Candida parapsilosis	*Saccharomyces marxianus*[a]
var. *intermedia*[a]	*Saccharomyces microellipsoides*[a,b]
Candida pseudotropicalis[b]	*Saccharomyces rosei*[a]
Candida saccharum n. sp.[a]	*Saccharomyces rouxii*[b]
Candida tropicalis[a,b]	*Saccharomycodes ludwigii*[a]
Endomyces magnusii[a]	*Schizosaccharomyces pombe*[a,b]
Hansenula anomala[a,b]	*Torulopsis candida*[b]
Hansenula minuta[b]	*Torulopsis glabatira*[b]
Kloeckera apiculata[a]	*Torulopsis glabrata*[a]
Pichia fermentans[a]	*Torulopsis globosa*[a,b]
Pichia membranaefaciens[a,b]	*Torulopsis saccharum* n. sp.[a]
Saccharomyces aceti[b]	*Torulopsis stellata*[a,b]
Saccharomyces acidifaciens[a,b]	*Torulopsis stellata*
Saccharomyces carlsbergensis[b]	var. *cambresieri*[a]

[a] El-Tabey Shehata (1960); [b] Parfait and Sabin (1975).
* The nomenclature used for micro-organisms in this review follows that of the original sources.

(w/v), decreasing with increasing alcohol content, and completely ceasing when the concentration of alcohol was 7.5% (v/v). Nemoto *et al.* (1975b) showed further that the butyric-acid bacterium together with the rum yeast, *Schizosaccharomyces pombe*, does not cause fermentation in molasses that contains more than 14% (w/v) glucose. Addition of 15–30% of a wash containing a high concentration of acids after fermentation with butyric-acid bacteria to rum wash enriches the aroma of the rum produced, although the ester content is increased only slightly. Aquarone *et al.* (1963) examined the effect of sulphuric acid, potassium penicillin and sodium pentachlorophenolate on fermentation by strains of *Saccharomyces cerevisiae* and *Sacch. carlsbergensis*. They found that sulphuric acid increased the rate of fermentation slightly and that all of the compounds decreased the formation of acids to some extent. Ammonium fluoride, sodium fluoride and formaldehyde are also used as bactericides (Kampen, 1974).

D. Distillation

Before being distilled, the fermented mixture is usually allowed to stand for some hours so that the yeast cells can settle out. The remaining insoluble material is finally separated by centrifugation.

Both pot-still and continuous distillation units are in general use. The pot-still method is used mainly in the English- and French-speaking areas of the West Indies for preparation of heavy rums. A major advantage is that it requires a relatively small capital outlay. The method is also quite flexible and yields a high-quality product. Continuous distillation is used to produce the lighter rums, for example Puerto Rican and Cuban rums (Brau, 1958).

1. Pot-Still Distillation

A diagram of the apparatus used in pot-still distillation is shown in Figure 1 (Kampen, 1967). The apparatus consists of three vessels.

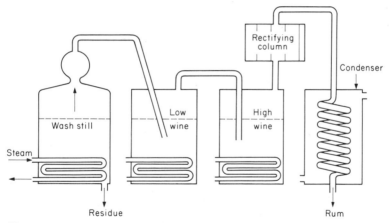

Fig. 1. A typical pot still distillation unit for rum production (Kampen, 1967).

The mixture to be distilled is first pumped to the copper wash-still distillation vessel, and the distillate from here is collected in a second vessel as low wines. The so-called high wines are obtained after a second distillation, and rum as the distillate from the high wines. Only the middle cut is taken as product. The initial low wines and final high wines are separated as fractions and returned to their respective vessels in the distillation of the following batch. Some Jamaican units do not have a rectifying column. Sometimes dunder is added to the wash to impart a particularly rich and fruity aroma to the distillate. Dunder is the lees from previous distillations that has been aged and ripened to varying degrees by bacterial action. It is commonly used in Jamaica but not in Guyana (I'Anson, 1971). Rums produced by pot-still distillation have the heavy, fruity aroma that is characteristic of Jamaica rum.

2. Continuous Distillation

Continuous distillation units consist of at least three columns (Brau, 1958). A diagram of a three-column unit is shown in Figure 2. The

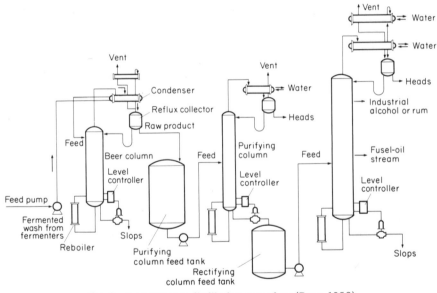

Fig. 2. A continuous distillation rum plant (Brau, 1958).

first column, known as the 'beer' or 'exhaustive' column, is used to remove all of the alcohol from the fermented wash. The vapour at the head of this column, containing volatile impurities and with an alcohol content of 40–65 (v/v), is condensed, part returning as reflux and the remainder being lead to the feed tanks for the purifying column. Before entering the purifying column, the raw distillate is suitably diluted with water, usually to 20–50 (v/v). Low-boiling impurities are taken off at the head of the purifying column, while the partially purified alcohol–water mixture is taken off at the bottom and lead to the rectifying-column feed tanks. The rectifying column is used to concentrate the alcohol to the desired strength and to remove the remaining impurities. Alcohol or beverage products are taken off from the upper trays of the column, while fusel oils

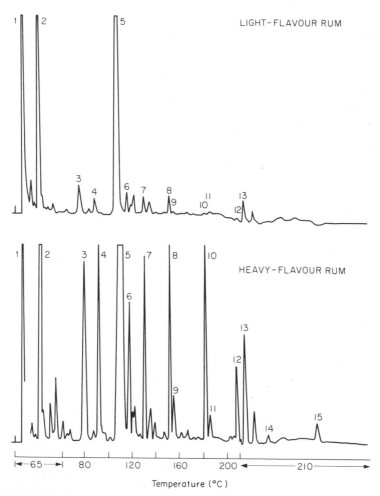

Fig. 3. Gas-liquid chromatograms of the aroma compounds of two types of white rum produced in the West Indies. Key to peak numbers: 1, Solvent; 2, ethyl acetate; 3, 2-methyl-1-propanol; 4, isoamyl acetate; 5, 3-methyl-1-butanol and 2-methyl-1-butanol; 6, ethyl hexanoate; 7, hexyl alcohol; 8, ethyl octanoate; 9, isoamyl hexanoate; 10, ethyl decanoate; 11, isoamyl octanoate; 12, ethyl laurate; 13, phenethyl alcohol; 14, ethyl myristate; 15, ethyl palmitate. From Suomalainen and Nykänen (1970).

accumulate in the intermediate plates and are removed as a side stream. Heads are removed from the top of the column.

Unger and Coffey (1975) have recently reported a modification of this distillation procedure in which the purifying column was made to act as an extractive column by feeding in water at the head. The use of extractive distillation can lead to the removal of almost all impurities.

The effect that the distillation process can have on the aroma composition of rum can be clearly seen by comparing the two gas-liquid chromatograms presented in Figure 3. These are of two West Indian rums, which contain substantially the same components but differ greatly in quantitative composition, the aroma fraction of light rum being only some 10% of that of the rum with the heavy aroma. Nemoto *et al.* (1975b) investigated the effects of distillation conditions, especially as they affect the content of acids and esters in the finished rum. They found that the amounts of acids rose 2–4-fold and the amounts of esters almost doubled when the pH value of the wash was lowered from 4.9 to 2.0. Supplementing the contents of acetic and butyric acids before distillation was shown to increase the formation of the corresponding ethyl esters during the distillation process.

E. Maturing

Freshly distilled rum often has a raw aroma, which can be improved by storing the liquor in oak casks. It is generally kept for two to ten years, although some heavy rums are matured for 10 to 12, or even 15 years. There is an English law, which was applicable in the former British colonies, that whisky, rum and brandy cannot be sold as such until they are three years old. The recent increase in the popularity and production of the lighter flavoured rums, which do not improve greatly with maturing, led to this rule being disregarded (I'Anson, 1971).

The ratio of the surface area of a cask to the volume of beverage it contains has an important effect on the course of the maturing. A capacity of about 150 litres is the most suitable (Paturau, 1969). The interior surfaces of the casks are usually charred to promote the maturing process, and the casks are kept upright during the maturing period.

The processes occurring during maturing are not known in detail. The oak walls of the cask are more or less permeable to easily volatile compounds depending on the temperature and relative humidity of the store. Another process occurring during maturing is extraction of wood components into the rum and their gradual decomposition. Additionally, it has been shown that esters are formed and that certain compounds are oxidized (M. Lehtonen and L. Nykänen, unpublished observations). Baldwin and Andreasen (1974) reported the changes occurring in quantity of aroma compounds in whisky and its colour during twelve years' maturing. More than half of the final level of acids and aldehydes was reached during the first four years, whereas the amount of esters continued to increase steadily throughout the whole period. Maturing had no noticeable effect on the concentration of higher alcohols.

III. AROMA COMPOUNDS OF RUM AND THEIR FORMATION

Rums can be divided into different groups according to both colour and aroma. Light and heavy rums are distinguished by their contents of aroma compounds. Aroma compounds include higher alcohols, fatty acids, fatty acid esters, carbonyl compounds, phenolic compounds and lactones. Rums can be classified by their so-called ester number, which is defined as the concentration of esters (mg) in 100 ml ethanol. Jamaican rums, for example, can be classified as follows: Common Clean rum, ester number 80–150; Plummer rum, 150–200; Wedderburn rum, 200–300; and Flavoured rum, 700–1,600 (Wollny, 1959). The concentration of higher esters is especially variable in both light and heavy rums; ethyl acetate is the only ester whose concentration is high in the lighter rums. In all, some 200 compounds have been identified in rum. They are listed in groups in Table 5.

A. Higher Alcohols

The fusel alcohols form quantitatively the largest group of aroma compounds in distilled alcoholic beverages, but their concentration in rum is lower than in most other distilled drinks. An average rum contains 0.6 g/l, whereas the concentration in Scotch whisky is 1 g/l

Table 5

Aroma compounds identified in rum

ALCOHOLS

Methanol[a]	1-Propanol[a, b, c]	1-Butanol[a, b, c]
2-Methyl-1-propanol[a, b, c]	2-Butanol[a, b]	1-Pentanol[a, b]
2-Pentanol[a]	3-Pentanol[a]	2-Methyl-2-butanol[a, c]
3-Methyl-1-butanol[a, b, c, d]	2-Methyl-1-butanol[a, b, c]	Methylbutenol[a]
1-Hexanol[a]	2-Hexanol[a]	2-Heptanol[c]
1-Octanol[e]	β-Phenethyl alcohol[a, d, e]	Menthol[a, d, e]
1-Hepten-3-ol[e]	1-Octen-3-ol[c]	

ACIDS

Acetic acid[a, b, f]	Propionic acid[a, b, f]	Butyric acid[a, b, f]
Isobutyric acid[a, f]	Valeric acid[a, b, f]	Isovaleric acid[a, f]
2-Methylbutyric acid[a]	Hexanoic acid[a, b, f]	4-Methylvaleric acid[a]
Heptanoic acid[a, f]	Heptenoic acid[a]	Octanoic acid[a, b, f]
6-Methylheptanoic acid[a]	Nonanoic acid[a, f]	Decanoic acid[a, f]
Undecanoic acid[f]	Lauric acid[f]	Tridecanoic acid[f]
Myristic acid[f]	Pentadecanoic acid[f]	Palmitic acid[f]
Palmitoleic acid[f]	Heptadecanoic acid[f]	Stearic acid[f]
Oleic acid[f]	Linoleic acid[f]	3-Ethoxypropionic acid[a]
Benzoic acid[a]	3-Furancarboxylic acid[a]	2-Furancarboxylic acid[a]
2-Ethyl-3-methylbutyric acid[n]		

ESTERS

Ethyl formate[a, b]	Isobutyl formate[a]*	Isoamyl formate[a]
Methyl acetate[a]*	Ethyl acetate[a, b]	Propyl acetate[a, b]
Butyl acetate[a, b]	Sec. butyl acetate[a]*	Isobutyl acetate[a]
Isoamyl acetate[a, b, c]	Hexyl acetate[a, b]	Phenethyl acetate[a, d, e]
Ethyl propionate[a, b]	Propyl propionate[a]	Isobutyl propionate[a]
Isoamyl propionate[a]	Ethyl butyrate[a, b]	Propyl butyrate[a, b]
Isobutyl butyrate[a]*	Isoamyl butyrate[a, b]	Ethyl isobutyrate[a, b]
Ethyl valerate[a, b]	Isobutyl valerate[b]	Isoamyl valerate[a]
Ethyl isovalerate[a, b]	Ethyl 2-methylbutyrate[a, b]	Ethyl hexanoate[a, b, d]
Propyl hexanoate[b]	Isobutyl hexanoate[b]	Isoamyl hexanoate[a, d]
Hexyl hexanoate[d]	2-Methylbutyl hexanoate[b]	Ethyl heptanoate[a, b]
Ethyl heptenoate[a]	Methyl octanoate[a]	Ethyl octanoate[a, b, d, e]
Isoamyl octanoate[a, d]	Phenethyl octanoate[a]	Ethyl nonanoate[a, b, d]
Methyl decanoate[a]	Ethyl decanoate[a, b, c, d, e]	Isobutyl decanoate[a]
Isoamyl decanoate[a, d]	Phenethyl decanoate[a]	Ethyl undecanoate[a]
Methyl laurate[a, e]	Ethyl laurate[a, d]	Isoamyl laurate[a, d]

ESTERS *(cont.)*

Ethyl dodecadienoate[a*]   Ethyl myristate[a,d]   Isoamyl myristate[a]
Ethyl pentadecanoate[a]   Methyl palmitate[a]   Ethyl palmitate[a]
Propyl palmitate[a]   Isoamyl palmitate[a,d]   Ethyl palmitoleate[a,d]
Ethyl heptadecanoate[a]   Ethyl stearate[a]   Ethyl oleate[a,d]
Ethyl linoleate[a,d]   Ethyl linolenate[d]   Ethyl lactate[a,b,d]
Monoethyl succinate[a]   Diethyl succinate[a,b,d]   Monoethyl citrate[a]
Ethyl benzoate[a,b,d]   Ethyl 3-hydroxybutyrate[b]   Methyl salicylate[a,c,d]
Ethyl 3-methoxy-4-hydroxybenzoate[h]   Ethyl 3-phenyl-propionate[a,d]   Ethyl 2-furancarboxylate[a]
Ethyl syringate[h]

PHENOLIC COMPOUNDS

Phenol[a,g,h]   *o*-Cresol[g]
m-Cresol[h]   *p*-Cresol[g]
Guaiacol[a,g,h]   Eugenol[a,b,g,h]
4-Ethylguaiacol[a,d,g,h]   4-Ethylphenol[a,g]
4-Methylguaiacol[a,b,g,h]   Isoeugenol[a,h]
4-Vinylguaiacol[h]   Propylguaiacol[d,g]
4-Ethyl-2,6-dimethoxyphenol[h]   2,6-Dimethoxyphenol[h]
Vanillin[a,h]   4-Vinyl-2,6-dimethoxyphenol[h]
Propiovanillone[h]   Acetovanillone[h]
Acetosyringone[h]   Syringaldehyde[h]
Coniferyl aldehyde[h]   Propiosyringone[h]
Scopoletin[i]   Sinapaldehyde[h]

NITROGENOUS COMPOUNDS

2-Methylpyrazine[a,j]   2,3-Dimethylpyrazine[j]
2,5-Dimethylpyrazine[a,j]   2,6-Dimethylpyrazine[a,j]
2-Methyl-3-ethylpyrazine[a]   2-Methyl-5-ethylpyrazine[j]
2-Methyl-6-ethylpyrazine[a,j]   2-Methyl-6-vinylpyrazine[j]
3,5-Dimethyl-2-ethylpyrazine[a]   2,5-Dimethyl-3-ethylpyrazine[a,j]
Trimethylpyrazine[j]   Pyridine[j]
α-Picoline[j]   β-Picoline[j]
Thiazole[j]

SULPHUR-CONTAINING COMPOUNDS   LACTONES

Dimethyl sulphide[a,k]   δ-Octalactone[a]
Methyl ethyl sulphide[a]   γ-Nonalactone[a]
Ethanethiol[k]   β-Methyl-γ-octalactone[d,i]

Table 5 (*cont.*)

SULPHUR-CONTAINING COMPOUNDS (*cont.*)   LACTONES (*cont.*)

Diethyl sulphide[k]   γ-Decalactone[a]
Dimethyl disulphide[k]   δ-Decalactone[a]
Diethyl disulphide[k]   γ-Dodecalactone[a]
                                                δ-Dodecalactone[a]

CARBONYL COMPOUNDS AND ACETALS

Formaldehyde[b]
Propionaldehyde[a,b]
Isovaleraldehyde[a]
Hexanal[b]
Furfural[a,b,d]
Benzaldehyde[a,b]
2-Ethoxypropanal[b]
Crotonaldehyde[b]
Acetone[a]
2-Butanone[a]
2-Pentanone[a]
2-Hexanone[a]*
3-Hexanone[a]*
Diacetyl[a]
2,3-Pentanedione[b]
3-Penten-2-one[a]
4-Methyl-3-penten-2-one[a]*
4-Ethoxy-2-butanone[a]
1,1-Diethoxy-2-propanone[a]
4-Ethoxy-2-pentanone[a]
Acetylfuran[a,b]
o-Hydroxyacetophenone[a]
2-Methyl-3-tetrahydrofuranone[a,b]
α-Ionone[a]*
Diethoxymethane[a,b]
1-Methoxy-1-ethoxyethane[a]
1,1-Diethoxyethane[a,b,d]
1-Ethoxy-1-propoxyethane[a]
1-Ethoxy-1-butoxyethane[a,b]
1-Ethoxy-1-(2-methylpropoxy)-
    ethane[a,b]
1-Ethoxy-1-pentoxyethane[a,b]
1,1-Ethoxy-hexoxyethane[b]
1-Ethoxy-1-(3-methylbutoxy)-
    ethane[a,b]
1-Ethoxy-1-(2-methylbutoxy)-
    ethane[a,b]
1,1-Dipropoxyethane[a]

1-Propoxy-1-(3-methylbutoxy)-
    ethane[a,b]
Acetaldehyde[a,b]
Isobutyraldehyde[a,b]
Valeraldehyde[b]
2-Methylbutyraldehyde[a]
5-Methylfurfural[a,b]
Hydroxymethylbenzaldehyde[a]*
3-Ethoxypropanal[m]
Acrolein[b,m]
1-Butoxy-1-(3-methylbutoxy)-
    ethane[a]
1,1-Di-(2-methylpropoxy)-ethane[a]
1-(2-Methylpropoxy)-1-(3-methyl-
    butoxy)-ethane[a,b]
1-Pentoxy-1-(3-methylbutoxy)-
    ethane[a]
1,1-Di-(3-methylbutoxy)-ethane[a,b]
1-(3-Methylbutoxy)-1-(2-methyl-
    butoxy)-ethane[a,b]
1,1-Butoxy-pentoxyethane[b]
1,1-Diethoxypropane[a,b]
1-Ethoxy-1-(2-methylpropoxy)-
    propane[a]
1-Ethoxy-1-(3-methylbutoxy)-
    propane[a]
1-Propoxy-1-(3-methylbutoxy)-
    propane[a]
1,1-Di-(2-methylpropoxy)-propane[a]
1,1-Diethoxybutane[a,b]
1,1-Diethoxy-2-methylpropane[a,d]
1-Ethoxy-1-propoxy-2-methyl-
    propane[a]
1-Ethoxy-1-(2-methylpropoxy)-
    2-methylpropane[a]
1-Ethoxy-1-(3-methylbutoxy)-2-
    methylpropane[a]
1-Propoxy-1-(2-methylpropoxy)-2-
    methylpropane[a]

CARBONYL COMPOUNDS AND ACETALS (*cont.*)

1-Propoxy-1-(3-methylbutoxy)-2-
methylpropane[a]
1,1-Di-(2-methylpropoxy)-2-
methylpropane[a]
1-(2-Methylpropoxy)-1-(3-methyl-
butoxy)-2-methylpropane[a]
1,1-Di-(3-methylbutoxy)-2-methyl-
propane[a]
1-Ethoxy-1-(2-methylpropoxy)-
pentane[a]
1,1-Di-(2-methylpropoxy)-pentane[a]
1,1-Diethoxy-3-methylbutane[a,d]
1-Ethoxy-1-(2-methylpropoxy)-3-
methylbutane[a]
1-Ethoxy-1-(3-methylbutoxy)-3-
methylbutane[a]
1,1-Dipropoxy-3-methylbutane[a]

1-Propoxy-1-(2-methylpropoxy)-3-
methylbutane[a]
1-Propoxy-1-(3-methylbutoxy)-3-
methylbutane[a]
1,1-Di-(2-methylpropoxy)-3-
methylbutane[a]
1-(2-Methylpropoxy)-1-(3-methyl-
butoxy)-3-methylbutane[a]
1,1-Di-(3-methylbutoxy)-3-
methylbutane[a]
1-Ethoxy-1-(3-methylbutoxy)-
butane[b]
1,1-Diethoxy-2-methylbutane[b]
1,1-Ethoxy-pentoxybutane[b]
1-Ethoxy-1-pentoxypentane[b]
1,1,3-Triethoxypropane[d]

MISCELLANEOUS

2-Methylfuran[a]
3,8,8-Trimethyltetrahydro-
naphthalene[a,d]
1,1,6-Trimethyl-1,2-dihydro-
naphthalene[a,c]

ar-Curcumene[d]
Methyl chavicol[d]
α-Terpineol[d]
2,2,6-Trimethyl-trans-crotonoyl-1-
cyclohexa-1,3-diene[d,e]

References: [a] Liebich *et al.* (1970); [b] Maarse and ten Noever de Brauw (1966); [c] Allan (1973); [d] de Smedt and Liddle (1975); [e] Dubois and Rigaud (1975); [f] Nykänen *et al.* (1968b); [g] Timmer *et al.* (1971); [h] Dubois and Brule (1972); [i] Otsuka and Zenibayashi (1974); [j] Wobben *et al.* (1971); [k] Dellweg *et al.* (1969); [l] Otsuka *et al.* (1974); [m] Dubois *et al.* (1973); [n] M. Lehtonen, B. Gref, E. Puputti and H. Suomalainen (unpublished data).

* Indicates that the compound was only tentatively identified.

and in cognac 1.5 g/l (Suomalainen and Nykänen, 1970). The fusel alcohol content of some rums is presented in Table 6.

The higher alcohols found in rum are largely the same as those appearing in other alcoholic beverages. Maarse and ten Noever de Brauw (1966) identified 1-propanol, 1-butanol, 2-methyl-1-propanol, 2-butanol, 2-methyl-1-butanol and 3-methyl-1-butanol in Jamaican rum. Later investigations showed that Jamaican rum also contains 2-methyl-2-butanol, 1-pentanol, 2-pentanol, 3-pentanol, 1-hexanol, 2-hexanol, 2-heptanol and phenethyl alcohol (Liebich *et al.*, 1970;

Table 6

Relative proportions of fusel alcohols in some types of rum

	Percent fusel oil in		
	Jamaican rum[a]	Martinique rum[a]	Guadeloupe rum[b]
1-Propanol	15.0	6.0	8.5
2-Butanol	5.0	traces	traces
1-Butanol	1.0	traces	0
2-Methyl-1-propanol	15.0	15.0	16.0
2-Methyl-1-butanol	10.0	12.0	8.5
3-Methyl-1-butanol	54.0	67.0	67.0
2-Pentanol	nd	nd	0

[a]Sihto et al. (1962); [b] Baraud and Maurice (1963).
nd indicates that the concentration was not determined.

Allan, 1973). 3-Methyl-1-butanol, 2-methyl-1-butanol, 2-methyl-1-propanol and 1-propanol are the major higher alcohol components.

Many of these alcohols have also been found in sugar-cane molasses and fermented molasses. Yokota and Fagerson (1971) identified ethanol, 1-propanol, 2-methyl-1-propanol, 2-methyl-2-butanol, 3-methyl-1-butanol and phenethyl alcohol in molasses. According to Komoda and Yamada (1968), fermented molasses contained 1-propanol, 2-methyl-1-propanol, 1-butanol, 2-methyl-1-butanol, 3-methyl-1-butanol, 1-hexanol, 1-octanol and phenethyl alcohol.

The fusel-alcohol fraction contains mainly saturated alcohols, but some unsaturated alcohols have also been found. Dubois and Rigaud (1975) identified 1-hepten-3-ol. It is not known with certainty how this alcohol is formed, but it is assumed that the mechanism is analogous to that by which methyl ketones are formed by moulds in cheese (Dubois and Rigaud, 1975). Allan (1973) has identified 1-octen-3-ol in the fusel-alcohol fraction of rum. 1-Octen-3-ol has been shown to be an important aroma component in fungi, where it is formed by oxidative decomposition of lipids (Forss, 1969).

The fusel-alcohol fractions of Jamaican rums are exceptional in that they generally contain a high concentration of 2-butanol, and almost as much 1-propanol as 2-methyl-1-propanol (Suomalainen and Nykänen, 1967; Mesley et al., 1975).

Attempts have been made to use the ratio of 2-methyl-1-butanol to 3-methyl-1-butanol to differentiate rum from other alcoholic beverages. de Smedt and Liddle (1975) found this ratio to be 0.195 for rum, 0.355 for whisky, 0.22 for cognac and 0.24 for armagnac. Calvados was the only beverage found to háve a lower value (0.18) than rum. Mesley *et al.* (1975) reported that the ratio of 2-methyl-1-butanol to 3-methyl-1-butanol is generally lower in rum than in whisky. Some other analytically measurable properties have been used to characterize different beverages. Rums with even the lightest aroma contain more 1-propanol than any type of vodka. The concentration of methanol in rums is usually lower than in brandies. The ratio of 1-propanol to 2-methyl-1-propanol is higher in rum than in most whiskies (Mesley *et al.*, 1975).

The fusel alcohols produced in fermentation can be formed in either of two different ways, by an anabolic, biosynthetic pathway from sugars or by a catabolic pathway from exogenous amino acids

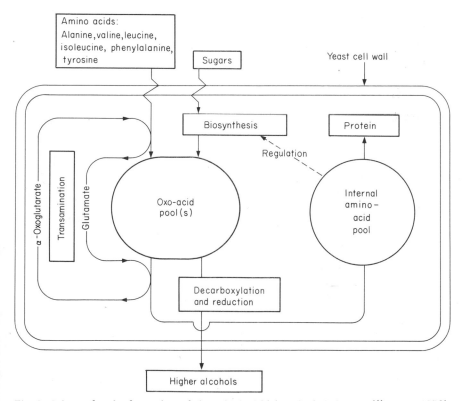

Fig. 4. Scheme for the formation of the principal higher alcohols in rum (Äyräpää, 1973).

(Äyräpää, 1973). In each case, oxo acids act as intermediates. A scheme showing the formation of fusel alcohols is presented in Figure 4.

Guymon *et al.* (1961) demonstrated that 1-propanol and the branched-chain C_4 and C_5 alcohols, all major components in alcoholic beverages, are formed by metabolism of valine, leucine and isoleucine. 2-Oxobutyric acid is an intermediate in the formation of 1-propanol, and it has also been found as an intermediate in the synthesis of isoleucine and in the formation of 2-methyl-1-butanol.

As has been stated, fusel alcohols can also be formed from sugars. According to Webb and Ingraham (1963), 2-methyl-1-propanol is formed from pyruvic acid by way of 2-oxo-isovaleric acid. In the mechanism presented in Figure 5, 2-methyl-1-butanol is formed from 2-oxo-isovaleric acid via 2-oxo-3-methylvaleric acid.

Reazin *et al.* (1973) examined the effect of threonine and isoleucine on synthesis of higher alcohols. They showed that, almost exclusively, 2-methyl-1-butanol was formed from isoleucine in fer-

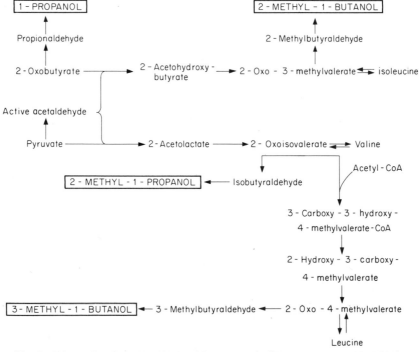

Fig. 5. Scheme for the biosynthesis of fusel alcohols (Webb and Ingraham, 1963).

mentations with *Saccharomyces cerevisiae*. In contrast, threonine gave 1-propanol, 2-methyl-1-butanol and 3-methyl-1-butanol. The biochemical reactions involved in the metabolism of threonine, leucine and isoleucine are presented in Figure 6. 1-Propanol is the

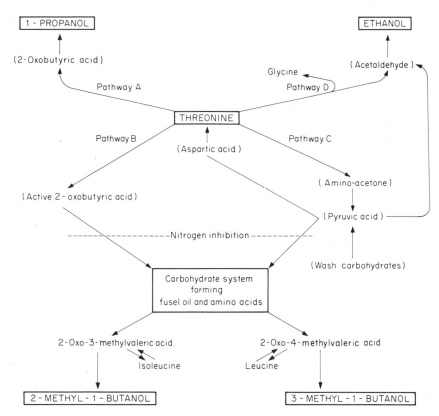

Fig. 6. Role of threonine and isoleucine in the biosynthesis of higher alcohols. From Reazin *et al.* (1973).

end product of pathway A. Threonine first forms 2-amino-2-butenoic acid by the action of threonine dehydratase. This compound is then deaminated to 2-oxobutyric acid, an intermediate in the formation of 1-propanol. Pathway B leads to the formation of 2-methyl-1-butanol. Activated 2-amino-2-butenoic acid is produced by the action of threonine dehydratase, and is deaminated to activated 2-oxobutyric acid. This compound reacts further with acetyl-coenzyme A to form acetohydroxybutyl-coenzyme A. This complex is a metabolic intermediate in the transformation of carbohydrates to 2-methyl-1-butanol and isoleucine. The oxo acid corresponding to isoleucine, namely 2-oxo-3-methylvaleric acid, acts as an intermediate in the formation of 2-methyl-1-butanol from isoleucine and threonine.

3-Methyl-1-butanol is the end product of pathway C. Labile 2-amino-3-oxobutyric acid, formed by the action of threonine dehydratase, is easily decarboxylated to form aminoacetone. This reacts to form methylglyoxal, which is oxidized to pyruvic acid. The pyruvic acid reacts with acetyl-coenzyme A to form 2-acetolactic acid, which acts as an intermediate in the formation of leucine and 3-methyl-1-butanol. All of the oxo acids appearing as intermediates in the formation of fusel alcohols have been identified in both yeast cells and fermentation solutions (Suomalainen and Linnahalme, 1966; Suomalainen and Keränen, 1967; Ronkainen et al., 1970).

Higher alcohols are also formed as metabolic products of bacteria. Maurel et al. (1965) have shown that 2-butanol can be formed in bacterial fermentations. 2-Butanol has also been identified in wines spoilt by bacteria or moulds (Hieke, 1972). Hieke and Vollbrecht (1974) showed that some Lactobacillus spp. produce 1-propanol and 2-butanol. 2-Butanol is presumably formed by direct reduction of a compound whose hydrocarbon chain remains unchanged; a possible precursor for 2-butanol would be 2,3-butanediol.

The type of yeast used for fermentation has a significant effect on the formation of alcohols. Schizosaccharomyces pombe, for example, produces relatively little of the higher alcohols (Parfait and Jouret, 1975). Mutations in yeasts can also affect formation of fusel alcohols. Guymon et al. (1961) showed that, whereas one mutant of a threonine-deficient strain of Saccharomyces cerevisiae produced neither 1-propanol nor 2-methyl-1-butanol, the remainder of the mutants examined could generate both of these alcohols. Webb and Kepner (1961) reported the same effect with pure cultures of Sacch. cerevisiae. Burgundy yeast produces large quantities of 1-propanol and correspondingly less 3-methyl-1-butanol. In contrast, Montrachet produces a normal amount of 1-propanol and relatively more 3-methyl-1-butanol. Like Burgundy yeast, Jerez yeast produces more 1-propanol and less 3-methyl-1-butanol. Arroyo (1945) showed that addition of Clostridium spp. to yeast fermentations decreased the amount of higher alcohols formed.

The amount and nature of yeast nutrients (ammonium sulphate

and urea are commonly used in production of rum) affect formation of alcohols. According to Äyräpää (1968), the amount of alcohols formed rises as a function of the nitrogen content at very low concentrations of nitrogenous nutrients. At higher concentrations of nitrogenous nutrients, but ones where yeast growth is still limited by the availability of these compounds, the amounts of alcohols formed decrease sharply as the nitrogen content of the medium increases. In the presence of excess nitrogen, formation of higher alcohols is low and relatively independent of the concentration of nitrogenous compounds. Formation of 1-propanol seems to obey no clear rules but, with limiting concentrations of nitrogenous compounds, it increases with the content of nitrogen and, at higher concentrations, large amounts are produced, largely independent of the concentration of nitrogenous compounds.

The fermentation temperature influences formation of alcohols. Merrit (1966) reported that the optimum temperature is 30°C. The amounts of 1-propanol and 2-methyl-1-butanol formed are influenced slightly by the temperature in the range 25–35°C. On the other hand, the amounts of 2-methyl-1-propanol and 3-methyl-1-butanol formed are relatively insensitive to environmental temperature (Parfait and Jouret, 1975). Äyräpää (1970) has reported that *Saccharomyces carlsbergensis* produces the largest quantity of higher alcohols at 20°C, but that the rate of production is maximum at 28°C.

B. Fatty Acids

In common with other distilled alcoholic beverages, rum contains volatile fatty acids. The total acid content varies greatly in different types of rum. The total acid content in light Puerto Rican rum is 100 mg/l, while the total acids in heavy Martinique rum can be as high as 600 mg/l (Nykänen *et al.*, 1968a). Acetic acid makes up some 75–85% of the total acids (Suomalainen, 1975). The relative composition of the volatile fatty acids in some rum types is presented in Table 7. The proportion of propionic and butyric acids is higher in rum than in other spirits. Propionic acid is one of the main acid components; in Jamaican rum, it is exceeded only by acetic acid. The concentrations of propionic, butyric, octanoic and decanoic acids in Martinique rum are approximately equal. Rum contains a certain

Table 7

Volatile acids higher than acetic acid in different types of rum. From Nykanen
et al. (1968b)

Acid	Per cent composition of acid fraction of		
	Martinique rum I	Martinique rum II	Jamaican rum
Propionic acid	15.7	14.5	30.2
Isobutyric acid	3.6	2.9	4.3
Butyric acid	15.3	8.5	8.0
Isovaleric acid	4.7	6.2	6.5
Valeric acid	6.5	1.7	1.8
Hexanoic acid	5.4	5.3	6.6
Heptanoic acid	traces	2.4	0.3
Octanoic acid	14.5	13.5	8.9
Nonanoic acid	traces	traces	0.5
Decanoic acid	17.5	26.1	16.6
Undecanoic acid	0.3	0.7	nd
Lauric acid	6.5	12.0	9.0
Tridecanoic acid	0.1	nd	traces
Myristic acid	1.1	1.5	1.7
Pentadecanoic acid	0.1	traces	0.1
Palmitic acid	4.0	3.2	2.9
Palmitoleic acid	1.0	0.6	0.9
Heptadecanoic acid	nd	nd	traces
Stearic acid	0.3	0.4	0.5
Oleic acid	1.2	0.5	0.5
Linoleic acid	2.2	nd	0.7

nd indicates that the composition was not determined.

amount of odd-numbered fatty acids, and more valeric acid than do
other beverages. Some unsaturated acids have been found in rum.
Liebich *et al.* (1970) identified heptenoic acid in Jamaican rum,
and Nykänen *et al.* (1968b) found palmitoleic, oleic and linoleic
acids in Jamaican and Martinique rums.

The relative proportions of fatty acids in whisky, cognac and rum
are presented in Figure 7. There is relatively much more propionic
and butyric acids in rum than in whisky and cognac. Compared with
rum, whisky and cognac contain very little n-valeric acid, but each
beverage contains similar proportions of the branched-chain C_4 and
C_5 acids. The proportions of hexanoic and higher acids were slightly
lower in rum than in the other beverages.

Acetyl-coenzyme A acts as starting material in the biosynthesis of

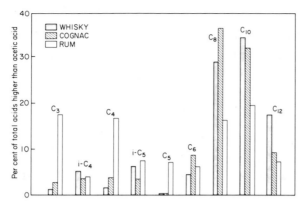

Fig. 7. Histograms showing the relative proportions of acids in whisky, cognac and rum. Unpublished results of E. Puputti.

fatty acids in yeasts. It is formed by oxidative decarboxylation of pyruvic acid in aerobic catabolism of carbohydrates (Lynen, 1973). Through the action of carboxylase, the reaction leads to the formation of malonyl-coenzyme A (Fig. 8). Long-chain fatty acids

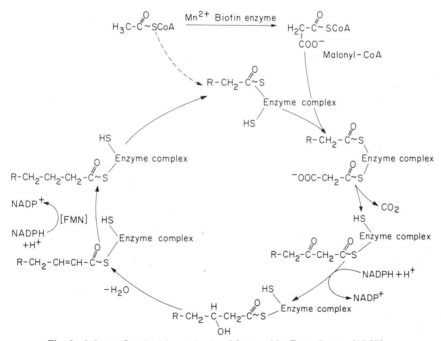

Fig. 8. Scheme for the biosynthesis of fatty acids. From Lynen (1967).

are formed with the help of acetyl-coenzyme A, malonyl-coenzyme A and NADPH. According to Lynen (1967), the reaction proceeds on a multi-enzyme complex that binds acetyl-coenzyme A and malonyl-coenzyme A. The enzyme complex continues to bind all of the intermediates until the fatty acids are formed. Acetyl-coenzyme A is replaced by propionyl-coenzyme A in the formation of odd-numbered fatty acids.

Unsaturated acids are formed from the corresponding saturated fatty acids by way of palmityl-coenzyme A and stearyl-coenzyme A in the presence of molecular oxygen and NADPH (Bloomfield and Bloch, 1960). The first step in the reaction is the activation of fatty acids to form acyl-coenzyme A. Desaturation at the 9–10 position occurs in the following stage. According to Bloomfield and Bloch (1960), the reaction goes as follows:

$$\text{palmitic acid} \quad \xrightarrow[\text{Mg}^{2+}]{\text{CoA, ATP}} \quad \text{palmityl-CoA}$$

$$\text{palmityl-CoA} \quad \xrightarrow{\text{O}_2,\ \text{NADPH}} \quad [\text{oxypalmityl-CoA}]$$

$$[\text{oxypalmityl-CoA}] \quad \xrightarrow{\hspace{2cm}} \quad \text{palmitoleyl-CoA}$$

$$\text{palmitoleyl-CoA} \quad \xrightarrow{\text{thiolase}} \quad \text{palmitoleic acid} + \text{CoA}$$

Bloomfield and Bloch (1960) also examined the role of biotin in these reactions. Biotin has no effect on the degree of unsaturation, but strongly modifies the course of lipid synthesis. Biotin deficiency decreases synthesis of fatty acids, and increases the amount of sterols formed. Suomalainen and Keränen (1963a) found that a deficiency of biotin under aerobic conditions increases synthesis of fatty acids up to C_{16} at the expense of C_{18}-acids.

As has already been stated, formation of unsaturated acids is an aerobic process. Suomalainen and Keränen (1963b) investigated the effect of anaerobic conditions on formation of fatty acids by baker's yeast. They found that the contents of the unsaturated fatty acids, oleic and palmitoleic acids, fell to less than half of their original values whether the medium contained biotin or not. The content of palmitic acid was found to increase as the level of palmitoleic acid fell, but no corresponding relationship was found between oleic acid and stearic acid.

Unsaturated fatty acids can be formed under anaerobic conditions by bacteria, as Goldfine and Bloch (1961) demonstrated with *Clostridium butyricum* and *Cl. kluyveri*. Scheuerbrandt *et al.* (1961) observed that octanoic and decanoic acids act as precursors for both saturated and unsaturated acids in *Cl. butyricum*. Lauric and longer-chain acids form exclusively saturated acids (Goldfine and Bloch, 1961). *Clostridium butyricum* is able to form palmitoleic acid and 11-octadecenoic acid from octanoic acid, and oleic acid and 7-hexa-decenoic acid from decanoic acid (Scheuerbrandt and Bloch, 1962). In the mechanism proposed (Fig. 9), the pathways leading to

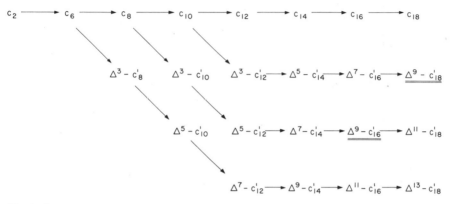

Fig. 9. Proposed anaerobic pathway leading to biosynthesis of mono-unsaturated fatty acids in bacteria (Scheuerbrandt and Bloch, 1962). The fatty acids underlined have been detected in rum.

formation of the saturated and unsaturated acids branch at C_8 and C_{10}. Palmitoleic and oleic acids are the dominating unsaturated fatty acids in plants, including fungi and yeast.

C. Esters

As regards aroma, the fatty-acid ethyl esters form the most inter-esting group. Nykänen *et al.* (1968a) determined the ester content, as ethyl acetate, in some rums. A light Puerto Rican rum contained 44 mg/l, whereas the ester content of a Martinique rum was as high as 634 mg/l.

The aroma components of rum can be divided into three fractions of different boiling ranges. Fatty-acid ethyl esters are major compo-nents in each group. The light aroma fraction, which comprises components up to 3-methyl-1-butanol, includes the lower fatty-acid ethyl, isobutyl and isoamyl esters (see Fig. 3, p. 605). These 'fruit esters' are particularly important aroma components. The middle fraction comprises components from ethyl caproate to 2-phenethanol, and includes hexanoic, octanoic, decanoic and lauric acid ethyl esters as main components, and a relatively large proportion of isoamyl isovalerate. The heavy fraction from rum contains few components, the most important being ethyl palmitate.

Unsaturated ethyl esters have been found in rum. Liebich *et al.* (1970) identified ethyl palmitoleate, ethyl oleate and ethyl linoleate in Jamaican rum; later, ethyl linolenate was identified (de Smedt and Liddle, 1975). Both of these papers also reported the presence of diethyl succinate in rum. According to Guymon and Crowell (1972), it originates from the oak casks.

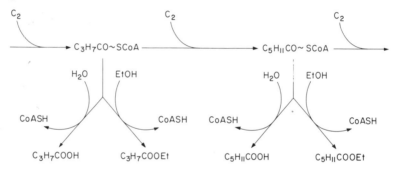

Fig. 10. Simplified scheme showing the biosynthesis of esters. From Nordström (1964).

The relative proportions of esters in different rums varies widely. Martin *et al.* (1974) examined the ester content of rums from the Caribbean and from New England, U.S.A. The concentration of ethyl esters of acids with six or more carbon atoms was found to vary between 0.1 and 0.5 p.p.m. in the Caribbean products and from 1.5 to 21.0 p.p.m. in the rums from New England. The Caribbean rums were found to contain more ethyl octanoate and the New England rums more ethyl decanoate.

The biosynthesis of esters is largely analogous to the synthesis of fatty acids. Nordström (1964) has shown that coenzyme A is an essential factor in the formation of esters (Fig. 10). Acyl-coenzyme A can be formed from activated fatty acids in the presence of ATP. Because of the low level of fatty acids appearing during fermentation, however, this reaction is of no great significance in the formation of esters. 2-Oxo acids can undergo oxidative decarboxylation in the presence of NAD^+ to form acyl-coenzyme A. As in the synthesis of fatty acids, most of the acyl-coenzyme A is formed by decarboxylation of pyruvic acid. The 2-oxo acids appearing as intermediates in the metabolism of sugars and amino acids are very few, so that formation of the corresponding esters is minimal. Acyl-coenzyme A and malonyl-coenzyme A can react together in the presence of NADH. This reaction leads to the formation of fatty acids in yeasts, and the complex also acts as a precursor for the ethyl esters of straight-chain, even-numbered fatty acids. Cleavage of the enzyme by alcoholysis of the acyl group finally leads to the formation of esters.

Nordström (1964) has shown that the straight-chain C_4-C_{11} acids produce their corresponding esters during fermentation, whereas formic, propionic and branched-chain C_4 and C_5 acids do not. According to Äyräpää (1973), unsaturated fatty acids with the *cis*-9 configuration decrease the formation of esters, while *trans*-9-octadecenoic acid has been found to have the opposite effect. Nordström (1964) reported that addition of 1-butanol, 3-methyl-1-butanol, 1-hexanol and 1-heptanol to the fermentation leads to the formation of the corresponding acetates. L. Nykänen and I. Nykänen (unpublished results) have shown with *Saccharomyces cerevisiae* that addition of 2-methyl-1-propanol and 3-methyl-1-butanol to a fermentation results in the formation of isobutyl acetate and isoamyl acetate in the same way. While investigating the reasons why esterification does not occur with acids higher than acetic, L. Nykänen and I. Nykänen (unpublished results) found that addition of 1-propanol to the fermentation so interrupted synthesis of fatty acids that acids higher than acetic were not formed.

Parfait *et al.* (1972), using *Pichia membranaefaciens, Hansenula anomala, Schizosaccharomyces pombe, Candida krusei* and *Saccharomyces cerevisiae*, examined the effects of different yeasts on the formation of esters. The use of *Schizosaccharomyces pombe* was found to yield the highest content of esters, and fermentations with *Hansenula anomala* and *Candida krusei* the lowest. While studying the effect of distillation on the aroma content of fermented sugar-containing solutions, Suomalainen and Nykänen (1966) found that distilling in the presence of the yeast increased the content of some esters, particularly esters of octanoic, decanoic and palmitoleic acids. Parfait *et al.* (1972) found the same effect when investigating the esters of rum.

D. Phenolic Compounds

Largely the same phenolic compounds are found in rum and whisky. Maarse and ten Noever de Brauw (1966) identified 4-methylguaiacol and eugenol in Jamaican rum. In addition to these two phenols, Liebich *et al.* (1970) isolated 4-ethylphenol, guaiacol, 4-ethylguaiacol and isoeugenol. Subsequently Timmer *et al.* (1971) found *o*- and *p*-cresol and propylguiacol. *Meta*-Cresol, 4-vinylguaiacol, propyl-guaiacol, 2,6-dimethoxyphenol and 4-ethyl-2,6-dimethoxyphenol have been isolated from rum matured in wooden casks (Dubois and Brule, 1972). de Smedt and Liddle (1975) identified 4-methyl-guaiacol, 4-ethylguaiacol and propylguaiacol in rum.

Besides volatile phenols, a number of phenolic aldehydes, including vanillin, syringaldehyde, coniferaldehyde and sinapaldehyde (Dubois and Brule, 1972), and scopoletin (Otsuka and Zenibayashi, 1974), have been found in rum. Hashizume *et al.* (1967) identified phenol, *m*-cresol, vanillin, and vanillic, salicylic, syringic and coumaric acids in cane molasses.

The phenols appearing in alcoholic beverages can be formed in two different ways, either during fermentation (Steinke and Paulson, 1964) or by alcoholic extraction from the oak casks. Steinke and Paulson (1964) showed that 4-vinylphenol and 4-vinylguaiacol are formed by thermal decarboxylation of *p*-coumaric acid and ferulic acid. Decarboxylation by yeasts and bacteria results in the formation of 4-ethylphenol, 4-ethylguaiacol and 4-methylguaiacol from, respectively, *p*-coumaric acid, ferulic acid and vanillin. Vinyl phenols occur as intermediates (Fig. 11). According to Whiting and Carr (1959), 4-ethylphenol can be formed from *p*-coumaric acid by the action of *Lactobacillus pastorianus*.

Phenolic compounds are extracted from the wood by gradual alcoholysis of lignin during the course of maturing an alcoholic beverage in wooden vessels. The volatile phenols extracted from oak include eugenol as a major component (Masuda and Nishimura, 1971) and smaller quantities of guaiacol, phenol, *m*-cresol and vanillin (M. Lehtonen and L. Nykänen, unpublished results). The compounds identified by Haeseler *et al.* (1972) in an ethanolic extract of oak included vanillin, syringaldehyde, coniferaldehyde and sinapaldehyde. The same compounds have been identified in rum (Dubois and Brule, 1972). Scopoletin has also been found in both

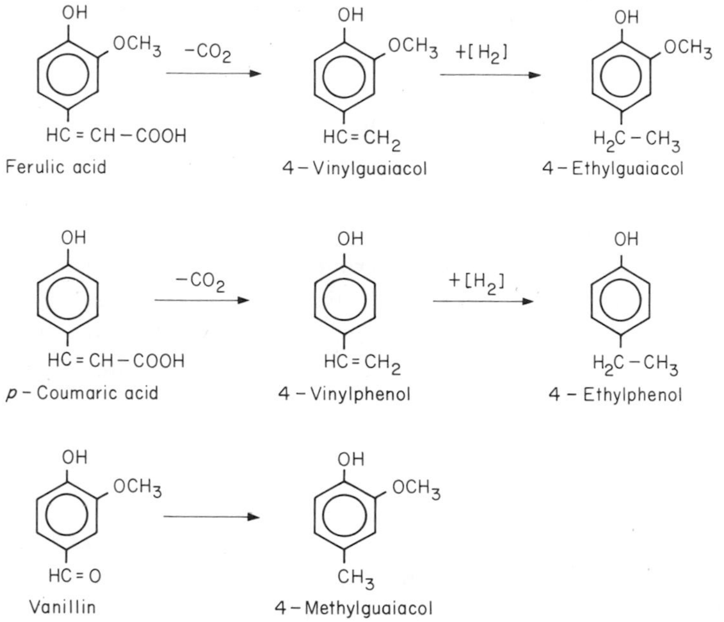

OH ⟨ring⟩ OCH₃ / HC = CH — COOH — Ferulic acid →(−CO₂) OH ⟨ring⟩ OCH₃ / HC = CH₂ — 4 − Vinylguaiacol →(+[H₂]) OH ⟨ring⟩ OCH₃ / H₂C − CH₃ — 4 − Ethylguaiacol

OH ⟨ring⟩ / HC = CH — COOH — p − Coumaric acid →(−CO₂) OH ⟨ring⟩ / HC = CH₂ — 4 − Vinylphenol →(+[H₂]) OH ⟨ring⟩ / H₂C − CH₃ — 4 − Ethylphenol

OH ⟨ring⟩ OCH₃ / HC = O — Vanillin → OH ⟨ring⟩ OCH₃ / CH₃ — 4 − Methylguaiacol

Fig. 11. Transformation of precursors to steam-volatile phenols. From Steinke and Paulson (1964).

rum and an ethanolic extract of oak (Otsuka and Zenibayashi, 1974). According to Baldwin *et al.* (1967), all of these phenols together with scopoletin can be formed by alcoholysis of lignin (Fig. 12).

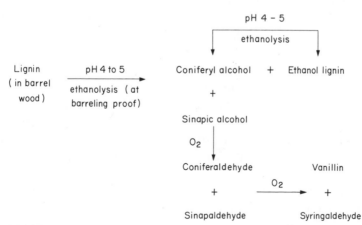

Fig. 12. Proposed pathway for lignin-derived congener formation. From Baldwin *et al.* (1967).

E. Nitrogenous Compounds

The nitrogenous compounds in rum are largely the same as those found in other distilled alcoholic beverages. Liebich *et al.* (1970) identified some alkyl-substituted pyrazines in Jamaican rum. Pyridine, α- and β-picoline and thiazole have also been found in rum (Wobben *et al.*, 1971; see Table 5, p. 609).

The basicity of most of the nitrogen-containing compounds found in rums and other distilled alcoholic beverages can vary greatly. As free bases, they have very powerful aromas. Because of the acid content of distilled beverages, however, they are mainly present as protonated cations, which have only weak aromas and have been shown to make only a small contribution to the bouquet of the beverage (Webb and Muller, 1972).

Pyrazines have been shown to be the products of reactions between sugars and amino acids. Dawes and Edwards (1966) found that pyrazines are formed by heating fructose with glycine or 2-phenylalanine. According to Koehler *et al.* (1969), sugars act as the carbon source in the formation of pyrazines, and amino acids as the source of nitrogen. There are two possible mechanisms for formation of pyrazines. In one, free ammonia is formed from the amino group of the amino acid and reacts with the carbohydrate. In the other, the amino-acid nitrogen atom is bound to the sugar or to a C_6-intermediate. The way in which the amino acid is bound to the sugar molecule depends on the structure of the amino acid. While investigating the nitrogen-containing compounds in roasted barley, Wang *et al.* (1969) arrived at a mechanism for the formation of pyrazines in which a reaction between amino acids and an α-dicarbonyl compound leads to a Strecker degradation and a subsequent condensation reaction. The reactions leading to formation of alkyl-substituted pyrazines by this mechanism are presented in Table 8. According to Wang *et al.* (1969), ammonia can react directly with α-dicarbonyls in the presence of catalysts to form pyrazines. Wiggins (1965) has reported that pyrazines are formed by heating ammonia and acid-hydrolysed molasses.

It seems certain that sugars and amino acids are intimately involved in the formation of the nitrogenous compounds, and molasses which contains both sugars and amino acids always gives rise to a certain quantity of pyrazines.

Table 8

Formation of some alkyl-substituted pyrazines that contribute to the flavour of rum. From Wang *et al.* (1969)

Starting materials		End product
Pyruvaldehyde + ethylglyoxal	+ amino acid	2-Ethyl-5-methylpyrazine
Pyruvaldehyde + 2,3-pentanedione	+ amino acid	2,5-Dimethyl-3-ethylpyrazine
Pyruvaldehyde + glyoxal	+ amino acid	2-Methylpyrazine
Pyruvaldehyde + diacetyl	+ amino acid	2,3,5-Trimethylpyrazine

F. Sulphur-Containing Compounds

Most alcoholic beverages contain some volatile sulphur-containing compounds. Liebich *et al.* (1970) identified dimethyl sulphide and methyl ethyl sulphide in Jamaican rum. Additionally, rum has been shown to contain ethanethiol, diethyl sulphide, dimethyl disulphide and diethyl disulphide (Dellweg *et al.*, 1969). According to Dellweg *et al.* (1969), the sulphur-containing compounds are formed by autolysis of the sulphur-containing amino acids in yeast proteins (cysteine and methionine; Maw, 1965). Wainwright (1972) has proposed the following schemes for decomposition of these amino acids:

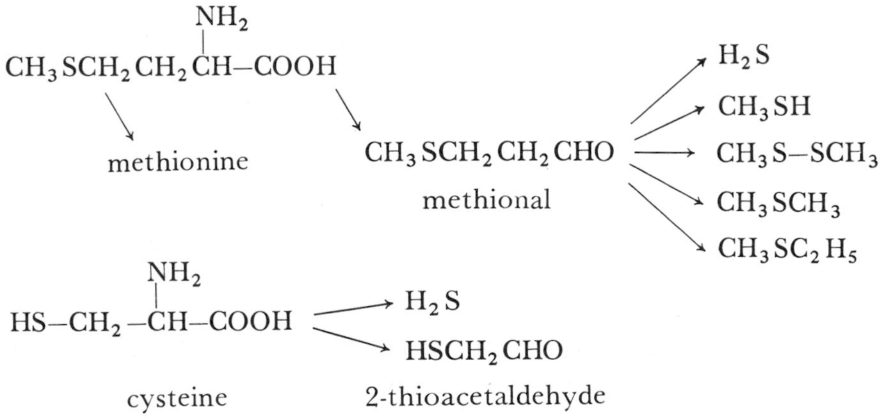

$$CH_3 SCH_2 CH_2 \overset{\overset{\displaystyle NH_2}{|}}{C}H-COOH$$

$$\searrow \qquad \qquad \searrow$$

methionine $\qquad CH_3 SCH_2 CH_2 CHO$

methional

$$\nearrow H_2 S$$
$$\nearrow CH_3 SH$$
$$\longrightarrow CH_3 S-SCH_3$$
$$\searrow CH_3 SCH_3$$
$$\searrow CH_3 SC_2 H_5$$

$$HS-CH_2-\overset{\overset{\displaystyle NH_2}{|}}{C}H-COOH \begin{array}{l} \nearrow H_2 S \\ \searrow HSCH_2 CHO \end{array}$$

cysteine $\qquad$ 2-thioacetaldehyde

Hydrogen sulphide formed during fermentation can react with ethanol during the distillation process to form ethanethiol (Tanner, 1969a, b). Ethanethiol can be oxidized by atmospheric oxygen to produce the particularly evil-smelling diethyl disulphide.

G. Lactones

Lactones are very important aroma compounds. Liebich *et al.* (1970) identified both γ- and δ-lactones in Jamaican rum (Table 5, p. 609). Later, Otsuka *et al.* (1974) found the *cis* and *trans* isomers of β-methyl-γ-octalactone in Jamaican rum. The *trans* isomer of this lactone had earlier been found by Suomalainen and Nykänen (1970) in Scotch whisky. Masuda and Nishimura (1971) showed that the *cis* and *trans* isomers of β-methyl-γ-octalactone originate from the oak casks. Guymon and Crowell (1972) showed that the *trans* isomer of this lactone is formed during the maturing of brandy in oak casks.

Most lactones are formed from unsaturated acids, hydroxy acids and oxo acids (Webb and Muller, 1972). *Gamma-* and *delta-*hydroxyalkanoic acids, generally found esterified as triglycerides, can act as precursors for the γ- and δ-lactones (Nawar, 1969). Heating the triglycerides liberates hydroxy acids, which immediately form lactones (Forss, 1969). Unsaturated acids with a double bond in the 3, 4 or 5 position easily form γ-lactones in the presence of dilute acids (Webb and Muller, 1972).

Not all lactones, however, are formed in this way. For example, in plants, β-methyl-γ-octalactone can be formed from the aldol condensation product of 2-heptanone and either acetyl-coenzyme A or pyruvyl-coenzyme A by isomerization and lactonization in the presence of acid (Kepner *et al.*, 1972). The mechanism is analogous to that by which α-oxo-β-methyl-γ-hexalactone is formed (Sulser *et al.*, 1967). Lactones can also be formed by pyrolysis of hexoses (Johnson *et al.*, 1969), a mechanism which is important in distilled beverages, especially in heavy rums (Webb and Muller, 1972).

H. Carbonyl Compounds

Almost all alcoholic beverages contain carbonyl compounds. Maarse and ten Noever de Brauw (1966) were the first to identify the C_1-C_6 alkanals, acrolein and crotonaldehyde, in Jamaican rum. Liebich *et al.* (1970) showed that rum contains acetaldehyde, propionaldehyde, 2-methylbutyraldehyde, furfural, 5-methylfurfural and benzaldehyde. Dubois *et al.* (1973) identified both acrolein and 3-ethoxypropanal in rum.

Aldehydes are intermediates in the formation of alcohols from sugars and amino acids, so they are also found in the fermentation solution (Suomalainen and Ronkainen, 1968). Furthermore, micro-organism can degrade amino acids to aldehydes. MacLeod and Morgan (1958) have shown that 2-methylbutyraldehyde can be formed from isoleucine and 2-methylpropionaldehyde from valine by *Streptococcus lactis*. Acrolein as well is probably produced by bacteria. 3-Ethoxypropanal is formed in a reaction between ethanol and acrolein. Rum also contains some ketones. Acetone, 2-butanone, 2-pentanone, 3-penten-2-one, 4-ethoxy-2-butanone, 4-ethoxy-2-pentanone, o-hydroxyacetophenone and 2-methyl-3-tetrahydro-furanone have been identified (Liebich *et al.*, 1970). Ketones can be formed by oxidation of lipids. Methyl ketones, for example, can be produced by decarboxylation of the 3-oxo acids appearing in triglycerides (Nawar, 1969).

Acetals are formed by the action of alcohols on aldehydes. More acetals have been isolated from Jamaican rums than from any other alcoholic beverage (Table 5, p. 610). Maarse and ten Noever de Brauw (1966) identified 100 components in rum, of which 16 were acetals. Moreover, 45 of the more than 200 components identified by Liebich *et al.* (1970) in rum were acetals. According to Misselhorn (1963), Jamaican rum contains 416 mg acetals/l pure alcohol and Martinique rum 43 mg/l. Misselhorn (1975) found that acetaldehyde diethyl acetal was the only acetal whose equilibrium concentration in rum was higher than would be expected from the aroma; higher acetals, on the other hand, tended to be greatly overestimated. He concluded that acetals make no substantial contribution to the aroma of rum.

IV. CONCLUSION

As has already been made clear, the aroma-producing components of rum do not differ greatly from those in other distilled alcoholic beverages. Some differences have been described, especially in the relative proportions of particular components, but none is so marked that rum can be obviously differentiated from other spirits. Because of this, rum has collected many definitions. Possibly the most apt is '. . . it must be produced by fermentation and distillation from sugar cane products in a sugar cane growing area, and it is further understood that it must have the organoleptic characteristics normally associated with rum' (Mesley et al., 1975).

REFERENCES

Allan, D. A. (1973). *Australian Wine Brewing and Spirit Review* 91, 42.
Aquarone, E., Brazzach, M. L. and Angelino, E. (1963). *Revista da Faculdade de Farmacia e Bioquimica da Universidade de Sao Paulo* 1, 141.
Arroyo, R. (1945). *Sugar* 40, 34.
Arroyo, R. (1949). *Sugar Journal* 11, 5.
Äyräpää, T. (1968). *Journal of the Institute of Brewing* 74, 169.
Äyräpää, T. (1970). *Brauwissenschaft* 23, 48.
Äyräpää, T. (1973). *In* 'Proceedings of the Third International Specialized Symposium on Yeasts' (H. Suomalainen and Ch. Waller, eds.), Part II, p. 31. Otaniemi/Helsinki.
Baldwin, S. and Andreasen, A. A. (1974). *Journal of the Association of Official Analytical Chemists* 57, 940.
Baldwin, S., Black, R. A., Andreasen, A. A. and Adams, S. L. (1967). *Journal of Agricultural and Food Chemistry* 15, 381.
Baraud, J. and Maurice, A. (1963). *Industries Alimentaires et Agricoles* 80, 3.
Binkley, W. W. (1966). *Zeitschrift für Zuckerindustrie* 16, 195.
Bloomfield, D. K. and Bloch, K. (1960). *Journal of Biological Chemistry* 235, 337.
Brau, H. M. (1958). Technical Paper 24, University of Puerto Rico. Agricultural Experiment Station, p. 98.
Burrows, S. (1970). *In* 'The Yeasts' (A. H. Rose and J. S. Harrison, eds.), Vol. 3, p. 349. Academic Press, London.
Clutton, D. W. (1974). *Flavour Industry* 5, 286.
Dawes, I. W. and Edwards, R. A. (1966). *Chemistry and Industry*, 2203.
Dellweg, H., Miglio, G. and Niefind, H. J. (1969). *Branntweinwirtschaft* 109, 445.
Dierssen, G. A., Holtegaard, K., Jensen, B. and Rosen, K. (1956). *International Sugar Journal* 58, 35.
Dubois, P. and Brule, G. (1972). *Industries Alimentaires et Agricoles* 89, 7.
Dubois, P., Parfait, A. and Dekimpe, J. (1973). *Annales de Technologie Agricole, Paris* 22, 131.
Dubois, P. and Rigaud, J. (1975). *Annales de Technologie Agricole, Paris*, 24, 307.
El-Tabey Shehata, A. M. (1960). *Applied Microbiology* 8, 73.
Forss, D. A. (1969). *Journal of Agricultural and Food Chemistry* 17, 681.
Garnier-Laroche, G. and Cottrell, R. H. (1975). Paper presented in 'International Symposium on Rums, Alcohols and Alcoholic Beverages from Sugar Cane' held in Martinique, 1975.
Goldfine, H. and Bloch, K. (1961). *Journal of Biological Chemistry* 236, 2596.
Guymon, J. F. and Crowell, E. A. (1972). *American Journal of Enology and Viticulture* 23, 114.
Guymon, J. F., Ingraham, J. L. and Crowell, E. A. (1961). *Archives of Biochemistry and Biophysics* 95, 163.

Haeseler, G., Misselhorn, K. and Underberg, P. G. (1972). *Branntweinwirtschaft* 112, 204.

Hashizume, T., Higa, S., Sasaki, Y., Yamazaki, H., Iwamura, H. and Matsuda, H. (1966). *Agricultural and Biological Chemistry, Tokyo* 30, 319.

Hashizume, T., Kikuchi, N., Sasaki, Y. and Sakata, I. (1968). *Agricultural and Biological Chemistry, Tokyo* 32, 1306.

Hashizume, T., Yamagami, T. and Sasaki, Y. (1967). *Agricultural and Biological Chemistry, Tokyo* 31, 324.

Hieke, E. (1972). *Allgemeine Deutsche Weinfachzeitung* 108, 24.

Hieke, E. and Vollbrecht, D. (1974). *Chemie Mikrobiologie Technologie der Lebensmittel* 3, 65.

I'Anson, J. A. P. (1971). *Process Biochemistry* 6 (7), 35.

Johnson, R. R., Alford, E. D. and Kinzer, G. W. (1969). *Journal of Agricultural and Food Chemistry* 17, 22.

Kampen, W. H. (1967). *Chemie und Techniek Revue* 22, 433.

Kampen, W. H. (1974). *Voedingsmiddelentechnologie* 7, 10.

Kepner, R. E., Webb, A. D. and Muller, C. J. (1972). *American Journal of Enology and Viticulture* 23, 103.

Koehler, P. E., Mason, M. E. and Newell, J. A. (1969). *Journal of Agricultural and Food Chemistry* 17, 393.

Komoda, H. and Yamada, M. (1968). *Nippon Nogei Kagaku Kaishi* 42, 413.

Liebich, H. M., Koenig, W. A. and Bayer, E. (1970). *Journal of Chromatographic Science* 8, 527.

Lynen, F. (1967). *Biochemical Journal* 102, 381.

Lynen, F. (1973). *In* 'Proceedings of the Third International Specialized Symposium on Yeasts' (H. Suomalainen and Ch. Waller, eds.), Part II, p. 7. Otaniemi/Helsinki.

Maarse, H. and ten Noever de Brauw, M. C. (1966). *Journal of Food Science* 31, 951.

MacLeod, P. and Morgan, M. E. (1958). *Journal of Dairy Science* 41, 908.

Martin, G. E., Dyer, R. H. and Buscemi, P. C. (1974). *Journal of the Association of Official Analytical Chemists* 57, 610.

Masuda, M. and Nishimura, K. (1971). *Phytochemistry* 10, 1401.

Maurel, A., Sansoulet, O. and Giffard, Y. (1965). *Annales des Falsifications et de l'Expertise Chimique* 58, 291.

Maw, G. A. (1965). *Wallerstein Laboratories Communications* 28, 49.

Merritt, N. R. (1966). *Journal of the Institute of Brewing* 72, 374.

Mesley, R. J., Lisle, D. B., Richards, C. P. and Wardleworth, D. F. (1975). *Annales de Technologie Agricole, Paris*, in press.

Misselhorn, K. (1963). *Branntweinwirtschaft* 103, 401.

Misselhorn, K. (1975). *Annales de Technologie Agricole, Paris*, 24, 371.

Nawar, W. W. (1969). *Journal of Agricultural and Food Chemistry* 17, 18.

Nemoto, S., Sugimoto, N. and Usui, T. (1975a). *Journal of the Society of Brewing, Tokyo* 70, 197.

Nemoto, S., Sugimoto, N. and Usui, T. (1975b). *Journal of the Society of Brewing, Tokyo* 70, 201.

Nordström, K. (1964). *Svensk Kemisk Tidskrift* 76, 510.

Nykänen, L., Puputti, E. and Suomalainen, H. (1968a). *Kemian Teollisuus* 25, 399.

Nykänen, L., Puputti, E. and Suomalainen, H. (1968b). *Journal of Food Science* 33, 88.

Olbrich, H. (1956). *Branntweinwirtschaft* 96, 27.
Oshmyan, G. L. (1961). Russian Patent No.140782.
Otsuka, K. and Zenibayashi, Y. (1974). *Agricultural and Biological Chemistry, Tokyo* 38, 1079.
Otsuka, K., Zenibayashi, Y., Itoh, M. and Totsuka, A. (1974). *Agricultural and Biological Chemistry, Tokyo* 38, 485.
Parfait, A. and Jouret, C. (1975). *Annales de Technologie Agricole, Paris* 24, 321.
Parfait, A., Namory, M. and Dubois, P. (1972). *Annales de Technologie Agricole, Paris* 21, 199.
Parfait, A. and Sabin, G. (1975). *Industries Alimentaires et Agricoles* 92, 27.
Paturau, J. M. (1969). *In* 'By-products of the Cane Sugar Industry', p. 153. Elsevier Publishing Company, New York.
Reazin, G., Scales, H. and Andreasen, A. A. (1973). *Journal of Agricultural and Food Chemistry* 21, 50.
Ronkainen, P., Brummer, S. and Suomalainen, H. (1970). *Analytical Biochemistry* 34, 101.
Scheuerbrandt, G. and Bloch, K. (1962). *Journal of Biological Chemistry* 237, 2064.
Scheuerbrandt, G., Goldfine, H., Baronowsky, E. and Bloch, K. (1961). *Journal of Biological Chemistry* 236, PC70.
Sihto, E., Nykänen, L. and Suomalainen, H. (1962). *Teknillisen Kemian Aikakauslehti* 19, 753.
de Smedt, P. and Liddle, P. (1975). *Annales de Technologie Agricole, Paris* 24, 269.
Steinke, R. D. and Paulson, M. C. (1964). *Journal of Agricultural and Food Chemistry* 12, 381.
Sulser, H., DePizzol, J. and Büchi, W. (1967). *Journal of Food Science* 32, 611.
Suomalainen, H. (1975). *Annales de Technologie Agricole, Paris* 24, 453.
Suomalainen, H. and Keränen, A. J. A. (1963a). *Biochimica et Biophysica Acta* 70, 493.
Suomalainen, H. and Keränen, A. J. A. (1963b). *Suomen Kemistilehti B* 36, 88.
Suomalainen, H. and Keränen, A. J. A. (1967). *Journal of the Institute of Brewing* 73, 477.
Suomalainen, H. and Linnahalme, T. (1966). *Archives of Biochemistry and Biophysics* 114, 502.
Suomalainen, H. and Nykänen, L. (1966). *Journal of the Institute of Brewing* 72, 469.
Suomalainen, H. and Nykänen, L. (1967). XXXVIe Congress International de Chimie Industrielle, Bruxelles, 1966. *Comptes Rendus* 3, 807.
Suomalainen, H. and Nykänen, L. (1970). *Näringsmiddelindustrien* 23, 15.
Suomalainen, H. and Ronkainen, P. (1968). *Technical Quarterly, Master Brewers Association of America* 5, 119.
Tanner, H. (1969a). *Alkohol-Industrie* 82, 187.
Tanner, H. (1969b). *Alkohol-Industrie* 82, 347.
Timmer, R., ter Heide, R., Wobben, H. J. and de Valois, P. J. (1971). *Journal of Food Science* 36, 462.
Unger, E. D. and Coffey, T. R. (1975). *Annales de Technologie Agricole, Paris*, 24, 469.
Wainwright, T. (1972). *Brewers Digest* 47, 78.

Wang, P. S., Kato, H. and Fujimaki, M. (1969). *Agricultural and Biological Chemistry, Tokyo* 33, 1775.

Webb, A. D. and Ingraham, J. L. (1963). *Advances in Applied Microbiology* 5, 317.

Webb, A. D. and Kepner, R. E. (1961). *American Journal of Enology and Viticulture* 12, 51.

Webb, A. D. and Muller, C. J. (1972). *Advances in Applied Microbiology* 15, 75.

Whiting, G. C. and Carr, J. G. (1959). *Nature, London* 184, 1427.

Wiggins, L. F. (1965). *In* 'Proceedings of the Congress of the International Society of Sugar-Cane Technologists' (9th), British West Indies, p. 525.

Wobben, H. J., Timmer, R., ter Heide, R. and de Valois, P. J. (1971). *Journal of Food Science* 36, 464.

Wollny, G. (1959). *Alkohol-Industrie* 72, 499.

Wollny, G. (1964). *Alkohol-Industrie* 77, 47.

Yokota, M. and Fagerson, I. S. (1971). *Journal of Food Science* 36, 1091.

10. Whisky

T. P. LYONS AND A. H. ROSE

Biocon Limited, Eardiston, Near Tenbury Wells,
Worcestershire, England and
Zymology Laboratory, School of Biological Sciences,
Bath University, Bath, England.

I. INTRODUCTION

Whisky is the potable spirit obtained by distillation of an aqueous extract of an infusion of malted barley and other cereals that has been fermented with strains of *Saccharomyces cerevisiae*. Various types of whisky are produced in a number of different countries in the World. They differ principally in the nature and proportion of the cereals used as raw materials along with malted barley, and also in the type of still used for distillation. The principal types of whisky are also characteristic of particular geographical regions of the World.

In Scotland, the characteristic product is manufactured using only malted barley as the raw material, and the fermented malt wort is distilled in batches in relatively small pot stills (see Chapter 1, p. 7). The product, known as Scotch malt whisky, is manufactured in relatively small distilleries of which there are over 100 in Scotland. Scotch malt whisky is marketed both as a straight malt whisky, many brands of which have recently become extremely popular throughout the World, and also as a blend with another type of whisky produced in Scotland, namely Scotch grain whisky, or because it is distilled continuously in Coffey-type patent stills, as patent-still whisky. Most Scotch whiskies available on the international market consist of blends with 30–40% malt whisky. Within the blend, there may be as many as 20–30 individual malt whiskies and grain whiskies. These blends are, by law, matured for at least three years and, in practice, this period is normally much longer. Unblended Scotch malt whiskies are usually matured for a minimum of eight years. Only one Scottish distillery, that at Cameronbridge, near Windeygates in Fife, retails bottled grain whisky. The cereals used in the manufacture of Scotch grain whisky are malted barley, together with a high proportion (up to 90%) of maize (known as corn in North America) and occasionally some rye. All whiskies are legally protected and defined, mainly because of the huge revenues which governments obtain from their sale. The 1952 Customs and Excise Act of Her Majesties Government in the United Kingdom (Clause 243 (1) (b)) defines Scotch whisky as follows: 'Spirits described as Scotch Whisky shall not be deemed to correspond to that description unless they have been obtained by distillation in Scotland from a mash of cereal grain saccharified by the diastase of malt and have been matured in warehouses in cask for a period of at least three years.' The word 'Scotch' is, in this definition, of geographical and not generic significance.

Irish whiskey (there they prefer the alternative spelling although, perversely the whisky distillers in Cork in Eire still adhere to the shorter spelling) is a distinctive product of either Eire or of Northern Ireland (Ulster). The legal definition of Scotch whisky, adopted in 1938, was extended in 1940 to Northern Ireland, and again embraced both pot-still and grain whisky. In Eire, more precise definitions were enacted by the Irish Parliament in 1950 in the Irish Whiskey Act, which distinguished pot-still whiskey from blends. The title 'Irish Pot-Still Whiskey' was reserved solely for spirits distilled in pot stills in Eire, from a mash of cereal grains normally grown in that country and saccharified by a diastase of malted barley. The legislation also dictated that spirits must be stored for at least three years before being retailed. While not possessing the 'smokey' taste and aroma of Scotch, Irish whiskey is usually more flavourful and has a heavier body than Scotch. It is unique among the major whiskies in that an uncooked cereal, namely barley, is used as a raw material. Moreover, the whiskey is distilled not twice, as in Scotland, but three times to give a very strong spirit of 150° proof (British) compared with the 125° proof whisky distilled in Scotland.

Whiskies distilled in U.S.A.—where the spelling 'whiskey' is also preferred—are more strictly defined in legal terms, with the regulations prescribing not only the proportion of various cereals that can be used to manufacture specific types of whiskey, but also limits of strength at which the spirit can be distilled. Title 27 of the Code of Federal Regulations, Subpart C, lists ten types of whisky which 'shall be deemed "American Type" whiskies'. Not all ten types are of major importance in the World-wide whiskey market, and only those that are widely encountered will be dealt with in this chapter. According to this definition, 'rye whiskey', 'bourbon whiskey', 'wheat whiskey' and 'malt whiskey' are potable spirits which have been distilled at not exceeding 160° proof U.S.A. (see Chapter 1, p. 35 for a discussion of the term 'proof') from a fermented mash which contained not less than 51%, respectively, or corn (i.e. maize) grain, rye grain, wheat grain or malted barley grain, and stored in charred new oak containers. In this legislation, 'corn whiskey' must be distilled from a fermented mash at or below 190° proof that contained not less than 80% corn grain and stored in uncharred oak containers or re-used charred oak containers. Beginning on 26th January, 1968, it was legal to produce in the United States 'light whiskey' at a strength of more than 160° proof, from any type of mash bill. Despite the breadth of the U.S.A. legislation, the bulk of the whisky distilled in America is bourbon whiskey, which is retailed either as straight single whiskey, the product of one distillery, or as a mixture of singles. There are no legal specifications regarding the cereals to be used to manufacture grain neutral spirit in the U.S.A. Straight whiskies in the U.S.A. must be aged for not less than four years. When blended with grain neutral spirit or light whiskey, the product is retailed as a 'blended whiskey'. There are laws governing the advertisement of blended whiskies, depending on the age of the whiskies in the blend.

Canadian whiskies are usually retailed as blends, very few being offered as straight whiskies. While Canadian whiskey (the shorter spelling is also widely used in Canada) is defined by the laws of Canada, the regulations governing its manufacture are far less stringent than those which apply to the manufacture of whiskies in the U.S.A. This leaves the distiller of Canadian whiskey free to select the optimum conditions to produce the desired product. Most Canadian whiskies are made using a mash that contains a high proportion of rye grain, together with malted rye and barley and some corn. Connoisseurs, on the whole, find that Canadian rye whiskies have a 'crisper' taste than the 'softer' and more flavourful bourbons from the U.S.A. Both old and new casks are used to store the whiskey, and most Canadian whiskies are stored for six years or more before being bottled, although the legal minimum is just three years.

The tremendous popularity of whiskies manufactured in Scotland, Ireland, U.S.A. and Canada—and particularly those coming from Scotland—has prompted several other countries to try their hand at manufacturing whiskies, usually ones which are designed to resemble Scotch. Indeed, the number of countries with minor but nevertheless significant whisky-distilling industries must now be well over a dozen. Some, notably Australia and Japan, have industries of a size and producing a sufficiently acceptable product for them to venture into the export industry. Other countries, including The Netherlands and Spain, have whisky-producing industries that cater mainly if not exclusively for home consumption. In yet other countries—New Zealand most recently—the whisky-distilling industry is only just getting off its feet. The measures which some of these industries have taken to imitate Scotch in their products are all too obvious when the spirits are sampled. One of the two whisky distilleries in Spain—that located in the Guadarrama Hills near Segovia, north-west of Madrid—produces a very acceptable Scotch-type whisky, the quality of which it attributes in part to the fact that the water used, which comes from the surrounding hills, closely resembles that used in highland Scotch-whisky distilleries.

Published information on the production of whiskies is almost entirely confined to the spirits manufactured in Scotland, Ireland, U.S.A. and Canada, so that, inevitably, the present account can only deal with these spirits. No book, text or extended review article has appeared which describes all four types of whisky. There are, however, a few short articles, notably those by Marrison (1957) and Packowski (1963), which furnish useful comparative accounts of the manufacture and properties of the four types of whisky. In addition, Johnson (1971) has given us brief but superbly presented cameos on Scotch and bourbon. Turning to the literature on each of the four types, that on Scotch is without doubt the most voluminous, although much of it has a decided emphasis on the history of Scotch whisky distilling, while not a few of the books published on Scotch can only be described as destined primarily for the coffee table. Recommended accounts of Scotch and its manufacture have come from Brander (1975), Daiches (1969), Dunnett (1953), Gunn (1935), Robb (1950), Ross (1970), Simpson (1968), Simpson *et al.* (1974) and Ross Wilson (1959, 1970, 1973). There are a few smaller books describing individual distilleries in Scotland, and recommended are those by McDowell (1975) and Wilson (1973, 1975). A fine account of Irish whiskey has come from McGuire (1973), and in short review articles by Court and Bowers (1970) and Lyons (1974).

II. HISTORY OF WHISKY PRODUCTION

The probable origins of the art of distilling potable spirits are recounted briefly in the first chapter of this volume (p. 6). The potency of distilled spirits caused many of them to be known as the 'water of life', a description which survives today in such names as *eau de vie* for French brandy and *akvavit* and *aquavit* for spirits in Northern Europe. The name *whisky*—or *whiskey*—is a corruption of *uisgebaugh*, the Gaelic word for water of life. *Uisge* was corrupted first into *usky*, which finally became whisky, but only after several centuries. Dr Johnson sang the praises of this potable spirit although, in his Dictionary of 1755, it is listed under 'u' and not 'w'.

Much to the chagrin of the Scotsman, it is likely that the first whisky was distilled not in Scotland but in Ireland. The spirit was known in Ireland when that land was invaded by the English in 1170-1172, and in the early hours an Irishman will confide to you that the secret of distilling was brought to Ireland by St Patrick. In all likelihood, the art of distillation was imported into Scotland by missionary monks from Ireland. Two of today's main centres of Scotch distilling, namely the island of Islay and the Speyside town of Dufftown, were the sites of early monastic communities.

Whisky—principally Scotch whisky—has for many years been one of the most popular drinks in the World, and it was in Scotland rather than Ireland, that its qualities came to be extensively appreciated. This has continued to the present, and in the intervening period many Scotsmen have felt compelled to record for posterity their thoughts and inspirations on the potable spirit. There are numerous histories of whisky distilling in Scotland, some more comprehensive than others. For good general accounts, the reader cannot do better than turn to the texts by Brander (1974), Daiches (1969), Ross (1970) and Wilson (1970).

Whisky distilling flourished in Scotland not least because consuming the spirit helped the inhabitants to withstand the climatic rigours of this northern region of Britain. The first recorded evidence of whisky production in Scotland is an entry in the Exchequeur Rolls for the year 1494-1495; it reads 'To Friar John Cor, by order of the King, to make aquavitae, VIII bolls of malt'. Production of whisky was therefore being controlled, and an Act of 1597 decreed that only earls, lords, barons and gentlemen could distil for their own use. To many of the Scots at this time, whisky was a medicine, and in 1506 King James IV of Scotland had granted a monopoly for manufacture of 'aqua vitae' to the Guild of Barber Surgeons in the City of Edinburgh. It was in the 17th Century that taxation on whisky production first appeared. Breaches of the monopoly regulations, and the need to raise money to send an army into England to help the English Parliament in its war against Charles 1st, led to the Act of 1644 which fixed a duty of two shillings and eight pence Scots on a pint of whisky (the Scots pint was then about 1.5 litres). But the tax was short-lived, and was replaced by a malt tax which later was also repealed.

At the time of the Treaty of Union between Scotland and England, in 1707, there was a tax on malt in England but not in Scotland. The English were irate and, in 1725 when Lord Walpole's

administration decided to enforce the tax in Scotland, the first of the
Malt Tax riots occurred, riots which were to recur over several years.
The English, meanwhile, had cultivated a taste for French brandy,
there being very little whisky consumed at that time outside
of Scotland. But around 1690, William IVth began to wage commercial war against the French, and imposed punitive taxes on imports
of French brandy into England. The English reacted by acquiring a
taste for gin, which was distilled locally. The scale of drunkenness
which developed following the popularity of gin had to be controlled
by law, which it was in the Acts of 1736 and 1743 which levied high
taxes on gin manufacturers. Both of these acts contained clauses
exempting Scotland. But not for long, for the Parliament in London
saw the prospect of a rich harvest of taxes in the distilleries of
Scotland and, in a series of acts starting in 1751, production of
whisky in Scotland was increasingly subject to taxation.

The outcome of these punitive measures was not surprising. An
extensive and thriving business in illicit distillation of whisky grew up
in Scotland, a delightful history of which has been written by Sillett
(1965). Curiously, illicit production of Scotch hardly extended over
the border into England, although there are a few records of the
operation of illicit stills in the Cheviot Hills west of Newcastle-upon-
Tyne in England. Following the Act of 1823, which introduced
much stiffer penalties for illicit distillation, and to some extent
because of the increased standards of living in northern Scotland,
illicit manufacture of whisky declined. Indeed, many erstwhile illicit
distillers emerged to become legal and registered distillers of Scotch
whisky.

In 1826, Robert Stein of the Kilbagie distillery in Clackmannan-
shire in Scotland patented a continuously operating still for
whisky production, an invention which was superseded in 1830 with
the introduction by Aeneas Coffey of an improved version of this
type of still. The appearance of continuous stills sparked off a period
of turmoil in the Scotch whisky industry, it being claimed that the
product from the continuous distillation of a mash that contained
unmalted grain—it was called neutral or silent spirit—could not be
called whisky since it had not been distilled in the traditional pot
still. The battle was waged for about three-quarters of a century, but
in 1908 a Royal Commission decided that malt whisky and neutral
spirit, when blended, could be labelled whisky.

The major factors which have affected the development of the whisky-distilling industry in Scotland in this century have been economic. The industry has had to endure the privations of two World wars, the economic depression in Great Britain during the 1920s, and prohibition in the United States from 1920 to 1933 which greatly affected export of Scotch to North America. Since 1945, however, the industry in Scotland has consolidated and expanded. When Barnard (1887) went on his superbly chronicled tour of whisky distilleries in Scotland in the late 19th Century, he visited all 129 of the distilleries then in operation. Twenty-one of these were in the small community of Campbeltown in Kintyre, where now just two of them survive. Most of these closures can be explained by the poor quality of the whisky produced. On the island of Islay, on the other hand, all but one of the nine distilleries visited by Barnard (1887) are still in operation. That the total number of distilleries now operating in Scotland (both malt and grain distilleries) totals, in the list compiled by Simpson et al. (1974), precisely 129, attests the buoyancy of the industry. The precise identity of the number of distilleries listed by Barnard (1887) and by Simpson et al. (1974) is entirely coincidence, for the number of distilleries currently operating in Scotland must now exceed 130. The 20th Century has also witnessed a considerable improvement in control of the quality of whisky distilled and blended in Scotland, which has been a result of the acceptance of blending malt with grain whisky and the amalgamation of numbers of smaller distilleries into combines, the largest of which is The Distillers Company Limited.

Scotch malt whiskies can be divided into highland, lowland, Islay and Campbeltown whiskies (Simpson et al., 1974). The highland line, which separates the areas in Scotland in which the first two types of spirit are distilled, is a straight line which runs from Dundee in the east to Greenock in the west. It then extends southwards, below the Isle of Arran. Any whisky produced north of this line, including those from Campbeltown and Islay, is entitled to be called a highland malt whisky, while whiskies which are distilled in areas below it are lowland whiskies. Of the 117 malt whisky distilleries in Scotland, 85 are highland malt whisky distilleries and, of these no fewer than 43 are situated in an area 50 miles east to west and 20 miles southwards from the Moray Firth. This area has been called the 'Kingdom of Malt Whisky' (Cameron Taylor, 1970), and the area is watered by five rivers, namely the Nairn, Findhorn, Lossie, Spey and Deveron, from each of which water is drawn for whisky manufacture. Classification of the four whiskies distilled on the islands of Jura, Orkney and Skye is disputed. Some authorities list them along with the Islay whiskies as 'island' whiskies, others as highland whiskies which in geographical terms they are. There are also 14 grain whisky distilleries in Scotland.

Whiskey distilling in Ireland was, as has been noted, recorded in the 12th Century. By 1556, it had become sufficiently widespread to warrant legislation to control it, seemingly because of its social evils. A statute in 1556 stated that a licence was required to manufacture the spirit; peers, gentlemen owning property worth £10 or more and borough freemen were exempt (McGuire, 1973). Taxation of whiskey distilling became more excessive and collection of taxes increasingly efficient but, in 1779, there was an important change in the distillery laws. An attempt was made to limit the extent of evasion of spirit duty by prescribing a minimum revenue to be exacted from the owner of each still. The effect of this legislation was dramatic. In 1779, there were said to be 1,152 registered stills in Ireland; by 1790, this number had fallen to 246 and this inevitably had fostered widespread illicit distilling (McGuire, 1973). This legislation lasted until 1823 when it was swept away by laws that taxed Irish whiskey on the volume of production, legislation that essentially is still in force today. Development of the Irish whiskey-distilling industry in the present century has inevitably been influenced by economic circumstances and by the political division of Ireland into Eire and Ulster that took place in 1922. Barnard (1887) visited 28 distilleries in Ireland, but closures and amalgamations followed so that, when McGuire (1973) prepared his account, there were only two whisky-distilling companies in Ireland, one with distilleries in Dublin and Cork in Eire, and the second with plants in Bushmills and Coleraine in Ulster. These two companies have since amalgamated, and have concentrated their operations in Cork, Bushmills and Coleraine. There has, too, been a move towards production of a lighter Scotch-type whisky in Ireland to replace the heavier and traditional Irish whiskey.

The Indians of North America almost certainly made some form of fermented drink from saccharine fruits and vegetables, although whether or not they acquired the art of distilling potable spirits is less certain. The first record of grain spirits being produced in North America was in 1640 in Staten Island by William Kieft, the Director General of the Dutch Colony of New Netherland. Although wines and brandies were imported from Europe on a small scale, the main distilled drink in early 18th Century America was rum. But, in 1733, the British Parliament passed the Molasses Act which effectively restricted importation of molasses from the West Indies. To replace molasses, it was natural for the early American settlers to turn to rye as a raw material, rye being a cereal which was successfully grown in Pennsylvania and Maryland. George Washington is credited with producing a rye whiskey.

All varieties of imported produce were subject to taxes, and flaunting of the British government's tax laws was a contributory factor in the events which led up to the War of Independence in 1776. But the new federal government also had to levy taxes, and a trial of strength took place in 1791 when Alexander Hamilton, Washington's Secretary of the Treasury, imposed an excise tax of 54 cents on each gallon of whiskey-still capacity and also of seven cents on each gallon produced. There was violent opposition to this law, and in 1794 at Parkinson's Ferry, delegates from five counties in Pennsylvania and from one Virginia county forgathered to voice their opposition. President Washington, accompanied by Hamilton, General Henry Lee and 15,000 militiamen, went to quell the rebellion, which quickly collapsed. This was the Whiskey Rebellion, and one outcome of it was that many of the dissenters packed their household effects, including their whiskey stills, and moved south west into what is now largely the State of Kentucky. In this area, maize, along with other cereals, was easy to cultivate, and so began the bourbon industry in the United States of America. The history of this industry has been graphically described by Carson (1963).

Exactly who distilled the first bourbon whiskey will never be known, although this has not prevented strong cases being advocated for various individuals. Arguments for this priority are confusing because of shifts in county boundaries as this region of the United States was settled. Before 1776, all of Kentucky was part of Fincastle County in Virginia. In that year, the region was renamed Kentucky but was still in the State of Virginia. Bourbon County covered a large part of the northern part of this area, and became one of the nine large counties organized by the Virginia legislature before

Kentucky acquired statehood in 1792. The name 'bourbon' com-
memorates the royal house of France, and is a legacy of the help
which was given to the settlers in that area during the American War
of Independence.

No matter who distilled the first bourbon—it may have been John
Ritchie at Linn's Fort, east of Bardstown in 1777 or as popular
legend favours the Reverend Elijah Craig of Georgetown in Scott
County—whiskey distilling largely from maize became popular, and
spread south and west as virgin territories were settled. Robinson's
(1951) novel, *Water of Life*, describes the importance of whiskey
distilling in the life of the American pioneer settlers. Distilling
remained concentrated largely in Kentucky, Pennsylvania, Maryland
and to some extent in certain southern regions; in 1811, Kentucky
had over 2,000 distilleries, many of them obviously very small. The
latter half of the 19th Century experienced the inevitable imposition
of heavier taxes on bourbon distilling, and the rise of active
temperance movements as the puritanical settlers saw the increase in
whiskey drinking as a pernicious social evil. The bourbon-distilling
industry also went through a 'what is whiskey?' crisis not unlike that
experienced by the industry in Scotland. This, too, centred around
the question of whether spirit not distilled in the traditional manner
could be called 'whiskey'. William Howard Taft took office as
President of the United States in 1909, and was determined to arrive
at a solution to this problem, which his administration did in favour
of accepting both types of spirit as whiskey.

The temperance movements, which had gained a foothold in the
United States in the late 19th Century, became even more powerful
after the First World War. Matters came to a head when Congress
passed, over a Presidential veto, the Volstead Act, which is the
18th Amendment to the United States Constitution. The United
States was legally dry as from January 17th, 1920. Prohibition was an
immensely damaging time for the bourbon-distilling industry in the
United States. With the exception from 1929 of small-scale production for medicinal purposes, production stopped completely—legal
production that is, for illicit distillation or 'moonshining' was
rampant. Prohibition ended with the adoption of the 21st Amendment to the Constitution on December 5th, 1933. Distilling was
resumed, but hundreds of smaller distilleries never re-opened. Almost
3,000 brands of bourbon are now retailed, and the distilleries which

produce this spirit are concentrated on a belt of limestone soil near the eastern seaboard of the United States, the limestone spring water being used in the production process. Well over half of these distilleries are in the State of Kentucky, the others being in Virginia, Maryland and Pennsylvania. While many of these distilleries are quite large, they can often trace their origins to well before prohibition times, and Kroll's (1968) book recounts several of these histories.

Comparatively little has been written on the history of whiskey distilling in Canada. Canada's first distillery was started in Quebec City in 1769, but this produced rum from molasses. Whiskey distilling developed in the 19th Century, and in 1850 there were some 200 distilleries operating in the State of Ontario alone, using largely the locally available rye. Amalgamations, mainly resulting from economic pressures on smaller producers but also influenced by prohibition in the United States, followed, and today there are only around 15 Canadian rye distilleries operating in Canada.

III. OUTLINE OF THE WHISKY-PRODUCING PROCESS

The definition of whisky given in the Introduction to the chapter clearly indicates the close relationship of this potable spirit to beer (see Chapter 1, p. 43). Whisky can indeed be considered as the product of distillation of an unhopped beer. Whiskies differ basically in the nature and proportion of the cereals used as raw materials, and on the type of still used in the distillation process. These differences in the production process are illustrated in the flow diagrams (Figs. 1 and 2) for production of Scotch malt whisky (production of Irish whiskey is very similar) and of American bourbon whiskey; Canadian whiskey and Scotch grain whisky are manufactured by a process basically similar to that used to produce bourbon. An additional feature shown in Figures 1 and 2 are the different names given by British (and Irish) and North American distillers to what is virtually the same unit process or item of plant. Detailed accounts of each of the unit processes in whisky production are given in subsequent sections of this chapter.

A characteristic of Scotch malt whisky is that the only cereal used

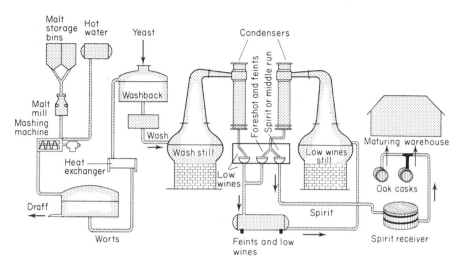

Fig. 1. Flow diagram showing the principal operations during production of Scotch malt whisky. See text for details.

in its manufacture is malted barley (Table 1). After milling, the *grist* is mashed in a *mash tun* (Fig. 1) similar to that used in beer production. During mashing or *conversion*, enzymes in the malt catalyse hydrolysis of starch and other components of the grain. In the manufacture of bourbon and Canadian whiskey—and this is true also of Scotch grain whisky and Irish whiskey—other cereals are used along with malted barley to provide additional starch in the *mash tub* (Fig. 2; Table 1). Owing to the high gelatinization point of their starches (see Chapter 2, p. 62), unmalted cereals must be precooked before they are incorporated into the mash.

The wort which leaves the mash tun is cooled, and fed into a vessel where it is mixed with yeast in proportions that differ in various countries (Table 1). In Scotland and Ireland these vessels have a relatively small capacity and are known as *washbacks* (Fig. 1), but in North America they are referred to as *fermenters* (Fig. 2). It is important to note that the worts are not boiled, nor are they hopped. Often, especially in North American distilleries, the whole mash is fermented ('in grains' fermentation); other distilleries filter their worts which however always contain a small proportion of grain husks. In Scotch malt-whisky distilleries, spent grains are usually sold as *draff* to farmers as a source of fodder.

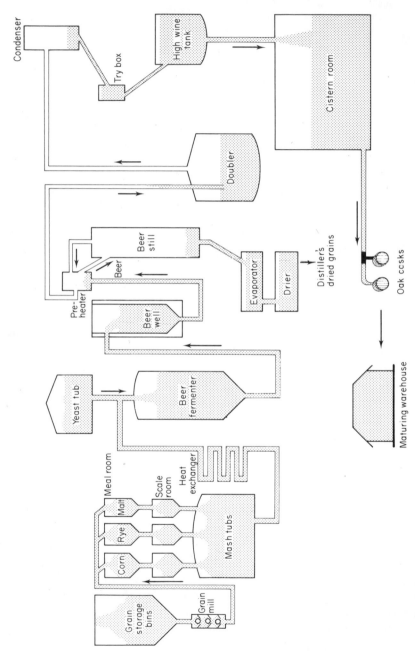

Fig. 2. Flow diagram showing the principal operations during production of bourbon whiskey. See text for details.

Table 1

Raw materials and unit processes used in the production of different types of whisky and grain spirit

	Scotch malt	Scotch grain	Irish	Bourbon	American grain	Canadian rye	Canadian grain
Raw Materials	Peated, malted barley	Maize and a small proportion of malted barley	Unmalted barley and unpeated, malted barley	Maize, rye and unpeated, malted barley	Maize, rye and unpeated, unmalted barley	Rye, maize, unpeated, malted barley, and malted rye	Rye, maize, unpeated, malted barley, and malted rye
Conversion	Infusion mash	Mash cook followed by conversion stand	Infusion mash	Mash cook followed by conversion stand	Mash cook followed by conversion stand	Mash cook followed by conversion stand	Mash cook followed by conversion stand
Fermentation	Distiller's yeast and brewer's yeast	Distiller's yeast	Distiller's yeast	Distiller's yeast	Distiller's yeast	Distiller's yeast	Distiller's yeast
Distillation Maturation	Two pot stills At 11° overproof in charred oak casks for at least three years	Patent still Up to 20° overproof in used sherry casks for at least three years	Three pot stills At 25° overproof in sherry casks or uncharred oak casks for at least three years	Patent still At 125° (U.S.) proof for at least one year	Patent still At or above 190° (U.S.) proof in oak containers for at least one year	Patent still Variable but always overproof (U.S.)	Patent still

Fermentation is conducted with strains of *Sacch. cerevisiae*, which usually are specially propagated for the purpose, although Scotch malt whisky distillers use some surplus brewer's yeast (Table 1). The process is allowed to proceed to a point at which the specific gravity of the fermented wort has usually dropped to below 1.000. In pot-still distilleries, the fermented wort or *wash* is fed directly to a still, known as the *wash still*, certain of the distillates from which are redistilled in the second or *low-wines still*. In Ireland, and in one Scotch malt-whisky distillery, a third distillation is carried out. In North America, the fermented wort is distilled in a continuous still of the Coffey type (Fig. 2; Table 1). The initial distillation process, carried out in the *beer still*, allows the distiller to separate and dry the spent grain, which is retailed for use as a cattle fodder (Fig. 2). Finally, the freshly distilled whisky is stored in charred or uncharred oak casks for minimum periods of time that depend on the legislation in the producing country (Table 1). Scotch malt, Irish, bourbon and Canadian rye whiskies are customarily matured for much longer than the legal minimum period.

IV. INDIVIDUAL OPERATIONS

A. Raw Materials

1. Malted Cereals

Malted barley is the principal malted cereal used in whisky production, although in the manufacture of Canadian rye whiskey a small proportion of malted rye is included. Like the brewer, the whisky distiller uses cultivars of *Hordeum vulgare* L. and *Hordeum distichon* (Hough *et al.*, 1971). Malted barley is employed primarily as a source of enzymes, principally amylolytic enzymes, that catalyse hydrolysis of barley-grain polymers, but also as a source of starch that is converted ultimately into ethanol. These two demands have to be finely balanced. In the manufacture of Scotch malt whisky, when only malted barley is used, care has to be taken that, in the malting process (see Chapter 2, p. 59), only a limited amount of enzyme activity is produced for this will be at the expense of the fermentable material in the grain, which both the brewer and the distiller determine as 'extract'. In the manfacture of other types of whisky, however, malted barley is used often as the only source of amylolytic enzyme in a grist that contains a high proportion of unmalted grain, so that the enzymic activity of the malted barley used must be greater than that used in Scotch whisky manufacture.

Traditionally, barley for use in production of Scotch malt whisky was malted on the distillery premises using a floor malting and dried over coke and peat fires in the pagoda-shaped kilns which are still a feature of these distilleries. To a large extent, these have now been superseded by mechanical maltings which produce malt for groups of distilleries. In order not to destroy enzyme activity which developed during malting, a balance has to be achieved in the kiln between drying the green malt to a suitably low level of moisture, curing to give the appropriate flavour, and retaining sufficient enzyme activity (Simpson, 1968). In maltings attached to the distillery, the kiln temperature is increased slowly over a 48-hour period to achieve an even rate of drying and the desired flavour. The latter character is achieved by stoking the furnace with peat during the early part of the kilning period when the green malt is moist and absorbs the peat smoke or 'reek'. In mechanical maltings, the green malt is dried at a faster rate with a forced-air draught, but a supplementary peat-fired kiln is used to produce a flavoured malt. The amount of peat used varies with different maltings. Some of the distilleries on Islay in Scotland specialize in producing a whisky with a very pronounced peat flavour, and they therefore use heavily peated malts. Malted barleys used in the manufacture of Scotch grain, Irish, Canadian and bourbon whiskies are not dried over a peat fire. In general, they have a greater enzyme activity so that the relatively small proportion of malted barley used in the mash (Table 1, p. 649) contains sufficient enzyme activity to convert the starch in the mash (principally supplied by unmalted cereals) into fermentable sugars. The greater enzyme activity in these malted barleys is reflected in their nitrogen contents. Malts used in production of Scotch grain whisky have a nitrogen content of 1.8% or higher (compared with a brewer's malted barley with a nitrogen content in the region of 1.5%; Hough *et al.*, 1971). In North America, where six-rowed barleys are used, the malts used have a higher nitrogen content, in the region of 2.2%. Malting acids, such as gibberellic acid and bromate, are not used in production of malted barley for whisky manufacture.

Because of the high cost of malted cereals, considerable effort has

been expended by the whisky distiller in attempting to devise
methods which will allow him to predict the yield of ethanol which
he can expect using different proportions of malted barley in the
grist. Unfortunately, the methods customarily used by the brewer,
such as those recommended in Great Britain by the Institute of
Brewing Analysis Committee (1975), have proved of limited value.
The brewer has used measurements of diastatic power, expressed as
the Lintner value which is a measure of the extent of saccharification
of soluble starch present in a cold-water extract of the malt (Lloyd
Hind, 1948), as an indicator of malt quality. Diastatic activity
measured in this way includes contributions from both α- and
β-amylases. However, Preece and his colleague (Preece, 1947, 1948;
Preece and Shadaksharaswamy, 1949a,b,c) have shown that high
β-amylase activity, as determined by the Lintner value, is not always
accompanied by high α-amylase activity. Pyke (1968) showed that
the Lintner value of a grist is only useful for predicting the spirit
yield in manufacture of Scotch grain whisky when the proportion of
malted barley in the grist is low (Fig. 3). Determination of α-amylase
activities of the grists gave a less satisfactory correlation than the
Lintner value, an observation which agrees with that made earlier by
Thorne *et al.* (1945). Further evidence for the unsuitability of

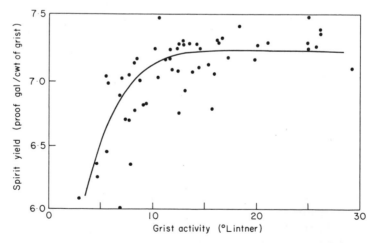

Fig. 3. Relationship between the diastatic activity of a Scotch grain-whisky grist and spirit
yield. Laboratory fermentations were conducted using grists containing different proportions of malt in a maize grind, and therefore with different Lintner values. It can be seen
that only when the proportion of malt in the grist is rate-limiting can spirit yield be
correlated with the Lintner value of the grist. From Pyke (1965).

employing traditional malt specifications for predicting performance in whisky manufacture has come from Griffin (1972).

Attempts are still being made to predict spirit yield from laboratory determinations on malted barley. A recent one (Dolan, 1976) emphasizes the individual character of these predictions since the formula used in the calculation includes a term which is characteristic of individual distilleries or types of distillery. According to Dolan (1976):

Predicted spirit yield (proof gallons/tonne) = $SE \times F(RG) \times \alpha$

where SE is the value for the standard hot-water extract of the malt, and $F(RG)$ is the fermentability of the wort calculated from the formula:

$$F(RG) = \frac{(OG - RG)}{OG + 1,000} \times 100$$

In this formula, OG is the original specific gravity, and RG the residual specific gravity, the specific gravity of water at 20°C being taken as 1.000. The term α in Dolan's equation is an empirical one values for which can be calculated for a particular distillery by inserting values for standard hot-water extracts of malts, fermentability and spirit yields over a period of time. He quotes a value for α of 0.1784 for a Scotch whisky distillery which uses traditional mash tuns, but states that the value is slightly higher for distilleries where lauter mash tuns are used.

Although the extent to which a malted barley has been peated can, to some extent, be assessed by smell, such is the importance of this character in malt that it must be determined in a more rigorous fashion. Peat smoke or 'reek' contains a wide range of compounds, but it is generally held that the peaty character is imparted to the malt largely as a result of absorption of phenols. For some years, Scots distillers used a method based on a reaction of phenols with diazotized sulphanilic acid. A lack of specificity in this method, coupled with the instability of the diazonium salt, prompted MacFarlane (1968) to recommend an alternative method involving extraction of phenols from malt with diethylether under acid conditions, and absorptiometric measurement of the colour developed when the phenols are reacted with 4-aminophenazone. He (MacFarlane, 1968) applied the method to a variety of malts, both peated and unpeated, and reported values ranging from zero (for an

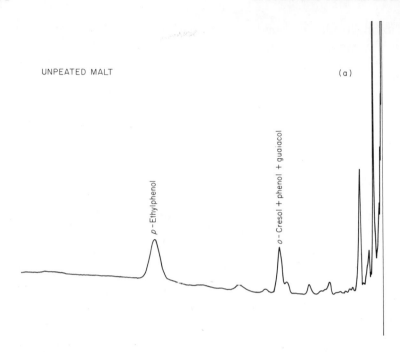

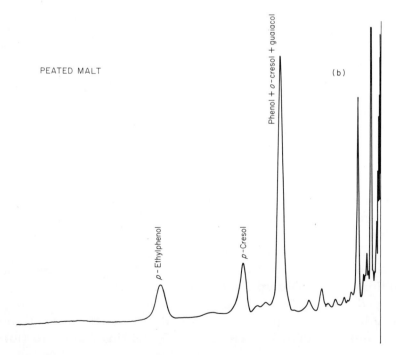

unpeated grain) to as high as 9.4 p.p.m. with a malt produced on Islay in Scotland. It has been calculated that, to obtain a malt with 10 p.p.m. phenols, one tonne of peat must be used for curing each tonne of malted barley.

Scotch whisky distillers have recently been concerned at the possibility that colourimetric methods, such as those recommended by MacFarlane (1968) and Kleber and Hurns (1972), may not assay all of the organoleptically important compounds that malt acquires as a result of peating. To examine this possibility, MacFarlane *et al.* (1973) produced peat smoke condensate on a laboratory scale, and separated the oil and aqueous phases from the wax fraction since only the two former would contain components that might appear in the distilled whisky. Six compounds, namely furfural, 5-methyl-furfural, guiacol, phenol, *p*-cresol and 5-xylenol, were detected in the aqueous fraction by gas–liquid chromatography. The peat-smoke oil was more complex and no fewer than 30 peaks, some of them created by more than one compound, were obtained by gas–liquid chromatography. The compounds included hydrocarbons, furfural derivatives, benzene derivatives and phenols. The authors stressed that, using their gas–liquid chromatographic techniques, 3,5-xylenol co-chromatographs with *m*-ethylphenol and *p*-ethylphenol, two compounds which are thought to make an important contribution to peat aroma and taste (T. P. Lyons, personal communication). Figure 4 shows gas–liquid chromatograms of extracts of malt that was peated and of a malt not so treated.

The small proportion of malted rye (*Secale cereale*) used in the grist for manufacture of Canadian rye whisky has a lower diastatic power than the malted barley used in the mash bill. Few data are available on the specifications required of malted rye. The principal amylolytic enzymes active during the mashing of this grist originate in the malted barley, and it is usually held that malted rye is included mainly to impart a characteristic flavour to Canadian whiskey.

Fig. 4. Gas–liquid chromatograms of extracts of unpeated (a) and peated (b) Scotch malt-whisky distillery malts, showing the contribution which peating makes to the content of phenols in the malt. Peating leads to an increase in the size of the peak corresponding to phenol, *o*-cresol and guiacol, and of the peaks which lie to the right of the mixed phenol peak and which are attributable to furfurals and hydrocarbons. *Para*-Cresol is also detectable on the chromatogram of extracts of peated malt. The ratio of the area of the total phenol peaks to that of *p*-ethyl phenol is used as an indication of the peatiness of the malt.

2. Unmalted Cereals

Fewer problems are encountered in arriving at specifications for the unmalted cereals used in whisky manufacture, namely maize, rye and barley.

The maize (or corn; varieties of *Zea mays*) used in grists for manufacturing Scotch grain, bourbon and Canadian rye whiskies (Table 1, p. 649) is usually of the American yellow-plate type. Occasionally, white maize is used, and it is reputed to give a higher alcohol yield. Maize is a popular grain because it has a high content of starch (67%, see Chapter 8, p. 545) which is readily extracted and converted into fermentable sugars. The United States of America and Canada have imposed controls on the quality of maize used for whisky manufacture. In the United States, there are three grades, with only grades 1 and 2 being used for spirit manufacture. In Great Britain, on the other hand, the maize used is normally grade 3 on the American scale.

In general, the distiller in North America pays considerable attention to the quality of the grain which arrives at the distillery. Test weights are determined on each grain shipment in accordance with recommendations issued by the U.S. Department of Agriculture (Bulletin No. 1065; May 18th, 1922). Sieving devices are used to assess the content of cracked corns and foreign material. The content of damaged kernels is also recorded, as is damage which may have been caused by heat arising from microbial action on the stored grain, or as a result of the grain sprouting. Most distilleries also carry out laboratory mashes to estimate the yield to be expected from each batch of grain.

Unmalted barley used in manufacture of Irish whiskey has a quality intermediate between that used for malting and grain used for cattle feed. In this way, the maltster can select the best barley available on the market at the time of purchase. In most distilleries, the quality of batches of unmalted cereal is again assessed using laboratory mashes to determine the yield of alcohol to be expected.

For many years, a small percentage (about 5% of the total) of unmalted oats (*Avena* spp.) was included in grists for manufacturing Irish whiskey. It was contended that these grains, with their large husks, improved the texture of the grain bed in the mash tun, and that oats influenced the flavour of Irish whiskey. Whether either or both of these effects were important probably will never be known, for oats are no longer used in the production of Irish whiskey (Court and Bowers, 1970).

B. Mashing and Cooking

Wort production in whisky distilleries involves a mashing process not unlike from that used to prepare wort in beer manufacture (see p. 59). However, where cereals other than malted barley are employed, mashing is preceded by a cooking process.

1. Mashing

Irrespective of whether the mash bill contains cereals other than malted barley, the main biochemical changes that take place during mashing are hydrolytic breakdown of starch, protein and other biopolymers in the grist to produce water-soluble low-molecular weight compounds that form a fermentable wort (see pp. 65 and 549). The major starch-liquefying and saccharifying enzymes are, respectively, α and β-amylases, while the limit dextrins formed by action of amylases on amylopectin are further hydrolysed by limit dextranases.

Barley malt used in the manufacture of Scotch malt whisky is coarsely ground in a roller mill, which is adjusted to give a grind no finer than the malt warrants. Too fine a grist can give rise to a 'set mash' which, settling on the bottom of the mash tun, blocks the plates and impedes drainage of the wort (Simpson, 1968). The mash tun is usually preheated with liquor (water) and the perforated plates at the bottom are flooded before mashing commences. The grist from overhead bins is mixed with hot liquor at 60-65°C in the proportion of one part grist to four parts liquor, and the mash is homogenized by action of revolving rakes. The mash is usually loaded into the tun to a depth of about one metre, and allowed to stand for about one hour, after which the wort is drained off from under the grain bed. This wort, which has a gravity of 1.070-1.060 (see Figure 5) is collected in an intermediate vessel, known as an underback, and then, after being cooled to around 25°C in a heat exchanger, is passed into the fermentation vessel. The bed of grains in the tun is then resuspended in liquor at 75°C, and a second batch of wort is drawn off, at a gravity of around 1.030, and passed into the underback. This process is known as the *first aftermash*, and is repeated a further two times, except that the dilute worts drawn off

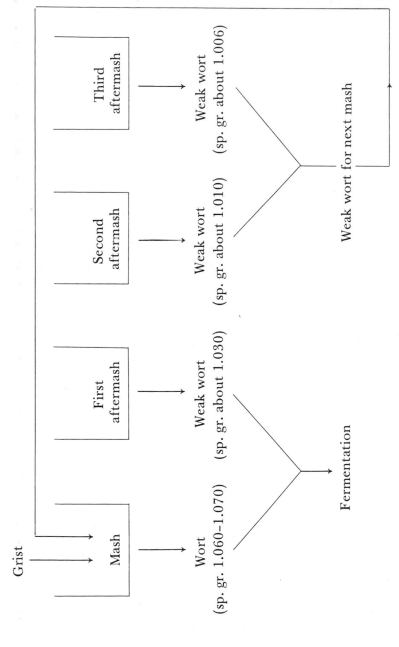

Fig. 5. Flow diagram showing the mashing cycle in a Scotch malt-whisky distillery.

are not passed to the underback but are returned to the hot-water tank to be used as liquor for the next mash (Fig. 5). The wort in the underback has a pH value of about 5.5, a gravity of 1.045–1.065, and an amino-nitrogen content of about 150–180 mg/litre. The spent grains or *draff* are removed from the mash tun, and sold as animal feed or processed to provide *dark grains* (see p. 678).

Wort production in the manufacture of Irish whiskey is very similar to that used in Scotch production, but there are certain differences. Use of a high percentage of raw barley in the mash bill (up to 60%) has necessitated the use of stone mills or hammer mills to achieve the required grind. The unmalted barley is sweated to give a moisture content of about 14% and then dried to around 4.5% moisture before grinding. The malted barley used is roller milled. Recently, a plant has been installed in Eire which uses a wet-milling process that eliminates the need for sweating and drying of the unmalted barley. Mash tuns used in Irish whiskey distilleries differ from those used to make Scotch in that they are larger simply because these distilleries have stills with a greater capacity than those in Scotland. Moreover, the mashing cycle differs in that the weak wort from the first aftermash is not passed to the underback, but is mixed with worts from the second and third aftermashes to provide a liquor for the subsequent mash (Lyons, 1974).

2. *Cooking Followed by Mashing*

The maize and rye used in production of whiskies in North America and of Scotch grain whisky must be cooked before being added to the mash containing malted barley (and malted rye in Canada) in order that the starch in these grains can become exposed to malt enzymes. Traditionally, cooking was carried out as a batch process, but this has now to a large extent been superseded by continuous processes especially in North America.

In batch cooking, the grain is freed from extraneous material by passage through a screen, and then ground either in a pin-type mill or a hammer still. It is then conveyed to the cooker and subjected to a cooking cycle involving high temperatures and pressures so designed to bring about complete gelatinization of the cereal. Inadequate cooking will sometimes leave starch granules intact in the mash, while excessive heating can cause caramelization, and therefore loss of sugar and decreased spirit yield. Pyke (1965) has provided a valuable account of the cooking of maize in production of Scotch grain whisky. The conventional cooker is a horizontal cylindrical vessel capable of working at pressures up to 90 p.s.i. (63×10^4 Pa), and fitted with stirring gear. A typical cycle in cooking maize might consist of 1-1.5 hours to reach a temperature of 120°C and a pressure of 15×10^4 Pa, after which the mash is held at this temperature and pressure for a further 1.5 hours. The liquor used for the mash is often that from the third aftermash (see p. 658). At the end of the cooking time, the pressure is released, and the hot cooked maize blown directly into a mash tun containing the malted barley suspended in liquor. Cold water is added to bring the temperature in the mash tun to around 60-65°C. Good mixing is also essential at this stage, and failure to achieve this can lead to the entire mash solidifying. The need for rapid cooling of the maize mash was emphasized by Murtagh (1970) who suggested that, at a temperature of around 82°C, lipid-carbohydrate complexes are formed which are not fermentable, a process that can lead to a loss of 1-2% in spirit yield. After a suitable mashing period, the mash may be filtered as already described, or the total mash may be pumped, via a heat exchanger, into a fermenter. In general, those distilleries that separate clear worts by filtration—Scotch grain and North American distilleries—obtain slightly lower spirit yields than those who operate in grains fermentations. Pyke (1965) has published the composition of a typical Scotch grain-whisky wort (Table 2).

In the manufacture of Scotch grain whisky, the proportion of malted barley in the mash bill is usually around 10-15%, which is a proportion far greater than that required merely to provide a source of amylolytic enzymes. This is a practice of long standing, and is done to obtain the required malt flavour in the grain whisky. It was noted upon as early as 1902 by Schidrowitz, and prompted further comment from Valaer in 1940.

Continuous cooking has been practised for many years in North America, and more recently in Scotland. Stark (1940) listed the advantages of using continuous cooking. Simpson (see page 546) has given a fairly full account of cooking procedures used in the manufacture of gin and vodka, and those used in the manufacture of whisky are basically similar. While practices vary to some extent in different distilleries, essentially the cereal is slurried at around 50°C, and then pumped into the cooking tubes, where the residence time is

Table 2
Chemical composition of a typical Scotch grain
wort. From Pyke (1965)

	%
Total soluble carbohydrate (as glucose)	9.00
Insoluble solids	2.20
Fructose	0.13
Glucose	0.29
Sucrose	0.28
Maltose	4.65
Maltotriose	0.96
Maltotetraose	0.15
Dextrin	2.54
Amino nitrogen (as leucine)	0.09
Ash	0.27
containing P_2O_5	0.09
K_2O	0.09
MgO	0.02
	$\mu g/ml$
Thiamin	0.46
Pyridoxin	0.61
Biotin	0.01
Inositol	236
Niacin	11.1
Pantothenate	0.71

normally 5–10 minutes. In N. America, liquor from the stills (see p. 648) is often used to slurry the maize. The pH value of the stillage is around 4.0, and using it to slurry the maize lowers the pH value of the mash from about 5.8 to 5.2, and helps to minimize infection. The continuous cooker has a narrow tube (6–16 cm in diameter) which avoids charring and carbon deposition. The mash passes through the tube at about 20 m/min, with the temperature reaching near 65°C and the pressure 65 p.s.i. (40×10^4 Pa).

C. Fermentation

The objectives in fermenting a whisky distillery wort with strains of *Sacch. cerevisiae* are the same as with a wort in beer brewing, namely to convert wort sugars to ethanol and carbon dioxide and at the same time produce quantitatively minor amount of other organic compounds which contribute to the organoleptic qualities of the final product, that is after distillation with whisky production (see Chapter 1, p. 1). Fermenting vessels vary considerably in volume depending on the distillery. The small Scotch whisky distillery at Edradour, near Pitlochry, for example, has washbacks with a capacity of only 4,500 litres, whereas other Scotch and Irish pot-whisky distilleries have washbacks with a capacity in the range 50,000 to 150,000 litres. Much larger fermenters are found in Scotch grain-whisky distilleries and in whisky distilleries in North America. Traditionally, the smaller pot-distillery washbacks were made of wood, usually of larch or Oregon pine, but in recent years they have been constructed of steel or aluminium. In some Scottish distilleries, timber is still used as a covering material.

When the fermenting vessel is partly filled, the wort is pitched with a suspension of *Sacch. cerevisiae* or in North American terminology 'yeasted'. The source of the yeast varies with the location and size of the distillery. North American distilleries invariably have special plants for propagating the yeast, as do a few of the larger distilleries in Scotland. An account of anaerobic and aerobic processes for propagating whiskey distillery yeasts in North America has been given by Andreasen (1949). A mixture of milled 'small' grains, consisting typically of about 90% rye and 10% malted barley, is mashed for 30 min at around 65°C. This mash is more concentrated (about 33% solids) than that used to make production worts in order that the wort so formed contains sufficient nutrients for both the propagating yeast and for lactobacilli that are added. After cooling to 40-50°C, a culture of a lactobacillus—often of *Lactobacillus delbrueckii*—is added, and the wort incubated for about four to six hours as a result of which the wort is supplemented with about 1.5% lactic acid (the traditional 'sour mash'). The acidified wort is then sterilized, cooled to 27°C, and the propagating yeast added. The temperature of the fermentation is maintained at around 30°C and, when the gravity of the wort has fallen to about half of its original value (typically from 22° to 10° Balling), the culture after cooling to around 15°C is used to inoculate the fermenters. The inoculating culture contains 90–150 million cells/ml, and 3% by volume is used as an inoculum. An alternative aerobic process may also be used, and it has the advantage of requiring less grain and producing a greater density of cells (about 600 million cells/ml).

Rye and malted barley are comparatively expensive cereals, while yeast cells grown in mashes made from these cereals die rapidly when the inoculum culture is stored at around 16°C. Accordingly, storage at this temperature has been restricted to 12-16 hours. To overcome these shortcomings, Van Lanen *et al.* (1972) have proposed preparing a mash containing 99% maize and only 1% malted barley, but including a mould glucamylase in the mash. This enzyme releases extra amounts of nitrogenous nutrients, particularly amino acids, and Van Lanen *et al.* (1972) attribute the much greater retention of viability of yeast cells grown in these mashes to the action of glucamylase.

No matter which propagation mashing system is used, all distilleries in North America employ pure cultures of yeast, that is plant mashes are inoculated from stock cultures of the yeast maintained in the laboratory. Previously, they were in the habit of using some of the inoculum mash to re-inoculate a new mash. This practice, known as *backstocking*, has been abandoned because of the dangers of uncontrolled bacterial contamination.

Distilleries outside North America, particularly the pot-whisky distilleries, rarely have their own yeast propagation plant. They rely on specially propagated pressed yeast for use in fermentations. In Scotch malt-whisky distilleries, this is augmented, often on an equal-weight basis, with surplus brewery yeast, supplied as a suspension in beer (known as barm; see Chapter 1, p. 1) from breweries that may be as far as 250 km from the distillery. Lactobacilli are not deliberately introduced into these supplies of yeast. Bacterial activity in Scotch malt-whisky fermentations originates from the grain used in the mashing, as indeed it can to some extent in North American distilleries.

The requirements demanded of a strain of *Sacch. cerevisiae* used in distillery practice have been described by Harrison and Graham (1970). Apart from the obvious need to have a strain that maintains a very high level of viability in the pressed state (containing 25% dry weight), a very important property of these strains is their ability to tolerate concentrations of ethanol of the order of 12-15 (v/v) and the capacity to hydrolyse oligosaccharides, such as maltotriose and maltotetraose, to glucose in order to maximize conversion of starch into ethanol and carbon dioxide.

Whisky worts usually have a specific gravity in the range 1.050-1.080, a pH value of around 5.0, a total acid content of 0.1% and an optical rotation of +30°. After inoculation, the yeast content is 5-20 million cells/ml. The bacterial count varies, in North American distilleries, on the extent of lactobacillus growth in the inoculum and, in Scotland and Ireland, on the cleanliness of the plant and the extent to which the raw materials were endowed with a microbial flora. In-grains fermentations, because of their large content of suspended solids, create little if any foam. However, in most Scotch malt-whisky fermentations, only a small proportion of the suspended solids of the mash is retained in the fermentation vessel. These fermentations tend to foam, and the distiller has resorted to the use of antifoams. Soap is used in some distilleries (Ross, 1970, McGuire, 1973) to combat foams, and it is conceivable that silicones, which have been recommended for control of foam in brewery fermentations (Evans, 1972; Vernon and Rose, 1976), might also be used.

The time-course of a typical fermentation in a Scotch malt whisky distillery is depicted in Figure 6. Fermentation proceeds vigorously for the first 30 h, during which time specific gravity falls to 1.000 or below, and the optical rotation to around zero. As in beer fermentations, the sugars in the wort are utilized in a particular sequence, glucose and fructose being fermented first, followed by maltose and then maltotriose. The removal of sugars during fermentation of a Scotch grain-whisky wort is shown in Figure 7 (Pyke, 1965). Over the first 30 h, the pH value, after declining to around 4.2, rises to about 4.5. During the first 30 h, the specific gravity drops at the rate of

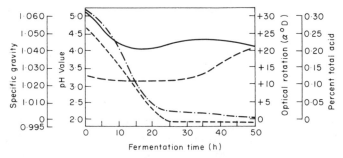

Fig. 6. Changes in specific gravity (– – –), optical rotation (–•–•–•), pH value (---) and acidity (———) during fermentation of a wort in production of Scotch malt whisky. From Dolan (1976).

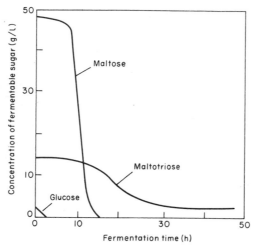

Fig. 7. Time-course of removal of fermentable sugars from a Scotch grain-whisky wort. From Pyke (1965).

about 0.5°/h, accompanied by a massive evolution of heat. While many of the larger distilleries have fermenters fitted with cooling coils, these are absent or if fitted are relatively inefficient in most pot-malt whisky distilleries, where the temperature of the fermentation can rise, by the end of the fermentation, to as high as 35-37°C. The distiller is concerned about the temperature rise during fermentation since this can cause the fermentation to arrest or 'stick'. Temperature rise can be controlled by employing a lower starting temperature or, because glycolysis of sugar is a heat-producing process, by using lower original gravities. Strains of *Sacch. cerevisiae* are well suited for malt-whisky distillery fermentations since they can ferment efficiently over a wide temperature range. Fermentation is usually continued for up to at least 36 hours and frequently longer at which time the ethanol content of the wash is 9-11% (v/v). In larger distilleries, particularly those in North America, the carbon dioxide evolved is collected, liquefied and retailed. Smaller distilleries, particularly the pot malt-whisky distilleries in Scotland, do not usually have this facility.

Reference has already been made to the differences between whisky and brewery fermentations. Since worts in whisky distilleries are not hopped, it follows that hop constituents cannot contribute to the organoleptic qualities of the final spirit. Two other differences in the processing of worts in whisky distilleries, as compared with those in breweries, also have important effects on the composition of the final whisky.

Worts in whisky distilleries are not boiled, so that any enzyme activity that can be manifested at the temperature of the mash, and any micro-organisms that can survive at that temperature, will continue to be active during the fermentation. The continued activity of limit dextrinases in unboiled distillery worts increases the concentration of sugars available for fermentation by the yeast. Hopkins and Wiener (1955) calculated that, in the presence of amylases alone, the yeast cannot degrade the equivalent of the final 12–16% of the starch.

Another important consequence of using non-sterile conditions in distillery fermentations is the activity of bacteria which pass over into the wort, an activity which is encouraged to some extent by the relatively high temperatures to which the fermentations can rise. In addition to lactic-acid bacteria, the flora can include other Gram-positive bacteria as well as Gram-negative strains. The size of the flora depends on a number of factors including the extent to which the lactic-acid bacteria grew during yeast propagation, the size of the flora on the cereal raw materials, and on the standard of hygiene in the distillery. There is no doubt, however, that the controlled activity of this bacterial flora, and particularly of the lactic-acid bacteria, is accompanied by excretion of compounds that contribute to the organoleptic qualities of the final whisky.

During the first 30 hours or so of a malt-whisky fermentation, there is a vigorous fermentation and the majority of the aerobic bacteria die. However, this provides ideal conditions for growth of anaerobic or micro-aerophilic bacteria, principally the lactic acid bacteria (mainly strains of *Lactobacillus brevis, L. fermenti* and *Streptococcus lactis*), with the result that the concentration of lactic acid in the final wash can be as high as 30 mg/l (MacKenzie and Kenny, 1965). Hardly any data have been published on the bacterial flora of whisky fermentations. Recently, however, Bryan-Jones (1976) identified *Lactobacillus fermentum, L. brevis, L. delbrueckii, L. plantarum, L. casei* and a bacterium resembling *L. collinoides*, from a Scotch distillery fermentation, in addition to *Leuconostic* spp., *Streptococcus lactis* and *Pediococcus cerevisiae*. Growth of lactic-acid bacteria is probably enhanced by excretion of nitrogenous nutrients by the yeast at the end of a vigorous fermentation. Kulka

(1953) demonstrated the ideal nature of yeast autolysate for growth of lactobacilli. Bacterial activity in the fermenting wort also leads to removal of some acids. Actively growing yeast secretes citric and malic acids, but MacKenzie and Kenny (1965) attribute the lower concentrations of these acids in malt distillery worts as compared to beer worts to their partial removal by bacteria.

Occasionally, the size of the bacterial flora in the fermenting wort can become too large, and this causes problems as a result of utilization by the bacteria of sugars that leads to an overall decrease in spirit yield. In addition, the bacteria may excrete organoleptically undesirable compounds, and also hydrogen ions which cause the pH value of the wort to fall too low, thereby providing suboptimal conditions for action of certain enzymes. Examples of noisome compounds that may be excreted by bacteria are hydrogen sulphide and other sulphur–containing compounds (Anderson et al., 1972). Lactobacilli can also metabolize glycerol, which is excreted by the yeast during fermentation, to produce β-hydroxypropionaldehyde, which subsequently breaks down on distillation to give acrolein (Harrison and Graham, 1970) that gives a pungent, burnt and often peppery odour to the whisky (Lyons, 1974). In a recent paper, Dolan (1976) concentrated on the problems which arise in malt-whisky distilleries when there is an unacceptably high concentration

Table 3

Changes in the concentration of bacteria during fermentation of a minimally infected and a heavily infected Scotch malt-whisky wash. From Dolan (1976)

	Minimally infected			Heavily infected		
	Bacteria/ml			Bacteria/ml		
Age (h)	Gram-negative rods	Gram-negative cocci	Lacto-bacilli	Gram-positive rods	Gram-positive cocci	Lacto-bacilli
At setting	2,000	3,700	n.d.	52,000	60	0.6×10^6
10	150	n.d.	n.d.	n.d.	n.d.	2.3×10^6
20	n.d.	n.d.	1.53×10^6	n.d.	n.d.	18.8×10^6
30	n.d.	n.d.	10.2×10^6	n.d.	n.d.	96×10^6
40	n.d.	n.d.	10.2×10^6	n.d.	n.d.	502×10^6
50	n.d.	n.d.	50×10^6	n.d.	n.d.	$1,000 \times 10^6$

n.d. indicates that the organism was not detected.

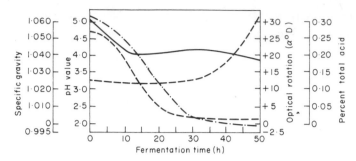

Fig. 8. Changes in specific gravity (– – –), optical rotation (–•–•–•), pH value (---) and acidity (———) during fermentation of a Scotch malt-whisky wort containing an unacceptably high concentration of bacterial infection. From Dolan (1976).

of bacteria in the wort. Table 3 shows changes in the concentrations of Gram-negative and Gram-positive bacteria and, separately, of lactobacilli, during fermentation of a minimally infected wort and of a heavily infected wort. The time-course of fermentation of an unacceptably infected malt-distillery wort (Fig. 8) shows, in comparison with similar data for fermentation of an acceptable wort (Fig. 6, p. 664), a greater rise in the acid content of the wash after about 35 h and a lower optical rotation of the wash after about 40 h. In the fermentations, there is often a difference of up to four hours from the time at which a rise in the acid content is detected to the point when the pH value of the fermentation begins to fall, which Dolan (1976) attributes to the buffering capacity of the wash. The data in Table 4 show the effect which different levels of infection after 30 h fermentation of a malt distillery wort have on spirit yield, and they indicate the associated financial losses to the distiller. Dolan

Table 4

Effect of the level of bacterial infection on the loss of spirit incurred following fermentation of a Scotch malt-whisky wort. From Dolan (1976)

Infection rating	Bacteria/ml in 30 h old wash (million)	Approximate loss in spirit yield (%)	Approximate financial loss £ sterling (thousands)	
			At filling	Duty paid
a	0–1	<1	<17	<238
b	1–10	1–3	17–51	238–714
c	10–100	3–5	51–85	741–1190
d	>100	>5	>85	>1190

An infection level designated 'a' is commonly encountered in washbacks constructed of stainless steel, while that designated 'b' is experienced in a wooden washback.

(1976) recommends limits of $\not> 1,500$ bacteria, $\not> 50$ Gram-positive and $\not> 10$ lactic acid-producing bacteria per 10^6 yeast cells in the wort at the start of fermentation.

Much less has been published on the effect of retaining solid material in the fermenting wort. However, marine microbiologists have long known that the presence of solid particles in a liquid medium can affect bacterial growth, probably because of the concentration of nutrients at the solid–liquid interface (Heukelekian and Heller, 1940; Zobell, 1943). Moreover, Crowell and Guymon (1963) found that formation of higher alcohols during fermentation of grape juice is stimulated by the presence of grape skins or inert solids. Beech (1972) made similar observations on cider fermentations. Merritt (1967), in the only detailed report on the role of solids in whisky-distillery fermentations, states that a dry solid concentration of 50 mg/100 ml might typically be expected, although much will clearly depend on the design of the mash tuns and tubs used in individual distilleries. He (Merritt, 1967) went on to report that a concentration of dry solids as low as 5 mg/100 ml causes an increase in yeast growth, and that suspended solids also enhance the rate of excretion of ethanol and glycerol. There was, too, an effect on excretion of higher alcohols by the yeast (Table 5). With the possible exception of n-propanol, excretion of all of the major higher alcohols was increased in the presence of solids, the effect being particularly noticeable with isobutanol and 2-methylbutanol. It is a pity that more research has not been published on this intriguing aspect of whisky distillery fermentations.

Table 5

Effect of including insoluble solids in the wort on excretion of higher alcohols during fermentation of a whisky wort. From Merritt (1967)

Wort	Insoluble solids content (mg per 100 ml)	Production of higher alcohols (mg per 100 ml)				
		n-Propanol	Isobutanol	2-Methyl-butanol	3-Methyl-butanol	Total
1	0	1.5	4.2	3.0	8.0	16.7
	25	1.5	6.5	4.4	8.8	21.2
2	0	2.8	4.5	2.7	9.5	19.5
	35	3.3	6.6	3.7	10.1	23.7
3	0	1.7	4.8	3.1	8.0	17.6
	50	1.7	6.8	4.6	9.5	22.6

D. Distillation

Whether the fermented wort is distilled in a pot still, as in production of Scotch malt and Irish whiskies, or in a continuous still based on the Coffey design as in the manufacture of other types of whisky, the objectives are to remove selectively volatile compounds, particularly the flavour-producing compounds or congeners, from non-volatile compounds, and to create additional flavour-producing compounds as a result of chemical reactions that take place in the still. Nevertheless, it is still most convenient to discuss whisky distillation under the separate headings of pot-still and continuous distillation.

1. Pot-Still Distillation

The copper pot still, which is the structural feature which dominates any Scotch malt or Irish whisky distillery, has changed hardly at all over the centuries, except of course in size. Traditionally, the onion-shaped stills were fired from beneath, and had the pipe or lyne arm from the still projecting through the distillery wall in the form of a coil or worm into a water tank fed from a local stream or burn (Fig. 9). Internal steam-heated coils are now preferred to direct firing, and this decreases the extent of pyrolysis of the still contents and results for example, in a lower concentration of furfural in the whisky. Variations in still design include expansion of the surface area of the column into a bulbous shape, water jacketing and return loops from the first stage of the condensation (Nettleton, 1913, provided a valuable account of early still design). In many distilleries, worms have been replaced by tubular condensers, which have the advantage that they are designed to conserve the heat extracted from the distillates. Yet other pot stills are fitted with 'purifiers' which consist of a circular vessel cooled by running water and which is interposed between the neck of the still and the condenser. In Irish pot stills, this purifier function is effected by a trough fitted round the lyne arm and through which running water is circulated. Pot stills in Scotch and Irish distilleries are traditionally constructed of copper. The reason for this adherence to copper is more than sentimental, since it has been established that copper fixes noisome volative sulphur-containing compounds which are produced during fermentation, but

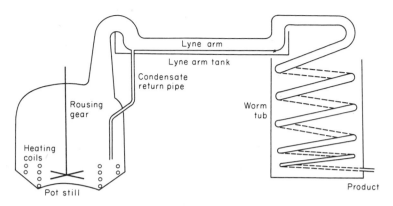

Fig. 9. Diagram of an Irish distillery pot still. Still design in Scotch malt-whisky distilleries is similar, except that the pot is onion-shaped, and the still usually has a shorter lyne arm which is not surrounded by a lyne-arm tank. From Lyons (1974).

whose presence is undesirable in the distilled spirit (see p. 563 and Thorne *et al.*, 1971).

Early distillers of spirit appreciated albeit empirically that, although the objective of distilling was to separate volatile constituents from the fermented wort, collecting the distillate not as a whole but in several fractions, and combining certain of these fractions, gave a much more acceptable product. Pot-still distillation in Scotland and Ireland differs not only in the smaller size of the stills in Scotland (25,000–50,000 litres) compared with those in Ireland (100,000–150,000 litres), but also in the different ways in which they collect fractions from the stills.

In Scotland, the wash is subjected to two distillations. In the first, carried out in the *wash still*, the fermented wort is brought to a boil over a period of 5–6 hours, and the distillate is referred to as *low wines*. This distillation effects a three-fold concentration of the alcohol in the wash (Fig. 10) and the residue in the wash still, known as *pot ale*, is either discharged to waste or converted into animal feed (Rae, 1967). Distillation of the low wines in the spirit still is more selective. The first fraction, which contains low boiling-point compounds, is rejected as *fore-shots* (Fig. 10). At a stage which is determined by continued hydrometric monitoring, and which usually takes place when the distillate has a gravity of approximately 25–30° overproof, there is a switch from fore-shots to distillation of whisky. This switch is one which traditionally has been made at the

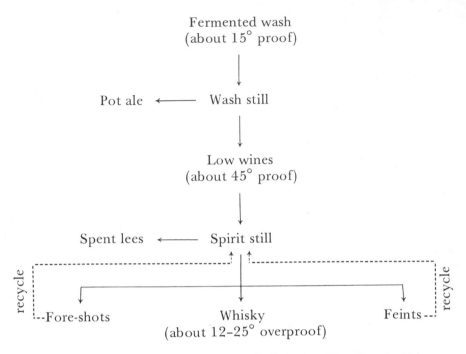

Fig. 10. Flow diagram showing the stages in distillation of Scotch malt whisky.

discretion of the distiller, and in which he has been aided by the disappearance of a bluish tinge when water is added to the distillate. The monitoring process takes place in a spirit safe, which is sealed with an Excise lock. Collection of the distillate is terminated when the gravity has fallen to a specified value, although distillation of the *feints* is continued until all of the alcohol has been removed from the low wines. The residue which remains in the spirit still is known as *spent lees*, and like pot ale is either run to waste or used to manufacture animal feed. The whisky distilled over in the middle fraction has a gravity of some 12–25° overproof.

In the manufacture of Irish whiskey, three rather than two distillations are carried out (Fig. 11). The fermented wash is heated in a wash still, and the first distillation, known as *strong low wines*, is collected until, at a predetermined gravity, the distillate, then known as *weak low wines*, is run into a separate vessel. The weak low wines are pumped into the low-wines still and are redistilled to produce two fractions termed *strong feints* and *weak feints*. Strong feints are mixed with the strong low wines in a spirit still the distillates from

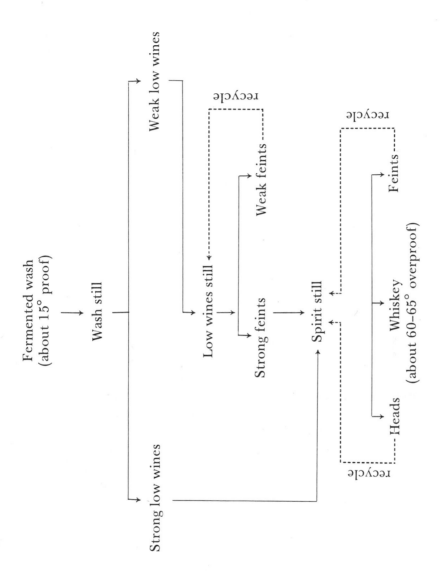

Fig. 11. Flow diagram showing the stages in distillation of Irish whiskey.

which are collected in the same fashion as in production of Scotch (Figs. 10 and 11). The whiskey collected is usually 60–65° over-proof.

2. Continuous Distillation

No fundamental changes have been introduced into the design of the patent or Coffey still over the past century. Automation, particularly of the wash feed, is now commonplace, as is continuous monitoring of other stages in the distillation process. Nevertheless, many Scotch and Irish grain distilleries continue to use a still which, like the original Coffey still, has just two columns—an analyser and a rectifier—although most distilleries operating in North America have more columns—up to five in number—it being maintained that only in this way can a distillate at or near the azeotrope, and of the required purity, be produced. Simpson, in Chapter 8 (p. 557), has given a comprehensive account of the design and use of different stills in the manufacture of gin and vodka, and those used to produce many whiskies are similar in design and operation.

A description of the operation of two-column continuous stills in the manufacture of Scotch grain whisky has come from Pyke (1965). In order to obtain whisky of high quality from these stills, they must be operated in such a manner that the alcohol concentration of the spirit drawn off at the spirit plate in the rectifier shall not be greater than 94.17% at 20°C. This is achieved by maintaining the 'bend temperature' at the spirit plate at about 48°C. Bends are the curved tubes between one rectifier plate and the next, and the temperature at any one plate will depend on the rate at which the wash is fed to the still, and quantity of steam being introduced into the analyser column. If, at any plate, the temperature is too high, the concentration of alcohol will increase, but the proportion of congenerics will drop and good whisky will not be obtained, and similarly when the temperature at a particular bend becomes too low. The manner in which precise control of still operation can affect the composition of the whisky is shown in Figure 12. It can be seen that, if the flow of wash and steam is changed in either direction on the abscissa, the concentration of congenerics in the whisky will alter so producing an adverse effect in the quality of the final spirit.

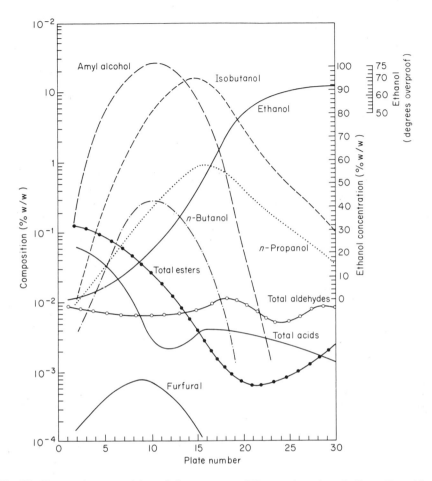

Fig. 12. Changes in composition of the vapour at different plates in a Coffey-still rectifier used in the manufacture of Scotch grain whisky. From Pyke (1965).

A five-column distillation unit for production of bourbon has been described by Packowski (1963), and is depicted in Figure 13. Fermented wash, containing about 7% (v/v) alcohol, is pumped into the whisky-separating column somewhere in between the 13th and 19th perforated plate from stripping. The residual mash is discharged at the base and pumped to a feed-recovery plant. The distillate then goes through a selective distillation column, a product-concentrating column, an aldehyde-concentrating column and finally a fusel oil-concentrating column. There are many variations on this basic design in distilleries in Scotland and in North America.

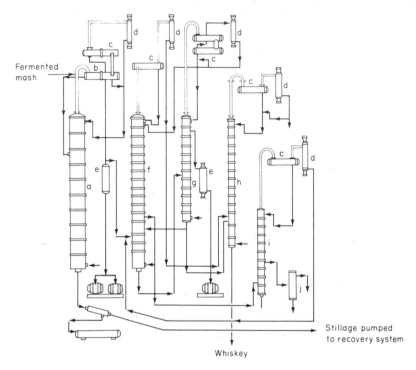

Fig. 13. Diagram of a five-column distillation unit used in the manufacture of bourbon. a indicates the whisky-separating column, b heat exchanger, c dephlegmator, d vent condenser, e product cooler, f selective distillation column, g product-concentrating column, h aldehyde-concentrating column, i fusel oil-concentrating column, j fusel oil decanter. From Packówski (1963).

E. Maturation and Ageing

Freshly distilled whisky, of any variety, is very different from the spirit which is later retailed, either singly or blended. The transformation is brought about by storing the whisky in oak casks for periods of time that depend on traditional practice and legal requirements. The data in Table 1 (p. 649) list these requirements. In general, whiskies are matured for far longer than the legally required period of time. The raw spirit is taken by pipeline from the distillation plant to the spirit stores, where it is diluted with water to the required strength and then stored in casks of various capacity.

Maturation and ageing in casks are accompanied by a loss of liquid by evaporation, and the relative rates of loss of water and of ethanol determine whether the aged whisky has a higher or lower alcoholic strength than that at filling. In Scotland, where the casks of whisky are stored in cool, unheated, but humid warehouses, the alcoholic strength decreases (Valaer, 1940), whereas Valaer and Frazier (1936) report that, in the United States, storage conditions cause an increase in alcoholic strength. Maturation in cask is also accompanied by changes in the chemical composition of the whisky, which are attributable to extraction of wood constituents from the cask, oxidation of components present in the original whisky as well as those extracted from the wood, and reactions between components in the whisky filled into the cask. Some of the earlier investigators reported on changes in the composition of the major classes of organoleptically important compounds during maturation and ageing in cask. Thus, Schidrowitz and Kaye (1905) found increased concentrations of volatile acids in aged whiskies, a trend that was also described in the report of the Royal Commission on Whisky and Other Potable Spirits (1909). Several reports followed, Liebmann and Scherl (1949), for example, reporting on increased concentrations of acids, furfural, tannins and colour with ageing in cask. The arrival of the gas–liquid chromatograph has, as already stated, greatly accelerated research on this topic, and more recent data on chemical changes that take place during maturation and ageing of whiskies are described in Section V.D. (p. 683) of this chapter.

Maturation of whisky in casks is an expensive process, and it is hardly surprising that consideration has been given to methods for speeding up the process. Jacobs (1947) described several of these methods, which include pretreatment of the wash with activated carbon, chemical treatment of the whisky to convert aldehydes into esters, and use of oxidation treatments. Such techniques are rarely used in the industry, mainly because of the traditional nature of the whisky-producing process.

F. Blending and Colouring

Whisky manufacturers take great pride in the quality of their straight or blended whiskies, and in their ability to maintain the quality of a particular product over the years. Blending is carried out by expert operators who advise manufacturers on mixing or blending large volumes of whisky after appropriate tasting sessions on experimental blends. After the whiskies have been blended, they are usually filled into re-used casks, either after dilution with water or not, and stored for a further six months or a year; this process is referred to as 'marrying'. The water used for dilution is soft or demineralized since water containing an appreciable concentration of salts can cause hazes in the whisky (Warricker, 1960). After marrying, and dilution if necessary, the colour of the whisky is adjusted to the desired value by adding caramel. Some brownish pigment is extracted from the casks, but this is never sufficient to provide the desired colour. Finally, the whisky is clarified for bottling by filtration through sheets of asbestos or cellulose, sometimes after pretreatment with charcoal (Simpson, 1968). Chill filtration is also often practised since it removes tannin material from the whisky and prevents subsequent appearance of chill haze.

G. Effluent Disposal and Spent Grains Recovery

Traditionally effluents from whisky distilleries were disposed of in the most convenient manner; spent grains were retailed, often quite cheaply, to local farmers as animal fodder, while pot ale and spent lees were simply discharged into the local sewer, stream or river. But no longer so, mainly because of the distiller's awareness of the nutritional value (largely the protein content) of some of these effluents, and the public awareness of problems that arise from uncontrolled disposal of effluents into waterways. Simpson (p. 564) has described production of 'distiller's dark grains' from effluents formed in the manufacture of gin and vodka, and these processes are widely used to dispose of effluents from whisky distilleries, especially where the traditional methods of disposal are forbidden or are considered to be uneconomic.

V. ORGANOLEPTICALLY IMPORTANT COMPONENTS OF WHISKY

Recent years have witnessed a major thrust in research on compounds responsible for the organoleptic properties of whiskies. However, the first reports on the nature of flavour-producing compounds in whiskies antedate the era of the gas–liquid chromatograph by nearly half a century. Two publications by Schidrowitz (1902) and Schidrowitz and Kaye (1905), dealing exclusively with Scotch whiskies, reported on the fusel-alcohol, acid and ether contents of some 50 different brands. They reported analyses of several Campbeltown malt whiskies from Scotland, whiskies that were soon to disappear from the market never to return. A report by Mann (1911), published a few years later, also quoted values for acidity and levels of furfural, aldehydes, ethers and alcohols in Scotch whiskies imported into Australia.

A. Concentrations of Organoleptically Important Compounds

Since the introduction of the gas–liquid chromatograph into distillery laboratories, several reviews have been published on the contents of the major flavour-producing compounds in whiskies—fusel alcohols, esters, carbonyl compounds, organic acids and aromatic compounds—and on identification of individual compounds that go to make up these fractions (see Suomalainen and Nykänen, 1970a, 1972, and Suomalainen and Lehtonen, 1976, for reviews of the subject). Fusel alcohols, which are still usually determined by modifications of the Komarowsky (1903) colour reaction, are quantitatively the most important. Bourbon and Scotch malt whiskies are richest in fusel alcohols, with contents often well over 2 g/l; the lighter flavoured Canadian, Japanese and Australian whiskies contain about a quarter of this concentration. Free fatty acids are relatively volatile, and make a major contribution to the organoleptic qualities of whiskies. Concentrations of acids in whiskies can be as high as 0.4–1.0 g/l absolute alcohol with some Scotch malt whiskies (Duncan and Philp, 1966); bourbons contain about the same concentration, but there is much less acid in corn and rye whiskies (Schoeneman and Dyer, 1968). Roughly comparable concentrations of esters are found in whiskies, although beverages produced with pot stills have, on the whole, higher concentrations than those from continuous stills. Concentrations in Scotch and Irish pot still whiskies have been reported in the range 0.27–0.87 g/l absolute alcohol (Valaer, 1940), while bourbons have been reported to have ester concentrations in the range 0.14–0.36 g/l absolute alcohol (Schoeneman and Dyer, 1968). Lighter whiskies contain lower concentrations of carbonyl compounds, although the concentration varies with the brand. Grain whisky may have as little as 20 mg aldehydes per litre, while in mature Scotch malt whisky the concentration may be as high as 80 mg/l (Duncan and Philp, 1966).

B. Chemical Nature of Organoleptically Important Compounds

A review of the chromatographic and other methods used to separate the various organoleptically important compounds from whiskies has come from Duncan and Philp (1966). The major problem in analysing whisky by gas–liquid chromatography is the overwhelming preponderance of ethanol and water. Only one volatile compound, namely isopentenyl alcohol, is likely to be present in a concentration exceeding 0.1%, while most others are present in concentrations that rarely exceed 50 p.p.m. Analyses are most conveniently conducted on extracted fractions of the different classes of compounds. When direct analysis of whiskies has been employed, only a limited number of components have been determined (Morrison, 1962; Bober and Haddaway, 1963; Singer and Stiles, 1965).

Some idea of the variety of compounds detected in whiskies came from the compilation made in 1969 by Kahn from both published and unpublished sources. Of the some 200 compounds listed, 25 are fusel alcohols, 32 acids, 69 esters and 22 phenolic compounds. Undoubtedly, this list could now be extended quite considerably. Of the fusel alcohols, isoamyl alcohol and optically active amyl alcohol predominate, accompanied by lower concentrations of isobutanol and n-propanol. Characteristically, there are usually only low concentrations of n-butanol and sec.-butanol. The principal organic acid in whiskies is acetic acid which can account for between 50 and 95% of the total content of volatile acids determined by titration. Of the remaining acids, caprylic, capric and lauric are quantitatively the most important (Suomalainen and Nykänen, 1970a). Some of the characteristic flavour and aroma of bourbon and Irish whiskies may be attributed to their containing somewhat higher concentrations of the odoriferous butyric acid. Compared with other types of whisky, Scotch whisky characteristically contains more palmitoleic acid (and its ethyl ester) than palmitic acid. Suomalainen (1971) has suggested that the typical stearin-like smell of Scotch malt whisky may be attributed to its containing long-chain fatty-acid ethyl esters. It is not surprising to find that ethyl acetate is the major whisky ester in view of the prevalence of acetic acid in these alcoholic beverages. Concentrations of 85 mg/l have been detected in a blended Scotch whisky, 98 mg/l in a Canadian whisky, and as much as 380 mg/l in a bourbon whiskey matured for eight years (de Becze *et al.*, 1967). Other esters, such as ethyl caprate, are present in much lower concentrations, of the order of 2–10 mg/l. Of the carbonyl compounds, acetaldehyde is the principal component, together with a range of other short-chain aldehydes. Furfural, with an aroma resembling that of grain, also occurs with as much as 20–30 mg/l in Scotch malt whiskies (Valaer, 1940). Acrolein, a pungent and lachrymatory compound, is also present, and it has been suggested that it may contribute to the 'peppery' smell of whisky. However, this idea has been refuted by Kahn and his colleagues (1969) who showed that acrolein reacts with ethanol to form 1,1-diethoxy-2-propene and 1,1,3-triethoxy-propane, and thereby is removed.

A variety of other organoleptically important compounds have also been detected in different whiskies, many of which are present as a result of maturing the whisky in charred oak barrels. Scopoletin and other aromatic aldehydes including vanillin were detected in bourbon by Baldwin and his colleagues (1967), compounds which had previously been found in ethanolic extracts of plain and charred American white oak by Black *et al.* (1953). A lactone, which has been dubbed 'whisky lactone', also appears in whisky following storage in oak barrels. This compound, β-methyl-γ-octalactone, was first isolated from Scotch whisky by Suomalainen and Nykänen (1970b), and it has since been reported that both *cis* and *trans* diastereomers of the compound occur in whisky (Nishimura and Masuda, 1971). Other compounds that have been detected in whisky include phenols (Salo *et al.*, 1976), glycerol and erythritol (Black and Andreasen, 1974), pyridine, α-picoline and various pyrazines (Wobben *et al.*, 1971).

C. Contribution of Compounds to Organoleptic Properties

Although there have been numerous studies on the contribution made by beer components to the flavour and aroma of that beverage (see Chapter 2, p. 113), other alcoholic beverages have received somewhat less attention from this standpoint. Published information on compounds responsible for the organoleptic qualities of whiskies is meagre, and very largely confined to reports by Suomalainen and his colleagues from the State Alcohol Monopoly in Helsinki, Finland. In order to assess the contributions made by whisky components to the odour of these spirits, Salo *et al.* (1972) concocted a synthetic whisky with components that chromatographic analysis had revealed were present in a light-flavoured Scotch whisky. It was made by dissolving 576 g of a mixture of fusel alcohols, 90 mg of acids, 129 mg esters and 17.4 mg carbonyl compounds in highly rectified grain spirit, which was diluted to 34% ethanol using water that had been ion exchanged and treated with activated charcoal. This imitation whisky contained 13 alcohols in addition to ethanol, 21 acids, 24 esters and 9 carbonyl compounds. Caramel colouring was used to give it the colour of a distilled and matured whisky. Odour thresholds of the individual compounds, and groups of compounds, were determined as described by Salo (1970). An experienced taste panel were easily able to distinguish the imitation whisky from a blended Scotch whisky but, when the concoction was mixed with an equal amount of the Scotch, only 6% correct judgements above chance were made, which suggested that the concentrations of, and interactions between, components of the synthetic whisky were not greatly dissimilar from that in the Scotch used for comparison.

Determinations of the odour thresholds of individual components in the imitation whisky showed that the contribution made by the mixture of alcohols and acids contributed only 10% of the total odour intensity, despite the fact that the alcohols themselves accounted for over 70% of the total concentration of organoleptically important compounds in the concoction. Esters and carbonyl compounds had a much greater influence, particularly butyraldehyde, isobutyraldehyde, isovaleraldehyde, diacetyl, and the ethyl esters of acetic, caproic, caprylic, capric and lauric acids. Since just three of the most important carbonyl compounds could substitute for the whole carbonyl fraction, there would seem to be considerable homogeneity in the odour contributions made by these compounds. Interestingly, the relative contributions made by the different classes of compounds are not very different from the contributions which Harrison (1970) reported they make towards the taste of beers.

Table 6
Threshold dilution levels for nine different types of
whisky. From Salo (1975)

Whisky	Threshold dilution ($\times 10^{-4}$)	One standard deviation range ($\times 10^{-4}$)
Scotch malt	0.56	0.2–1.3
Scotch, old blend	0.87	0.5–1.5
Scotch, blend	1.20	0.3–4.2
Irish	1.30	0.4–2.0
Bourbon	2.40	0.6–11.5
Irish	4.50	2.7–7.5
Canadian	10.40	3.0–37.0

Threshold values can be assessed not only for individual components in whisky but for the total aroma of the beverage. Salo (1975) followed the latter by diluting different whiskies with water until the characteristic whisky aroma could only just be recognized. Values for the threshold dilution of several commercial whiskies shown in Table 6 reflect the differences in aroma strength for several different commercial whiskies.

D. Origin of Organoleptically Important Compounds

The two main sources of the organoleptically important compounds in whisky are the yeast used to ferment the wort, and the charred oak barrels in which the whisky is matured. Excretion of organoleptically important compounds by yeast during alcoholic fermentation has been demonstrated for several alcoholic beverages as indicated in other chapters in this volume. Suomalainen and Nykänen (1966) fermented a sucrose-containing nitrogen-free medium with a strain of *Sacch. cerevisiae*, and distilled the fermented medium either after removing the yeast by centrifugation or with the yeast remaining in the medium. Gas chromatographic analyses of these distillates are reproduced in Figure 14 which also shows a chromatogram of a Scotch whisky for comparison. There is clearly a similarity between all three analyses, although differences, such as the higher proportion of isoamyl alcohol in the distillate from the fermented medium, can be detected. Also worth noting is the greater concentration of ethyl caprate in the distillate from the

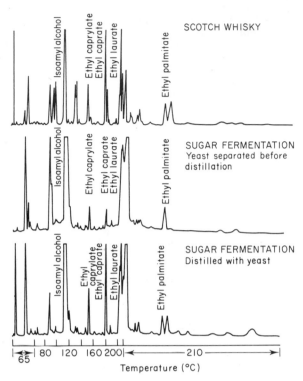

Fig. 14. Gas–liquid chromatograms of aroma compounds produced by yeast in a nitrogen-free sugar fermentation, with a trace for comparison of the aroma compounds detected in a sample of Scotch whisky. From Suomalainen and Nykänen (1966).

yeast-containing spent medium compared with that obtained by distilling medium from which yeast had been removed. It would be interesting to learn of the importance of yeast strain in production of organoleptically important compounds in whisky. Unfortunately, there is a complete lack of published data on this matter.

Rather more has been published on those organoleptically important compounds which arise, either directly or indirectly, from the oak barrels in which whisky is matured. The increase in colouring and in tannin, dissolved solids and acid concentrations are not observed when whisky is stored in glass, which is proof of the importance of the oak barrels in the maturation process. An analysis of heartwood of the American oak (*Quercus albus*) gave cellulose (49–52%), lignin (31–33%), pentosans (or hemicelluloses, 22%), and compounds extracted with hot water and ether (7–11%; Ritter and

Fleck, 1923). However, when charred oak-wood sawdust was directly extracted with water or 192° proof (U.S.) ethanol, the extracts obtained differed markedly in odour from aged whisky. Moreover, none of the various fractions of ethanol-soluble oak-wood extractives contained flavours that resemble mature whisky (Baldwin *et al.*, 1967). As a result, it is now generally held that the maturation process involves not only extraction of compounds from the oak wood but also chemical modifications of at least some of the compounds extracted from the wood.

Most of the work reported on this aspect of maturation of whisky has come from the laboratories of Joseph E. Seagram and Sons in the U.S.A. Changes in the concentrations of organoleptically important compounds during a 12 year storage of a 109° proof (U.S.) bourbon, on a 100° proof basis, are shown in Figure 15. The nature and origin of some of these compounds have been examined in some detail. Among the aldehydes, scopoletin and the aromatic aldehydes syringaldehyde, sinapaldehyde, coniferaldehyde and vanillin are important. According to Baldwin *et al.* (1967), these compounds could be formed by ethanol reacting with lignin in the oak wood to produce coniferyl alcohol and sinapic alcohol. Under mildly oxidizing conditions, these alcohols could be converted into coniferaldehyde and sinapaldehyde, respectively. Vanillin could then arise from coniferaldehyde, and syringaldehyde from sinapaldehyde. The increase in

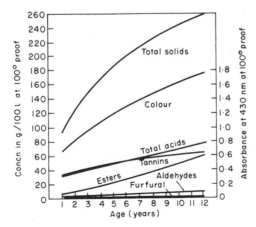

Fig. 15. Changes in the concentration of some organoleptically important compounds during a 12-year storage of a 109° proof bourbon whiskey calculated on a 100° proof basis. From Baldwin and Andreasen (1973).

aldehyde content during maturation is also attributable in part to formation of acetaldehyde by oxidation of ethanol. Formation of ethyl acetate probably accounts for the steady rise in the ester content of whisky during maturation (Fig. 15).

Several other groups of compounds not described in Figure 15 are also important in the maturation process. Monosaccharide sugars are found in mature whisky, and probably arise from the pentosans and other polysaccharides in the oak wood. Otsuka et al. (1963) reported that a mature Japanese whisky contained xylose, arabinose, glucose and fructose, while Black and Andreasen (1974) added rhamnose to this list when they analysed a mature bourbon. The latter workers found that the concentrations of arabinose and glucose increased at a faster rate than those of xylose and rhamnose over a 12-year maturation period. Salo et al. (1976) also detected low concentrations of mannose and galactose in a matured Scotch malt whisky, in addition to the sugars already referred to. The concentrations of sugars in mature whiskies—of the order of 100 mg/l—are too low to suggest that they have any sweetening effect on the beverage. Phenols are also detectable in mature whisky, although some of these probably arise during mashing (Steinke and Paulson, 1964), or from malt produced using peat-fired kilns (MacFarlane, 1968). However, Salo et al. (1976) reported an increase during a one-year maturation of a Scotch malt whisky in the concentration of eugenol, which is a major phenol extracted from oak chips by ethanol (Suomalainen and Lehtonen, 1976). Also present in mature whiskies are sterols, which may precipitate in bottled whisky stored at room temperature. Black and Andreasen (1973) found campesterol, stigmasterol and sitosterol in mature bourbon, in addition to sitosterol-D-glucoside, although the possibility that some of these were formed during mashing cannot be excluded. Finally, reference has already been made to the whisky lactone, β-methyl-γ-octalactone, and its origin.

Not surprisingly, the nature and amounts of compounds extracted from charred oak wood depend on the ethanol concentration of the whisky. It is to some extent an advantage to mature whisky at a high proof, since this requires fewer barrels and is economic on storage space. Up to 1962, the Treasury Department in the U.S.A. limited the barrelling proof of whisky to a maximum of 110° (U.S.). In anticipation of this limit being raised—which it was to 125° in 1962—Baldwin and Andreasen, who reported in 1973, initiated a series of experiments to establish the importance of barrelling proof on changes in colour and concentrations of organoleptically important compounds during maturation of bourbon whiskies. The colour intensity and congener concentration of whiskies matured for 12 years decreased as the entry proof was raised from 109° to 155°, the one exception being the fusel alcohol content which remained approximately constant.

VI. WORLD-WIDE PRODUCTION OF WHISKIES

Production of different types of whisky throughout the World is increasing, and has been so for several years, although the extent of the increase varies with the whisky. Data on whisky production are freely available. Those for Scotch malt and grain whisky are published annually in the Statistical Report of the Scotch Whisky Association in Edinburgh, Scotland, for bourbons by the Bourbon Institute in New York, U.S.A., while data on whisky production in Canada are obtainable from the Association of Canadian Distillers in Montreal. Irish Distillers, who own all of the whiskey distilleries in Eire and Northern Ireland, can supply data on production of Irish whiskey.

Figure 16 shows data for production of Scotch malt and grain whiskies over the period 1964-1974. With the exception of the years 1967-1969, there has been a steady increase in the volumes distilled of both beverages. The data in Figure 16 also show the proportionate increase in the volume of Scotch malt whisky produced, which is attributable mainly to the increased popularity throughout the World of straight Scotch malt whisky over the past 5-10 years. Production of straight bourbon is probably running at about 70 million proof gallons, per annum, while approximately 57 million proof gallons of blended bourbon are produced each year. Production of straight bourbons has not increased much during the past few years, reflecting the trend towards 'lightness' in the spirit industry. Another feature in whiskey production in North America has been the introduction onto the market, starting in 1972, of two new whiskies. The first of these was a 'light' whiskey, distilled at between 161 and 189° proof (in contrast to the traditional bourbon which is distilled at 160° proof or lower) and aged in re-used cooperage (rather than new charred oak barrels), and the second a 'blended light' whiskey

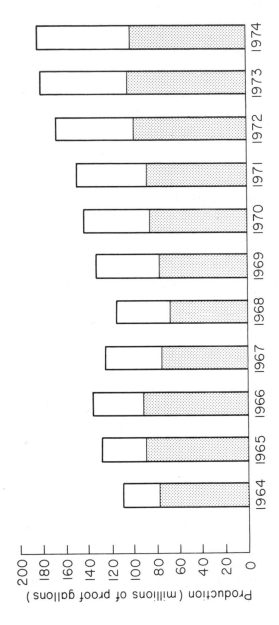

Fig. 16. Histograms showing changes in the annual production of Scotch malt (upper non-hatched) and Scotch grain whisky (lower hatched areas). Data from the Statistical Report of The Scotch Whisky Association (1974).

which is mixed with less than 20% by volume of straight bourbon. In Canada, whiskey production is at about 15 million proof gallons annually, while in Ireland the level of production is around 5 million proof gallons per annum. In Japan, the largest of the newer whisky-producing countries, production is at about four million gallons each year.

VII. ACKNOWLEDGEMENTS

We wish to thank our friends and colleagues in whisky production in many countries of the World for their co-operation and willingness to supply information on the processes of whisky production.

REFERENCES

Anderson, R. J., Howard, G. A. and Hough. J. S. (1972). 'Proceedings of the European Brewing Convention, Vienna', 253.

Andreasen, A. A. (1949). *American Brewer* 82 (4), 30.

Baldwin, S. and Andreasen, A. A. (1973). *Journal of the Association of Official Analytical Chemists* 57, 940.

Baldwin, S., Black, R. A., Andreasen, A. A. and Adams, S. L. (1967). *Journal of Agriculture and Food Chemistry* 15, 381.

Barnaud, A. (1887). 'The Whisky Distilleries of the United Kingdom', 457 pp. Proprietors of Harper's Weekly Gazette, London.

de Becze, G. I. (1967). 'Encyclopaedia of Industrial Analysis', Vol. 4, pp. 462. Interscience Publications, New York.

Beech, F. W. (1972). *Progress in Industrial Microbiology* 11, 178.

Black, R. A. and Andreasen, A. A. (1973). *Journal of the Association of Official Analytical Chemists* 56, 1357.

Black, R. A. and Andreasen, A. A. (1974). *Journal of the Association of Official Analytical Chemists* 57, 111.

Black, R. A., Rosen, A. A. and Adams, S. L. (1953). *Journal of the American Chemical Society* 75, 5344.

Bober, A. and Haddaway, L. W. (1963). *Journal of Gas Chromatography* 1 (12), 8.

Brander, M. (1975). 'A Guide to Scotch Whisky', 96 pp. Johnson and Bacon, Edinburgh.

Bryan-Jones, G. (1975). *In* 'Lactic Acid Bacteria in Beverages and Foods', Proceedings of the Fourth Long Ashton Symposium (J. G. Carr, C. V. Cutting and G. C. Whiting, eds.), pp. 165–175. Academic Press, London.

Cameron Taylor, I. B. (1970). 'Whisky Export', 2nd issue, June-Sept. Aldiffe Publishing Co. Ltd., Wilmslow, Cheshire.

Carson, G. (1963). 'The Social History of Bourbon', 280 pp. Dodd, Mead and Co., New York, N.Y.

Court, R. E. and Bowers, V. H. (1970). *Process Biochemistry* 5 (10), 17.

Crowell, E. A. and Guymon, J. F. (1963). *American Journal of Enology and Viticulture* 14, 214.

Daiches, D. (1969). 'Scotch Whisky, Its Past and Present', 168 pp. Andre Deutsch, London.

Dolan, T. C. S. (1976). *Journal of the Institute of Brewing* 82, 177.

Duncan, R. E. B. and Philp, J. M. (1966). *Journal of the Science of Food and Agriculture* 17, 208.

Dunnett, A. (1953). 'The Land of Scotch', 179 pp. Scotch Whisky Association, Edinburgh.

Evans, J. I. (1972). *Process Biochemistry* 7 (4), 29.

Griffin, O. T. (1972). *Process Biochemistry* 7, 17.

Gunn, N. M. (1935). 'Whisky and Scotland', 198 pp. Routledge, London.

Harrison, G. A. F. (1970). *Journal of the Institute of Brewing* 76, 486.

Harrison J. S. and Graham, J. C. J. (1970). *In* 'The Yeasts' (A. H. Rose and J. S. Harrison, eds.), vol. 3, pp. 283–348. Academic Press, London.

Heukelekian, H. and Heller, A. (1940). *Journal of Bacteriology* 40, 547.

Hopkins, R. H. and Wiener, S. (1955). *Journal of the Institute of Brewing* 61, 493.

Hough, J. S., Briggs, D. F. and Stevens, R. (1971). 'Malting and Brewing Science', 678 pp. Chapman and Hall Ltd., London.

Institute of Brewing Analysis Committee, Recommended Methods of Analysis. (1975). *Journal of the Institute of Brewing* 81, 368.

Jacobs, M. B. (1947). *American Perfumery and Essential Oil Review*, 157.

Johnson, H. (1971). 'The World Atlas of Wine', 272 pp. Mitchell Beazley, London.

Kahn, J. H. (1969). *Journal of the Association of Official Analytical Chemists* 52, 1166.

Kahn, J. H., Shipley, P. A., Laroe, E. G. and Conner, H. A. (1969). *Journal of Food Science* 34, 587.

Kleber, von W. and Hurns, N. (1972). *Brauwissenschaft* 25, 98.

Komarowsky, A. (1903). *Chemiker Zeitung* 27, 807.

Kroll, H. H. (1967). Bluegrass, Belles and Bourbon. 224 pp. A. S. Barnes & Co., New York.

Kulka, D. (1953). *Journal of the Institute of Brewing* 59, 285.

Liebmann, A. J. and Scherl, B. (1949). *Industrial and Engineering Chemist* 41, 534.

Lloyd Hind, H. (1948). 'Brewing Science and Practice', vol. 1, 505 pp. Chapman and Hall, London.

Lyons, T. P. (1974). *The Brewer*, 634.

McDowell, R. J. S. (1975). 'The Whiskies of Scotland', 3rd edit., 166 pp. John Murray, London.

MacFarlane, C. (1968). *Journal of the Institute of Brewing* 74, 272.

MacFarlane, C., Lec, J. B. and Evans, M. B. (1973). *Journal of the Institute of Brewing* 79, 202.

McGuire, E. B. (1973). 'Irish Whiskey', 462 pp. Gill and MacMillan, Dublin.

MacKenzie, K. G. and Kenny, M. C. (1965). *Journal of the Institute of Brewing* 71, 160

Mann, E. A. (1911) *Government Analyst for Western Australia*, pp. 1–12. Perth, W. Australia

Marrison, L. W. (1957). 'Wines and Spirits', 320 pp. Pelican Books, London.

Merritt, N. R. (1967). *Journal of the Institute of Brewing* 73, 484.

Morrison, R. L. (1962). *American Journal of Enology and Viticulture* 13, 159.

Murtagh, J. E. (1970). M.Sc. Thesis: University College of North Wales, Bangor.

Nettleton, J. A. (1913). 'The Manufacture of Whisky and Plain Spirit', 616 pp. Cornwall and Sons, Aberdeen.

Nishimura, K. and Masuda, M. (1971). *Journal of Food Science* 36, 819.

Otsuka, K., Morinaga, K. and Imai, S. (1963). *Nippon Jozo Kyokai Zasshi* 59, 448.

Packowski, G. W. (1963). Alcoholic Beverages, Distilled. *In* 'Encyclopaedia of Chemical Technology' (R. E. Kirk and D. F. Othmer, eds.), vol. 1, pp. 501–531. John Wiley and Sons, New York.

Preece, I. A. (1947). *Journal of the Institute of Brewing* 53, 154.

Preece, I. A. (1948). *Journal of the Institute of Brewing* 54, 141.

Preece, I. A. and Shadaksharaswamy, M. (1949a). *Journal of the Institute of Brewing* 55, 298.

Preece, I. A. and Shadaksharaswamy, M. (1949b). *Biochemical Journal* 44, 270.

Preece, I. A. and Shadaksharaswamy, M. (1949c). *Journal of the Institute of Brewing* 55, 373.

Pyke, M. (1965). *Journal of the Institute of Brewing* 71, 209.

Rae, I. J. (1967). *Process Biochemistry* 1 (8), 407.

Ritter, G. J. and Fleck, L. C. (1923). *Industrial and Engineering Chemistry* 15, 1055.

Robb, J. M. (1950). 'Scotch Whisky', 197 pp. W. and R. Chambers, London.

Robinson, H. M. (1951). 'Water of Life', 608 pp. Macdonald, London.

Ross, J. (1970). 'Whisky', 158 pp. Routledge, and Kegan Paul, London.

Royal Commission on Whisky and Other Potable Spirits (1909). Appendix Q, p. 229.

Salo, P. (1970). *Journal of Food Science* 35, 95.

Salo, P. (1975). 'Proceedings of the International Symposium on Aroma Research', Central Institute for Nutrition and Food Research, TNO, Zeist, Netherlands, 121.

Salo, P., Nykänen, L. and Suomalainen, H. (1972). *Journal of Food Science* 37, 394.

Salo, P., Lehtonen, M. and Suomalainen, H. (1976). 'Proceedings of the Fourth Symposium on Sensory Properties of Foods', Skövde, Sweden.

Schidrowitz, P. (1902). *Journal of the Chemical Society*, 814.

Schidrowitz, P. and Kaye, F. (1905). *Journal of the Chemical Society*, 585.

Schoeneman, R. L. and Dyer, R. H. (1968). *Journal of the Association of Official Analytical Chemists* 51, 973.

Sillett, S. W. (1965). 'Illicit Scotch', 121 pp. Beaver Books, Aberdeen.

Simpson, A. C. (1968). *Process Biochemistry* 3 (1), 9.

Simpson, B., Troon, A., Grant, S. R., MacDiarmid, H., MacKinlay, D., House, J. and Fitzgibbon, T. (1974). 'Scotch Whisky', 120 pp. MacMillan, London.

Singer, D. D. and Stiles, J. W. (1965). *Analyst* 90, 290.

Stark, W. H. (1954). *In* 'Industrial Fermentations' (L. A. Underkofler and R. J. Hickey, eds.), vol. 1, pp. 17–72. Chemical Publishing Company, New York.

Steinke, R. D. and Paulson, M. C. (1964). *Journal of Agricultural and Food Chemistry* 12, 381.

Suomalainen, H. (1971). *Journal of the Institute of Brewing* 77, 164.

Suomalainen, H. and Lehtonen, M. (1976). *Kemia-Kemi* 3 (2), 69.

Suomalainen, H. and Nykänen, L. (1966). *Journal of the Institute of Brewing* 72, 469.

Suomalainen, H. and Nykänen, L. (1970a). *Naeringsmidelidustrien* 23, 15.

Suomalainen, H. and Nykänen, L. (1970b). *Process Biochemistry*, July, 1.

Suomalainen, H. and Nykänen, L. (1972). *Wallerstein Laboratories Communications* 35, 185.

Thorne, C. B., Emerson, R. L., Olsen, W. J. and Paterson, W. H. (1945). *Industrial and Engineering Chemistry* 37, 1142.

Thorne, R. S. W., Helm, E. and Svendsen, K. (1971). *Journal of the Institute of Brewing* 77, 148.

Valaer, P. (1940). *Industrial and Engineering Chemistry* 32, 935.

Valaer, P. and Frazier, W. H. (1936). *Industrial and Engineering Chemistry* 28, 92.

Van Lanen, J. M., Maisch, W. F. and Smith, M. B. (1972). *Proceedings of the Division of Microbial Chemistry, American Chemical Society*, 46.

Vernon, P. S. and Rose, A. H. (1976). *Journal of the Institute of Brewing* 82, 335.

Warricker, L. A. (1960). *Journal of the Science of Food and Agriculture* 11, 709.

Wilson, J. (1973). 'Scotland's Malt Whiskies. A Dram by Dram Guide', 109 pp. Famedram Ltd., Gartochan, Dunbartonshire, Scotland.

Wilson, J. (1975). 'Scotland's Distilleries. A Visitor's Guide', 104 pp. Famedram Ltd., Gartochan, Dunbartonshire, Scotland.

Wilson, Ross (1959). 'Scotch Made Easy', 336 pp. Hutchinson Ltd., London.

Wilson, Ross (1970). 'Scotch: The Formative Years', 502 pp. Constable, London.

Wilson, Ross (1973). 'Scotch, Its History and Romance', 184 pp. David and Charles, Newton Abbot, Devon, England.

Wobben, H. J., Timmer, R., ter Heide, R. and de Valois, P. (1971). *Journal of Food Science* 36, 464.

Zobell, C. E. (1943). *Journal of Bacteriology* 46, 39.

AUTHOR INDEX

Numbers in italic are those pages on which References are listed

A

Accree, T. C., 363, *379*
Acker, L., 241, *293*
Acree, T. E., 251, *293*
Adachi, K., 462, *470*
Adamow, M., 399, 403, 410, *419, 420*
Adams, A. M., 179, 252, 262, *293*
Adams, S. L., 554, *590*, 625, *630*, 681, 685, *689*
Agabal'janc, G. G., 399, *419*
Agulhon, R., 335, *380*
Ahlburg, H., 440, *468*
Ahmad, K. U., 33, *37*
Ahmad, M., 33, *37*
Aida, K., 261, *309*
Aitken, R. A., 110, *126*
Akai, Y., 435, 437, *468*
Akasaka, K., 434, *470*
Akimvo, Y. A., 572, *590*
Akiyama, H., 434, 438, 441, 444, 445, 447, 448, 449, 451, 458, 460, 462, *468, 469, 470, 472, 474*
Alas, G., 10, *40*, 505, *535*
Alford, E. D., 628, *631*
Alfredsson, M., 582, *590*
Ali, A. M., 13, 14, *39*
Alizade, M. A., 367, *379*
Allan, A. M., 120, *128*
Allan, D. A., 611, 612, *630*
Allan, H. M., 525, *533*
Allcott, E. S., 145, *294*

Allen, H. W., 320, 321, 322, 323, *379*
Alley, C. J., 329, 338, *379, 383*
Almenar, J., 104, 112, *134*
Althausen, D., 565, 566, 567, *593*
Amaha, M., 103, 118, *126, 130*, 250, *303*
Amemiya, S., 291, *294*
Amerine, M. A., 263, *294*, 334, 336, 337, 338, 339, 341, 342, 343, 357, 359, 362, 364, 365, 366, 368, 370, 371, *379, 382, 383, 385*, 388, 394, *419*, 479, 482, 508, 521, 522, 527, 529, 533, *533, 534, 535*
Amos, W. M. G., 50, *135*
Amphoux, M., 335, *380*
Andersen, K., 118, *129*
Anderson, E., 17, *38*
Anderson, F. B., 62, *126*
Anderson, R. G., 92, 97, *126*, 268, *294*
Anderson, R. J., 6, 12, 21, 32, *37*, 81, *126*, 271, *294*, 667, 686, *689*
Ando, F., 446, *469*
Ando, N., 438, *469*
Andreasen, A. A., 358, *379*, 607, 614, 615, 625, *630, 632*, 662, 681, 685, *689*
Andrews, J., 121, *126*
Anerzoni, M. E., 251, *313*
Angelino, E., 602, *630*
Anon, 141, 143, 147, 218, 232, 238, 245, 253, 269, 271, 274, 276, 291, *294*, 316, 317, 326, 331, 335, 337,

C

M

SUBJECT INDEX

A

716

F

Fat, changes in content of during polishing of rice, 435

Fatty acids
biosynthesis of in rum, 617
in molasses, nature of, 598
occurrence of in table wines, 355

Feints, nature of in whisky distillation 672

Fennel seed, as a botanical in gin manufacture, 565

Fermentation
alcoholic, of grape juice, 342
by yeasts, microbiology of, 9
continuous, of beer, 99
efficiency of brewing yeasts
definition of, 12
nature of, 83, 84
extent of and formation of ethyl acetate by brewery yeasts, 92
growth of yeast during cider, 214
in yeasts, biochemistry of, 21
of apple juice, 183
technology of, 256
of brewery worts, 81
of fruit in pulp, 404
of fruit musts, 402
of honey, 415, 417
of molasses in rum manufacture, 600
of musts in fortified wine production, 499
of whisky worts, time-course of, 664
of worts in gin manufacture, 551
of worts in whisky manufacture, 661
preparation of fruit must for, 398
systems in beer brewing, 96
time in saké brewing, 425
velocity of brewing yeasts, definition of, 12
yeasts, use of in fortified wine manufacture, 502

Fermenters
tower, in beer production, 100
use of in Scotch production, 647

Fermenting ability of strains of Saccharomyces cerevisiae, 11

Ferric ions in beer brewing liquor, 61

Ferrocyanide, use of to clarify fruit wines, 410

Fertilizers, use of in the vineyard, 493

Fibre content of apple pomace, 236

Film yeasts
growth of in ciders, 209, 216

Filter aid, barley husk as a, 50

Filtration
of fruit wines, 411
of saké, 458
of table wines, 364
of whisky, 678

Fining
of beers, 104
of sherries, 513

Finishing of gin and vodka, 589

Finland, production of cider in, 163

Fino character, responsibility of yeasts for in sherry production, 505

First
aftermash, in whisky mashing, 657
saké, classification of, 430

Fish bladders, use of to clarify fruit wines, 410

Five-column stills, used in continuous distillation of bourbon, 675

Flakes, barley, use of in beer brewing, 62

Flash pasteurization of beers, 109

Flavobacterium spp., appearance of in moto, 447

Flavonal glycosides, presence of in apple juices, 175

Flavour
of beer, nature of, 113
of table wines, changes in during malo-latic fermentations, 366

Flavour profiles, use of in beer assessment, 115

Flavoured
fortified wines, manufacture of, 529
vodkas, popularity of, 542

Flavouring of fruit wines, 408

Flocculating
ability of brewery yeasts, importance of, 84
yeasts, classification of, 95

I

J

Turbidity, decrease in during mellowing of fruit wines, 407
Two-column stills
use of in gin manufacture, 561
use of in whisky distillation, 674
Types of dry sherry, 505

U

Uisgebaugh, as an ancient name for
whisky, 639
Ulster, history of whiskey production
in, 643
Uncinula necator, infections caused by
in vineyards, 334
Underback, use of in beer brewing, 70
United States of America
vine plantings in, 332
wine consumption in, 317
Unmalted cereals
in beer brewing, 62
use of in manufacture of whiskies,
656
Unsaturated
acids as sources of lactones in rums,
628
ethyl esters, presence of in rum,
622
fatty acids, biosynthesis of in rum
manufacture, 620

V

Vacuoles, yeast, as a location for lytic
enzymes, 16
Vacuum, use of in fruit must desulphiting, 398
Valine as a source of higher alcohols
found in rums, 614
Vanilla, use of to flavour meads, 416
Vanillin, presence of in whiskies, 681
Vapour changes in composition during
whisky distillation, 675
Varieties
apple, high-yielding, in cider manufacture, 218
grape, used to produce fortified
wines, 489
Vermouth
manufacture of, 529
production of, 479

Vertical
pack press, use of in apple juice
manufacture, 231
type rice mill, diagram of, 436
Vesicles, intracellular in yeast, as a
location for lytic enzymes, 16
Viability of strains of *Saccharomyces
cerevisiae*, 14
Vicinal diketones, formation of by
brewery yeasts, 91
Vico system for continuous fermentation of grape juice, 360
Vines, age of, in production of
fortified wines, 492
Vins ordinaires, future for production
of, 377
Vintage
nature of in production of fortified
wines, 494
port wines, shipment of, 518
Virgin Islands, rum production in, 596
Virginia, production of bourbon in the
State of, 646
Virus infections of the grape vine, 336
Virus-free rootstocks, use of in production of fortified wines, 492
Viruses in *Saccharomyces cerevisiae*, 19
Vitaceae, properties of as a plant
family, 326
Vitamin B content of beers, 117
Vitamin content of beer wort, 69
requirements of *saké* yeasts, 444
Vitamins
B group
changes in content of in fermenting apple juice, 197
in cider apples, 177
content of in Scotch grain wort,
661
in molasses, concentrations of, 597
Viticulture in early Italy, 319
Vitis labrusca, cold tolerance of strains
of, 339
V. vinifera
age of cultivated strains of, 327
use of to make table wines, 325
use of to produce fortified wines,
489
Vodka
composition of, 584

Zosimos of Pabopolis, treatise on
brewing by, 4
Zubrovka, nature of as a spirit, 542
Zymomonads, resistance of to sulphur
dioxide, 207
Zymomonas sp., occurrence of in
apple juices, 181
Z. strains, properties of in relation to

cider disorders, 206
Z. anaerobia
as a causative organism of cider
sickness, 205
effect of sulphur dioxide on, 248
source of in cider making, 207
spoilage of beers by, 120